If You're Trying to
Get Better Grades
& Higher Test Scores in
Social Studies

You've Gotta Have This Book!

Grades 4-6

By Imogene Forte
& Marjorie Frank

Incentive Publications, Inc.
Nashville, Tennessee

Illustrated by Kathleen Bullock
Cover by Geoffrey Brittingham
Edited by Patience Camplair

ISBN 0-86530-647-8

1   2   3   4   5   6   7   8   9   10   08   07   06   05

PRINTED IN THE UNITED STATES OF AMERICA
www.incentivepublications.com

Contents

GET SHARP . . . on World Geography 97

GET SHARP . . . on U.S. Geography 133

GET SHARP . . . on World History 155

GET SHARP . . . on U.S. History, Government, & Citizenship   185

Get Ready

Get ready to get smarter in social studies. Get ready to be a better student and get the grades you are capable of getting. Get ready to feel better about yourself as a student. Lots of students would like to do better in school. Lots of students CAN do better. But it doesn't happen overnight. The first part of getting ready is: **wanting** to do better—motivating yourself to get moving on this project of showing how smart you really are. The **Get Ready** part of this book will help you do just that: get inspired and motivated. It also gives you some practical ways to organize yourself, your space, your time, and your social studies homework. And there's more! It gives tips you can use right away to make big improvements in your study habits.

Get Set

Once you have taken a hard look at your goals, organization, and study habits, you can move on to other skills and habits that will help you be more successful at learning. The **Get Set** part of this book starts out with an overview of the themes of social studies. Then, it gives a quick tune-up on the thinking skills that will help you get the most out of your brain, followed by a reminder about good places to find information for your social studies lessons. Top this off with a great review of skills you need for good studying. It is all right here at your fingertips—how to listen well, read carefully, study for tests, and take tests. Take this section seriously, and you will start improving in social studies right away.

Get Sharp

Now, you are ready to mix those good study habits and skills with the social studies that you need to learn. The **Get Sharp** sections of this book contain all kinds of facts, people, places, events, lists, definitions, and how-to information. These sections cover the basic areas of social studies that you study—social and cultural concepts, map skills, world and U.S. geography, world history, U.S. history, U.S. government and citizenship, and economics. The pages of the **Get Sharp** sections are loaded with information you need to understand social studies homework and get it done right. This part of the book is a great reference tool PLUS a *how-to* manual for many topics and assignments. Keep it handy whenever you do any social studies assignment or project. It is sure to help you keep all those concepts, definitions, dates, places, persons, and events clear.

How to Use This Book

Students

This can be the ultimate homework helper for your social studies instruction and assignments. Use the *Get Ready* and the *Get Set* sections to improve your attitude and sharpen your organizational and study skills. Then, have the book nearby at all times when you have social studies work to complete at home, and use the *Get Sharp* sections to . . .

   . . . reinforce a topic you have already learned.

   . . . get different and fresh examples of something you've studied.

   . . . check up on a fact, definition, event, skill, process, or detail of social studies.

   . . . get a quick answer to a social studies question.

   . . . get clear on something you thought you knew
      but now aren't so sure about.

   . . . guide you in social studies thinking, research, or projects.

   . . . review a topic to get ready for a test.

Teachers

This book can serve multiple purposes in the classroom. Use it as . . .

   . . . a reference manual for students to consult during learning activities or assignments.

   . . . a reference manual for yourself to consult on particular events, facts, or concepts.

   . . . an instructional handbook for a specific social studies topic.

   . . . a remedial tool for anyone needing to sharpen a particular social studies concept.

   . . . a source of advice for parents and students regarding homework habits.

   . . . an assessment guide to help you gauge student mastery of social studies concepts.

   . . . a source of good resources for bridging home and school.

     (Use the letter on page 17 and any other pages as take-home pieces for parents.)

Parents

The *Get Ready* and *Get Set* sections of this book will help you to help your child improve study habits and sharpen study skills. These can serve as positive motivators for the student while taking the burden off of you. Then, you can use the *Get Sharp* sections as a source of knowledge and a guide for yourself. It's a handbook you can consult to . . .

   . . . refresh your memory about a person, place, event, era, or idea in social studies.

   . . . get a clear definition of a social studies term.

   . . . end confusion about concepts, facts, dates, changes, processes,
      and many other social studies questions.

   . . . provide useful homework help to your child.

   . . . reinforce the good learning your child is doing in social studies class.

   . . . gain confidence that your child is doing the homework correctly.

GET READY →

Get Motivated

Dear Student,

Nobody can make you a better student. Nobody can even make you WANT to be a better student. But you CAN be. It's a rare kid who doesn't have some ability to learn more, do better with assignments and tests, feel more confident as a student, or get better grades. You CAN DO THIS! You are the one (the only one) that can get yourself motivated.

The first question is this: "WHY would you want be a better student?" If you don't have an answer to this, your chances of improving are not so hot. If you do have answers, but they're like the ones on page 15, your chances of improving still might be pretty slim. Now, we don't mean to tell you that it's a bad idea to get a good report card, or get on the honor roll, or please your parents. But—if you really are going to improve as a student, the reasons need to be about YOU. The goals need to be YOUR goals for your life right now. In fact, if you are having a hard time getting motivated, maybe it is just BECAUSE you're used to hearing a lot of "shoulds" that seem to be about what other people want you to be. Or maybe it's because the goals are so far off in some distant future that it's impossible to stay excited about them.

Why try to be a better student? Consider these reasons:

- to make use of your good mind (Don't miss out on something you could learn to do or understand.)

- to get involved—to change learning into something YOU DO instead of something that someone else is trying to do TO you

- to take charge and get where YOU WANT TO GO (It's YOUR life, after all.)

- to learn all you can for YOURSELF (The more you know, the more you think, and the more you understand—the more possibilities you have for what you can be in your life RIGHT NOW and in the future.)

Follow the "Get Motivated Tips" on the next page as you think about this question. Then list a few reasons of your own. These will inspire you to put your brain to work, show how smart you are, and get even smarter.

Sincerely,

Imogene and Marjorie

Hmmmmm,

Why should I be a better student?

To please my parents?
To please my teachers?
To impress other kids?
To impress my parents' friends?
So people will like me better?
To keep from embarrassing my parents?
To do as well as my older brother?
To do better than my sister?
So teachers will treat me better?
To get the money my parents offer
for good grades?
To be well-prepared for high school?
To make a lot of money when
I finish school?
To get a good report card?
To get into college?

None of these reasons motivate me that much.

Get Motivated Tips

1. Think about why you want to do better as a student.

2. Think about what you would gain now from doing better.

3. Set some short-term goals *(something you can improve in a few weeks).*

4. Think about what gets in the way of doing your best as a student.

5. Figure out a way to change something that keeps you from improving.

(Use the form on page 16 to record your thoughts and goals.)

What changes could I make in the near future?

Write two short-term goals—things that you could improve in the next month.

1. _____

   _____

2. _____

   _____

What gets in the way of good grades or good studying for me?

Name the things that most often keep you from doing your best as a student.

1. _____

   _____

2. _____

   _____

What distraction can I eliminate?

Choose one thing from above that you will try to change or get rid of for the next month.

1. _____

   _____

   _____

Get Ready Tip #1

Set realistic goals. Choose something you actually believe you can do. Also, you'll have a better chance of success if you set a short time frame for your goal.

These are my **Get Motivated Goals.**

Dear Parent:

How can you help your child get motivated to do the work it takes to be a better student? You can't do it for her (or him). But here are some ideas to help students as they find it within themselves to get set to be good students:

- Read the letter to students (page 14). Help your son or daughter think about where she or he wants to go, what reasons make sense to her or him for getting better grades, and what benefits he or she would gain from better performance as a student.

- Help your child make use of the advice on study habits. (See pages 18–26.) Reinforce the ideas, particularly those of keeping up with assignments and turning in work on time.

- Provide your child with a quiet, comfortable, well-lit place that is available consistently for study. Also, provide a place to keep materials, post reminders, and display schedules.

- Set family routines and schedules that allow for good blocks of study time, adequate rest, relaxing breaks, and healthy eating. Include some time to get things ready for the next school day and some ways for students to be reminded about upcoming assignments or due dates.

- Keep distractions to a minimum. You may not be able to control the motivations and goals of your child, but you can control the telephone, computer, Internet, and TV. These things actually have on-off switches. Use them. Set rules and schedules.

- Demonstrate that you value learning in your household. Read. Show excitement about learning something new yourself. Share this with your kids.

- Help your child gather resources for studying, projects, papers, and reports. Try to be available to take her or him to the library, and offer help tracking down a variety of sources. Try to provide standard resources in the home (dictionary, thesaurus, computer, encyclopedia, etc.).

- DO help your student with homework. This means helping straighten out confusion about a topic (when you can), getting an assignment clear, discussing a concept or skill, and perhaps working through a few problems along with the student to make sure he or she is doing it right. This kind of help extends and supports the teaching done in the classroom. Remember that the end goal is for the student to learn. Don't be so insistent on the student "doing it himself" that you miss a good teaching or learning opportunity.

- Be alert for problems, and act early. Keep in contact with teachers and don't be afraid to call on them if you see any signs of slipping, confusion, or disinterest on the part of your child. It is easier to reclaim lost ground if you catch it early.

- Try to keep the focus on the student's taking charge for meeting his or her own goals, rather than on making you happy. This can help get you out of a nagging role and get some of the power in the hands of the student. Both of these will make for a more trusting, less hostile relationship with your child on the subject of schoolwork. Such a relationship will go a long way toward supporting your child's self-motivation to be a better student.

Sincerely,

Imogene and Marjorie

Get Organized

Anna has done plenty of studying about the surface features of Africa. However, since she is so disorganized, she is not able to show what she learned. Don't repeat Anna's mistakes.

Get Ready Tip #2

Set up your study space before school starts each year. Make it cozy and friendly—a safe refuge for getting work done.

Get Your Space Organized

Find a good place to study. Choose a place that . . .

      is always available to you.

    . . . is comfortable and uncluttered.

    . . . is quiet and as private as possible.

    . . . has good lighting.

    . . . is relatively free of distractions.

    . . . has a flat surface large enough to spread out materials.

    . . . has a place to keep supplies handy. *(See page 19 for suggested supplies.)*

    . . . has some wall space or bulletin board space for posting schedules and reminders.

Get Your Stuff Organized

Gather things that you will need for studying or for projects, papers, and other assignments. Keep them organized in one place, so you won't have to waste time looking for them. Here are some suggestions:

Handy Supplies

a good light
a clock or timer
bulletin board or wall
 (for schedule and reminders)
pencils, pens, erasable pens
erasers
colored pencils or crayons
markers, hightlighters
notebook paper, typing paper
scratch paper
drawing paper
index cards, sitcky notes
posterboard
folders, report folders

glue, glue sticks
ruler, compass, tape, scissors
paper clips, push pins
stapler, staples
standard references:
 globe
 world atlas
 history textbook
 geography textbook
 encyclopedia (books, CD)
 homework hotline numbers
 homework help websites
 good social studies websites

Get set with a place to keep supplies.

(a bookshelf, a file box, a paper tray, a drawer, a carton, a plastic dishpan, a plastic bucket, or a plastic crate)

  Keep everything in this place at all times.
  Return things to it after use.

Get Ready Tip #3

Have a place to put school things by the door, so important stuff doesn't get lost in the house or used up by other family members.

Also have:

  an assignment notebook *(See page 21.)*
  a notebook for every subject
  a book bag or pack to carry things back and forth
  a schedule for your week (or longer)

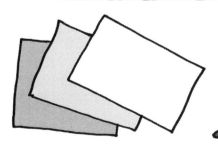

Get Your Time Organized

It might be easy to organize your study space and supplies. But it might not be quite as easy to organize your time. This takes some work. First, you have to understand how you use your time now. Then you will need to figure out a way to make better use of your time. Here is a plan you can follow right away to help you get your time organized.

Get Ready Tip #4
When you plan your week's schedule, don't make it too tight or too rigid. Leave room for unexpected events.

I notice that I forgot to take my social studies homework to school twice this week.

I forgot about the geography quiz on Tuesday, and I left my notes at school.

I watched 2 hours of TV on three nights.

I left my colored pencils at school, too.

I talked on the phone over an hour every school night.

I usually leave my science and social studies homework until last.

1. Think about how you use your time now.

For one week, pause at the end of each day, think back over the day, and write down what you did in each block of time for the whole day. Then, look at the record you have kept to see how you used your time. Ask yourself these questions:

Did I have any goals for when I would get certain things done?

Did I even think ahead about how I would use my time?

How did I decide what to do first?

Did I have a plan or did I just get things done in any old order?

Did I get everything done or did I run out of time?

How much time did I waste?

Notice the patterns that helped you get your work done and the patterns that didn't.

2. Make a plan for the next week.

Get a fresh start. Plan your time for next week. Skip the bad habits or poor use of time from last week and plan to do some things differently. Get a notebook and make a schedule for each day.

Include:

. . . time that will be spent at school

. . . after-school activities

. . . meals

. . . study time

. . . family activities

. . . fun, sports, or recreational activities

. . . social activities or special events

. . . time for rest and sleep

Better Grades & Higher Test Scores / SOCIAL STUDIES gr. 4–6

Get Your Assignments Organized

You can't do a very good job of an assignment if you don't have a clue about what it is. You can't possibly do the assignment well if you don't understand the things you are studying. So if you want to get smarter, get clear and organized about assignments. Follow these eight steps:

1. Listen to the assignment.

2. Write it down in an assignment notebook. *(Make sure you write down the due date.)*

3. If you don't understand the assignment—ASK. *(Do not leave the classroom without knowing what it is you are supposed to do.)*

4. If you don't understand the material well enough to do the assignment—TALK to the teacher. *(Tell him or her that you need help getting it clear.)*

5. Take your assignment book home.

6. Write major assignments onto a calendar at home. This way, you can be reminded of projects and other assignments that are coming up.

7. Make a Daily To-Do List *(For each day, write the things that must be done by the end of that day. Make this list a day or two ahead of time.)*

8. Look at your assignment book every day and check your To-Do list to make sure you know what needs to be done that day.

Get Ready Tip #5

At all times—keep a copy of class outlines, schedules, or long-range class assignments at home.

Thursday To-Do List

study for economics quiz

get supplies for history project

find Internet source for U.S. Civil War history timeline

math. Ch 6 review problems

return library books

grammar exercise #21

wash soccer uniform

Lang.	choose biography, write report	2/6	
Spanish	description of my town	2/9	
Math	Ch 6 review (pgs. 112–114)	2/9	
Math	Ch.6 test	2/13	
Science	project—ocean currents	2/14	
Lang.	Spelling Test, Unit 6	2/10	
Soc. St.	quiz on economics	2/9	
Lang.	grammar, Pg. 99, 1–20	2/10	
Soc. St.	Civil War time line	2/16	

Get Ready Tip #6

Don't count on anyone else to listen to the assignment and get it down right. Get the assignment yourself.

Better Grades & Higher Test Scores / SOCIAL STUDIES gr. 4–6
Copyright ©2005 by Incentive Publications, Inc., Nashville, TN.

Get Ready: Get Organized

Get Yourself Organized

Okay, so your schedule is on the wall—all neat and clear. Your study space is organized. Your study supplies are organized. You have written down all your assignments, and you've made all of your lists. Great! But do you feel overloaded or stressed? Take some time to think about the behaviors that will help YOU feel as organized as your stuff and your schedule.

Before you leave school . . .

STOP—take a few calm, unrushed minutes to think about what books and supplies you will need at home for studying. ALWAYS take your assignment notebook home.

When you get home . . .

FIRST—Put your school bag in the same spot every day, out of the way of the bustle of your family's activities.

STOP—after relaxing, or after dinner, take a few calm, unrushed minutes to look over your schedule and review what needs to be done. Review your list for the day. Plan your evening study time and set priorities. Don't wait until it is late or you are very tired.

Before you go to bed . . .

STOP—take a few calm, unrushed minutes to look over your assignment notebook and to-do list for tomorrow one more time. Make sure everything is done.

THEN—put everything you need for the next day IN your book bag. Don't wait until the morning. Make sure you have all the right books and notebooks in your bag. Make sure your finished work is all in the bag. Also, pack other stuff (for gym, sports, etc.) at the same time. Put everything in one place consistently, so you don't have to look for it.

In the morning . . .

STOP—take a few calm, unrushed minutes to review the day one more time.

THEN—eat a good breakfast.

Oh, no!

Michael finally finished his diagram of the structure of the U.S. government. It's due today. He worked on it all week. It shows how much he learned about the government. He added creative cartoons and many interesting facts.

He remembered to take his lunch and gym bag to school. He remembered the DVD he promised to lend to his friend Max. **Guess what Michael forgot to take to school today?**

Get Ready Tip #7
You learn from doing your homework. If you leave it at home, you'll miss out on sharing what you've learned.

Get Healthy

If you are sick, tired, droopy, angry, nervous, weak, or miserable, it is very hard to be a good student. It is hard to even use or show what you already know. Your physical and mental health is a basic MUST for doing well in school. So, don't ignore your health. Pay attention to how you feel. No one else can do that for you.

> I got plenty of sleep last night. After school, I went on a long bike ride with my best friend and stopped at the library for a book on my way home. I ate a healthy snack, and when I finish practicing on my guitar, I'll be in great shape to study for my geography test tomorrow.

Get plenty of rest.

If you're tired, nothing works very well in your life. You can't think, concentrate, pay attention, learn, remember, or study. Try to get eight hours of sleep every night. Get plenty of rest on weekends. If you have a long evening of study ahead, take a short nap after school.

Eat well.

You can't learn or function well on an empty stomach or when your nutrition is poor. Junk food (soda, sweets, chips, snacks) actually will make you more tired. Plus, it crowds the healthy foods out of your diet—the foods your brain needs to think well and your body needs to get through the day with energy. So eat a balanced diet, with lean meat, whole grains, vegetables, fruit, and dairy products. Oh, and drink a lot of water—eight glasses a day is good.

Exercise.

Everything in your body works better when you get a chance to move. Don't let your life become inactive. Do something every day to get exercise—walk, play a sport, play a game, or run. It's a good idea to get some exercise before you sit down to study, too. Exercise helps you relax, unwind, and de-stress. It's good for stimulating your brain.

Relax. Find stress relief.

Your body and your mind need rest. Do something every day to relax. Pay attention to signs of anxiety and stress. Are you nervous, worried, angry, sad, tense? Stress can lower your success in school and interfere with your life. Find a way to relieve the stress. Start with exercise and rest. Also, try these: stretch, take a hot bath or long shower, laugh, listen to calming music, write in a journal. If you are burdened with worries, anger, or problems, talk to someone—a good friend, a teacher or parent, or another trusted adult.

Get a Grip (on Study Habits)

Here is some good advice for getting set to improve your study habits. Check up on yourself to see how you do with each of these. Then set goals where you need to improve.

. . . in school:

1. Get to school on time.

When you are late, you get off to a slow start. Sometimes you miss important instructions. Show up on time. Take your book, your notebook, your pencil and other supplies.

2. Choose your seat wisely.

Sit where you won't be distracted. Avoid people with whom you'll be tempted to chat. Stay away from the back row. Sit where you can see and hear.

3. Pay attention.

Get everything you can out of each lesson. Listen. Stay awake. Your assignments will be easier if you've really been awake and aware during class.

4. Take notes.

List main points. Record examples of problems, solved correctly. If you hear something AND write it, you will be likely to remember it.

5. Ask questions.

It's the teacher's job to see that you understand the material. It's your job to ask if you don't.

6. Use your time in class.

Get as much as possible of the next day's assignment done before you leave school. Use your time during class, between classes, or during study period.

7. Write down assignments.

Do not leave school until you understand the assignment and have it written down clearly.

8. Turn in your homework.

If you turn in every homework assignment, you are a long way toward doing well in a class—even if you struggle with tests.

Better Grades & Higher Test Scores / SOCIAL STUDIES gr. 4–6
Copyright ©2005 by Incentive Publications, Inc., Nashville, TN.

It's a good thing I started early on this globe-making project. It takes a long time for each layer of paste to dry.

. . . at home:

1. Gather your supplies.

Before you sit down to study, get all the stuff together that you will need: assignment book, notebook, notes, textbook, study guides, paper, pencils, etc. Think ahead so that you have supplies for long-term projects.

2. Avoid distractions.

Think of all the things that keep you from concentrating. Figure out ways to remove those from your life during study time. Keep your study time uninterrupted.

3. Turn off the TV. Phone later.

No matter now much you insist otherwise, you cannot study well with the TV on. Plan your TV time before or after study time, not during it. The best way to avoid the distraction of the telephone is to study in a room with no phone. Call your friends when your work is done.

4. Hide the computer games.

Stay away from video game playing stations, computer games, e-mail, and Internet surfing. Plan time for these when studies are done, or before you settle into serious study time.

5. Plan your time.

Think about the time you have to work each night. Make a timeline for yourself. Estimate how much time each task will take, and set some deadlines. This will keep your attention from wandering and keep you focused on the task.

6. Start early.

Start early in the evening. Don't wait until just before bedtime to get underway on any assignment. When it is possible, start the day before or a few days before.

7. Do the hardest things first.

It is a good idea to do the hardest and most important tasks first. This keeps you from avoiding procrastination on the tough assignments. Also, you will be doing the harder stuff when your mind is the most fresh. Study for tests and do hard problems early, when your brain is fresh. Do routine tasks later in the evening.

8. Break up long assignments.

Big projects or test preparations can be overwhelming. Break each long task down into small ones. Then, take one small task at a time. This will make the long assignments far less intimidating. And you'll have more successes more often. Never try to do a long assignment all in one sitting.

9. Take breaks.

Plan a break for your body and mind every 30-45 minutes. Get up, walk around, or stretch. Do something active or relaxing.

10. Plan ahead for long-range assignments.

Start early on long-range assignments, big projects, and test preparations. Don't wait until the night before anything is due. You never know what will happen that last day. Get going on long tasks several days before the due date. Make a list of everything that needs to be done for a long-range assignment (including finding information and collecting supplies). Then, start from the due date and work backwards. Make a timeline or schedule that sets a time to do each of the tasks on the list.

11. Cut out the excuses.

It is perfectly normal to want to avoid doing school work. Remember, however, that excuses take up your energy. In the time you waste convincing yourself or anyone else that you have a good reason for avoiding your studies, you could be getting some of the work done. If you want to be a better student, you will need to dump your own list of excuses.

12. Don't get behind.

Keeping up is good. Many students slip into failure, stress, and hopelessness because they get behind. The best way to avoid all of these is—NOT to get behind. This means DO your assignments on time. If you do get behind because of illness or something else unavoidable, do something about it. Don't get further and further into the pit! Talk to the teacher. Make a plan for catching up. Getting behind is often caused by procrastination. **Don't procrastinate.** The more you do, the worse you feel, and the harder it is to catch up!

13. Get on top of problems.

Don't let small problems develop into big ones. If you are lost in a class, missed an assignment, don't understand something, or have done poorly on something—act quickly. Talk to the teacher, ask a parent to help, find another student who has the information. Do something to correct the problem before it becomes overwhelming.

14. Ask for help.

You don't have to solve every problem alone or learn everything by yourself. Don't count on someone noticing that you need help. Tell them. Use the adults and services around you to ask for help when you need it. Remember, it is the teacher's job to teach you. Most teachers are happy to help a student who shows interest in getting help.

15. Reward yourself for accomplishments.

If you break your assignments down into manageable tasks, you will have more successes more often. Congratulate and reward yourself for each task accomplished—by taking a break, getting some popcorn, going for a walk, bragging about what you have done to someone—or any other way you discover. Every accomplishment is worth celebrating!

GET SET →

Get Familiar with Social Studies Themes

Social studies includes many different areas of study—all of them related to people. Without people, there can be no study of anything *social*! The subject of social studies describes, examines, and explains how, where, and when people live, and their groups, relationships, and institutions. To get an overview of the social studies, you can divide the subject into these themes, or big ideas.

Culture

... *the features that contribute to cultural traits*
... *how culture is learned*
... *characteristics of specific cultures*
... *similarities in cultures and differences between cultures*
... *the multicultural nature of a country and the world*
... *how cultures change*
... *how cultures affect other cultures*

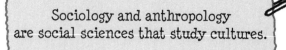

Sociology and anthropology are social sciences that study cultures.

People in Societies

... *how personal identity is shaped*
... *various kinds of social interaction and groups*
... *how individuals function in groups and institutions*
... *the role of institutions in the lives of individuals*
... *the need for rules, laws, and authority in groups*
... *changes in institutions and how institutions change society*

Psychology and sociology are social sciences that study the growth, development, and behavior of people.

Places

... *the different places and regions of the world*
... *physical and human characteristics of different regions*
... *why people live where they do*
... *interrelationships between people, cultures, and places*
... *reasons for movement of people and materials*
... *how technology affects places*

History is a social science that focuses on time and the changes that occur over time in human societies and institutions.

Time and Change

... *the location of people, cultures, and events in time*
... *chronological relationships between events*
... *important contributions of individuals and groups to historical events*
... *causes and effects of historical events*
... *what has happened in the past, and how it has affected people*
... *things that have changed over time; things that have stayed the same*
... *relationships between past and present conditions, events, or institutions*
... *differing interpretations of historical events and issues*
... *the role of science and technology in changes*

Geography and anthropology are social sciences that study the relationships between people and places.

Power, Authority, and Government

Political science, sociology, and history are social sciences that study power, authority, and government.

. . . structures of power, authority, and government
. . . different forms of power, government, and political systems
. . . the origins, purposes, functions, and formations of governments
. . . the function of power and authority in social groups
. . . individual rights within political systems
. . . features of American democracy

Citizenship

Political science and history are social sciences that study the roles of citizens in political systems.

. . . individual participation in society
. . . rights and responsibilities of citizens
. . . the principles and origins of different governments
. . . the electoral process and importance of voting
. . . role of individuals as citizens of cities, states, nations, and the world

Economics

. . . the dilemma of scarcity, and why decisions must be made about the use of resources
. . . benefits and consequences of choices about the use of resources
. . . the wants and needs of individuals and societies
. . . what different individuals, groups, and societies consume
. . . the relationship between production and consumption
. . . how goods are produced and distributed
. . . how different economic systems make use of resources
. . . how different economic systems produce, distribute, and exchange goods and services
. . . the results of trade and economic interdependence

Economics, political science, and sociology are social sciences that study the role of economics in the lives of individuals and societies.

History, economics, political science, anthropology, sociology, and geography are social sciences that study global connections.

Global Connections

. . . how nations and cultures interact, cooperate, and clash
. . . issues that concern many or all nations
. . . problems that affect the globe
. . . different kinds of world connections
     (political, economic, cultural, environmental)
. . . political and military divisions, clashes, and alliances
. . . roles of international institutions and agreements

Get Tuned-Up on Thinking Skills

Your brain is capable of an amazing variety of accomplishments! There are different levels and kinds of thinking that your brain can do—all of them necessary to get you set for good learning. To answer social studies questions, your brain must use many different processes. Here are some of the thinking skills that will freshen up your mental flexibility and keep your mind sharp as you learn concepts and investigate events in the many areas of social studies.

Recall — To **recall** is to know and remember specific facts, names, processes, categories, ideas, generalizations, theories, or information.

Examples: *Recall helps you remember such things as the branches of the U.S. government, the location of Afghanistan, the meanings of symbols for maps, the date of the French Revolution, the latitude of the South Pole, or the length of a senator's term of office.*

Classify — To **classify** is to put things into categories. When you classify ideas, events, topics, or things, you must choose categories that fit the purpose and clearly define each category.

Elaborate — To **elaborate** is to give details about a situation (to explain, compare, or give examples). When you elaborate, you might use words or phrases such as these: *so, because, however, but, an example of this is, on the other hand, as a result, in addition, moreover, for instance, such as, if you recall, furthermore, another reason is.*

Example: *A law is a rule established by an authority. Furthermore, there are usually specific consequences or punishments given to those who break a law.*

Get Set: Thinking Skills

Recognize Cause and Effect

Recognize Cause and Effect — When one event occurs as the result of another event, there is a **cause-effect relationship** between the two. Recognizing causes and effects takes skill. When you read or hear about an event or group of events, pay careful attention to words or symbols that give clues to cause and effect (*the reason was, because, as a result, consequently, so*).

Example: *Because of the steep mountains, many people in Peru use pack animals for transportation.*

Distinguish Fact from Opinion

Distinguish Fact from Opinion — A **fact** is a statement that can be proven true. An **opinion** expresses personal attitudes or beliefs. Many opinions tell what a person wishes or believes to be so. It is not always easy to tell the difference between fact and opinion. Good thinkers will analyze statements carefully in order to keep from accepting opinions as fact. Opinions often use the words *ought, should,* or *must.*

Predict

Predict — To **predict** is to make a statement about what will happen. Predictions are based on some previous knowledge, experience, or understanding.

Example: *In December of 2004, a huge tsunami killed thousands of people in southeast Asia. Jessica predicts that, because of the horrible devastation, nations around the world will develop better systems for warning their citizens of a coming tsunami.*

Get Set Tip #1

Thinking skills are rarely used in isolation from one another. For example: In order to predict, you'll need to make inferences.

Infer

Infer — To **infer** is to make a logical guess based on information.

Example: *Alex has noticed that stock prices have fallen steadily for the last several months. He infers that buyers have lost confidence in the stock market.*

Generalize — To **generalize** is to make a broad statement about a topic based on observations or facts. A generalization should be based on plenty of evidence (facts, observations, and examples). Just one exception can prove a generalization false.

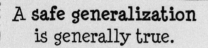

A **safe generalization** is generally true.

Climates at high latitudes are likely to be cooler than those at low latitudes.

Invalid generalizations are untrue. A **faulty** generalization is invalid because there are exceptions.

Average temperatures at latitudes of 45° are lower than temperatures at latitudes of 25°.

A **broad** generalization suggests something is always or never true about all or none of the members of a group. **Most broad generalizations are untrue.**

The climate is hot and dry at all locations between 0° and 10° latitude.

Draw Conclusions — A **conclusion** is a general statement that someone makes after analyzing examples and details. A conclusion generally involves an explanation someone has developed through reasoning.

Example: *Louisa notices that most of the largest cities in the United States are located along coastlines or major rivers. She concludes that cities developed in areas where goods and people could be transported by water.*

Extend — To **extend** is to connect ideas or things together, or to relate one thing to something different, or to apply one idea or understanding to another situation.

Example: *A group of students read all parts of the U.S. Constitution. They extended their knowledge by writing a "Student's Bill of Rights." This Bill of Rights for their school was based on the principles in the "U.S. Constitution's Bill of Rights."*

Think Logically (or Reason)

Think Logically (or Reason) — When you think **logically**, you take a statement or situation apart and examine the relationships of parts to one another. You reason **inductively** (*start from a general principle and make inferences about the details*) or **deductively** (*start from a group of details and draw a broad conclusion or make a generalization*).

I did some research on the average February temperatures in several locations along the 75⁰ W line of longitude. I found temperatures averaging from well below zero⁰ to around 100⁰. There were many average temperatures in between these two extremes.

From looking at these different details, I **deduce** that longitude has no effect on the climate of a particular location.

Identify Faulty Arguments

Identify Faulty Arguments — An **argument** is **faulty** when it is based on an error in logic. This means the information is misleading, or there are exceptions to the statement, or the statement is not supported by evidence.

Examples: *Once you see the museums of Paris, you will want to move to the city.*
Any business that does not display a flag has owners that are unpatriotic.
People who invest in the stock market have a lot of money.

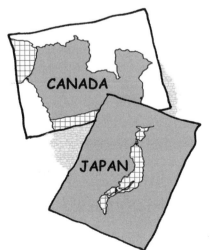

Compare & Contrast

Compare & Contrast — When you **compare** things, you describe similarities. When you **contrast** things, you describe the differences.

Examples: *Compare: Canada and Japan are countries with long coastlines. Fishing is an important activity in the economy of both countries. Both countries border the Pacific Ocean.*

Contrast: Canada is a large country on the North American continent. Japan is a smaller country, made up of several islands.

Analyze — To **analyze,** you must break something down into parts and determine how the parts are related to each other and how they are related to the whole.

Examples: *You must analyze to . . .*
> . . . *describe the ethnic groups within a society.*
> . . . *explain the difference between characteristics of a strait and an isthmus.*
> . . . *discuss the role of each house of Congress in making a law.*

Let's analyze the job Luke is doing in his role as president of our club.

Hey, who needs to analyze? Let's just agree that I am awesome.

Synthesize — To **synthesize,** you must combine ideas or elements to create a whole.

Examples: *You must synthesize to . . .*
> . . . *describe the process by which a president is elected in the United States.*
> . . . *understand how factors and events combined to start World War I.*
> . . . *create a map to show the average monthly rainfall on the continent of Europe.*

Evaluate — To **evaluate** is to make a judgment about something. Evaluations should be based on evidence. Evaluations can include opinions, but these opinions should be supported or explained by examples, experiences, observations, and other forms of evidence.

Examples: *When you evaluate an argument, an explanation, a decision, a proposal, a prediction, an inference, a conclusion, or a generalization, ask questions such as these:*
> • *Are the conclusions reached based on good facts?*
> • *Is there evidence for the generalization or inference?*
> • *Is the evidence substantial? (Is there enough?)*
> • *Does the explanation make sense?*
> • *Are the sources used to make the decisions reliable?*
> • *Did the writer or speaker give clear examples?*
> • *Is the argument effective?*
> • *Is it realistic?*

I'm a native Californian. Your proposal about breaking California into two states is certainly interesting. However, you have not convinced me that this is a good idea. The sources you've used are mostly opinions of citizens. You have not told what percentage of the citizens favor this idea. You have not given enough evidence to show that this is needed. You have not explained exactly how the separation would work.

You have a long way to go to convince me!

34

Get Set: Thinking Skills

Identify Biases

Identify Biases — A **bias** is a one-sided attitude toward something. Biased thinking does not result from facts, but from feelings or attitudes. Learn to recognize biases. Biased information may not be reliable, especially if it is presented as fact or nonfiction.

Example: *I just know that anyone who has a tattoo is a person of low moral standards.*

Identify Propaganda

Identify Propaganda — **Propaganda** is a form of communication intended to make listeners or readers agree with the ideas of a group. Unlike ordinary persuasive writing, propaganda often focuses on an appeal to emotions. Propaganda often uses faulty arguments, exaggeration, or information that distorts or confuses the truth. To identify propaganda, look for faulty arguments, exaggeration, manipulation of facts, manipulation of emotions, or unsupported claims.

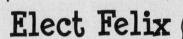

Elect Felix for Student Body President!

He always shows up. His opponent is often late or absent. Felix has never missed a day of school and he won a prize for punctuality!

It's hard to decide whose propaganda is more effective. Felix is always on time, but he can be quite bossy. Muriel is certainly popular, but she has no experience as a leader.

VOTE FOR MURIEL FOR **STUDENT BODY PRESIDENT**

Everybody likes her. She is much nicer than Felix.

Hmmm. I wonder who else is running?

Identify Stereotypes

Identify Stereotypes — A **stereotype** is an oversimplified opinion or belief about a group, person, or event. A stereotype makes a generalization (often faulty or broad, or both) about someone or something as a group, without paying attention to individual circumstances or characteristics. A stereotype is often negative or critical in nature.

Examples: *People of that religion are untrustworthy. Dog owners don't care about the privacy of other people.*

Teenagers don't care about important issues. They only think about themselves.

Wait a minute! You shouldn't **stereotype** ALL teenagers like that!

Get Brushed-Up on Information Skills

If you're going to get set to be a good student, you need sharp skills for finding and using information. You are fortunate to live in a time and place of almost unlimited resources for finding information. However, you cannot make use of those resources well unless you know what they are and what is in them.

Here is a quick review of some of the most common sources of information available for students. Get to know these references well.

Which Reference is Which?

Almanac: a yearly publication that gives information, basic facts, and statistics on many topics. Almanacs are organized with lists of information by topics. They have an alphabetical index. Much of the information is about current or recent years, but some of it is historical. Almanacs cover current events, famous people, sports, countries, geographic records, and many other categories. They usually have an index that lists information by categories.

Atlas: a book of maps. Atlases give geographical information in the form of maps, tables, graphs, and lists. They include information about geography, including population, climate, weather, elevation, vegetation, regions, topics, topography, and much more. Some maps in atlases show political information such as countries and cities.

Bibliography: a list of books, articles, and other resources about a certain topic. Often a bibliography is found at the end of a book or article, giving a list of the sources used in the publication.

Biographical Dictionary or Biographical Reference: a book that gives a brief summary of the lives and accomplishments of famous persons. Entries are listed alphabetically. *Contemporary Authors, The Dictionary of American Biography*, and *Who's Who in America,* are examples of this kind of reference.

Dictionary: a book that lists the standard words of a particular language alphabetically, and gives their meanings and pronunciations. Many dictionaries also provide other information about the word, such as the part of speech, uses, antonyms, and etymologies.

Special Dictionaries: dictionaries of words related to one subject only. There are many special dictionaries, listing such things as slang, scientific terms, historical terms, geographical features, biographies, foreign words, or abbreviations.

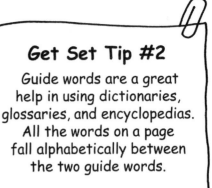

Get Set Tip #2

Guide words are a great help in using dictionaries, glossaries, and encyclopedias. All the words on a page fall alphabetically between the two guide words.

Glossary: a listing of the important terms used in a specific book or article, accompanied by their definitions. A glossary is arranged alphabetically and generally is located at the end of the book or article.

Encyclopedias: a set of books providing information on many branches of knowledge. Usually there are many volumes. Information is presented in the form of articles, and consists of a survey of the topic. The information is arranged alphabetically according to the topic or name of a person, place, or event. It is best to use key words to search for a topic in an encyclopedia.

Special Encyclopedias: There are many encyclopedias that contain information about one subject rather than about many subjects. Individual volume encyclopedias or whole sets cover such topics as science, art, music, history, and sports. (Don't miss this one: *The Encyclopedia of American Facts and Dates.*)

Get Set Tip #3
Use key words to look for information in encyclopedias.

When I use the encyclopedia, I know I can find the information on dolphins somewhere between the guide words "dollar" and "Dominican Republic."

To find out about . . .	look under key word . . .	instead of under . . .
the natural resources of the islands in Oceania	Oceania	natural resources or islands
how Egyptians preserved mummies	mummy	Egypt, death, or preservation

Famous First Facts: a book that lists facts about firsts (first events, accomplishments, discoveries, and inventions) of many kinds in America, listed alphabetically. There is also an international version.

Some famous firsts:

first human to survive a trip over Niagara Falls
- Annie Edison Taylor, 1901
first female skydiver
- Georgia "Tiny" Broadwick
first of the modern Olympic Games
- 1896, in Athens, Greece
first president to appear on TV
- Franklin D. Roosevelt, 1939
first credit card
- Diners' Club, issued in 1950
first First Lady
- Martha Washington
first woman in space
- Valentina Tereshkova
first animal in space
- a dog, Laika, 1957
first use of an atomic bomb
- in Japan, 1945
first to fly solo across the Atlantic Ocean
- Charles Lindbergh, 1927

Some noteable lasts:

Custer's Last Stand - 1876
last Model T Ford built - 1927
last planet discovered, Pluto, - 1930
last play written by Shakespeare,
   The Tempest, - 1611
last (and first) voyage of *Titanic* - 1912
last time Halley's comet was
   visible from Earth - 1991
last time an elephant hanged for
   murder - 1916

Gazetteer: a geographical dictionary, listing information about important places in the world. Subjects and places are listed alphabetically.

The Guinness Book of World Records: a collection of information about the best and worst, most and least, biggest and smallest, longest and shortest, and other facts and records. This reference is also found on the Internet.

Index: a list of information or items found in a book, magazine, set of books, set of magazines, or other publications. The index is generally located at the end of the resource. Information is listed alphabetically. Sometimes a resource has an index that is a separate book. A specific magazine or journal sometimes has its own index, as do most encyclopedia sets. To find the volume and page location of information in a set of encyclopedias, you would consult the encyclopedia index accompanying the encyclopedia set. When a reference is online or on CD, a CD or online index accompanies the reference.

Internet: an extensive computer network that holds a huge amount of information from organizations and groups around the world as well as government agencies, libraries, schools and universities, educational organizations, and businesses. Information can be located by browsing through categories and sites assembled by your Internet service provider and by searching the Web with the help of a good search engine. The Internet can connect you to information on a vast number of topics related to all sorts of subject areas.

Library Catalog: a computer file or database of author, title, and subject listings for all books (and other materials) in the library. The computer system usually allows you to search by title, author, subject, or key words. It shows a list of materials on your subject or by your author available in the library, and the current status of the item (whether it is checked out or available for you to check out). Often the computer system also connects to databases of articles or books online that you can read or print. Some libraries have their catalogs in a card file. There are three different cards for each item in the library. Each kind of card is filed in a separate set of drawers. For each book or item, there is an author card (filed alphabetically by the author's last name), a subject card (filed alphabetically according to the subject of the book), and a title card (filed alphabetically according to the title of the book).

Periodicals: publications that are issued at regular intervals, such as daily, weekly, monthly, quarterly, or annually. Magazines, newspapers, and scholarly journals are types of periodicals. Periodicals are an excellent source of current news and information.

Periodical Index: a book or computer database that lists the subjects and titles of articles in a particular magazine or newspaper, or a particular group of magazines or newspapers.

Newspapers: periodicals published frequently, containing current information on national, international, and local news. Newspapers provide a wealth of information on sports, financial trends and figures, weather, book reviews, editorial comments, reviews of film, theater, and other entertainment events. Other features (such as classified ads, comics, puzzles, restaurant reviews, recipes, horoscopes, and listings for TV, radio, and movie programs) add to the list of information available in newspapers.

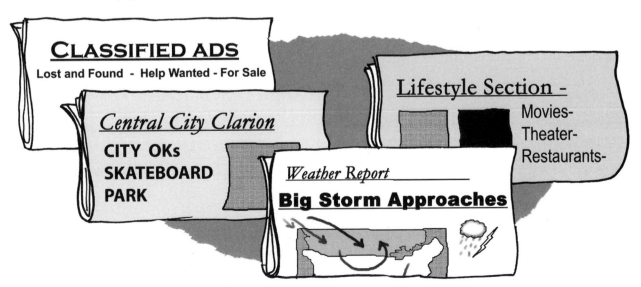

Quotation Index: a compilation of famous quotations and the persons who said them, listed alphabetically by the first word of the quotation and by the last name of the person. A popular quotation index is *Bartlett's Familiar Quotations.*

I'm looking for a few good quotes to spice up my report on the Revolutionary War.

The trouble with the rat race is that even if you win, you're still a rat.
- Lily Tomlin

Don't fire until you see the whites of their eyes.
- General Putnam, Revolutionary War

If you can't feed a hundred people then feed just one.
- Mother Teresa

Cheer up! The worst is yet to come!
- Mark Twain

History is the version of past events that people have decided to agree upon.
- Napoleon

Whoever gossips **to** you will gossip **about** you.
- Spanish proverb

The secret of being boring is to tell everything.
- Voltaire

Make the most of yourself for that is all there is of you.
- Ralph Waldo Emerson

Never hold a dust-buster and a cat at the same time.
- Kyoya, age 9

When you come to a fork in the road - take it!
- Yogi Berra

There never was a good war or a bad peace.
- Benjamin Franklin

Anyone who has never made a mistake has never tried anything new.
- Albert Einstein

The pen is mightier than the sword.
- Edward George Bulwer Lytton

The pen is mightier than the sword, and considerably easier to write with.
- Marty Feldman

Table of Contents: an outline of the information contained in a book, listed in the order that the information occurs in the book. The Table of Contents is found at the beginning of the book.

Thesaurus: a reference book that groups synonyms or words with similar meanings. A thesaurus is sometimes organized by idea or theme with an alphabetical index. Other versions organize the words like a dictionary. Some thesaurus editions contain antonyms as well as synonyms.

little

synonyms: small, tiny, short, brief, scanty, unimportant, insignificant, slight, weak, trivial, paltry, petty, diminutive

antonyms: big, large, monstrous, giant, enormous, full, much, long, huge, serious, important, generous

Yearbook: a book that gives up-to-date information about recent events or findings, or that reviews events of a particular year. One such yearbook is the *World Book Yearbook of Facts*. Many encyclopedia sets publish a yearbook to update the set each year. This reduces the need to update the entire set to keep information current.

Don't forget about these other resources.
They can add information you could not easily find elsewhere.

textbooks	museums	CDs & DVDs
classroom supplies	diagrams	librarians
advertisements	timelines	neighbors
maps	filmstrips	teachers
video tapes	tables & graphs	parents
illustrations	TV & radio programs	grandparents
movies	professional people	experts

Better Grades & Higher Test Scores / SOCIAL STUDIES gr. 4–6
Copyright ©2005 by Incentive Publications, Inc., Nashville, TN.

Get Set: Information Skills

Finding Information on the Internet

It's a skill to use the Internet well for finding reliable information. It takes practice. Here's some good advice for smart use of the Internet.

GOOD QUESTIONS TO ASK ABOUT A WEBSITE

Is the page sponsored by an established organization?

Is there plenty of useful information?

Are sources given for the facts?

Is the material on the site up to date?

Does the author appear to be qualified?

Is the information easy to use and understand?

Browse — Your Internet provider gathers pages on general topics. These give you quick access to information on several of the most popular topics, such as news, weather, health, travel, music, and sports. Most providers also offer links to kids' pages and reference materials.

Search — For a more advanced search, use a good search engine such as google.com or yahoo.com. Try different engines until you find your favorite. To use a search engine, type in a key word (such as *climbing*). To make your search more specific, type in a phrase (such as *mountain climbing*) or more than one word connected by AND (*mountain* AND *climbing* AND *equipment*).

Be selective — Use your time wisely to get the best information by choosing reputable sites. Sites from the government, established companies or organizations, and universities are usually reliable (*Examples: National Hockey League* **www.nhl.com**; *Field Museum of Natural History* **www.fmnh.org**; *NASA* **www.nasa.gov**; *National Geographic for Kids* www.nationalgeographic.com/kids).

Be smart — Learn to evaluate the websites you visit, and don't waste time on sites that won't yield information that is reliable.

Be cautious — If you download information, beware of viruses. Download information only from sites that seem reputable. If you are going to download software, it is safest to do it directly from the company that publishes the software. Be very careful what you download from individuals. Never open an e-mail or download a file unless you know the source of the document. Keep a good anti-virus program and a good spyware program on your computer, and keep these updated.

Be safe — NEVER give away any personal information on the Internet (your name, age, address, phone number).

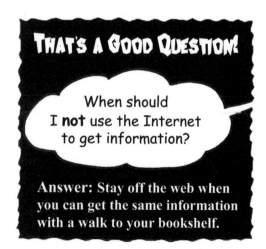

THAT'S A GOOD QUESTION!

When should I **not** use the Internet to get information?

Answer: Stay off the web when you can get the same information with a walk to your bookshelf.

Good Stuff on the Web

The Internet has wonderful social studies facts, explanations, and discussions, all available for your use if you know where to look. There are hundreds of good sites. Check out a few of these to find fascinating information related to culture, society, geography, economics, civics, or history.

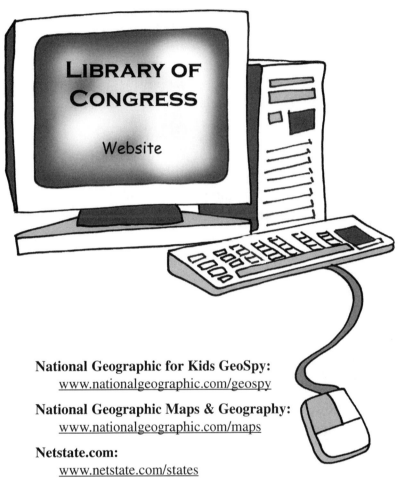

American Memory, Library of Congress:
www.memory.loc.gov

American Museum of Natural History, Ology:
www.ology.amnh.org

Angelfire Hands On History:
www.angelfire.com/ma4/handsonhistory

Atlapedia Online (World Maps Online):
www.atlapedia.com

BBC History for Kids:
www.bbc.co.uk/history/forkids

Ben's Guide to U.S. Government for Kids:
www.bensguide.gpo.gov

CIA Kids Page:
www.cia.gov/cia/ciakids

CIA Kids Page History:
www.cia.gov/cia/ciakids/history

FirstGov for Kids:
www.kids.gov

Geography 4 Kids:
www.geography4kids.com

History Channel:
www.historychannel.com

H4K (History for Kids):
www.historyforkids.org

Infoplease.com:
www.infoplease.com

The Internet Public Library: States Facts:
www.ipl.org/div/kidspace/stateknow

Library of Congress Geography & Maps:
www.lcweb.loc.gov/rr/geogmap

NASA's Visible Earth:
www.visibleearth.nasa.gov

National Geographic Kids:
www.nationalgeographic.com/kids

National Geographic for Kids GeoSpy:
www.nationalgeographic.com/geospy

National Geographic Maps & Geography:
www.nationalgeographic.com/maps

Netstate.com:
www.netstate.com/states

Smithsonian Institute:
www.si.edu

U.S. Geological Survey Education Site:
www.usgs.gov/education

U.S. Census Bureau Fact Finder Kids' Corner:
www.factfinder.census.gov/home/en/kids/kids.html

U.S. Mint Site for Kids:
www.usmint.gov/kids

U.S. Treasury for Kids:
www.ustreas.gov/kids

The United Nations:
www.un.org

Welcome to the White House:
www.whitehouse.gov

Get Serious About Study Skills

Let's face it–good learning and good grades don't happen without some sharp study skills. Take advantage of every opportunity you get to strengthen skills such as those described on pages 44–58.

Better Listening

Keep your ears wide open! You can increase your understanding of social studies facts and concepts if you listen well. Here are some tips for smart listening. They can help you get involved with the information instead of letting it buzz by your ears.

1. Realize that the information is important.

Here's what you can get when you listen to someone who is giving you information about social studies:

. . . details about a social studies concept or event

. . . help answering social studies questions

. . . examples of projects done correctly

. . . difficulties you might face when completing a social studies project

. . . meanings of terms used in social studies questions or assignments

. . . directions for certain assignments

Get Set Tip #4
Stop talking!
(You can't listen
while you talk.)

I listened
well!

2. Be aware of the obstacles to good listening.

Know ahead of time that these will interfere with your ability to listen well. Try to avoid them, change them, or manage them, so they don't get in the way.

. . . tiredness . . . wandering attention

. . . surrounding noise . . . too many things to hear at once

. . . uncomfortable setting . . . missing the beginning or ending

. . . talking . . . personal thoughts or worries

3. Make a commitment to improve.

You can't always control all obstacles (such as the comfort of the setting or the quality of the speaker's presentation), but there are things you can control. Put these to work to gain more from your listening.

Get enough rest.

Do your best to be comfortable while you listen.

Cut out distractions. Keep your mind focused on what is being said.

Look directly at the speaker.

Take notes. Write down examples that the speaker gives.

As the speaker talks, think of examples or relate the information to your life.

Pay special attention to opening and closing remarks, and anything that is repeated

Careful Reading

There is plenty of reading in social studies. Textbooks and other materials explain concepts and processes. Many social studies lessons include details from lists, maps, charts, graphs, or captions that you need to read closely and interpret. All social studies questions or assignments include some sort of instructions to follow.

Before you read a social studies article or assignment, have a clear idea of the purpose for reading.

Are you reading to find directions for the assignment?

Are you reading to gain general understanding of a concept?

Are you reading to answer a question?

Are you reading to find a particular fact?

You can accomplish some purposes by skimming quickly. For other purposes, you need to read closely, paying attention to every detail. In some cases you may need to read the information more than once—possibly even several times.

> **Latin America** is a broad region that includes land on two continents and many islands. Mexico, Central America, and the Caribbean islands (all of North America), and all the countries on the continent of South America are part of the region.
>
> The name "Latin America" comes from the name of the language spoken in ancient Rome. Spanish and Portuguese are two languages that developed from the ancient Latin. In the 1500s, Spain and Portugal started many colonies in the region, bringing their languages with them. Because of the Latin languages spoken, this region became known as Latin America.
>
> This region is a land of varied landscapes. The longest mountain range in the world, the Andes, runs down the west side of South America. The Amazon River system drains thousands of miles in South America. In addition to mountains and river plains, "Latin America" is a region of tropical islands, rainforests, and vast grasslands.

Skimming — By skimming the passage, a reader can quickly gain the main ideas:

- *Latin America includes land on two continents and several islands.*
- *The region's names come from the languages spoken there.*
- *The region has a variety of landscapes.*

Reading Closely — With closer, slower reading, the reader will discover specific details, such as:

- *the places included in the region*
- *the origin of the name "Latin America"*
- *some of the languages spoken in the region*
- *the time period of colonization*
- *the name of the major mountain range*
- *the name of the major river*
- *some kinds of land in Latin America*

It is interesting to read about skateboarding legend and my hero, Tony Hawk.

Summarizing & Paraphrasing

WHAT'S THE DIFFERENCE?

Hey Marty! I have to **summarize** some stuff for economics class. Then, I'm supposed to write a **paraphrase** of the information, too. What's the difference between a **summary** and a **paraphrase**?

Well, Joe, a summary is a short statement of the **MAIN IDEAS** of something (such as a speech, movie, or piece of writing).

A paraphrase is a restatement of someone else's ideas in your own words. It covers **ALL** the ideas from the original statement.

Can You Trade Your Dollars for Gold?

The U.S. dollar used to be backed by gold and the country's money system was called the *gold standard*. This was a system of currency in which paper money can be exchanged for a fixed amount of gold. The purpose for this system was to be sure that the money was worth something.

As the U.S. government and economy got stronger, the money was strengthened also. The need for gold to back the money was not so strong. So, the United States gave up the gold standard in 1971. Without the gold standard, the amount of money in circulation does not have to depend on the amount of gold in storage.

The U.S. government still has billions of dollars worth of gold. It is stored at Fort Knox, Kentucky, in a bomb-proof building. Alarm systems and many armed guards keep the building and gold secure. No one has ever broken into Fort Knox.

There was a time when you could bring your paper money to a bank and exchange it for gold; but that time is gone!

Summary:

At one time, the U.S. dollar was backed by a gold standard, where each dollar was worth a fixed amount of gold. Though the government still has billions of dollars worth of gold, the gold-backed system is no longer in use.

Paraphrase:

The United States had a money system that used gold to back each dollar. To assure the value of the paper money, it could be exchanged at a bank for a fixed amount of gold. As the government and economy grew stronger, the need for a gold-backed system disappeared. The gold standard ended in 1971. Even though the gold standard is gone, the government still keeps billions of dollars worth of gold in heavily-guarded storage at Fort Knox, KY.

Now the amount of money in circulation is not related to the amount of gold the government has. You can no longer trade your dollars for gold at a bank.

Better Grades & Higher Test Scores / SOCIAL STUDIES gr. 4–6
Copyright ©2005 by Incentive Publications, Inc., Nashville, TN.

Outlining

An outline is a way to organize ideas or information into main ideas and supporting details. If you want to get set to improve as a student, it's a good idea to polish your outlining skills. An outline can be formal or informal. It can contain single words, phrases, or sentences—depending on its purpose. You will find outlining very helpful for many study situations.

You can use an outline to:
- organize ideas to prepare a speech
- organize ideas for a piece of writing
- plan a project
- record and review information from a textbook
- get ready to re-tell a story
- take notes in class
- take notes from a textbook assignment
- prepare to give or write a report
- write a story
- write a speech
- study a passage

I wrote this outline as I read a section from my geography textbook.

Writing the outline also helped me process and remember the information.

Doing the outline helped me find the main points in the assignment.

Scandinavia

I. What is Scandinavia?
   A. Countries on Scandinavian Peninsula, Jutland Peninsula, and surrounding area
   B. Norway, Sweden, Denmark, Finland, Iceland

II. Physical Geography
   A. Rugged mountains
   B. Long coastlines, lakes, fjords
   C. Cold climate
   D. Scarce resources

III. History
   A. Warlike people
   B. Vikings
      1. Skilled shipbuilders
      2. Raided other areas in Europe
   C. After Vikings, turned to farming, fishing

IV. People
   A. Live in or near small cities
   B. Close-knit families
   C. Similar languages throughout region

V. Economy
   A. Diverse
      1. Oil
      2. Lumber
      3. Fishing and farming
      4. Crafts—wood products
   B. Known for cooperatives
   C. High standard of living

VI. Government
   A. Sweden, Norway, Denmark—Constitutional Monarchies
   B. Iceland, Finland—Republics
   C. Welfare states

Taking Notes

Knowing how to take notes and use them well is an important study skill. If you are trying to improve as a student, good notes taken from classes and from reading will help you. A lot of learning goes on while you're taking notes. You may not even realize it's happening!

When you take notes . . .

1. You naturally listen better. (You have to listen in order to get the information and write it down!)

2. You listen differently, so you naturally learn and understand the material better. Taking notes forces you to focus on what is being said or read.

3. You sort through the information and decide what to write. This means you naturally think about the material and process it—making it more likely that you will remember it.

4. The actual act of writing the notes fixes the information more firmly in your brain.

5. You end up with good notes in your notebook. When you can actually look at written examples of definitions, facts, events, processes, or characteristics, you are way ahead in your efforts to review and remember important information.

Here's the basic process for taking notes:

1. Listen or read for a main idea, key formula, or important process. Write it down.

2. Write examples, problems, definitions, and details to support each key idea.

3. Review your notes. This will help to fix the information in your mind.

Tips for Wise Note Taking

. . . in class

- When the class begins, write the topic for the day at the top of a clean page.

- Write the date at the top of the page.

- Use an erasable pen for clear notes, not a pencil.

- Record examples of situations or problems.

- Write notes to yourself about explanations for different events or situations.

- Write neatly so you can read your notes later.

- Leave a big margin to the left of the outline. Use this space to mark important items or write key words.

- Leave a blank space after each main idea section.

- Pay close attention to the opening and closing remarks.

- Listen more than you write.

- ASK about anything you do not understand.

Get Set Tip #6

When you take notes in class, watch for signals from the teacher about important ideas. Write down anything the speaker (or teacher). . .
. . . writes on the board.
. . . gives as a definition.
. . . emphasizes with his/her voice.
. . . repeats.
. . . says is important.

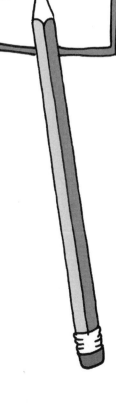

. . . from a textbook assignment

- Skim through one section at a time to get the general idea. (Use the textbook divisions as a guide to separate sections, or read a few paragraphs at a time.)

- After skimming, go back and write down the main ideas.

- Write a few supporting details or examples for each main idea. If a social studies term, event, or concept is explained, write down a summary of the explanation or a correct example.

- Notice bold or emphasized words or phrases. Write these down with definitions.

- Read captions under pictures. Pay attention to facts, tables, charts, graphs, and pictures, and the explanations that go along with them. If information is very important, put it in your notes.

- Don't write too little. You won't have all the main points or enough examples.

- Don't write too much. You won't have time or interest in reviewing the notes.

Preparing a Report

Students are always being asked to do a report of some kind. When you hear the word, you might immediately think of a book report or a long written paper. But there are many kinds of reports. They can be papers, posters, demonstrations, speeches, audio or visual presentations, computer projects, or art projects (to name a few). They can be assigned for any subject area to cover just about any topic.

Whatever the subject or the type, reports all have some things in common. First, you need some raw material (facts and information) as the basis for the report. To get that, you need to do some research. Then, for any report, you must select and organize the information so that it can be communicated. Finally, a report is presented. This means you need to find a way to share with someone else what you learned about the topic.

Here are some steps to follow for any report of any kind on any topic. Page 53 gives some suggestions for creative or out-of-the ordinary kinds of reports. This will get you thinking beyond the standard written report.

Step 1: Choose a topic.

Your topic might be assigned, but usually you will have some choice. There are dozens of possibilities within any one subject or topic. When you do have a choice, follow these tips.
- Pick something that interests you.
- Make sure your topic is not too broad. If it is, there will be too much information to manage.
- Make sure your topic is not too narrow. If it is, you won't be able to find enough information to create a substantial report.

> I've chosen a topic that interests me.

Don't choose a topic that is. . .
too broad: Settlements in America
too narrow: The Last Railroad Spike
Choose a topic that is just right:
The Westward Movement in America

The Westward Movement

I. Railroads
   A. Need for transcontinental railroad
   B. Process of building the railroad
   C. Last spike - Promontory Point, UT
   D. Changes resulting from railroad

II. Indian Wars
   A. Reasons for wars
   B. Move of Indians to reservations
   C. Unrest after resettlement

III. Western Settlements & economy
   A. Miners
   B. Cattle drives from Texas to east
   C. Homestead Act (1862)

Step 2: Identify the subtopics.

- Make a list of subtopics.
- For each subtopic, note details you will need to find to explain or support that subtopic. Ask:
   What do I need to know about this topic?
   What kinds of details should I learn or understand?
- You might use a rough outline for this step.

50

Step 3: Find information.

- Use as many resources as you can to find solid information on your topic. Don't limit yourself to just one source or one kind of source.

- As you observe, read, or listen to the sources, take notes. Write ideas, key words or phrases, and examples. Use a separate note card for each source and each major idea or fact you find. Use your subtopics as labels for the cards.

> **Changes Resulting From Railroads**
>
> The completion of transcontinental railroad made travel across America much more possible. It enabled people to hurry west to take part in the Gold Rush.
>
> Sour

> **Transcontinental Railroad**
>
> 1869 - Building of the first transcontinental railroad
> - The Golden Spike put in where railroads met in Promotory, Utah.
>
> S

> **Cattle Drives**
> Late 1800s - Cowboys rounded up Texas Longhorn cattle for drives to Abilene, Kansas. Cows were shipped from there by rail to east coast markets.
>
> Source: Beyer, Barry, et al. _United States and Its Neighbors_

> On each card write the source of the information.

Step 4: Organize the information.

- Organize the information by grouping your cards into subtopics and placing them in a logical sequence. Decide what fits where.

- If you have too much information, or if some of your information doesn't quite fit, this is the time to eliminate it.

- If you have subtopics that are not well supported with examples or details, this is the time to do more research and collect more information.

Step 5: Decide on the format.

- If you have been asked to write a paper or give a speech, then the format is already decided.

- If you are free to choose a format or product, do this now.

- How will you show what you have learned? Will it be a paper, a speech, a demonstration, a dance, a musical production, a broadcast, an interview, a painting, a slide show, a mime?

- Decide now! The steps you follow from this point depend greatly on the format you choose.

Step 6: Put the report together.

- If your report will be spoken or written, you will begin writing sentences and paragraphs, making sure each paragraph covers a subtopic with supporting details.

- If your report follows a different format, you still need to decide how to communicate each idea and its supporting examples or details.

Step 7: Review and edit your work.

- This is the time to look at your work. This is also a time to ask someone else to give you a response. (Exactly how you review the work will depend on the format of the report.)
- Ask questions such as these about the "rough draft" of your report, whatever form it takes:

  Are the main ideas covered?
  Is the information clear?
  Is the information complete?
  Does the manner of presentation make sense?
  Does the report have a clear introduction and conclusion?
  Is there a logical order for the presentation?
  Is the material interesting? Is the presentation interesting?
  If written, does the piece flow along well?
  If written, are the mechanics and grammar correct?

- After you and another person (or persons) have reviewed it, make revisions that are necessary.

> ### Get Set Tip #7
> Avoid these common problems with reports:
> ✓ topic too broad
> ✓ topic too narrow
> ✓ missing some subtopics
> ✓ not enough information on some subtopics
> ✓ poor presentation of final report

Step 8: Put the final product together.

- Whatever the format, this is the time to prepare the final product. Add extra materials at this stage (drawings, diagrams, charts, maps, graphs, timelines, tables, surveys, music, etc).

Step 9: Present the report.

- How will you share the information? Turn it in? Hang it up? Sing it? Dance it? Show it? Read it? Perform it? Mail it? Publish it? This is the time to do it!

Creative Reporting

There are many ways a report can be structured and shared. It might take a little creativity (or a lot), but nearly any information can be presented in a number of different or unexpected ways. Here are just a few options for preparing and giving a report or presentation of your work.

Written or Spoken Reports

- clues to unravel a mystery
- phrases cut from magazines
- fictionalized account of an event
- book of crossword puzzles
- series of interview questions
- radio or TV broadcast
- series of riddles
- cause-effect account
- group of short poems
- series of e-mails

- The Fact Book About ____
- The ABC Book of ____
- Things You've Never Heard About ___
- A Top 10 List of ____
- 10 Facts & 10 Fables About ____
- A Day In the Life of ____
- The Truth About ____
- Myths About ____ Debunked
- 20 Questions & Answers About ____
- Strange & Amazing Facts About ____
- Future Predictions About ____

- viewpoint
- differing viewpoints
- one or more letters
- editorial
- diary entries
- narrative poem
- timeline
- protest
- dialogue
- argument

Reports That Combine Writing and Art

- children's picture book
- advertisement
- original CD
- travel brochure
- one or more maps
- cartoons
- timeline
- original game
- original songs or an album
- book cover
- music album cover
- slide presentation
- instructive poster
- *How-To* Handbook
- video presentation
- illustrated guide book
- word & picture collage
- illustrated dictionary of terms

I used my collection of baseball cards as part of my presentation on the history of baseball.

BASEBALL HALL OF FAME

Other Reports:
mime performance
dance
drawings or paintings
campaign speech
3-D model
series of recipes
demonstration
drama
plan for reality TV show
scavenger hunt
sculpture
rap performance

How to Prepare for a Test

Good test preparation does **not** begin the night before the test. The time to get ready for a test starts long before this night. Here are some tips to help you get ready—weeks before the test and right up to test time.

1. **Start your test preparation at the beginning of the year—or at least as soon as the material is first taught in the class.**

   The purpose of a test is to give a picture of what you are learning. That learning doesn't start the night before the test. It starts when you start attending the class. Think of test preparation this way, and you'll be less overwhelmed or nervous about an upcoming test.

   You'll be much better prepared for a test *(even one that is several days or weeks away)* if you . . .

   > *. . . pay attention in class.*

   > *. . . work out sample problems.*

   > *. . . keep your notes and class handouts organized.*

   > *. . . read all your assignments.*

   > *. . . do your homework regularly.*

   > *. . . make up any work you miss when you're absent.*

   > *. . . ask questions in class about anything you don't understand.*

   > *. . . review notes and handouts regularly.*

2. **Once you know the date of the test, make a study plan.**

   - Look over your schedule and plan time to start organizing and reviewing material.

   - Allow plenty of time to go through all the material.

   - Your brain will retain more if you review it a few times and spread the studying out over several days.

3. **Get all the information you can about the test.**

   - Record everything the teacher says about the test.

   - Get clear about what material will be covered.

   - If you can, find out about the format of the test.

   - Make sure you get all study guides the teacher distributes.

   - Make sure you listen well to any in-class reviews.

The big test on all of South America is next Friday. I'll review each country's history on Tuesday night, summarize their economics and natural resources on Wednesday, and study the geography on Thursday.

I'm confident I'll do well on the test.

4. Use your study time effectively.

Dos & Don'ts

Do gather and organize all your notes and handouts.

Do review your text. Pay attention to bold words, bold statements, and examples, operations, or problems.

Do identify the kinds of problems in the section being tested; practice solving a few of each kind.

Do review the questions at the end of text sections; practice answering them.

Do review the study guides provided by the teacher.

Do review any previous quizzes on the same material.

Do make study guides and aids for yourself.

Do make sets of cards with key vocabulary words, terms and definitions, main concepts, and types of problems.

Do ask someone (reliable) to quiz you on the main points and terms.

Don't spend your study time blankly staring at your notebook or mindlessly leafing through your textbook.

Don't study with someone else unless doing so with that person actually helps you learn material better.

Don't study in blocks of time so long that you get tired, bored, or distracted.

5. Get yourself and your supplies ready.

Do these things the night before the test (not too late):

Gather all the supplies you need for taking the test (good pencils with erasers, erasable pens, scratch paper, calculator with batteries).

Put these supplies in your school bag.

Gather your study guides, notes, and text into your school bag.

Get a good night of rest.

In the morning:

Eat a healthy breakfast.

Look over your study guides and note card reminders.

Relax, and be confident that your preparation will pay off.

I'm so ready for this test!

How to Take a Test

Before the test begins . . .

- Have supplies ready: take sharpened pencils, scratch paper, calculator, and eraser.

- Try to get a little exercise before class to help you relax.

- Go to the bathroom and get a drink.

- Arrive at the class on time (or a bit early).

- Get settled into your seat; get your supplies out.

- If there is time, you might glance over your study guides while you wait.

- To relax, take some deep breaths; exhale slowly.

When you get the test . . .

- Put your name on all pages.

- Before you write anything, scan over the test to see how long it is, what kinds of questions it has, and generally what it includes.

- Think about your time and quickly plan how much time you can spend on each section.

- Read each set of directions twice. Circle key words in the directions.

- Answer all the short-answer questions. Do not leave any blanks.

- If you are not sure of an answer, make a smart guess.

- Don't change an answer unless you are absolutely sure it is wrong.

Get Set Tip #9
Research shows that your first answer is correct more often that not. So stick with it unless you are positive about another answer.

Josie is not sure of the answer, so she makes a smart guess. She puts an **X** by the question so she will remember to come back to it later.

When she comes back to the question, she is still not sure, so she stays with her first answer.

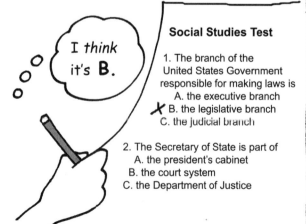

Get Set: Study Skills

Better Grades & Higher Test Scores / SOCIAL STUDIES gr. 4–6

More Test-Taking Tips

Tips for Answering Multiple Choice Questions

Multiple choice questions give you several answers from which to choose.

- Read the question twice.
- Before you look at the choices, close your eyes and answer the question. Then, look for that answer.
- Read all the choices before you circle one.
- If you are not absolutely sure, cross out answers that are obviously incorrect.
- Choose the answer that is most complete or most accurate.
- Or, choose an answer that has not been ruled out.
- Do not change an answer unless you are positive about the correct answer.

Tips for Answering Matching Questions

Matching questions ask you to recognize facts or definitions in one column that correspond to facts, definitions, answers, or descriptions in a second column.

- Read both columns to get familiar with the choices.
- Do the easy matches first.
- Cross off answers as you use them.
- Match the leftover items last.
- If you do not know the answer, make a smart guess.

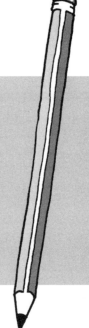

Tips for Answering Fill-in-the Blank Questions

Fill-in-the-blank questions ask you to write a word that completes the sentence.

- Read each question. Answer it the best you can.
- If you don't know an answer, **X** the question and go on to the ones you do know.
- Go back to the **X**'d questions. If you don't know the exact answer, write a similar word or definition—come as close as you can.
- If you have no idea of the answer, make a smart guess.

Tips for Answering True-False Questions

True-False questions ask you to tell whether a statement is true or false.

- Watch for words like *most, some,* and *often.*
  Usually statements with these words are TRUE.
- Watch for words like *all, always, only, none, nobody,* and *never.*
  Usually statements with these words are FALSE.
- If any part of a statement is false, then the item is FALSE.

Even More Test-Taking Tips

Tips for Answering Essay Questions

Essay questions ask you to write a short answer (usually a few paragraphs) about a subject.

- Make sure you are clear about what the question is asking.
- Think ahead to your answer. Sketch a rough outline of the main points you will make and details supporting each point.
- Write an introduction which briefly states a summarized version of your answer.
- Write a body that states the main ideas clearly.
- Reinforce each main idea with details and examples.
- Write a summarizing sentence that restates the main idea.

Tips for Answering Reading Comprehension Tests

Reading comprehension tests ask you to read a piece of writing and answer questions about it.

- Read through the questions before you read the passage.
- Keep the questions in mind as you read the passage.
- Read each question carefully.
- Skim back through the passage to look for key words that are related to the question.
- Reread that section carefully.
- Eliminate any answers that cannot be correct.
- Choose the correct answer.

Get Set Tip #10

On all questions, on all tests—
always read
the directions twice.

I know this!

58

Get Set: Study Skills

GET SHARP →

on

CULTURE & SOCIETY

Culture

Culture is the way of life of a group of people—a system of their values, beliefs, habits of conduct, and material goods. Every society is composed of one or more cultures. The term *nonmaterial culture* refers to the beliefs, values, and behaviors of a society. *Material culture* refers to the things that are created by a society.

Influences on Culture

These are some of the factors that affect the way a culture develops or changes:

- geography (things such as weather, climate, latitude, altitude, landforms, rivers and other water)
- availability of natural resources
- availability of food
- political boundaries
- natural disasters
- migrations
- neighboring countries
- wars or other conflicts
- technology and inventions
- past experiences of the society

Some Things to Know About Culture

- Culture is a set of learned behaviors. Older members of the culture pass it on to the younger generation.

- Families, groups, and institutions play a part in passing on culture.

- Many different influences help to shape a culture.

- Culture is expressed in many different ways. These expressions are called *traits*.

- Cultures differ from each other in many ways.

- Cultures are similar to each other in many ways.

- Cultures often cross political or national lines.

- Most nations include different cultural groups.

- Current expressions of culture are affected by the culture's history.

- Cultures borrow from, share with, and spread traits to other cultures.

- Cultures benefit from communication and interaction with different cultures.

Welcome to the Culture Cafe

The United States is a nation influenced by many cultures. Dozens of different languages are spoken in America. The English language borrows many words from other languages.

ORDER HERE:

I'll have the cheese souffle, pie a la mode, and two enchiladas.

MENU

In some cultures, people revere cows. In other cultures, people eat them.

I'll have the hamburger sandwich, but hold the beef.

MENU

More Things to Know About Culture

Enculturation is the process by which members of a group learn the culture. As children grow up in a culture, they learn the cultural patterns and behaviors by watching, listening, and imitating.

Diffusion is the process by which cultural traits and patterns spread from one society to another.

Acculturation is the process that takes place when cultures having contact with each other exchange or blend patterns of the two cultures.

Assimilation is the process by which people give up the ways of their culture and become part of a different culture.

Civilization generally refers to a culture or society that has advanced social systems such as political, economic, governmental, and educational systems.

A **subculture** is a group within a culture that holds to beliefs and behaviors that are a variation of the wider culture's beliefs and behaviors.

International culture describes a situation in which cultural traditions extend beyond the boundaries of one nation.

Multiculturalism describes a situation in which a society includes many different, distinct cultures.

Pop culture (popular culture) is the part of culture that is expressed in its current arts and entertainment. This includes such things as television, radio, sports, music, visual and performing arts, fashion, fads, hobbies, leisure activities, movies, and other media.

Cultural lag is the process that takes place when certain parts of a culture don't keep up with the changes in the rest of the culture.

Cultural relativism is the idea that one culture should not be judged by the rules of another culture.

Culture shock is the discomfort people feel when they come into contact with an unfamiliar culture.

Ethnocentrism is the attitude that one culture is superior to other cultures.

Due to *cutural diffusion*, Russians can buy French fries and American-style fast food from restaurants in Moscow.

Emil's mom experiences *culture shock* every time she comes in contact with her son's *subculture*. She can't get used to his slang, music, and fashions.

Members of some Amish groups in the U.S. don't use motor-powered vehicles for transportation. This is an example of *cultural lag*.

Patterns & Expressions of Culture

There are thousands of different expressions of culture—endless varieties of behaviors.
These are some of the categories or traits that are examples of cultural behaviors or systems:

architecture
art
beliefs and values
celebrations
childcare practices
clothing for everyday life
clothing for special occasions
customs
dance, drama, and theater
economic systems
entertainment
fads
family structure
fashions
forms and uses of money
forms of entertainment
forms of power, rule, or authority
funeral and burial customs
hobbies
holidays
institutions and organizations
inventions
kinds of homes and shelter
kinds of technology
kinds of work
languages
laws and rules
leisure activities
music
patterns of movement
political systems
religious systems
rituals
rules and laws
symbols
taboos
traditions

ways of eating
ways of getting goods
ways of keeping safe
ways of learning and teaching
ways of preparing food
ways of providing services
ways of settling disputes
ways of travel
wedding customs
wedding ceremonies

Get Sharp Tip #1
Anthropology is the study of human cultures.
Archaeology is the study of past cultures.

In some cultures, it is a form of entertainment to charm snakes.

Ancient Egyptians practiced the custom of mummifying dead people to safeguard their souls in the afterlife.

Sometimes cats and other pets were mummified also, but probably not snakes.

62

Some cultural patterns defined . . .

Symbol — an object that represents an idea, event, or concept important to a culture.

Customs — patterns of behavior that are common to a culture or society.

Mores — customs or patterns of behavior that are extremely strong or that result in strong punishment if they are violated.

Taboo — the prohibition of a certain behavior, under threat of serious punishment; an act or behavior that is strictly forbidden.

Totem — an object that is honored or revered by members of a group because it represents something sacred or special about the group.

The totem is often an animal or plant. A symbol of the totem is sometimes engraved or painted on a mask or totem pole, or tattooed on the body.

Rituals — ceremonies and other events or behaviors that are significant to a culture.

Rituals are repeated regularly, generally according to some schedule. Rituals are often connected to religious beliefs or practices. They also are used to commemorate special events in the lives of the citizens. Birthdays, wedding ceremonies, religious confirmations, baby dedications, baptisms, and funerals are examples of rituals.

Rite of passage — a special ritual or ceremony that celebrates the transition from childhood to adulthood for members of the society.

Some Middle Eastern cultures have a taboo against women uncovering their faces or other parts of their bodies in public.

Hindus believe that the Ganges River is sacred. Many perform a ritual of bathing in the river to purify their bodies and souls.

All nations have a flag, which is a symbol of the country. Often the flag itself contains colors or icons which symbolize some value or characteristic of the country.

The flag of the island nation of Kiribati has blue and white bands that represent the Pacific Ocean. The bird flying above the rising sun is said to symbolize strength and power at sea. The bird is taken from the nation's coat of arms.

Totem poles include many symbols. They are often created to symbolize the history, status, or rights of a family, tribe, or clan.

Cultural Interactions

Many different influences help to shape the traits (characteristics) of a culture. Cultures are constantly developed and changed by interactions with the land, the climate, the past, new technological development, and exposure to other cultures. As a culture develops, it may also affect other cultures or bring changes to the land its people occupy. Here are a few examples of the ways cultures develop certain traits, change due to a particular influence, affect the environment, or influence other cultures.

Encountering Culture

Different cultures meet a need in similar ways.

Example:
All over the world, people carry babies in backpacks, front packs, and slings. Though the style and fabric may differ, parents of many cultures have found a similar answer to the need of carrying a small child while leaving their hands free to do other tasks.

Different cultures develop different ways of meeting a need.

Example:
Some Australians greet each other affectionately by sticking out their tongues. In America or China, such a greeting would be considered rude, embarrassing, or insulting. In those cultures, people greet each other with other gestures, such as a bow, a kiss, a handshake, or a hug.

A culture develops customs that honor its historical heritage.

Example:
There are two official languages in the Canadian province of Quebec: French and English. This honors the area's heritage, which was settled by people of both cultures.

A social situation sometimes leads a culture to develop a custom or set of behaviors.

Example:
In some African cultures, people stretch their lips by wearing a large disc inside the edge of the mouth. The practice is said to have developed to keep neighboring cultures from taking these people as slaves.

A cultural group assimilates the ways of a new (different) culture.

Example:
For centuries, arranged marriages have been a custom in some cultures of India. Many people of these cultures who live in America have relaxed these rules. This allows young people to choose their own mates, as is the usual custom in America.

The physical geography of an area contributes to the culture's economy.

Example:
Thrill-seeking tourists come to Venezuela to parachute off the top of Angel Falls, the world's highest waterfall. These tourists spend money in the country, helping Venezuela's economy.

A culture develops behaviors in response to the geographic environment.

Example:
In the high Andes Mountains, the geography is too rough for transporting goods with vehicles. Peruvian Indians have adapted to the problem by using llamas to carry goods and supplies around the rocky terrain.

Example:
In wet jungle areas of South America, some people build their riverside homes on stilts to protect them from rising water.

Example:
Many inhabitants of northern Africa wear long, loose clothing to keep cool and a head covering (called a *kaffiyeh*) to shield them from the hot desert sun.

A culture meets some of its needs by making use of natural resources.

Example:
The tundra of Siberia is a natural habitat for reindeer. Because of this, the people of the area hitch sleds to reindeer for transportation. Reindeer meat and skin also provide clothing, food, and shelter for the people.

The natural resources of an area contribute to the culture's economy.

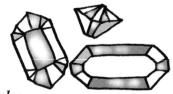

Example:
Rare pink diamonds and beautiful opals are found in fields and mines of Australia. The country's economy benefits from worldwide sale of these precious and semi-precious stones.

Example:
The economies of many middle Eastern nations are based on the selling of oil. The area is rich in this natural resource, and provides much of the world's oil supply.

A culture's economic needs or wants sometimes harm or deplete natural resources.

Example:
For many years, forests around the world have been cut for timber sales. People use the wood to build homes or other structures. As a result of the cutting, the natural habitat of some species (such as the panda bear) is shrinking. This loss of habitat even threatens the survival of some species.

Example:
Poaching (illegal hunting) is decreasing the number of tigers and other animals, such as orangutans. The poachers make money by selling young orangutans for pets or selling the tiger skins for decorations.

A culture's behavior can cause changes in the environment over a small or large area.

Example:
When rain forests are cut for lumber to build dwellings or to sell timber to other countries, the ecology of the area and of the entire globe changes. Erosion increases in the local area, causing loss of valuable soil and changing rivers and streams. Habitat is lost for many species of plants and animals. In addition, global temperatures are affected.

Example:
A culture may build dams on rivers as a way to use running water to generate electricity at a good price for large numbers of customers. Dam building causes many changes. Some of these are: changes in the flow of rivers, flooding of river valleys, creation of lakes, interference with migration of fish, change in fish habitat, change in economic practices (such as fishing) that took place on the river.

New technology changes the way of life in a culture.

Example:

In recent years, lumber mills in the Pacific Northwest of the United States have become so automated that fewer people are needed to do the work which many mill workers used to do. As a result, many mill workers have lost their jobs.

Example:

Digital technology makes it possible to take a picture in China, scan and print it with a computer, and send it by the Internet to Argentina in a matter of seconds.

A culture's need leads to the development of new technology.

Example:

People in the British Isles and on the European mainland across the English Channel had a need for transportation across the channel that was faster than boats. So they built the *Chunnel*, a tunnel beneath the English Channel. Using the *Chunnel*, a high speed *Eurostar* train can take a passenger from Paris to London in just three hours.

New technology can contribute to a culture in a harmful way.

Oops! Gotta go! I think I need to call 911!

CRASH! CRUNCH!!

Example:

An increasing number of auto accidents are occurring because people are using cell phones while they drive.

New technology can make positive contributions to a culture's development.

Example:

Since the invention of the jet airplane, people in different cultures living thousands of miles apart are able to visit and interact with one another with a relatively short travel time.

Example:

Water purification technology supplies clean water to many cultures, reducing health problems. This improves people's lives, decreases the death rates, and boosts the economy.

Societies & Social Groups

A *society* is a nation, community, or other broad group of people with common institutions and traditions. Every society has a number of smaller groupings within it. *Socialization* is the process by which one learns to adapt to the behavior patterns of the surrounding society.

A *social group* is a number of individuals that have some sort of common relationship, purpose, or interest. In a social group, two or more people interact or identify with each other. Members in most social groups share a common purpose that involves personal contact that will be repeated or ongoing. In other groups, there is a shared characteristic, but the group members do not necessarily have contact with one another. There are literally thousands of different kinds of social groups within a society.

Some Examples of Social Groups

- members of the International Star Trek Fan Association
- women attending a Mothers of Triplets Association meeting
- flute players in the Boston Symphony Orchestra
- members of the Albany, NY, Chamber of Commerce
- members of the Community Church in a town in Ohio
- members of the Brown University women's soccer team
- members of a particular rap singer's fan club
- members of the American Birding Association
- engineers in the design department at a car company
- the computer club at Asheville Middle School
- the film crew on a movie
- competitors at a dance contest
- a neighborhood homeowners' association
- member countries in the United Nations
- fans of the Tennessee Titans football team
- a bridge club in Norwich, Vermont
- people at a family reunion
- the staff in a doctor's office
- teachers at North Shore High School
- Arizona's state legislators
- the U.S. Olympic Committee
- your family
- a city police force's SWAT team
- Mr. Wilson's sixth grade history class
- the Crater High School marching band
- members of a SCUBA diving class in Santa Barbara

I'm a flute-playing, football-loving, scuba-diving, ballet-dancing, soccer-playing, bird-watching, Star Trek-loving triplet.

Social Roles

During each person's life, he or she will belong to many social groups. In every group, each individual plays or fills some kind of *role* or part in the group. Different roles serve different purposes in groups. There are numerous roles, and they vary from group to group. In many groups, there are differing levels of responsibility or power. Often, one or more individuals fill some kind of leadership or authority role. At any one time in your life, you will probably be a member of several groups, filling several different roles.

Meet Max

Max is a guitar player and the lead singer in a band that he formed with three friends. He writes most of the music for the band. He is an eighth grader at Lone Pine Middle School, where he belongs to a chess club. One afternoon a week, he volunteers to tutor younger kids in math. Besides music, his hobbies include skateboarding, wakeboarding, and snowboarding. He is a member of the school's snowboard team. Max is the oldest of four children. He lives with his mom and stepdad (and two cats) and visits his dad on weekends. As often as possible, he reads to his blind grandfather.

What are my roles right now, you might ask? Hmmm, let's see . . .
son
stepson
brother
grandson
band leader
guitar player
songwriter
student
tutor
team member
athlete
pet owner
volunteer

My roles right now? Let's see . . .
mother
wife
sister
aunt
daughter-in-law
accountant
board member
cook
housekeeper
caretaker
volunteer
pet lover
teacher
church member
athlete
knitter

Pardon me if I knit and run!

Meet Caroline

Caroline works as an accountant for a large accounting firm. She serves on the company's social committee. She donates ten hours a month to handle finances for a local animal shelter. Caroline has three children and she is an aunt to her sister's boys. She serves on the local school board and helps to take care of her husband's aged parents. Along with her husband, she cooks and takes care of the family's house. In her free time, Caroline runs in marathons and teaches knitting classes at her church.

Institutions

An ***institution*** is a particular set of organizations, patterns, customs, groups, or activities that meets the basic needs of a society. The social institutions of a society are some of its most important features. You might think of an institution as a school or a bank, but sociologists (scientists who study the patterns of human social interaction) describe institutions in a wider way. They have identified five basic categories of institutions that exist in all societies. The purpose of these institutions is to satisfy the basic functions and needs of the society.

The 5 Basic Social Institutions

Family   Religion   Economy

Political Order   Education

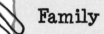

Marriage License

Baptisimal Certificate

Savings Bond

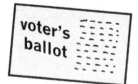

voter's ballot

Graduation Diploma

Institutions satisfy basic societal needs and functions, such as:

- *preparing workers for jobs*
- *keeping law and order*
- *providing recreation*
- *offering worship opportunities*
- *providing transportation*
- *passing on skills to individuals*
- *settling disputes*
- *supporting individuals*
- *teaching appropriate social behaviors*
- *arranging to distribute goods*
- *contributing to reproduction to ensure the continuation of the society*
- *helping people find answers to questions about life's meaning*
- *helping people in emergencies*
- *helping needy citizens*
- *nurturing children*
- *supervising and managing flow of money*
- *keeping people safe*
- *teaching religious values*
- *providing justice*
- *carrying on traditions*
- *arranging to produce goods*
- *arranging to provide services*

A sampling of groups, patterns, and organizations that make up institutions:

a church

a temple

a mosque

Britain's monarchy

a system of religious schools

a national sports league

a state's prison system

a government's system of regulating businesses

a nation's armed forces

marriage

a university

a banking system

a school district

a nation's court system

a world court system

a religious denomination

a child care system

a nation's railway system

a nation's government

political parties

a county government

a nation's economic practices

a health care system

a nation's emergency response program

Laws & Rules

A law
is a rule that is established by an authority or society. In many cases, there are specific punishments given by a governmental authority to those who break a law.

A rule
is a direction, set of principles, or standard for behavior or conduct in a certain group or situation. Generally, a rule is less binding than a law.

Every society has rules and laws. Rules and laws serve these purposes: controlling, ordering, or protecting the people in the group, or ensuring that the group functions to accomplish its purpose. Some rules and laws are written down, others are unwritten but understood by the society members. Most social groups also have rules or laws or both. In groups, many of the rules are unwritten. Generally, a law is more binding to an individual or group than a rule. However, societies and groups have ways of giving punishment to those who do not follow certain rules, as well as to those who break laws.

Examples of Laws:

Examples of Rules:

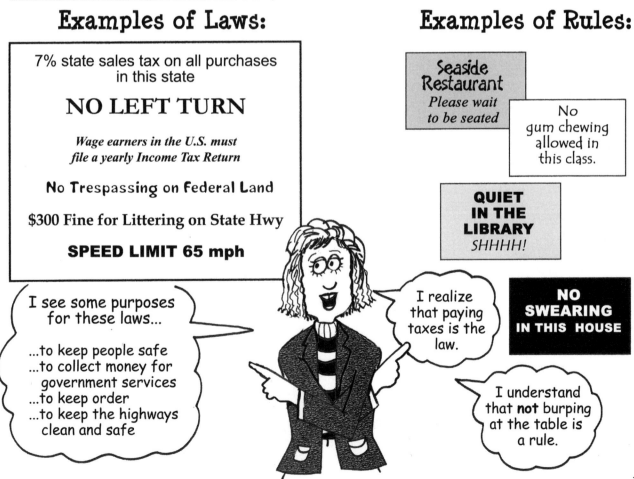

7% state sales tax on all purchases in this state

NO LEFT TURN

Wage earners in the U.S. must file a yearly Income Tax Return

No Trespassing on Federal Land

$300 Fine for Littering on State Hwy

SPEED LIMIT 65 mph

Seaside Restaurant
Please wait to be seated

No gum chewing allowed in this class.

QUIET IN THE LIBRARY *SHHHH!*

NO SWEARING IN THIS HOUSE

I see some purposes for these laws...

...to keep people safe
...to collect money for government services
...to keep order
...to keep the highways clean and safe

I realize that paying taxes is the law.

I understand that **not** burping at the table is a rule.

Get Sharp: Society

Authority & Power

Most social groups and institutions have an ***authority*** figure—someone who holds the most power in the group, or someone who is "in charge." In some cases, the authority rests in the hands of one person. In other groups, the authority is shared. Usually the authority serves some purpose such as leadership, keeping order, or seeing that proper rules are followed.

The Group	The Authority	The Purpose
tourists on a cruise ship	cruise director or captain	keep order and explain rules structure activities keep people safe
group of firefighters battling a fire	captain	keep firefighters safe get the job done
members of the United States Senate	president of the Senate	keep order see that work gets done set schedules
drivers on an Interstate Highway in Idaho	state of Idaho Idaho state police	keep people safe keep order on the highway
middle school soccer team	coach team captain	guide the practice keep order teach soccer skills
fans attending a high school football game	school officials	keep order keep people safe assure that rules are followed
group of riders on a city bus	bus driver	ensure safety keep order get people to their destinations
school board	chairperson	keep order ensure that everyone gets a chance to speak get the board's work done
shoppers in a department store	store manager store security team	keep people safe help the shoppers make sure goods are not stolen

Political Systems

Some nations have a king or queen. Some have a sultan. Some countries have a prime minister or a president, while others have a shah. In some countries, a dictator is in charge. A *political system* is a power structure and a whole set of laws, practices, institutions, and organizations that accomplish the purpose of running the government. Here is an overview of some of the political systems throughout the world.

A **parliamentary government** is headed by an assembly of persons who make the laws of a nation. In some cases, the members of parliament are elected. In other cases, some or all of the members gain their positions by other means, such as appointment or family inheritance. In addition to the parliament, there may be an elected president or a prime minister.

A **monarchy** is a nation that is ruled by a sovereign such as a king, queen, or emperor whose power is inherited. The sovereign holds the highest power in some monarchies. In a *constitutional monarchy* (such as Great Britain), the sovereign is the head of state but holds no political power. The country is ruled by another form of government.

A **republic** is a nation whose leaders are elected by the people for a specific length of time. The leaders are expected to represent the interests and wishes of the citizens. The head leader of a republic is generally a president.

A **dictatorship** is a system controlled by a person who has absolute power. The dictator position is not inherited. Sometimes a dictator takes power by force or gains power because he or she controls the armed forces of the nation.

A **federation** is a joint federal government formed by a group of independent states. A federation is formed to meet needs (such as foreign affairs or national defense) that can be managed more successfully by a larger group.

A **territory** is a country that is not under its own rule, but is owned and governed by another nation.

A **co-principality** is a country that is ruled jointly by two other countries or authorities.

> To understand a political system well, ask questions such as these:
>
> Who holds the power?
>
> Who leads the government?
>
> How is the leader elected?
>
> How is the government structured?
>
> Who makes the rules and laws?
>
> How are laws enforced?
>
> What rights do all citizens hold?

Myanmar's government is a dictatorship. A military group controls the government. The senior general holds all the power and serves as the prime minister.

The United Arab Emirates is a group of seven Arab states that has formed a federation. Each state is ruled separately, but the federation manages foreign affairs and economic development.

India has a parliamentary government. A prime minister is the head of state. The lawmaking body is a parliament whose members are elected by the people.

Andorra is a co-principality. It is ruled jointly by the president of France and the bishop of Spain.

Religions

A *religion* is a belief in or worship of some sort of higher power or principle outside the human. Some cultures worship one God. Others worship many gods. For some religions, there is no god. Some cultures believe that animals or trees are sacred. Statues and icons are a part of worship in some cultures. The people of the world have many different beliefs and ways to worship. In all cases, religious beliefs help people make sense of the world around them. Religion helps people answer questions about the meaning of life, the purpose for living, and the mysteries of death.

About six billion people in the world follow some type of organized religion.

Here is a description of some of the world's major religions.

Get Sharp Tip #2
Monotheism is a belief in one God.
Polytheism is a belief in many gods.

Buddhism

Number of believers: approximately 360 million

Beginnings: Siddhartha Gautama, known as the Buddha, founded Buddhism around 525 B.C.

Beliefs: Buddhists believe that the life of all beings includes suffering. They believe that suffering occurs because of desire, and that to escape suffering, believers must give up attachment to worldly life and belongings. They believe that this escape comes through leading a disciplined life of self-denial that can bring a person to *nirvana*, or perfect peace.

Holy writings or teachings: the sacred teachings of Buddha, known as the *Tripitaka*.

Christianity

Number of believers: approximately 2 billion

Beginnings: Jesus, a Jew born about 7 B.C.; his followers founded Christianity.

Beliefs: Christianity is a monotheistic religion. Its followers believe that Jesus Christ is the Son of God, and that he was sent by God to live among humans and offer them a way to be forgiven of their sins and join the kingdom of God. Jesus Christ was executed by crucifixion on a cross. Christians believe that he rose from the dead, and that belief in him and his resurrection is a way to gain salvation. The believers have spread Christianity across the globe. There are three major divisions of Christianity. (1) **Roman Catholics** follow the authority of the Pope. (2) **Protestants** reject the idea that a pope, priest, or other higher person must speak to God for them. Protestantism began when reformers broke away from the Roman Catholic Church in the mid-1500s. There are many different sects or denominations of Protestantism. (3) **Orthodox Christians** follow most of the teachings of the Roman Catholics, but follow a patriarch rather than the Pope.

Holy writings or teachings: the Old Testament and the New Testament of the *Bible*.

Hinduism

Number of believers: approximately 785 million

Beginnings: The Hindu religion has no founder. It is considered the oldest religion in the world, and dates back as far as prehistoric times.

Beliefs: Hinduism is the major religion of India. There is no one belief that is held by all Hindus. There is freedom to believe in one god, many gods, or no god. The central belief is that a divine intelligence, called *Brahman*, is in all beings. Hinduism is based on the idea of reincarnation—the concept that all living beings are in a cycle of death and rebirth, and that human beings are reborn several times in different forms or bodies. For Hindus, the goal of life is to escape the cycle and become a part of the *Brahman*. Hindus believe that to achieve this goal, one must lead a pure life. The practice of Hinduism includes many rituals and ceremonies for purification.

Holy writings or teachings: the *Vedas* and many other religious writings and poems

Islam

Number of believers: approximately 1.2 billion

Beginnings: Muhammad founded the religion in Arabia in 610 A.D. The followers of Islam are called Muslims. They refer to Muhammad as the Prophet.

Beliefs: Islam is a monotheistic religion. They worship the God, *Allah*, whom they believe determines the fate of humans, and follow the teachings of Muhammad, whom they believe is the one true prophet of Allah. Beliefs include the duties of praying five times a day, giving money to the poor and to their church (mosque), fasting during the day in the month of Ramadan, and making a pilgrimage to Mecca once in their lifetime if it is possible.

Holy writings or teachings: the *Koran*

Judaism

Number of believers: approximately 17 million

Beginnings: It is believed that Abraham was the first Jew. He lived in the 1300s B.C.

Beliefs: Judaism is the oldest of the monotheistic religions. It centers on the existence of one god, Yahweh, who created the universe and rules it. The Jews believe that Yahweh entered into a covenant with them, promising to be present with them throughout their history. Followers of Judaism believe that they are "God's Chosen People." They also believe they should keep God's commandments and worship God faithfully.

Holy writings or teachings: the *Torah*, which is the first five books of the Old Testament of the *Bible*

Sikhism

Number of believers: approximately 16 million

Beginnings: Sikhism began under guru Nanak around 1500 A.D. but was influenced by other gurus who have shaped the religion since.

Beliefs: The Sikhs accept the Hindu concept of the cycle of birth, death, and rebirth, but reject the idea of many gods. They pursue *moksha*, which is release from the cycle. They believe that *moksha* can only be attained with the help of a spiritual teacher, or guru, and that it can be gained by ritual spiritual devotions of singing, praising, and repeating God's name. For Sikhs, following a strict ethical code is part of the process of attaining this release.

Holy writings or teachings: the *Adi Granth*, a book of teachings about the Sikh faith and practice

Celebrations

All over the world, people celebrate! This is one of the wonderful things humans have in common. No matter what the culture, time in history, geographical setting, language, political system, religion, or economic system, all people seem to find ways to commemorate and rejoice in special occasions. Everyone loves to dance and sing, parade and feast, and take part in the traditions and rituals that are meaningful to them. Births, deaths, marriages, religious anniversaries, the seasons, the harvest, and so many other human events are all good reasons to celebrate—and we do!

The **warrior dance** has very specific steps that the boys do with joy and exuberance during the N'cwala festivities.

N'cwala

The Zambian festival of N'cwala celebrates the end of harvest time in February. A dance is a central part of the celebration. In the traditional ritual, the best dancers are singled out by the Ngoni chieftain as great warriors.

The word **carnival** means "goodbye to meat." This refers to the 40 days of fasting that is practiced during Lent.

Carnival

Before the beginning of Lent (the season of penance before Easter), a great carnival takes place in Rio de Janeiro, Brazil. Everyone takes part, even the children. People wear magnificent costumes, ride on fancy floats, and dance the samba. Everyone enjoys taking advantage of this last chance to feast before Lent begins.

A **piñata** is a papier-mâché toy filled with candy and small surprises. Blindfolded children make a game of smashing the piñata to get the treats inside.

Cinco de Mayo

In Mexico, and among Mexican people around the world, May 5th is the day for a grand celebration. It marks the victory of the Mexican Army over the French at the Battle of Puebla.

Kodomono-Hi

This Japanese Children's Day Festival takes place on May 5th. Young boys display colorful fish kites and streamers on poles in their gardens and on their rooftops. The boys bathe with iris leaves to protect them from evil influences, and eat tiny rice cakes called *chimaki*. Girls have their own holiday. **Hina Matusun** is the day when they float special dolls down the rivers in boats.

Carp kites symbolize energy and determination for Japanese boys. The kites come in different sizes, but the largest always flies on top. It represents the father.

Maligawa Tusker is the elephant that carries a replica of Buddha's sacred tooth in a golden casket on its back.

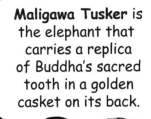

Muslim children eat a special cookie called a **ma'moul**. The cookies are made of flour, dates, and pistachio nuts. They are pressed into molds to make them more decorative.

Esala Perahera

The August festival of Esala Perahera in Sri Lanka includes ten days and nights of singing, dancing, and feasting. It ends on the night of the full moon with a parade of a hundred elephants in honor of Buddha.

Eid ul-Fitr

During the month of the Islamic religious holiday called **Ramadan**, Muslims do not eat or drink between sunrise and sunset. To mark the end of Ramadan, they have a 3-day feast called Eid ul-Fitr. During this celebration, they also exchange presents and give food to the poor.

Hanukkah

Hanukkah is a Jewish holiday meaning the festival of lights. It commemorates the time when the Temple of Jerusalem was recaptured in 164 B.C. Each of eight candles is lit from the central candle, which symbolizes the drop of oil used to light the reclaimed temple. Families celebrate with feasting, gifts, and games.

The **menorah** is a candelabrum that represents the eight days of Hanukkah.

Christian children often take part in Christmas plays that re-enact the **Nativity** (the birth of Jesus Christ).

St. Lucia's **crown** is made of evergreen lingonberry leaves and candles. It symbolizes the promise of rebirth after the long winter season.

Christmas

Many countries, including America, celebrate Christmas on the 25th of December to honor the birth of Christ. It evolved from a purely religious holiday into one that is also secular. Today, children wait for Santa Claus to come on Christmas Eve and fill their stockings with presents and candy. Many families put up Christmas trees and share presents with family and friends.

The Feast of St. Lucia

On the darkest day of winter in December, the people of Sweden celebrate the festival of St. Lucia, the patron saint of light. Each community chooses a young girl to represent St. Lucia in a procession of candlelight and carol-singing.

Chinese New Year

This is one of the most spectacular and colorful of the world's celebrations. The Chinese New Year festival begins on the first day of the Chinese calendar, and lasts for 15 days. This occurs near the beginning of February. The celebrations include parades with colorful costumes, banners, and wonderful long dragons. The Chinese Dragon is called **Gum Loong**, or Golden Dragon. He comes at the end of the parade to wish everyone good luck, prosperity, and peace.

Make this **Gum Loong** long enough to circle the whole room!

How to make a paper dragon:

1. Start with a piece of construction paper 11" x 17" (28 x 43 cm) for each segment.

2. Fold the paper in half. Cut the unfolded edges into the shape of a pattern (as shown above).

3. Cut scales from bright bits of wrapping paper, colored tissue, or colored foil.

4. Create a collage of scales with scraps of the decorative paper on each segment. Use glue and plenty of glitter.

5. When the glue is dry, staple colorful crepe paper streamers to the bottom of each segment.

6. Punch a hole 1 inch (3 cm) from the center fold of each segment. Tie varying lengths of string (1–3 feet or 30–90 cm) onto the segments.

7. Tie each segment to a string or clothesline. Let the segments hang at varying lengths to imitate the undulating movement of a dragon.

How to make the dragon's head:

1. Use 2 pieces of 11" x 17" paper. Draw a head, using the picture as a model. Cut both pieces exactly the same.

2. Draw matching eyes, nostrils, and teeth on both sides.

3. Create a collage of bright scales and glitter to match the scales on the body.

4. Punch 2 holes in the center of one side of a small cereal or raisin box. Thread and knot a 2-foot (60 cm) string through the holes.

5. Glue the pieces of the head to both sides of the box. Hang this from the line.

Get Sharp: Cultural Celebrations

Languages

There are thousands of different ways to say "Hello," "Happy Holidays," or "Merry Christmas." About 6,500 different languages are spoken in the world today. Two-thirds of those languages have more than 1,000 native speakers.

> The most popular language in the world is Mandarin Chinese. There are 885 million people in China and over one billion worldwide who speak that language.

The Top 15 Spoken Languages in the World

What's the language?	How many speak it? (approximate number of speakers for whom the language is their native, or first, language)	Where is it spoken?
Chinese (Mandarin and other major Chinese dialects)	1.1 billion	China, Taiwan
Hindi	366 million	India
Spanish	358 million	Spain, Central America, South America, U.S.
English	341 million	Britain, U.S., Canada, Australia
Arabic	280 million	Arabian Peninsula, Iraq, Syria, Jordan, Lebanon, northern Africa, Ethiopia
Bengali	207 million	Bangladesh
Portuguese	176 million	Portugal, Brazil
Russian	167 million	Russia and other countries that were part of the former Soviet Union
Japanese	125 million	Japan
German	121 million	Germany, Austria, Switzerland
Korean	78 million	Korea
French	77 million	France, Belgium, Switzerland, Canada

GET SHARP

on

GLOBES & MAPS

Using Globes & Maps

You have probably never stopped to count the number of times you use a map in a week or month or year. *Globes* and *maps*, which are visual representations of some part of the world or universe, are more a part of life than we often realize. It's a good thing, too!

Without maps, we would be at a loss for finding our way around a lot of places such as stores, parks, malls, museums, subway systems, cities, countries, or continents. Without maps, we'd be missing a great deal of information about our world.

Globe Map

As our cities, towns, and world get more complicated, we rely more and more on maps. For example, if you need to get to a library across the city this afternoon, you can log onto the Internet and get a bus route custom-made just for you. It will tell you when to leave, what buses to catch, and how long your trip will take!

Political Map

Atlas

route map on the web

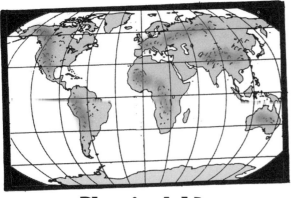

Physical Map

Weather Map

3-D Map

Relative Location Map

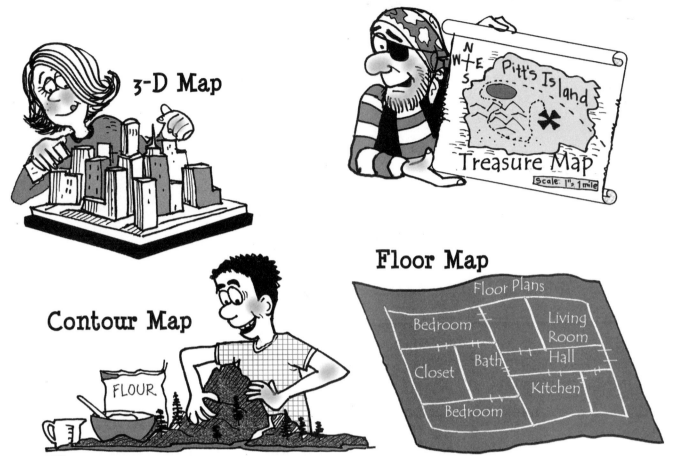

Treasure Map

Scale: 1"= 1 mile

Pitt's Island

Contour Map

FLOUR

Floor Map

Floor Plans

Bedroom

Living Room

Closet

Bath

Hall

Kitchen

Bedroom

Distribution Map

Maps and Locations of Worldwide Scuba Diving Sites

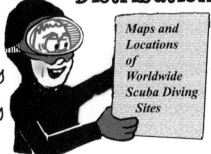

Relative Location map

Water Dunk

Slip-n-side

Bumper Cars

Loop-de-Loop

Ferris Wheel

you are here

Info

Restrooms

Fun Town Amusement Park

Grid Map

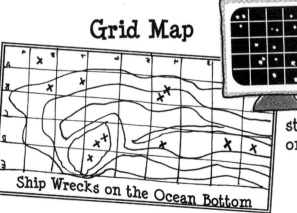

Ship Wrecks on the Ocean Bottom

star grid map on the computer

Get Sharp: Globes & Maps

Globes

Earth is shaped like a sphere. A photograph or other flat representation of Earth can only show half (a *hemisphere*) of Earth's surface at any one time. A **globe** is a sphere that represents the Earth, so a globe is useful to show the whole Earth at once. Globes show the land masses and bodies of water on Earth's surface. Some globes also show other features, such as land elevations, ocean depths, the political divisions (countries) of the world, ocean currents, or major cities.

Northern Hemisphere

Eastern Hemisphere

Southern Hemisphere

Western Hemisphere

I notice that all the continents except Australia and Antarctica show up in the Northern Hemisphere.

All the continents except North and South America show up in the Eastern Hemisphere.

The ancient Greeks made the first globes to show relative locations of things on Earth. They divided the globe into the 360 equal segments that are used to measure circles (called *degrees*). They used vertical and horizontal lines to mark off each of the 360 segments from north to south and east to west. These lines became known as the lines of *longitude* and *latitude*.

What a good idea those Greeks had! A globe gives you an idea of what the whole world looks like from space.

Better Grades & Higher Test Scores / SOCIAL STUDIES gr. 4–6
Copyright ©2005 by Incentive Publications, Inc., Nashville, TN.

Longitude & Latitude

Longitude

The *lines of longitude*, imaginary lines called *meridians,* run north and south from the North Pole to the South Pole. The first meridian, or *prime meridian*, is at 0° longitude. It passes through the Royal Naval Observatory in Greenwich, England. The *longitude location* of a place is the distance measured east or west of this line. 180°E longitude and 180°W longitude are the same location, exactly halfway around the Earth from the prime meridian. The 180° meridian is known as the *International Date Line*.

Latitude

The *lines of latitude*, imaginary lines called *parallels,* run east and west around the Earth. The line at 0° latitude is the *equator.* The *latitude location* of a place is the distance in degrees north or south of the equator. These are other specific lines of latitude:

- the *Tropic of Cancer* at 23.5°N latitude
- the *Tropic of Capricorn* at 23.5°S latitude
- the *Arctic Circle* at 66.5°N latitude
- the *Antarctic Circle* at 66.5°S latitude
- the *North Pole* at 90°N latitude
- the *South Pole* at 90°S latitude

The equator passes through several countries and three continents.

Two continents are completely *south* of the equator. Two continents are completely *north* of the equator.

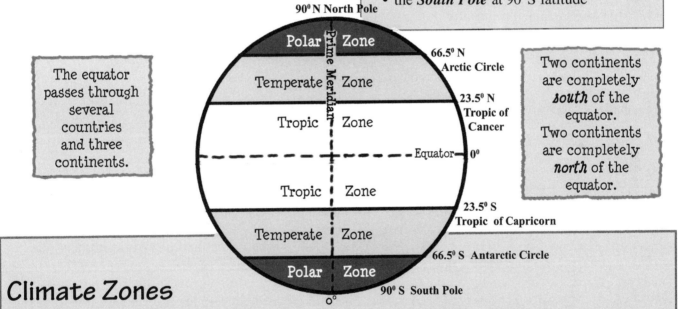

Climate Zones

The latitude of a region is related to its climate, because the Sun's rays do not fall at the same angle at all locations north or south of the equator.

The **tropical zone** of the Earth lies between the Tropic of Cancer and the Tropic of Capricorn. This area receives the most direct rays of the Sun.

The **temperate zones** of the Earth lie between the Tropic of Cancer and the Arctic Circle in the Northern Hemisphere and the Tropic of Capricorn and the Antarctic Circle in the Southern Hemisphere. Since the Sun's rays are less direct in these zones than in the tropical zone, climates are cooler.

The **polar regions** of the Earth lie north of the Arctic Circle and south of the Antarctic Circle. Polar regions receive the most indirect rays of the Sun, and are therefore the coldest areas on Earth.

Latitude

This map shows the major lines of latitude running through North America, South America, and part of Antarctica. From looking at this map, you can learn some things such as:

- No part of the North American continent reaches the North Pole.

- Fort Yukon, Alaska, is on the Arctic Circle.

- All of the continental United States lies between the Tropic of Cancer and the Arctic Circle.

- The southern tip of South America has a latitude similar to the northern tip of Antarctica.

- The city of Houston is close to 30°N latitude.

- Most of Antarctica is south of the Antarctic Circle.

- Most of Greenland is north of the Arctic Circle.

- The equator crosses South America.

- Mexico is not on the equator.

- Quito, Ecuador is on the equator.

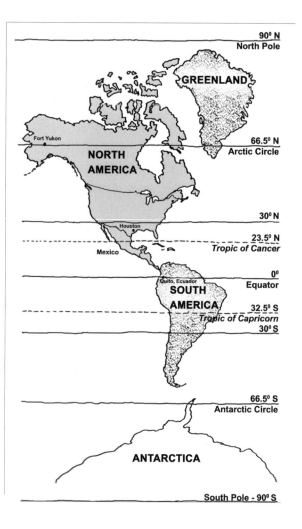

Longitude

This map shows lines of longitude through four continents. By reading the map, you can learn some things such as:

- The prime meridian passes through the continent of Africa.

- Some locations in Africa are east longitude; others are west longitude.

- Most of Australia lies between 120°E and 150°E longitude.

- Europe stretches from about 10°W to 65°E longitude.

- Beijing and Calcutta are about 30° apart in longitude.

- The International Date Line crosses the continent of Asia.

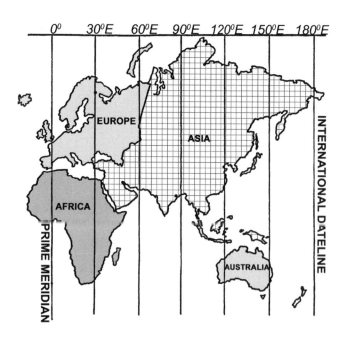

Earth's Grid

The lines of longitude and latitude form a ***global grid*** (system of parallel and perpendicular lines). This grid is very helpful in locating points on Earth's surface. You can find any place on Earth if you know its latitude and longitude. The location of St. Petersburg, Russia, for instance, is 59°N, 30°E. To find St. Petersburg, place your finger on the spot where the equator and the prime meridian meet. This is 0°, 0° on the global grid. Move your finger north and stop just below the 60° parallel (line of latitude). Now, move your finger east to the 30° meridian (line of longitude).

This global grid can help you locate these places:

- The continent located approximately between 50°E and 10°W and 35°N and 35°S is Africa.
- The city at 38°N, 77°W is Washington D.C., USA.
- The city at 15°S, 47°W is Brasilia, Brazil.
- The city at 30°N, 31°E is Cairo, Egypt.
- The city at 38°N, 23°E is Athens, Greece.
- The city at 55°N, 37°E is Moscow, Russia.
- The city at 28°N, 77°E is New Delhi, India.
- The city at 6°S, 106°E is Jakarta, Indonesia.
- The city at 33°S, 151°E is Sydney, Australia.

Get Sharp Tip #3

The first number in a location is its **latitude** and the second number is its **longitude**.
77°N, 15°E reads
77° north latitude,
15° east longitude.

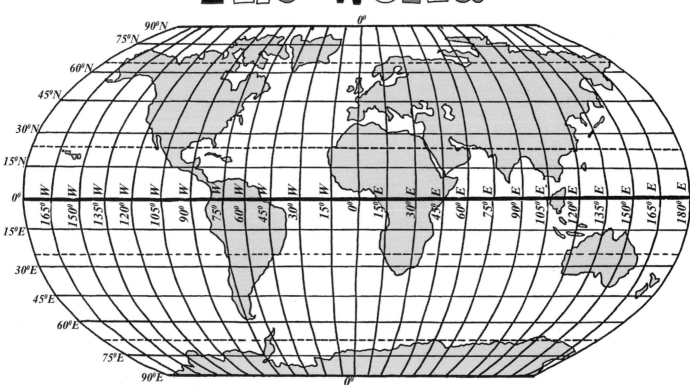

The World

Better Grades & Higher Test Scores / SOCIAL STUDIES gr. 4–6
Copyright ©2005 by Incentive Publications, Inc., Nashville, TN.

Get Sharp: Longitude & Latitude

Maps

A *map* is a representation of a place on Earth presented on a flat surface. Maps can also be made of places beyond Earth. A map can represent something as simple as the top of your desk or the arrangement of food on a plate, or a map can represent something as complex as the entire world or a piece of the solar system.

Maps are grouped according to the kinds of information they provide. Most maps fall into one of the three groups: physical, political, or cultural.

Physical Maps

Maps that show natural features of Earth's surface are called *physical maps*. These maps show features such as oceans, lakes, rivers, mountains, islands, deserts, and plains. They may also show natural occurrences or patterns such as vegetation or climate patterns, winds, or ocean currents. This map shows the location of the major physical features of the country of Mexico.

Political Maps

Maps that show political divisions within an area are called *political maps*. These maps show boundaries and names of nations, countries, states, provinces, territories, or counties. They may also show locations of other political divisions such as cities, towns, or neighborhoods.

This map shows the location of the main political divisions (the countries) of Europe.

Better Grades & Higher Test Scores / SOCIAL STUDIES gr. 4–6

Cultural Maps

Maps that show human features within an area are called **cultural maps**. These maps show such things as population, language, customs, or economic activity. They may also show locations of particular cultural features that humans have added to the world.

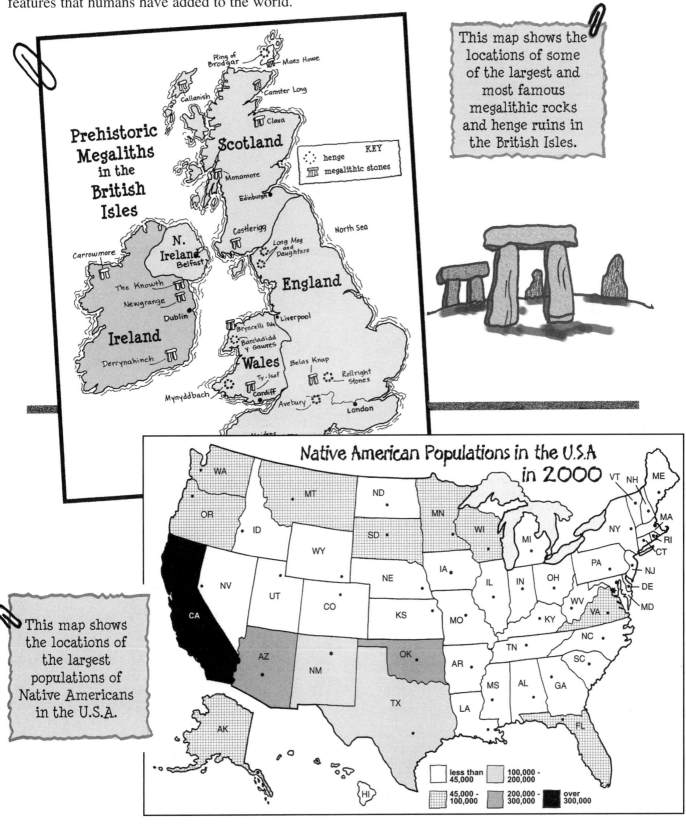

This map shows the locations of some of the largest and most famous megalithic rocks and henge ruins in the British Isles.

Prehistoric Megaliths in the British Isles

KEY
henge
megalithic stones

Ring of Brodgar
Maes Howe
Callanish
Camster Long
Clava
Scotland
Monamore
Edinburgh
Castlerigg
North Sea
Long Meg and Daughters
Carrowmore
N. Ireland
Belfast
England
The Knowth
Newgrange
Dublin
Ireland
Bryncelli Ddu
Liverpool
Barclodiad y Gawres
Belas Knap
Rollright Stones
Derrynahinch
Ty-Isaf
Wales
Mymyddbach
Cardiff
Avebury
London

Native American Populations in the U.S.A in 2000

This map shows the locations of the largest populations of Native Americans in the U.S.A.

less than 45,000
100,000 - 200,000
45,000 - 100,000
200,000 - 300,000
over 300,000

Parts of a Map

In order to use maps effectively, it is important to know how to "read" them. A map has several parts, made up of words, symbols, pictures, lines, or photographs. All these parts help to present information to the map reader.

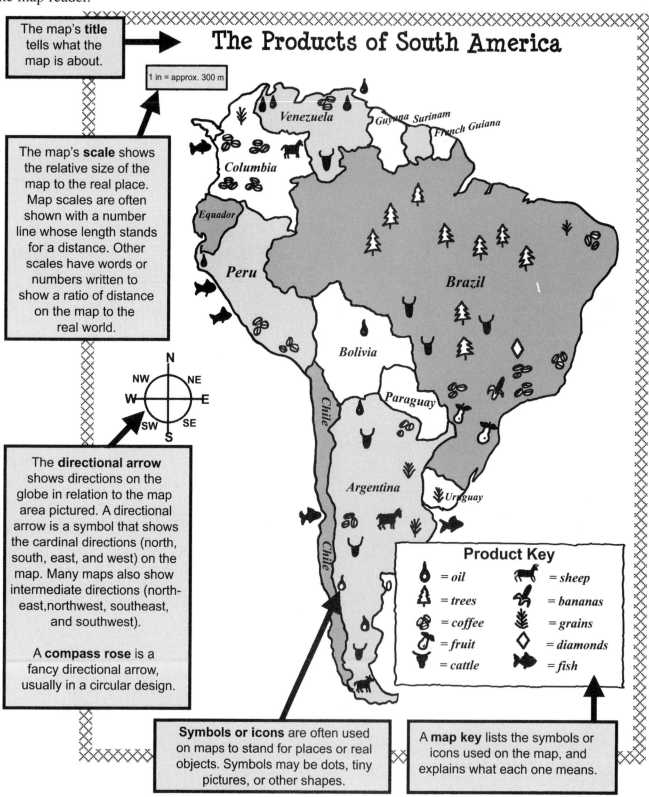

The map's **title** tells what the map is about.

The map's **scale** shows the relative size of the map to the real place. Map scales are often shown with a number line whose length stands for a distance. Other scales have words or numbers written to show a ratio of distance on the map to the real world.

The **directional arrow** shows directions on the globe in relation to the map area pictured. A directional arrow is a symbol that shows the cardinal directions (north, south, east, and west) on the map. Many maps also show intermediate directions (northeast, northwest, southeast, and southwest).

A **compass rose** is a fancy directional arrow, usually in a circular design.

Symbols or icons are often used on maps to stand for places or real objects. Symbols may be dots, tiny pictures, or other shapes.

A **map key** lists the symbols or icons used on the map, and explains what each one means.

The Products of South America

1 in = approx. 300 m

Venezuela Guyana Surinam French Guiana Columbia Equador Peru Brazil Bolivia Paraguay Chile Argentina Uruguay Chile

Product Key

= oil		= sheep	
= trees		= bananas	
= coffee		= grains	
= fruit		= diamonds	
= cattle		= fish	

90

Special Purpose Maps

Maps that give information about specific subjects or are designed for a unique purpose can be called *special purpose maps*. There are literally hundreds of different kinds of maps created for giving specialized information or helping people find various locations. This page and pages 92–96 will give you examples of some special purpose maps.

Weather or Climate Maps

Weather or *climate* maps give information about the climate or weather patterns of an area.

> This map shows the average annual rainfall in Australia.

Average Rainfall in Australia

Elevation Maps

Elevation maps are physical maps that show how the surface varies from place to place. (These are sometimes called *landform maps*.) Differences in elevation can be shown on a map with color, shading, pictures, or lines. A *contour map* uses a series of lines to show change in elevation. A *contour line* on the map is a line that connects areas of the same elevation.

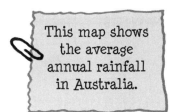

> This contour map shows the elevation on these small islands. When you see lines close together on a contour map, you can assume the land has a sudden elevation increase. This alerts you to a hill, mountain, or cliff on the land.

Elevation Key
≈≈≈ sea level

— each line represents a rise of 500 feet

The Flotsam and Jetsam Islands

Get Sharp: Special Purpose Maps

Grid Maps

A **grid map** is a map that has lines drawn over it to form a grid. The purpose of the grid is to make it easier to find the locations of places or items on the map. You read the map grid by looking at the letters or numbers in the margins of the map. Generally, letters run along one edge of the map and numbers run along another side. You identify a location by a combination of a letter and a number.

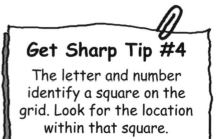

Get Sharp Tip #4

The letter and number identify a square on the grid. Look for the location within that square.

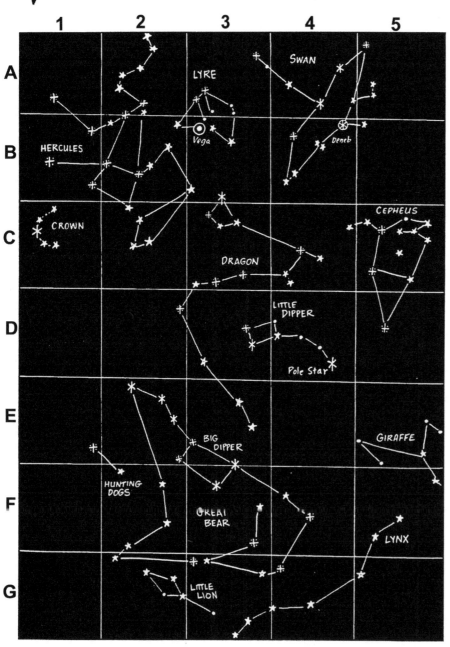

The Northern Night Sky

Magnitudes of Stars
brightest to faintest

⊙ ⊛ ✳ ✢ ★ •
0   1   2   3   4   5

From looking at this constellation grid map. you can see that...

...the location of the Little Dipper is **D-3 and D-4.**

...the Crown constellation is found in **C-1.**

the Giraffe constellation is **E-5 and F-5.**

Better Grades & Higher Test Scores / SOCIAL STUDIES gr. 4–6
Copyright ©2005 by Incentive Publications, Inc., Nashville, TN.

Road or Route Maps

Road maps or *route maps* help people find their way to and from many places.

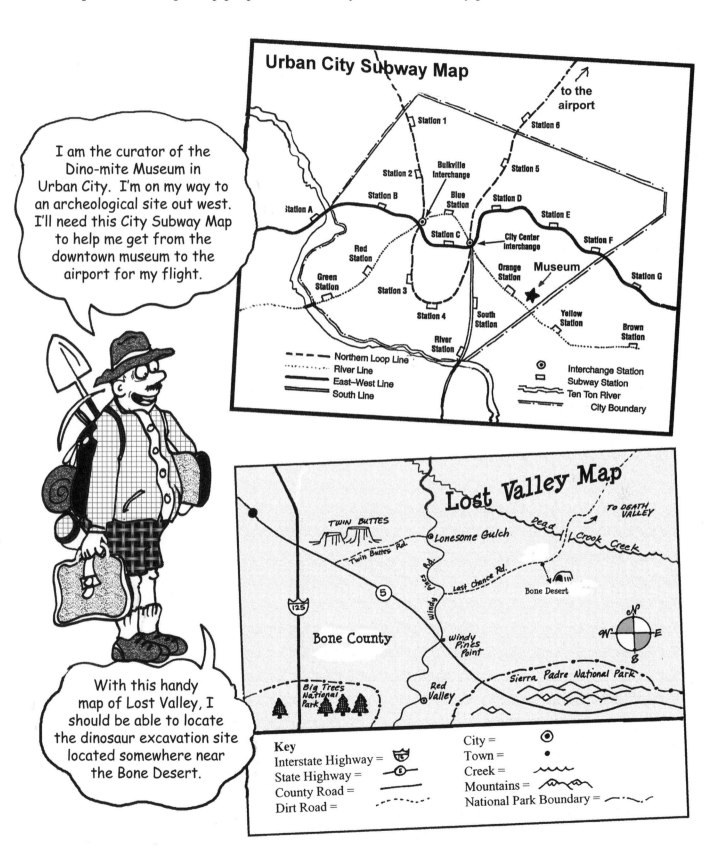

Floor Maps

A *floor map* or *floor plan* is a map that shows the way around a room, building, shopping center, or other structure. This kind of a map uses lines, shapes, and sometimes color or shading to show such things as the layout of the structure, the position of the rooms or furniture, the halls or walkways, the doors, and the windows.

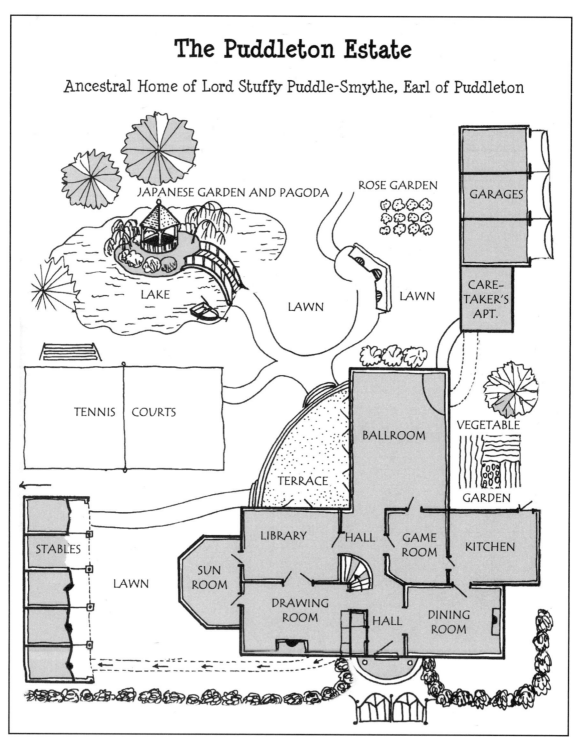

The floor plan of this English manor shows a visitor the features and layout of the first floor of the main house. It also shows the floor plans of the outbuildings and the outside landscape.

Relative Location Maps

A *relative location map* shows the position of a person, place, or object in relation to its surroundings. You can find relative location maps at most shopping centers, malls, museums, and other large public places. These maps help people figure out exactly where they are and where a specific spot or item is located.

1. OUTDOOR STORE
2. OPTOMETRIST
3. SPORTS SHOP
4. CHOCOLATE SHOP
5. COSTUME SHOP
6. BOOK STORE
7. PHOTOCOPY STORE
8. BAGEL SHOP
9. DEPARTMENT STORE
10. MUSIC SHOP
11. COMPUTER STORE
12. COMIC BOOK STORE
13. GAME STORE
14. PET SHOP
15. HAIR SALON
16. VIDEO STORE
17. CANDLE BOUTIQUE
18. JEWELRY STORE
19. SKI SHOP
20. CANDY STORE

Distribution Maps

Some maps show how a cultural or physical feature is distributed in different parts of the world, country, or other area. Maps that show how something is spread out across an area are called *distribution maps*. This kind of a map could use symbols, icons, or colors to show the locations of bus stations throughout a city, where diamond mines are in a country, how population is distributed on a continent, what kind of vegetation grows around the world, or all the places in a county where someone can donate blood.

This is an example of a distribution map made by a group of campers who wanted to find out how many bears were seen at various campsites during the previous year.

GET SHARP →

on

WORLD GEOGRAPHY

Five Themes of Geography

Geography is such a broad subject that it is often divided into two parts. *Physical geography* is the study of the kinds of land and water that make up Earth's surface. *Cultural geography* is the study of the people who live on Earth—their ways of life, how they have used and changed the Earth, and how the physical geography has affected their ways of life. The study of geography examines different themes, known as the *Five Fundamental Themes of Geography*.

PLACE

No one place on Earth is exactly like any other place. To describe any one place, you need to show its uniqueness. Geographers look at the specific physical characteristics of a place, such as shape of the land, kinds of landforms, elevations, variations in elevation, bodies of water, plant and animal life, natural resources, climate, and soil. They also look at the human characteristics of a place: where the people live, how close together they live, how they make a living, their social and cultural practices and traditions, their languages, their political systems, and their relationships with the land and their neighbors.

> **Get Sharp Tip #5**
> Geography is not just about the land, water, and weather. Geography is also human. It includes a study of the world's people and how they interact with the places where they live.

What is geography?

> **Geography** is the study of the world and everything in it.

> The word *geography* has Greek roots. *Geo* means "earth." *Graph* means "writing."

LOCATION

Location is the specific spot where something can be found. *Absolute location* is the exact spot on the Earth. Geographers make use of maps, globes, and cardinal directions (north, south, east, and west) to describe the absolute location of a place. The lines of latitude and longitude allow anyone to give a very precise description of the absolute location.

Relative location is the relationship of one place, person, or thing in comparison to some other spot. Knowing or finding relative location helps us find our way around parts of the world dozens of times a day. Relative location allows you to explain that you live 300 miles from the Pacific Ocean, 6 blocks from school, 9 miles from the zoo, or 40° north of the equator.

HUMAN and ENVIRONMENT INTERACTION

The physical environment affects the way people live and the way cultures develop. It affects many (if not most) of the human activities of an area. The activities of humans, in turn, have effects on the natural environment. Geographers are interested in knowing how these two factors interact with one another. There are thousands of examples of these interactions. People in Africa may build homes from stones because there are no trees to provide wood. In the islands of the southern Pacific Ocean, many people earn a living from fishing because fish are plentiful. Herds of buffalo used to roam the Great Plains in the center of the United States, but humans have turned so much of this land into farms that there is no longer room for the large herds.

HUMAN MOVEMENT

Patterns of movement affect the way human cultures develop. Movement of large groups of people is of great interest to geographers. These movements, called *migrations*, have been caused by many factors such as natural disasters (floods, volcanoes, earthquakes, droughts), famine, war, or displacement by a government (such as the relocation of Native American tribes to reservations). There are other kinds of movement that geographers study: movement of individual people or families, movement of goods, movement of ideas, or movement of information.

> **GPS**, the **Global Positioning System**, is a great way to find a location. It's a system that shows the exact position of any person or object, any time, anywhere on Earth, in any kind of weather. 24 GPS satellites orbiting the Earth transmit radio signals that can be detected by anyone with a GPS receiver.

Get Sharp Tip #6

Each theme connects with all other themes. The five components interact with each other in many ways.

REGIONS

A *region* is an area that has some common features that set it apart from other areas. These features might be physical, cultural, or a combination of both. Separating parts of the world into regions allows geographers to study areas more closely and understand them better.

For purposes of studying world geography, the world is often divided into these physical-cultural regions:
- North America
- Latin America
- Western Europe
- Eastern Europe
- the Middle East and North Africa
- Sub-Saharan Africa
- Southern and Eastern Asia
- the South Pacific (which includes Australia and Oceania—the islands of the South Pacific Ocean).

The World's Land & Water

Earth's surface is made up of land and water. The largest bodies of land are called ***continents***. There are seven continents on Earth: North America, South America, Europe, Asia, Africa, Australia, and Antarctica. Europe and Asia share the same land mass. Large bodies of water, called ***oceans***, separate the continents. Most of the large bodies of water are connected, but this huge covering of water is divided into four oceans: the Atlantic Ocean, the Pacific Ocean, the Indian Ocean, and the Arctic Ocean.

The World

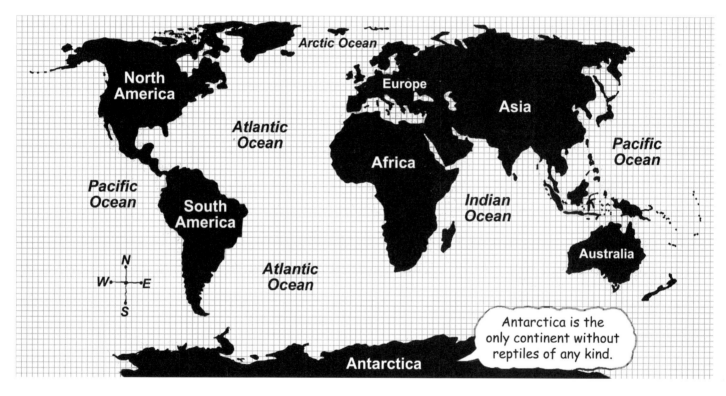

Antarctica is the only continent without reptiles of any kind.

Fascinating Facts . . .

- The world has more water than land. Almost two-thirds of Earth's surface is covered with water.

- About 98% of Earth's water is in the sea. Most of the rest is locked up in ice in the Arctic and Antarctica. A fraction of a percent is in groundwater, lakes, rivers, and the atmosphere.

- The Pacific Ocean is the largest body of water. It covers 64,200,000 square miles and has an average depth of 12,900 feet.

- The Atlantic Ocean is saltier than the Pacific Ocean.

- Together, Europe and Asia cover about 20,800,000 square miles.

- The lowest point of dry land, Death Valley in California, USA, is 282 feet below sea level.

- The highest point of land, Mt. Everest in Nepal and Tibet, is 29,035 feet above sea level.

Better Grades & Higher Test Scores / SOCIAL STUDIES gr. 4–6

The Physical World

The physical world is an amazing collection of ups and downs. Here is an overview of the major physical features of the world.

Western Hemisphere

World's Longest Rivers		
River	*Length in Miles*	*Continent*
Nile	4,160	Africa
Amazon	4,000	South America
Yangtze	3,960	Asia
Huang Ho	3,400	Asia
Ob-Irtish	3,360	Asia
Amur	2,740	Asia
Lena	2,730	Asia
Congo	2,720	Africa
Mackenzie	2,640	North America
Mekong	2,600	Asia
Niger	2,590	Africa
Yenisey	2,540	Asia
Parana	2,480	South America
Mississippi	2,340	North America
Missouri	2,320	North America
Volga	2,290	Europe
Purus	2,100	South America
Madeira	2,010	South America
Yukon	1,980	North America
Rio Grande	1,900	North America
Darling	1,750	Australia
Zambezi	1,700	Africa

World's Tallest Mountains		
Mountain	*Height in Feet*	*Location*
Everest	29,035	Nepal-China
K2	28,238	Pakistan-China
Kangchenjunga	28,208	Nepal-India
Lhotse	27,923	Nepal-China
Makalu I	27,824	Nepal-China
Lhotse Shar II	27,504	Nepal-China
Dhaulangiri I	26,810	Nepal
Manaslu I	26,760	Nepal
Cho Oyu	26,750	Nepal
Nanga Parbat	26,660	Pakistan

Eastern Hemisphere

Earth's Amazing Surface

The surface of Earth is a wonderful collection of peaks and troughs, dry lands and wet lands, rippling streams and wild seas, breathtaking panoramas and curious formations. Here is a brief, illustrated overview of landforms and water forms that spread across Earth's surface.

archipelago – large group or chain of islands

atoll – ring-shaped coral island or string of islands, usually surrounding a lagoon

bay – part of a large body of water that extends into the land

beach – gently sloping shore of ocean or other water body

butte – flat-topped hill; smaller than a mesa

canal – waterway built to connect two other bodies of water

canyon – deep, narrow valley with steep sides

cape – coastline that projects into the water

channel – narrow strip of water between two land bodies

cliff – steep rock face

delta – land formed by deposits at the mouth of the river

desert – dry, sandy region of little rainfall, extreme temperatures, and sparse vegetation

dune – mound, hill, or ridge of sand heaped by wind

fjord – deep narrow inlet of the sea between steep cliffs

foothills – hilly area at the base of a mountain range

glacier – large sheet of ice that moves slowly over a land surface

gulf – part of an ocean or sea that extends into the land; larger than a bay

hill – rounded, raised landform; lower than a mountain

island – body of land completely surrounded by water

isthmus – narrow strip of land (bordered by water) joining two larger bodies of land

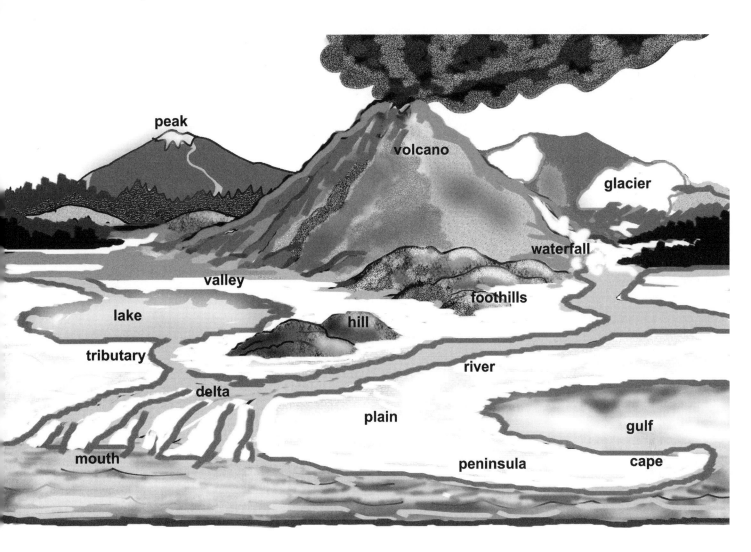

Labels on diagram: peak, volcano, glacier, waterfall, valley, foothills, lake, hill, tributary, river, delta, plain, gulf, mouth, peninsula, cape

lake – body of water completely surrounded by land

lagoon – shallow water area enclosed within an atoll or cut off from sea by a strip of land

mesa – high, flat landform rising steeply above surrounding land; smaller than a plateau

mountain – high, rounded or pointed landform with steep sides

mountain range – row or chain of mountains

mouth – place where a river empties into a body of water

oasis – a place in a desert where a supply of water makes the land fertile

ocean – one of Earth's four largest bodies of water

peak – pointed top of a mountain or hill

peninsula – body of land almost completely surrounded by water

plain – large area of level or gently rolling land

plateau – area of high, flat land; larger than a mesa

river – large stream of water that flows across land and empties into a larger water body

sea – large bay of water partly or entirely surrounded by land

strait – narrow waterway or channel connecting two bodies of water

tributary – river or stream that flows into a larger river or stream

valley – V-shaped depression between mountains or hills

volcano – mountain created by volcanic action

waterfall – flow of water falling from a high place to a low place

Get Sharp: Physical Geography

World Extremes

The extremes on Earth's surface make geography especially fascinating. Around the world, there are breathtaking highs, lows, depths, and widths. Some of them are easily seen; others are too high or deep beneath water to view easily. Here is a list of some of the most spectacular record-holding extremes in the world.

Highest

Highest mountain – Mount Everest in Nepal and Tibet: 29,035 feet.

Highest active volcano – Guallatiri in Chile: 19,882 feet

Highest waterfalls – Angel Falls in Venezuela: 3,212 feet

Deepest

Deepest ocean – Pacific Ocean: 35,937 feet (water at deepest point)

Deepest sea – Caribbean Sea: 22,788 feet

Deepest lake – Lake Baikal in Russia: 1.02 miles

Deepest ocean trench – Marianas Trench in the Pacific Ocean: 35,840 feet (That's almost 7 miles deep!)

Deepest cave – Lamprechtsofen-Vogelschacht in Austria: 5,354 feet

Deepest canyon – Kings Canyon in California: 8,199 feet

Lowest

Lowest point of dry land – Death Valley in California, USA: 282 feet below sea level

Biggest

Biggest sea – Arabian Sea: 1,492,000 square miles

Biggest lake – Caspian Sea in Europe and Asia: 143,244 square miles

Biggest freshwater lake – Lake Superior in North America: 31,761 square miles

Biggest river delta – Ganges River and Brahmaputra River delta: 30,000 square miles

Biggest island – Greenland in the North Atlantic Ocean: 840,000 square miles

Biggest island in fresh water – Marajo, in the mouth of the Amazon River in Brazil: 18,500 square miles

Biggest desert – Sahara Desert in Africa: 3,500,000 square miles

Biggest glacier – Lambert-Fischer Glacier in Antarctica: 320 miles long

Biggest area of glaciers – Antarctica: 4,610,610 square miles of ice

Biggest iceberg – North Atlantic Ocean in 1987: 208 miles long and 60 miles wide

Biggest ocean – Pacific Ocean: 64,200,000 square miles

Biggest meteorite crater – Sudbury Crater in Ontario, Canada: 87 miles wide

Longest

Longest underwater mountain range – Mid-Atlantic Range: 7,022 miles

Longest above-water mountain range – The Andes Mountains in South America: 4,500 miles

Longest cave system – Mammoth Cave System in Kentucky, USA: 352 miles

Longest canyon – Grand Canyon in Arizona: 277 miles

Longest reef – Great Barrier Reef in waters off Australia: 1,260 miles

Longest fjord – Nordvest Fjord in Greenland: 194 miles

Longest river – The Nile River in Egypt and Sudan: 4,160 miles

Tallest

Tallest mountain that rises out of the ocean – Mauna Kea: 33,480 feet from the floor of the Pacific Ocean (Mauna Kea forms the island of Hawaii.)

Tallest underwater mountain – The Great Meteor Tablemount, North Atlantic Ocean: 13,123 feet

Tallest sand dunes – found in the Sahara Desert in Africa: as tall as 1,500 feet

Tallest iceberg – 550 feet, seen off Greenland in 1958

Highest wave (aside from a tsunami) – recorded in 1933 in the Pacific Ocean: 112 feet

Highest tsunami (tidal wave) – recorded in 1968 in Lituya Bay, Alaska: 1,700 feet

Other Extremes

Greatest outflow of any river – Amazon in Brazil, discharges 2.5 cubic miles of water in a minute

Saltiest sea – Dead Sea (in the Middle East, west of Israel)

Oldest lake – Lake Baikal in Russia: 25 million years old

Fastest-moving glacier – Quarayaq Glacier in Greenland: flows up to 70–80 feet a day

Windiest spot ever recorded – Port Martin, Antarctica: 65 mph for a month

Sunniest place – Eastern Sahara Desert: Sun shines 97% of the time

Least sunny place – North Pole: 182 days a year with no sunshine

Wettest spot in the world – Mt. Waialeale (Kuai, Hawaii): about 500 inches a year, falling 350 or more days a year

Driest spot – Atacama Desert in Chile: about 0.02 inches a year of rain

The coldest temperature ever recorded – Vostok, Antarctica: –128.6° F

The highest temperature ever recorded in the shade – Aziziyah, Libya: 136° F

The water in the Great Salt Lake of Utah, in the USA, is four times saltier than the water in any ocean.

Lake Baikal, in Siberia, holds one-fifth of the world's fresh water.

World Time Zones

If the time were the same around the world, there would be sunlight at noon in some places and darkness at noon in other places. Earth makes a complete 360° turn every 24 hours; therefore different parts of Earth are facing the Sun at different times in the day. To keep the time in an area related to the position of the Sun, Earth is divided into 24 time zones, each of them 15° in size. A *time zone* is an area within which the time is the same at a given moment. The base location for determining time is the prime meridian, which runs through Greenwich, England, at 0° longitude.

How to Figure Out Time Around the World, or
When in Doubt—Phone a Friend

Paris, France

Bon jour, mon ami. It's noon here in Paris. What time is it in Tokyo?

Tokyo, Japan

Well, Tokyo is 8 time zones east of you, so you need to add an hour for each of the zones. It's 8:00 PM here.

SU NAMI'S SUMO SCHOOL

Greenwich, England

Hello, Pepe? It's 6:00 AM here in Greenwich, England. What time is it there in Uruguay?

Ecuador

Grrr! It's 3:00 AM! Everybody knows the Earth rotates from east to west, so one hour of time is subtracted for each time zone to the west of 0°. Uruguay is 3 time zones to the west of you, so subtract one hour for each zone.

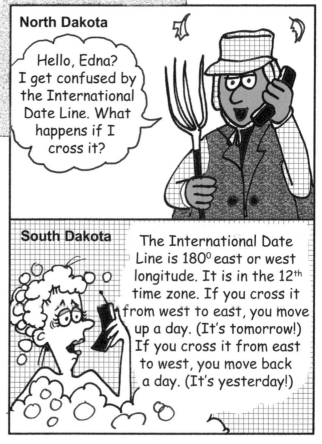

North Dakota

Hello, Edna? I get confused by the International Date Line. What happens if I cross it?

South Dakota

The International Date Line is 180° east or west longitude. It is in the 12th time zone. If you cross it from west to east, you move up a day. (It's tomorrow!) If you cross it from east to west, you move back a day. (It's yesterday!)

Better Grades & Higher Test Scores / SOCIAL STUDIES gr. 4–6

Take the Time Zone Challenge

Find the right answer on the checkerboard. Use the Time Zone map as a reference.

1. It's 6:00 AM on Friday in Perth, Australia. Joe calls his cousin in Rio de Janeiro, Brazil, to wish her a happy birthday. What time is it now in Rio?

2. A bear on loan to a New York zoo from Moscow, Russia is shipped from Moscow Saturday at 9:30 AM. She travels 14 hours. What time does the bear arrive in New York?

3. Zelda left Anchorage, Alaska, at noon on Monday for a trip to London, England. She arrives on Tuesday at 2:30 PM. How long was the trip?

4:00 PM, Saturday	18 hours	7:00 AM, Thursday
7:00 PM, Thursday	22 hours	4:40 PM, Saturday
17 hours	8:00 AM, Sunday	7:00 PM, Friday

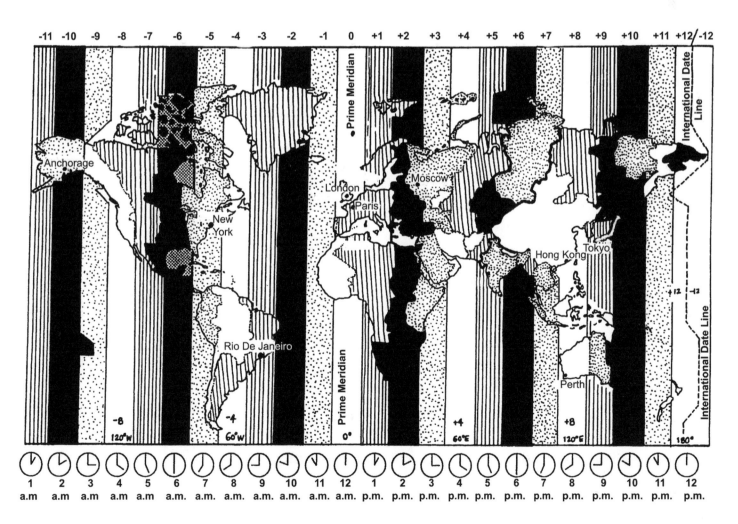

Get Sharp: Physical Geography

The World's Nations

The world is divided into different political areas. Some of these are independent countries or nations. Others are territories or other areas governed by another nation. This list shows the name of each of the world's 193 self-governing nations, along with its location, size, population (in 2004), and capital city. Maps showing these nations can be found on pages 118–123.

Three-quarters of the country of Austria is covered by the Alps Mountains.

Nation	Location	Area *in square miles*	Population *in 2004*	Capital City
Afghanistan	Southern Asia	251,737	29,547,078	Kabul
Albania	Eastern Europe	11,100	3,544,808	Tirane
Algeria	Northern Africa	919,590	33,357,089	Algiers
Andorra	Western Europe	181	69,865	Andorra La Vella
Angola	Southern Africa	481,350	10,978,552	Luanda
Antigua & Barbuda	In the Caribbean Sea, east of Puerto Rico	171	68,320	St. John's
Argentina	South America	1,068,296	39,144,753	Buenos Aires
Armenia	Western Asia	11,500	3,325,307	Yerevan
Australia	In the South Pacific Ocean, south of Asia	2,967,893	19,913,144	Canberra
Austria	Central Europe	32,375	8,174,762	Vienna
Azerbaijan	Western Asia	33,400	7,868,385	Baku
The Bahamas	In the Atlantic Ocean, east of Florida	5,380	299,697	Nassau
Bahrain	In the Persian Gulf, east of Qatar	257	656,397	Manama
Bangladesh	Southern Asia	55,598	141,340,476	Dhaka
Barbados	In the Atlantic Ocean, east of Puerto Rico	166	278,289	Bridgetown
Belarus	Eastern Europe	80,154	10,310,520	Minsk
Belgium	Western Europe	11,781	10,348,276	Brussels
Belize	Central America	8,865	272,945	Belmopan

For three hundred years, Barbary pirates used Algiers as their home base.

The tiny island country of Barbados is famous for its 5,000 green monkeys.

There are more than 700 islands in the Bahamas. People inhabit only about 40 of them.

Nation	Location	Area in square miles	Population in 2004	Capital City
Benin	Western Africa	43,483	7,7250,033	Porto-Novo
Bhutan	South-Central Asia	18,147	2,185,569	Thimphu
Bolivia	South America	424,162	8,724,156	La Paz
Bosnia & Herzegovina	Southern Europe	19,741	4,997,608	Sarajevo
Botswana	Southern Africa	231,800	1,561,973	Gaborone
Brazil	South America	3,286,470	184,101,109	Brasilia
Brunei	In the southern Pacific Ocean on the island of Borneo	2,228	365,251	Bandar Seri Begawan
Bulgaria	Eastern Europe	42,822	7,517,973	Sofia
Burkina Faso	Western Africa	105,870	13,574,820	Ouagadougou
Burundi	Central Africa	10,745	6,231,221	Bujumbura
Cambodia	Southeastern Asia	69,900	13,363,421	Phnom Penh
Cameroon	Central Africa	183,567	16,063,678	Yaoundé
Canada	North America	3,851,788	32,507,874	Ottawa
Cape Verde	In the Atlantic Ocean, west of the tip of Africa	1,557	415,294	Praia
Central African Republic	Central Africa	240,534	3,742,482	Bangui
Chad	Northern Africa	495,752	9,538,544	N'Djamena
Chile	South America	292,258	15,827,180	Santiago
People's Republic of China	Eastern Asia	3,705,386	1,294,629,555	Beijing
Columbia	South America	439,733	42,310,775	Bogotá
Comoros	In the Indian Ocean, east of Mozambique, Africa	838	651,901	Moroni

You can find the Kalahari Desert in Botswana.

Canada has the longest coastline in the world. It is 155,000 miles long. It is long enough to wrap around the world 6 times.

The lush Amazon rainforest in Brazil is home to almost half of the animal and plant species on Earth.

The Galapagos islands of Ecuador have only non-human residents. It is a refuge to thousands of birds, seals, giant turtles, and iguanas.

Nation	Location	Area in square miles	Population in 2004	Capital City
Democratic Republic of the Congo	Central Africa	905,562	58,317,930	Kinshasa
Republic of the Congo	Central Africa	132,046	2,998,040	Brazzaville
Costa Rica	Central America	19,730	3,956,507	San Jose
Cote d'Ivoire (Ivory Coast)	Western Africa	124,502	17,327,724	Yamoussoukro
Croatia	Southern Europe	21,829	4,435,960	Zagreb
Cuba	In the Caribbean Sea, south of Florida	42,803	11,308,764	Havana
Cyprus	In the Mediterranean Sea, west of Turkey	3,572	775,927	Nicosia
Czech Republic	Central Europe	30.450	10,246,178	Prague
Denmark	Northern Europe	16,639	5,413,392	Copenhagen
Djibouti	Northern Africa	8,80	466,900	Djibouti
Dominica	In the Caribbean Sea, east of Puerto Rico	290	69,278	Roseau
Dominican Republic	Shares an island with Haiti in the Caribbean Sea, east of Cuba	18,815	8,833,634	Santo Domingo
East Timor	In the southern Pacific Ocean, north of Australia	5,814	1,019,252	Dili
Ecuador	South America	109,483	13971,798	Quito
Egypt	Northeastern Africa	386,660	76,117,421	Cairo
El Salvador	Central America	8,124	6,587,541	San Salvador
Equatorial Guinea	West Africa	10,830	523,051	Malabo
Eritrea	Northeastern Africa	46,842	4,447,307	Asmara
Estonia	Northern Europe	17,462	1,401,845	Tallinn
Ethiopia	Eastern Africa	435,184	67,851,281	Addis Ababa
Fiji	In the southern Pacific Ocean, east of Australia	7,054	856,346	Suva

A village in Denmark has a very short name. The village is named A. This is even shorter than the Scottish town, Ae.

Ecuador is named after the equator (which runs through the country).

Fiji is made up of more than 300 islands.

Nation	Location	Area in square miles	Population in 2004	Capital City
Finland	Northern Europe	130,127	5,214,512	Helsinki
France	Western Europe	211,208	60,424,213	Paris
Gabon	Central Africa	103,347	1,355,246	Libreville
The Gambia	Western Africa	4,363	1,546,848	Banjul
Georgia	Western Asia	26,911	4,909,633	Tbilisi
Germany	Central Europe	167,846	82,424,609	Berlin
Ghana	Western Africa	92,456	20,757,032	Accra
Greece	Southern Europe	50,942	10,647,529	Athens
Grenada	In the Caribbean Sea, north of Venezuela	133	89,357	Saint George's
Guatemala	Central America	42,042	14,280,596	Guatemala City
Guinea	Western Africa	94,925	9,246,462	Conakry
Guinea-Bissau	Western Africa	13,946	1,388,363	Bissau
Guyana	South America	83,000	705,803	Georgetown
Haiti	Shares an island with the Dominican Republic in the Caribbean Sea, east of Cuba	10,714	7,656,166	Port-au-Prince
Honduras	Central America	43,278	6,823,568	Tegucigalpa
Hungary	Central Europe	35,919	10,032,375	Budapest
Iceland	In the northern Atlantic Ocean, west of northern Europe	39,768	282,151	Reykjavik
India	Southern Asia	1,269,338	1,065,070,607	New Delhi
Indonesia	In the southern Pacific and Indian Oceans, south of Asia	741,096	238,452,952	Jakarta
Iran	Southwestern Asia	636,293	69,018,924	Tehran

There are more than 100 volcanoes in Iceland. That's one volcano for every 2,822 people!

Indonesia is made up of more than 13,000 islands. If you count the water between the islands, the country spans about two million square miles.

Nation	Location	Area in square miles	Population in 2004	Capital City
Iraq	Southwestern Asia	168,753	25,374,691	Baghdad
Ireland	In the Atlantic Ocean, west of Great Britain	27,136	3,969,558	Dublin
Israel	Middle East	8,020	6,199,008	Jerusalem
Italy	Southern Europe	116,305	58,057,477	Rome
Jamaica	In the Caribbean Sea, south of Cuba	4,244	2,713,130	Kingston
Japan	in the Pacific Ocean, east of Asia	145,882	127,333,002	Tokyo
Jordan	Middle East	34,445	5,611,202	Amman
Kazakhstan	Central Asia	1,049,150	16,798,552	Astana
Kenya	Eastern Africa	224,960	32,021,856	Nairobi
Kiribati	In the mid-Pacific Ocean, northeast of Australia	313	100,798	Tarawa
Kuwait	Southwestern Asia	6,880	2,257,549	Kuwait City
Kyrgyzstan	Western Asia	76,641	4,965,081	Bishkek
Laos	Southeastern Asia	91,429	6,068,177	Vientiane
Latvia	Central Europe	24,938	2,332,078	Riga
Lebanon	Middle East	4,015	3,777,218	Beirut
Lesotho	Southern Africa	11,720	1,865,040	Maseru
Liberia	Western Africa	43,000	3,390,635	Monrovia
Libya	Northern Africa	679,358	5,631,585	Tripoli
Liechtenstein	Southern Europe	62	33,436	Vaduz
Lithuania	Northern Europe	25,174	3,584,836	Vilnius

The city of Venice, Italy, is built on 118 islands in a lagoon. Parts of the city are connected by as many as 400 bridges.

A moat surrounds Riga, the capital city of Latvia.

Nation	Location	Area in square miles	Population in 2004	Capital City
Luxembourg	Western Europe	999	462,690	Luxembourg
Macedonia	Southern Europe	9,781	2,071,210	Skopje
Madagascar	In the Indian Ocean, east of Africa	226,660	17,501,871	Antananarivo
Malawi	Southern Africa	45,745	11,906,855	Lilongwe
Malaysia	Southwestern Asia and the South China Sea on the Island of Borneo	127,316	23,552,482	Kuala Lumpur
Maldives	In the Indian Ocean, south of India	116	339,330	Male
Mali	Western Africa	478,764	11,956,788	Bamako
Malta	In the Mediterranean Sea, south of Italy	122	403,342	Valetta
Marshall Islands	In the Pacific Ocean, northeast of Australia	70	57,738	Majuro
Mauritania	Western Africa	397,953	2,998,563	Mouakchott
Mauritius	In the Indian Ocean, east of Africa	788	1,220,481	Port Louis
Mexico	North America	761,600	104,959,594	Mexico City
Micronesia	In the Pacific Ocean, northeast of Australia	271	108,155	Palikir
Moldova	Eastern Europe	13,067	4,446,455	Chisinau
Monaco	Western Europe	0.75	32,279	Monaco
Mongolia	Central Asia	604,250	2,751,314	Ulaanbaatar
Morocco	Northwestern Africa	172,413	32,209,101	Rabat
Mozambique	Southern Africa	309,494	18,811,731	Maputo
Myanmar (Burma)	Southern Asia	261,969	42,720,196	Yangon
Namibia	Southern Africa	318,694	1,954,033	Windhoek
Nauru	In the western Pacific Ocean, northeast of Australia	8.2	12,909	Yaren district

The capital of Mexico is sinking about 6 inches a year because it is built on an underground water reservoir.

Monaco is the world's most densely-populated country.

Mongolia is the world's least densely-populated country.

Get Sharp: World's Nations

The
deepest
freshwater
lake in the
world, Lake
Baikal, is
in Russia.

Pakistan is
home to the
world's second
highest peak,
K-2.

K-2

Nation	Location	Area *in square miles*	Population *in 2004*	Capital City
Nepal	Central Asia	54,363	27,070,666	Kathmandu
Netherlands	Northern Europe	16,036	16,318,199	Amsterdam
New Zealand	In the southern Pacific Ocean, east of Australia	103,737	3,993,817	Wellington
Nicaragua	Central America	50,000	5,232,216	Managua
Niger	Northern Africa	489,189	11,360,538	Niamey
Nigeria	Western Africa	356,700	137,253,133	Abjua
North Korea	Eastern Asia	46,540	22,697,553	Pyongyang
Norway	Northern Europe	125,181	4,574,560	Oslo
Oman	Southwestern Asia	82,030	2,903,165	Muscat
Pakistan	Southwestern Asia	310,400	153,705,278	Islamabad
Palau	In the northern Pacific Ocean, southeast of the Philippines	177	20,016	Koror
Panama	Central America	30,193	3,000,462	Panama City
Papua New Guinea	Shares an island in the southern Pacific Ocean with Indonesia, northeast of Australia	178,703	5,420,280	Port Moresby
Paraguay	South America	157,046	6,191,368	Asuncion
Peru	South America	496,223	28,863,494	Lima
Philippines	In the northwestern Pacific Ocean, east of southeastern Asia	115,830	86,241,697	Manila
Poland	Central Europe	120,727	38,626,349	Warsaw
Portugal	Southern Europe	35,672	10,084,245	Lisbon
Qatar	Middle East	4,416	840,290	Doha
Romania	Southern Europe	91,700	22,355,551	Bucharest
Russia	Spans from eastern Europe across the whole of northern Asia	6,592,735	144,112,353	Moscow

Better Grades & Higher Test Scores / SOCIAL STUDIES gr. 4–6
Copyright ©2005 by Incentive Publications, Inc., Nashville, TN.

Nation	Location	Area in square miles	Population in 2004	Capital City
Rwanda	Central Africa	10,170	7,954,013	Kigali
Saint Kitts and Nevis	In the Caribbean Sea, east of Puerto Rico	100	38,836	Basseterre
Saint Lucia	In the Caribbean Sea, north of Venezuela	240	164,213	Castries
Saint Vincent	In the Caribbean Sea, north of Venezuela	150	117,193	Kingstown
Samoa	In the southern Pacific Ocean, east of Australia	1,100	177,714	Nicosia
San Marino	Southern Europe	24	28,503	San Marino
Sao Tome and Principe	In the Atlantic Ocean, west of central Africa	386	181,565	Sao Tome
Saudi Arabia	Western Asia	756,981	25,100,425	Riyadh
Serbia and Montenegro	Eastern Europe	39,517	10,663,022	Belgrade
Senegal	Western Africa	75,750	10,852,147	Dakar
Seychelles	In the Indian Ocean, east of Africa	176	80,832	Victoria
Sierra Leone	Western Africa	27,700	5,883,889	Freetown
Singapore	In the southern Pacific Ocean, off the tip of southeastern Asia	267	4,767,974	Singapore
Slovakia	Eastern Europe	18,860	5,423,567	Bratislava
Slovenia	Eastern Europe	7,820	1,938,282	Ljubljana
Solomon Islands	In the western Pacific Ocean, northeast of Australia	10,985	523,617	Honiara
Somalia	Eastern Africa	246,200	8,304,601	Mogadishu

Singapore means "City of Lions." A lion has never been seen in Singapore.

Volcanoes National Park in northwestern Rwanda is home to half of the remaining mountain gorillas in the world.

Nation	Location	Area in square miles	Population in 2004	Capital City
South Africa	Africa	471,010	42,718,530	Pretoria and Cape Town
South Korea	Eastern Asia	38,023	48,598,176	Seoul
Spain	Western Europe	194,896	40,280,780	Madrid
Sri Lanka	In the Indian Ocean, southeast of India	25,332	19,905,165	Colombo
Sudan	Northern Africa	967,500	39,148,162	Khartoum
Suriname	South America	63,040	436,935	Paramaribo
Swaziland	Southern Africa	6,704	1,169,241	Mbabane
Sweden	Northern Europe	173,730	8,986,400	Stockholm
Switzerland	Central Europe	15,940	7,450,867	Bern and Lausanne
Syria	Northwestern Asia	71,500	18,016,874	Damascus
Taiwan	In East China Sea-Pacific Ocean, east of China	13,890	22,749,848	Taipei
Tajikistan	Western Asia	55,300	7,011,556	Dushanbe
Tanzania	Eastern Africa	364,900	36,588,225	Dar-es-Salaam
Thailand	Southeastern Asia	198,000	64,865,523	Bangkok
Togo	Western Africa	21,930	5,556,812	Lome
Tonga	In the southern Pacific Ocean	290	110,237	Nuku'alofa
Trinidad and Tobago	In the Caribbean Sea, north of Venezuela, South America	1,980	1,096,585	Port-of-Spain
Tunisia	Northern Africa	63,170	10,032,050	Tunis
Turkey	Eastern Europe and partly in western Asia	301,380	68,893,918	Ankara
Turkmenistan	Western Asia	188,500	4,863,169	Ashgabat
Tuvalu	In the southern Pacific Ocean, east of Australia	10	11,468	Funafuti Atoll
Uganda	Eastern Africa	91,140	26,404,543	Kampala
Ukraine	Eastern Europe	233,100	47,732,079	Kiev
United Arab Emirates	Middle East	32,000	2,523,915	Abu Dhabi

Sri Lanka is home to one of the most poisonous snakes in the world, the carpet viper. On the average, two people are killed each day by poisonous snakes in Sri Lanka.

The Vatican City is the smallest independent state. Its birthrate is zero, because the citizens are Roman Catholic priests, who are not allowed to marry.

Nation	Location	Area in square miles	Population in 2004	Capital City
United Kingdom (Great Britain)	In the Atlantic Ocean, west of the European mainland	94,525	60,270,708	London
United States	North America	3,717,810	293,027,571	Washington, D.C.
Uruguay	South America	68.040	3,440,205	Montevideo
Uzbekistan	Central Asia	172,740	26,410,416	Tashkent
Vanuatu	In the southern Pacific Ocean, east of Australia	5,700	202,609	Port-Vila
Vatican City	Within the city of Rome, Italy	0.2	890	no capital
Venezuela	South America	352,140	25,017,387	Caracas
Vietnam	Southeastern Asia	127,240	82,689,518	Hanoi
Yemen	Southwestern Asia	203,850	20,024,867	Sanaa
Zambia	Southern Africa	290,580	10,462,436	Lusaka
Zimbabwe	Southern Africa	150,800	12,671,860	Harare

About 10 million people in the world live in places that are not independent. These places are dependent territories ruled by the UK, the US, Denmark, France, Portugal, Norway, Australia, or New Zealand.

North America — Political Divisions

North America is a vast continent that includes three large countries and twenty smaller ones, some of them tiny islands.

Key
scale: 1 in = 900 mi
● represents capitals of countries

Island Nations
1. St. Kitts & Nevis
2. Antigua & Barbuda
3. Dominica
4. St. Lucia
5. Barbados
6. Grenada
7. St. Vincent & the Grenadines

South America – Political Divisions

Caribbean Sea

Trinidad & Tobago

Venezuela

Columbia

Guyana

Suriname

French Guiana

Amazon River

Ecuador

Peru

Brazil

Pacific Ocean

Bolivia

Key
Scale: 1 in = 545 mi
● *represents capitals of countries*

Chile

Paraguay

Atlantic Ocean

Argentina

Uruguay

South America was colonized by Spanish conquerors except for the land that is now Brazil, which was settled by the Portuguese. As a result, most of the countries are Spanish-speaking, but Portuguese is the main language in Brazil.

Falkland Is.

Get Sharp Tip #7

The bottom edge of South America comes closer to the continent of Antarctica than any other continent.

Antarctica is the only continent with no political divisions. Since it has no permanent residents, there is no governmental unit on the continent.

Europe – Political Divisions

Key
scale: 1 in = 400 mi
● represents capitals of countries
Small Countries
1. Andorra
2. Monaco
3. Liechtenstein
4. Luxembourg
5. San Marin
6. Vatican City

Iceland

Atlantic Ocean

Norwegian Sea

North Sea

Baltic Sea

Sweden

Norway

Finland

Russia

Estonia

Denmark

Latvia

Ireland

United Kingdom

Lithuania

Netherlands

Poland

Blarus

Belgium

Germany

4

Czech. Rep

Ukraine

Bay of Biscay

France

3

Slovakia

Switzerland

Austria

Moldova

Slovenia

Hungary

Romania

Croatia

1

2

Portugal

Spain

5

Italy

Bosnia

Yugo-slavia

Bulgaria

Corsica

6

Macedonia

Majorca

Albania

Turkey

Sardinia

Greece

Black Sea

Mediterranean Sea

Sicily

Istanbul, Turkey, is the only city that is in two continents–Asia and Europe. The continental boundary goes right through the city!

Asia – Political Divisions

Asia is the largest continent. It is home to the ten highest mountain peaks, the lowest place on Earth (the Dead Sea), and over 65% of the world's people.

Key
scale: 1 in = 1100 mi
● represents capitals of countries

Get Sharp Tip #8
Though Europe and Asia are named as two different continents, they share the same large land mass.

Better Grades & Higher Test Scores / SOCIAL STUDIES gr. 4–6
Copyright ©2005 by Incentive Publications, Inc., Nashville, TN.

Get Sharp: World's Nations

Africa – Political Divisions

Africa is often described in two regions. North Africa is the region of the Sahara Desert. The people are primarily Arabic-speaking Muslims. South of the Sahara desert is a region of many different cultures and languages.

Mediterranean Sea

Morocco
Tunisia

Western Sahara

Algeria

Libya

Egypt

Cape Verde

Mauritania

Mali

Niger

Chad

Sudan

Nile River

Red Sea

Eritrea

The Gambia

Senegal

Guinea Bissau

Guinea

Burkina-Faso

Benin

Nigeria

Chad

Djibouti

Somalia

Sierra Leone

Ghana

Cote D'Ivoire

Togo

Ethiopia

Liberia

Atlantic Ocean

Central African Rep.

Cameroon

Equatorial Guinea

Uganda

Kenya

Key
scale: 1 in = 670 mi
● *represents capitals of countries*

Gabon

Rep. of the Congo

Democratic Republic of the Congo

Rwanda Burundi

L. Victoria

Indian Ocean

Sao Tome & Principe

Tanzania

Seychelles

Get Sharp Tip #9
Africa is the only continent that lies on both sides of the equator (0° latitude) and on both sides of the prime meridian (0° longitude).

Angola

Zambia

Malawi

Comoros

Mozambique

Madagascar

Namibia

Zimbabwe

Botswana

Swaziland

South Africa

Lesotho

Australia & Oceania – Political Divisions

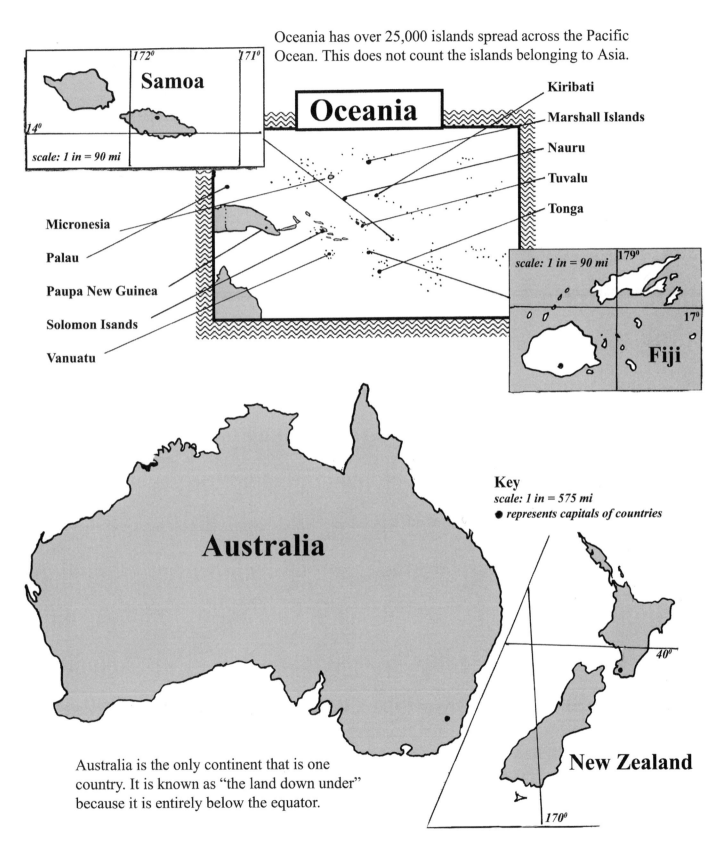

Oceania has over 25,000 islands spread across the Pacific Ocean. This does not count the islands belonging to Asia.

Samoa

scale: 1 in = 90 mi

Oceania

Kiribati

Marshall Islands

Nauru

Tuvalu

Tonga

Micronesia

Palau

Paupa New Guinea

Solomon Isands

Vanuatu

scale: 1 in = 90 mi

Fiji

Australia

Key
scale: 1 in = 575 mi
● represents capitals of countries

New Zealand

Australia is the only continent that is one country. It is known as "the land down under" because it is entirely below the equator.

World Population

Population is the number of people in a given area. *Population density* describes how close together people live. An area with high population density is very crowded.

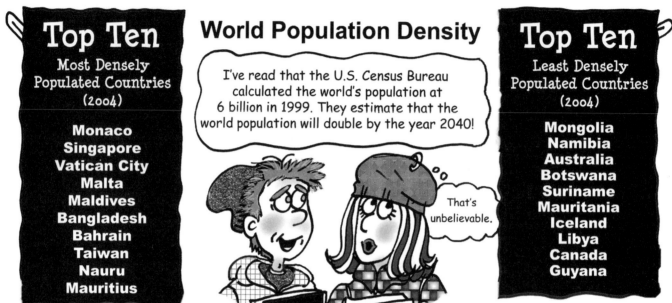

Top Ten
Most Densely Populated Countries (2004)

Monaco
Singapore
Vatican City
Malta
Maldives
Bangladesh
Bahrain
Taiwan
Nauru
Mauritius

World Population Density

I've read that the U.S. Census Bureau calculated the world's population at 6 billion in 1999. They estimate that the world population will double by the year 2040!

That's unbelievable.

Top Ten
Least Densely Populated Countries (2004)

Mongolia
Namibia
Australia
Botswana
Suriname
Mauritania
Iceland
Libya
Canada
Guyana

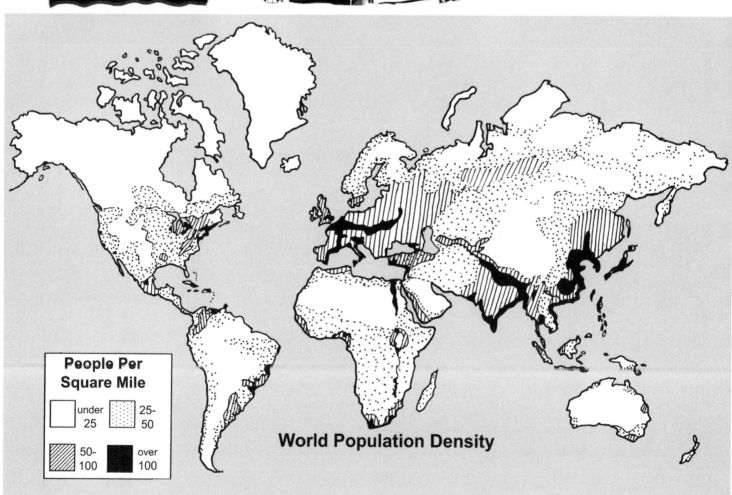

People Per Square Mile

under 25
25–50
50–100
over 100

World Population Density

How World Population Has Changed

World Population . . .

in 1950	2,556,000,053
in 1960	3,039,451,023
in 1970	3,706,618,163
in 1980	4,453,831,714
in 1990	5,278,639,789
in 2000	6,082,966,429
in 2005	6,413,001,357

Top 10 Populations of Countries

(Countries with Most People in 2004)

Population to nearest 1,000

1.	China	1,298,848,000
2.	India	1,065,071,000
3.	United States	293,028,000
4.	Indonesia	238,453,000
5.	Brazil	184,101,000
6.	Pakistan	159,196,000
7.	Russia	143,782,000
8.	Bangladesh	141,340,000
9.	Nigeria	137,253,000
10.	Japan	127,333,000

Top 10 Most Populous World Cities

(2004)

Population to nearest 100

1.	Shanghai, China	13,278,500
2.	Mumbai (Bombay), India	12,622,000
3.	Buenos Aires, Argentina	11,928,400
4.	Moscow, Russia	11,273,400
5.	Karachi, Pakistan	10,899,100
6.	Delhi, India	10,400,900
7.	Manila, Philippines	10,330,100
8.	Sao Paulo, Brazil	10,260,100
9.	Seoul, South Korea	10,165,400
10.	Istanbul, Turkey	9,631,700

Stay up-to-the-minute with the world population as it grows. Visit the **World Population Clock** at http://www.census.gov/main/www/popclock.html

Pop Trivia

The country of Niger has the highest birth rate in the world.

The country of Angola has the highest death rate in the world.

The people of the United Kingdom are the world's top consumers of baked beans.

The people of Lebanon eat the most vegetables per person.

The top butter consumers in the world are the people of New Zealand.

The people of Finland drink more coffee per person than anywhere else in the world.

The French are the world's top consumers of fat.

The Swiss people are the world's top consumers of chocolate, eating an average of 26 pounds a year each.

The people of Somalia are the most undernourished in the world.

Remarkable Creations

Humans have made some amazing additions to the world's landscape. These are just a few of the astounding, creative cultural landmarks that have been designed and built on Earth over the course of human history. See page 127 for the locations of these structures.

Some Remarkable Creations in the Western Hemisphere

The **Panama Canal**, completed in 1914, is a waterway built across the Isthmus of Panama. It allows ships to pass between the Atlantic and Pacific Oceans.

The **Gateway Arch** is a 630-foot arch overlooking the Mississippi River in St. Louis, Missouri. It was built to honor the Louisiana Purchase.

Christ the Redeemer is a tall statue of Jesus Christ that overlooks the harbor in Rio de Janeiro, Brazil.

Mt. Rushmore, in South Dakota, depicts the faces of several American presidents carved into the rock.

The **Statue of Liberty** is a tall statue of a lady standing in the harbor of New York City, welcoming visitors to a free land.

Chichen Itza, the ruins of a powerful city of the ancient Mayan empire, is found in eastern Mexico.

The **Space Needle** looks like a needle. It was the centerpiece of the 1962 Seattle World's Fair.

Machu Picchu is known as the "Lost City of the Incas." It is a collection of ruins of an ancient Incan city, found high in the Andes Mountains of Peru.

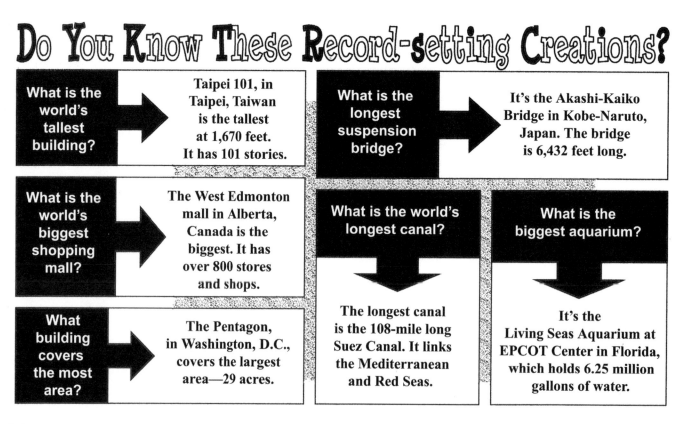

Do You Know These Record-setting Creations?

What is the world's tallest building? → **Taipei 101, in Taipei, Taiwan is the tallest at 1,670 feet. It has 101 stories.**

What is the longest suspension bridge? → **It's the Akashi-Kaiko Bridge in Kobe-Naruto, Japan. The bridge is 6,432 feet long.**

What is the world's biggest shopping mall? → **The West Edmonton mall in Alberta, Canada is the biggest. It has over 800 stores and shops.**

What is the world's longest canal? → **The longest canal is the 108-mile long Suez Canal. It links the Mediterranean and Red Seas.**

What is the biggest aquarium? → **It's the Living Seas Aquarium at EPCOT Center in Florida, which holds 6.25 million gallons of water.**

What building covers the most area? → **The Pentagon, in Washington, D.C., covers the largest area—29 acres.**

Remarkable Creations
in the Western Hemisphere

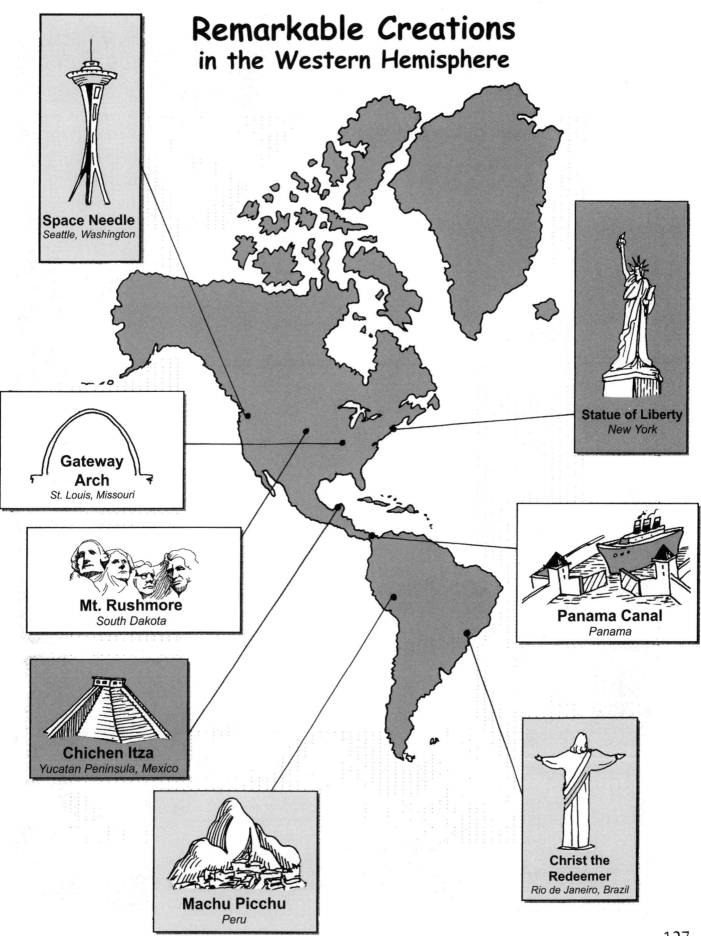

Space Needle
Seattle, Washington

Statue of Liberty
New York

Gateway Arch
St. Louis, Missouri

Mt. Rushmore
South Dakota

Panama Canal
Panama

Chichen Itza
Yucatan Peninsula, Mexico

Machu Picchu
Peru

Christ the Redeemer
Rio de Janeiro, Brazil

Get Sharp: World Creations

Some Remarkable Creations in the Eastern Hemisphere

The **Parthenon** is an ancient Greek temple overlooking the city of Athens, Greece. It sits on top of a hill called the "Acropolis."

St. Basil's Cathedral is a beautiful Russian Orthodox church built at the southern end of the Red Square in Moscow, Russia.

The **Leaning Tower of Pisa** is an Italian bell tower in the town of Pisa. Because it was built on unstable soil, the tower is leaning about 14 feet out of alignment.

Notre Dame is a famous and beautiful two-towered cathedral in Paris. Its name means "Our Lady."

Stonehenge is a mysterious stone circle built in ancient times in southwestern England.

The **Tower of London** is a group of buildings along the Thames River in London. The buildings have been a prison and a castle. It is now an arsenal and a museum which houses the British crown jewels.

The **Eiffel Tower** is a steel and iron tower built in Paris for the World's Fair of 1889.

The **Sydney Opera House**, in Sydney, Australia, is a huge performance center of unusual architecture. It has a roof of overlapping shells that looks like two huge sails.

The **Great Wall of China** is the longest human-built structure, stretching 4,500 miles across China.

The **Taj Mahal** is a huge white marble structure built as a tomb for the wife of Shah Jahan.

The **Great Sphinx**, a great monument with the head of a human and the body of a lion, sits near the great pyramids in Egypt.

The **Egyptian Pyramids** are large stone tombs built for Egyptian pharaohs. Ruins of 35 pyramids are still standing along the Nile River.

The ***Mona Lisa***, completed in 1506 by Leonardo da Vinci, is probably the most famous painting in the world. It hangs in the Louvre Museum in Paris, France.

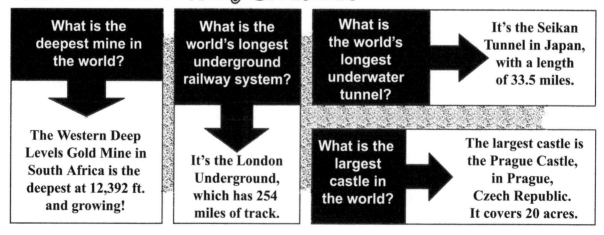

More Record-setting Creations

What is the deepest mine in the world?

The Western Deep Levels Gold Mine in South Africa is the deepest at 12,392 ft. and growing!

What is the world's longest underground railway system?

It's the London Underground, which has 254 miles of track.

What is the world's longest underwater tunnel?

It's the Seikan Tunnel in Japan, with a length of 33.5 miles.

What is the largest castle in the world?

The largest castle is the Prague Castle, in Prague, Czech Republic. It covers 20 acres.

Better Grades & Higher Test Scores / SOCIAL STUDIES gr. 4–6
Copyright ©2005 by Incentive Publications, Inc., Nashville, TN.

Remarkable Creations in the Eastern Hemisphere

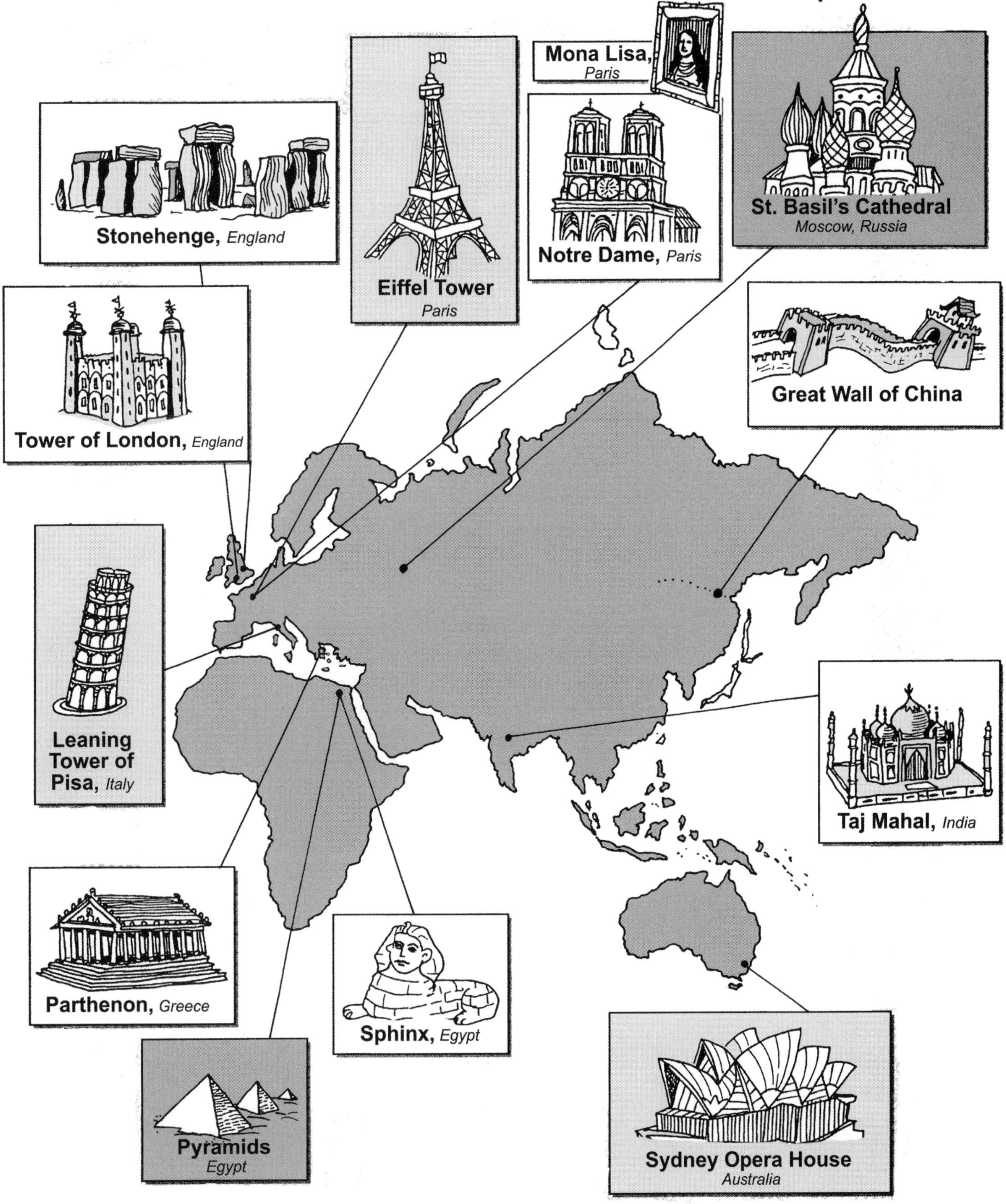

Mona Lisa, *Paris*

Stonehenge, *England*

Eiffel Tower
Paris

Notre Dame, *Paris*

St. Basil's Cathedral
Moscow, Russia

Tower of London, *England*

Great Wall of China

Leaning Tower of Pisa, *Italy*

Taj Mahal, *India*

Parthenon, *Greece*

Sphinx, *Egypt*

Pyramids
Egypt

Sydney Opera House
Australia

Get Sharp: World Creations

World Connections

The distance around Earth is thousands of miles, and the world's peoples are from hundreds of different cultures. Yet today, the world seems small. A traveler can speed from one continent to another in a few hours. In just seconds, you can communicate by Internet with a friend halfway around the world. In addition, the issues, needs, problems, and lives of people all over the world are connected by the fact that we all share the same home—planet Earth. Here are some types of connections that bring us together.

Big Problems

All humans on Earth share the same kinds of problems. These things affect us all, and affect the world we share.

global warming
pollution
deforestation
poor air quality
terrorism
natural disasters
poverty
shrinking resources
food shortages
population increases
wars
political conflicts
hunger

Cultural Connections

Geographical borders do not confine cultures. Many cultures have spread all over the world. Cultures have shared and exchanged ideas with one another. The world is a multicultural habitat for humans.

Religious Connections

Geographical borders do not confine religion. Ideas from most religions have spread all over the world. Wherever a person lives, the understanding and tolerance of many religious ideas is a part of life as a world citizen.

Economic Connections

In today's modern world, economic systems, patterns, and institutions tie nations and cultures together. Any country's economic policies are affected by the economic status and practices of other countries.

Needs and Wants Connections

All humans have similar needs for things such as food, shelter, safety, space, and relationships. Humans have wants, too, although these differ among people and cultures. Meeting needs and satisfying wants for people in one part of the world affects people in other parts of the world. This happens because Earth's resources are limited. Filling wants and needs uses resources, and often leaves some sort of impact on the world's environment (air, water, or land).

Environmental Connections

All of the world's peoples share the Earth's environment. A healthy environment or an unhealthy environment eventually affects us all. Deforestation in South America affects the climate worldwide. Air pollution in China is carried across oceans by winds. Depletion of coal and oil supplies in North America puts extra demand on those resource supplies elsewhere in the world.

Travel & Communication Connections

Technology has caused the world to "shrink." Jet airplanes, fast trains, telephones, computers, and the Internet have made it possible to visit or connect with someone else just about anywhere in the world. It is possible to get a message to someone at the top of Mt. Everest, on a subway underground, deep in a cave, or in the Amazon rainforest.

World Organizations

Many organizations have sprung up to meet the needs of the world or a part of the world. These organizations have the support and cooperation of more than one nation and fill a variety of needs: social, political, military, economic, or humanitarian.

> These are a few of the organizations in which several nations cooperate to meet some kind of need that crosses national borders.

CIS Commonwealth of Independent States

Purpose: an agreement among nations that were once a part of the Soviet Union, formed to help the new countries work together

Commonwealth Commonwealth of Nations

Purpose: an organization of countries that have been under British rule, formed to cooperate in economic and foreign affairs

EU European Union

Purpose: an agreement of several European countries to cooperate in many economic and political areas

IAEA International Atomic Energy Agency

Purpose: to work for peaceful and safe uses of atomic energy

ILO International Labor Organization

Purpose: to promote the welfare of workers worldwide

IMF International Monetary Fund

Purpose: to help nations cooperate on financial matters that affect the world's nations

IMO International Maritime Organization

Purpose: to promote marine safety, prevent pollution from ships, and set high standards for shipping

NATO North Atlantic Treaty Organization

Purpose: a military alliance of U.S., Canada, and many European countries, formed to keep peace in Europe and protect one another

OAS Organization of American States

Purpose: for a group of North American and South American countries to work together for peace, self-defense, and cooperation

OPEC Organization of Petroleum Exporting Countries

Purpose: to increase revenue from the sale of oil

UN United Nations

Purpose: an organization of most of the world's nations, formed to work for world peace and security and the bettering of humans

UNICEF United Nations Children's Fund

Purpose: to help children get the care and stimulation they need; to reduce illness and death in children; to protect children in war or natural disasters

WHO World Health Organization

Purpose: to promote health and health education

WTO World Trade Organization

Purpose: to oversee international trade

The United Nations

The United Nations (UN) is a community of nations joined together to work toward making the world a better place. The UN began in 1945 at the end of World War II. Representatives of 50 nations gathered in San Francisco, California, and wrote an agreement called the *UN Charter*. By the year 2004, the UN had 191 member nations. The UN headquarters is in New York City, New York. The World Court is located at The Hague, Netherlands.

UN Day is celebrated around the world on October 24. Concerts, speeches, parades, and other events commemorate the day the UN Charter was signed.

The Purposes of the United Nations

- to maintain international peace
- to develop friendly relations among nations
- to cooperate in solving international problems
- to promote respect for human rights and basic human freedoms
- to help countries achieve their goals for meeting these purposes

UN Agencies & Programs

The UN operates several agencies and programs to deal with many world concerns. The organization is active in working on issues, problems, and concerns such as:

peacekeeping

humanitarian needs

human rights

needs of children

environmental protection

disease prevention

treatment of diseases

poverty

consumer protection

safe travel

stopping terrorism

stopping drug trafficking

clearing land minds

helping refugees

fighting against AIDS

The Structure of the United Nations

The **General Assembly** includes all members of the UN, with each country having one vote. The assembly discusses world problems, appoints the secretary-general, agrees on the budget, and admits new members.

The **Security Council** has five permanent members (China, France, Great Britain, Russia, and the U.S.) and ten members elected by the General Assembly for 2-year terms. The council discusses and votes on matters of world peace and security.

The **Economic and Social Council** has 54 members, each elected for a term of 3 years. The council discusses and acts on issues related to economic development, trade, and a variety of social issues such as health, human rights, children, education, food, and population.

The **International Court of Justice** (World Court) has 15 judges, each elected for a 9-year term. The judges are all from different countries. The court settled disputes between countries.

The **Secretariat** is a part of the organization that operates the day-to-day business of the UN. This organ of the UN is headed by the secretary-general, who is appointed by the General Assembly.

Better Grades & Higher Test Scores / SOCIAL STUDIES gr. 4–6
Copyright ©2005 by Incentive Publications, Inc., Nashville, TN.

GET SHARP →

on

U.S. GEOGRAPHY

U.S. Land and Water

This map shows some of the major physical features of the United States.

The United States is a land of great variety in physical features. If you travel around the country, you will see an amazing, breath-taking assortment of tall mountains, rolling hills, flat plains, rushing rivers, vast forests, deep canyons, high plateaus, wide valleys, rocky cliffs, long beaches, and lakes of all sizes.

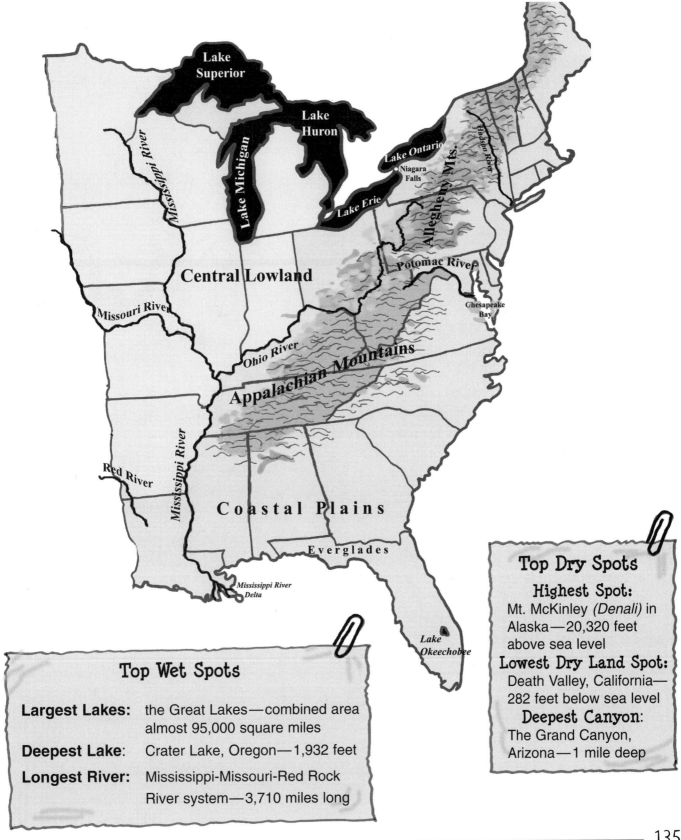

Top Wet Spots

Largest Lakes: the Great Lakes—combined area almost 95,000 square miles

Deepest Lake: Crater Lake, Oregon—1,932 feet

Longest River: Mississippi-Missouri-Red Rock River system—3,710 miles long

Top Dry Spots

Highest Spot: Mt. McKinley *(Denali)* in Alaska—20,320 feet above sea level

Lowest Dry Land Spot: Death Valley, California—282 feet below sea level

Deepest Canyon: The Grand Canyon, Arizona—1 mile deep

U.S.A. — Vital Statistics

Capital: Washington, D.C.

Size: 3,717,796 square miles

Relative size: the 4th largest country in area

Location: North America, between Canada and Mexico, with one state northwest of Canada and another state in the central Pacific Ocean

Latitude range: 19°N – 71°N

Longitude range: 67°W – 172°E

Span: stretches from the Atlantic Ocean to the Pacific Ocean across the whole of the North American continent

Northernmost point: Point Barrow, Alaska

Southernmost point: Ka Lae, Hawaii

Easternmost point: West Quoddy Head, Maine

Westernmost point: Cape Wrangell, Alaska

Geographic center of the 50 states: Butte County, South Dakota

Length of coastline: 12,380 miles

Natural resources: forests, coal, natural gas, oil, minerals, salt, silver, gold, and many others

Average temperatures: range from 10° below zero in parts of Alaska to almost 80° above zero in Death Valley, California

Precipitation levels: range from less than 2 inches a year in Death Valley to over 450 inches a year on Mt. Waialeale, Hawaii

Climate: mostly moderate with variation in temperatures and precipitation, except for Alaska (cool summers and long cold winters) and Hawaii (mostly warm with high levels of precipitation)

Political divisions: 50 states and several territories

Economy: a free enterprise system

Economic output: highest production of goods and services in the world; one of the highest standards of living in the world

Products: a wide variety of agricultural goods, timber, power, domesticated farm animals, electronic equipment, and other manufactured goods, along with many services

Here is a quick overview of some basic facts about the United States— its land, location, and people.

For Your Information...

In addition to the 50 states, the United States governs several territories and outlying areas. These are mostly located in the Pacific Ocean and the Caribbean Sea.

Puerto Rico
Guam
U.S. Virgin Islands
Northern Mariana Islands
American Samoa
Midway Islands
Wake Island
Johnston Atoll
Baker Islands
Howland Islands
Jarvis Islands
Kingman Reef
Navassa Island
Palmyra Atoll

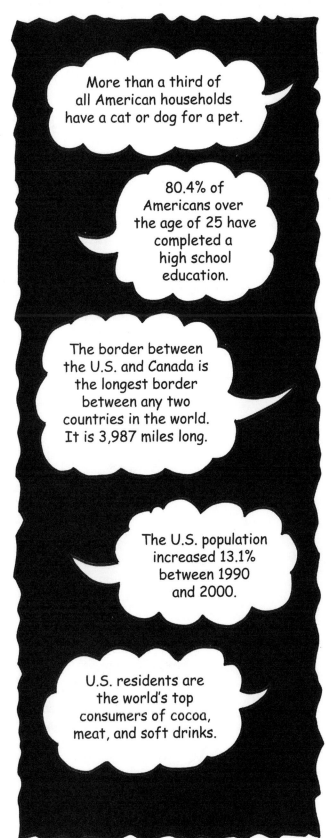

More than a third of all American households have a cat or dog for a pet.

80.4% of Americans over the age of 25 have completed a high school education.

The border between the U.S. and Canada is the longest border between any two countries in the world. It is 3,987 miles long.

The U.S. population increased 13.1% between 1990 and 2000.

U.S. residents are the world's top consumers of cocoa, meat, and soft drinks.

Population: 281,421,906 *(2000 census)*

Male/female population ratio: 49.1% male; 50.9% female

Population density: 79.6 persons per square mile

Number of families: 71,787,347

Average family size: 3.14 persons

Median age: 35.3 years

Population under 18 years old: 72,293,812

Population 85 years and older: 4,239,587

Life expectancy: average 76.9 years (men: 74.1, women 79.5)

Way of life: 80.3% urban; 19.7% rural

Number of people age 3 and older enrolled in school: 76,632,927

Number of universities: 5,758

Households with no telephone service: 2,570,705

Major religions practiced: Protestant Christian, Roman Catholic, Christian Orthodox, Judaism, Islam, Buddhism, Anglicanism, and Hinduism

Main languages spoken: English, Spanish, French, German, Italian, and Chinese

Number of persons who speak a language other than English at home: 46,851,595

Most populated state: California, population 35,484,453

Least populated state: Wyoming, population 501,242

Most densely populated state: New Jersey, 1,124 persons per square mile

Least densely populated state: Alaska, 1.1 persons per square mile

Most populated city: New York City, population 8,085,742

Get Sharp Tip #10
Visit this website to look at the U.S. population clock, and find up-to-the-minute population statistics.

www.census.gov/population/www/popclockus.html

The 50 States

The United States of America is divided into fifty states and the capital, Washington, D.C., which is a city that is not within any state. The first state to enter the union was Delaware. It became a state on December 7, 1787. The last state, Hawaii, entered the union on August 21, 1959.

Washington
Olympia

Oregon
Salem

Idaho
Boise

Montana
Helena

North Dakota
Bismark

South Dakota
Pierre

Wyoming
Cheyenne

Nevada
Carson City

Utah
Salt Lake City

Nebraska
Lincoln

California
Sacramento

Colorado
Denver

Kansas
Topeka

Arizona
Phoenix

New Mexico
Santa Fe

Oklahoma
Oklahoma City

Texas
Austin

Alaska
Juneau

Hawaii
Honolulu

Northernmost City: Barrow, Alaska, 71°17' N
Southernmost City: Hilo, Hawaii, 19°43' N
Easternmost City: Eastport, Maine, 66°59' W
Westernmost City: West Unalaska, Alaska, 63°32' W
The largest state: Alaska, 591,004 square miles
The smallest state: Rhode Island, 1,212 square miles

● represents capitals of states

The States — Vital Statistics

Visitors can keep the diamonds they find in Crater of the Diamonds State Park near Murfreesboro, Arkansas.

Battle Creek, Michigan, is the **Cereal Capital of the World.**

A Diamond in the Rough

State *postal abbreviation and nickname*	Capital	Some Other Large Cities	Neighbors *bordering states*	Area *in square miles*	Population *2003*
Alabama - AL *The Heart of Dixie* *Cotton State* *Yellowhammer State*	Montgomery	Birmingham Huntsville Mobile	Florida, Georgia, Tennessee, Mississippi	52,237	4,500,752
Alaska - AK *The Last Frontier*	Juneau	Anchorage Fairbanks	Canada	615,230	648,818
Arizona - AZ *Grand Canyon State*	Phoenix	Tucson Mesa Glendale Scottsdale	California, Nevada, Utah, Colorado, New Mexico	114,006	5,580,811
Arkansas - AR *Razorback State* *Natural State*	Little Rock	Fort Smith North Little Rock	Oklahoma, Missouri, Tennessee, Mississippi, Texas, Louisiana	53,182	2,725,714
California - CA *Golden State*	Sacramento	Los Angeles San Diego San Jose San Francisco	Arizona, Nevada, Oregon	158,869	35,484,453
Colorado - CO *Centennial State*	Denver	Colorado Springs Aurora Lakewood	Utah, Wyoming, Nebraska, Kansas, Oklahoma, Arizona, New Mexico	104,100	4,550,688
Connecticut - CT *Constitution State* *Nutmeg State*	Hartford	Bridgeport New Haven Hartford Stamford	New York, Massachusetts, Rhode Island	5,544	3,483,372
Delaware - DE *First State*	Dover	Wilmington Newark	Maryland, New Jersey, Pennsylvania	2,396	817,491

State postal abbreviation and nickname	Capital	Some Other Large Cities	Neighbors bordering states	Area in square miles	Population 2004
Florida - FL Sunshine Sate	Tallahassee	Jacksonville Miami Tampa St. Petersburg	Georgia, Alabama	59,928	17,019,068
Georgia - GA Peach State	Atlanta	Augusta Columbus Savannah	Florida, Alabama, North Carolina, South Carolina, Tennessee	58,977	8,684,715
Hawaii - HI Aloha State	Honolulu	Hilo Kailua Kaneohe	none	6,459	1,257,608
Idaho - ID Gem State	Boise	Nampa Pocatello	Washington, Oregon, Nevada, Utah, Wyoming, Montana	83,574	1,366,332
Illinois - AL Prairie State	Springfield	Chicago Rockford Aurora Peoria	Wisconsin, Iowa, Missouri, Kentucky, Indiana	57,918	12,653,544
Indiana - IN Hoosier State	Indianapolis	Fort Wayne Evansville South Bend Gary	Illinois, Ohio, Michigan, Kentucky	36,420	6,195,643
Iowa - IA Hawkeye State	Des Moines	Cedar Rapids Davenport Sioux City	Nebraska, Missouri, Minnesota, Illinois, South Dakota, Wisconsin	56,276	2,944,062
Kansas - KS Sunflower State	Topeka	Wichita Kansas City Overland Park	Colorado, Nebraska, Missouri, Oklahoma	82,282	2,723,507
Kentucky - KY Bluegrass Sate	Frankfort	Lexington Louisville	Tennessee, Missouri, Indiana, Illinois, West Virginia, Virginia, Ohio	40,411	4,117,827

Hawaii was the last state admitted to the United States. It gained statehood in 1959.

The Everglades Swamp in Florida is a huge swamp, covering 1.5 million acres. But that's only a fifth of the swamp's size before it was drained to gain land for development.

State *postal abbreviation and nickname*	Capital	Some Other Large Cities	Neighbors *bordering states*	Area *in square miles*	Population *2004*
Louisiana - LA *Pelican State*	Baton Rouge	New Orleans Shreveport	Texas, Arkansas, Mississippi	49,651	4,496,334
Maine - ME *Pine Tree State* *Chickadee State*	Augusta	Portland Lewiston Bangor	New Hampshire	33,741	1,305,728
Maryland - MD *Free State* *Old Line State*	Annapolis	Baltimore Frederick Gaithersburg	Delaware, Virginia, West Virginia, Pennsylvania	12,297	5,508,909
Massachusetts - MA *Bay State*	Worcester	Springfield Lowell	New Hampshire, Vermont, Maine, New York, Connecticut, Rhode Island	9,241	6,433,422
Michigan - MI *Great Lakes State* *Wolverine State*	Flint	Detroit Grand Rapids Warren	Ohio, Indiana, Wisconsin	58,216	10,079,985
Minnesota - MN *North Star State*	St. Paul	Minneapolis	North Dakota, South Dakota, Iowa, Wisconsin	86,943	5,059,375
Mississippi - MS *Magnolia State*	Jackson	Gulfport Biloxi	Alabama, Tennessee, Arkansas, Louisiana	48,286	2,881.281
Missouri - MO *Show Me State*	Jefferson City	Kansas City St. Louis Springfield	Arkansas, Iowa, Tennessee, Kentucky, Illinois, Kansas, Nebraska, Oklahoma	69,709	5,704,484

Rayne, Louisiana, is the Frog Capital of the World.

Michigan is the only state with two geographical parts. It is made of two peninsulas. Both parts are surrounded by Great Lakes on three sides.

Better Grades & Higher Test Scores / SOCIAL STUDIES gr. 4–6
Copyright ©2005 by Incentive Publications, Inc., Nashville, TN.

The States – Vital Statistics, continued

Nevada is a Spanish word meaning "snow-clad."

| State
postal abbreviation and nickname | Capital | Some Other Large Cities | Neighbors
bordering states | Area
in square miles | Population
2004 |
|---|---|---|---|---|---|
| **Montana - MT**
Treasure State | Helena | Billings
Missoula
Great Falls | Idaho, Wyoming, North Dakota, South Dakota | 147,046 | 917,621 |
| **Nebraska - NE**
Cornhusker State | Lincoln | Omaha | Wyoming, South Dakota, Iowa, Missouri, Kansas, Colorado | 77,358 | 1,739,291 |
| **Nevada - NV**
Sagebrush State | Carson City | Las Vegas
Reno | California, Arizona, Utah, Idaho, Oregon | 110,567 | 2,241,154 |
| **New Hampshire – HN**
Granite State | Concord | Manchester
Nashua | Vermont, Maine, Massachusetts | 9,283 | 1,287,687 |
| **New Jersey - NJ**
Garden State | Trenton | Newark
Jersey City
Paterson | Delaware, Pennsylvania, New York | 8,125 | 8,638,396 |
| **New Mexico – NM**
Cactus State | Santa Fe | Albuquerque
Las Cruces | Arizona, Texas, Oklahoma, Utah, Colorado | 121,598 | 1,874,614 |
| **New York – NY**
Empire State | Albany | New York
Buffalo
Rochester | Vermont, New Jersey, Massachusetts, Connecticut, Pennsylvania | 53,989 | 19,190,115 |
| **North Carolina – NC**
Tar Heel State | Raleigh | Charlotte
Greensboro
Durham
Winston-Salem | South Carolina, Virginia, Tennessee | 52,672 | 8,407,248 |

North Carolina got its nickname, the "Tar Heel" State, from a Civil War story. Supposedly, many Confederate soldiers ran away during a tough battle and left Carolina soldiers to fight alone. So they threatened to put tar on the heels of those soldiers in the next battle, so they would "stick" to the fight.

New York City has 162 skyscrapers. That's more than any other city in the world.

Better Grades & Higher Test Scores / SOCIAL STUDIES gr. 4–6
Copyright ©2005 by Incentive Publications, Inc., Nashville, TN.

Get Sharp: U.S. States

The States – Vital Statistics, continued

State *postal abbreviation and nickname*	Capital	Some Other Large Cities	Neighbors *bordering states*	Area *in square miles*	Population *2004*
North Dakota - ND *Peace Garden State Flickertail State*	Bismarck	Fargo Grand Forks	Montana, South Dakota, Minnesota	70,704	633,837
Ohio - OH *Buckeye State*	Columbus	Cleveland Cincinnati Toledo Akron	Michigan, Indiana, Pennsylvania, Kentucky, West Virginia	44,828	11,435,798
Oklahoma - OK *Sooner State*	Oklahoma City	Tulsa Norman Lawton	New Mexico, Colorado, Kansas, Missouri, Arkansas, Texas	69,903	3,511,532
Oregon - OR *Beaver State*	Salem	Portland Eugene	Washington, California, Idaho, Nevada	97,132	3,559,596
Pennsylvania - PA *Keystone State*	Harrisburg	Philadelphia Pittsburgh Allentown Erie	New York, Ohio, New Jersey, Delaware, Maryland, West Virginia	46,058	12,365,455
Rhode Island – RI *Little Rhody Ocean State*	Providence	Warwick Cranston Pawtucket	Massachusetts, Connecticut	1,231	1,076,164
South Carolina – SC *Palmetto State*	Columbia	Charleston North Charleston Greenville	Georgia, North Carolina	31,189	4,147,152
South Dakota – SD *Coyote State*	Pierre	Sioux Falls, Rapid City	North Dakota, Montana, Wyoming, Nebraska, Iowa, Minnesota	77,121	764,309
Tennessee – TN *Volunteer State*	Nashville	Memphis Knoxville Chattanooga	Mississippi, Alabama, Georgia, Virginia, North Carolina, Kentucky, Missouri, Arkansas	42,146	5,841,748

South Dakota was the first state to have an official state animal. In 1949, the state adopted the coyote as its state animal.

Oklahoma was the first state to choose a flower. In 1893, mistletoe became the official state flower.

The States – Vital Statistics, continued

State *postal abbreviation and nickname*	Capital	Some Other Large Cities	Neighbors *bordering states*	Area *in square miles*	Population *2004*
Texas - TX *Lone Star State*	Austin	Houston Dallas San Antonio El Paso Fort Worth	New Mexico, Oklahoma, Arkansas, Louisiana	267,277	22,118,509
Utah - UT *Beehive State*	Salt Lake City	West Valley City Provo	Nevada, Idaho, Wyoming, Colorado, New Mexico, Nevada	84,904	2,351,467
Vermont - VT *Green Mountain State*	Montpelier	Burlington Essex	New Hampshire, New York, Massachusetts	9,615	619,107
Virginia - VA *Old Dominion*	Richmond	Virginia Beach Norfolk Chesapeake	Maryland, West Virginia, Kentucky, Tennessee, North Carolina	42,326	7,386,330
Washington - WA *Evergreen State*	Olympia	Seattle Spokane Tacoma	Oregon, Idaho	70,637	6,131,445
West Virginia – WV *Mountain State*	Charleston	Huntington Wheeling	Pennsylvania, Ohio, Kentucky, Virginia, Maryland	24,231	1,810,354
Wisconsin – WI *Badger State*	Madison	Green Bay Kenosha Racine	Minnesota, Iowa, Illinois	65,499	5,472,299
Wyoming – WY *Cowboy State*	Cheyenne	Casper Laramie	Idaho, Utah, Montana, North Dakota, South Dakota, Colorado	97,818	501,242

Washington has the highest high school graduation rate in the country. 92% of residents over age 25 have a high school education.

Cody, Wyoming, is known as "The Rodeo Capital of the World." The Cody Nite Rodeo puts on an event every night from June 1- August 31.

U.S. Regions

The United States is such a large country that its land, climate, and resources vary widely. In order to learn about the country, it is helpful to divide it into areas smaller than the whole span of thousands of miles. The continental United States can be divided into eight different regions. The states that make up each region of the United States share similar landforms, natural resources, and climate.

Get Sharp Tip #12

A region is a large area that has common features.

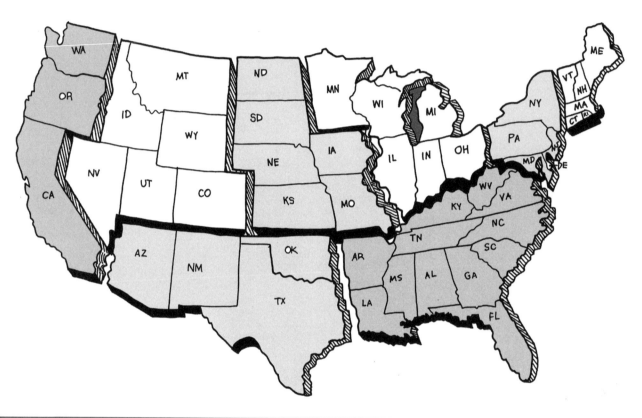

The New England States

This small region in the northeast corner of the country has a rural landscape, small villages, rugged ocean coastlines, sandy beaches, and beautiful scenery. The area is famous for its maple syrup and beautiful autumn leaves. Its land is too rocky and hilly for much agriculture, but the region produces many dairy and poultry products. The climate is cold in the winter, with frequent snow or rain. The summers are warm and humid.

Largest cities:
Boston, Hartford, Providence

Economic activities:

industry	manufacturing
dairy farming	poultry farming
fishing	tourism

In Connecticut, it is illegal to walk across a street on your hands.

The Mid-Atlantic States

This is the most densely populated region in the country; it is home to several large cities. Its many harbors make it a worldwide trade center. There is coal mining in the Appalachian Mountain region. These mountains also attract hikers and vacationers. The region is filled with farms, lakes, scenic forests, and sandy beaches along its Atlantic coast. The big cities, historic sites, and ocean beaches attract many tourists. The winters are cool or cold and wet. Summers are humid and warm or hot.

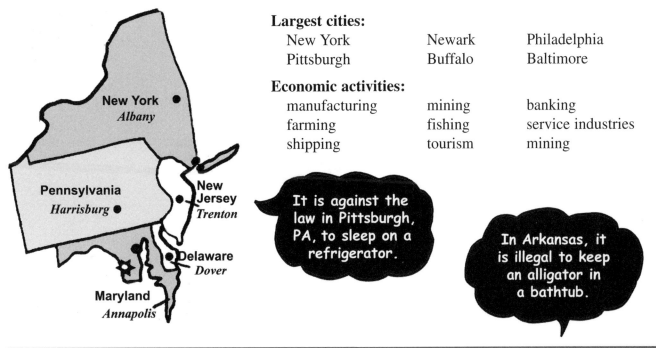

Largest cities:

New York	Newark	Philadelphia
Pittsburgh	Buffalo	Baltimore

Economic activities:

manufacturing	mining	banking
farming	fishing	service industries
shipping	tourism	mining

> It is against the law in Pittsburgh, PA, to sleep on a refrigerator.

> In Arkansas, it is illegal to keep an alligator in a bathtub.

The Southern States

This region has been a major agricultural area for the country. The tourist business is also healthy because of the rolling hills, beautiful mountains, and Atlantic and Gulf beaches. West Virginia, in the Appalachian Mountains, has some of the most rugged terrain of any state. Most of the state is covered with mountain chains. The region's warm climate makes it an attractive place to live, do business, and vacation. Winters are mild; springs and summers are hot and humid.

Largest cities:

New Orleans	Nashville
Miami	Atlanta

Economic activities:

agriculture	dairy farming
mining	industry
tourism	

Get Sharp: U.S. Regions

The Great Lakes States

Every state in this region touches one of the Great Lakes. (The Great Lakes hold almost one-fourth of all the fresh water in the world.) The water affects the climate and economy of the whole region. The Great Lakes are a part of an extensive water transportation system. Thanks to a series of locks, canals, and rivers, ships can travel from the region to the Atlantic Ocean or the Gulf of Mexico. Many ports and harbors are found in the region, allowing ships to carry away the products of mining and manufacturing. This area also has many dairy farms. The climate is cold in the winter with rain and snow. The summers are warm or hot with moderate rain.

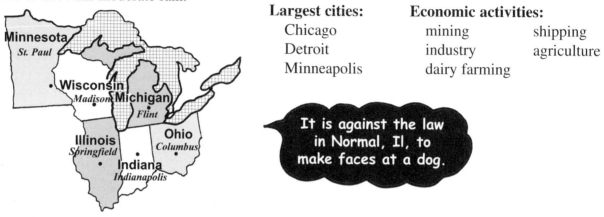

Largest cities:
Chicago
Detroit
Minneapolis

Economic activities:
mining   shipping
industry   agriculture
dairy farming

It is against the law in Normal, Il, to make faces at a dog.

The Midwestern States

This region is primarily a plains region, covering much of the central part of the country. With its rich soil, this is a main region for producing wheat, corn, and livestock. The winters are cold in the northern plains, and mild in the southern parts of the region. Summers are hot and dry, with some thunderstorms.

Largest cities:
St. Louis
Kansas City
Omaha

Economic activities:
agriculture (corn, soybeans, wheat)

The Rocky Mountain States

The centerpiece of this region is the Rocky Mountains. The region also has plains, plateaus, forests, and deserts. It is a rich ranching and mining area. Its beauty attracts many tourists. The climate is greatly affected by the mountains; there is cold weather and snow at the higher elevations.
At lower elevations, the climate is semi-dry.

Largest cities:
Denver
Salt Lake City

Economic activities:
mining   ranching
tourism   farming

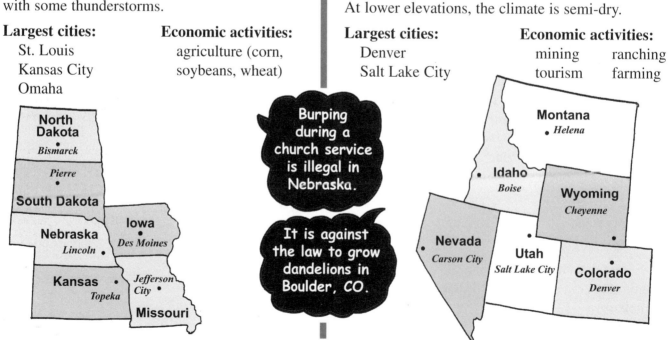

Burping during a church service is illegal in Nebraska.

It is against the law to grow dandelions in Boulder, CO.

148

The Southwestern States

This is a region of large cattle ranches and fields of crops (such as cotton), which spread over vast areas. The plentiful oil and natural gas beneath its surface has made the region wealthy. The southwest is also a region of pleasant weather that attracts tourists and permanent residents alike. Winters are mild and dry. Summers are hot and dry. It is the home to the Grand Canyon and other areas of great beauty.

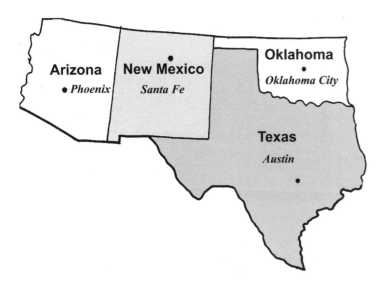

Largest cities:

Phoenix	Houston
Dallas	Oklahoma City

Economic activities:

ranching	oil drilling
tourism	oil refineries
mining	

In Texarkana, Texas, no one may ride a horse at night unless the horse has a taillight.

The Pacific Coast States

This region borders the Pacific Ocean. It has a long, beautiful coastline, dense forests, and mountains. The coasts supply fish; the forests supply timber; and the valleys produce fruits, wine, and vegetables. It is also a region of manufacturing and technological development, with a computer and electronics industry that has grown rapidly in recent years. Due to the effects of the ocean, the climate is mild. Irrigation and a long growing season allow for plentiful agriculture in the long coastal valleys and valleys between mountain ranges. (Alaska and Hawaii are sometimes considered a part of this region. They border the Pacific, though they are not attached to the other 48 states.)

It is against the law in Los Angeles, CA, to tickle a toad.

Hawaii has a law against putting coins in your ears.

In Alaska, it is unlawful to push a moose out of a moving airplane.

Largest cities:

Los Angeles	San Francisco	Seattle

Economic activities:

timber	high technology	tourism
entertainment	agriculture	mining
fishing		

See the U.S.A.

Come and tour the U.S.A.!
From north to south, from east to west,
it is full of fascinating sights.

Don't forget to send a postcard home!

Spectacular **Niagara Falls**
Visit this natural wonder
on the U.S. and Canadian border.
See Horseshoe Falls,
2,600 feet wide, and
the American Falls,
1,000 feet wide.

The Empire State

The Empire State Building
in New York City was once
a wonder of the world. After 70
years it still inspires
awe at 1250 feet tall
and 102 stories!

CARLSBAD CAVERNS New Mexico

The Carlsbad Caverns are some of the biggest
underground limestone caverns in the world.
The largest cave, called the Big Room, is
1,800 feet long
with a 225-foot
ceiling.

Cliff Dwellings

Some cliff dwellings in the Southwest
were built by Anasazi Indians over
800 years ago. They were carved
into the mountainside and
were inhabited
until recent years.

See The **Grand**ness
of the Grand Canyon in Arizona.

*It was gouged out of rock
over thousands
of years by
the Colorado River.
It is a mile deep at
its deepest point.*

The Cowboy Hall of Fame
Ye-ha!
Oklahoma City is home
to the Cowboy Hall of
Fame. It has a life-size
replica of an
early cowboy.

The Baseball Hall of Fame
in
Cooperstown,
New York

Rock 'n Roll Hall of Fame
in Cleveland, Ohio
See the musical
greats of a whole generation.

GRAND OLD OPRY

Nashville, Tennessee is the
country music capital of the world.

The Audubon Aquarium of the Americas

New Orleans

See an amazing display of underwater creatures from North and South America.

CRAZY HORSE MEMORIAL

A huge sculpture is being carved into a mountain side in South Dakota. Crazy Horse was a brave Lakota chief.

ROLLER COASTER RIDE

You can ride one of the world's largest roller coasters, **Superman: The Escape**, at Six Flags Magic Mountain, in Valencia, California.

See the
Dinosaur National Monument
in Colorado.

Mardi Gras
in New Orleans

The **Mardi Gras** celebration lasts for a week before the fasting begins in Lent. Parties, parades, and colorful costumes make Mardi Gras week a favorite tourist attraction.

The Magic Kingdom
at Walt Disney World in Florida

The Magic Kingdom is the most visited theme park in the world with 15.5 million visitors a year.

See glaciers in the world's largest national park, **Wrangell-St. Elias**, in Alaska. **Mt. McKinley** in Alaska is 20,320 ft. tall.

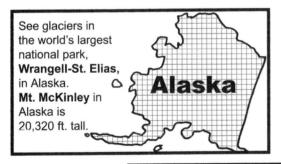

Alaska

Seattle
Space Needle

The Space Needle was considered very futuristic for its day. It was built for the 1962 World's Fair.

THE GOLDEN GATE

The Golden Gate Bridge in San Francisco, is one of the longest suspension bridges in the world.

Surf Hawaii

Waves in Hawaii can rise to 50 feet and higher!

Record-Setting Wonders

Here are a few of the highest, longest, biggest, deepest, tallest, lowest, and otherwise most spectacular natural and human-created features of the United States.

Tallest

Tallest active volcano: Mt. Mauna Loa, Hawaii – 13,681 feet above sea level
(32,000 feet from its base on the floor of the Pacific Ocean)
Tallest building: Sears Tower, Chicago – 1,454 feet tall *(with spires: 1,707 feet)*
Tallest structure: a television tower in Blanchard, North Dakota – 2,063 feet
Tallest statue: Chief Crazy Horse, Black Hills of South Dakota – 563 feet
Tallest monument: Gateway Arch, St. Louis, Missouri – 630 feet
Tallest active geyser: Steamboat Geyser, Yellowstone National Park – more than 300 feet

Highest

Yodel-lay-dee-hoo...

Highest mountain: Mt. McKinley (Denali), Alaska – 20,320 feet
Highest island: Akutan, Alaska – 13,698 feet
Highest waterfalls: Yosemite Falls, California – 2,425 feet
Highest town: Climax, Colorado – 11,560 feet.
Highest bridge: Royal Gorge, Colorado – 1,053 feet above water

Lowest & Deepest

Hello -ello -ello- ello

Lowest town: Calipatria, California – 185 feet below sea level
Lowest point: Death Valley, California – 282 feet below sea level
Deepest cave: Lechuguilla Cave in Carlsbad Caverns, New Mexico – 1,521 feet
Deepest lake: Crater Lake, Oregon – 1,932 feet
Deepest gorge: Hell's Canyon, Snake River, Idaho – 7,900 feet

Most

State with the most tribal land: Arizona – 20,087,538 acres
State most visited by U.S. tourists: Florida – over 6 million a year
State with most lakes: Alaska – over 3 million lakes
State with the most geysers: Wyoming – over 300
Most spectacular geyser: Old Faithful, Yellowstone National Park – erupts every 30 seconds
Most damaging hurricane: Hurricane Andrew in 1992 – $25 billion damage
Most visited city: New York City – 5 and one-half million visitors a year
Most common U.S. city name: Fairview

Longest

Longest river: Mississippi-Missouri-Red Rock River system –
3,710 miles

Longest cave: Mammoth Cave System – 352 miles

Longest suspension bridge: Verrazano Narrows, New York – 4,250 feet

Longest steel arch bridge: New River Gorge, Fayetteville, Virginia –
1,700 feet

Longest cantilever bridge: Commodore Barry, Pennsylvania – 1,644 feet

State with longest shoreline: Alaska – 33,904 miles

Why is New York City called the BIG APPLE?

The phrase was first used in a book, **The Wayfarer in New York,** in 1909. The author, Edward S. Martin, explained that New York was one fruit of a tree that spread across all of America—but New York seemed to get a larger share of the tree's sap (meaning the national wealth), making it the Big Apple.

Biggest

Biggest lake: Lake Superior – 31,820 sq. mi.

Biggest island: Hawaii – 4,037 sq. mi.

Biggest island in a lake: Isle Royal, Lake Superior – 209 sq. mi.

Biggest meteorite found: Canyon Diablo, Arizona – 30 tons

Biggest city: New York City – population 8,008,278

Biggest waterfalls: Niagara Falls – two falls, total of 3,600 feet wide

Biggest canyon: Grand Canyon, Arizona – 277 miles long, 1 mile deep at
deepest point

Biggest Native American Reservation: Navajo, in Utah-Arizona-N. Mexico – 230,000 population

Biggest university: University of California – 157,400 students

Biggest library: Library of Congress, Washington DC – 24,000,000 books

Other Record-Setters

Oldest city in the 50 states: St. Augustine, Florida – settled in 1513

Oldest U.S. city: San Juan, Puerto Rico – settled in 1508

Coldest city: International Falls, Minnesota – average temperature, 36.8° F

Hottest city: Key West, Florida – average temperature, 77.8° F

Hottest temperature: 134° F, recorded in Death Valley, California

Coldest temperature: –80° F, recorded in Prospect Creek, Alaska

Wettest spot: Mt. Waialeale, Hawaii – 460 to 500 inches annually

Driest spot: Yuma, Arizona – 2.17 inches annually

Oldest national park: Yellowstone National Park – established in 1872

Smallest park: Mills End Park, Portland, Oregon – a circle 2 feet in diameter

Busiest airport: JFK International, New York – 17,378,000 passengers per year

Busiest seaport: South Louisiana Port, New Orleans, Louisiana – 245 million tons of
cargo in the year 2000

Busiest underground railway: New York Subway – over 1 trillion passengers per year

153

U.S. Time Zones

When you travel across the United States, you need to keep track of the time! That is because the country is so wide that it crosses six time zones. Get to know the U.S. time zones, so you can always be sure what time it is wherever you are!

Time Zones in the U.S.A.

12:00 PM
Alaska Time

11:00 AM
Hawaii Time

1:00 PM
Pacific Time
(PT)

2:00 PM
Mountain
Time (MT)

3:00 PM
Central Time
(CT)

4:00 PM
Eastern Time
(ET)

Time Zone Challenges - Going to Colorado for the Holidays

Hello, Julie? I hope I didn't wake you. I'm organizing a family ski trip for the holidays. It's 8:30 AM here in Alaska. **What time is it at your house in Georgia?**

Answer: It's 12:30 PM in the state of Georgia.

Cousin John has to fly from Hawaii to the ski resort in Colorado. He'll leave Honolulu at 9:15 AM and arrive in Denver at 8:15 PM. **How long is the trip?**

Answer: Denver is three time zones east of Hawaii, so he'll actually leave at 12:15 PM Denver time. That makes it an 8 hour trip.

Aunt Susie wants to come for the holiday, but she has to be back home in Boston by noon on the 27th. It's a 3-hour flight from Denver to Boston. **What time will she need to leave Denver?**

Answer: Denver is two time zones west of Boston. Add two hours to the trip time—making five hours. She'll need to leave at least 5 hours before noon: 7 AM Denver time.

GET SHARP →

on

WORLD HISTORY

What's the story here?

Prehistory

People have lived on earth for a long time. Many scientists believe that archaeological evidence shows that humans may have existed as far back as two million years ago. Archaeologists are scientists who study past cultures. They have learned about early history by studying things that were left behind: tools, bones, utensils, weapons, fossils, ruins of buildings, and artwork. Such things left behind by a culture or group of people are called ***artifacts.***

The Old Stone Age

The Old Stone Age dates from approximately two million years ago to about 10,000 years ago. The outstanding feature of the Old Period is the appearance of humans, perhaps around 35,000 to 40,000 B.C. It is believed that these prehistoric people lived mainly in Europe, Africa, and Asia. They lived by gathering food and hunting prehistoric animals, made crude implements and tools of stone and bones, and used the skins and furs of animals to make clothing. Artifacts show that more humans began to live in communities in the later years of the Old Stone Age. As they joined in groups, new cultures grew. They built shelters, made tools that were more effective, developed belief systems centered around the supernatural, created jewelry, and left simple drawings on cave walls. Artifacts also suggest that some cultures expanded their activities to hunting reindeer and fishing.

stone age cave art

The New Stone Age

early Mesopotamian farmer

The New Stone Age, dating from about 10,000 B.C., is characterized by the use of stone tools, the existence of settlements dependent on farming and domestication of animals, and the presence of arts or crafts. Because they found ways to produce food without wandering to follow herds of wild animals, people were able to settle down into villages. The earliest known settlement was in southwestern Asia about 8000 B.C. Scientists have found evidence of primitive, independent farming communities in the Tigris and Euphrates River Valleys, the Nile River Valley, the Indus Valley, and the Huang He Valley in China. By 2000–1500 B.C., groups were cultivating crops and domesticating animals in Southeast Asia, Mexico, and South America.

Early Civilizations

Civilization generally refers to a culture or society that has advanced social systems (such as political, economic, governmental, and educational systems). Agriculture changed the lives of early people. Once they were able to grow food, they no longer needed to wander to find food. As the nomadic (wandering) life ended, people settled into one area and formed permanent settlements, usually in areas where land was fertile. Civilizations developed quickly. With a settled life, cultures were able to become more complex. About 3500 B.C., the first traces of writing appeared. From then on, humans could keep records that told others of their cultures and stories. These are some of the early civilizations that developed in Asia, the Middle East, Africa, Europe, and the Americas.

Get Sharp Tip #14

Periods of history are usually described in years before the birth of Christ (**B.C.**) and after Christ's death (**A.D.**). Another description uses the term common era (**C.E.**), beginning A.D. 0-6, and before common era (**B.C.E.**).

It's a wheel.

Sumer

One of the earliest civilizations grew up in an area that stretched from the Eastern shores of the Mediterranean Sea between the Tigris and Euphrates Rivers to the Persian Gulf. The crescent-shaped area had very rich soil, so it was known as the *Fertile Crescent*. Cultures developed from about 4000 B.C. in the area of Mesopotamia (meaning *land between the rivers*). The Sumerian culture in southern Mesopotamia grew rapidly from about 3500 to 2000 B.C. Here, the people farmed, raised cattle, developed trade, and created crafts. The people of Sumer are credited with inventing the wheel and a form of writing known as *cuneiform*. They built a pyramid-like temple known as a *ziggurat*.

Babylonia

In about 2000 B.C., the city of Babylon was built along the Euphrates River. A powerful Babylonian king, Hammurabi, was a good administrator. He created a set of laws to take care of his people. *Hammurabi's Code* set fair prices, fair taxes, rights for all citizens, and a system of punishment.

Assyria

Beginning in about 1800 B.C., the Assyrians lived in southern Mesopotamia. Their culture was based around the capital city of Nineveh on the Tigris River. The Assyrian empire grew wealthy from the lands captured by their fierce armies. A king of Assyria founded the first library, which contained writings on many subjects preserved on clay tablets. The first Assyrian Empire flourished from 1814 to 1754 B.C. The second empire lasted from 911 to 609 B.C.

Hebrews

The Hebrews are the ancestors of modern-day Jews. The earliest Hebrews were from the land of Canaan, between the Jordan River and the Mediterranean Sea. A shortage of food forced them to go to Egypt, where they were taken as slaves and lived in slavery for many years. The Hebrews, led by the prophet Moses, escaped from Egypt in about 1250 B.C. The Hebrew people wandered in the desert for over 200 years, enduring many wars and hardships. Finally, they arrived in Canaan and settled in Palestine. In about 1000 B.C., the Hebrews made Jerusalem their capital. After that, Palestine was invaded many times by different groups.

Phoenicians

From about 1200–800 B.C., the Phoenicians lived in the Fertile Crescent area, in the region that is now Lebanon. They were some of the first and most successful sailors and traders. They sailed around the Mediterranean Sea, building cities and colonies at places such as Carthage, Byblos, Beirut, and Tyre. The successful trade brought them great wealth. They are also known for their artistic skills and their alphabet, which formed the basis for Greek, Latin, and modern Roman writing.

Phoenician

Persians

Another culture of the ancient Middle East was Persia, which began in the area that is now Iran. A powerful king, Cyrus II, united Persia with the kingdom of Media and expanded his empire by conquering areas west to the Fertile Crescent. A later king, King Darius I, expanded the empire further. He built a strong government that established a fair legal system and built roads throughout the entire empire. The Persian Empire flourished from about 700 to 330 B.C.

Minoans & Mycenaens

The first-known European civilization developed between in Crete between 2500 and 1450 B.C. It was named after King Minos. The Minoans were traders in the Mediterranean Sea. They built well-planned towns and huge palaces. They developed a form of writing known as *Linear A*. Another culture, the Mycenaen civilization, developed in Greece from 1600 to 1200 B.C. Like the Minoans, these people were traders in the Mediterranean area. They developed a form of writing known as *Linear B*.

Minoan bull

Hittites

The Hittites lived in the mountains north of the Mediterranean Sea. Their empire was a chief power and cultural influence in western Asia from about 1400 to 1200 B.C. They were one of the first cultures to successfully smelt iron, giving them the ability to make stronger tools and weapons. They were also one of the first civilizations to establish a treaty. They agreed with Egypt to respect each other's borders, not to attack one another, and to help each other if attacked by someone else.

Indus Valley Civilization

The Indus Valley civilization flourished in India along the Indus River from 2500 to 1800 B.C. The people built large cities such as Mohenjo-Daro and Harappa. Archaeologists have found remains of hundreds of cities. The Indus people are known for the organization of their cities, well-developed drainage and sewage systems, farms with complex irrigation systems, and advanced tools and crafts. About 1500 B.C., this civilization mysteriously disappeared.

What happened to the people of the Indus Valley?

There are several theories . . .

- The land was over-farmed and no longer yielded enough food, so the people moved.

- The people scattered due to an invasion.

- A big flood destroyed the civilization.

- Drought caused widespread famine, and the civilization died out.

Egypt

A very complex and successful civilization grew up along the banks and delta of the Nile River, where the flooding of the river created rich soil. The ancient Egyptian civilization began about 3300 B.C. and lasted almost 3,000 years. The Nile River provided transportation, food, and work for the people. Warrior kings (*pharaohs*) conquered a vast empire. The Egyptians produced amazing works of architecture and feats of engineering. They are known for their development of a calendar, for a system of weaving cloth, for building boats and temples, and for making paper and many objects of art. Their paper and system of writing (*hieroglyphics*) enabled them to become the first civilization with a written history.

The ancient Egyptians are perhaps best remembered for their pyramids. The religion gave great honor to the dead; they wanted to make sure the dead had a good life in the next world. They built huge and magnificent stone tombs (*pyramids*) for their kings and other important people. They filled the pyramids with valuable items and food for the dead to use in the next life. The bodies were preserved by *mummification*. Many of the great pyramids remain, displaying the skills of the Egyptian engineers and builders.

SOME OF THE EGYPTIAN GODS

AMUN-RE' the chief god of the new kingdom

HATHOR goddess of love, music, and dancing

MA'AT goddess of harmony, truth and law

ANUBUS jackal-headed god of embalming

HORUS falcon-headed god of death

Classical Greece

Alexander the Great

Alexander the Great was a brilliant military leader who ruled in northern Greece. His father, King Philip II of Macedonia, defeated the Greek city-states that had been weakened by fighting among themselves. Alexander became king at age 20 when his father was murdered. He built a great empire—the largest one in the ancient world. His empire stretched from Greece to India. He established cities and spread Greek ideas and language over a wide area.

During the period of 500 to 330 B.C., Greece was divided into great *city-states*. Each city was like a separate nation. This is known as the ***Classical Period*** in Greek history. During this period, the Greeks made developments in politics, art, science, and philosophy that left their influence on Europe and the rest of the world for hundreds of years to come. Athens and Sparta were two particularly prosperous and influential city-states. Sparta was a military city-state that conquered many people and made slaves. The Spartans became rich from the trade and the work of the slaves. In Athens, great learning, writing, and art flourished. Thinkers such as Plato, Aristotle, and Socrates discussed ideas that became the basis for modern philosophy. The Athenian system of government was the beginning of *democracy*, a form of government in which citizens rule. The Greeks are also credited with great advances in medicine, drama, architecture, literature, and poetry. Eventually, rivalries between the city-states ended the classical period in Greece.

Rome

The city of Rome began as a group of small villages in Italy built along the edge of the Tiber River. By about 750 B.C. the villages had grown into one great city, Rome. This city became the center of one of the greatest ancient civilizations and the largest empires in the ancient world. Kings ruled Rome until 510 B.C. when the people set up a republic. A ***republic*** is a form of government where citizens choose representatives to run the government. Under a series of generals and emperors, the Roman Empire conquered all the lands around the Mediterranean Sea and spread from North Africa and the Middle East to England. The achievements of the Romans include a system of representative law that is a foundation of many democratic societies today, great roads and aqueducts, spectacular architecture and sculpture, and advances in literature and poetry. The Roman Empire lasted until around A.D. 476, when Germanic tribes and Mongol people (***Huns***) invaded and conquered parts of the empire.

The Development of Christianity

During the era of the Roman Empire, a Jewish boy named Jesus was born in the Roman province of Judea. He grew up to become a religious teacher who claimed to be the Son of God. His followers called him *Christ*, which means *the anointed one*. His teachings became very popular and spread throughout the empire, even though the Romans tried to stop it. Christians, including Jesus, were persecuted and even killed, but the religion continued to spread. In A.D. 337, the Roman emperor Constantine became a Christian and made the religion legal. After that, Christianity became a prominent religion in the empire.

China

Civilizations grew up along two large rivers in China: the Hauang He (Yellow River) and the Chang Jiang (Long River). The history of ancient China is the story of a succession of dynasties. China had over ten major dynasties before the revolution in 1911 that put an end to dynastic rule. Some dynasties are credited with cultural, artistic, and societal advances. Some were warlike; others ruled periods of peace. The first known dynasty, the Shang dynasty, ruled China from 1766–1027 B.C. During this time, writing was invented, art flourished, and silkworms were cultivated. The Great Wall of China was built under the Qin (or Ch'in) dynasty (221–206 B.C.) to protect China from invaders. Some important achievements of the ancient Chinese civilizations were the invention of gunpowder and paper, advances in astronomy and engineering, and the development of acupuncture.

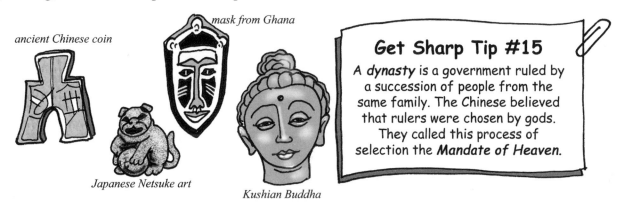

ancient Chinese coin

mask from Ghana

Japanese Netsuke art

Kushian Buddha

Get Sharp Tip #15

A **dynasty** is a government ruled by a succession of people from the same family. The Chinese believed that rulers were chosen by gods. They called this process of selection the **Mandate of Heaven**.

Japan

The early history of Japan is mostly legend. Supposedly, Japan was founded in 660 B.C. under Emperor Jimmu, a descendent of the Sun goddess. Reliable records only date back to A.D. 400, however. In the early centuries, Japan was inhabited by many clans or tribes ruled by priests. The first control over some of Japan came in the 5th century with the power of the Yamato clan. The Yamato chief priest took the position of emperor. The society developed rapidly over the next 300 years, with strong Chinese influence on the culture.

Kush

The Kush civilization was one of the first in Africa. From about 2000 B.C. to A.D. 350, the Kush people lived along the Nile River south of Egypt. They raised crops and cattle, and mined copper and gold. For many years, the Egyptians invaded Kush and took slaves, gold, and other resources. In 752 B.C., the Kush invaded and conquered Egypt, ruling Egypt for about 100 years, until the Assyrians pushed them back. The Kush moved their capital to Meroe and developed their iron-making skills. The city became one of the ancient world's major centers for the production of iron.

Ghana

One of the first empires of Africa was the Ghanaian Empire, located on the grasslands of western Africa. Ghana became a great, wealthy trading empire. Although Ghana had little of the valuable metal resources gold and iron, it acted as an agent in the exchange of these metals between other cultures. Ghanaians used the iron to make weapons and built a powerful army. The empire of Ghana lasted from about A.D. 700 to 1200.

Adenas and Hopewells

The Adena people made up one of the first known civilizations in North America. They lived in small groups, farming from about 300 to 100 B.C. in what is now the Ohio River Valley. They were skilled pottery makers. In addition, the Adena are known as the *Mound Builders* because they built large mounds of earth to cover the graves of the important members of their society. The Hopewell people lived in the Ohio and Mississippi River valleys from 2000 B.C. until A.D. 400. They were influenced by the Adena, and also built mounds of many different shapes and sizes.

Mayans

The Mayan culture was one of the most sophisticated ancient civilizations in the Americas. The culture lasted from about 300 B.C. until A.D. 900 in the Yucatan Peninsula of Central American. The Mayan people were farmers who built many cities deep in the jungles. Some their civilization centers were the great cities of Copán El Tikal, Uaxactún, and Uxmal in the regions that are now Honduras, Mexico, and Guatemala. They developed a calendar, a system of writing, and a system of numbers. They were skilled mathematicians and astronomers. Mayan architects built splendid buildings and monuments, and their artists produced elaborate murals, paintings, and carvings.

Chavins and Moches

The Chavin civilization was the first in South America, developed in the Andes Mountains of Peru and lasting from about 1200–300 B.C. The people were skilled stoneworkers who built large temples and spectacular sculptures. They were the first people in South America to make things from gold. The Moche civilization also developed in the Andes of Peru. From about A.D. 200 to 800, its people built pyramids from adobe bricks. The most famous of these is the *Temple of the Sun.*

Olmecs

The Olmec people developed one of the first civilizations in the Americas. This civilization grew up along the coast of the Gulf of Mexico between 1500 B.C. and A.D. 200. The Olmecs were farmers ruled by priests. They developed a system of hieroglyphic writing, began a counting system, and created calendars. They are known for their great temples, monuments, and pyramids built to honor their rulers. They carved huge heads from stone that are believed to be representations of their rulers.

Toltecs

The Toltec civilization flourished in the Valley of Mexico beginning in about 900 and lasting into the 1200s, with their capital at Tollan. Their culture had been influenced by the Olmec culture. The tools and arts of the Toltecs were advanced; they smelted metals and worked with highly developed stonework. (The name Toltec means *master builders*.) They also had a well-developed system for studying astronomy. The Toltecs worshiped many gods, and human sacrifice was a part of their religious practice.

Toltec chieftain artifact

Aztecs

The Aztec civilization replaced the Toltecs as the dominant culture in central Mexico. The capital of the Aztec Empire was the magnificent city of Tenochtitlan, near the site of present-day Mexico City. The Aztecs had well-developed engineering skills—building roads, irrigation channels, and a water system for the city. The Aztec arts of weaving, metalwork, sculpture, and music were also highly developed. The organization of the society was also highly organized, with one ruler, nobles that ruled cities, and priests to perform religious duties. Religion was a major part of the lives of the Aztecs. They built grand pyramids and ornate temples to honor their gods. They are known as Sun worshippers; their main god was a god of Sun and war. Human sacrifice was a part of the religious practice of the Aztecs. They believed that the shedding of blood was necessary for agricultural bounty and strength of the civilization. With a strong army and years of conquests, they conquered their neighbors. By about 1400, the Aztecs ruled a mighty empire throughout central and southern Mexico.

Incas

Incan artifact

In the 1300s and 1400s, the Inca civilization gained control of the Peruvian area in South America. By the early 1500s, they controlled a huge empire, stretching along the coast of South America in the Andes Mountains. The Incas were skilled agricultural engineers, building terraces for farming and ditches and canals for drainage and irrigation. Their engineering also extended to construction of buildings, temples, and an elaborate network of roads and bridges. They domesticated animals such as llamas and alpacas. The Incas were also fine artists and metal workers. They mined copper, gold, silver, and tin, and made extensive use of metals in their artistic designs and temples. The Incas are also known for using many different kinds of fiber to produce beautiful multicolor tapestries.

Get Sharp: Early Civilizations

40,000–35,000 B.C. – The Old Stone Age begins; humans emerge in southern Europe.

15,000 B.C. – The first people migrate to the North American continent, crossing from Asia on land and ice.

10,000 B.C. – Agriculture begins in the Fertile Crescent.

9000–5000 B.C. – Towns, such as Jericho and Catal Huyuk, grow up in the Fertile Crescent.

5000 B.C. – Farming begins in Egypt.

5000–4000 B.C. – Groups of people settle in the Huang Ho and Yangtze River Valleys in China.

4500–1500 B.C. – Large stone monuments, called *megaliths*, are built in areas of Europe. These structures are temples, tombs, and stone circles (*henges*) used for ceremonies.

Stonehenge, a huge megalith, is built between 3000 and 1500 B.C. in Britain.

4000–3000 B.C. – Sumerians build the first cities in Mesopotamia.

4000 B.C. – People settle in communities in the Indus River Valley in India.

3500–3300 B.C. – The Sumerians invent the wheel and a system of writing called *cuneiform*.

3300 B.C. – A strong Egyptian civilization grows along the banks of the Nile River.

3100 B.C. – Egyptian culture begins a form of writing called *hieroglyphics*.

2686–2181 B.C. – The pyramids are built in Egypt.

In the 2500s B.C., the Great Sphinx is built to line up with the Pyramid of Khafre.

2500–1800 B.C. – A strong civilization flourishes in the Indus River Valley in India.

2500–1200 B.C. – The Minoan and Mycenaean civilizations flourish in southern Europe.

2000 B.C. – Horses are used in Europe.

2000 B.C. – The city of Babylon is built.

2000 B.C. – The kingdom of Kush arises in Africa, south of Egypt.

1800–1200 B.C. – The Assyrian Empire grows and flourishes in the Middle East.

1766 B.C. – The first known dynasty, the Shang dynasty, rules China.

1792 B.C. – Babylonians develop the first system of written laws: the *Code of Hammurabi*.

1500 B.C. – A.D. 200 – The Olmec culture thrives in Mexico.

The Olmecs carve heads of stone, possibly replicas of their rulers. Cobata, the largest one discovered, stands 111 feet tall.

Get Sharp: World History Timeline

1250 B.C. – The Trojan Wars between the Greek Mycenaens and Trojans from Troy, Turkey, bring the destruction of Troy.

According to the story of the Trojan War, the Greeks deceive the Trojans to get their army into the enemy's city. They build a huge wooden horse, hide warriors inside it, and leave it as a gift outside the gates of Troy. While the Trojans are sleeping, the Greek soldiers come out and conquer the city.

1200–300 B.C. – The Chavin civilization is the first in South America.

1200 B.C. – The Hebrew people settle in Palestine after fleeing captivity in Egypt.

1200 B.C. – The Hindu religion begins to spread throughout India.

1200–1000 B.C. – The Phoenician civilization arises and thrives in Lebanon.

1010 B.C. – The Hebrews unite in one kingdom under King David.

1000 B.C. – The Hebrews make Jerusalem their capital.

776 B.C. – The first Olympic Games begin in Greece.

753 B.C. – Rome is founded.

700–300 B.C. – The Persian Empire flourishes and grows under King Cyrus II and King Darius I.

600–200 B.C. – The Adena civilization flourishes in North America. The people construct burial mounds and earthen buildings.

563 B.C. – Siddhartha Gautama is born in India. He establishes the Buddhist religion and becomes known as the *Buddha.*

510 B.C. – Rome becomes a republic. A Senate is established as the ruling group.

508 B.C. – In Greece, reforms in the political system lead to the establishment of a democracy in Athens.

500–338 B.C. – A classical period thrives in Greece; important ideas and advancements develop in politics, literature, architecture, arts, drama, science, and philosophy.

500 B.C. – The Nok civilization develops in Nigeria, West Africa.

The Noks make unique terracotta sculptures of heads, the earliest known African sculptures.

336 B.C. – Alexander becomes king in Macedonia. He begins a great empire, spreading Greek culture through a wide area.

300 B.C.–A.D. 900 – The Mayan civilization rises to its peak on the Yucatan Peninsula of Mexico.

214 B.C. – The Qin leader of China, Shi Huangdi, begins building the Great Wall of China.

27 B.C. – Augustus becomes emperor of Rome. His rebuilding and organization leads to a long period of peace (200 years) called *Pax Romana.*

6 B.C. – Jesus Christ is born in Bethlehem. His teachings become the basis of the Christian religion.

Get Sharp: World History Timeline

A.D.

1–100 – Buddhism spreads throughout Asia.

100 – Paper is invented in China.

100–552 – Buddhism spreads to China and from China to Japan.

29 – Jesus Christ is crucified in Jerusalem. Afterward, Christian followers spread the teachings of Jesus.

50 – Teotihuacan is built in Central America, in the area of present-day Mexico City. It becomes a center of civilization.

Great pyramids are a part of the city. The largest is the Pyramid of the Sun. At 216 feet, it is the tallest pyramid in present-day Mexico.

300–1200s – Ghana has great power in western Africa, controlling the trade in gold.

300–349 – Constantine the Great rules and reunites the east and west Roman Empires, with a capital at Constantinople.

350–399 – The Huns (Mongols) invade Europe from central Asia.

400 – The first towns appear in sub-Saharan Africa.

400–1500 – *The Middle Ages* begins in Europe. This is generally understood to be the time from after the fall of Rome until the Renaissance. This period is marked by a system of *feudalism,* in which powerful lords rule areas of land and give lands to nobles in exchange for their military service. Peasants work fields in large estates owned by lords.

400s–500s – The legendary King Arthur supposedly lives and fights with his Knights of the Round Table during this time period.

In medieval history, knights are private armed warriors that give service to nobles. Knights wear protective plates of armor, shields, helmets, and suits of mail.

410 – Barbarian tribes from northern Europe, including the Visigoths, invade and conquer lands throughout Europe that are part of the Roman Empire.

476 – The Roman Empire falls.

527–565 – The Byzantine Empire, the eastern half of the Roman Empire, survives long after the fall of Rome with its capitol in Constantinople (now Turkey). Under the leadership of Justinian, the empire extends its power into Italy, North Africa, and Spain.

594 – The plague subsides after killing almost half the population in Europe.

611 – The prophet Muhammad of Mecca dictates the *Koran.* These teachings of Muhammad begin and spread the religion of Islam.

618–907 – The Tang dynasty rules in China, bringing a period well known for poetry, art, music, and silk trade.

632 – Muhammad, founder of Islam, dies. By this time, Islam is spreading rapidly across North Africa and Arabia.

632–850 – Through conversion and conquering, a vast Islamic empire is established across Asia.

700s – The Mississippi Valley civilization develops in North America.

768 – Charlemagne becomes King of the Franks, ruling a large kingdom in northern Europe.

800 – Feudalism begins to rise as a system of control in Europe.

800–1000 – Viking warriors invade Britain, France, and other parts of Europe.

900 – The Vikings discover Greenland.

The Vikings are warriors, traders, and farmers. Some Vikings raid and loot because of food shortages at home. Others are skilled shipbuilders traveling in search of new homes.

900–1200 – The Toltec civilization controls much of Mexico.

1000 – The Anasazi people establish settlements called *pueblos*, or *cliff dwellings*, in the southwestern part of North America.

1000 – The Samurai people gain control in Japan.

1000 – The Chinese invent gunpowder.

1000 – Maori people settle in New Zealand.

1000–1600 – Inhabitants of Easter Island in the southern Pacific build huge stone monuments in the shape of heads.

Giant stone monoliths, known as "maoi," dot the coastline of Easter Island.

1066 – William of Normandy (known as *William the Conqueror),* invades England, takes power after winning the Battle of Hastings, and proclaims himself king.

1096 – A group of kings in Europe sends armies to the Middle East to try to capture the city of Jerusalem. The purpose of these invasions, or *Crusades*, is to regain areas for Christianity and stop the spread of the Islam religion into Europe. A series of crusades continues until 1291. Jerusalem is recaptured in the First Crusade, but it is later lost. The eight Crusades have limited military success.

1150 – A magnificent temple, Angkor Wat, is completed by the powerful Khmer civilization in Cambodia.

Angkor Wat is the largest of many temples built by the Khmers over a period of 300 years.

1170 – Oxford University is established in England. Universities are established in Bologna in 1119 and in Paris in 1150.

1162 – The Archbishop of Canterbury, Thomas Becket, is murdered under instructions from King Henry II.

1179 – The great Mayan city of Chichen Itza in Mexico is destroyed.

1200s – The Mongols, warlike nomadic tribes, form a large empire and seize control of large areas of Asia. In 1206, a Mongol warrior is named Genghis Khan (meaning *the Great One*). Khan leads the Mongols in many conquests.

1210 – The Mali Kingdom becomes powerful in North Africa. Its capital is Timbuktu.

1215 – Nobles of the court of King John of England force the king to sign the *Magna Carta*, an agreement limiting the king's powers and giving the nobles a right to be involved in decisions.

1275 – Parliamentary government takes hold in England.

1290 – The Ottoman Empire, under the control of Muslim Turks, expands and controls large areas of the Middle East and Europe.

1300 – The Incan people settle in Peru around Cuzco. Machu Picchu, the *Lost City of the Incas*, is built as a religious retreat some time in the 1400s.

The ruins of Machu Picchu can still be seen high in the Andes Mountains of Peru.

1325 – The Aztec Indians in Mexico build the city of Tenochtitlan, which becomes the center of a huge and powerful empire.

1337 – The Hundred Years' War begins between France and England, lasting until 1453.

1347–1353 – A terrible disease, known as the *Black Death* or the *plague*, strikes Europe and kills as much as one-third of the population.

1350 – The Renaissance (meaning *rebirth*) begins in Italy, starting a period of renewed interest in the arts, learning, and literature, and blossoms into new scholarship, invention, and discovery. The Renaissance spreads throughout all of Europe over the next 150–200 years.

1400s – Europeans begin explorations around the globe that continue for more 200 years. In this *Age of Exploration*, new territories for commerce develop rapidly.

1440 – Portuguese explorers, by taking African slaves, begin hundreds of years of slave trade.

1429 – Jeanne d'Arc, a French peasant girl, leads the French against the English at Orleans, France. She is burned at the stake in 1431.

1452-1519 – Leonardo da Vinci lives a life full of long-lasting artistic accomplishments. He is famous for many pieces of art, in particular, the painting of the *Mona Lisa*.

1455 – Johann Gutenberg develops printing presses and prints the first book in Europe, the *Gutenberg Bible*.

1478 – Russian Ivan II frees Moscow from Mongol rule and becomes the first Czar of Russia.

1492 – Christopher Columbus, an Italian explorer, sails from Europe to the Caribbean Sea, founding the first European settlements in the Americas.

1498 – Spanish explorer Vasco da Gama sails around Africa.

1503 – Leonardo da Vinci paints the Mona Lisa.

1508–1512 – Michelangelo paints the ceiling of the Sistine Chapel.

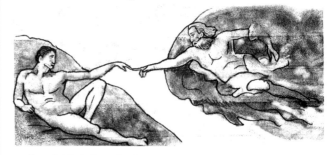

It took Michelangelo 4 years to paint several fresco scenes on this arched ceiling. A poem that he wrote about the experience revealed that he did the work standing on a scaffold, not lying on his back as some historians thought.

1517 – The Reformation begins as an attempt to reform the Roman Catholic Church, but results in a church split—leading to the formation of Protestant sects.

Martin Luther, a Catholic monk, posts 95 theses on a church door, objecting to some practices and beliefs of the Catholic Church.

1519 – Portuguese explorer Ferdinand Magellan sets out on a journey to sail around the world. Natives in the Philippines kill him, but one of his ships completes the circumnavigation of the globe in 1522.

1543 – Nicolaus Copernicus publishes his theory that Earth revolves around the Sun.

1588 – Spain tries to invade England, but the English navy defeats the entire fleet of warships (*the Spanish Armada*)

1593 – Spanish explorer Ponce de Leon discovers Florida.

1607 – English colonists settle in Jamestown, Virginia, in North America.

1608 – Quebec is founded by the French.

1619 – African slaves arrive in North America for the first time.

1620 – The Pilgrims land at Plymouth Rock in North America after a 3-month voyage on the *Mayflower*.

1632 – Italian astronomer Galileo publishes ideas about his discoveries in science, math, and astronomy.

1650 – Dutch settlers, known as *Boers*, arrive in the southern part of Africa.

1665 – A great plague sweeps London. 75,000 people die from disease.

1666 – A great fire sweeps through London for five days. The fire virtually destroys the city.

1600s –1700s – China has a heavy trade business, exporting fine fabrics, porcelain, and tea to Europe.

1750 – The Industrial Revolution begins in England and, over the next century, spreads to Western Europe and the United States.

The invention of machines, such as the spinning Jenny and steam-powered engines, helped industries speed up production of goods.

1762 – Catherine the Great becomes the Empress of Russia. The Russian Empire thrives and expands under her leadership.

1775–1783 – The American colonists, dissatisfied with the British rule, plan and declare independence from England.

1783 – In the Treaty of Paris, Britain recognizes the 13 colonies in North America as an independent country: The United States of America.

1789–1799 – The French Revolution begins with the storming of the Bastille Prison and spreads quickly through France. During the *Reign of Terror* that follows, anyone suspected of being against the revolution is executed by guillotine.

1799 – Napoleon Bonaparte becomes dictator of France. Under his brilliant military leadership, France conquers much of Europe by 1812.

Who Said It? Quotations from History

The unexamined life is not worth living.

Socrates, 469 - 399 BC

Nature does nothing without purpose, or uselessly.

Aristotle, 384 - 322 BC

Eureka! I have found it!

Give me but one firm spot on which to stand, and I will move the earth.

Archimedes, 287 - 212 BC

Veni, vidi, vici. (I came, I saw, I conquered.)

Julius Caesar, 100 - 44 BC

"Know Thyself!"
Anonymous, Ancient Greece

"Nothing in excess."
Anonymous, Ancient Greece

I want there to be no peasant in my kingdom so poor that he is unable to have a chicken in his pot every Sunday.

Henri IV, France, 1553 - 1610

Cogito, ergo sum. (I think, therefore I am.)

Decartes, 1596 - 1650

To no man will we sell, or deny, or delay, right or justice.

Magna Carta, AD 1215

All that glitters is not gold.

To thine own self be true, and it must follow as the night the day, thou can not be false to any man.

I know I have the body of a weak and feeble woman; but I have the heart and stomach of a king, and a King of England, too.

Elizabeth I, England, 1568 - 1603

William Shakespeare, 1564 - 1616

If I have seen further it is by standing on the back of giants.

Sir Isaac Newton, 1642 - 1727

170

1800s – The century sees a mad rush on the part of European countries to increase their influence in other continents. In this *Age of Imperialism*, Britain, Belgium, Spain, France, Italy, Portugal, and Holland colonize most of Africa, as well as large portions of southeastern Asia and islands in the South Pacific Ocean. The imperialism provides more raw materials for the new manufacturing and opportunities for people to move to new lands.

1802–1803 – English explorer Matthew Flinders is one of the first Europeans to explore Australia. Australia becomes a place where Britain "dumps" criminals.

1808–1825 – In Central and South America, Argentina, Venezuela, Paraguay, Colombia, Uruguay, and Chile fight wars to gain independence from Spanish and Portuguese rule.

1810 – Colombian Simon Bolivar leads a revolt against Spanish control. After many years, ten South American countries gain independence from Spain.

1814–1815 – Napoleon is forced from power to exile on the island of Elba. He escapes and retakes power, but is defeated in a battle at Waterloo.

1823 – In the *Monroe Doctrine*, the U.S. president warns European nations not to interfere in the Western Hemisphere.

1830–1832 – British navigator John Biscoe circumvents and explores Antarctica.

1841 – David Livingston, from Scotland, is the first European to cross Africa on foot.

1843 – Samuel Morse develops an effective code for sending telegraph signals.

The Morse Code is a system of short and long sounds, called dots and dashes.

1845–1848 – A long famine in Ireland causes thousands of Irish to emigrate to the U.S. from their homeland.

1848 – Karl Marx and Friedrich Engels release the *Communist Manifesto*.

1848 – A *Year of Revolutions*: people in many European countries rise up to protest food shortages, harsh rule, or economic problems. The rebellions are mostly unsuccessful, but leaders do make some changes.

Mid to late 1800s – Westward movement and settlement in the U.S. leads to wars with Native American populations. Large portions of the Native American populations die from war and disease.

Thousands of people followed the Oregon Trail west. The trail began in Independence, Missouri and stretched to Ft. Vancouver (now in Washington).

1853 – American Naval officer Matthew Perry sails into Tokyo harbor with gunboats, forcing Japan to open its ports to outside trade.

1857–1858 – In the Indian Mutiny, people in India rise up against the British. The British regain power.

1861 – Southern states in the U.S. break away from the union and form the Confederate States of America. A civil war breaks out.

1865 – The American Civil War ends.

1869 – The transcontinental railroad is finished, making faster travel across the North American continent possible. The last spike is made of gold and driven into the railroad in Promontory, Utah.

1869 – Discovery of diamonds in South Africa leads to a rush of settlers and explorers hunting for diamonds.

1876 – The telephone is invented by Alexander Graham Bell.

1880 – Construction begins on the Panama Canal to connect the Atlantic and Pacific Oceans.

1880s – Jewish immigrants from Europe begin migrating to Palestine, with the purpose of returning to their historic homeland.

1885 – The first motorized car is built in Germany by Karl Benz.

The Benz auto has an internal-combustion engine, 3 wheels, electric ignition, differential gears, and a water-cooling system.

1886 – The Statue of Liberty, given to the U.S. by France, is set up in New York City harbor.

1889 – The Eiffel Tower is built in Paris.

1890 – The last uprising of Native Americans, the *Battle of Wounded Knee*, ends in their tragic defeat.

1896 – The first modern Olympic Games are held in Athens, Greece.

1898 – Spain loses some of its colonies to the U.S. in the Spanish-American War.

1903 – The Wright brothers succeed with the first powered flight at Kitty Hawk, North Carolina, U.S.

1908 – In the U.S., Henry Ford begins the first mass production of automobiles.

1912 – The *Titanic* sinks on its maiden voyage across the Atlantic.

1914 – World War I begins.

1915 – Mahatma Gandhi begins a long nonviolent campaign to win rights for the common people in India.

1917 – The Russian Revolution overthrows the czar, leaving the communists (called *Bolsheviks*) to take control.

1919 – World War I ends with a peace treaty signed in Versailles, France.

1922 – The U.S.S.R. is formed.

1927 – Charles Lindbergh successfully completes a solo flight across the Atlantic Ocean.

The flight took 33$\frac{1}{2}$ hours in Lindbergh's single-engine, propeller plane named "The Spirit of St. Louis."

1929 – The Great Depression begins.

1933 – Adolf Hitler becomes dictator of Germany.

1939 – World War II begins in Europe. Germany invades Poland and France.

1941 – Japan attacks the U.S. Naval Fleet at Pearl Harbor; U.S. enters into World War II.

1941 – Hitler sets up extermination camps to get rid of Jews.

1942 – In the *Manhattan Project*, U.S. scientists go to work to create an atom bomb.

1945 – The U.S. drops nuclear bombs on the Japanese cities of Nagasaki and Hiroshima.

1945 – World War II ends.

1945 – After World War II, a long period of tension develops between the U.S. and the Soviet Union, beginning a period called the *Cold War*.

1945 – The United Nations is established, replacing the League of Nations.

1948 – Mahatma Gandhi is assassinated.

1948 – The state of Israel is created.

1948 – Several Arab states attack the new country of Israel, beginning the first Arab-Israeli war.

1948 – South Africa established the policy of *apartheid*, separating black and white citizens.

1948–1949 – The Soviet Union blockades West Berlin in an attempt to force it to be part of Eastern Europe; Britain and the U.S. airlift supplies into West Berlin; West Germany and East Germany become separate states.

1949 – Mao Zedong takes control of the Communist Party in China, forms the Communist Peoples' Republic of China.

1949 – The U.S. and 11 European nations form NATO (*the North Atlantic Treaty Organization*), signing agreements to protect each other against Soviet aggression.

1950s–1970s – The era of colonialism ends and most colonies in Africa gain independence.

1950–1953 – The U.S. and other nations join South Korea to fight against a North Korean invasion.

1953- Scientists Francis Crick and James Watson discover the structure of DNA.

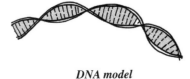

DNA model

1954–1973 – Civil war rages in Vietnam. Pro-communist forces fight against anti-communist forces in South Vietnam. The U.S. eventually becomes involved in supporting the South Vietnam government.

1955 – In the U.S., Martin Luther King, Jr., leads a bus boycott in Alabama in a protest against segregation, expanding the American Civil Rights Movement.

A national holiday in the U.S. honors the work of Dr. King each February.

1956 – In the *Suez Crisis*, Egypt nationalizes the Suez Canal, triggering action by Israel, Britain, and France to retake control of the canal. International pressure ends the crisis. The canal is closed for six months.

1957 – The U.S.S.R. launches *Sputnik I*, the first satellite in space.

Sputnik I carries the first living creature in space, a small dog named Laika.

1958 – Fidel Castro takes power in Cuba and installs a communist government aligned with the Soviet Union.

1961 – Soviet Cosmonaut Yuri Gagarin becomes the first human to fly in space, orbiting Earth in his space ship, *Vostok I*.

1961 – The Berlin Wall is built around East Berlin to keep Germans on the east side from escaping to West Germany.

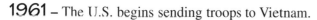

1961 – The U.S. begins sending troops to Vietnam.

1962 – In the *Cuban Missile Crisis*, the U.S. and Cuba have a standoff over Soviet nuclear weapons in Cuba.

In response to Soviet military shipments to Cuba, Soviet bases in Cuba, and the presence of Soviet nuclear missiles there, the U.S. blockades Cuba and threatens war. For a few dangerous days, the world seems on the brink of nuclear war, before Russia backs down and gives in to U.S. demands.

1963 – U.S. President John F. Kennedy is assassinated.

1966 – The Seven-Day War between Israel, Egypt, and Syria ends with a victory for the Israelis.

1966 – Mao Zedong, leader of China, begins the Cultural Revolution. The Cultural Revolution is a period of time when any capitalist influences in China are brutally crushed and all citizens are encouraged to keep Communism pure. The period ends in 1976 with the death of Zedong.

1967 – Israel captures territory from Egypt, Syria, and Jordan in the Six Days War.

1969 – The U.S. successfully lands the first human on the Moon.

When U.S. astronaut Neil Armstrong set foot on the moon, he said: "That's one small step for man, one giant leap for mankind."

1969 – The peace movement grows in the U.S. with major demonstrations against the Vietnam War.

1971 – Pakistan gives up the control of East Pakistan, allowing it to become the independent state of Bangladesh.

1971 – The first space station, *Salyut I*, is launched by the U.S.S.R.

1972 – Israeli athletes are murdered at the Olympic Games in Munich by an Arab terrorist organization, *Black September*.

1972 – President Richard Nixon is the first U.S. president to visit Communist China.

1972 – The U.S.S.R. and the U.S. sign the SALT to reduce arms. (SALT is *the Strategic Arms Limitation Treaty.*)

1973 – The U.S. withdraws its troops from Vietnam.

1974 – U.S. President Richard Nixon resigns amidst the Watergate Scandal.

1975 – North Vietnam defeats and occupies South Vietnam.

1976 – The *Concorde*, a supersonic passenger plane designed by Britain and France, takes its first transatlantic flight. The *Concorde* flies at a speed of 1,350 mph (twice the speed of sound) and holds 100 passengers. Twenty of the planes are built, at a cost of about $46 million each.

1978 – Israel and Egypt agree to terms of peace in the *Camp David Agreement*.

1978 – The U.S. begins diplomatic relations with China.

1980s – The Cold War tensions between communist and noncommunist countries decrease.

1980 – The Iran-Iraq war begins.

1982–1985 – Israel invades Lebanon in an attempt to drive the Palestine Liberation Organization out of the country.

Get Sharp: World History Timeline

1986 – The U.S. and other nations begin economic sanctions against South Africa because of its *apartheid* policies.

1986 – The first major disaster at a nuclear power plant occurs in Chernobyl, U.S.S.R.

1986 – The Space Shuttle *Challenger* explodes immediately after liftoff.

1989 – Chinese students protest their government policies and march for democracy in Beijing's Tiananmen Square; the Chinese army crushes the protest.

1989 – The Berlin Wall is knocked down; Germany is reunified in 1990.

1990 – The Hubble Space Telescope is launched.

Hubble is the size of a school bus, and transmits enough data every day to fill 10,000 computer diskettes. It takes 97 minutes to circle the Earth at a speed of 17,500 mph.

1990 – *Apartheid* ends in South Africa. Activist Nelson Mandela is released from prison after 27 years.

1991 – The Soviet Union collapses.

1991 – The U.S. and a coalition of Allies go to war with Iraq to push back Iraq's 1990 advances on its neighbor Kuwait.

1991 – A cyclone kills 125,000 people in Bangladesh and leaves many more homeless.

1993 – The European Union is established.

1994 – Nelson Mandela becomes the first black president in South Africa.

1997 – The British return control of Hong Kong to China.

1997 – The first animal is cloned from the cells of another adult animal.

1998 – The European Union (except the U.K.) adopts a single currency, the *Euro*.

1999 – Northern Ireland wins the right to govern itself.

2000 – The first crew arrives at the International Space Station.

2001 – Terrorists crash planes into buildings in the U.S. on September 11, killing about 3,000 people.

2002 – The U.S. and allies go to war with Afghanistan to overthrow the ruling Taliban party and search for members of Al Qaeda, the group responsible for the September 11 attacks.

2002 – Scientists and researchers complete a draft of the human genome sequence.

2002 – The first synthetic virus is created.

2003 – The United States and allies topple the Iraq government of Saddam Hussein.

2004 – The of true age of the galaxy is discovered (13.6 billion years).

2004 – A huge tsunami hits countries in the southern Pacific and Indian Oceans, killing over 150,000 people and leaving millions homeless.

2004 – NASA lands two rovers on the surface of Mars.

The Mars Exploration Rover Mission uses robotic rovers to look for answers about the history of water on Mars.

Who Said It?

Quotations from Modern History

The future belongs to those who believe in the beauty of their dreams.
Eleanor Roosevelt (1884-1962)

Democracy is the worst form of government—except for all the rest.
Winston Churchill (1874-1965)

The human race has one really effective weapon—and that is laughter.
Mark Twain (1835-1910)

The hunger for love is more difficult to remove than the hunger for bread.
Mother Teresa (1910-1997)

The only tyrant I accept is the still voice within.
Gandhi, (1869 - 1948)

Men, their rights and nothing more; women, their rights and nothing less.
Susan B. Anthony (1820-1906)

We are not amused.
Queen Victoria (1819-1901)

The ballot is stronger than the bullet.
Abraham Lincoln (1809-1865)

Power tends to corrupt and absolute power corrupts absolutely.
Lord Acton (1834-1902)

The great question, which I have never been able to answer- is, "What does a woman want?"
Sigmund Freud (1856-1939)

Let every nation know, whether it wishes us well or ill, that we shall pay any price, bear any burden, meet any hardship. support any friend, oppose any foe, to assure the survival and success of liberty.
John F. Kennedy (1917-1963)

Somewhere out in this audience may even be someone who will one day follow my footsteps and preside over the White House as the President's spouse. I wish him well.
Barbara Bush (1925-   )

Get Sharp: World History Quotes

World History Personalities

An army marches on its stomach.
-Napoleon Bonaparte

Here are just a few of the people who made specific contributions to the amazing history of the world.

Alexander the Great (356–323 B.C.) – King of Macedonia; conqueror of Greece and Persia

Alexander II (1818–1888) – Russian Czar from 1855-1881; abolished serfdom

Anaan, Kofi (1838–) – UN Secretary-General from 1987 to present; born in Ghana; winner of the 2001 Nobel Peace Prize

Antoinette, Marie (1755–1793) – Queen of France from 1774–1792; killed by guillotine in the *Reign of Terror* during the French Revolution

Arafat, Yasir (1929–2004) – leader of the Palestine Liberation Organization (PLO) who signed 1993 Peace Accord with Israel; president of Palestine since 1994; recipient of 1994 Nobel Peace Prize

Aristotle (382–332 B.C.) – philosopher of Ancient Greece; made important contributions to mathematics

Balboa, Vasco de (1475–1517) – Spanish explorer who first reached the Pacific by crossing Panama (1513)

Begin, Menachem (1913–1992) – Israeli prime minister who signed the Camp David Peace Accord (1978)

Benedict (480–543) – Italian monk who organized monasteries

Bolivar, Simon (1783–1830) – Venezuelan leader who drove Spanish out of northern South America

Bonaparte, Napoleon (1769–1821) – French emperor and military conqueror from 1804–1815

Brezhnev, Leonid (1906–1982) – head of the Communist Party of the U.S.S.R. from 1964 until his death

Caesar, Julius (100–44 B.C.) – Roman general, statesman, and historian

Calvin, John (1509–1564) – French-born Swiss Protestant reformer; one of the founders of Protestantism

Castro, Fidel (1927 –) – Cuban revolutionary who took control of the country in 1959 and headed the country under a Communist government

Catherine the Great (1729–1796) – Russian empress who poisoned her husband to gain control and greatly expanded Russia's territory; reigned from 1762–1796

Chaing Kai-shek (1886–1975) Chinese national leader; led fight against the Communists in 1930s and 1940s

Charlemagne (724–814) – Frankish king who spread Christianity through Europe; emperor from 768–814

Churchill, Winston (1874–1965) – British prime minister from 1951–1955; led Britain during World War II

Cleopatra (69–30 B.C.) – powerful Egyptian queen during the rule of Caesar

Columbus, Christopher (1446–1605) – Italian explorer who arrived in the Americas in 1492

Confucius (551–479 B.C.) – Chinese philosopher whose teachings spread through China, beginning the philosophy-religion of Confucianism

Get Sharp: Persons in World History

Constantine (280–337) – Roman emperor from 312–337; legalized Christianity in the Roman Empire

Cook, James (1728–1779) – British explorer who first explored Australia

Copernicus, Nicolaus (1473–1543) – Polish astronomer who made many important discoveries in astronomy and argued that the Sun is the center of the solar system

Da Gama, Vasco (1469–1542) – Portuguese explorer; found a water route to the Indies

Da Vinci, Leonardo (1452–1519) – successful Renaissance painter and inventor

DeKlerk, F. W. (1936-) – South African president from 1989 to 1994 who led the country during the end of apartheid; lifted the ban on the African National Council, and released Nelson Mandela from prison

Drake, Francis (1540–1596) – English military leader who led the defeat of the Spanish Armada in 1588

Einstein, Albert (1879–1975) – German scientist who published the *Theory of Relativity* in 1905

Eisenhower, Dwight D. (1879–1975) – supreme commander of Allied forces who organized the D-Day invasion in 1944; became U.S. president in 1953

Elizabeth I (1533–1603) – powerful Queen of England from 1558–1603 who reinstated the Anglican Church as the Church of England

The past cannot be cured.
-Elizabeth I of England

Ferdinand, Franz (1863–1914) – heir to the Austria-Hungary throne whose murder by a Serbian nationalist triggered World War I

Frank, Anne (1929–1945) – young Jewish girl who recorded a diary of her experiences hiding from the Nazis and, after being caught, died in a concentration camp

Galileo Galilei (1563–1642) – Italian astronomer and mathematician who made use of a telescope to observe the solar system and published new findings about astronomy

Gandhi, Mohandas (1869–1948) – Indian leader who taught civil disobedience and led India's independence movement (1920)

Gautama, Siddhartha (563–483 B.C.) – founder of Buddhism; known as the *Buddha*

Gorbachev, Mikhail (1933–) – leader of the Soviet Union from 1985–1991; began reforms that led to the fall of Communism in the U.S.S.R.

Gutenberg, Johann (1400–1468) – German printer credited with the invention of the printing press; published the first book made on printing presses, the *Gutenberg Bible*

Hammurabi (1800–1750 B.C.) – Babylonian ruler famous for first system of laws called *Hammurabi's Code* (1792 B.C.)

Hidalgo, Miguel (1752–1811) – Mexican priest who led a revolt that began the Mexican fight for independence

Hitler, Adolf (1889–1945) – German Nazi leader and dictator who led Germany into World War II

Ho Chi Minh (1890–1969) – North Vietnamese leader who led communist troops in the takeover of South Vietnam

Homer (950–900 B.C.) – Greek poet; writer of famous epic poems, *The Odyssey* and *The Iliad*

Jesus Christ (6 B.C.–A.D.29) – Jewish carpenter and teacher whose teachings led to the establishment of Christianity, and whose followers became known as Christians

Lenin, Vladimir (1870–1924) – Russian communist leader who founded the Soviet Union

Livingston, David (1813–1873) – Scottish missionary who ventured into the deepest parts of Africa where no white person had traveled

Louis XIV (1638–1715) – French king from 1643–1715; advanced French culture, adopting the sun as his emblem

> I took control of the French Government in 1661 and ruled with absolute power. My friends and enemies called me the "Sun King."
> -Louis XIV of France

Louis XVI (1754–1793) – French king from 1774–1792; executed by guillotine during the *Reign of Terror* in the French Revolution

Luther, Martin (1483–1546) – German monk who demanded reforms in the Roman Catholic Church and whose efforts eventually led to the Protestant Reformation

Mandela, Nelson (1918-) – South African lawyer who led the struggle against the policies of *apartheid*; jailed from 1964–1990; became South Africa's first black president in 1994

Marcos, Ferdinand (1917–1989) – Philippine leader who became a dictator and was forced into exile in 1986 by the people of his country

Marx, Karl (1818–1883) – German writer whose ideas formed the basis for socialism and communism

Meir, Golda (1898–1978) – Zionist leader who helped to found Israel and served as Israel's prime minister from 1969–1974

Michelangelo (1475–1654) – Italian Renaissance painter and sculptor

Muhammed (570–632) – founder of the Islamic religion

Nasser, Gamal Abdel (1819–1970) – Egypt's first president

Nehru, Jawaharlal (1889–1964) – India's first prime minister; follower of Gandhi's teachings

Newton, Isaac (1642–1727) – English scientist who discovered the law of gravity, and formulated other laws about energy and motion

Peter the Great (1672–1725) – Russian czar from 1682–1725; built the capital at St. Petersburg

Plato (428–347 B.C.) – Greek philosopher who studied under Socrates

Roosevelt, Franklin (1882–1945) – U.S. president from 1933–1945; led the country during World War II

San Martin, Jose de (1778–1850) – South American leader of armies that won independence from Spain for Argentina and Chile

Shakespeare, William (1564–1616) – well known Renaissance English poet and playwright whose work has endured for centuries

Sharon, Ariel (1928–) – Israeli general who sparked controversy by visiting the Temple Mount in Palestinian East Jerusalem in 2000, triggering Arab demonstrations and derailing progress toward peace; prime minister of Israel since 2001

Socrates (470–399 B.C.) – famous philosopher and scholar of ancient Greece

Stalin, Joseph (1879–1953) – harsh Soviet dictator from 1924–1953; turned the U.S.S.R. into a totalitarian nation

Walsea, Lech (1943–) – factory worker who led 1988 Polish protests against the communist government; won a Nobel Peace Prize in 1985 and became president of Poland in 1990

Zedong, Mao (1893–1976) – Chinese communist leader who founded the Cultural Revolution in China with the purpose of purging all noncommunist influences from China

Spectacular Inventions & Discoveries

Remarkable discoveries and amazing inventions have punctuated the story of human life on Earth. Over and over, new understandings, ideas, and technologies keep changing the way people live, think, work, and interact.

In the air . . .

The **propeller airplane** was invented by the American brothers, Orville and Wilbur Wright, in 1903.

Fortunately for early aviators, the **parachute** had already been invented in 1785 by Frenchman, Jean Pierre Blanchard.

Igor Sikorsky (U.S.) thought the **helicopter** was a good idea in 1939. This is the same year that Hans van Ohain of Germany was busy inventing the **jet airplane.**

On land . . .

Englishman George Stephenson invented the **steam locomotive** in 1829. Before the century ended, travel by rail would become the fastest, safest, mode of transcontinental transportation.

Frank and Charles Duryea (U.S.) developed the **gasoline-powered automobile** in 1892. Henry Ford introduced his **assembly-line creation** in 1908. He sold it for a whopping $850.

The **bicycle** (James Starley, England) and the **motorcycle** (Gottlieb Daimler, Germany) were both invented in 1885. Almost 100 years later, in 1980, Scott Olsen invented a truly innovative mode of personal transportation—**rollerblades.**

Transportation really advanced when Mary Anderson (U.S.A.) invented the windshield wiper in 1903.

At sea . . .

Transatlantic ocean travel was revolutionized when American Robert Fulton invented the **steamboat** in 1807.

Artist and inventor, Leonardo da Vinci envisioned the **submarine** in the 15th century. But the first **modern submarine** was not devised until 1894 (by Simon Lake, U.S.).

Person to person . . .

Paper was invented in China in the second century, and the art of letter writing was born.

Samuel Morse invented the **telegraph** in 1837, allowing messages to be sent and received quickly.

Alexander Graham Bell really pulled telecommunication into the modern age with his invention of the **telephone** in 1876 (earning the everlasting gratitude of teenagers everywhere).

The area of interactive communication advanced again with the introduction of the **cell phone** by the Swedish company, Ericsson, in 1979.

Far-out theories and inventions . . .

Credit is usually given to the Italian genius, Galileo, for inventing the **telescope** in 1609, but some believe that Hans Lippershey of Holland may have been the first to view the heavens through a lens in 1600.

The launching of the **Hubble Space Telescope** in 1990 greatly expanded our knowledge of the universe.

The German astronomer, Johannes Kepler (1571–1630) correctly theorized that the force of **gravity** controls the orbits of the planets around the Sun.

Albert Einstein (1879–1955) developed the **Theory of Relativity,** which explains some relationships between time, energy, matter, and space.

Lise Meitner (1878–1968) discovered **nuclear fission**, and theorized about the kind of chain reaction that would lead to the release of power in a nuclear bomb.

Down to Earth inventions . . .

Spectacles for reading date back to the 13th century, but Benjamin Franklin (UI.S.) had the right idea when he invented **bifocals** in 1780.

The **sewing machine** seemed like a good idea when Elias Howe (U.S.) invented it in 1846. The **zipper** (invented by Whitcomb L. Judson) came along in 1891, and **Velcro** (Georges de Mestral, Switzerland) was introduced in 1948.

Englishman Jacob Perkins invented **refrigeration** in 1834 and the American Clarence Birdseye invented **prepackaged frozen food** in 1924. Another American, Frederick Jones, **developed refrigerated trucks** at about the same time.

Major Conflicts

War is a major theme in the history of the world. Conflicts and wars have been motivated by economic needs, desire for power and territory, human greed, self-defense, religious differences, and clashes in ideas.

The Crusades (1095–1291) – For almost 200 years, European Christians launched a series of military actions to win the Holy Land (Palestine) back from Muslims. In the *First Crusade* (1096–1099), the crusaders took back Jerusalem, but the territories gained were later lost. Many other *Crusades* followed, but the Christians did not succeed in gaining and holding the Holy Land for themselves. In 1212, a group of children tried to accomplish what the older crusaders could not. This was called the *Children's Crusade*. The crusade failed miserably, with many of the children dying from disease or hunger, and many others taken into slavery.

Hundred Years' War (1337–1453) – War began between England and France when William the Conqueror (of Normandy, France) conquered England, creating a state that included English and French land. The French wanted control of their own territory and the English believed they controlled France. A struggle for power and land continued for over a hundred years.

The American Revolution (1775–1783) – After years of dissatisfaction with British rule in the American colonies, representatives from the colonies signed the *Declaration of Independence*, beginning a war with the British (1776). The war ended in 1783 with the *Treaty of Paris*, in which Britain recognized the independence of the colonies and the United States of America was formed.

1212
Children's Crusade
DOOMED TO FAILURE

The French Revolution (1789) – In the late eighteenth century, the citizens of France rebelled against the poor living conditions, shortages of food, heavy taxes, and unfair government of the kings and his nobles. In 1789, the Commoners formed their own National Assembly, which put forth the *Declaration of the Rights of Man*. Riots against the government began, and a mob stormed the Bastille Prison on July 14, 1789. The revolution continued and became more violent, even after France became a republic. During the *Reign of Terror* in 1793–1794, many leaders were put to death by guillotine.

Boer War (1899–1902) – The South Africa Republic (Transvaal) and the Orange Free State formed an alliance to protect their independence since they believed that Great Britain was threatening to take over their territories. Control of the diamond and gold mines was a part of the struggle in the area. A long guerrilla war waged, with many deaths on both sides. The Boers could not hold out against the more powerful British forces. The war ended in 1902 with the *Treaty of Vereeniging*.

The Philadelphia Indepe[...]

1783
American War for Independence is a Success

The South Afrikaner Gazette

1902
War Ends
Boers Fall to British Forces

The Russian Revolution (1917) – The people of Russia, oppressed for years by czars who held absolute power, followed the leadership of Lenin (the head of the communist Bolshevik party) and overthrew the czar. The new government killed the czar and his family and centralized control of land and services.

1989

Berlin Wall Comes Down

World War I (1914–1918) – The war began when Archduke Francis Ferdinand, the prince of Austria-Hungary, was killed in Sarajevo in 1914. The murderer was a Serbian, so Austria declared war on Serbia. Russia joined in to defend Serbia. Greater causes of the war were the intense economic and territorial rivalries between the powers of Europe. In just a few weeks, the Central Powers (Germany, Austria-Hungary, Turkey, and Bulgaria) were at war with the Allies (Russia, France, and Britain). Fierce fighting took place for four years, with Italy, Japan, the United States, Turkey, and Bulgaria joining. About 17 million people were killed in the war, which ended with the signing of several treaties.

World War II (1939–1945) – The war began when Germany, under Adolf Hitler, invaded Poland. Britain and France, who were part of an alliance with Poland (the Allied Powers), declared war on Germany. Over the next five years, the war moved across Europe and into northern Africa. Japan joined with the German alliance (the Axis Powers), and began taking control of areas in southeastern Asia and the Pacific. In 1942, the U.S. joined the Allies after Japan attacked the U.S. Naval fleet at Pearl Harbor, Hawaii. The Allies landed in Europe (at Normandy) in 1944 and turned the tide of the war against Germany. The U.S. dropped two atomic bombs in Japan in 1945, and the Axis powers were defeated both on the European and Pacific fronts in the same year.

The Arab-Israeli Wars (1948–Present) – Soon after the establishment of the state of Israel in 1948, conflicts arose between the Jews and the Arabs. Frequent wars, border raids, and other clashes have continued ever since.

In 1948, several Arab nations invaded the new country until the UN established a truce. Fighting erupted again in 1956 (*the 1956 War*), when Israeli forces moved into Egypt's Sinai Peninsula. Israel withdrew from these positions in 1957.

In the *Six Day War* in 1967, Egypt closed Israel off from the Gulf of Aqaba in response to Israeli raids across the borders of neighboring countries. In 1973–1974, Egypt attacked Israel on a Jewish holy day (*the Yom Kippur War*). This brutal siege ended through diplomatic efforts from the U.S. In 1979, Israel and Egypt signed the *Camp David Peace Accords*.

In 1982, Israel launched an attack to destroy Palestinian bases in Lebanon. Under international pressure, Israel retreated and cease-fire agreements were reached. In 1988, Yasir Arafat, leader of the PLO (*Palestine Liberation Organization*) signed an accord with Israel leading to limited Palestinian self-rule in Jericho and the Gaza Strip. Further agreements to finalize borders and solve the dispute over Jerusalem were signed, but new violence, attacks, and suicide bombings that began in September of 2000 stalled progress on these issues. With the death of Arafat in 2004, there was some optimism that the peace process might move forward.

Korean War (1950–1953) – At the end of World War II, Korea was divided into two zones at the 38th parallel. In 1950, communist North Korean forces invaded noncommunist South Korea. Forces from the U.S. and UN joined under the command of U.S. General Douglas MacArthur to aid South Korea. After much brutal fighting with heavy casualties, a cease-fire agreement was signed in 1953. There was no official treaty ending the war, and U.S. troops still occupy the area near the North Korea-South Korea border. Tensions between the two countries continue.

Vietnam War (1950–1975) – After Vietnam won its independence from French colonial control in 1954, the U.S. began to support anti-communist efforts in South Vietnam. In this *Cold War* period, the U.S. had a belief in the *Domino Theory,* a fear that the North Vietnam's fall to Communism could result in the spread of Communism throughout the area. The anti-communist efforts grew into full-blown American military involvement in Vietnam, with thousands of U.S. troops taking part in a war against the communist forces. Even with heavy bombing and its military might, the U.S. was unable to stop the communists. Forces on both sides suffered heavy casualties, while inside the U.S., opposition to the war grew strong. American troops withdrew from Vietnam in 1973. South Vietnam surrendered to North Vietnam in 1975, and the country was reunited.

Iran-Iraq War (1980–1988) – This conflict began with an Iraqi invasion of Iran in 1980 following a dispute over a waterway that forms the Iran-Iraq border. Clashes continued for years, bringing huge death tolls and devastation to the countries, economies, and people of both countries. After Iran attacked Kuwaiti oil tankers in 1988, the UN forced a cease-fire. In 1990, Iraq withdrew its troops from Iran, but a formal peace treaty has never been signed.

Persian Gulf War (1991) – The war was sparked by Iraq's August, 1990 invasion of long-disputed territory in Kuwait. The U.S. and a coalition of allies launched *Operation Desert Storm* on January 18, 1991, and liberated Kuwait in February. Iraq withdrew from Kuwait, but Iraq's leader, Sadaam Hussein, remained in power.

Afghanistan War (2002–) – The war was sparked by the 2001 terrorist attacks on the World Trade Center in New York City and the Pentagon in Washington, D.C. The group that was apparently responsible for the attacks, Al Qaeda, had major bases in Afghanistan. The United States believed that the governing group in Afghanistan, the Taliban, was supporting and hiding Al Qaeda. When the Taliban refused to expel Al Qaeda terrorists from their country, the United States invaded Afghanistan to topple the Taliban control and hunt for Al Qaeda terrorists.

Iraq War (2003–) – Leaders of the U.S. government believed that the government of Sadaam Hussein was supporting the kinds of terrorists that were responsible for the September 11, 2001 attacks. In addition, the U.S. government believed that Hussein was building nuclear weapons and other weapons of mass destruction. Troops of the U.S. and allies invaded Iraq and toppled Hussein's government. Much guerrilla fighting continued after Hussein was removed. Troops remained in Iraq, trying to make the country safe enough for the Iraqi people to run their own country.

Better Grades & Higher Test Scores / SOCIAL STUDIES gr. 4–6
Copyright ©2005 by Incentive Publications, Inc., Nashville, TN.

GET SHARP →

on

U.S. HISTORY, GOVERNMENT, & CITIZENSHIP

Vote For Class President Here

Early Americans

Today, the North American continent is separated from Asia by the Bering Strait. Thousands of years ago, during the Ice Age, glaciers froze so much of the water that the level of the oceans dropped. This exposed dry land (a land bridge) between the two continents, and allowed humans to migrate into America.

Early Cultures

By the 13th century, about a million people lived in the area that is now the United States and Canada. Cultures differed because of the land, climate, and resources in the areas where they lived. Some cultures were based on agriculture. Others were hunting cultures. Each group had to adapt to their particular environment, finding ways to get food, provide shelter, and meet the other basic needs of life. Most of the societies had little contact with other groups unless their trading and food-gathering needs brought them into contact or conflict with other groups.

The Eastern Woodlands

The native people of the Northeast lived between the Atlantic Ocean and the Mississippi River. The area extended to the Great Lakes and above the lakes into Canada. Cultures grew up in densely wooded areas. Their way of life included deer hunting, fishing, and farming. A group of tribes joined together in a tribal association known as the *Five Nations* or the *League of the Iroquois* in the area that is now New York. (These tribes were the Seneca, Mohawk, Onondaga, Cayuga, and Oneida.) Other tribes of the Eastern Woodlands were the Ojibwa (Chippewa), Potawatomi, Miami, Illinois, Shawnee, Ottawa, Algonquin, Powhatan, Huron, Penobscot, Susquehanna, Delaware, Narraganset, Massachuset, and Mohegan.

The Southeast

South of the Eastern Woodlands was a region stretching from the Ohio River to the Gulf of Mexico. This area, some of it in the Ohio River Valley, was rich with fertile soil and deep forests. Tribes that inhabited this area lived by hunting, fishing, farming, and gathering food. Some of them made pottery. After the year 500, some of the cultures in this area became *Mound Builders*, building earthen mounds in the shape of humans, birds, or other animals for burying their dead. This region was the home of several tribes: the Choctaw, Creek, Cherokee, Natchez, Timucua, and Chickasaw. The Calusa and Seminole tribes lived in the southernmost parts of the region.

The Great Plains

The Plains area extended from the Canadian border south to what is now Texas and spread from the Mississippi River to the foothills of the Rocky Mountains. The main tribes that lived in this area were the Crow, Cheyenne, Mandan, Dakota (Sioux), Arapaho, Pawnee, Osage, Kiowa, and Comanche. The people of some tribes were farmers who lived in permanent dwellings. Others tribes were nomadic, traveling to hunt buffalo. The horse, introduced to the region in the 18th century, changed life for the Indians. Horses made it easier for them to travel and hunt. It also brought them into more frequent contact with other tribes.

The Southwest

The people of the Southwest lived in an area that extended over present day Arizona, New Mexico, and parts of Utah and Colorado. The earliest Southwest people lived in pit dwellings or stone slab houses. Later, the Pueblo Indians created large community houses built in terraces on ledges of canyons (*cliff dwellings*). These tribes lived by farming and hunting. They were skilled potters and basket weavers. Water was scarce in the region, so people had to find ways to keep a water supply. Some tribes brought water to their fields through irrigation ditches. The tribes that inhabited these areas were the Pueblo, Zuni, Hopi, Navajo, and Apache.

The Plateau

The Plateau area extended from above the Canadian border through the plateau area of the southwest, part of California, and the mountainous area of the Rockies. Tribes that lived in the area were the Cayuse, Nez Perce, Flathead, Chumash, Spokan, Paiute, and Pomo. They lived by hunting and gathering.

The Great Basin

In the Great Basin region (the area that is now Nevada, Utah, and parts of southern Oregon and Idaho), the land was harsh and dry. The Shoshone and Ute tribes were wanderers, hunting small animals and gathering seeds and plants. Other tribes were the Klamath, Modoc, and Paiute.

The Northwest

The inhabitants of the Northwest lived along the Pacific coast from northern California to Alaska. The area was thickly wooded with heavy rainfall. The natives fished for salmon and hunted land animals and sea mammals. In addition, they gathered fruit and berries. They used wood from the forests to build houses and canoes. The plentiful trees also supplied wood for totem poles. The tribes that lived in this area were the Maidu, Hupa, Yurok, Chinook, Satish, Kwakiutl, Haida, Tsimshian, and Nootka. In northern Canada and Alaska, ancestors of today's Eskimos lived from the bountiful animal life in the sea: walruses, seals, whales, and salmon. In the summer, they also hunted caribou.

30,000–10,000 B.C. – The first people arrive on the North American continent, crossing from Asia on land and ice.

1000 B.C.–A.D. 1492 – Many different Native American cultures develop throughout North America.

1492 – Italian explorer Christopher Columbus reaches the West Indies and the Bahamas.

1499–1502 – Italian Amerigo Vespucci explores the South American coast.

1507 – The New World is named *America*, after Amerigo Vespucci.

1513 – Spanish explorer Juan Ponce de Leon explores Florida.

1524 – Italian explorer Giovanni da Verrazano explores the North American east coast and enters New York Harbor.

1540–1541 – Spanish explorer Francisco de Coronado discovers the Grand Canyon and the Mississippi River.

1565 – The Spaniards establish the first European settlement at St. Augustine, Florida

1585 – Sir Walter Raleigh establishes the first English colony in America on Roanoke Island off the coast of North Carolina. By 1591, the colony is mysteriously deserted.

1607 – Captain John Smith founds the first permanent English settlement in North America at Jamestown, Virginia.

1609 – English-Dutch explorer Henry Hudson sails into New York Harbor and explores the Hudson River.

1619 – Virginia establishes the House of Burgesses, the first representative legislature in America.

1619 – Virginia imports slaves from West Africa, the first slaves brought to America.

1620 – Arriving on the *Mayflower* from England, Pilgrims found the colony of Plymouth, Massachusetts. They draw up the *Mayflower Compact* as the legal basis for governing themselves.

1622 – Colonists leaving Massachusetts found the colony of New Hampshire.

1624 – The colony of New Netherland (which later becomes New York) is established on the Hudson River.

1626 – Peter Minuit, a representative of the Dutch, buys Manhattan Island from the Manahata Indians for trinkets worth $24. The island is named New Amsterdam.

1626 COLONIAL TIMES
GREAT BARGAIN!
MANHATTAN ISLAND PURCHASED FROM NATIVES

1630 – Colonists from Massachusetts, led by John Winthrop, found the city of Boston.

1630–1640 – Twenty thousand settlers join the Massachusetts Bay Colony.

1632 – Maryland is founded as a Catholic colony with religious tolerance for all.

1636 – Harvard, the first college in the colonies, is founded.

1636 – After leaving Massachusetts, Roger Williams founds the colony of Rhode Island as a haven for religious freedom.

1636 – Thomas Hooker and followers, driven from Massachusetts, found the colony of Connecticut.

1638 – The colony of New Sweden (which later becomes Delaware) is founded on the Delaware River.

1647 – Massachusetts establishes the first colonial public school system.

1649 – Rhode Island becomes the first colony to outlaw slavery.

1660 – The British Parliament passes the first *Navigation Act* to regulate colonial commerce.

1663 – The colony of the Carolinas is founded.

1664 – The English take control of New Amsterdam from the Dutch and give the city a new name: New York.

1664 – The colony of New Jersey is founded on the land between the Hudson and Delaware Rivers.

1673 – French explorers Marquette and Joliet reach the headwaters of the Mississippi River.

1682 – The colony of Pennsylvania is founded by William Penn.

1699 – French settlements are established in Mississippi and Louisiana.

1703 – Delaware becomes a colony.

1704 – The first successful colonial newspaper, *The Boston Newsletter*, begins publication.

1729 – North Carolina and South Carolina become separate colonies.

1732 – Benjamin Franklin publishes the first issue of *Poor Richard's Almanack*.

1732 – The colony of Georgia is founded.

1740 – The Great Awakening, a great religious revival and force for religious tolerance, spreads through the colonies.

1750 – The Enlightenment spreads the belief that human reason will prevail—that by increasing their knowledge, people can improve themselves and the world.

1752 – Benjamin Franklin flies a homemade kite during a storm, proving that lightning is a form of electricity.

1754–1763 – The French fight against the English in the French and Indian War. They lose land to the English.

1763 – The *Proclamation of 1763* bans settlement beyond the Appalachian Mountains. Colonists dislike the limits on their westward expansion.

1764 – The British Parliament passes the *Sugar Act of 1764*, placing duties on lumber, foodstuffs, molasses, and rum in the colonies.

1765 – The spinning jenny, a mechanical spinning wheel, is invented; this leads to greatly increased cloth production.

1765 – The British Parliament passes the *Stamp Act*, taxing newspapers, legal documents, and other printed matter in the colonies. The act leads to protests in the colonies and a boycott of British imports.

DAILY BULLETIN_ – 1649

Rhode Island Colonists Say
"NO" to Slavery

1766 – The British parliament repeals the *Stamp Act* and passes the *Declaratory Act*, declaring that the colonies are subordinate to the control of Parliament and Parliament can pass any law it desires.

1767 – The British government's *Townsend Acts* levy taxes on glass, painter's lead, paper, and tea in the colonies.

1770 – In the Boston Massacre, British troops fire on colonists protesting English taxes.

1773 – The British Parliament passes the *Tea Act*. Colonists stage the Boston Tea Party to protest a tax on tea, dumping British tea into Boston Harbor.

1774 – The *Coercive Acts* (or *Intolerable Acts*) increase the power of the British government in the colonies, close Boston Harbor, and take other steps to punish the colonists.

1774 – The First Continental Congress meets in Philadelphia to condemn the *Intolerable Acts*.

1775 – *The Revolutionary War* begins between the colonists and the British with fighting at Lexington and Concord, MA.

1775 – The Second Continental Congress meets in Philadelphia to create an American army and make decisions about the war.

1776 – The *Declaration of Independence* is adopted, forming the United States of America.

1777 – The Second Continental Congress forms a government and drafts the *Articles of Confederation*, the first document of the U.S. central government.

1780 – Pennsylvania is the first state to abolish slavery.

1783 – The *Treaty of Paris* officially ends the Revolutionary War and recognizes the United States of America as an independent nation.

1787 – The Constitutional Convention begins writing the *U.S. Constitution*.

1789 – The *U.S. Constitution* is approved by all the states.

1789 – George Washington is chosen as the first U.S. President.

1790s–1900 – The Industrial Revolution leads to mass production of goods, a move toward an urban society, and a great change in the way of life for Americans.

1790s – The first U.S. political parties develop; a two-party system develops in 1796.

1791 – The Bank of the United States is established. It issues paper money.

1791 – The *Bill of Rights* becomes law.

1792 – White House construction begins.

1793 – Eli Whitney invents the cotton gin, which leads to great increase in the production of cotton.

1793 – Congress passes a law requiring the return of runaway slaves.

1798 – Congress passes the *Alien and Sedition Acts* to protect the country against influence and danger from foreigners.

1862 – The *Homestead Act* gives land to any settler who farms it for five years. This leads to an increase in movement to the Great Plains and western U.S.

1863 – President Lincoln issues the *Emancipation Proclamation*, declaring freedom for all slaves in Confederate-held territory.

1863 – In the bloody Battle of Gettysburg, the Confederate and Union forces fight on northern soil. Thousands of soldiers are killed and wounded before the Confederates retreat. After the battle, President Lincoln delivers the *Gettysburg Address*.

1865 – Confederate General Robert E. Lee surrenders to Union General Ulysses S. Grant at Appomattox Court House in Virginia, ending the Civil War.

1865 – President Abraham Lincoln is assassinated by John Wilkes Booth at Ford's Theater in Washington, D.C.

1865 – The *13th Amendment* outlaws slavery throughout the U.S.

1865–1867 – A period of Reconstruction follows the Civil War. Congress passes legislation and amendments giving African-Americans rights and protections of law.

1866 – The *Civil Rights Act*, passed over the veto of President Andrew Johnson, makes African-American people citizens of the U.S.

1866 – The Ku Klux Klan is formed secretly. By 1867, there are units of the Klan in every southern state.

1867 – The U.S. buys Alaska from Russia.

1868 – The House of Representatives impeaches President Andrew Johnson for removing the Secretary of War without Senate approval. There are not enough votes in the Senate to remove him from office.

1868 – The *14th Amendment* guarantees equal protection by the law to all Americans.

1869 – The Transcontinental Railroad is completed.

1869 – The Knights of Labor union is founded in Philadelphia, becoming one of the first powerful labor unions in the U.S.

1870 – The *15th Amendment* gives African-American males the right to vote.

1872 – Congress establishes Yellowstone as the first national park.

1875 – Congress passes the *Civil Rights Act of 1875*, guaranteeing citizens of every race access to public places.

1876 – At the Battle of Little Bighorn, Sioux Indian Chief Sitting Bull is victorious over U.S. military officer, General Custer.

1876 – Alexander Graham Bell invents the telephone.

1881–1889 – States pass Jim Crow laws (laws that promote segregation in states).

1884 – Construction of the world's first skyscraper begins in Chicago.

1886 – The American Federation of Labor is founded. This becomes one of the most powerful labor unions in U.S. history.

1890 – The Battle of Wounded Knee, the last major battle between U.S. troops and Indians, is fought in South Dakota.

1890 – Congress passes the *Sherman Antitrust Act*, banning monopolies.

1893–1896 – A depression leads to severe unemployment.

1896 – The Supreme Court hears the case of *Plessy v. Ferguson* and gives a decision that makes segregation legal, even in public schools.

1898 – The U. S. defeats Spain in the Spanish-American War, gaining control of Guam, Puerto Rico, and the Philippines.

1900–1915 – During this period known as the Progressive Era, many Americans work to improve society (protect workers, protect children, regulate businesses, check the growth of monopolies, encourage prosperous people to share their wealth, expose evils of factories and city slum conditions, and reform corrupt city governments).

1903 – The Wright Brothers make the first successful motor-powered airplane flight at Kitty Hawk, North Carolina.

1908 – Henry Ford begins mass production of the Model T car.

1909 – William Du Bois and several white liberals form the National Association for the Advancement of Colored People (NAACP) to stop lynching and speak out for the rights of African-Americans.

1912 – The *Titanic* sinks on its maiden voyage across the Atlantic.

1913 – The *16th Amendment* allows the federal government to collect income taxes.

1914 – The Panama Canal is completed.

1914 – World War I begins in Europe.

1917 – The U.S. enters World War I, declaring war on Germany after the sinking of ships carrying Americans in particular the 1915 sinking of the *Lusitania*.

1918 – World War I ends with the German surrender and signing of an armistice.

1919 – The *18th Amendment* prohibits the manufacture, sale, or transportation of intoxicating liquors. The amendment is repealed in 1933 by the *21st Amendment*.

1920s – The decade is known as the *Roaring Twenties* because of a surge in entertainment and recreation such as music and dancing, a boom in spectator sports, advances in motion pictures and radio, and the mass production of automobiles.

1920 – The *19th Amendment* gives all citizens, including women, the right to vote.

1920 – The League of Nations is formed as an organization for keeping peace among the world's nations.

1921 – In an isolationist mood, Congress passes the *Emergency Quota Act* to limit the number of immigrants by nationality.

1921 – The heightened fear of foreigners is demonstrated in the Sacco-Venzetti murder trial of two Italian immigrants. They are convicted and executed with little evidence against them.

1924 – Congress passes another immigration quota law, the *National Origins Act*, to limit the number of immigrants that can enter the U.S.

1925 – The Scopes Trial in Dayton, Tennessee, upholds the right of a state to ban the teaching of evolution in public schools.

194

Who Said That? Quotations from American History

Liberty, when it begins to take root, is a plant of rapid growth.
-George Washington U.S. President (1732-1799)

Do not put such unlimited power into the hands of the husbands.
-Abigail Adams, First Lady (1744-1818)

A single twig breaks, but the bundle of twigs is strong. Someday I will embrace our brother tribes and draw them into a bundle and together we will win our country back from the whites.
-Tecumseh, early Shawnee Leader (1768-1813)

I know not what course others may take; but as for me, give me liberty, or give me death.
-Patrick Henry patriot (1736-1799)

The mass of men live lives of quiet desperation.
-Henry David Thoreau philosopher (1817-1862)

Enthusiasm is the yeast that makes your hopes rise to the stars.
-Henry Ford automobile manufacturer (1863-1947)

". . . all men are created equal."
–Declaration of Independence

I never said, "There's a sucker born every minute." But I did say, "Every crowd has a silver lining."
-P.T. Barnum showman (1810-1891)

Go west, young man.
-Horace Greeley (attributed) newspaperman (1811-1872)

"We the people of the United States, in order to form a more perfect union, . . . do ordain and establish this Constitution of the United States of America."
–American Constitution

The woman who can create her own job is the woman who will win fame and fortune.
-Amelia Earhart aviatrix (1898-1937)

There are two ways of exerting one's strength: one is pushing down, the other is pulling up.
-Booker T. Washington educator (1856-1915)

That government is best which governs least, because its people discipline themselves.
-Thomas Jefferson U.S. President (1743-1826)

Hope is a thing with feathers That perches in the soul And sings a tune without words And never stops at all.
-Emily Dickinson poet (1830-1886)

Success is getting what you want. Happiness is wanting what you get.
-Dale Carnegie, philanthropist (1888-1955)

I have ploughed and planted and gathered into barns, and no man could best me - and ain't I a woman?
-Sojourner Truth (attributed) ex-slave and Freedom Fighter (1797-1883)

195

Black Tuesday
Stock Market Crashes

1927 – Charles Lindbergh is the first to fly nonstop across the Atlantic Ocean alone.

1929 – The stock market crashes on October 29, bringing thousands of investors to financial ruin. This day, known as *Black Tuesday*, sparks the Great Depression.

1930s – The U.S. suffers through the Great Depression.

1931 – The Empire State Building opens in New York City.

1933 – President Franklin D. Roosevelt begins the New Deal. Its three aims are: relief, recovery, and reform. He proposes legislation to end the depression, help people hurt by the depression, and stabilize the economy.

1935 – Congress passes the *National Labor Relations Act*, guaranteeing the right of workers to organize and bargain collectively.

1937 – Aviator Amelia Earhart and her co-pilot Fred Noonan are lost somewhere in the Pacific on a flight around the world.

1939 – World War II begins in Europe with Hitler's invasion of Poland.

1941 – The U.S. enters World War II after Japan attacks the U.S. Naval Fleet at Pearl Harbor, Hawaii, on December 7.

1944 – The U.S. and Allied forces invade Europe at Normandy on D-Day, June 6.

1945 – The U.S. drops the first atomic bombs used in warfare on Hiroshima and Nagasaki, Japan.

1945 – Japan and Germany surrender, ending World War II.

1945 – The United Nations is formed as an organization to foster world peace.

1945 – At the Yalta Conference, the Big Three (Roosevelt of the U.S., Churchill of Britain, and Soviet Joseph Stalin) meet to decide the fate of Europe after the war.

1945 – Tensions rise between communist and anticommunist ideologies after the war. This period is called the *Cold War*.

1947 – President Truman announces the *Truman Doctrine*, pledging American aid to nations threatened by Communism.

1947 – The *Marshall Plan* offers American money for European nations affected by the war.

1947 – Congress passes the *Labor Management Relations Act* (*Taft-Hartley Act of 1947*), restricting strikes that endanger the health, safety, or welfare of the nation.

1948 – The Soviets blockade roads leading to Berlin in an effort to force the Allies to give up their zones in the city. The U.S. and Allies respond with the *Berlin Airlift*, bringing supplies into West Berlin by plane.

1949 – The U.S. and several western European nations form the North Atlantic Treaty Organization (NATO) to protect each other in the event of Soviet attack.

1949–1950 – A number of Cold War events produce a widespread fear of Communism (called the *Red Scare*) within the U.S.

1933...Metropolitan Herald
FDR Calls for New Deal

December 7, 1941
War!
Japanese Bomb Pearl Harbor
U.S. Enters World War

The Times 1945
Atomic Bombs Crush Japan
Hirohito Surrenders
World War Ends

COURT REVIEW...........1954

SEGREGATION ENDS

Highest Court Rules that Segregated Schools are Unconstitutional

1950 – Senator Joseph McCarthy of Wisconsin charges that the state department is full of traitors, setting off a "hunt for communists" known as *McCarthyism.*

1950s–1960s – The country sees a major population shift from cities to suburbs.

1950–53 – The U.S. supports South Korea against North Korean communist forces in the Korean War.

1954 – In the case known as *Brown v. Board of Education of Topeka*, the Supreme Court rules that school segregation is unconstitutional.

1955 – Rosa Parks, an African-American woman, is arrested for refusing to give up her seat on a city bus to a white man in Montgomery, Alabama. This sparks the year-long Montgomery Bus Boycott.

1955 – Martin Luther King, Jr. begins organizing a movement to protest discrimination against African-Americans.

1957 – The space race begins with the Soviet launch of the first satellite, *Sputnik I.*

1957 – The Governor of Arkansas calls out the National Guard to prevent the Little Rock schools from admitting African-American students to a white high school. President Eisenhower sends 10,000 soldiers to enforce the desegregation ruling of the Supreme Court.

1958 – *Explorer I*, the first U.S. satellite to go into orbit, is launched in Florida.

1960 – In the *U-2 Affair,* a U.S. plane spying over the Soviet Union is shot down.

1960 – John F. Kennedy becomes president.

1961 – The *Bay of Pigs* invasion, a U.S.-backed plan by Cuban refugees to overthrow Fidel Castro fails miserably.

1961 – Astronaut Alan B. Shepard, Jr. becomes the first American in space.

1962 – In the *Cuban Missile Crisis*, President Kennedy demands that the Soviet Union remove missiles from Cuba. The standoff puts the world on the brink of nuclear war until the Soviets back down.

1962 – Cesar Chavez organizes the National Farm Workers Association to fight for improvement in working and living conditions for migrant workers.

1963 – President John F. Kennedy is assassinated on November 22; Lyndon Johnson becomes president.

1963 – Martin Luther King, Jr. leads a campaign against segregation in Alabama. The rough treatment of demonstrators by police sets off nationwide protest. Soon afterwards, 200,000 people demonstrate peacefully for civil rights in the March on Washington.

1963 – The publication of *The Feminine Mystique* by Betty Friedan, attracts widespread attention to the Women's Liberation Movement.

1964 – Congress passes the *Civil Rights Act of 1964* prohibiting racial discrimination in restaurants, hospitals, hotels, theaters, and all kinds of public facilities, and making it safer for southern African-Americans to register and vote. The act bans discrimination on the basis of gender as well as race.

1965 – American combat troops enter the Vietnam War.

Daily Tidings-----November 22, 1963

JFK SLAIN!

The nation is stunned when the 35th President is shot in Texas.

Chronicle 1969

Touchdown – Moon!
American Astronauts Walk on the Moon

Midwest Monitor
1970
Thousands Protest Vietnam War

1981
Hostages Freed After 444 Days
The Iranian hostages are finally freed just before the presidential inauguration.

1966 – Betty Friedan helps found the National Organization for Women (NOW).

1968 – Martin Luther King, Jr. is assassinated on April 4; Senator Robert F. Kennedy is assassinated on June 5.

1969 – Astronauts Neil Armstrong and Edwin Aldrin walk on the Moon.

1970 – National Guard Troops kill 4 students during a war protest at Kent State University in Ohio. Police at Jackson State kill 2 students during protests.

1971 – The *26th Amendment* lowers the voting age to 18.

1972 – In the Watergate Affair, members of the Republican Party are involved in a break-in to the campaign headquarters of the Democratic candidate for president.

1972 – Richard Nixon becomes the first U.S. president to visit Communist China.

1972 – Congress passes the *Equal Rights Amendment*, stating that equal rights cannot be denied to anyone because of gender. Opposition blocks its ratification.

1973 – Several suspects in the Watergate Affair are put on trial; most plead guilty.

1973 – American Indian Movement (AIM) members hold the town of Wounded Knee, South Dakota, in a protest that lasts several weeks.

1973 – The U.S. removes the last of its troops from Vietnam.

1974 – Nixon becomes the first American president to resign from office after members of Congress take steps to impeach him over the Watergate Affair.

1975 – The Vietnam War ends with North Vietnam defeating and occupying South Vietnam. The country of Vietnam is united.

1976 – The U.S. celebrates its bicentennial.

1978 – President Jimmy Carter brings rival nations Israel and Egypt together and helps to form a peace agreement between the two countries (the *Camp David Accords*).

1979 – In Iran, a mob holds 53 Americans hostage for 444 days.

1981 – The Iran hostages are released.

1981 – Congress agrees to provide weapons to a counter-revolutionary group in Nicaragua (the Contras) who are seeking to overthrow the procommunist controlling party (the Sandinistas).

1981 – Sandra Day O'Connor is the first woman appointed to the Supreme Court.

1984 – Congress passes the *Boland Amendment*, banning aid to the Contras and other such counter-revolutionary groups. This amendment is violated when Colonel Oliver North uses profits from the sale of arms to aid the Contras in Nicaragua.

1986 – The U.S. space shuttle *Challenger* explodes, killing all 7 members of the crew.

1988 – The U.S. and the U.S.S.R. sign a treaty eliminating some nuclear missiles.

1989 – The Berlin Wall falls, signaling the end of the Cold War.

World Events ----------------------------------1989

The End of the Wall

The Berlin Wall comes down. Fifty years of Communist rule ends in East Germany

1990 – The *Americans with Disabilities Act* outlaws discrimination against the handicapped.

1991 – The U.S. allies attack Iraq, beginning the Persian Gulf War in response to Iraq's 1990 invasion of Kuwait.

1992 – Riots break out in Los Angeles following the acquittal of 4 white policemen whose beating of African American Rodney King was caught on videotape.

1993 – President Bill Clinton signs the *North American Free Trade Agreement* (NAFTA) to reduce trade barriers among the U.S., Canada, and Mexico.

1993 – The World Trade Center in New York City is bombed.

1993 – U.S. troops join a UN peacekeeping force in Bosnia.

1995 – A truck bomb kills 168 people in the Federal Building in Oklahoma City.

1995 – The U.S. reestablishes diplomatic relations with Vietnam.

1998 – The House of Representatives votes to impeach President Bill Clinton. Clinton is acquitted in 1999.

1998 – Terrorists bomb the U.S. Embassies in Tanzania and Kenya.

1999 – In Littleton, Colorado, 2 students kill 12 other students, 1 teacher, and themselves at Columbine High School.

2000 – Elian Gonzales, a 6-year old Cuban boy whose mother died trying to get him into the U.S. illegally, returns to Cuba with his father after a federal raid removes him from the home of his Miami relatives.

2000 – George W. Bush is declared the winner of the contested presidential race after the Supreme Court stops the recount.

2000 – 2 Russians and 1 American arrive at the new International Space Station.

2000 – Officials of the U.S. government and representatives of a private company announce that they have completed mapping the DNA sequence of the human genome.

2001 – On September 11, over 3,000 people are killed in terrorist attacks on the Pentagon in Washington, D.C., and the World Trade Center in New York City.

2001 – Letters containing anthrax are sent to different government and media offices. Several people, including postal workers, die after handling the letters.

2002 – U.S. and Afghan troops launch Operation Anaconda—a war in Afghanistan aimed at ending the Taliban control and finding al-Qaeda terrorists.

2002 – Under pressure from the U.S., the UN Security Council passes a resolution demanding that Iraq disarm or "face serious consequences."

2003 – The United States and allies begin a war that ends the power of Saddam Hussein in Iraq.

2004 – NASA lands two rovers on the surface of Mars.

September 11, 2001

Twin Towers Collapse

The World Watches in Horror as 3000 Lives Are Lost

Wise Words from Americans

There is nothing to fear but fear itself.
Franklin D. Roosevelt
32nd U.S. President
(1882-1945)

Our flag is red, white, and blue, but our nation is a rainbow--red, yellow, brown, black, and white--and we are all precious in God's sight.
Rev. Jesse Jackson
politician (1941-   )

Those who dwell among the beauties and mysteries of the earth are never alone or weary of life.
Rachel Carson, environmentalist
writer (1907-1964)

Sometimes I think we're alone in the universe; and sometimes I think we're not. In either case the idea is quite staggering.
Arthur C. Clark
science fiction writer (1917-   )

Income tax has made liars out of more Americans than golf.
Will Rodgers, humorist
(1879-1935)

The buck stops here.
Harry S. Truman
33rd U.S. President
(1884-1972)

A nickel ain't worth a dime anymore.
Yogi Berra, baseball player
(1925-   )

That's one small step for man, one giant leap for mankind.
Neil Armstrong, astronaut
(1930-   )

Ask not what your country can do for you. Ask what you can do for your country.
John F. Kennedy
35th U.S. President
(1917-1963)

Always do the right thing. This will gratify some people and astonish the rest.
Mark Twain (Samuel Clemens)
author, humorist
(1835-1910)

Never go to a doctor whose office plants have died.
Erma Bombeck,
author, humorist
(1927-1996)

Love is the only force capable of transforming an enemy into a friend.
Dr. Martin Luther King, Jr.
minister, civil rights leader
(1929-1968)

There is nothing wrong with America that cannot be fixed by what is right in America.
William J. Clinton
42nd U.S. President
(1946-   )

Don't ever take a fence down until you know why it was put up.
Robert Frost, poet
(1874-1963)

United States Presidents

Number	President	Vice President	Party	Term
1st	George Washington	John Adams	None	1789–1797
2nd	John Adams	Thomas Jefferson	Federalist	1797–1801
3rd	Thomas Jefferson	Aaron Burr, George Clinton	Republican	1801–1809
4th	James Madison	George Clinton, Elbridge Gerry	Republican	1809–1817
5th	James Monroe	Daniel D. Tompkins	Republican	1817–1825
6th	John Quincy Adams	John C. Calhoun	Republican	1825–1829
7th	Andrew Jackson	John C. Calhoun, Martin Van Buren	Democrat	1829–1837
8th	Martin Van Buren	Richard M. Johnson	Democrat	1837–1841
9th	William Henry Harrison	John Tyler	Whig	1841
10th	John Tyler		Whig	1841–1845
11th	James K. Polk	George M. Dallas	Democrat	1845–1849
12th	Zachary Taylor	Millard Fillmore	Whig	1849–1850
13th	Millard Fillmore		Whig	1850–1853
14th	Franklin Pierce	William R. King	Democrat	1853–1857
15th	James Buchanan	John C. Breckenridge	Democrat	1857–1861
16th	Abraham Lincoln	Hannibal Hamlin, Andrew Johnson	Republican	1861–1865
17th	Andrew Johnson		Republican	1865–1869
18th	Ulysses S. Grant	Schuyler Colfax, Henry Wilson	Republican	1869–1877
19th	Rutherford B. Hayes	William A. Wheeler	Republican	1877–1881
20th	James A. Garfield	Chester A. Arthur	Republican	1881
21st	Chester A. Arthur		Republican	1881–1885
22nd	Grover Cleveland	Thomas A. Hendricks	Democrat	1885–1889
23rd	Benjamin Harrison	Levi P. Morton	Republican	1889–1893
24th	Grover Cleveland	Adlai E. Stevenson	Democrat	1893–1897
25th	William McKinley	Garret A. Hobart	Republican	1897–1901
26th	Theodore Roosevelt	Charles W. Fairbanks	Republican	1901–1909
27th	William H. Taft	James S. Sherman	Republican	1909–1913
28th	Woodrow Wilson	Thomas R. Marshall	Democrat	1913–1921
29th	Warren G. Harding	Calvin Coolidge	Republican	1921–1923
30th	Calvin Coolidge	Charles G. Dawes	Republican	1923–1929
31st	Herbert C. Hoover	Charles Curtis	Republican	1929–1933
32nd	Franklin D. Roosevelt	John Nance Garner, Henry A. Wallace, Harry S. Truman	Democrat	1933–1945
33rd	Harry S. Truman	Alben W. Barkley	Democrat	1945–1953
34th	Dwight D. Eisenhower	Richard M. Nixon	Republican	1953–1961
35th	John F. Kennedy	Lyndon B. Johnson	Democrat	1961–1963
36th	Lyndon B. Johnson	Hubert Humphrey	Democrat	1963–1969
37th	Richard M. Nixon	Spiro T. Agnew	Republican	1969–1974
38th	Gerald R. Ford	Nelson A. Rockefeller	Republican	1974–1977
39th	Jimmy Carter	Walter Mondale	Democrat	1977–1981
40th	Ronald Reagan	George Bush	Republican	1981–1989
41st	George Bush	J. Danforth Quayle	Republican	1989–1992
42nd	William J. Clinton	Albert Gore, Jr.	Democrat	1992–2001
43rd	George W. Bush	Richard B. Cheney	Republican	2001–____

Important Places & Spaces

Events in history can be labeled with dates to show **when** they happened. In addition to being set in time, events are set in places and spaces; they all happened **somewhere**. Refresh your knowledge about the locations of some of America's historical events.

Alabama – home to the first Confederate capital

Alaska – state bought from Russia for $7 million

Arizona – home state to the Navajo National Monument and preserved cliff dwellings of the Anasazi culture

Arkansas – home state of Maya Angelou, Bill Clinton, and Johnny Cash

California – site of a major gold discovery in 1848

Connecticut – home of the nation's oldest newspaper still being published, *The Hartford Courant*

Delaware – first state to join the union

Florida – site of St. Augustine, the oldest city in the U.S.

Georgia – home state of Martin Luther King, Jr.

Hawaii – site of the Japanese attack on Pearl Harbor (December 7, 1941)

Idaho – part of the Louisiana Purchase, explored by Lewis and Clark in 1805–1806

Illinois – state to see Lincoln's boyhood home and the country's tallest building (Sears Tower)

Indiana – site of many Indian uprisings, including battles at Fallen Timbers in 1794 and Tippecanoe in 1811

Iowa – home to Effigy Mounds National Monument, a prehistoric Indian Burial Site at Marquette

Kansas – state that earned the name *Bleeding Kansas* because of the pre-Civil War disputes over slavery

Kentucky – state caught in the middle in the Civil War, supplying soldiers to both sides

Louisiana – site of the Battle of New Orleans and magnificent Mardi Gras celebrations

Maine – site of the first naval action of the Revolutionary War

Maryland – site of a colony formed by Catholics for religious freedom

Massachusetts – home to Plymouth Rock and the Salem Witch Trials

Michigan – home to the Mackinaw Bridge and the Sault Ste. Marie locks and canals

Minnesota – state settled by fur traders and French explorers

Mississippi – one of the country's largest producers of cotton throughout its history

Missouri – starting point of the Oregon Trail and home to the Gateway Arch

Montana – state famous for The Little Bighorn Battlefield and Glacier National Park

Nebraska – home of William James Bryan, Willa Cather, Buffalo Bill Cody, and Dick Cheney

Nevada – site of discovery of the Comstock Lode in 1869, the richest-known deposit of silver

New Hampshire – state whose delegates were the first to vote for the *Declaration of Independence*

New Jersey – site of Princeton, one of the oldest universities in the nation

New Mexico – state acquired by the U.S. in the Mexican War (1848) and by the Gadsden Purchase (1853)

New York – home to the Empire State Building and the Statue of Liberty

North Carolina – the site of pirate raids in its early days as a colony

North Dakota – home to the Garrison Dam, Theodore Roosevelt National Park, and the Badlands

Ohio – site of severe fighting with the Indians in the 1790s

Oklahoma – site of the 1995 bombing of the Federal Building in Oklahoma City

Oregon – the end of the Oregon Trail

Pennsylvania – where both the *Constitution* and the *Declaration of Independence* were written

Rhode Island – site of Dorr's Rebellion in 1842, protesting property requirements for voting

South Carolina – where the first shots of the Civil War were fired

South Dakota – home of Mt. Rushmore, the Crazy Horse Monument, and Wounded Knee battlefield

Tennessee – site of federal reservoirs on the Tennessee River, built to bring affordable electricity to citizens

Texas – place to remember the Alamo

Utah – where the last spike was hammered into the Transcontinental Railroad

Vermont – Ethan Allen and the Green Mountain Boys captured Ft. Ticonderoga from the British in 1775

Virginia – George Washington's home state

Washington – site of the most recent major volcanic eruption (Mt. St. Helen's)

West Virginia – state that split off from Virginia when 40 delegates disputed the secession from the union

Wisconsin – the first state to enact an unemployment compensation act (1932)

Wyoming – home to the nation's first national park, Yellowstone

Important Documents

The Declaration of Independence

By 1776, the colonists in America had given up hope of persuading England to treat them more fairly, and many Americans had been killed fighting the British on American soil. The Continental Congress met to draft a document explaining why independence was necessary. The document, mostly written by Thomas Jefferson, was called the *Declaration of Independence*. Congress officially approved it on July 4, 1776.

The Main Points of the Declaration of Independence . . .

- All people are born with certain rights, including life, liberty, and the pursuit of happiness.

- Governments are formed to protect these rights.

- When a government does not protect these rights, it is the right of the people to end or change the government.

- The colonists have been patient a long time with the unfair treatment, taxes, and insults of the British king and government.

- The British government has not been willing to listen or adjust to the complaints of the colonists.

- The people of the colonies claim independence from Britain and their right to set up a separate state.

Get Sharp Tip #16

Not all Americans supported the *Declaration of Independence*. Loyalists to England (Tories) believed that those in favor of it were traitors.

When, in the Course of human events, it becomes necessary for the people to dissolve the political bonds which have connected them with another, and to assume, among the powers of the earth, the separate and equal station . . . .

The Articles of Confederation

The first government of the United States was called a ***confederation***. It consisted of the first thirteen states. After the Revolutionary War, the new government had the task of turning the colonies into states and joining the states under one central government. The first constitutional document, written in 1777, was called *The Articles of Confederation*. This document put into writing the processes and powers the Continental Congress was already using. It gave each state one vote, required laws to be approved by at least nine of the thirteen states, and gave the national government several powers (to declare war and make peace, to make and borrow money, to operate post offices, and to make foreign policy). It did not give the national government power to levy taxes, to form armies, to enforce laws, or to establish a court system.

The Constitution

Problems that developed in the early years of the new nation brought many leaders to believe that the United States needed a stronger central government in order to maintain better order, gain more unity, and increase prosperity. In May of 1787, delegates from every state except Rhode Island met in Philadelphia to write a new constitution. The meeting became known as the Constitutional Convention. The *Constitution* was ratified in 1788 and went into effect in 1789. With this change, the thirteen states truly became one nation.

The **Preamble** is a short statement beginning the *Constitution*, stating clearly the intention to exist as a unified nation.

We the people of the United States, in Order to form a more perfect Union, establish Justice, insure domestic Tranquility, provide for the common defense, promote the general Welfare, and secure the Blessing of Liberty to ourselves and our Posterity, do ordain and establish this Constitution for the United States of America.

The **Articles** describe the structure and procedure of the government. The articles establish a government with *three branches*. They also establish a system of *checks and balances*. The powers of each branch can be controlled by the other two branches. The Articles also describe the processes for ratifying and amending the *Constitution*. There are seven articles.

Article I   The Legislative Branch *(creates the two houses of Congress and describes their powers and functions)*

Article II   The Executive Branch *(creates the office of the President and the Electoral process)*

Article III   The Judicial Branch *(creates the Supreme Court; defines powers and processes of courts)*

Article IV   Relations Among States *(describes the states' powers and the relationship between states)*

Article V   Amending the Constitution *(describes how the Constitution can be changed)*

Article VI   Role of the National Government *(makes the Constitution the supreme law over state laws)*

Article VII   Ratification *(describes the process for approving the Constitution)*

The **Amendments** are changes or additions to the *Constitution*, added after the *Constitution* was ratified. The first ten amendments are known as the *Bill of Rights*. Twenty-seven amendments have been added between 1791 and the present.

The Bill of Rights

The first ten amendments were added to the *Constitution* because the people demanded them. Many people in the new country feared that the central government would have too much power. The people wanted safeguards to assure their rights and liberties. These amendments, which guarantee basic liberties, are known as the *Bill of Rights*. It was ratified in 1791, three years after the *Constitution*.

What Does the Bill of Rights Mean to You?

The 1st **Amendment** gives me the freedom to practice any religion I choose.

The 1st **Amendment** gives me the right to speak or publish my thoughts and opinions freely.

The 1st **Amendment** gives me the right to speak out against my government if I don't agree with something it does.

The 2nd **Amendment** guarantees me the right to own and keep a gun.

The 3rd **Amendment** allows me to choose whether or not I want to keep soldiers in my home.

The 4th **Amendment** says that the government cannot search me or my home, or take away my property, without a good cause.

The 5th **Amendment** protects my rights if I am on trial for a crime.

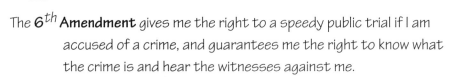

The 6th **Amendment** gives me the right to a speedy public trial if I am accused of a crime, and guarantees me the right to know what the crime is and hear the witnesses against me.

The 7th **Amendment** assures me the right to a trial by jury if someone sues me for more than $20.

The 8th **Amendment** protects me from being required to pay excessive amounts of money for bail or fines.

The 9th **Amendment** says that any rights stated in the *Constitution* cannot be used to deny other rights that are not listed.

The 10th **Amendment** gives all powers to the states and the people that are not specifically given to the federal government by the *Constitution*.

Get Sharp: U.S. Documents

Better Grades & Higher Test Scores / SOCIAL STUDIES gr. 4–6
Copyright ©2005 by Incentive Publications, Inc., Nashville, TN.

Some Other Amendments

The **13**th **Amendment** prohibits slavery in the United States.

The **14**th **Amendment** guarantees equal protection of the law for all citizens, and guarantees that the *Bill of Rights* protects citizens' rights against actions taken by a state.

Get Sharp Tip #17

In order to pass, an amendment must be approved by a two-thirds majority in the House of Representatives and in the Senate. After that, the amendment must be approved by three-fourths (38) of the states.

The **15**th **Amendment** guarantees that no person (including me) can be denied the right to vote because of race or color.

The **16**th **Amendment** gives the federal government the power to collect tax on my income.

The **17**th **Amendment** specifies that any state I live in will be represented in the Senate by two Senators.

The **19**th **Amendment** assures me and all other female citizens the right to vote.

The **22**nd **Amendment** says that, if I am elected president, I can serve no more than two 4-year terms of office.

The **24**th **Amendment** makes it illegal for anyone to charge me a poll tax in a federal election.

The **25**th **Amendment** gives the president the power to appoint a new vice president if a vice president dies or leaves office in the middle of a term. The appointment must be approved by Congress.

The **26**th **Amendment** gives me—an 18-year old—the right to vote. (It lowers the voting age from 21 to 18.)

The **27**th **Amendment** says that any pay increases Congress members give themselves will not take effect until after the next election.

The Legislative Branch

The chief responsibility of the legislative branch of the government is ***to make laws for the country***. This branch is also responsible for deciding how money will be collected and spent. The legislative branch is made up of two groups, or houses: the House of Representatives and the Senate. The members of the two houses meet in different chambers on opposite sides of the Capitol Building. In order to pass, a law must receive a majority of votes in each of the two houses of Congress.

General powers of Congress:

- decide on all federal laws

- provide for the common defense and general welfare of the United States

- make all laws which shall be "necessary and proper" for carrying out other duties given to Congress

- impose and collect taxes and duties

- borrow money

- regulate trade among states and with foreign nations

- coin and print money

- establish post offices

- declare war

- raise armed forces

- control funds for use by armed forces

Limits on the power of the legislative branch:

- The President can veto a bill passed by the Congress.

- The court system can decide that a law passed by Congress is unconstitutional.

- Supreme Court Justices are appointed for life. Congress cannot remove any of them.

The Capitol building was built in 1783. Since then, it has been burned, rebuilt, expanded, and restored.

The Capitol dome was finished in 1866. It stands 287 feet tall and has 108 windows.

What if someone thinks the president has committed a crime or is violating the oath of office? ***Impeachment*** means charging an official with serious crimes in order to remove him or her from office. The House of Representatives is the only government body that can vote to impeach an official. Once someone is impeached, the Senate acts as a jury for trying the case. The chief justice of the Supreme Court acts as the judge. A vote of two-thirds of the members of the Senate is needed for impeachment.

The House of Representatives

The House of Representatives is the largest house of Congress. The number of representatives each state sends to the House of Representatives depends on the population of the state; each state has at least one. There are currently 435 members in the House of Representatives.

Requirements for a Representative:
- must be 25 years or older
- must be a U.S. citizen
- must be a resident of the state he or she is representing

Representative's term:
- 2-year term; no limit on number of terms

Presiding officer in House of Representatives:
- the Speaker of the House, selected by the members of the House, usually a member of the majority party

Duties and powers of the House of Representatives:
- vote on laws
- begin impeachment proceedings on government officials

> The first Chinese congressman was David Wu, elected to the House of Representatives in 1998.

> Joseph Rainey, elected to the House of Representatives in 1870, was the first African-American congressman.

The Senate

The Senate has two members from each state, with a total of 100 members.

Requirements for a Senator:
- must be 30 years or older
- must be a U.S. citizen
- must reside in the state he or she is representing

Senator's term:
- 6-year term; no limit on number of terms

Presiding officer in the Senate:
- the Vice President of the United States
  (The Vice President can vote only if there is a tie between the senators.)

Duties and powers of the Senate:
- vote on laws
- approve people the president appoints for jobs such as federal judges, Supreme Court justices, cabinet members, and ambassadors
- approve all treaties *(by a two-thirds vote)*
- act as jury in the impeachment process

> The first Hispanic U.S. Senator, Octavio Larrazolo, was elected in 1928.

> In 1931, Hattie W. Caraway was the first woman appointed to the U.S. Senate.

How a Bill Becomes a Law

Step 1: A member of Congress proposes a *law.* This proposal is called a *bill.* The person who proposes it is the *sponsor.*

Step 2: The bill is introduced into both houses of Congress.

Step 3: The bill is sent to committees for discussion. Both houses of Congress have several committees, each specializing in a particular area of government.

Step 5: The committees vote on the bill.

Step 4: Committees in each house of Congress discuss the bill and change it if they wish.

Step 6: If the committee has approved a bill, it goes to the full House of Representatives or Senate for debate and vote.

Step 7: The bill is debated in both houses of Congress. A majority in both houses of Congress passes the bill.

Step 8: If the House and Senate pass different versions of the same bill, members of the two bodies meet in a conference committee and agree on one version.

Step 10: If both houses pass the bill, it is sent to the president.

Step 9: The bill, with final changes, goes back to the houses for a vote.

Step 11: If the president signs the bill, it becomes a law.

Step 13: Members of both houses of Congress may vote on the bill again. If two-thirds of the votes in both houses are in favor of the bill, it can *override* the president's veto.

Step 12: The president can *veto* the bill. The vetoed bill does not pass.

Get Sharp Tip #18

Revenue bills (bill to raise money) can only come from one source: the House of Representatives.

Step 14: The bill then becomes law without the president's signature.

Powers & Limits on Power

The *Constitution* grants many important powers to the Congress (such as the power to coin money, declare war, and fund armed forces). The *Constitution* also says that there are some things Congress cannot do.

Officer, you can't arrest me. When I tied my alligator to the fire hydrant last week, it wasn't against the law. That law was just passed yesterday.

- Congress may not take away a person's right of *Habeas Corpus*. This is the right of a person charged with a crime to be seen and heard in a courtroom by a judge (except in cases of rebellion or invasion).

- Congress may not pass *bills of attainder* (laws that convict a person of a crime and punish them without a trial).

- Congress may not pass *ex post facto laws*. These are laws that punish someone for a crime that was not a crime when the person did it.

- Congress cannot tax products from a state.

- Congress cannot spend money without passing a law.

- Congress cannot issue titles of nobility.

Enumerated powers are powers that are specifically given to Congress by the *Constitution*.

Implied powers are general powers that are stated in the *Constitution* but are not clearly outlined.

Inherent powers are unlisted powers that Congress must have simply because it is a government and needs to run its affairs smoothly.

Delegated powers are powers specifically given to the federal government (such as the power to declare war).

Concurrent powers are powers that are shared by the federal and state governments (such as the power to levy taxes).

Reserved powers are powers that are held only by the states (such as the power to create school systems).

Is ex post facto a crime against the post office?

Some powers reserved for the states:

- establish public schools
- conduct of elections
- maintain public schools
- make marriage laws
- establish local governments
- creation of corporation laws
- regulate business within the state
- provide for public safety
- assume other powers not delegated to the federal government or prohibited to the states

The Executive Branch

The chief responsibility of the executive branch is *to enforce laws*. The president heads the executive branch of the federal government. This branch also includes the vice president, the staffs of the president and vice president, and several departments and agencies. The cabinet is made up of the heads of major departments. The president, vice president, and many of their staff members work in the White House. The president and his family, called the first family, also live in the White House.

Requirements for president:
- must be 35 years or older
- must be a natural-born U.S. citizen
- must be a U.S. resident for at least 14 years

President's term:
- A limit of two 4-year terms

President's duties:

- **Commander-in-Chief of the armed forces**
    acts as top military person
    makes decisions regarding the use of armed forces
    can call the National Guard from individual states

- **Chief Executive**
    chooses people to head up departments that run the government
    oversees the operations of the government
    appoints judges and ambassadors

- **Chief of State**
    takes charge of foreign relations
    represents the U.S. to foreign nations
    hosts foreign dignitaries visiting the U.S.
    makes treaties with foreign governments

- **Chief Legislator**
    can suggest laws to Congress
    can veto laws passed by Congress

- **Chief of the Party**
    leads his or her own political party

What happens if a president cannot complete a term?

If a president dies in office or is not able to complete a term, the vice president becomes president. This might be temporary if the president is able to take over the job again. After the vice president, the next person in line for the presidency is the Speaker of the House of Representatives.

The White House was completed in 1780. The first president to move in was President John Adams.

There are 6 floors, 132 rooms, 412 doors, 147 windows, 35 bathrooms, 8 staircases, and 3 elevators in the White House.

Limits on the powers of the executive branch:
- Congress can override a presidential veto.
- Congress must approve funds for armed services.
- Congress is the only body that can declare war.
- The Senate must confirm presidential appointments.
- The Senate must approve treaties with foreign governments.
- The House of Representatives can impeach the president or vice president.

The Cabinet

The *cabinet* is a group of people that advise the president. It is made up of the vice president, heads of departments, and other top officials. The heads of most cabinet departments have the title of *secretary* of their department.

Cabinet Departments

Commerce
(business, trade)

Agriculture
(farming)

Interior
(U.S. Lands)

Transportation
(roads, transportation systems)

Veterans Affairs
(services for war veterans)

Energy
(research on energy, energy use)

Homeland Security
(protection against terrorism)

Justice
(court system, legal issues)

Health and Human Services
(health, welfare)

State
(foreign affairs)

Education
(public schools)

Labor
(workers, working conditions)

Housing and Urban Development
(housing, cities)

Treasury
(money, taxes)

Defense
(armed forces)

Agencies & Organizations

Over two hundred different agencies or organizations make up the executive branch. Here are a few of the many agencies that administer programs that touch many areas of American life.

NASA *(National Aeronautic Space Administration)* – oversees space research

IRS *(Internal Revenue Service)* – collects taxes

FBI *(Federal Bureau of Investigation)* – investigates crimes against U.S. government

CIA *(Central Intelligence Agency)* – gathers clues about international crimes

FTC *(Federal Trade Commission)* – regulates trade and commerce

FHA *(Federal Highway Administration)* – plans and builds interstate highways

BIA *(Bureau of Indian Affairs)* – oversees matters to do with Native Americans

BLM *(Bureau of Land Management)* – manages national lands

FDA *(Food and Drug Administration)* – regulates quality and safety of food and drugs

FAA *(Federal Aviation Administration)* – ensures safety in air travel and at airports

DEQ *(Department of Environmental Quality)* – oversees environmental clean-up

INS *(Immigration and Naturalization Service)* – oversees immigrants and those who become citizens

The Judicial Branch

The chief responsibility of the judicial branch is to ***interpret the laws***. The Supreme Court is the highest and most important court in the country. A decision of the Supreme Court is final. (This means that the decision cannot be appealed to any other court.) The nine justices of the Supreme Court are appointed by the president and confirmed by the Senate. The Supreme Court meets in the Supreme Court Building. In addition to the Supreme Court, there are 91 District Courts, 12 Courts of Appeal, the Court of Military Appeals, the United States Claims Court, and the United States Tax Court that are all parts of the federal judicial system.

Supreme Court Justice's term:
- appointed for life

Presiding officer in the Supreme Court:
- the Chief Justice (one of the nine justices)

Duties of the Chief Justice:
- preside over all meetings of the Supreme Court
- act as judge in impeachment proceedings

Duties and powers of the Supreme Court:
- review and decide cases involving federal law
- review and decide cases involving treaties of the U.S.
- review and decide cases that involve actions of presidents
- review and decide the constitutionality of state laws

Limits on the power of the Supreme Court:
- Congress can make new laws after a law is found unconstitutional.
- Justices must be appointed by the executive branch.
- Justices must be confirmed by the Senate.
- The House of Representatives can impeach a Supreme Court Justice.

Do you think that the Supreme Court will hear any of these cases?

- I was arrested in Baltimore for taking a lion to a movie. I didn't know that was illegal.
- How was I supposed to know it's against the law in Tennessee to sell hollow logs?
- I took my French poodle to the opera in Chicago, and now I have to pay a fine.
- In Vermont, it's against the law to whistle underwater. I guess I didn't see the sign.
- A Florida law says an unmarried woman cannot go parachuting on Sunday. Will I go to jail?
- Was I supposed to know that it's against the law to tease a skunk in Minnesota?

Better Grades & Higher Test Scores / SOCIAL STUDIES gr. 4–6
Copyright ©2005 by Incentive Publications, Inc., Nashville, TN.

Historic Supreme Court Decisions

Some court decisions stand out in history because of their impact on the society. These are a few of the better-known cases that have come before the Supreme Court.

In the 1954 case of **Brown v. the Board of Education of Topeka,** the Supreme Court ruled that school segregation is unconstitutional. This overturned the previous Supreme Court decision of **Plessy v. Ferguson.**

Marbury v. Madison (1803) – This ruling stated that the Supreme Court can overrule a law of Congress. It was the first time the court struck down an act of Congress.

Dred Scott v. Sandford (1857) – The Supreme Court ruled that, whether slave or free, an African-American person had no right to bring a lawsuit.

Plessy v. Ferguson (1896) – The Supreme Court declared that requiring African Americans to ride in separate railroad cars did not deprive them of their rights under the 14th amendment, so long as the facilities were equal. This was called the "separate but equal" ruling.

Engel v. Vitale (1962) – This case ended with a Supreme Court decision to forbid prayer in public schools.

Miranda v. Arizona (1966) – The Supreme Court ruled that anyone arrested must be read a statement of their rights before being questioned, or their statements can't be used as evidence against them. These rights have come to be known as *Miranda rights*.

Tinker v. Des Moines School District (1969) –High school students who wore black armbands to school to protest American participation in the Vietnam War had been suspended from school. The Supreme Court overturned the suspension, declaring that students cannot be asked to leave their constitutional rights to freedom of speech or expression at the door of the school.

U.S. v. Nixon (1974) – The Supreme Court ruled that executive privilege for the president has limits. President Nixon was ordered to turn over tapes of personal conversations as evidence in the Watergate investigation.

Board of Education v. Pico (1982) – The Supreme Court ruled that a public school board couldn't ban a book from a school library because someone doesn't agree with the ideas in the book.

Texas v. Johnson (1989) – The Supreme Court ruled that a state government couldn't stop a person from a dissenting view or action because it finds it offensive. In this case, the offensive action was desecration (burning) of an American flag in Texas.

Bush v. Palm Beach County Canvassing Board – (2000) The Supreme Court refused to rule on issues related to the Florida recount of votes in the 2000 presidential election. This decision led to the victory of George W. Bush in the election.

Get Sharp: U.S. Government

Citizenship & Voting

The people, or citizens, are a powerful force in a representative democracy like the United States. In order for democracy to work, the citizens must participate. Voting is the one of the most important ways for a citizen to take part in the democratic process.

Some good things for citizens to do:

Get Sharp Tip #19
A President can win the election without getting the majority of the popular vote. This happened in 1876 (Hayes), 1888 (Harrison), and 2000 (Bush).

Be informed! Learn about political issues, both in Washington, D.C., and in your own backyard. Pay attention to the news, ask questions, and read about things that affect your life. Find out what's going on in the world, the nation, your state, and your community. Think about your own views on the issues. Discuss them with friends and family members. Get to know some facts about the elected officials who represent you in your city, county, state, and country.

Vote! It is the primary right of a citizen. A person cannot have a voice in the choices or operations of the city, state, or nation if he or she does not vote. Even if you are too young to vote, you can think about how you would vote on an issue or which candidates you would support.

Get involved! Volunteer for a community service or other organization that you think deserves help and attention. A good citizen gives something of herself or himself to make the country or local area a better place. When you become an adult, think about running for a public office. You can run for president, mayor, or a position in the U.S. Congress, state government, city council, school board, or many other government offices.

How a President is Elected

Every four years, American voters elect a president and vice president. This election is somewhat different from elections for other officials, in that the president and vice president are not chosen directly by the people. In the presidential election, the votes people cast actually choose electors. The president is then chosen by these electors (the Electoral College).

The *Electoral College* is a group of 538 members (called *electors*) that have been chosen by the states. Each state has a number of electors equal to its total number of U.S. senators and representatives. In December, after the election, the Electoral College members meet to cast their votes for the president. Usually, the party that got the most votes in the November election wins all the electoral votes for the state. In January, the votes are presented during a session of Congress. To win the presidential election, a candidate must get a majority (270) of the electoral votes. If no candidate wins a majority, the House of Representatives chooses the president. This happened in 1800 (with the election of Thomas Jefferson) and 1824 (with the election of John Quincy Adams).

VOTE HERE

Some good things for citizens to know:

- A **democracy** — a government that is governed by its people, all of whom have the same basic rights and freedoms

- A **representative democracy** — a democracy in which the people vote for officials to represent them in certain government positions

- A **constitution** — document that describes the structure of the government and assures and protects citizens' rights

- **Political parties** — organizations that put candidates forward for political offices

- The **platform of a political party** — a statement of the party's policies and principles for voters to consider

- An **election** — the process of voting to choose public officials.

- A **primary election** — an election to choose candidates for the main election

- **Candidates** — people who are running for political offices

- To **register** — to officially sign up to vote

- A **residency requirement** — a length of time that someone must live in a state before being able to vote there

- A **ballot** — a list of candidates used by the voter to place his or her vote

- A **voting district** — the place where a citizen lives and is registered to vote

- A **polling place** — the location people go to vote in their district

- **Absentee ballots** — votes mailed in by people who cannot be present at the polls on the election date

- The **popular vote** — the number of votes cast by individual voters in a presidential election

- **Electoral College votes** — votes cast in a presidential election by electors chosen by each state

- The **turnout** — the number or percentage of eligible voters who actually vote in an election

- An **initiative** — an issue placed on the ballot for citizens to decide by vote

- A **recall election** — held to decide whether to remove an elected public official from office before the end of his or her term

- A **recount** — a second counting of the ballots when the outcome of an election is very close

- A **referendum** — a vote on a specific issue, such as a city's budget or a building project

Good Citizens Vote for:

president
vice president
U.S. senators
U.S. representatives
governor
state senators
state representatives
county commissioners
state district attorney
mayor
city council members
school board members
parks commissioner
judges
sheriff

Harrison Middle School students vote for:

student body president and officers
class president
school mascot
homecoming king and queen
cheerleading squad
extra-curricular activities
best cafeteria food

Better Grades & Higher Test Scores / SOCIAL STUDIES gr. 4–6
Copyright ©2005 by Incentive Publications, Inc., Nashville, TN.

Get Sharp: U.S. Citizenship

Symbols & Traditions

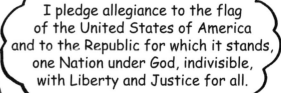

I pledge allegiance to the flag of the United States of America and to the Republic for which it stands, one Nation under God, indivisible, with Liberty and Justice for all.

The pledge (to the flag) is a promise of allegiance to the United States. Francis Bellamy of Boston wrote the original pledge. Public school children first recited it in 1892. In 1942, Congress made the pledge part of its code for use of the flag.

The American Flag

The *Stars and Stripes* is the popular name for the red, white, and blue national flag of the United States. Francis Scott Key first called this flag the *Star-Spangled Banner* in 1814 when he wrote the poem that later became the national anthem. A Massachusetts sea captain, William Driver, gave the name *Old Glory* to the United States flag in 1824.

The flag represents the land, the people, the government, and the ideals of the United States. The seven red and six white stripes represent the thirteen original colonies. The stars represent the states. In 1777, Congress stated that the flag have thirteen stars. In 1795, Congress directed that the flag should have stars on a blue field and fifteen stripes. In 1818, Congress resolved that the flag have thirteen stripes and that a new star be added for each new state. Today, the flag has 50 stars.

Flag Terms to Know:

badge – an emblem or design, usually on the fly

battle flag – carried by armed forces on land

bunting – cloth decorated with stripes of the national colors

canton – the upper corner of a flag where a special design appears

color – a special flag carried by a military unit or officer

field – the background color of a flag

fly – the free end of a flag, farthest from the staff

halyard – a rope used to hoist and lower a flag

national flag – the flag of a country

pennant – a triangular or tapering flag

staff – the pole on which the flag hangs

standard – a flag around which people rally

What do the colors mean?

Red stands for hardiness and courage.
White stands for puity and innocence.
Blue stands for vigilance, perseverance, and justice.

The Great Seal

The Continental Congress adopted the Great Seal in 1782 as a symbol of the nation. The eagle is a symbol of sovereignty. The eagle holds a ribbon in its mouth with the Latin words *e pluribus unum*, meaning *out of many, one*. The olive branch stands for peace. The arrows stand for war. The constellation symbolizes the nation as a sovereign republic. The pyramid on the back of the seal represents strength. The eye on the pyramid represents the eye of Providence. The Great Seal is kept in the U.S. Department of State and its image is printed on many government documents.

The National Anthem

The national anthem of the United States comes from a poem, "The Star Spangled Banner." The poet, Francis Scott Key, was inspired by the U.S. flag flying during a battle in the War of 1812. Mr. Key's poem was later set to music composed by John Stafford Smith. Congress officially approved the song as the national anthem in 1931. The song has four verses.

O say, can you see, by the dawn's early light,
What so proudly we hailed at the twilight's last gleaming?
Whose broad stripes and bright stars, through the perilous fight,
O'er the ramparts we watched, were so gallantly streaming!
And the rockets' red glare, the bombs bursting in air,
Gave proof through the night that our flag was still there:
O say, does that star-spangled banner yet wave
O'er the land of the free and the home of the brave?

The Eagle

The United States chose the bald eagle as its national bird in 1782. The bald eagle has powerful wings, and its white head feathers give it the appearance of baldness. Its tail is also white.

The Liberty Bell

The Liberty Bell is a symbol of American independence. The bell was made in England in 1752 and sent to the State House in Philadelphia. It broke after its arrival and was recast. The bell was rung along with other church bells on July 8, 1776, to announce the adoption of the *Declaration of Independence*. The Liberty Bell was rung each year until 1835, when it cracked as it was ringing during the funeral of Chief Justice John Marshall. The bell is no longer rung. It is housed in Liberty Bell Pavilion, just north of Independence Hall in Philadelphia.

The Statue of Liberty

The Statue of Liberty is a 151-foot tall copper statue located in New York Harbor. It is a symbol of American liberty under a free form of government. France presented the monument to the United States in 1884 as a symbol of friendship, and in commemoration of the two countries' alliance during the American Revolution. The statue's title is "Liberty Enlightening the World." It has become a symbol of freedom for oppressed people everywhere.

Better Grades & Higher Test Scores / SOCIAL STUDIES gr. 4–6
Copyright ©2005 by Incentive Publications, Inc., Nashville, TN.
Get Sharp: U.S. Citizenship

Holidays

The United States Congress has established several federal holidays. They are holidays for Washington, D.C. and for federal offices and buildings, banks, and some schools. Each state decides on its own holidays. Many states honor several or all of the federal holidays.

Americans Celebrate a Year of Federal Holidays: ■ ■ ■ ■ ■ ■ ■ ■ ■ ■

New Year's Day
(January 1st)

In the U.S., the first day of the new year is commemorated. Most work places are closed on this day.

Martin Luther King, Jr. Day (the third Monday in January)

This holiday honors the birthday (Jan. 15, 1929) of Dr. Martin Luther King, Jr., African-American Civil Rights leader.

President's Day
(the third Monday in February)

This day celebrates the birthdays of Presidents George Washington (Feb. 22, 1732) and Abraham Lincoln (Feb. 12, 1809).

Memorial Day
(the last Monday of May)

Originally known as Decoration Day, this holiday honors the men and women who died while serving their country in the military.

Independence Day
(July 4th)

This day is regularly celebrated as a day to honor and remember American independence and the events that made it possible. July 4th is the anniversary of the 1776 adoption of the *Declaration of Independence.*

Labor Day
(the first Monday in September)

This day honors America's workers with a day off work for many citizens.

Columbus Day
(the second Monday in September)

This is the anniversary of the day Chrisopher Columbus supposedly arrived in the Americas (October 12, 1492).

Election Day
(the first Tuesday after the first Monday in November)

Election Day is the day designated for voting in federal elections. Americans vote every four years for their president.

Veterans Day
(November 11th)

Also called Armistice Day, this holiday honors veterans who fought in world wars. It celebrates the armistice that ended World War I on Nov. 11, 1918.

Thanksgiving Day
(the fourth Thursday in November)

The Pilgrims celebrated the first Thanksgiving in 1621. It was, and still is, a day to give thanks for the harvest and for other blessings.

Christmas Day
(December 25th)

This is a religious holiday of the Christian religion, honoring the birth of Jesus Christ. It has also become a secular holiday.

Get Sharp: U.S. Citizenship

Better Grades & Higher Test Scores / SOCIAL STUDIES gr. 4–6
Copyright ©2005 by Incentive Publications, Inc., Nashville, TN.

GET SHARP

on

ECONOMICS

Money

Money is bills and coins, right? Not necessarily! Throughout history, many other things have been used as money around the world. People have exchanged things like shells, beans, stones, feathers, and even cows or camels for the goods and services they need or want.

Money is a ***medium of exchange*** (anything that a society or group of people accepts in exchange for goods or services). *Goods* are things you want or need, such as clothing, food, toys, and vehicles. A ***service*** is work that someone does for you—such as fixing plumbing, serving food, giving haircuts, or providing medical care. A country's ***currency*** is any kind of money used as a medium of exchange in the country.

Today, coins and paper bills serve as the medium of exchange for most countries. In 1792, the U.S. Congress established a money system using the ***dollar*** as the main unit of currency. In 1793, the government began minting coins. To ***mint*** a coin means to stamp it out of metal. A ***mint*** is also a place where coins are made.

> ### Get Sharp Tip #20
> A medium of exchange can be anything that the group agrees has a certain value.

Coins

Over thirteen billion coins are minted in the U.S. each year. All the coins are produced at two government mints: The U.S. Mint in Philadelphia and the U.S. Mint in Denver. At one time, there were also mints in San Francisco and New Orleans. The first coins minted in the U.S. were made of gold and silver, but coins are no longer made from these precious metals. Today's coins are made from nickel and copper alloys. Metal is melted and poured into bars called ***ingots***. After the ingots are flattened, the coin shapes are cut from the flat sheets. Machines then add edges and stamp designs on the coins.

> Dimes and quarters are ***milled coins*** (coins with ridges around the edges). When coins were made of silver and gold, people would shave the edges off them and sell the scraps. The ridges were added to stop this practice.

> Look for a tiny letter on any coin. This will tell you where the coin was minted.
> P stands for Philadelphia.
> D stand for Denver.
> S stand for San Francisco.
> O stands for New Orleans.

> Every coin minted in the U.S. has two sayings on it. One saying is in Latin: *E Pluribus Unum*, which means, **Out of many, one.**
> The English saying is: **In God We Trust.**

Paper Money

The official unit of paper currency in the U. S. is the ***dollar***. All the paper currency in the country is produced in Washington, D. C., at the Bureau of Engraving and Printing. Each bill is called a ***Federal Reserve Note***, and is issued by one of the branches of the ***Federal Reserve***, the government's bank. Dollars are made in several ***denominations*** (or specific values): one, five, ten, twenty, fifty, and hundred dollar bills are currently printed in the U.S.

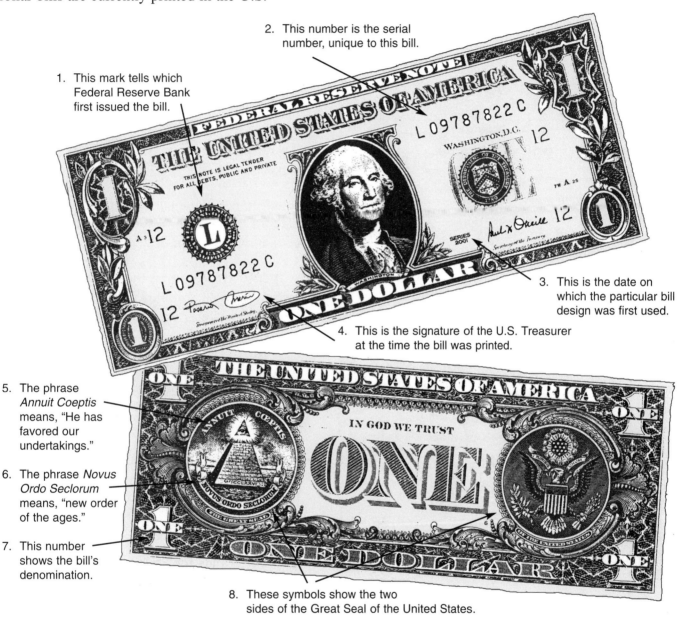

2. This number is the serial number, unique to this bill.

1. This mark tells which Federal Reserve Bank first issued the bill.

3. This is the date on which the particular bill design was first used.

4. This is the signature of the U.S. Treasurer at the time the bill was printed.

5. The phrase *Annuit Coeptis* means, "He has favored our undertakings."

6. The phrase *Novus Ordo Seclorum* means, "new order of the ages."

7. This number shows the bill's denomination.

8. These symbols show the two sides of the Great Seal of the United States.

Whose Face is That?

$1	George Washington
$5	Abraham Lincoln
$10	Alexander Hamilton
$20	Andrew Jackson
$50	Ulysses S. Grant
$100	Benjamin Franklin

To discourage people from making counterfeit (fake) money, the government uses special tricks such as individual serial numbers, secret formula inks, color-shifting inks, watermarks, microprinting and invisible fibers.

Paper money is not really paper. U.S. dollars are made from a blend of 25% cotton and 75% linen. These fabrics are stronger and last longer than paper.

Getting Money

People can get money in several ways. Money can be gained by earning interest on savings or investments. Some people inherit money; it is passed to them from a family member. Some people get money from the government. Most people, however, get most of their money by doing some kind of work. Here are a few things to know about getting money.

Will Chip's Business Be a Success?

Chip wonders if his new business venture, "Chip's Chocolate Chip Cookie Co." will make a profit.

Chocolate "Chip"

Will I earn more in a year if I bake 500 dozen chocolate chip cookies per month and sell each dozen for a $6 profit, or if I work as a chef on a yearly salary of $31,000?

I guess it depends on how many cookies I eat.

How should Chip market and sell his product?

Sell to big stores.

Sell door-to-door.

Take orders on the Internet.

Advertise for sale on radio, TV, or newspapers.

- **Income** is money earned or received from someone else. It can be gained from working or from investments.

- An **employer** is a person who runs a business of some kind.

- An **employee** is a person who works for someone else.

- A **wage** is the amount of money someone is paid for doing a job. Wages are often paid at a certain rate per hour of work.

- A **minimum wage** is the lowest amount of money per hour that the laws of a state allow a worker to be paid.

- A **salary** is a fixed sum of money that an employer pays to an employee.

- **Benefits** are additional awards, other than pay, given to workers by an employer.

- An **investment** is the risk of money or time taken for the hope of getting something in return (such as a profit).

- **Interest** is money earned when a bank or other borrower pays someone for use of their money.

- A **dividend** is a share of a company's profits that is paid to stockholders.

- A **profit** is money made on an investment or money a business makes after all the expenses are paid.

- **Welfare** is income given by the government to some people who are not able to earn enough money to live.

Using Money

There are so many things to do with money once you have it! You have to decide whether to spend it or whether to save it. If you spend it, you must choose how, when, and where to spend. Here are a few things to know about using money.

- A **need** is something necessary for survival or a healthy life, such as food, clothing, or housing.

- A **want** is something that you would like to have but don't really need.

- A **consumer** is someone who uses or consumes goods and services. If you buy anything or pay for any services, you are a consumer. Consuming costs money.

- A **producer** is someone who makes goods or provides services. If you are a producer, you are hopefully earning money or making a profit. Usually a producer must spend some money in order to create a product or offer a service.

- **Advertising** is any method used to convince consumers to part with their money to buy something, invest, lend, or donate.

- A **donation** is a contribution of money, time, services, or goods that is given to a charity or other worthy cause.

- **Interest** is an amount of money paid to borrow money.

- **Disposable income** is money earned that is left over after you've paid for necessities.

- **Saving** is holding on to money (not spending it), usually by putting it somewhere so that interest is earned.

- **Investing** is risking some money for the possibility of making a profit.

- A **budget** is a plan for keeping track of all the money coming in going out.

- A **balanced budget** is a budget in which the money going out is equal to or less than the money taken in.

Where Does All the Money Go?

housing
food and clothing
electricity
water
gas or heating oil
telephone
cell phone
homeowner's or renter's insurance
car payments and insurance
education and school supplies
medical care
health insurance
business expenses
entertainment
travel and vacations
child care
pet care
furniture

$200 a month for flour!

$300 a month for sugar!

$1000 a month for chocolate chips!

HELP! The money goes out faster than it comes in!

$250 a month for gas and electricity!

Banking

A bank is a place that keeps money for people and businesses. It's a safe place to keep money that you are planning to use soon, or money that you want to save for later. Your money doesn't just sit in the bank. Like any business, banks try to make a profit. They use their customers' money in many ways to bring in profit for the business.

Chip made a $2,000 **profit** selling his chocolate chip cookies last month. He needs a safe place to keep his money so he decided to open an **account** at a bank. He put half of the money into a **checking account** and the other half into a **savings account**.

Chip can use the checking account to pay bills, buy things, or **withdraw** money by writing **checks**. **Most checks look like this:**

A **check** is a written order that tells the bank to pay a specific amount of money to a person, or a business named on the first line of the check. Chip's check will not be valid unless he puts his **signature** on the bottom line.

Banking Know-How

> I've really learned a lot about banking and how to manage my money.

Chip D. Baker
1943 Truffle Dr.
Cookiville, AK   13563
Date: *Jan. 21, 05*
Pay to: *The Chocolate Factory* $ *253.61*
Two hundred + fifty-three + 61/100 Dollars
Cookiville Bank
Brownie Rd.
1-800-555-2020   *Chip D. Baker*
3322557390--228734 0001

He must be careful to keep a true **account** of every check he writes in a **register book**, and subtract the amounts from his **balance**. If he forgets, he might write a check for more money than he actually has in his account. This is called being **overdrawn**, and banks usually charge a fee for covering **bounced checks.**

Some of Chip's customers pay him with a check. He can **deposit** these checks into his checking account, or his savings account. He is careful to **endorse** (sign) the customer's check on the back side. In order to deposit a check, Chip has to fill out a **deposit slip.**

Chip's **savings account** or **CD** (*certificate of deposit*) is a good place for him to put the money that he doesn't need to use right away. The bank will pay him **interest** on the money he keeps in a savings account. That means that Chip will earn a **profit** on his savings over time (provided that he doesn't withdraw the money too soon).

Sometimes, Chip needs small amounts of cash in a hurry. He can use an **ATM** (*Automatic Teller Machine*) to withdraw cash from a machine at his bank, or in shopping centers and other convenient locations. In order to use an ATM, he has a special card and a **PIN** (*a Personal Identification Number*).

226

More things that Chip has learned about banking...

Any business I do at a bank is called a **transaction**. Basically, there are two kinds of transactions: **Deposits** (putting money in the bank) and **withdrawals** (taking money out of the bank). **Debit** is another word used to describe the removal of money from my account. I can do transactions at the bank in person, at an ATM machine, over the phone, or over the Internet.

Every month, my bank sends me a **bank statement** for each account. The statement is a monthly summary of all the transactions on the account. I also keep my own records of all my accounts.

I can purchase special checks from the bank. One kind of check is a **cashier's check**, where the money comes from the bank's account after I've given them the money. **Traveler's checks** are other special checks I can purchase. A traveler's check works just like money, but it can only be used with my signature. Use of traveler's checks is a safe way to carry money on a trip.

There are different kinds of **loans** available at my bank. A loan is sum of money that someone borrows for a certain amount of time. The bank offers **credit cards** to its customers, too. With a credit card, I can buy things now and pay for them later. The bank charges interest and other fees for this privilege of using a **credit card**.

I rent a **safe-deposit box** for a small fee at my bank. This is a box that is kept locked in the bank's vault. I keep valuable possessions such as important papers and insurance policies in mine. Two keys are needed to open a safe-deposit box. I have one key and the banker keeps the other. The bank provides me with a room where I can have plenty of privacy to put things in or take things out of my safe-deposit box.

Checks & Balances

Christine took her friends out for ice cream and wrote a check for $30.00.

The ice cream shop sent her check back! They wanted the original $30 and another $25 for a total of $55!

What's going on here?

Christine's bank "bounced" her check (would not pay the shop the money). This is because she did not have enough money in her account to cover the $30. The ice cream shop got NO money from her. They want the $30 and they are charging a $25 penalty for their trouble.

I guess I've learned my lesson! If I'm going to write a check, I'd better make sure I have enough money in the bank to cover it.

Credit

Credit is a way to get money when you don't have it. It is also a way to buy things without money at all. It's not exactly free, though. Having credit means someone is willing to lend you money and let you pay it back later, usually charging a fee or interest for the use of the money.

What's Happening Here?

A bank has agreed to loan Charlie the money to buy a ski chalet, but they are holding the title to his house until the loan has been paid off.

→ *Charlie has been given a **mortgage** (a loan given for a house or building). He put his house up for **collateral** against the loan. This means that if Charlie doesn't pay the loan, the bank will keep his house.*

Charlie went to his bank and borrowed $6,000 by giving only a credit history and his signature.

→ *Charlie has been given an **unsecured loan**. This means he does not have to give the bank something valuable in return for the loan.*

Charlie paid $2,000 to the car dealer for his new car. The car company will loan him the remaining $13,000 for 5 years at 6% interest. He'll pay about $250 a month.

→ *Charlie made a **down payment** of $2,000. He now has a **debt** of $13,000 to the car company. The $250 is a **monthly payment**. The 6% interest is the **finance charge** on his loan.*

Charlie's bank has signed an agreement with Charlie that he can borrow up to $5,000 from the bank whenever he needs money.

→ *Charlie has just arranged for a **line of credit**.*

When Charlie gets his credit card bill, he sees that the bank is requiring him to pay at least $50 on the account.

→ *The bank has set $50 as the **minimum payment** due on his credit card balance for this month.*

Boating is fun, but I'll be paying a boat-load of interest on my debt for years to come.

Charlie's friend, Abigail, needs a loan. Because her income is low, the bank is reluctant to loan her the money. Charlie agrees to sign for the loan along with her.

*Charlie has just **cosigned** a loan for Abigail. This means that he has agreed to pay the loan if Abigail can't.*

Charlie has been paying for two years on his motorcycle. He owes $668 on the loan. $88 of this amount is interest.

*The **balance** on Charlie's loan is $668. The **principal** is $580. (That's the amount he owes that does not include interest.)*

Charlie has failed to pay his car payments according to the agreements of his car loan.

*Charlie has **defaulted** on his debt to the car company.*

Charlie could not pay for his boat all at once. After paying a down payment of $500, he arranged to pay the rest of the cost in monthly payments.

*Charlie has just agreed to make **installment payments**, or small monthly amounts, on his purchase. Interest will be charged for this privilege of paying for most of the boat later.*

Hey, Sam. Can you believe it? My credit card was refused. The credit card company won't let me charge my fishing trips any more. Why not?

Well, Sam, I do believe you must have reached your credit limit. That is the total amount of money the bank thinks you will be able to pay back, and not a penny more!

In that case, can you loan me 30 bucks?

Get Sharp Tip #21
There is always a cost when you buy on credit. Watch out for interest— it adds up fast.

Money & the Government

The Fed

The United States government collects, controls, and spends a huge amount of money. All this money is managed by the Federal Reserve System, known as **The Fed**, which is the bank of the U.S. government. The headquarters of the Fed is in Washington, D.C. The Fed has 12 regional banks across the country. The biggest of the branches is the Federal Reserve Bank of New York. All the checks written in the country pass through the Federal Reserve System.

The Fed's main job is to control the amount of money in circulation. It controls the flow of money by requiring banks to hold more money in reserve, or by making more money available for loans. The Federal Reserve can raise or lower interest rates. This affects the amount of money people borrow, so it is a tool to control the flow of money.

In periods of rapid economic expansion, the Fed would probably raise interest rates to slow down the flow of money and keep inflation from rising. In periods of recession, the Fed is likely to lower interest rates. This loosens up the flow of money and encourages people to buy and businesses to grow. The Fed works to keep just the right balance between having too much money in circulation and too little money in circulation.

The **FDIC (Federal Deposit Insurance Corporation)** is a U.S. government agency that acts as a huge insurance company for banks. This corporation assures bank customers that their money will be safe in any bank in America. All banks must insure each customer account for an amount up to $100,000. If the bank goes out of business, runs out of money, or gets robbed, the bank customers will not lose their money.

The **GDP (Gross Domestic Product)** of a country is a measure of the amount of goods and services produced within a country in a given period, even those produced by companies that are not owned by citizens of the country.

The **GNP (Gross National Product)** of a country is a measure of all the production of goods and services by businesses owned by the nation's citizens during a given period, even if the businesses are not located within the country.

The **balance of trade** is the relationship between the value of a country's imports and its exports. A country has a *favorable balance of trade* if the value of the exports is greater than the cost of the imports.

The U.S. has by far the highest **GDP** in the world. In the year 2003, the worth of goods and services produced in the country was almost *11 trillion dollars!*

That's an awesome number!

Better Grades & Higher Test Scores / SOCIAL STUDIES gr. 4–6
Copyright ©2005 by Incentive Publications, Inc., Nashville, TN.

Making Choices

You can't have anything to do with money without making choices. Since most people do not have unlimited money, they have to choose when to say, "yes" or "no" to different purchases. They also have to choose between saving and spending.

For every decision you make about earning, spending, saving, investing, or donating money, there is a *cost* or *consequence* (something you give up) and a *benefit* or *gain* (something you get). The costs and benefits might not always be financial.

Everywhere you turn, there are strong influences trying to convince you to spend, save, invest, or give away money. These influences that encourage you to make one kind of choice are called *incentives*. There are *positive incentives* (incentives that cause you TO DO something with your money) and *negative incentives* (incentives that cause you NOT TO DO something with your money). Some incentives come from outside. Others come from inside yourself.

> Lucy is excited about getting a new ski jacket. She finds a great jacket for $180. The jacket is advertised as being very warm and made with an ultra-waterproof fabric. The color is one of the season's new colors, and the style is the same one that her friends are buying.
>
> Then she sees another jacket on sale for $90. It's last year's style and last year's color, and it's not rated quite as high for being waterproof. Though it is not quite as warm, it is still a good jacket for cold weather skiing. It fits her perfectly. Her mother tells her she should not waste her money on the more expensive jacket. She needs $200 to buy her season pass to the ski hill.

The choice: Lucy chooses the more expensive jacket.

The benefits of this choice:
- She will look as stylish as her friends on the ski hill.
- This jacket that will keep her drier and warmer than the cheaper one.

The consequences of this choice:
- She spends twice as much money.
- She won't have the extra $90 to put towards her season pass.
- She pays $90 extra for something that will go out of style in a year.

The positive incentives to buy the expensive jacket:
- her need to have the latest style and color (internal)
- her pressure to be as "in style" as her friends (internal)
- advertising about the warmth and waterproof rating of the jacket (external)

The negative incentives to buy the expensive jacket:
- her mother's pressure to buy the cheaper jacket (external)
- her desire for money to buy a season pass (internal)

Economically Speaking

What's the answer?

Get Sharp Tip #22
The rate of employment is very important in an economy. A high rate of unemployment can mean that the economy is weak. People need jobs in order to produce and buy goods and services.

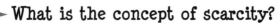

What is the economy?

It's the way the people in a society use resources and work together to produce the goods and services that they need and want.

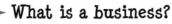

What resources are used in an economy?

There are natural resources (such as land, water, minerals, and wood), human resources (such as people's time, energy, and ideas), and financial resources (such as money).

What is the concept of scarcity?

This is a key idea in economics; it is the idea that there is a limit to all resources. If a resource is heavily used for one purpose or group, there will be less of that resource available for other uses or for other groups.

The frost caused a scarcity of oranges this year. I'll either have to charge more for my homemade marmalade, or make something else.

What is a business?

A business is any enterprise that brings in money from selling goods or services.

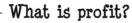

What is capital?

Capital usually refers to the money an investor puts into starting a business. Sometimes capital is not financial. The investment of time and energy that people put into starting a business venture is called ***human capital***.

What is profit?

It's the goal of most businesses—an amount of money earned that exceeds the expenses of running the business. Some businesses exist to provide a service, but do not intend to make a profit. A business that makes no profit is called a ***non-profit business***.

What is an entrepreneur?

An entrepreneur is the person who has an idea for a business, creates the business, and operates it.

What is a market economy?

This is the term used to describe an economy in which making a profit is the main incentive for producing goods or offering services.

Speech bubbles: "I'm so confused about all these economic ideas. I can never remember which is which." / "Just stick with me! I'm a genius when it comes to matters of the economy."

What's the difference...

...between producers and consumers?

Producers are people or businesses that create or provide goods and services. **Consumers** are people who buy and use goods and services. Just about everybody in an economy is a consumer.

...between the private sector and the public sector?

The **public sector** is the part of the economy that is produced or controlled by the government. The **private sector** is the part of the economy produced by businesses or individuals.

...between supply and demand?

Supply is the amount of goods and services that are available in the economy at any one time. **Demand** is the amount of desires consumers have for goods and services. In general, prices fall when supply is high, and prices increase when demand is high. If the price of a product or a service gets too high, it is likely that the demand will decline.

...among recession, depression, and inflation?

Recession is a condition in the economy when the flow of money slows down. Generally, unemployment rises and demand for goods and services declines. **Depression** is a severe form of recession, when business declines to an extreme low and unemployment is very high. In periods of **inflation**, prices show a continued increase.

...between monopoly and competition?

A company has a **monopoly** on a product or service when it is the only source of that product or service. **Competition** occurs when more than one business supplies the same product or service. In general, competition leads to lower prices and more varied products.

...between stocks and bonds?

A **stock** is a part ownership of a company that is available for sale to the public. Owners of stock are called *stockholders*. A **bond** is a certificate showing that someone has loaned money to a business or to the government. People buy bonds because of the promise of a profit, or dividend, on the money they loan.

Get Sharp: Economic Terms & Concepts

INDEX

G

gain, 231
Gagarin, Yuri, 173
Galileo, 169, 181
Gandhi, Mahatma, 173 178
Garrison, William Lloyd, 191
Gateway Arch, 126, 127
Gautama, Siddhartha, 74 165 178
gazetteer, 38
geography, 97–154
    cultural, 64–66,
    human, 99
    physical, 98
    themes, 98–99
    U.S., 133–154
    world, 97–132
Gettysburg Address, 193
geysers, 152
Ghana, ancient, 161
glacier, 102, 104, 105
global connections, 29, 130–132, 184
globes, 82, 84
glossaries, 37
goals, setting, 15–16
Golden Gate Bridge, 151
Gold Rush, 192
Gonzales, Elian, 199
goods, 222, 233
Gorbachev, Mikhail, 178
government, 29, 73, 204–217
GPS, 99
Grand Canyon, 150
Grant, Ulysses S., 193
Great Awakening, 189
Great Depression, 172, 196
Great Lakes States, 148
Great Seal, U.S., 219
Great Sphinx, 128–129 164
Great Wall of China, 128–129, 131
Greece, classical, 160, 165
Greeley, Horace, 195
grid,
    Earth's, 87
    maps, 83, 92
gross domestic product (GDP), 230
gross national product (GNP), 230
groups, social, 68–72
Guinness Book of Records, 38
gulf, 102, 103
Gutenberg, Johann, 168, 178

H

habits, study, 24–27
Hammurabi, 157, 164, 178
Hammurabi's Code, 157 164
Hanukkah, 78

Harvard, 189
health, 23
Hebrews, 158, 165
hemispheres, 84
Hidalgo, Miguel, 178
hieroglyphics, 159, 162, 164
hill, 102
Hinduism, 75, 165
Hiroshima, Japan, 173, 196
historical events,
    U.S. timeline, 188–199
    world timeline, 164–176
history,
    U.S., 185–203
    world, 155–184
Hitler, Adolf, 172, 178, 183, 196
Hittites, 158, 164
Ho Chi Minh, 178
holidays, U.S., 220
Homer, 178
Homestead Act, 193
Hopewells, 162
House of Representatives, U.S., 208–211
Howe, Elias, 181
Hubble Space Telescope, 175, 181
Hudson, Henry, 188
human,
    genome, 175
    geography, 64–66, 98
    interaction with environment, 65–66, 99
    migration, 99
    movement, 99
Hundred Years' War, 168, 182
Huns, 160, 166
hurricane, 152
Hussein, Sadaam, 184

I

iceberg,
    biggest, 104
    tallest, 105
immigrants, 194
impeachment, 193, 199, 208
Incas, 163, 168
incentives, 231
income, 224
independence,
    African, 173
    America, 169, 182, 190
    Latin American, 171
index, 38
Indian Mutiny, 171
Industrial Revolution, 169
Indus Valley Civilization, 159, 164
infer, 31
inflation, 233

ingots, 222
initiative, 217
institutions, 70
integration, 197
interest, 224,225, 227, 228, 229
International Atomic Energy Association (IAEA), 131
international culture, 61
International Date Line, 85, 86
International Labor Organization (ILO), 131
International Maritime Organization (IMO), 131
International Monetary Fund (IMF), 131
International Space Station, 198, 199
Internet, 39, 42–43
Interstate Commerce Act, 193
Intolerable Acts, 190
inventions, 180–181, 189, 190, 191, 192, 194
investment, 224, 225
Iran Hostage Crisis, 198
Iraq Wars, 184
Irish famine, 171
island, 102
    biggest in a lake in U.S., 153
    biggest in freshwater in world, 104
    biggest in U.S., 153
    biggest in world, 104
    highest in U.S., 152
Islam, 75, 166, 167, 169
Israel, 173
isthmus, 102–103
Ivan II, 168

J

Jackson, Jesse, 200
Jackson State protests, 198
Japan, 161, 171, 172, 173, 183
Jefferson, Thomas, 195 201
Jesus, 74, 178
Jewish migration, 172
Jews, 75, 158, 172
Jim Crow laws, 193
Joliet, 189
Jones, Frederick, 181
Judaism, 75
judicial branch, U.S. government, 208, 214–215
Judson, Whitcomb, 181

K

Kansas-Nebraska Act, 192
Kennedy, John F., 174, 197, 200
Kent State protests, 198
Kepler, Johannes, 181
Khan, Genghis, 167
Khmer dynasty, 167
King Arthur, 166
King Henry II, 167
King John, 168
King Louis, XIV, 179
King Louis XVI, 179
King, Martin Luther, Jr., 173, 197
Koran, 75, 166
Korean War, 184, 197
Kodomono-Hi, 77
Kush, 161, 164

L

Labor Management Relations Act, 196
lag, cultural, 61
lagoon, 102, 103
lake, 103
    biggest in U.S., 153
    biggest in world, 104
    biggest freshwater in world, 104
    deepest in U.S., 152
    deepest in world, 104
    oldest in world, 105
Lake, Simon, 180
landmarks,
    U.S., 150–153
    world, 104–105, 126–130
languages, 80
latitude, 84–87
laws, 71, 208–211
    how bills become, 210
League of Nations, 173, 194
Leaning Tower of Pisa, 128, 129
least sunny spot, 105
Lee, Robert E., 193
legislative branch, U.S. government, 208–211
Lenin, Vladimir, 179, 183
Lewis and Clark Expedition, 191
Liberty Bell, 219
library,
    biggest in U.S., 153
    card catalog, 39
    computer catalog, 39
Lindbergh, Charles, 172, 196
Lincoln, Abraham, 192, 193
Linear A writing, 158
Linear B writing, 158
Lippershey, Hans, 181

ADVANCE KNOWLEDGE. LET PREJUDICE PERISH. LET JUSTICE AND CHARITY ENCIRCLE THE EARTH AND EXTEND TO THE MEN OF EVERY CREED.

THIS IS NUMBER ONE HUNDRED AND NINETY-TWO
IN THE SECOND NUMBERED SERIES
OF THE MIEGUNYAH VOLUMES
MADE POSSIBLE BY THE MIEGUNYAH FUND
ESTABLISHED BY BEQUESTS UNDER THE WILLS OF
SIR RUSSELL AND LADY GRIMWADE.

'MIEGUNYAH' WAS RUSSELL GRIMWADE'S HOME FROM 1911 TO 1955
AND MAB GRIMWADE'S HOME FROM 1911 TO 1973.

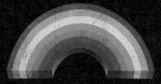

UNDER THE RAINBOW

The life and times of EW Cole

RICHARD BROINOWSKI

THE
MIEGUNYAH
PRESS

SONG OF THE BOOK ARCADE
(Tune "Mary had a little lamb")
Cole's Book Arcade Cole's Book Arcade
It is in Melbourne town
Of all the book stores in this land
It has the most renown.

2 It was the first first book arcade
That in the world was found,
'Tis still the finest book arcade
In all the world around.

3 A lovely rainbow sign appears
Above the book arcade,
And 'tis the very grandest sign
Was ever yet displayed.

4 A million, yes! a million books
Are stored within its walls
Which can be seen looked at or bought
By any one that calls.

5 The book you wish the book you want
Is almost sure to be
Found somewhere in the book arcade
If you will call and see.

CONTENTS

ACKNOWLEDGEMENTS

In writing this book, I have relied on a large number of sources, the most important of which has been *Cole of the Book Arcade,* the first comprehensive, but little known, biography written by Edward Cole's grandson Cole Turnley and published by Cole Publications in 1974. Turnley was the son of Cole's eldest daughter, Linda, and while she and he were still alive she regaled Turnley with many anecdotes about her father. In the absence of corresponding primary written material, these have become an invaluable source on many aspects of Cole's life and his family.

I have also been fortunate to receive much information and wise advice from a wide circle of friends and acquaintances. Among them are Melbourne researcher Abigail Belfrage; New South Wales historian Peter Hack, who is especially knowledgeable about Chinese-Australian history; Melbourne collectors Ian Armstrong, OAM, and Hank Ebes; Associate Professor Jay Johnston, Chair of the Department of Studies in Religion at the University of Sydney; Ken Orchard of the Art Gallery of South Australia; playwright Hilary Bell; historian Geoffrey Blainey; and Cole's grandson, Bill Rudd, and *his* son, Tony Rudd.

I have been greatly assisted with research on Cole's early life in Kent and his year in South Africa by Lisa Mendes and another South African, Michael Truter.

Mari Minami, Mariko Yamamoto and Kazuhiro Tsunoda have been extremely helpful with Japanese history and in helping me gain access to Japanese Ministry of Defence and Foreign Ministry archives. The Gaimusho research staff and those of the Peacekeeping Training and Research Centre at the Japanese Ministry of Defence in Tokyo were particularly helpful, as were the wonderfully cooperative research staff at both State Library Victoria and the Mitchell Library in Sydney. I also acknowledge the helpful service of three historical societies in Victoria: Castlemaine, Echuca and Albury.

I thank Cathy Smith of Melbourne University Press for her counsel; Katie Purvis for her intelligent and thoughtful input and amiable ways; and Tony Balfe and Ron Male, Trustees of the E.W. Cole Foundation, for their support and encouragement. Also, importantly, Caroline Verge, my Sydney-based copyright solicitor, without whose advice this book may never have been completed.

Finally, my thanks to two members of my own family for their advice and encouragement: my sister Dr Helen Caldicott's partner, Mary Cunnane, a former vice president of Norton Books in New York; and, as in all my writing endeavours, my wife Alison, an enduring source of enthusiasm, humour and encouragement.

PREFACE

Like the rainbows he used as trademarks, Edward William Cole lit up Victorian Melbourne with his Book Arcade and the ways he promoted it.

From the start, fortune was against him. He was born into an impoverished family in Kent, where his father, Amos Cole, was frequently absent and his mother, Harriet, struggled to provide enough food, clothes and shelter for Edward and his brother Richard, plus the nine half-brothers and three half-sisters she had by her second husband, John Watson. Edward received a stern education in Christian values from Watson, a Wesleyan, before leaving home at eighteen to become a costermonger on the mean streets of London. He spent a year in South Africa, where he learned about racial violence, before moving to Australia in 1851 at the tender age of nineteen.

Trying his luck on the Victorian goldfields in Castlemaine, Edward realised he could never make his fortune from gold. His claim was far from a stream to sluice his pans, which after a long backbreaking day were usually full of mud. But he found he *could* earn a living from selling things—first, lemonade to miners, then pies to Melbourne's nightlife, and finally, books, second-hand and new, to the city's reading public.

Cole began selling books from a barrow in the Eastern Market, then moved to a small arcade in Bourke Street above Swanston Street, before settling in a much larger arcade on Bourke Street between Swanston and Elizabeth streets.

He had the characteristics of a marketing genius. He equipped his third arcade with skylights, brass columns and light-filled galleries. At its entrance, two little mechanical sailors advertised what was for sale within. He designed open-plan shelving where customers could help themselves to books, and he made them feel welcome by providing sanctuaries where they could rest their tired feet and read his books without being obliged to buy.

ABOVE Cole's arcade on Bourke Street between Elizabeth and Swanston streets, looking east towards Parliament House

OPPOSITE A quiet place to sit and read without being obliged to buy

He scattered coins around city streets advertising his books and bearing morally uplifting slogans. He entertained Melbourne's reading public with outrageously exaggerated advertisements about his arcade. He ran a serialised story about a newly discovered race of human beings in New Guinea equipped with tails. He advertised for a wife in the Melbourne *Herald*, and found a good one.

In his arcade he provided diversions to attract children and their mothers, such as funny mirrors, a mechanical hen that laid eggs, live monkeys and an aviary. He filled the arcade with the sound of light classics and hymns played by a live orchestra. He attracted more customers with a high-quality tearoom with murals of oriental splendour, a gallery of fine art and a beauty parlour. He sold everything from fine writing instruments to china ornaments, cosmetics and soap.

The arcade became a carnival, a place to see and be seen. But its main business remained the selling of books, and by the early 1890s it stretched from Bourke Street through to Collins Street and was one of the biggest and most splendid bookshops in the world—as he frequently reminded his customers.

In person, Cole was not a vulgar huckster but thoughtful, quietly spoken and well mannered. Beneath the surface was a steely determination to succeed. He employed hundreds of staff, treating them with concern and sympathy without getting too close or, with a few exceptions, too involved with their problems. He hated to delegate responsibility for the running of the arcade to any but his wife, and was fiercely determined to run things his way. He avoided mortgaging his holdings, preferring leaseholds or outright purchases, which saved his business from the disastrous foreclosures prevalent during the 1890s depression.

Cole was not only a bookseller but an autodidact, a writer and philosopher. He was driven to express his opinions on a wide range of moral issues—the evils of drink and tobacco, the power of positive thinking, the virtue of hard work and self-discipline. He held unconventional views about religion that earned him a degree of notoriety among Melbourne's clerics. He was strongly opposed to racism, which he found common among miners on the goldfields, especially towards the Chinese. His fervent opposition to the Immigration Restriction Act of 1901 led him on a moral crusade to Japan, where he found at least superficial agreement among writers, philosophers, journalists, politicians and the aristocracy that the White Australia policy was wrong, and would, in the long run, damage Australia's national interests.

What Cole was known and admired for more than anything was his love of children and his sense of the absurd. This found expression in his Funny Picture Books, the first of which was published in 1879. Full of rhymes, cartoons, picture puzzles and morally uplifting sayings, they were enormously entertaining to children from five to fifty, not just in Melbourne but throughout Australia and in New Zealand and Great Britain. The original volume, a collector's item, was reprinted at least seventy times. The second volume was followed by another published after Cole's death by his grandson Cole Turnley. They are still fondly remembered by older generations.

Associated with his child-oriented humour was Cole's love of his own family—his Tasmanian wife, Eliza, whom he attracted by newspaper advertisement, and the six children they had together, two sons and four daughters, one of whom, Ruby, died tragically of scarlet fever in 1890 aged eight. Cole surrounded his family with love and indulgence. None of his children inherited his business flair and, lacking direction, the great arcade he had created deteriorated and died little more than a decade after his own death in 1918.

Cole's legacy lives on in the memories of countless Australians. My hope is that this book will provide an understanding of a man who inspired much affection and entertainment among those of his generation, so that his imprint on Australian society will endure.

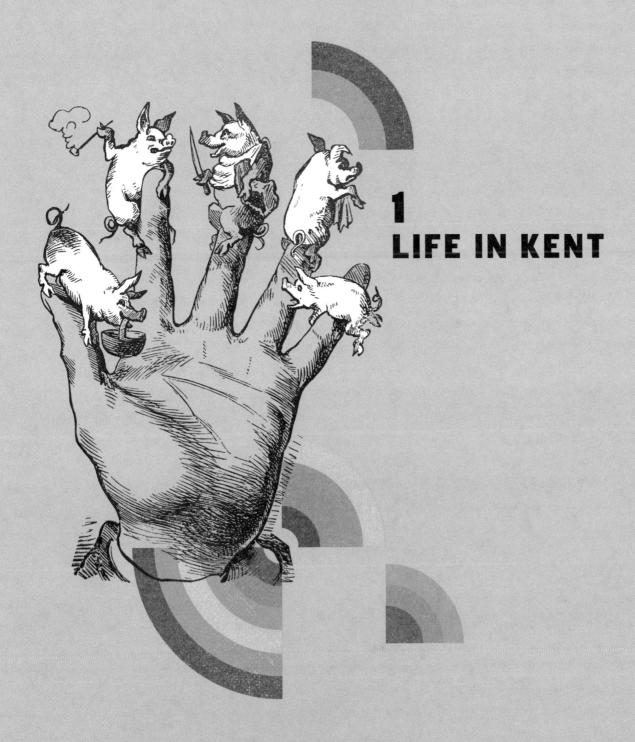

1
LIFE IN KENT

Windmill in Woodchurch, Kent

Edward William Cole was born on 4 January 1832 in Woodchurch, a village in south-west Kent near the High Weald, an area once populated by dense woodlands, and the Rother Levels, which slope down towards sheep-grazing areas on the Romney Marshes. Woodchurch is surrounded by settlements with names that could have come out of Tolkien's hobbit shire: north-east of Woodchurch lie Ashford and Appledore; close by are Tenterden, Frights Bridge, Cold Blow, Rough Lands, Frogs Hole and High Lands Hatch.

Woodchurch mirrored England's class divisions of the time. It boasted two substantial 'gentleman's residences'—Henghurst and Court Lodge—together with a small number of substantial farmhouses occupied by the families of forty or so better-off artisans and farmers, and a collection of smaller cottages set around the village green housing the families of around 230 agricultural labourers. For the inhabitants' spiritual needs, Woodchurch was the location of All Saints—an Anglican church of imposing proportions—and two nonconformist chapels, one for Wesleyans, the other for O'Brienites, an Irish protestant sect.

In 1974, Cole Turnley, a grandson of Edward, published a biography entitled *Cole of the Book Arcade*.[1] Chief among those who helped him with recollections were his mother, Ada Belinda, Cole's eldest child; Cole's two sons, Edward and Valentine; some other family descendants; and a few former employees of the Book Arcade. Turnley's version of his grandfather's biography is no doubt accurate in parts, but in others it tends towards the romantic, hiding some harsh truths. Turnley's version of his grandfather's birth is one example. He has it that Cole was born in a cosy thatched cottage, and the book even shows a photograph of the cottage covered in ivy and roses.[2] The midwife who delivered Edward was said to have been delighted to discover that he was enveloped in a caul, which at the time was regarded as a phenomenon signalling good fortune. The story is embroidered by

LEFT Cole's grandmother's rose-covered cottage, a poignant figment of his imagination
OPPOSITE The church where Cole was christened—both the church and its baptismal font remain today as they then were

Edward Cole himself, who described the cottage as 'Our Old Home on a Quarter Acre of Ground'.[3] In the same article he claims that when he was a child, his grandmother 'loved flowers dearly, and had a beautiful garden with an immense variety'.

Further, Cole's alleged father, Amos, while not well-to-do, is described by Turnley as a conscientious labourer who died tragically at the age of thirty-two when Edward was only four. Amos is said to have left to his wife, Harriet, the princely sum of £40 (£3200 in today's money) to be divided equally between their two surviving children, Edward and Richard.

These versions are inaccurate about Edward's parentage and gloss over the family's abject circumstances. Amos was almost certainly not his father, and their living conditions, if they followed the average pattern of the rural life of landless labouring families in Kent in early Victorian England, were probably very rough.

Most agricultural labourers shared small cottages with other families. If lucky, a family of two adults and several children may have occupied two rooms, and possibly shared with their co-tenants a scrap of adjacent land on which they grew vegetables and perhaps fattened a pig to feed the family over the lean winter months. Meals would have been basic— breakfast a simple porridge made from flour, butter and water, lunch bread and cheese, supper bread or potatoes and sometimes a piece of bacon. At harvest time, a labourer might receive a jug of beer made from local hops from his master, or drink cider, ale or wine he made himself from fruits such as elderberries and apples.[4]

The wives of most farm labourers shared such backbreaking tasks as clearing ground of stones and weeds, spreading manure, hoeing turnips and lifting potatoes. At harvest time they would have followed the harvesting men by raking up hay and binding and stook-ing cut corn, mothers and children working together. The kids would also have served as mobile scarecrows in newly sown fields, often in bitterly cold and rainy weather. When Queen Victoria came to the throne in 1837 (her coronation was a year later, in June 1838), the average weekly wage of a farm worker was about 13 shillings (approximately £50 in 2019), which could be increased to £1 if the worker's wife and children also worked the fields. Children earned around a penny a day.

In nineteenth-century England, children's learning came a poor second to helping the family budget. Most received only a cursory education, if any, until the Education Act of 1870 made primary education compulsory for children under twelve. Most rich children were tutored at home by governesses until the age of about ten; the boys were then sent to private schools while the girls learned domestic skills, such as sewing and playing the piano, at home. For poor children there were three choices: pick up whatever education they could at Sunday school, such as Bible reading; attend ragged/charity schools, which were often based in one room of a house and financed by the local parish; or seek entry at a 'dame' school run by one woman with a bit of education who doubled as a child-minder.

[*Continues on page 9*]

Woodchurch Church.

THE COUNTY OF KENT

Kent, one of Britain's seven home counties,[5] is south-east of London with water on three sides—the Thames Estuary and North Sea to the north, the Dover Strait to the east, and the English Channel to the south. To the west is Sussex. The French town of Calais is within sight just across the Channel from Dover and Folkestone.

Modern-day Kent has a prosperous population of two million people, many of them commuting to day jobs in London. It enjoys generally warmer weather than the rest of Britain, and a casual daily influx of tourists from Calais and further afield. In early summer, the high streets of Canterbury and other towns are alive with French schoolchildren as well as Britons. Its industries include haulage, logistics, tourism, building materials, printing and scientific research. When nuclear power was held to be the ultimate in sophisticated electricity generation in the 1960s, two nuclear reactors were built at Dungeness near Dover, one of which is still in operation.[6] The county's tranquil prosperity contrasts with its troubled past of war, invasion, plague, and agricultural and industrial upheaval.

Kent was the preferred invasion route for continental armies invading Britain, including the Romans under Julius Caesar in AD 54, and the Normans under William the Conqueror in 1066. The Spanish tried to land there in 1588, but the wind gods moved their armada on. The French planned to invade Britain, mainly through Kent, in 1744, 1759 and 1779. The Germans would have landed in Kent in Operation Sea Lion in 1940, but the invasion was ruled impractical when RAF Spitfires and Hurricanes defeated Goering's Luftwaffe in the Battle of Britain.

Like many English counties, Kent was blighted in the Middle Ages by the black death, a bubonic pandemic caused by *Yersinia pestis* bacteria carried by flea-infected rats. It wiped out a large proportion of the artisan and agricultural classes, causing serious labour shortages. These led in turn to riots against measures to peg wages at artificially low levels.

In the eighteenth and nineteenth centuries, a conjunction of new laws, a military victory and bad weather had disastrous economic effects on the rural population of Britain, not least in Kent. Between 1760 and 1820 over 2.8 million hectares of open fields where peasants traditionally supplemented their meagre diet with wild game became private property under a series of Enclosure Acts.

Wellington's defeat of Napoleon in the Battle of Waterloo in 1815 resulted in a horde of demobbed English soldiers sweeping across Kent looking for work. But few jobs were available as a series of devastatingly cold winters had reduced harvest yields.

The Corn Laws enacted between 1815 and 1846 kept corn prices at artificially inflated levels, which protected the vested

of mechanical threshers. It was aimed at rich tenant farmers who were replacing human labourers with threshers. 'Swing letters' calling for the destruction of threshing machines and a rise in wages were sent to wealthy farmers, magistrates and parsons, the arbiters of the Poor Laws, who decided which of the poor should be consigned to workhouses.

The Poor Laws were designed to punish lazy malingerers, as the rich suspected most paupers to be.[8] In medieval England, monasteries and parishes had looked after the poor when poverty was seen as an affliction, not a vice. But Henry VIII closed the monasteries, and a series of laws enacted from 1349 to 1834 inflicted increasing misery on the less well-off. The Act of Settlement of 1662 was particularly harsh: designed to prevent paupers from overrunning towns and parishes, it inhibited mobility and forced the unemployed to remain in their original places of 'settlement'. In 1776, economist Adam Smith described it as 'cruel oppression' in his *Wealth of Nations*.

By 1832, payments to the poor were costing Britons £7 million a year (£275 million today). A royal commission set up in 1832 led to an Act of Parliament in 1834 that made poor relief more punitive. Relief would not be available to those unwilling to enter workhouses, which were often privately run for whatever profit owners could extract from workers by utilising their free labour. Dark and sordid housing combined with poor food and sanitation added to the social stigma of the inmates— miserable and punitive conditions captured by Charles Dickens when Oliver dares to ask the Beadle for more gruel in *Oliver Twist*.

interests of large English grain producers but severely affected smaller landholders, tenant farmers and labourers, who could not afford to buy continental grains now subject to tariffs. Many had to spend the bulk of their income on staples just to survive. Prime Minister Sir Robert Peel repealed the laws in 1846, but this had reverse consequences: while some merchants and workers benefited from the improvement in trade and the lower cost of living, many small farmers could not compete with cheaper imports or afford to employ farm labourers.

Then came mechanised farming as the industrial revolution gathered momentum across Britain and steam-driven machines began to replace human labour. Agitation against mechanisation began in the early nineteenth century among textile workers in the Midlands. It spread to agricultural workers in the Elham Valley of East Kent and across the whole of southern England in the summer of 1830. Called Swing Riots,[7] the agitation involved the systematic destruction

8

In *Oliver Twist*, Dickens describes the Field Lane Ragged School as the den of the villain Fagin, a school I had actually visited in London:

> A dirtier and more wretched place he had never seen. The street was very narrow and muddy, and the air was impregnated with filthy odours. There were a good many small shops; but the only stock in trade appeared to be heaps of children, who, even at that time of night, were crawling in and out at the doors, or screaming from the inside.

Ragged schools in the rural counties were probably marginally less crowded and fetid than in London or the industrial cities of Manchester and Birmingham, but conditions would have still been quite wretched.

How did Edward and his family in Kent cope in this depressing situation? He may have been born in a caul, but it is doubtful that his early life was idyllic. A more forensic examination of the family undertaken in 2017 by researcher Lisa Mendes presents a rather different story—that of the grinding poverty and hardship typical of agricultural labourers at the time.

Lisa reckons that the family may have lived in their own cottage, but it was probably very tiny; it does not appear to have survived in its original form today. Poverty was real and brutal, as illustrated by the fate of Edward's maternal grandmother, Grace Gilbert. Born and baptised in the village of Pluckley in April 1784, she was an illiterate unmarried woman ground down by the relentless task of trying to care for her two illegitimate children, Harriet and Richard. Grace collapsed and died in a street of the nearby village of Great Chart in 1810 at the age of twenty-six. According to the *Kentish Chronicle*:

> On Thursday the 11th instant, Grace Gilbert, who lived in the Workhouse at Great Chart, was found dead in that street, lying under a faggot which she had stolen from a neighbour. It appeared to the Coroner's Jury that the deceased had been in a weak state for some time past, and it is supposed that she fell with the faggot, and being unable to extricate herself from it, the weight occasioned her death. Verdict—Died in a fit by the visitation of God.[9]

Grace's daughter, Harriet Wall Gilbert, was Edward Cole's mother. Harriet was born in April 1803 and baptised on 1 May in Great Chart, Kent. She married Amos Besor Cole in the nearby village of Shadoxhurst on 24 September 1824. Her illiteracy is confirmed by her signing the marriage certificate with an 'X'; Amos signed his name. Edward Cole said he had four brothers: Amos, George, Henry and Richard. Of these, two died in infancy—George at three, Amos at one. Henry's survival and whereabouts remain a mystery. Richard survived along with Edward.[10] The older Amos was said to have died at the age of thirty-six, when Edward was four.

But—and it is a big but—Amos did *not* die when Edward was four, or anytime shortly thereafter. Instead, he committed a series of thefts, probably in a desperate attempt to put food on the family table. According to the Criminal Registers of England and Wales, he was found guilty of petty theft by the Easter sitting of the West Kent Quarter Sessions in April 1820. The wonderful language in the charge sheet demonstrates the iron control of the monarchy over the church, the law and English life in general:

> The Jurors for our Lord the King, upon their Oath present, That Amos Cole late of the Parish of Woodchurch in the County of Kent Labourer on the sixth Day of April in the first year of the Reign of our Sovereign Lord George the Fourth by the Grace of God, of the United Kingdom of Great Britain and Ireland King, Defender of the Faith with Force and Arms, at the Parish aforesaid, in the County aforesaid, one round Frock of the value of one Shilling one Jacket of the value of three pence one pair of Trousers of the value of six pence and one Book of the value of one shilling of the Goods and Chattels of William Wells feloniously did steal, take and carry away, against the Peace of our Lord the King, his Crown and Dignity.

The court did not agree with Amos's plea of not guilty, and he was sentenced to six months' imprisonment at Maidstone jail.

Amos was convicted again, in April 1825, of three counts of larceny by the West Kent Circuit Court. One section of the charge sheet[11] alleged that he 'did feloniously steal, take and carry from Thomas Kingsnorth one handkerchief of the value of one shilling'. If he had escaped with it, he could have pawned the handkerchief for the price of a joint of meat. Instead, he was convicted and sentenced to seven years' incarceration.

Amos is listed on the register of prisoners on the prison hulk *Retribution* moored in Woolwich on the Thames, then on the prison ship *Captivity* in Devonport, near Plymouth. According to Jeff James, chief executive of the British National Archives, who did his academic dissertation on a group of hulk prisoners, inmates were shackled in irons and rose daily at 5 a.m. before typically undertaking around ten hours of hard labour in summer and seven in winter; they were put down at 7 each night. In wet weather and on Sundays, they were excused from working and would sit around bemoaning their fate and reminiscing about past misdemeanours.

Amos was pardoned after serving five years and released towards the end of 1831. This shows rather conclusively that he and Harriet could not have conceived Edward William Cole, who was born in January 1832. Nor was Amos able to attend Edward's baptism at All Saints Church in Woodchurch on 26 February 1832, because he was once more on board a prison hulk for theft. Who Edward's natural father was remains a mystery.

In 1833 and 1836, Amos Cole was found guilty of other indictable offences and, after the second trial, sentenced to fourteen years' transportation. He was first imprisoned on the prison hulk *Fortitude* moored at Chatham docks and then, according to the 'Naval Intelligence' section of *The Globe* of 22 April 1836, transported in chains to Van Diemen's Land on the *Lord Lyndoch* from Sheerness in the Thames Estuary. He arrived in Van Diemen's Land on 20 August 1836.

Amos again got into trouble with the law, this time in May 1839 in Australia, for 'making penury false statements of his master Thomas Archer' in a letter to the governor-general, for which he was sentenced to twelve months' hard labour. He served eleven and a half years of his fourteen-year transportation sentence and was then pardoned and given his ticket of leave in 1847. Research shows that he married (bigamously)[12] another convict, Ann Newman, in December 1843.[13]

Like Amos, Ann had been a repeat felon in England. On 26 October 1840 she was convicted at the Liverpool Borough Sessions of stealing a gold watch, and sentenced to twelve months' imprisonment. On 14 December 1841 she was convicted in the same court of picking the pocket of a Mrs Hannah Carter and stealing four shillings and sixpence, and sentenced to ten years' transportation. Along with 204 fellow women convicts, she boarded the convict ship *Royal Admiral* in Woolwich, London, and set sail in May 1842, arriving in Hobart on 24 September the same year.[14]

Ann married Amos Cole on 23 December 1843 and obtained her ticket of leave in February 1845 and a conditional pardon in January 1849. After gaining final freedom, Amos was employed as a sawyer in Tasmania and lived with his bride at Longford, Cressy and Deloraine, where they raised five children. In 1851, the family sailed to Melbourne on the schooner *Alice* only a year before the alleged younger son of Amos's first marriage, Edward William, similarly sailed up Port Phillip Bay. In Victoria, Amos and Ann had three more children. They first lived in Collingwood and then moved to Ballarat, where Amos died of chronic bladder and kidney disease on 14 March 1870. Ann wasted no time and remarried six weeks after his death; her new husband was Thomas Wilkinson, an Irishman from Naas near Kildare.

It is certain that Edward William and his 'dead' father, Amos, were both in Melbourne at the same time: Edward arrived there from South Africa in September 1852. But even if the two had met in Australia, it is doubtful they would have recognised each other.

Bringing in the stock, Ashford, Kent

During the years of separation from Amos in Kent, Harriet had a very hard time. Her name was on the local paupers' list of 1833 and 1834. She (and her two surviving children) may have been consigned to a poorhouse, or to a farm such as Robhurst Farm, leased in 1821 for £130 a year by the parish from a local landowner, Sir Edward Knatchbull, for the purpose of putting paupers to work in a more healthy outdoor environment.

According to Cole Turnley, two years after Amos's 'death', Harriet remarried—in 1838, the year Queen Victoria was crowned. Her second husband was another farm labourer, Thomas Watson,[15] from the nearby village of Tenterden. He was a steady and reliable worker, and a prominent, stern and principled member of the local Wesleyan Church.[16]

Harriet presented Thomas with a new baby each year until there were eleven children in the extended family, including Richard and Edward. Of Harriet's nine children with Thomas, two died at a very young age, adding to the heartbreak of the loss of her two earlier children. But infant mortality rates were very high in Victorian times: in 1840s England, one in every six children died before they were a year old. The most commonly cited causes of death were convulsions, diarrhoea and 'atrophy', the latter being a polite term for starvation.

It is probable that Harriet's second marriage to Thomas, though bigamous like Amos's one to Ann Newman, saved her from further manual labour. Thomas kept Harriet and their children off the streets and out of the workhouse. Once the children had left home, Harriet and Thomas moved around from the 1860s on, first to nearby Cranbrook, where Thomas appears to have been promoted to the position of 'farm bailiff' at a farm called 'Shavenswer'. By the 1880s they were living in West Ashford, perhaps to be closer to Harriet's brother Richard Gilbert and his family. The 1881 census shows them living in a cottage on Parsonage Farm in Westwell, West Ashford, along with a woman called Jane Jamie, aged fifty-eight, who is described as a servant and housekeeper, perhaps for the farm—however, it is equally possible that she was hired by the family to take care of Harriet, who was now in her dotage. Harriet's death certificate reveals that she died on 7 May 1881, aged seventy-eight. Her cause of death is listed as 'gradual asthenia', which meant general weakness and debility.

In sum, Edward was raised in a deprived, unstable and overcrowded environment. His step-father, Thomas, may have instilled in him the basic skills of reading and writing, if not a degree of flexibility about religion. Edward may also have benefited from the wisdom of his teachers in Rolvenden, if indeed he had any.

Who else influenced him? He did not have the stimulus of a well-stocked library, nor, apparently, the companionship of educated young friends. Where did he acquire the qualities he displayed in his adult life, including a voracious appetite for learning, an independent way of thinking, a shrewd business sense, a capacity for self-promotion, an idealism about humanity and the natural universe, a distaste for alcohol and tobacco, an intense curiosity about technology, and a strong antipathy towards prejudice and racism?

We start with his mother, Harriet. Despite her poverty, heartache at losing four of her children, and lack of any emotional support from her first husband, Harriet must have given Edward maternal love and encouragement. But she had no education, nor probably any understanding of the world outside her parochial environment in Woodchurch and the poorhouse at Rolvenden where she occasionally worked. Hardly inspirational.

Nor could Amos have added much of substance or value to Edward's upbringing. Amos had agricultural skills—including as a ploughman, farm labourer and shepherd—and, later in life, skills as a sawyer of wood and in carpentry. But he contributed little to his family or the upbringing of the two sons he had with Harriet.

Edward's stepfather, Thomas Watson, is another possibility. He held a rebellious set of Christian convictions somewhere towards the purist end of the Protestant scale. Indeed, Rolvenden, Tenterden and Woodchurch were inhabited by a substantial number of people with strong nonconformist religious views, which may explain why John Wesley, an evangelical Anglican cleric who founded Methodism, was able to free many Anglicans and some Catholics from priestly mummery during the 1760s. Thomas probably taught his two stepsons to read alongside the older of his children with Harriet, including Edward's half-brother John. Turnley says Thomas treated them as if they were his own, and part of this may have been to educate them. But Thomas also displayed a degree of religious rigidity: Edward is said to have approached him one day to question the Bible's simple explanation of the immensity of the universe but was told not to doubt the word of God or to question it again in the house. Thomas's absolutism may well have encouraged resentment in young Edward that led to his later scepticism about religious dogma.

The same rigid thinking did not affect another of Edward's possible mentors: a liberal-thinking teacher, William Smeeth, who came to Woodchurch in 1819 and became the local schoolmaster and churchwarden of All Saints, where he remained for over thirty-five years. A regular preacher for the Wesleyans, Smeeth seems to have been an open-minded individual dedicated to educating the young sufficiently for them to be able to read the Bible. But Edward was only four when he moved with his mother and brother to Rolvenden for Harriet's second marriage. Smeeth could therefore hardly have had an influence on Edward before the move, although he may have done so indirectly through Richard, who may have passed on to Edward what he learned from Smeeth.

The family certainly had another connection with Smeeth: Amos broke into Smeeth's school around 1835 and stole textbooks worth 40 shillings, a crime for which he was sentenced to fourteen years' transportation on 5 January 1836, the year he is supposed to have died. Whether Amos was simply after the money the books may have generated, or planned to read the books himself and pass the knowledge on to his sons, will never be known.

Did Edward go to school in his new home in Rolvenden? Possibly. According to Turnley, Edward was taught by a freethinker, an unnamed scholar interested in astronomy, who taught him to gaze up into the summer sky and wonder about the immensity of the universe.[17] A dame school cum day care centre was run by a schoolmistress, Mary Austin, who may have taught him the rudiments of reading and writing. Another possible influence was James Oxley, a schoolmaster in Rolvenden. Oxley's brother William emigrated to Australia in 1839, three years after Edward arrived in the village, and kept sending letters back to James about his Australian adventures. Was Edward one of James's students, and did James infect Edward with a desire to escape the suffocating environment of rural Kent for the wider world of Australia? James was quite entrepreneurial and had many interests; he worked as an insurance agent and a tax collector, and was the church organist and choirmaster. Was he an inspiration to young Edward? Possibly. There is no evidence one way or the other.

Other influences on the young Edward Cole may have come from his naval and military heritage. Edward's paternal grandfather was George Cole. Born around 1775, George was an ordinary seaman on two ships, HMS *Shannon* and HMS *Salvador*. Engaged in the Napoleonic Wars, *Shannon* was captured in 1804 and its crew, including George, imprisoned at Valenciennes until they were repatriated in April 1806 under what was known as the cartel system. A register of mariners from the British Board of Trade shows lots of other Coles involved in the maritime life, many from Essex and Sussex. Some may have been Edward's forebears, and some may even have known him. In any event, Edward was never attracted to a life at sea: on the contrary, he was repelled by the dangers he associated with a seafaring life and only reluctantly embarked on his voyage to South Africa in 1850 at the age of eighteen.

There were also Coles in the army, some of whom may have been related to Edward. Members of the Essex branch of the Cole family may have joined up at Colchester to fight the war against Napoleon, and then been posted to Kent for artillery and rifle training at Lydd, the southernmost Kentish town on the Romney Marsh. Many of them were garrisoned to man Kent's coastal defences, including in Martello watchtowers along the shoreline. Some may have been involved in digging the Royal Military Canal between Romney and Hythe. Edward's uncle George Pearson was attested in Bexhill near Brighton in Sussex on 1 October 1818, and served in the 35th Regiment of Foot until he was discharged in 1840 and became a Chelsea pensioner. Whether he had any influence on his young nephew is not known.

Edward's brother Richard also joined the army. Leaving home at the age of twenty in 1849, he claimed to his family that he was bound for the Californian goldfields. The only news Harriet ever received was a half-page letter saying he was well and expressing the hope that he would soon become rich; it gave no details of his life or where he was. Meanwhile, it is doubtful that he ever left Britain. Instead of heading for London and then California, he appears to have gone to Devon, where he enlisted in the 11th Regiment of Foot based in North Devon; it was later known as the 'Devonshires' when it merged with several other units.

The registered marriage is recorded of one Richard, son of Amos Cole, born in May 1830, to Elizabeth Pinckham at St Peter's Church, Farnborough, on 23 July 1859.[18] The adult Richard's profession is listed as a sergeant in the 11th Regiment, 1st Battalion of the British Army. Corroboration of this evidence is found in the official British census of 1851, which shows one Richard Cole as a patient in a military hospital in Rochester, Kent, although he is now reduced in rank to private. Beyond that, details of Richard's life and fate are lost to us.

According to his twentieth-century biographer, Turnley, Edward left his mother and their overcrowded environment in Rolvenden in 1850 to try his fortune in London, a few months after his brother had departed. He must have been seventeen. Turnley gives an imaginative and sentimental account of his departure:

> He was seen off by the family at the garden gate. His mother, moist-eyed, kissing his young bearded cheek. There was a chill wind and a spit of rain, and two babies could be heard crying in the house. All Harriet could find to say was, 'Don't squander your

Pentonville, Islington, near where
a prison was constructed in 1842
for prisoners awaiting deportation

Prince Albert's idealistic vision: the Great
Exhibition, held in 1851 at the newly
constructed Crystal Palace, may have
inspired Cole's ambitions for his book arcade

money, Eddy. Remember it's all you've got to get a start with.' He tossed his carpet bag
up onto the dray of a neighbour who had offered him a lift as far as the village before he
need begin to walk.[19]

Much excitement had been generated in London by the construction of the Crystal Palace
in Hyde Park, with the enthusiastic support of Queen Victoria and Prince Albert. The prince
was determined to make the Great Exhibition of the Works of Industry of all Nations, to
be held from 1 May to 15 October 1851, a resounding success. And so it was, under the
guidance of its driving supervisor, the philanthropist Sir Henry Cole of the Royal Society
for the Encouragement of Arts, Manufactures and Commerce (unfortunately no relation to
Edward), and Joseph Paxton, landscape architect of the 6th Duke of Devonshire.

The Crystal Palace was a gigantic glass house blazing with light, full of the most intricate and
amazing exhibits from Britain's far-flung empire. Did the young Edward see it? Did he remember its soaring glass ceilings and vaulted cast-iron buttresses, and did he attempt to mimic
them in his own Book Arcade opened in Bourke Street, Melbourne, thirty-two years later?

Possibly, although he would also have read about the Crystal Palace in newspapers and
seen illustrations. But although the project generated much employment among skilled
workers, none filtered down to unskilled rural labourers freshly arrived from the counties.

The dreary fact was that in London, Edward, like thousands of other labourers, struggled
to survive by hawking goods in the streets. He was one of around 30,000 costermongers
who sold everything from oysters to hot eels and fried fish, pies and puddings, sheep's trotters, pickled whelks, gingerbread, baked potatoes and crumpets; or bought bottles, bones,
fat dripping and silver spoons. Many costermongers made a fair living, but apparently not
Edward. According to Turnley,[20] he earned around 3s 6d in a good week selling sandwiches,
of which he had to pay 1s 9d for a bed in a room shared with seven other men that had
a slop bucket in the middle. No evidence exists that he found other more lucrative work,
but Turnley claims that as a last throw of some rather desperate dice, he went to Chatham
Barracks to enlist in the military. The jovial recruiting sergeant is said to have told him that
he was a quarter-inch (6 millimetres) too short, and that if he returned when less tired the
next morning and stood up straight, he might gain it back.

But did he go to Chatham Barracks, which is not in London but in one of the Medway towns in northern Kent? And if he did, which arm of the military did he try to join? Chatham was home to the Royal Marines, the Corps of Royal Engineers (the Sappers), Kitchener Barracks, Brompton Artillery Barracks and Melville Barracks. Or did he try to enlist in an army barracks within London itself? Did he go to South Africa as part of the British Army, or did he go as a civilian?

Certainly, advertisements were appearing at the time in newspapers in London and the counties inviting civilians to go to South Africa as part of an official emigration scheme. This would be consistent with a claim by Turnley that Edward found an advertisement about migration to South Africa and, overcoming an apparent fear of shipwreck and drowning, took passage in 1850 to Port Elizabeth.[21] Research by Lisa Mendes goes a long way to confirm this speculation: Edward most likely sailed to South Africa in mid-April, probably on the sailing ship *Dalhousie* from Plymouth, arriving in Table Bay (Cape Town) in late June 1850.[22]

2
CAPE
WITHOUT
HOPE

ABOVE Four men looking far and wide in different conveyances for an elusive flying machine
OPPOSITE Market Square in Port Elizabeth, around the time of Cole's arrival

British colonisation in the Victorian era was an early example of modern globalisation—moving people around to reinforce the control of the mother country's far-flung empire. This occurred across Africa as well as in Canada, Australia, South-East Asia and the Pacific.

In 1806 Britain wrested control of much of the Cape Colony from the Dutch, whose homeland had been annexed by Napoleon. Whitehall was prompted to take it to prevent Napoleon, with whom Britain was at war, from doing so. In 1819 British authorities offered settlers 100 acres (40 hectares) of land in the Cape Colony free of taxes for ten years, plus seed and implements at cost. Three thousand English men and women accepted the offer, but their settlement was less than satisfactory because most were not farmers, the climate was more suitable to grazing than farming, blight destroyed crops, and the parcels of land offered were often too small for viable farms. Also, when the Slavery Abolition Act of William Wilberforce came into force in 1833, settlers were prohibited from owning slaves. Despite such setbacks, the English continued to arrive; the Dutch moved north and east until a substantial number settled in what became known as the Orange Free State.

It is likely that Edward Cole was prompted by a British government scheme to migrate to the Cape in 1850, and that he went there as an agricultural labourer. One advertisement in the *Illustrated London News* of July 1850 called for shepherds, herdsmen and 'country mechanics', such as blacksmiths, wheelwrights, carpenters and masons, between the ages of fourteen and forty, and female domestic servants.[1] Another advertisement concerning an official migration scheme appeared in the *Western Times*, a local paper in the Devon area. Given his miserable circumstances, Edward was very likely to have been attracted by such advertisements and applied to emigrate in order to change his life.

His attention may also have been drawn to South Africa by his schoolmaster at Rolvenden, James Oxley, whose brother William had advised him in 1839 that 'the Cape was indeed a great place to start afresh', even if the voyage out from England could be rough. Certainly prospects of adventurous employment in South Africa would have been much talked about among young men leaving school and facing unemployment in the villages of England at the time. It would have been a popular topic of conversation among Edward and his friends.

Compelling evidence that Edward went to the Cape as a labourer is found on a shipping manifest of a vessel called the *Dalhousie*,[2] which arrived in Cape Town on 23 June 1850. An Indiaman built of teak in the British colony of Burma in 1848, *Dalhousie* was a full sailing ship, not particularly fast. Constructed during a period of revolutionary change in shipbuilding when passenger vessels were being fitted with steam engines to add speed and reliability to their schedules, *Dalhousie* had no engine. Commanded by Captain John Butterworth and owned by Mr John Allan of Leadenhall Street, London, it was a 'wet' vessel. The voyage in question was apparently a rough one. The ship floundered its way south in stormy seas on a long voyage, well beyond the usual sailing time of forty-five days. Royal Mail steamers (with sails and engines) made the voyage in around forty days unless hindered by severe weather. As poignant proof of its unseaworthiness, *Dalhousie* sank during a subsequent voyage near Beachy Head in the English Channel just off Eastbourne in October 1853, with the loss of the captain, sixty passengers and most of the crew.

On landing cold and miserable at Cape Town in June 1850, Edward appears to have immediately taken passage eastwards on another ship to Algoa Bay, Port Elizabeth. This may have been the *Phoenix*, a steamer from Table Bay (Cape Town).[3] *Phoenix* was carrying soldiers, and if Edward was a passenger he would have been either fascinated or appalled by their stories of fighting—both real and imaginary. Whatever the ship, he would again have faced stormy weather judging from other distressed vessels as reported in the 'Shipping Intelligence' column of the *Cape Exchange Gazette* at the time.[4] As Cole Turnley put it: 'finally at Port Elizabeth when with other passengers he was put ashore in a surf boat, (Cole) was so weak and emaciated that he had to be admitted to the settlement's white-washed stone hospital.'[5]

According to authoritative sources, a whitewashed stone hospital was not built in Port Elizabeth until 1856.[6] But research by Lisa Mendes found that a military hospital existed in 1850 at the old barracks building below Fort Frederick, and Edward may have been treated there. The fort underlined the strategic importance of Port Elizabeth on the eastern seaboard. It was an ideal landing place for visitors wishing to travel into the southern African interior, including to Grahamstown (now known as Makhanda) and Bathurst. It was the main point of entry for immigrants to the eastern districts, military forces charged with their protection, and missionaries seeking to propagate their faith among local tribes. It became the main route to the Kimberley diamond fields. By 1860, Port Elizabeth had become the colony's most significant port and its second-largest city.

Whether he went to hospital and whichever one he went to, Edward could hardly have landed in Port Elizabeth at a more unstable and dangerous time. Conflict had been raging in frontier wars between white settlers and Indigenous tribes, the Khoi and Xhosa, since 1779. The Seventh Frontier War, the 'War of the Axe', had occurred between 1846 and 1847 with horrendous loss of life on both sides. It was ignited when a Khoi soldier in the pay of the British was attacked and killed by Xhosa raiders while a group of Khoi men were escorting a manacled Xhosa chief to Grahamstown to be tried for stealing an axe.

The Eighth Frontier War began at the end of December 1850, when white farmers in border regions had invited Xhosa neighbours into their houses for Christmas festivities only for the Xhosa to fall on the settlers and slaughter them. The Xhosa followed this up with further assaults, which Sir Harry Smith, the heavy-handed governor of the Cape Colony, was unable to resist. Smith had alienated many allies, including burghers, Boer commandos, Khoi warriors, even the Cape Mounted Police. Reinforcements under a Colonel Mackinnon arrived from Cape Town in January 1851 to relieve Fort White, Fort Cox and Fort Hare. Led by an outstanding Xhosa warrior chief named Maqoma, the Xhosa retreated to the forested Waterkloof on Mount Misery, a natural fortress. The Eighth War resulted in the comprehensive defeat of the Xhosa in the Transkei and Ciskei.

How did Edward cope in such an environment? It would certainly have made its mark on his psyche. He would have experienced fear, apprehension, dread—even, if he had been in a more buoyant frame of mind, a sense of adventure. The following summarises Turnley's account of what took place.

During the several days he remained in the military hospital at Port Elizabeth in 1850, Edward supposedly met another young Englishman, Charles Kent. Kent was apparently recovering from a spear wound inflicted during some 'trouble with the natives' near his family sheep farm, which was 'well inland, close to the frontier of white settlement'. Two white men had been killed by 'kaffirs' and at least one of these had to be replaced urgently. The smilingly serious Eddy Cole might be a first-rate applicant.

Charles's father, a tall, genial man with a 'happy little wife', took Edward on as an overseer and he earned the natives' trust by being fair and unprejudiced in his dealings with them. When not on duty, Edward would wander through the karoo, the kloofs and the mountains in the neighbourhood, admiring the scenery and gathering wildflowers. It was for him a welcome relief from the violence and confrontation of an environment in which he was

A warrior of the Ama-Xhosa, a civilisation that
was as highly organised as that of the white
man seeking to take their lands

compelled to survive—a spiritual renewal that drew him above the depressing violence of his day-to-day existence. Although the land was dry and thorny, the Cape Colony was host to a wide variety of botanical specimens. To his delight, Edward later found a similar abundance of exotic flora in Australia, and to observe and catalogue its richness was a fascination and source of comfort that endured throughout his life.

Although Edward's activities are not precisely delineated in Turnley's biography, Turnley speculates that he probably gained some experience as an armed overseer on Kent's farm. According to an anecdote told by Edward to his children, he was once nervously standing watch when he heard a suspicious rustling in the bush and blazed away with his rifle only to discover with relief that he had grazed a cow, not a marauding 'kaffir'.

In 1852, Sir George Cathcart replaced the autocratic Smith as governor of the Cape Colony. Cathcart warned the colonial settlers that his soldiers were taking heavy casualties as the frontier war progressed, and unless the settlers assisted by providing their own commandos, the military might be withdrawn altogether. This may have well been the final straw for Charles's father, who had become tired of all the danger and tension surrounding his farm. He sold up the same year, and with his wife embarked for England. He left Edward with a bonus on top of his wages to remain at the farm to see in the new owners, which Edward did. But Edward had heard the excited rumours of gold discovered in Australia and, with around £300 in his kitty, he decided to embark for the great southern land.[7]

Several elements of this story are vague and lack accuracy. What was Charles Kent's father's name? Where precisely was his farm? Having Edward wandering across the karoo and through the kloofs does not help us locate it.[8] Who were these 'kaffirs'—a term with racist overtones used generically to describe black men? They were probably Xhosas, but were not clearly identified. And Cathcart did not replace Smith as governor until February 1852, by which time Edward had probably already left for Australia.

Researcher Lisa Mendes did, however, manage to find a likely Charles Kent through the South African Genealogical Society—and even his diary, at the Albany Museum in Grahamstown. According to these records, Charles was born on 10 August 1827 in Trappe's Valley near Bathurst in the Eastern Cape, the second son of a James Kent. James was one of the original English settlers who emigrated from Liverpool on 13 January 1820. His family formed part of the Hayhurst party who settled on the frontier near Fish River close to Cawood's Post, a fortified farm in the Bloukrans Valley known previously as Kaffir's Drift. James set up as a farmer and shoemaker on a property known as 'Kent's Wood', located close to Roundhill, where he lived until 1832, then moved to Wiggils Mill close to Grahamstown. There his wife, Ellen, died in 1833. James then moved with his family to the King William's Town area where he ran a general trading store on behalf of two local merchants.

But James himself could not have been the genial landowner who offered Edward Cole the job of overseer of his farm in 1850, because James Kent was killed on Christmas Eve 1834 during a dispute with some local Xhosas at the start of the Sixth Frontier War—sixteen years before Edward arrived in Port Elizabeth. As a result, all his children were orphaned, including Charles. According to Charles Kent's diary:

> Now the war of thirty-four and thirty-five breaks out. The Kaffirs kill my father and plunder the shop. Me and my two sisters are taken to Missionary Ross for refuge by some kaffir maids said to be loyal. Trekked by first escort of soldiers with Mr Ross to Grahamstown. There we were cast lots for. My lot fell to be Mr John Cawood's adopted son, much against my will and sorrow.[9]

Further on in his diary, Charles writes:

> So we moved to the Fish River Mouth and opened a boarding house on the west side. There was a large camp on both sides by and by. Then the Governor Maitland encamped on the east side with a large army. I broke my arm for the second time and had to go to the military hospital for two weeks. It was broken by a fall from a horse. Pato was then Paramount Chief of the country, now Peddie district.[10]

We know there was a military camp near Grahamstown and the Fish River during the Seventh Frontier War (1846–47), and that there was a military hospital at Fort England in Grahamstown.[11] But Edward did not arrive in South Africa until June 1850, so it is unlikely he met Charles at the Fort England hospital.

A further clue about where Edward met a Charles Kent is provided by another entry in Charles's diary. In late 1850 Charles helped take a load of salted beef from Waterloo Bay to Port Elizabeth for his adoptive family, the Cawoods, who enjoyed a monopoly on the supply of meat and groceries in the Eastern Cape at the time. This was just before 1851, so the dates of Edward's landfall there and Charles's whereabouts fit.

Another puzzle is whether Edward actually worked as an overseer on any farm owned by Charles's adoptive father, John Cawood, or, indeed, for Charles himself. Charles owned and rented farms, including one called 'Collingham' on the Peddie Road near Grahamstown. But he rented Collingham the same year he got married, 1853—so probably too late for Edward to have worked there.

It is more likely that Edward actually worked for the Cawoods. Certainly their holdings were more extensive than Charles'. Charles' stepfather, John Cawood, together with his brothers William, Samuel and Joseph—all second-generation 1820 settlers—had extensive business interests throughout the Eastern Cape region. John owned a butchery in Grahamstown, and the brothers owned trading posts as well as holding a monopoly on supplying meat and other provisions to the British Army. They also had cotton and livestock farms, including a sheep farm and wool washery.[12] The only problem—an insurmountable one in establishing Edward's activities at the time—is that according to Charles Kent's diary, John 'died of the dysentery' in 1846, four years before Edward's landfall in the Cape.[13]

Another possible employer of Edward was John's brother William Cawood. He and his wife, Sarah, were well-off, respected members of society, and may match the description of the tall, genial man with a happy wife who 'made an overseer of young Cole':[14]

> Their ten-bedroom home in Cradock was in keeping with their status in the town. Grand old English mahogany furniture and fine carpets throughout gave the home a touch of spacious elegance. They were a happy couple. He lived to a good old age, nearly 77, and his funeral was the largest ever seen in Cradock.[15]

The fact that William Cawood did not sell his farm around 1851, or anytime soon after that, weakens the speculation that Edward worked for him. Edward is supposed to have migrated to Australia in 1852 when his employer sold his farm, staying long enough to see in the new owner.

Yet another piece of evidence possibly linking Edward and the Cawood family concerns religion. Edward was brought up by his stepfather, Thomas Watson, to value nonconformist traditions, including strict teetotalism. The Cawood clan, who were Wesleyans, had similar values: did this predispose him towards them, or them to him? But then the bulk of British settlers in South Africa in 1820 were Wesleyans, and a nonconformist ethos pervaded the region.[16]

The only conclusion a historian can make from these stories is that it is all speculative and provides no firm evidence of what Edward did in the Cape Colony between 1850 and 1852.

What about the possibility of his having led a military life? Turnley speculates about this, but provides no convincing evidence.[17] All that we know for certain is that his older brother, Richard, was in the military and possibly served in South Africa. Richard's name crops up on the 1861 census as a sergeant in Her Majesty's 11th Regiment, 1st Battalion, with his residence recorded as North Camp, Farnborough. His father is listed as Amos Cole, deceased (actually alive and transported, but possibly described by his wife Harriet as deceased to avoid scandal at her bigamous marriage to Watson in 1836). Richard may have served in Ireland and possibly further afield.

One clue about Edward is from a genealogy website called Findmypast. It lists a Private Edward Cole, born circa 1834 (pretty close to Edward's real birthday in 1832), in the Cape Mounted Rifles—a cavalry force used to reinforce regular troops in both the seventh and eighth frontier wars.[18] But according to his pay records, this Edward Cole was pensioned off and in 1865 was based in London again. Very likely a different Cole.

Another possibility is an Edward Cole of the 7th Dragoon Guards who received the South African medal for active service in the seventh and eighth frontier wars. We know from Charles Kent's diary that the 7th Dragoons were based in Fort Beaufort and the Amatola regions during these wars, so it's the right time and place for our Edward Cole. But this Cole is recorded as having enlisted between 1842 and 1855 in Bigglesthwaite, Bedfordshire. Another blank.

A third and final possibility is a Private Edward Cole of the 59th Infantry Regiment who was discharged at Chatham in 1862. But he came from Kimbolton in Cambridgeshire, and his discharge was well after our Edward Cole went to Australia in 1852.

All that can be confidently asserted is that in whatever employment he undertook in the Cape Colony between 1850 and his departure for Australia in 1852, Edward William Cole would very likely have witnessed violence and bloodshed—either as a volunteer armed sentry at a farm, or as part of a team supplying rations to regular troops in the Eighth Frontier War, or even as an irregular soldier dragooned to augment regular forces under Sir Harry Smith in his attempts to quell Xhosa warriors. These experiences may have caused him to have an aversion for conflict and convinced him to leave the Cape.

In an interview with a local reporter from the *Essendon Gazette and Keilor, Bulla and Broadmeadows Reporter* published on 21 March 1918, Edward recalled that he arrived in Port Phillip Bay from South Africa 'in a small 110-ton boat called the *Sebim*'. Turnley also claims that Edward left South Africa for Australia on a schooner, the *Sebim*, on 29 September 1852.[19] Whether this was a detail remembered by Turnley's collaborators or backed up by hard research is unclear, but Mendes has found newspaper and shipping details of *Sebim* and its voyage from Algoa Bay to Port Phillip with only minor discrepancies from Turnley's account. *Sebim* was a brigantine, not a schooner,[20] and its entry is on the 'Passengers in History' section of the South Australian Maritime Museum website. If Edward did travel on the *Sebim*, it seems that his bad luck on sea voyages continued on this one. According at least one news report, *Sebim* ran into foul weather, was dismasted, and forced to return to the Cape for repairs. It embarked again twenty days later and dropped anchor in Melbourne on 11 November the same year. If Edward was an original passenger on this interrupted voyage, he must have had an anxious time of it.[21]

SS *Great Britain*, 1852

We cannot be certain that Edward sailed from South Africa to Melbourne on the *Sebim* in 1852, as he is not listed on the manifest. But that must not be allowed to spoil the good story Turnley relates:

> One diarist wrote of the jubilation experienced on sighting the Victoria coast. Men chased each other along the deck, shouted, leaped, and seemed nearly frantic.
>
> The smoke of a steamship appeared astern of the *Sebim*, and presently a six-masted liner was identified as the mighty ship Cole had so naively hoped to sail on himself, the *Great Britain*.
>
> Seth Doane, the *Sebim*'s master, clapped on full sail, and for a time the battered little schooner gave the world's largest and fastest ship a 'race' across the bay, provoking wild cheers from the passengers and crews of both ships until, inevitably, *Great Britain* steamed ahead.
>
> She was next sighted at anchor at the edge of an cvcr-crossing seascape of masts, a panorama of some 200 ships anchored in Hobson's Bay. In many cases these ships were virtually stranded, their crews having deserted for the diggings. The pugnacious Seth Doane tacked right up the Yarra River; and in the warm shadows of late afternoon he successfully tied up at Cole's Wharf.

Cole's landfall at Queen's Wharf in Melbourne: 'Cole's Wharf' had nothing to do with Edward Cole, but he took it as a good omen

Though he was sure there would be no family connection, sight of his own name lettered large across a storage shed inevitably suggested to Cole a good augury for his future in this vast, exciting new land.[22]

A related story, no doubt true, is that George Robertson and Samuel Mullen, both destined to make a substantial mark on the Australian book trade, arrived in Melbourne on the *Great Britain* on the same day as the *Sebim*. *Great Britain* raced past *Sebim* on its way to the Melbourne docks, but all three men arrived there on the same day in 1852.

If Edward did have a 'good augury' about Melbourne, it certainly came true—but probably not in the way he expected at the time.

3
EARLY
MELBOURNE
AND THE
GOLDFIELDS

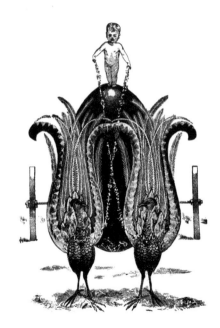

Castlemaine in 1858, a photograph by
Richard Daintree, slightly better established than
when Cole arrived there in November 1852

The extraordinary thing about Melbourne is the precocity of its beginnings. Within less than fifty years, it ceased to be the exclusive territory of the Koori people and became a sprawling infestation of European settlers drunk on speculation and visions of wealth.

In the words of EM Curr, a pioneer squatter on the Murray, it was 'a bustling, stirring sort of place from the very pip, a youngster in a hurry, very much on a par with a three-day-old baby declining its pap and clamouring busily for beefsteak and bottled ale'.[1] Speculation over land was insane, houses were of brick, weatherboard, and wattle and daub, some hugging the footpath, others standing back from the street, amid trees and stumps in semi-rural retirement. No attempt had been made to macadamise the road surfaces, with gullies 8 feet (2.4 metres) deep and 15 feet (4.5 metres) wide excavated by the rains for drainage. The streets held few women and old men, but many young men—hirsute and swaggering, garbed in blue serge suits in lieu of coats, cabbage-tree hats, belts supporting leather tobacco pouches and in some few cases a pistol, and often breeches, boots and spurs.

The Koori in the area were the Wurundjeri people, who had occupied the Birrarung (Yarra River catchment) for more than 40,000 years.[2] They were in alliance with others collectively known as the Kulin people, and spoke the language Woiwurrung. The territory of this alliance extended from north of the Great Dividing Range, east to Mount Baw Baw, south to Mordialloc Creek and west to the Werribee River. Like their compatriots, the Wurundjeri had led a comfortable life fishing, hunting and gathering around what became Port Phillip Bay and the surrounding grasslands. They held their corroborees near the Yarra and Maribyrnong rivers. Some of their sacred sites were near what are now Burnley Park, Jolimont, Fitzroy Gardens and Fawkner Park.

With the beginnings of white settlement, the Indigenous people's peaceful existence ended. They were forcefully displaced in favour of English farms and sheep runs, and their numbers were quickly reduced by the multiple scourges of alcohol, venereal disease, small-pox, dysentery and heartbreak.

They tried to resist this encroachment. Two notable examples occurred in 1840 and 1842. The first was precipitated when settlers started a potato farm on Wurundjeri land at Warrandyte. Shots were fired by the settlers, and the Wurundjeri leader Jaga Jaga was captured. The second occurred when two Tasmanian Aboriginal people, Tunnerminnerwait and Maulboyheenner, who had been brought to Melbourne in 1839 by the 'Protector' of Aborigines, George Augustus Robinson, were involved in a brief guerilla war around Western Port. They were caught and publicly executed at the Queen Victoria Market in 1842.

There were other skirmishes, but the locals were no match for British infantry. Newcastle historian Professor Lyndall Ryan has developed a digital online mapping service showing over 150 massacres (where six or more Aboriginal people were killed) in Tasmania, Victoria, New South Wales and Queensland between 1788 and 1872.[3]

The white invasion of Victoria began in 1802, when a seaman and explorer, John Murray, dispatched from Sydney's Port Jackson to explore the southern part of the continent, entered Port Phillip Bay in the armed 60-tonne brigantine *Lady Nelson*. Murray was followed in January 1803 by Charles Grimes, deputy surveyor-general of New South Wales. Grimes entered the heads in *Cumberland*, a schooner built at Port Jackson in 1801, and landed at what is now Frankston. On his return to Sydney he recommended against a settlement, but Governor Philip Gidley King, fearing French occupation of Port Phillip, sought London's help in occupying the bay. Colonel David Collins was dispatched on HMS *Calcutta* from London with five officials, a detachment of marines and 307 convicts to establish a settlement. He landed at what became Sorrento on the Mornington Peninsula, but, finding no water, sailed on to Van Diemen's Land and established a settlement at what became Hobart.

The bay was originally dubbed Port King by John Murray in 1802, but Governor King overruled this presumption and renamed it Port Phillip in 1805 after Admiral Arthur Phillip, commander of the First Fleet. Nearly twenty years passed, with a gradual increase in European settlers—whalers, sealers, farmers, convicts. In 1824, the explorers Hamilton Hume and William Hovell came overland from Sydney, ending up at what became Corio Bay, a marine alcove on the western side of Port Phillip Bay. White settlement spread. In 1834, a Tasmanian grazier, Edward Henty, established a sheep run near Portland in western Victoria.

In 1835, John Batman, a farmer from northern Tasmania and partner in a business syndicate, came up the Yarra and pronounced that this would be the place for a village, declaring the area 'Batmania'. He signed a treaty with eight Wurundjeri elders for 600,000 acres (2400 square kilometres) in what became the city of Melbourne, and 100,000 acres (400 square kilometres) in Geelong. In exchange for the land, he gave the Wurundjeri 40 blankets, 30 axes, 100 knives, 50 pairs of scissors, 30 mirrors, 200 handkerchiefs, 100 pounds (45 kilograms) of flour and six shirts. It is doubtful the Indigenous residents knew what they were giving in exchange for this bounty, and they would have been extremely suspicious of Batman and his motives if they'd known of his slaughter of many of their brethren in preceding months and years in Tasmania while leading 'roving parties' to do them in. Another farmer, John Fawkner, had similar designs on land around the settlement.

In October 1835, the New South Wales government annulled Batman's treaty, restoring the lands he had obtained from the Wurundjeri elders to the Crown. But an official blind eye was cast at what was now trespass, and settlements were allowed to continue. In September 1836, Governor Sir Richard Bourke established the Port Phillip District of New South Wales and appointed Captain William Lonsdale as police magistrate and chief agent of the government. Lonsdale travelled to Port Phillip as a passenger on HMS *Rattlesnake*, an Atholl-class 28-gun sixth-rate corvette commanded by Captain William Hobson, who himself went on to become governor of New Zealand.

The settlement continued to grow without identity until 1837, when Governor Bourke finally gave it a formal name: Melbourne, after British prime minister William Lamb, 2nd Viscount Melbourne, friend and confidant of the young Queen Victoria.[4] In the same year, Robert Hoddle completed the first survey and a grid-patterned town plan. And in 1842, by Act 6 Victoria No. 7 of the Governor and Legislative Council of New South Wales, Melbourne became an official 'town'.

Matching the city's early growth was the dawning realisation that parts of the colony were rich in gold. The Polish explorer Paul Edmund de Strzelecki had reached Sydney from Europe in 1839, walked 11,000 kilometres to and fro across the country, and discovered gold in silicate near Hartley in New South Wales. In 1841, the Reverend WB Clarke found it at Cox's River on the road to Bathurst. More gold was discovered at Hill End. The New South Wales authorities suppressed the news, fearing an exodus of labourers and convicts from their jobs in Sydney. But when news came through of gold in California in 1848, they decided to release news of the gold in New South Wales to keep those affected by gold fever in their home country. More gold was discovered and, invoking a sixteenth-century lawsuit, *Queen Elizabeth v. The Earl of Northumberland*, the colonial government claimed all gold found to be the property of the Crown.

Of much greater consequence than these were discoveries of gold further south near Melbourne. In early 1849, Thomas 'Tommy' Chapman, a shepherd and former prison delinquent, claimed he'd found 38 ounces (1 kilogram) of gold on Glenmona, or Daisy Hill station, near the town of Amhurst, 160 kilometres north-west of Melbourne. The story goes that he clandestinely took his find to Melbourne and engaged the interest of three ex-convicts—the Collins Street jewellers and silversmiths Charles Bretani, Joseph Forrester and Alexandre Duchene. Not having a clue about the alluvial extraction of gold by sluicing water and dirt around in a dish, the trio travelled up to Daisy Hill and used sledgehammers to break quartz rock from the ground near Tommy's find, piled it into heaps and set it on fire to melt and extract the gold seams they could see in the quartz.[5] Other diggers used fire to ignite thick vegetation and expose geological formations, sometimes inadvertently creating disastrous bushfires in the hot, dry spring and summer scrub around Mount Macedon, Ballarat, Bendigo and Castlemaine. On 6 February 1851 these fires joined up in an enormous conflagration north-west of Melbourne that became known as Black Thursday. Five million hectares were burnt and twelve people died, along with one million sheep and thousands of cattle. In the evening, the glow of the fire was seen far out to sea, and cinders fell on ships in Port Phillip Bay. The colonial government promised a royal commission, but in the mayhem that followed the gold rush, that promise was quickly forgotten.

Chapman's 1849 find may have been kept under wraps, but it did not discourage other spruikers and chancers, such as Edward Hammond Hargraves, an English settler who had returned to New South Wales from the Californian goldfields in January 1851 with knowledge of the alluvial method of separating gold from mud using dish and cradle, from trumpeting their real and imagined gold finds in the bars and brothels of Sydney and Melbourne. Fevered rumours of alluvial gold nuggets created an exodus to the fields of Clunes, Buninyong, Fryer's Creek, Forest Creek, Campbell's Creek, Sailor's Gully and Cobbler's Gully—a spread of around 390 square kilometres at the foot of Mount Alexander, 100 kilometres north-west of Melbourne. By September 1851, 1000 men were digging there and at adjacent fields at Ballarat, Bendigo and Maryborough, and that number quickly grew to 2500.

One consequence of the rush was dislocation of Melbourne's law enforcement. The colony had a mere forty-four soldiers and was initially unable to get reinforcements from New South Wales or Tasmania. Thirty-three ships in Port Phillip Bay remained stranded in the absence of crews.

As easy pickings of alluvial nuggets on or near the surface were snapped up in 1851 and 1852, gold became more difficult to find.[6] Miners had to dig down to underground rivers and creeks buried by prehistoric lava flows. It became hard and dangerous work sinking shafts, shoring them up against collapse, bucketing out the water. The shafts became giant barometers: in gathering storms as air pressure fell, carbon dioxide would drift up from old watercourses like a poisonous mist. It became a lottery whether the miners sinking their shafts

The first gold escort against highwaymen,
William Street, Melbourne, 1852

would find their targets of gold buried by prehistoric lava flows, or miss the seam altogether. An Italian miner, Raffaello, wrote: 'This Balaarat, a nugget eldorado for the few, a ruinous field of hard labour for many, a profound ditch of Perdition for Body and Soul to all'.[7]

Many claims were abandoned and then taken over by a growing number of Chinese settlers, who were only allowed to dig where miners had left their claims. The Chinese, mainly a homogeneous Cantonese-speaking people from the thirteen counties around Guangzhou in Guangdong Province,[8] worked patiently and assiduously and uncovered more gold. To the fierce resentment of the former owners, the Chinese miners repatriated their riches home.

The white miners became angry. They scorned and resented the Chinese. The white miners themselves were bullied by the overseers and had no political rights, no vote, no way of getting the colonial authorities to address their grievances—especially the exorbitant fees they had to pay for mining. Inspired by the Chartist-influenced Ballarat Reform League,[9] a protest began against general government maladministration and injustice. The league called for manhood suffrage, abolition of the mining fee, the opening-up of the land to small farming settlements, and an end to government corruption.

In the winter of 1853, a peaceful agitation against the fees was held in Bendigo. Before he retired in May 1854, the lieutenant governor of the new colony of Victoria, Charles Joseph La Trobe, temporarily lowered the fee, but the miners remained unsatisfied. La Trobe was replaced by Captain Sir Charles Hotham, a competent administrator but an autocratic and unimaginative man who had little sympathy for miners' grievances. On the night of Sunday 3 December 1854, British troops attacked miners in their Ballarat redoubt called the Eureka Stockade, built by rebels led by an Irish engineer, Peter Lalor, over which flew the Southern Cross flag. Reputedly designed by Captain Henry Ross, a Canadian miner, the flag depicted a white cross joining five stars on a blue background: the cross represented unity and defiance, the blue background the colour of the miners' shirts. The fighting lasted less than an hour, but around thirty miners and five soldiers were killed. The troops tore down the stockade, set fire to tents and fired on unarmed miners nearby.

In response to the confrontation, the Victorian government reformed the goldfield laws. In the winter of 1855 it abolished the diggers' fees and introduced a £1 per annum fee entitling miners to work on the diggings, gave them a vote in parliament, and collected a standard fee of 2s 6d on each troy ounce of gold exported—a duty of around 3 per cent.

Meanwhile, the hunt for gold went further afield. Deposits were found in north-eastern Victoria at Chiltern and Beechworth, and in the Gippsland mountains at Omeo and Woods Point. Prospectors went upstream along the spurs, deep gullies and ridges of the Goulburn and Ovens rivers and across to Walhalla, now a semi-ghost town with an old rotunda for a long-departed brass band, in the fastness of a remote walled valley. Walhalla's gold rush population was 4000 but in the 1960s, when I visited it as a boy with my parents, it had twenty permanent residents and was a place of echoes and fascination for weekend tourists from Melbourne eager to share the romance of gold rush days.

As historian Geoffrey Blainey has written, no other country in the world was so quickly transformed by minerals, especially gold, and especially in Victoria. A comparison between the value of gold extracted from Victoria and New South Wales is reflected in the size of the state buildings and respective art collections of Melbourne and Sydney. Melbourne's buildings are grand and stately, especially its parliament house, town hall, treasury and public hospitals; Sydney's are smaller and less pretentious. Melbourne still calls its art gallery the National Gallery of Victoria, reflecting the wealth of its collection and bequests originally founded on gold. But the populations of both colonies trebled in the first twelve years of the gold discovery. Gold sales stimulated agriculture as well as factories and workshops in the cities. The goldfields themselves became a vast market for timber, candles, boilers, engines, pumps. For the time of the rush, Australia exported to the mother country and elsewhere a greater value in gold than wool.[10]

Edward William Cole landed in the middle of this Victorian maelstrom in Melbourne around the end of October 1852, a year after the frenzy had begun. In a double coincidence, his actual point of disembarkation in Melbourne was Cole's Wharf (no relation), at the mouth of the muddy Yarra River and not far from where his alleged father, Amos Cole, had landed after being transported from England in 1836.

Melbourne's population was approximately 76,000, a number that kept growing unevenly as the hundreds of new arrivals pouring off the ships were offset by hundreds more deserting their jobs and heading for the goldfields. Within a year the population had doubled, and by 1857 it had risen to 200,000. The town was a dusty, fly-blown and toxic place with no sewerage or piped water. Hotels had been thrown up on the four corners of most intersections to sell beer to thirsty settlers and rent them rooms at astronomical prices. Rooms were going for £3 a week upwards, excluding washing, which varied from sixpence to one shilling per dozen items. In the dining room a bowl of soup cost 1s 6d, a glass of ale 6d, pork or mutton chops 3s 6d, cauliflower 1s, potatoes 6d. Lunch was an expensive meal, beyond the reach of most new arrivals. Those without friends or contacts in the hotel trade crowded into tents along the banks of the Yarra, swimming, washing and defecating into the river's already turgid waters. If they couldn't find a tent to share, they slept in doorways, on wharves or under trees. Dysentery and other enteric diseases were rife.[11]

Edward had gained a friend on the *Sebim*: another Englishman, Henry Smith. The pair milled around the Melbourne crowds trying to find their land legs and get their bearings. They had sufficient funds to pay the inflated price of at least one night's accommodation, and successfully bargained for a room at Hockin's Hotel on the corner of Elizabeth and La Trobe streets. Over the next few days they ditched their lice-infested clothes in favour of mining gear, including moleskin trousers, stout boots and cabbage-tree hats. These were plaited from the broad leaves of the *Livistona australis,* or cabbage-tree palm. The hat became distinctively Australian, ideal for keeping the burning sun off the heads of pale new settlers. Edward and Henry bought fly nets, blankets, and a rifle and ammunition for protection against real and imagined robbers, but not heavy items such as picks, shovels or sluicing dishes, which they calculated they could buy at the diggings.

Wishing to save their not very substantial funds for sustenance and lodgings on the fields, the two men decided to walk the 130 kilometres to Forest Creek. They set off north up

"Diggers on road to Bendigo.

OPPOSITE ABOVE Diggers on their way to the goldfields, 1869
OPPOSITE BELOW Sluicing for gold, 1864
RIGHT Lola Montez, whose 'spider dance' set the miners aflame

Elizabeth Street but their muscles were weak after the long sea voyage from South Africa, and they managed only about 10 kilometres the first day, stopping at a timber-frame hostelry called the Bridge Inn, Tulip Wright's pub (perhaps in the vicinity of Essendon). But they were young and their fitness soon returned, and on the second day they stepped up the pace to walk 20 kilometres, pausing overnight at a pub hastily thrown up at a place called Digger's Rest. The third night they reached Jackson's Creek on the edge of Gisborne. They kept going over the next few days through hills and rough country, passing beneath Mount Macedon and the mystic shadow of Hanging Rock, through sparse settlements at what are now towns called Woodend, Kyneton, Taradale and Elphinstone. After ten days, in November or December 1852, they reached their goal of Forest Creek, later renamed Castlemaine.

It was the beginning of summer. What they found was a hot and dry expanse of mullocky clay and rocks, stripped of trees by axe and fire, littered with huts and tents—a human ant colony. The air was blue with wood smoke, fragrant with the smell of damper, frying meat and onions, and noisy with the sound of barking dogs. The nights were accompanied by singing—some of it extraordinarily harmonious from Welsh miners—punctuated by the occasional drunken brawl or the discharge of a rifle. There were few women around, but the male community was on one spectacular occasion treated to the appearance of Lola Montez. Otherwise known as Marie Dolores Eliza Rosanna Gilbert, Countess of Landsfeld, Lola was an Irish dancer and actress, and one-time courtesan and mistress of King Ludwig of Bavaria (not Ludwig II, the 'mad' King of Bavaria, but his predecessor Ludwig I). Just arrived from Melbourne, she performed her notorious 'spider dance' one Saturday night at the local hall, reportedly without undergarments. In general, the miners observed the Sabbath as a time of recovery, rest and repair after six days of relentless labour. They especially needed the break after the stimulation and excitement of Lola's spider dance quite wore them out.

Probably well before Lola's appearance, but the dates are uncertain, Edward and Henry bought miners' licences for 30 shillings each from the local officials, many of whom were standover merchants, foul-mouthed hoodlums recently released from convict bondage in Van Diemen's Land. They located their claim, which was disappointingly far from a creek in which to sluice their pans for gold. Undaunted, they bought the essentials for mining: picks, shovels, a puddling dish, a barrow, some hand tools, and a tent for accommodation.

Not all the miners were unfriendly. Edward and Henry weregood-naturedly invited to join a shooting party, but Edward was upset when a miner shot a kangaroo as it squatted by a tree looking quietly curious. The death of such a gentle creature left a lasting impression on him.

Kangaroo hunting, 1863

But he had to eat, and the meat, although tough, was fresh and wonderful in comparison with the flyblown sides of beef and mutton hanging outside butchers' tents.

In truth, like the more crowded parts of Melbourne, Forest Creek was an unsanitary place. Drinking water was found only in a few wells, or carted in from distant creeks through the summer heat. Toilets were randomly dug holes surrounded by canvas flaps. The diggings were a breeding ground for enteric diseases such as typhoid and dysentery (the latter also known as 'colonial fever'). Governor La Trobe had forbidden drinking alcohol, but sly grog was available throughout the area.

The work was backbreaking and the rewards sparse—a few grains of gold at the end of each long hot day, sometimes not even that. Within weeks, Henry succumbed to a bout of colonial fever, not correctly diagnosed as typhoid until the 1870s. Edward found a peddler dispensing a nostrum called Holloway's Pills, promoted as a cure not only for stomach complaints but for gout, rheumatism, incontinence, an impure liver and fevered blood. Unsurprisingly, it did not work on Henry, who got progressively weaker and then died from dehydration after several days.

Edward wanted to tell the authorities of Henry's death but his neighbours talked him out of it, saying they'd probably accuse him of causing it and demand all kinds of extortionate fees for a death certificate and Henry's burial. Instead, late at night as the digging grounds slept, a group of them helped Edward carry Henry's body up a nearby hill, where they dug a shallow grave and buried him under loose clay to stop the dingoes getting at his remains. This may have been at what was locally known as the Pennyweight Flat Cemetery, also called the Forest Creek, Wesley Hill or Children's Cemetery, but no records exist, and Henry's death pre-dates official records.[12] According to Cole Turnley, Edward quietly reflected through that star-filled night:

> It always appeared to me that there must be in this vast, illimitable, and beautiful universe, myriads of beings, superior to our weak mortal selves, and at the head of all and over all, an immortal Being of infinite perfections, which thinking men in all countries and ages have called GOD. And shall not we, immortal souls, increase in knowledge and wisdom, and as the ages roll on, more and more perceive and understand this mighty universe and its Author? I firmly believe we shall, and as yet we are only beginning to live and think and understand and appreciate.[13]

Edward was now twenty-one, alone and untutored in bush survival, but not unnecessarily discouraged. He had survived as a peddler on the streets of London, and beneath a quiet exterior was tough, and agile in thought and movement. Around him, a few miners still

Forest Creek, Mt Alexander, 1852

occasionally made spectacular strikes, but he observed that most worked long and cruel hours for little if any reward. Easy pickings of alluvial gold on or near the surface were long gone, but, like habitual gamblers, the rank and file still hoped for the great strike. Edward noticed that throughout the diggings at Castlemaine, Campbell's Creek and Maryborough, those who continued to make money were the army of vendors who supplied food, mining equipment, tents and clothing that they had hauled in bullock drays up from Melbourne. Maybe he could make some money by joining them and supplying a commodity the miners desperately needed: clean drinking water. And why not make it palatable by selling it as lemonade?

So Edward sold his and Henry's claim to some new arrivals, and with his dwindling supply of money bought at extortionate cost a big iron cauldron, a hessian bag of sugar, a case of lemons and a dozen shiny new pannikins. He hammered and sawed planks together into a long wooden table from which to serve his cordial. He boiled water in the cauldron and mixed it with sugar and lemon juice and, as it cooled, lined it up with his pannikins on the table. He acquired the largest, blackest iron frying pan his money could buy, wrote on it in whitewash the legend 'Cole's Cordial', nailed it to a nearby gum tree at the diggings in Maryborough, and began his trade. He wrote to his mother: 'The diggers come back day by day and many say it was the nicest they had tasted, and it is selling even better than I had hoped.'[14]

Edward made some money, but demand for his cordial slackened during 1853 as several good wells were sunk at the diggings and more clean water became available. Timber houses were also being built with their own water tanks. It was time to move on. He noted that land was selling at £10 to £20 a square foot on a rising market. On top of his original capital he had 'inherited' around £100 from Henry Smith, which together with his takings from cordial gave him in excess of £1000 by the end of 1853. This enabled him to buy five town lots in a government sale in Forest Creek in early 1854. He thought that with rapidly rising real estate prices, he could build on his blocks and make a profit when he sold them, or he could sell three of them and with the additional capital build brick houses on the other two.

What he did not foresee, however, was an unanticipated fall in the gold price in 1854, a resultant drop-off in jobs in the larger diggings now employing labour, and the culmination of digger unrest in December of that year at the Eureka Stockade in Ballarat. He pressed on against the bad economic news, using the proceeds of selling the three blocks to purchase bricks and other building materials. Ever optimistic, he pitched a tent on the site of his first brick house and painstakingly laid bricks with mortar, using a line of string to keep them straight. (Spirit levels had been in use in Europe since the eighteenth century, but history does not relate whether they had yet found their way to the goldfields.) Edward finished his house, neat and square, at the end of the year. He was convinced conditions would improve, and persuaded his bank manager to advance him a loan to build another brick house and shop on his second block. But he ran out of money, could not convince the bank to lend him more, and ended up being foreclosed on his first house. According to Turnley, he managed to hold on to his partially completed brick shop but was now completely broke.

Records at the Castlemaine Historical Society are disappointing in some respects. They have nothing about Edward's mining activities, stating that official records only exist where a person sent gold by escort or deposited it in the Gold Office. Nor do records exist of a mining licence issued to Edward or to Henry Smith. No duplicates of such licences were ever held in Castlemaine, and paper records of those years had a very limited shelf life and have likely disappeared. The society does not have records of Edward's lemonade-selling activities as these pre-dated the start of the local newspaper, in which they would surely have been reported.

In respect of Edward's land holdings, however, the society holds some documents of resounding authenticity.

Victoria
Town Lot
Grantee Edwd Wm Cole
Date 11 June 1853

To all to whom these Presents shall come, Greetings:-

Whereas in conformity with the Laws now in force for the Sale of Crown Lands in our Colony of Victoria, and Our Royal Instructions under Our Signet and Sign Manual, issued in pursuance thereof,

Edward William Cole of Forest Creek has become the Purchaser of the Allotment or Parcel of Land hereinafter described for the Sum of Twenty four pounds Sterling; Now Know Ye, That, for and in consideration of the Said Sum for and on Our behalf, well and truly paid into the Colonial Treasury of Our said Colony, before these Presents are issued, And in further consideration of the Quit-Rent hereinafter reserved, WE HAVE GRANTED and for Us, Our Heirs and Successors, DO HEREBY GRANT unto the said Edward William Cole his Heirs and Assigns, Subject to the several and respective Reservations hereinafter mentioned, ALL THAT Allotment or Parcel of Land in Our said Colony contained by Admeasurement One Rood be the same more or less situated in the County of Talbot, Parish of Castlemaine being Allotment No. Three of section eleven Township of Castlemaine bounded on the North by Allotment Four being a line bearing West two chains etc., etc.

In its records of the Castlemaine Municipal Council, the Historical Society has further evidence of Edward's holdings. The council held its first meeting in 1856 and its rate notices issued that year record that Edward owned blocks in Barker Street, including a 'ruinous' weatherboard slab cottage on part of Allotment 2. He appears to have owned two (part)

A fist fight on the goldfields, 1852

allotments in Section 11 of a subdivision that encompassed Barker Street. Both, however, were land only, with no improvements. In 1860, he still owned land but had not paid rates on it. He apparently continued to hold some land in Castlemaine until at least 1904, when conversion documents from the old law title system transferred to the Torrens title system (still in force). In that year, Edward, an absentee landowner now back in Melbourne, apparently realised £350 for one block in Barker Street.

Undaunted by the mess surrounding his land dealings, Edward kept looking for ways to make a living in Castlemaine. He was having a rough time, being frequently prostrated by illness. Undaunted, he made occasional but unprofitable forays to new diggings, including to one at Back Creek in Maryborough. He worked sporadically as a carpenter, and attempted to develop a fruit and vegetable round. According to an advertisement in the *Mount Alexander Mail* of 18 June 1860, he also attempted to start a sausage business.

Sausage House
Opposite Talbot Drug Store
Hargreave Street
The undersigned having for some time been impressed with the fact of the toughness and tastelessness of Castlemaine sausages, begs to inform the public that he has commenced to manufacture them from prime meat alone, and trusts by strict attention and care to merit their support.
Beef sausages 9d per pound
Pork ditto 1s 6d per pound.
NO CREDIT
E W Cole

Castlemaine Municipal Council accepted Edward's tender for £200 to light the city's lamps for one year, and to paint the lampposts for a further £15.[15] His more adventurous imaginings included setting up factories in Castlemaine, Bendigo and Ballarat to make moleskin trousers for sale to diggers, but he was never able to accumulate sufficient capital. So he returned to his lemonade business—but with a twist. Edward was a teetotaller and he decided to make cider, but not of the alcoholic sort:

Millions of gallons of cider have been made in the world without a single apple being used! Large quantities of it were sold on the goldfields. A man who had done well at selling it offered me his recipe for £30. I experimented with dried apples and a number of other things, but could not get the correct thing …

'Well,' I thought, 'tartaric or citric acid and cane sugar will do; water can be got anywhere, burnt sugar will give a splendid colour.'

I tried many things to get the flavour, but could not succeed until one day I asked a chemist, 'Have you got anything that will give or make the flavour of apples?'

He said 'I have the essence of Ripstone Pippin; will that do?'

I cried, 'Eureka! My fortune is made!', and I took the essence home, adding it to the mixture, and sold many thousands of gallons of beautifully flavoured and coloured cider.

Now, this manufactured cider, artificial as it is, is generally tastier and healthier than the real cider, which through its fermentation contains alcohol. In the hot summer of 1857, at the Havelock diggings' rush, I sold 800 gallons [3600 litres] in eight days of this and a similar mixture, under an old gum tree, and the thirsty diggers were glad to get it.[16]

As cooler weather coincided with the abatement of the Havelock rush, Edward's cider business declined, but he had accumulated enough money to complete his brick shop and dwelling on Barker Street. According to Turnley, he rented it to a butcher, Robert Fisher, who lived in it rent free while he helped Edward finish it, and then at a very modest rent thereafter in anticipation of Edward leaving Castlemaine.

Claims of some of Edward's other activities must be treated with caution. Memories can be defective. A view held by some early denizens of Castlemaine was that Mr EW Cole of the Bourke Street arcade had conducted a stationery business in Castlemaine 'in the early days'. Mr R Thimbleby, an old resident, had unhesitatingly declared that Edward kept a bookshop on the site where Messrs Tonks Bros now carried on business in Barker Street just north of Templeton Street (Section 11 of the subdivision plan). Another of the town's oldest residents, Mr HNL Kentish, Clerk of Courts in the 1850s, said just as unhesitatingly that Mr Cole's shop was on the site of Mr W Wilson's ironmongery in Barker Street, south of Lyttleton Street (a Section 15 allotment). When questioned regarding the inconsistency, both gentlemen became choleric and each ridiculed the other. Thimbleby was most emphatic about the Tonks Bros site, stating that he had frequently purchased books and papers from the shop and minutely describing it, even to the kind of signboard Edward had installed. With increasing acerbity, Kentish declared Thimbleby an idiot and asserted that he had purchased stationery every week from Edward's shop, frequently chatted to Mr Cole, and procured books from his lending library. The researcher was in a quandary, and sought clarification from Edward himself in Melbourne, who stated categorically that he had never kept a shop in Castlemaine.[17]

Some old-timers have strong if incorrect memories, but perhaps there is a connection, however tenuous, between the recollections of Mr Thimbleby and Mr Kentish and Edward's bookstore. The fact is that Edward, now a young man in his twenties, was fascinated with technology, particularly steam engines, railways, printing and the electric telegraph. He had joined a discussion group in Castlemaine headed by Mr RT Vale, a bookseller and one of the founders of the local mechanics' institute, later a politician in Victoria. A colleague of Vale was Charles Glass, another bookseller. The two old gentlemen could have confused Vale's and Glass's activities with Edward's.

At any rate, Edward's discussion group debated many issues of the time, including social improvements such as Victoria's new eight-hour day. Race issues were also discussed, including the growing public antagonism to the Chinese miners who had taken over abandoned claims on the goldfields and were regarded by many as 'soulless heathens' who deserved whatever ill will other settlers felt towards them. Edward apparently argued vociferously against such prejudices, asserting that the Chinese were human beings like the rest of Castlemaine's society and deserved compassion and friendship. (His strong conviction found amplification in his later written objections to Australia's restricted immigration law, one of the first pieces of legislation passed by the newly established federal parliament in Melbourne in 1901 when popular anti-Chinese sentiment, spurred on by the Boxer Rebellion, was at its height. Fancy those pagan Chinese barbarians roaming the countryside slaughtering Christians!)

It was now 1861 and Edward had struggled to survive in Castlemaine for nine years, with varying degrees of success. He was still looking for a lasting job prospect, a project not dependent on seasonal vagaries or the absence of potable water in the goldfields, that might reliably make him some money. The opportunity came when he met George Burnell, a bearded young man with deeply held religious views whose father was an elder of the Congregational Church in Adelaide.[18] Like Edward, George had been lured to the goldfields to make some easy money, but, also like Edward, he had not succeeded. Instead, with a wife and two small children to support, George lived in a shack made from beaten-flat kerosene tins and eked out an existence driving a water cart, collecting firewood, and managing a hay and corn store a kilometre or so out of Castlemaine.

Edward's initial connection with George was at a meeting at the mechanics' institute, during which the two had argued about the Bible. George argued passionately that every word of it was literally true; Edward argued with equal passion that it was not. Edward was attracted to George over more than theological disagreement: he was also fascinated by George's grasp of a new technique for recording what people said at the same speed at which they said it. It was known as Pitman's shorthand. What a boon this would be for officials

George Burnell, a pedantic Christian, was Cole's fellow crewmate on their trip down the Murray

gathering evidence, or court or parliamentary reporting, or recording a public speech. Edward persuaded George to teach him the skill.

The preoccupations of the two men changed one morning when a traveller in a spring trap came to town. Rejoicing in the name Golightly, the man carried with him a strange and fantastic machine: a camera. Setting it up on a tripod and hiding it from view with a black cloth, Mr Golightly would point his lens at men and women he had persuaded to be photographed. They would become rigid and unsmiling before his camera but were invariably awestruck by the result: black-and-white photographs produced from beneath the voluminous folds of the black cloth that had faithfully recorded their faces, their clothes, their stature and mien in a way that even the most accomplished artist could not hope to achieve over many days of sittings.

Golightly persuaded George that this was the coming thing and a lot of money could be made from such a lucrative profession. George was hooked and so was Edward. They quickly decided to become partners, and between them bought Golightly's trap, his horse, and a second camera and tripod that he just happened to be carrying with him. It was similar to one developed in 1850 by the English sculptor Frederick Scott Archer, an improvement of a camera invented in the 1830s by another Englishman, William Henry Fox Talbot. Talbot impregnated paper with light-sensitive silver nitrate and then developed the exposed image in a solution of gallic acid and silver nitrate and fixed it with hypo (sodium thiosulphate). The negative that resulted could be used to make any number of positives simply by shining light through it onto light-sensitive paper. Archer improved this process by forming the image on a glass plate coated with an emulsion of silver iodide mixed with a viscous substance called collodion. Exposure time was cut to as little as half a second, although the plate had to be used wet and then developed instantly. It was a messy process that stained clothes and hands, but it was effective.[19]

Edward and George's camera was also equipped to take stereoscopic images, which were sometimes referred to as 'solid pictures'. They had a three-dimensional effect that, when viewed through a stereoscope, gave the viewer a sense of actually being present at the scene depicted.

Where to start their exciting new business? By persuading publicans of the numerous drinking establishments in and around Castlemaine to let them take photographs of themselves standing proudly before their hotels—a compelling talking point for drinkers if put up behind the bar. The publicans were less enthusiastic when it became clear that neither George nor Edward would themselves purchase even one cleansing ale, but the two made a few pounds out of it. They made further profit by persuading town locals and members of the neighbourhood squattocracy to have photographs taken of themselves and their families. At least one matron objected, however, and would not pay the requested fee, claiming Edward and George were a pair of crooks who kept likenesses of their subjects under the black cloth and each time found one that looked like the person being photographed.

After exhausting the pickings around Castlemaine, Edward and George decided to take their business elsewhere. George persuaded his wife and children that his absence would be rewarded by income and that he would come back eventually to collect them with sufficient funds to pay for their return to Adelaide. So with a new horse, and a logo on their canvas-covered trap proclaiming, 'Cole and Burnell, photographic artists, portraits and likenesses taken', they bravely headed north-east up a bush track towards Albury.

4
VOYAGE DOWN
THE MURRAY

The rowing boat used on the Cole–Burnell expedition down the Murray from Echuca to Goolwa in 1862

In 2019, one of the shortest routes from Castlemaine to Albury was up the Midland Highway to Shepparton, east across to Benalla on the A300, then up the Hume to Wodonga and Albury—a distance of 326 kilometres. It took me three quiet and restful hours in an air-conditioned and automatic SUV, through country towns and pleasant, undulating grazing country and vineyards, with rest stops along the way.

In the year 1861, 29-year-old Edward Cole and his partner George Burnell, 32, took considerably longer in their spring trap with one horse. There were few settlements, no sealed roads, no convenience stores or motels, and no rest stops with drinking water or toilets. They traversed rutted dirt tracks through flat dry country barely known to European settlers, camping where they could find the shelter of trees, or beside a stream. As well as their precious camera, tripod, hood and associated bottled chemicals, they carried basic pioneering supplies—flour, tea, salt, sugar, perhaps some jam as a treat, with a billy and maybe a flat piece of heavy-gauge iron to cook their damper over a camp fire—and forage for the horse and a spade to bury their waste. Precisely when they left Castlemaine is not clear, but they must have reached Albury around June 1861, in time to backtrack west to reach Echuca before the end of the year.

Albury was a settlement on the Murray, Australia's longest river. Hamilton Hume and William Hovell had been the first European explorers to discover the river, in 1824, when Hume named it after his father, Andrew Hamilton Hume, who came to Australia in charge of convicts in 1790 and was later to become a farmer at Appin, west of Wollongong. In 1830 Captain Charles Sturt renamed it after the British secretary of state for war and the colonies, Sir George Murray.

By 1861, Albury had grown from a likely cattle crossing into a sizeable town. It had stores and market gardens, several pubs, a flour mill, a primary school, a courthouse and a jail.

The spring trap used by Cole and Burnell on their photographic safari from Castlemaine to Echuca via Albury in 1861

Since 1855, it had been connected by paddle-steamer to towns stretching west as far as Goolwa in South Australia. The Union Bridge had just been constructed across the Murray to connect Albury to Wodonga on the Victorian side of the border. Something about the town and its environment must have strongly impressed Edward, because later in the century he became an enthusiastic advocate for its suitability as the nation's capital:

> The site is the most beautiful in Australasia. Albury, the New South Wales town, and Wodonga, the Victorian town, with the river running between them, lie on a plain a few miles wide, surrounded by hills in the shape of an amphitheatre, forming, as it were, a little world of itself. The space between the present towns, with its fertile soil, its river and lagoons, could by the hand of man be made into a Federal park similar to, and as beautiful as, the famous botanic gardens of Kandy; whilst the higher, yet fertile, ground, with gently rising hills all around, would furnish thousands of beautiful sites for gardens and residences.[1]

Edward was not alone. Other advocates of Albury included the member for Sydney in the New South Wales Legislature, Henry Parkes. A great boost was given to Albury's claim in

1876 when the governors of New South Wales and Victoria, Sir Hercules Robinson and Sir George Bowen, visited the town and symbolically walked together across the Union Bridge. In January 1891 locals formed a Federal Capital Association, and in 1899 a commission was granted to Alexander Oliver, president of the New South Wales Land Appeal Court, to investigate sites presented by different interest groups for the new capital city. Over the next five years he examined twenty-three possibilities and held inquiries at fourteen of them. Debate continued through Federation in 1901, with no decision among the dozen or so sites still in contention. Albury's chances suffered a blow in February 1902 when a delegation of senators from the new federal parliament in Melbourne visited the town. The weather, always trying at that time of year, was extremely hot and blustery, and senators were heard to remark that it was a 'nice position for a federal cemetery' and 'hot as a stokehole'.[2] (The final decision to build the national capital on pasture land at Yass–Canberra, encompassing Lake George, was taken in 1908. Little did those making the choice realise that Canberra could get as hot as Albury in summer.)

Did Edward and George's 1861 visit make a mark on Albury? Cole Turnley claimed they took scenic photographs along the riverbanks and pinned them on the side of their cart, resulting in several profitable commissions.[3] But neither the Albury and District Historical Society nor the Murray Art Museum has records of their stay. Nor do photographs attributed to them exist in the well-stocked municipal archives.

The Riverina was now a vast grain, cattle and sheep run, and Echuca and Moama were the closest points on the Murray for its produce to be assembled and sent on to Melbourne—a much closer and more convenient maritime port than distant Sydney. Travel-stained and weary, Edward and George arrived from Albury in this rambunctious and alcohol-sodden settlement in December 1861. Its pubs, cafes, music halls and brothels held no attraction for the earnest young men, whose idea of a stimulating evening was to debate whether the Bible was literally true or not (Edward thought not) over a pot of tea. And the purpose of their arrival was not to explore Echuca, but to secure passage on a paddle-steamer and make their way westward towards Adelaide, where George would assess prospects for setting up a photography business before committing his family in Castlemaine to a permanent move back to Adelaide.

On seeking bookings at the riverfront, they were told that at the end of a long, dry spring the river was too low for ferries. They were urged to drive their trap on to Wentworth, a town 450 kilometres further west at the confluence of the Murray and Darling rivers, where there was plenty of water and steamers could navigate all year round.

[*Continues on page 63*]

Echuca depicted in 1865

ECHUCA

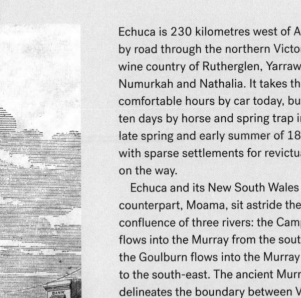

Echuca is 230 kilometres west of Albury by road through the northern Victorian wine country of Rutherglen, Yarrawonga, Numurkah and Nathalia. It takes three comfortable hours by car today, but it was ten days by horse and spring trap in the late spring and early summer of 1861, with sparse settlements for revictualling on the way.

Echuca and its New South Wales counterpart, Moama, sit astride the confluence of three rivers: the Campaspe flows into the Murray from the south, and the Goulburn flows into the Murray slightly to the south-east. The ancient Murray delineates the boundary between Victoria and New South Wales, the actual border being on the southern, Victorian bank. The region was home to thousands of generations of original settlers, a dignified and cautious people sympathetically and knowledgeably observed in 1841 by Edward Micklethwaite Curr in his *Recollections of Squatting in Victoria, Then Called the Port Phillip District (from 1841 to 1851)*, first published by George Robertson in 1883 and later abridged and reprinted in 1965. Curr identified many sub-tribes in the area at the time, all part of two larger groups: the Wongatpan and Towroonban, collectively known as the Bangerang.[4] They had intimate knowledge of the rivers that provided their sustenance, diving for fish and hunting for ducks in the waters beneath the magnificent river red gum forests, floating on bark canoes with fires kept burning on a hearth of wet clay in the bows both to grill freshly caught fish and for warmth. Opossums, kangaroos, wombats and emus provided additional protein, while yams and native carrots were their vegetables. A mild climate and abundant food meant the Murray natives enjoyed a life of comparative ease.[5]

As happened throughout Australia, the lives of the original inhabitants were shattered by the coming of white people and their alcohol and alien diseases, and by the seizure of hunting grounds and the destruction of sacred and ceremonial places. As Curr observed:

> There was, however, no doubt, a tendency to disease consequent on the partial abandonment of their traditional ways of life for others less healthy, for, after my settlement in their country, the Bangerang gave up in great measure their wholesome and exhilarating practices of hunting and fishing, and took to hanging about our huts in a miserable objectless frame of mind and underfed condition, begging and doing trifling services of any sort. To this course they were mainly led by their desire to obtain from the newcomers various commodities, such as iron tomahawks, tobacco, and especially flour, mutton, sugar and other articles of food for which they quickly acquired a keen relish, and preferred to the game, fish and roots on which they and their ancestors had subsisted.[6]

Passing through the area for a second time in 1838, the explorer Charles Sturt noted of the Indigenous inhabitants:

> Many were pitted as if by smallpox. The disease, which was raging among them on the Darling in 1828 and the Murray in 1829 must have committed dreadful havoc, since on this journey I did not see hundreds to the thousands I had formerly met. I could not contemplate without a feeling of melancholy the remnant of these unfortunate people. A new era was dawning, and a fearful change was coming upon them, whether for good or evil God only knows.[7]

Following repeated unequal clashes with pastoralists—muskets and swivel guns against spears—the Bangerang were forced out of the settlement of Echuca by the late 1850s to subsist as best they could on its fringes with little or no recognition. Meanwhile, overland droving of cattle destined for meat-hungry southern and western markets passed through Echuca in increasing numbers. Among the early drovers were Charles Bonney and Joseph Hawdon, the pioneers in 1838 of a safe stock route from the Riverina to Adelaide. They were closely followed by Sturt, who left Sydney on his second major expedition in April 1838 with 400 head of cattle.

Two entrepreneurs stand out as early developers of Echuca and Moama.

James Maiden was convicted at the Lancaster Assizes on 8 March 1834 of theft: he did 'feloniously and burglariously (sic) steal take and carry away' silverware from a private house—sugar tongs, teaspoons, castor tops and a mustard pot to the value of nine shillings—plus two candles, each worth a penny. King William IV 'was pleased to extend His Royal Mercy' and commuted the sentence to seven years' transportation to New South Wales. Maiden sailed on the *Bengal Merchant*, arriving in Sydney on 30 January 1835.[8] A compact, energetic man, he became a stockman after gaining his ticket of leave, and built a punt on Long Swamp Run on the Goulburn River. In 1845, he installed a larger punt on the Murray at Moama. With takings from ferrying cattle, he built a pub, the Junction Inn, which was licensed in July 1846 and became a changing station for a coach service between Deniliquin and Bendigo. He also acquired a postal service and several properties. The gold rush at Bendigo, Ballarat and Castlemaine dramatically increased the demand for meat, and on acquiring an abattoir, Maiden became the largest carcass butcher in the district. By 1855 he had bought seventeen properties and was widely regarded as a very wealthy man, the 'owner' of Moama. As a cattle market, Moama became known as the Chicago of Australia (Chicago being the notorious centre of the US meat trade at the time).

Across the border in Echuca, similar developments were taking place through the energy of Henry Hopwood. Born in Bolton, Lancashire in 1813, he was transported to Van Diemen's Land in 1834 for receiving a bolt of stolen silk. He was literate and charming, with much energy and a lively mind, and amassed a fortune by developing a monopoly of punts and bridges on all river crossings in and out of Echuca. In April 1853, Hopwood was granted a licence to occupy part of Wharparilla Run, known as Junction Paddock, lying east of the Murray-Campaspe Junction; today it is Echuca's Victoria Park. In 1858 he built the Bridge Hotel, described by Helen Coulson as the jewel in his crown.[9] At the time of writing, the building still stands.

Instead, they embraced a radical change of plan. At the waterfront they exchanged their horse and trap for a boat owned by a local lounger: an ungainly, heavy, 18-foot (5.5-metre) craft made from planks of river red gum. They knocked up foot lockers on either side of the boat, a navigating table up front, and a canopy over the top, and transferred in their camera, tripod, bottles of chemicals, trays and boxed sheets of glass; the boat would double as a camp kitchen and darkroom. They augmented their remaining stores from the trap with salted beef, flour and vegetables bought locally. They faced a voyage of just under 1700 kilometres to the entrance to Lake Alexandrina, which they estimated would take them until around the middle of 1862, about six months. In fact, it took them four months.

Others had navigated parts of the Murray before them. The most extensive exploration had been conducted by Sturt, who in 1830 had solved the mystery of where the west-flowing Murray–Darling river system ended up. Did it go into a vast inland lake, or end up in the sea? Using a whaleboat with convict oarsmen, he travelled all the way to Lake Alexandrina in South Australia and was disappointed to find not a navigable outlet to the Southern Ocean but a vast freshwater lagoon, which was separated from the Southern Ocean by sandbars. He and his party then faced the unenviable task of rowing back up the river in summer heat against the current. They made it as far as Narrandera before abandoning the river and heading overland back to Sydney.

In 1849 Daniel Bunce, an English-born botanist and nurseryman, travelled down the Murray Valley from north of Melbourne to Adelaide, and in 1853 Baron Sir Ferdinand Jakob Heinrich von Mueller, an eminent pharmacist and botanist, collected seeds and other specimens from the river country around Mildura for the herbarium and botanical gardens he was establishing in Melbourne. Edward Cole later sent von Mueller seeds of plants he had collected along the Murray, some of which the latter planted when he was director of Melbourne's Botanic Gardens, a position he held until 1873 when he was replaced by the horticulturalist William Robert Guilfoyle.

In 1857, the naturalists William Blandowski and Gerard Krefft led an expedition financed by the Victorian colonial government to explore the river system and its flora around Mildura. They established a semi-permanent camp below the cliffs of present-day Merbein, and assisted by Yaree Aboriginal residents at the Yelta Mission Station, collected many botanical and zoological specimens. Both were competent artists, and they produced watercolours and sketches of Aboriginal people, fauna and environs around Merbein. Another botanist, John Dallachy, curator of Melbourne's Botanic Gardens from 1849 to 1857 (preceding Mueller's appointment as director in 1857), undertook an expedition between Wentworth and Mount Murchison on the Darling River in 1858, resulting in a wealth of botanical specimens.[10]

Less scientifically minded adventurers had spilled out from abandoned diggings on the goldfields of Ballarat, Bendigo and Castlemaine and rowed along parts of the Murray. But none of these had undertaken a photographic survey as Edward and George were contemplating. Blandowski and Krefft had been equipped with photographic equipment, but its technical demands had defeated them and they did not use it, relying instead on their paintbrushes and skills as artists.

Edward and George departed Echuca on New Year's Day, 1862. Waved off by locals from the wharf, they faced the river without even a shakedown cruise. They had a pair of oars for propulsion and a long pole to fend things off, but neither of them could handle these with any confidence: they either dipped their oars too deeply or feathered them, catching air and falling flat on their backs. They nearly turned the boat over when they changed positions, and got caught in snags, which proliferated in the river, or drifted aimlessly from one bank to the other. After a few days of travail, it occurred to them to go with the flow, to drift with the current, simply keeping the boat in the centre of the stream by using one oar as a rudder. At Edward's insistence (opposed by the dour and unimaginative George), they even rigged up a sail at one stage, which added to their speed—although Edward almost capsized the boat when turning too quickly around a river bend, the wind suddenly coming from the opposite direction. It did not occur to them to fit a centreboard, so tacking across the stream was not possible.

Many stations and settlements existed along the Murray by 1862, and the Murray–Darling Basin Commission in Canberra lists fifteen of the more prominent.[11] Edward and George called in at many of them to get information about local conditions and advice about Aboriginal communities, and to collect botanical specimens. In his diary of the voyage, Edward made special mention of what he took to be wild cherry bushes, box plants and blackwood trees along the banks and the spectacular sandbanks they passed, some rising 12–15 metres above the river. The pair were generally welcomed and treated with hospitality by station owners and their families: their bizarre and sudden arrival, especially their photographic gear, broke the silent tedium of bush life along the river.

It took them till March 1862 to reach Wentworth, the regular paddle-steamer terminal from South Australia at the confluence of the Murray and Darling rivers. Suddenly the river was a lot wider, with a larger volume of water and more currents and eddies. Wentworth was the one place at which, according to Turnley, they offered their photographic services without success. It was said to be a notoriously puritanical Calvinist settlement where photography was regarded as catering to men's vanity and a sin.[12] This perception offended their professional sensibilities, although as a fervent biblical literalist, George was not put out too much. Nor, to Edward's chagrin, did George have any difficulty refusing a succulent lamb roast at another settlement because the wood for the oven had been chopped on the Sabbath.

The Cole–Burnell rowing boat on a vast and lonely stretch of the Murray—it was hot, heavy and ungainly

As winter set in, the flies and heat abated somewhat, and they reached Mannum, where they photographed on stereographic plates the paddle-steamer *Mary Ann*, which had been operated since 1853 by Captain William Randall. The hull of *Mary Ann* was later incorporated as the left hull of a twin-hulled steamer, the PS *Gemini*, operating today as a survivor of the river's fleet.

In describing Edward and George's encounters with Aboriginal people, it is instructive to compare them with those of other European explorers. When Captain James Cook sailed into Botany Bay in April 1770, he and his crew encountered several indigenous people but their exchanges were superficial, fleeting and varied. Sometimes they were threatening and menacing with spears and clubs; at other times they seemed aloof and more interested in spearing fish from their canoes than observing what must have seemed like creatures from outer space. Sometimes the locals shouted at the invaders, a clear assertion of defiance that was interpreted by the Englishmen as meaning 'Go away'. Sometimes they launched spears, usually aimed over English heads. At least one crew member fired a musket at what looked like a war party; the locals were surprised, but continued their signs of defiance. The visitors, seeking reconciliation, left presents of beads and cloth at the entrance to dwellings, but these were seldom accepted and were left where they were. Provisioning parties looking for fresh water were usually unmolested when they went ashore. After these desultory contacts, the *Endeavour* left Botany Bay without clear communications having been established with the Indigenous people.[13]

In 1841, the pioneer settler Edward Curr encountered similar reactions from the Aboriginal people on the Murray. Accompanied by an Aboriginal man, Tommy, who spoke some English, he recounts:

> I soon found that they were both surprised and displeased at finding a pale-faced stranger invading their fastnesses without having sent them word. It so happened that the party was rather a defenceless one, consisting principally of women, old men, and children, the young men being out hunting, so that on seeing us, a general stampede took place to the shore; whilst yells of every variety of shrillness, from voices of every age, burst on our ears. Tommy laughed heartily at the scamper, and tried to reassure his kinsfolk, shouting to them at the top of his voice 'to sit down; that I was friendly and would not injure them', and so on. But his assurances were without avail. The *sauve qui peut* [rush to escape] was general, all paddling their canoes in hot haste to a point at which the banks, which were of some height, sloped gradually to the water's edge …
>
> To this precipitate retreat, however, there was one exception, in the person of a very old man—the identical Warri's father, of whom Tommy had spoken. From what I afterwards knew of him, I think he must have scored his ninety summers. This poor wreck

of humanity, disregarding the many and vociferous entreaties of his friends, refused to retire. Somewhat emaciated and bent, with bald head and long white beard, he stood naked and defiant by the stream on whose banks he had seen the best part of a century pass by. He had never before seen a white man. His fishing spear quivered in his hand, and, after an abortive attempt at a warlike caper, he howled, abused, and spat at me in senile fury, asking, as Tommy afterwards explained, why I came to the Moira? What I wanted? That I was a demon from the grave! That the water, the fish, and the ducks belonged to his tribe. That he spat at me and hated me. That I was Pekka (a ghost), but that man or devil, he would spear me![14]

On the Murray twenty-one years later, Edward and George witnessed a subtle but depressing change. Acts of defiance were fewer, as was feigned indifference. Many Aboriginal people had been herded into mission settlements and made to wear cast-off European clothes to cover their nakedness. Others, still free of such forced confinement, appeared reasonably friendly. Edward even contemplated undertaking a census of the various tribes they encountered, but found little cooperation for such an ambition. Reactions of the locals to the rowing boat's arrival ranged from wariness to muted hostility, but without white-hot indignation. Several times Edward persuaded the locals to pose for photographs, but according to Turnley, once made the mistake of getting an Aboriginal man to put his head under the black hood of the camera. This brave soul was traumatised when he saw his companions upside down through the lens, and he and they quickly vanished into the surrounding bush.[15] Once, some locals helped free the boat from snags. On another occasion, Edward gave a bunch of locals joy rides to and fro across the river, to their uproarious amusement.

In sum, meetings with original Australians continued to be desultory, unpredictable, sometimes cordial, other times tinged with suspicion—deservedly so if the locals had received news of how whites had peremptorily shouldered their brothers and sisters off their lands in other parts of the country.

Before closing our account of this epic river journey, let us put Edward and George into a time machine and fast-forward them into the beginning of the twenty-first century to let them see what the complex and beautiful Murray–Darling river system has become. We use as our comparator the epic voyage of *Bismarck*, a slightly tongue-in-cheek expedition undertaken in 2006 by the Australian environmentalist Dr Tim Flannery and comedian John Doyle (of Roy and HG fame). Their voyage was recorded by the ABC for the television series *Two Men in a Tinnie*.

Bismarck was a battered, mud-stained, 14-foot (4.2-metre) open aluminium skiff with an inordinately large outboard motor attached to its stern that allowed for improbable speeds

Photograph by Cole or Burnell of paddle
steamers, thought to be *Gemini* and *Bunyip*,
at Mannum, 1862

on straight parts of the course. Flannery and Doyle took fifty days to traverse parts of the Darling and then the Murray. They described the avarice of cotton growers on the upper Darling in Queensland who starved settlers of water lower down the river. They filmed the hot silence of abandoned towns, the rusting machinery in shearing sheds, and the grand squatter mansions with broken pianos and stained-glass windows, testament to the frustrated hopes of pastoralists who had succumbed to the ravages of drought, rabbits and heat. They wryly noted Henry Lawson's indecision about whether to describe the Darling as a muddy gutter where men lived like dogs at the tail end of a drought, or a second Mississippi.

They marvelled at fossils of giant wombats and kangaroos preserved in the steep clay banks of the rivers, and the ancient paintings and scars on the river gums where Aboriginal people had stripped bark for canoes. They deplored the infestation of blue-green algae and of the alien, bottom-feeding carp, which were interfering with the breeding capacity of native Murray cod, golden and silver perch, and smelt—even crayfish, yabbies, turtles and platypus. They worried over rising salt levels in the lower Murray due to excessive irrigation. Said Doyle laconically, 'The river is buggered. They oughta stop the rivalry of state bureaucrats and introduce a coordinated national management scheme.'

Towing their tinnie and film crew overland to the upper reaches of the Murray to the east, Doyle and Flannery relaunched their boat at Tom Groggin Station near the river's headwaters in the Snowy Mountains. Flannery noted that the waters from there west almost down to Albury ran clean and unsullied, but when they got to Albury, things changed: hoons on jetskis played dangerous games of brinksmanship, and lazy pleasure seekers boozed their days away on luxurious houseboats.

Doyle and Flannery then headed west through a bewildering system of locks, dams and reservoirs past Echuca, Swan Hill, Robinvale, Mildura and Wentworth and vast irrigated fruit blocks to the South Australian border. They took a sharp southward turn at Morgan and sailed through South Australia towards the river mouth at Goolwa. They paused in awe to view gigantic pumping stations at Morgan, Swan Reach, Mannum and Murray Bridge, constructed to pump yet more water out of the river and pipe it hundreds of kilometres to the thirsty inhabitants of Port Pirie and Port Augusta at the top of Spencer Gulf, to people living on the Eyre Peninsula and in settlements on the Yorke Peninsula, and the million inhabitants of Adelaide. The river, if not buggered, was extremely taxed.

In the autumn of 1862, Edward Cole and George Burnell continued their voyage down the last stretches of the as yet unbuggered river from Murray Bridge and Tailem Bend and out into Lake Alexandrina at the Murray mouth. They had covered 1700 kilometres in four months. Rowing out onto the enormous freshwater expanse, they made their way to a

Congregational mission station at Point McLeay run by the Reverend George Taplin, who had married George's sister Martha. Taplin was enthusiastic about the epic river voyage and wondered whether the two explorers could mount a show like the one an American artist had put on in New York and London about a trip he had made down the Mississippi. Instead of sketches, he suggested they display photographs they had captured of the fauna and local inhabitants. This they eventually did.

The 'Stereoscopic Views of the River Murray' series that George and Edward later produced of their voyage was marketed under the title *Stereograms of River Murray Scenery* and put on public display for sale at Rigby's Bookshop in Hindley Street, Adelaide, in June 1862. Customers were intrigued by the exhibition, which filled a void in visual representations of the riverine environment of the period. It graphically showed aspects of Aboriginal settlements, the residences of some of the more prominent pastoralists who by 1850 occupied almost the entire length of the Murray River, and the growing townships and infrastructure such as Hopwood's pontoon bridge over the river at Echuca. Upon viewing the stereographic series, a journalist for the *South Australian Register* wrote:

> the various pictures of Murray scenery are such as to convey to persons who have never visited the river a vivid and correct idea of its scenery. The rocks near Moorundee, the rugged reefs of shingle, the calm surface of deep water, the noble breadth of the river, its acute zigzag bends, the monstrous gumtrees on its banks, the wild savages in their little canoes, are all so true to nature as to carry one back in imagination to the scenes themselves.[16]

During the pair's brief sojourn at Point McLeay before heading on to Adelaide, the Reverend Taplin accidentally reignited a radical suspicion Edward had held for much of his youth about comparative religious beliefs: that many of the world's religions had common narratives. After dinner one night, Taplin told him of a conversation he had had in the local (Narrinyere) language with Billy, one of the elders at the mission:

> Billy: How do you know that Bible is Jehovah's book? Did he give it to you? Did he tell you it? Did not whitefellow make it?
> Taplin: No, Jehovah gave it to my fathers a long time ago.
> Billy: Well and our God told my fathers our customs a long time ago, and so we must do them.
> Taplin (aside): I could see that there was a more thoughtful opposition to the Divine Word than I had expected to find.[17]

A Burnell photograph of an Aboriginal family, uncomfortable
in western clothing, somewhere along the Murray, 1862

Edward also showed great interest in Taplin's account of the local Aboriginal legend of
Nurundere, the Supreme Being who had made all things on earth:

> When he was ready to leave what he had made to mortal man, Nurundere first
> descended beneath the sea where there was a great fire which he had to avoid before he
> ascended to a land in the western sky, there to reside forever in sunset-hued glory. And
> all spirits which depart the bodies of the dead must go similarly beneath the sea; and
> those who are not fine enough souls to be able to avoid the fire must remain confined
> down there for eternity while all others ascend to glory with Nurundere.
> Thunder is the angry voice of Nurundere; the rainbow his sign of pleasure.

He was for a time represented on earth by another splendid hunter named Wyungare, who had no father but was mystically born of a mother only. Among his many great adventures on earth Wyungare once fed his people in a famine by tearing a giant kangaroo to pieces and scattering those pieces upon the plain—whereupon they miraculously became the host of comparatively small kangaroos whose descendants exist today.

Killed by the treachery of a fellow hunter, Wyungare ascended directly to Nurundere by driving a vast and barbed spear into the sky in the west and climbing up it.[18]

After several days gathering their strength, George and Edward left the hospitality of the Taplins and rowed across Lake Alexandrina to Goolwa, where they took a stagecoach to Adelaide. There they stayed with George's parents at Hindmarsh. According to Turnley, this family was heavily dominated by 'the Old Man', John Burnell, a fellmonger and tanner with a two-storey concrete factory in the suburb, and a deacon of the Hindmarsh Congregational Church.

Edward spent a few weeks in Adelaide heavily immersed in whatever books he could find on comparative religions.[19] His interest had been aroused by Billy's tale at the mission station at Point McLeay, and he wanted to explore whether religions other than Billy's had the same striking similarities to Christian beliefs: the great fire beneath the sea was hell; how Nurundere, the Supreme Being, had at one stage been represented on earth by Wyungare, born of a mother only; how Wyungare was killed by a Judas-like hunter who had betrayed him; how Wyungare had performed miracles with kangaroos as Jesus had with loaves and fishes; and how Wyungare had ascended to heaven after death as Jesus had. Edward found other similarities, and was determined to undertake further extensive research on his return to Melbourne, where he and George now planned to go, the latter en route to Castlemaine to rescue his family.

In midwinter of 1862, the pair embarked from Port Adelaide on the *Coorong,* a coastal steamer bound for Melbourne. On landfall, Edward bid farewell to George. Turnley's account of the separation was probably accurate enough:

He saw Burnell off on a stage coach for Castlemaine, and despite their too-long-together antipathy there was inevitably a moment of softer emotion between them at this finale of their long adventure. However, as the coach clattered away, Cole knew an echo of that sense of release he had experienced following Henry Smith's burial on the Mount Alexander goldfields. Again, at last, he was in the 'ever-agreeable company of one'.[20]

5
POVERTY
AND HERESY

Looking west down Bourke Street
from Spring Street, 1858

So here is Edward William Cole, alone in the cold rainy Melbourne spring of 1862, hard-up and looking for affordable lodgings. He is just thirty years old. According to Cole Turnley's speculative and anecdotal evidence, he has £7.7.9 in his pocket, with no rent coming in from his butcher tenant in Castlemaine, nor any expected.[1] He finds a room in a terrace building in St Kilda Road where, unable to pay for a doctor's diagnosis, he self-medicates his way through a heavy and persistent cold.

The city is marginally more civilised than its gold-fevered predecessor Edward landed in ten years earlier. It now has a population of 200,000, including many staid burghers and a regularly paid workforce of reliable artisans and tradespeople seeking stability in their lives. Bushmen still swagger around town taking a break from their lonely sheep and cattle runs, but they are outnumbered by citified flaneurs and Hooray Henrys, as well as serious businessmen and traders. Wealth from the goldfields has financed some fine public buildings: Melbourne now has a railway station, a general post office, a trades hall, an art gallery, a secular university, a public library, several mechanics' institutes and the beginnings of a botanical garden run by the Victorian government botanist Baron Ferdinand von Mueller.

Melburnians are informed about their rapidly spreading metropolis through a set of directories published by Sands & McDougall, printers who see value in listing streets, banks, companies, societies and institutes, traders and professional men and women. The map of the city itself is set in a symmetrical grid pattern with a church—Roman Catholic, Anglican, Methodist or Presbyterian—standing on many street corners. Sands & McDougall also list fifteen new suburbs as the city spreads north and east across flatlands and gentle hills away from the Yarra River, including North Melbourne, Brunswick, Fitzroy, Carlton, East Melbourne, Footscray, Preston, Northcote, Emerald Hill, Prahran and Richmond, and the working-class inner suburb of Collingwood where, had Edward known it, his allegedly dead father, Amos, has bigamously settled with his second wife, Anne, and their children.

English mail day at the post office, Melbourne, 1862

Victorian terraces grace the streets of East Melbourne and Carlton. Mansions of the rich are beginning to line the streets of other suburbs, especially Toorak and Hawthorn, and along the northern bank of the Yarra at Kew, overlooking the dusty flour mills of Burnley and the backyard industries of Fitzroy and Collingwood.

The Eastern Market is located on a 2-acre (0.8-hectare) block at the corner of Bourke Street and Stephens (later Exhibition) Street. It is one of three markets gazetted by the New South Wales government in 1846, and is administered by the Melbourne Town Council. From its establishment in the 1850s, the market has primarily been a venue for the sale of fresh produce from market gardens in Moorabbin, Plenty, Heidelberg, Northcote, Kew, Hawthorn, Richmond and as far away as Keilor in the west and Dandenong in the east.

It receives 1,200 drays of fresh produce a week, and all kinds of livestock—geese, turkeys, ducks and fowl, suckling pigs, rabbits, wild fowl, guineafowl and pigeons—plus honey and half a tonne of butter. It is proudly called by those most closely associated with it Melbourne's 'Covent Garden' after the famous market established in London by the Duke of Bedford in the 1600s. It also contains a lively public space—a people's forum—for open-air church services, meetings, lectures and political demonstrations. It was used to celebrate the extension of voting rights to all white men in 1858, and to host public debate about the opening-up of Crown land for selection in 1860.

It is in this busy commercial space that Edward first plants the tentative roots of his mercantile skills, which will later spread and dominate the book trade of Melbourne. But as winter turns to spring in 1863, he is less concerned about books and more about his immediate survival. In an earlier letter written to his mother and stepfather, he admits ruefully that although he has followed many callings, including miner, builder's labourer, umbrella repairer, land agent, glassblower, county court bailiff, wood splitter, cider, beer, wine and lemonade maker, gaslighter, sausage and pork butcher, photographer, sauce and jam maker, carpenter, painter and fencer, he is proficient in none of them, and has no money:

> If I had commenced at one trade eight years ago and kept at it and made myself proficient in it instead of running from one thing to another I might now be one of the richest men in the country. You say I do not prosper because I do not read the Bible. This may be so … But in this city and in fact in every city of the civilised world there is a class of men who do not read the Bible—a most heartless dishonest lying cheating lazy and despicable race of men and yet in proportion to their number they have by far a greater amount of wealth than any people in the world … Once more and finally, if I enter into a trade with which I am little acquainted with a small (and perhaps borrowed) capital in a place where there is brisk competition carried on by men well versed in it and redundant of capital, it is evident to an intelligent man, if he puts it to the thought, that whether I read the Bible or no, I shall fail. From your affectionate son. EW Cole.[2]

The melancholy fact is that Edward is unemployed and desperately poor, and although he has followed many callings, he has few marketable skills. He scavenges for food, steals apples from orchards (although, constrained by his moral scruples, only those that have fallen off the trees), even boils a concoction of grass and plants to stave off hunger. For twelve months he wanders the streets looking for work. One man takes him in to weave baskets in exchange for meals of scraps and a corner of a shed to sleep in, but when he asks for a wage, his boss shouts at him, 'Money? For an unskilled tucker job like this? It's cadging loafers like you who make the depression worse!'[3] His employer is exaggerating: apart from slight fluctuations in unemployment, there is no major depression in Melbourne until the end of the 1880s.

Despite such brutal disparagement, Edward is buoyant and tough-minded enough not to sink into apathy. He finds a job at five shillings a day clearing rubble from a building site, and with a small accumulation of capital tries to revive the lemonade business that was moderately successful on the goldfields at Castlemaine. But Melburnians do not have to endure the backbreaking manual labour of gold-diggers, and their thirst is more for a cool lager or pilsener in a corner pub than lemonade of questionable provenance from a nondescript street vendor pushing a barrow.

So Edward switches from selling lemonade to become a baker—not of sweet concoctions of fruit, cream and puff pastry, but robust meat pies, which are to become a staple Australian fast food and the cause of many a burnt tongue at Saturday afternoon Australian Rules football matches. Edward's pies pre-date Australia's first factory-made pies, mass-produced in Sydney by Sargent's in Darlinghurst in 1893, and later in Melbourne by assembly-line bakeries such as Four'n Twenty and Noon. But the recipe would have been similar: ground beef or mutton seasoned with salt and pepper in a brown gravy, encased in a short-crust pastry shell strong enough to contain the molten meat sauce. Edward adds an economical and delicious kicker: wild rabbit purchased from itinerant trappers who hawk their wares around the city streets at a penny a carcass (cleaned and skinned). Twenty-four of these creatures were originally imported from England in 1859 by the settler Thomas Austin, who wanted them as quarry for the pleasure of visiting sportsmen on his property Barwon Park. But the rabbits encountered no natural enemies in the recently cleared colonial paddocks and enthusiastically bred to plague proportions across Victoria and further afield.

Edward installs himself on the footpath on Bourke Street outside the Eastern Market, baking his pies in a kerosene-fuelled oven set into a wheelbarrow. The pies have a hole in the top into which the customer can pour additional gravy at no extra cost. Edward's sign announces: 'Cole's Delicious Mixed Meat Pies, None so Nice, 3d Extra Gravy Free!'

He is now onto a sustainable if meagre income-producing business. And selling pies guarantees him steady customers, for it is a night-time trade, in which he fills the stomachs of the customers of Melbourne's entertainment quarter after they have satisfied their more carnal appetites in the brothels in nearby Flinders Lane, drunk their fill at neighbouring pubs, or doubled or lost their weekly wages in the gambling and opium dens in China Town around Little Bourke Street. After lively nights spruiking his pies, he sleeps beneath the barrow from early dawn.

With his new trade, Edward joins a vast army of spruikers and hawkers on Melbourne streets selling everything from bootlaces and matches to coffee, peanuts, potatoes and

The Eastern Market, 1863

saveloys. There are also fortune tellers and phrenologists, and the telescope man who, according to writer Marcus Clarke, 'shows Saturn's rings for a penny and describes Jupiter's moons for a glass of gin'.[4]

But Edward does not sleep for long. His mind is in a ferment. Although he has no formal education beyond primary school, he is emerging as a man with an unusual degree of intellectual energy and curiosity about science, technology, nature, the universe, race, the uses and curses of alcohol and tobacco—in fact, about every aspect of the human condition and its environment. He is part of a colonial society where anything is possible, where a settler can escape from the suffocation of a hierarchical British society—monarchy, wars, class, the repressive rule of Albion's fiat.

Like so many autodidacts of his day, Edward is voraciously driven to assemble the facts, and *all* the facts, on whichever subject attracts his volatile imagination. He holds a strong Victorian belief in the availability of absolute knowledge, which presupposes the positive relationship of knowledge to virtue. This compulsion makes some of his later writings prolix to the point of unreadability, although he shows occasional signs of recognising this tendency. For example, when enumerating Catholic miracles in his 1867 work *The Real Place in History of Jesus and Paul*, he writes: 'it may not be improper in this place to warn the reader that the remainder of this chapter being simply a collection of a number of similar evidences respecting miracles, reads somewhat monotonously; therefore, he can just glance over it, or plod through it as best suits his humour.'

At this stage in his existence, religion has become a subject of consuming fascination. Driven by a conviction that if he puts his views to fair-minded men, logic and truth will prevail, Edward is developing a passion for analysing and comparing religious beliefs, including different Christian sects and major world religions. Whether this compulsion arises from his early rudimentary Christian upbringing at the hands of his stepfather in Kent, arguments about the literal veracity or otherwise of the Bible with George Burnell during their long weeks drifting down the Murray, or Aboriginal beliefs that he absorbed from Reverend Taplin and his missionary work at Point McLeay on Lake Alexandrina, is unclear.

What is very likely, however, is that his stepfather's brutal admonition to him as a child never to question the literal truth of the Bible in their house would have left Edward with an abiding resentment of the dogmatism of his stepfather's beliefs, which he would have transferred thereafter towards the closed-minded arrogance of the clergy. As in so many things, he is slightly ahead of his time. Among many thinking people, Charles Darwin's *On the Origin of Species*, published in 1859, has destroyed Biblical chronology and literal faith in creation. And geologists, archaeologists and anthropologists are providing evidence of the antiquity of humans.

An atheistic secularist movement begins in Melbourne around the same time as Edward completes his *Real Place in History of Jesus and Paul*, and gains momentum in the 1880s. As Edward observes in his 1868 pamphlet *A Discourse in Defence of Mental Freedom*:

> This stifling of free inquiry in matters of religion is one of the still lingering relics of a barbarous age and a manifest sign of the present weakness of orthodoxy … for no man who is thoroughly convinced beyond all doubt that his faith is the absolute truth, unassailable by adverse arguments, should shirk or attempt to stifle inquiry … 'Whoever,' says Milton 'knew truth to be put to the worse in a free and open encounter?'[5]

Edward's perspective is shared by many humanist intellectuals in the post-Darwinian nineteenth century, and he finds Melbourne a rewarding environment in which to pursue his quest. For the city has acquired an active intellectual life in which land reform, education and the efficacy of trade tariffs are legitimate subjects of exploration and debate. So are wider social issues, such as religion and the nature of human existence. Public platforms in parks and gardens compete with the pulpit, the press and pamphleteering as the main means of communicating ideas.

And so, more exclusively, do societies for the intelligentsia. In 1867, Edward joins the Eclectic Association founded by Henry Keylock Rusden, an atheist and rationalist stimulated by, among others, Darwin and his theories on evolution. Other joiners are future Australian prime minister Alfred Deakin; BS Naylor, a spiritualist and socialist; journalist Charles Bright; and another journalist, the ubiquitous James Smith of *The Argus*. The society is ill-regarded by the Christian establishment and with jaundiced cynicism by some of the press. Such mixed views persisted well after Edward joined it. On 17 June 1873, *The Herald* commented on the views of another Melbourne journal:

> The *Victorian Independent* of this month endeavours to electrify its readers with the announcement that a Society of Atheists exists in our midst, viz, the Eclectic Society. It urges upon the church members to come out of their cushioned pews, and fight. In the next breath it tells them that there is nothing to fight; for Atheism is an expiring old lion, and a toothless, clawless dotard. The members of the Eclectic Society are informed that they are launching themselves upon a stormy sea, without compass or rudder—a form of expression which is lifted bodily from the good book for such occasions. This rhetorical finery, however, rather suggests a writer who wants to show off in his own little garden than a man speaking conviction to his fellow man. Ecclesiastical sailors are probably paid by the column or line, just like profane ones, and have to rack their brains for sensational topics with which to make up their quantum stuff. Still, they might as well be logical. The answer to the alarmist in this case seems to be that, if Atheism be a toothless, clawless old lion, the wisest plan is to let him rip.

Even before he joins the Eclectic Association, Edward has embarked on his own compulsive mission. He spends many hours each day combing through every book on religious texts he can find in the newly established Melbourne Public Library on Swanston Street and the library of the equally new Mechanics' Institute in Collins Street.

The result is his first published writing, in 1866: a substantial pamphlet of twenty-six pages priced at sixpence and entitled *Cole's Information for the People on the Religions of the World*. It is, declares Edward, an impartial, equally fair portrayal of all major religious sects, written in the simple and untechnical language of everyday life. He writes it, he says, 'to annihilate sectarian prejudices'. It summarises what he believes to be the essence of

Looking west down Bourke Street, 1860

Buddhism, Christianity (Roman Catholic, Protestant and Greek), Hinduism, Islam, Taoism and Judaism; of Confucius, of Sintoos (followers of the Japanese religion Shinto), Sikhs and Parsees; and of the scriptures of the Druze, Mandaeans and Pagan. His survey is neither comprehensive nor discursive, but he writes so that his readers may, through his thumbnail sketches, become acquainted with the beliefs, hopes and aspirations that sway the human race. Inchoate in his thinking is the view that all religions are basically the same, of equal validity and of common moral principle. His 'globe' design accompanying the pamphlet proclaims his belief that the publication will change the world.

Edward's information pamphlet gets some favourable reviews, including on page 2 of the *Ballarat Star* of 7 September 1866:

> Mr E.W. Cole of Melbourne, has published the first number of a series to be called 'Cole's Information for the People on the Religions of the World', to be completed in about twenty issues. The present contains sketches of the religious sects and the sacred scriptures of all nations. Both are intellectually and concisely complied, and accompanied by a cloud of authorities—the latter affording to the theological student plenty of sources for enlarging his information on such matters.

But it is a sales flop, tedious and boring.

Religions of the World is a dry run for Edward's first substantial book, *The Real Place in History of Jesus and Paul*, which he self-publishes in 1867, a year after *Religions* and the same year as the founding of the Eclectic Society. He dedicates the book to 'rational Christians of all denominations', signs himself as EDWIC (short for Edward William Cole), and hires the printer Robert Bell of Little Collins Street East. He prices the book at one shilling or, later, sixpence for a briefer pamphlet covering the same material.

In Chapter One, Edward asks some perceptive questions. If Christ raised the dead and healed the sick in the presence of adoring multitudes throughout Judea, why was there no popular outrage when the Jews urged Pontius Pilate to put him to death as an imposter? And when he died on the cross, and there was darkness at midday with earthquakes and the dead rising, why did the people not panic, or express the least concern at such extraordinary phenomena? Why was such an eclipse not recorded in neighbouring regions? And when a brilliantly effulgent angel descended from heaven to roll back the stone from Christ's sepulchre, why did the Roman guards not panic, or at least report to their centurion such an extraordinary visitation?

Because, Edward surmises, these events did not happen. None of the miracles Jesus is said to have wrought were mentioned by any of the Greek, Roman or Jewish writers who were contemporaries of Jesus. Even the Pharisee Josephus, the great Jewish historian who lived in the countryside of Roman Judea and wrote of the time of Jesus, who enumerated and discoursed on the various Jewish sects, never mentioned the miracles of Jesus. Edward argues, as do other sceptics, that 'It is evident that what is said of the universal renown acquired and the great miracles wrought by Jesus are not facts, or certainly Josephus would have referred to them.'[6] He goes on to remind his readers (those who have not by this time given up in outrage) that Jesus himself refused to perform miracles to prove his own divinity, even when tempted by the devil to do so. This, asserts Edward, he has in common with Guru Nanak Dev, founder of the Sikh faith, and with Muhammad, Zoroaster and Moses.

He gets further under the skin of the Melburnian ecclesiastical establishment by describing the scorn Protestants hold towards the miracles of Catholic saints, and the equal intolerance of Catholics towards Protestant miracles. Drawing on *Lives of the Principal Catholic Saints* written by the English Catholic priest Alban Butler (1710–1773), Edward estimates that down through the ages, 30,000 Catholic saints performed on average four miracles each—120,000 altogether, a huge number, mostly unremarked, forgotten or, if remembered, derided by Protestants. He enumerates in detail those of fifty saints and says he could go on, but would exhaust the reader's patience.

Edward also describes the intolerant condescension of the priests and laypeople of Christian faiths towards the miracles and legends of other faiths. For each, he observes, belief in the validity of their own culture and religion is sacrosanct, against which the beliefs of other faiths are to be discounted. He goes on to enumerate miracles allegedly performed by Buddhists, Muslims and Parsees, and compares them to the councils of illiterate bishops and clergy who made authoritative decisions about Christian doctrine, dogma and alleged miracles. He asserts that the miracles of Jesus, such as feeding 9000 people with a few loaves and fishes, stilling the winds, walking on water, withering a fig tree with a curse, and raising the dead, were grossly exaggerated by superstitious and ignorant men. Also, that the gospels of Matthew, Mark, Luke and John, as well as their epistles and those of other prophets, are frequently contradictory and conjectural. He describes their writings as a jumble of history that make accepting their literal truth a nonsense.

Miracles, Edward asserts, cannot be believed without doing violence to reason. They are not evidence of the truth of any doctrine, which can only be authenticated by virtue of the doctrine's inherent force, beauty and truthfulness. He declares:

> He who would attempt to explain the character of Jesus and define his real historical position should deal with his character in every important aspect, and this is a most important one; in fact, the real point in question is whether Jesus was God or man— whether the Christians, like the Buddhists, Taoists, Sintooists, and others, have merely deified the man who founded their faith, and now worship him as God—or, whether he was God in reality from the beginning. For if Jesus, like them, was only a frail man, similar to ourselves, the sooner that mankind cease to pay him the honours which can be only due to a Supreme Being of infinite attributes the better. We see in the relation of the divine incarnation of Jesus but one story of a class—a story exactly similar to hundreds of others that have arisen in other countries under similar conditions; and the presumption is strong upon our mind that it, like them, is utterly fictitious, and consequently unworthy of the belief of mankind.[7]

Edward goes on to discuss the commonality of claimed divinity of most religious founders: Christ, the Buddha, Menu (founder of Hinduism), Muhammad, Lao-tze (founder of Taoism), Confucius, Zoroaster, Nanak Dev, Mexitli or Huitzilopochtli (supreme deity of Mexico), the founders of the Druze religion, and the Islamic mystics Hamza ibn Ali ibn Ahmad and Al-Hakim bi-Amr Allah. Many founders, he asserts, were said by their followers to have been miraculously conceived, and miracles supposedly accompanied their birth. He would very much have empathised with Monty Python's satire *The Life of Brian*.

What Edward attempts to do is look at Jesus and his teachings from a humanistic set of principles by which people can live in harmony without the associated superstitions. He also suggests that prophets of all major religions emphasise the same principles. The Christian golden rule of doing unto others as one would have them do unto oneself has universal application. To question the divine origin and alleged miracles of prophets should not be seen as degrading such humanistic principles.

Some of Edward's scepticism about religion is later shared by others, including his friend Deakin, who explores the divinity of Christ following a famous lecture by Victorian Supreme Court judge George Higinbotham that outraged conservative opinion when it was delivered on 1 August 1883.[8] In a supportive article on the divinity of Christ published ten days later, Deakin asks of what Christ's divinity consisted, as described by historian of religion Al Gabay:

> It was not his body, confessedly human, nor his miracles, for he was only one of a host of wonder workers, nor even his mind. Though he was 'pure, royally unselfish, intuitively wise, simple and yet profound', and though his was patently 'an intense devotion, an exalted faith, and a resplendent course of conduct', other men had approached if not equalled him in these virtues. His divinity is unprovable, but if Christ is divine, Deakin concludes, 'then is humanity divine too in diverse degrees'? Here then is a lasting image, a Gnostic conception of Jesus as the zenith of human development, that rejects the Trinitarian man-god for the moral and spiritual Master of Wisdom whom mankind in the mass might seek to emulate.[9]

Edward appears to have given little forethought to how his views will impact on Melbourne's Christian establishment, or to the indignation and excoriation his book will attract. Many lay readers are either indifferent or strongly hostile to it. Few clergy are intellectually equipped for rational debate, and many lash out rancorously. What particularly outrages them is how this unqualified upstart with no formal education has the temerity to question Christian texts.

More broadly, the outrage of Melbourne's clerics underlines a prevailing Christian prejudice, particularly of Anglo-Saxon Protestants, that had existed long before, existed during and has existed since Edward listed his own views about religion. This prejudice found particular expression in the World's Parliament of Religions, organised in the United States to coincide with the Chicago World Fair in 1893. An aggressively Christian event born of American Protestant arrogance, the Parliament showcased all the world's religions on the unquestioned but unstated basis of the superiority of the Protestant Christian faith. It was governed by a set of Christian assumptions that effectively reduced all other religions to inadequacy, making them quaint sideshows relegated to the corridors of discussion.

Of the representatives of other countries and religions invited to the Parliament, the Japanese refused to be sidelined with regard to either their cultural and technical achievements or the validity of their religious beliefs. The Japanese government built the magnificent Hōden (Phoenix) Pavilion in the centre of the fair to showcase the country's material and cultural attainments, and at the concurrent Parliament of Religions, Japanese Buddhists argued for the centrality of Buddhism alongside Christianity. As the Australian scholar Judith Snodgrass points out:

> Buddhism held a unique place at the World's Parliament of Religions. More than any other non-Christian religion it was the 'other' of Christianity. Its function was not *xenos,* the radically different and totally 'not-us' of the 'heathen', 'idolatrous' Hinduism of missionary rhetoric, or of Islam, which at this event remained beyond the pale, but that of alterity. Buddhism was recognizably similar, a religion comparable with Christianity, but differing from it precisely on those points at issue in the debates of the time.[10]

It had been agreed among religious scholars by the time of the 1893 Parliament that Buddha was an atheist who denied the existence of an immortal soul; that Buddhists were self-taught, not reliant on the existence of a saviour; and that Northern Buddhism, Mahayana Buddhism, was based on Sanskrit texts and founded by the atheist Sakyamuni, a historical figure who taught a system of ethical philosophy that only later developed features of a religion, the written word coming from Sanskrit. Sakyamuni's views would have accorded with Edward's that religious leaders should be celebrated for their moral truths, not the fictitious miracles with which their followers insisted on investing them.

After Buddhism was introduced to Japan in the sixth century, a new religion called Shugendo emerged. Based on a form of mountain worship, it worships the mountain itself as where spirits of ancestors return after death, and blends imported religions such as esoteric Buddhism, Confucianism and Taoism with native Shintoism. Anyone who has had the experience of walking through the deep fastnesses of the cypress forests surrounding the ancient Kumano Kodo trail on the Kii Peninsula south of Osaka in Japan can comprehend the strength of emanations that inspire Japanese religious spiritualism. Edward would have understood.

At the Chicago Parliament, American Presbyterian mission administrator Dr FF Ellinwood condescendingly dismissed Japanese spiritual Buddhism as nothing more than the bastardisation of 'real' Buddhism. A Japanese abbot tried to correct the Americans' assumptions but to little avail. Throughout the Parliament, in a kind of religious colonisation, the white hosts, while not crass enough to spell out their prejudices, left their foreign guests in no doubt that Western scholars knew as much as or more than did they about their own religions, and that Christianity was the only true faith.

During his beginnings in Melbourne, Edward was a universalist, an idealist—a position he maintained through his life. He did not discount the existence of a Divine Watchmaker, but wanted to put Him in a much broader context than simply as the creator of a tiny planet and its parochial earthly religions. In *God and the Universe*, an undated article he published in Melbourne sometime in the 1880s, he observed that:

> these many millions of suns and worlds and systems (in the universe) and all their parts are clearly working together, like the most exquisitely designed clockwork. Look at the marvellous mechanisms of the human brain, the human eye, the human hand, the human heart, and, in fact, the whole human structure and composition; they all prove the truth of the affirmation that man is 'fearfully and wonderfully made' … It always appeared to me that there must be in this vast, illimitable, and beautiful universe, myriads of beings, superior to our weak mortal selves, and at the head of all and over all an immortal Being of infinite perfection, which thinking men in all countries and ages have called *God*. And shall not we, immortal souls, increase in knowledge and wisdom, and as the ages roll on, more and more perceive and understand this mighty universe and its Author? I firmly believe we shall, and that as yet we are only beginning to live and think and understand and appreciate the infinite truth.

Although he threw a bomb into the calm religious complacency of nineteenth-century Melbourne, Edward was only a minor player among the growing number of religious sceptics in the English-speaking world. For example, in his work *Anacalypsis: An Attempt to Draw Aside the Veil of the Saitic Isis: or an Inquiry into the Origin of Languages, Nations and Religions* (posthumously published in London in 1836), the British writer Godfrey Higgins (1772–1833) asserted that 'one thing is clear—the mythos of the Hindus, the mythos of the Jews and the mythos of the Greeks, are all at bottom the same; and what are called their early histories of humankind are but contrivances under the appearance of histories to perpetuate doctrines'.[11] Rationalist and spiritualist Kersey Graves (1813–83) was popular in the American free thought circuit of the late nineteenth century. He listed sixteen crucified saviours who lived before Christ, died on a cross or tree and allegedly ascended into heaven.

They included Thulis of Egypt (1700 BC), Krishna of India (1200 BC), Indra of Tibet (725 BC), Jimmu of Japan (660 BC) and Quetzalcoatl of Mexico (587 BC). Like Edward, Graves was an autodidact and had humanist beliefs—he was an abolitionist, an anti-slaver, a health reformer and social utopianist.

The evolutionary theories of Darwin in *On the Origin of Species* gave the sceptics intellectual weight. His views about evolution cast doubt on the veracity of those who took the Bible literally, particularly the creationists. He postulated that humans had evolved over many thousands of years, and the fittest of these had survived because they adapted to their environment. The more agile adaptive Christian clerics accepted Darwinism, arguing that God's creative seven days and seven nights should not be taken as literal truth but were an elastic time frame of millennia. God, they argued, still 'created' humans in His own image, even if He baked them in His celestial oven for unimaginably longer periods than a mere week. Miracles were more part of the rich imaginary tapestry of ancient scribes than records of fact. And religions other than Christianity should not be dismissed as superstition but a valid part of humans' attempt to explain His existence. For there were elements of truth in every religion.

The philosopher and orientalist Max Muller (1823–1900) gave intellectual weight to such theories by studying and popularising religions other than Christianity, especially Eastern religions, in his Sacred Books of the East. A scholar, he neither advocated beliefs nor challenged Christianity. What drew him to the study of religions was his theory of the parallel evolution of language and religious thought. The value of Indian religions for him was also that they offered a written record that extended through millennia. Muller and Edward had much in common.

Later in his life in Melbourne, Edward turned to spiritualism, but perhaps more because of his wife Eliza's enthusiasm for seances than because of his own beliefs. If we had the technical capacity to teleport him from the late nineteenth century into the second decade of the twenty-first, we would see a man delighted by science fiction, by the possibilities of interstellar travel it offers. In his short essay God and the Universe, Edward wrote about the millions and millions of stellar bodies that exist, roll, revolve and travel through space, about the multitude of suns and worlds around us in every direction and at such immense distances that a person travelling at the speed of light would take 10,000 years to reach them. In the present, he would see that by 2019 humankind still does not have the capacity to reach them, being restricted to the limited efforts of reaching the moon and sending space probes to a few planets in our solar system. But he would be intrigued by the breadth and scope of the science fiction industry and by such filmic sagas as *Star Wars*, *Star Trek* and *Stargate*, *Alien*, *Avatar* and *Passengers*, in which space crews are put into 'hyper sleep' as their ships travel at light speed to distant planets.

6
THE ART OF SELF-PROMOTION, OR HOW TO SELL BOOKS

OPPOSITE Cole's first book arcade at 158 Bourke Street
RIGHT Eliza Cole keeping an eye on things

In 1862 and 1863, Edward Cole was occupied with two things: baking and selling his meat pies from a barrow in the Eastern Market among the denizens of Russell Street and China Town, and finding a publisher for *The Real Place in History of Jesus and Paul,* the manuscript he had just written in his painfully untidy longhand outlining his unconventional views about Christ and one of his disciples.

Most of Melbourne's clergy who knew about Edward's book were untutored in handling religious sceptics and resented having to find answers to questions they raised. Some of the city's Christian laity reacted the same way. George Robertson, now a robust and prosperous Melbourne publisher and a pillar of Melbourne's Congregational Church, threw Edward out when he approached him to publish the manuscript. Undaunted, Edward decided to try his luck in Sydney. He had enough money for the passage, so he took a coastal steamer and called on a leading Sydney bookseller and publisher, William Maddock of 838 George Street. Unknown to Edward, Maddock had recently purchased Robertson's Sydney business and had similar religious convictions to George. The few lines of Edward's manuscript he bothered to read he found heretical, and he impatiently asked Edward to leave.

Despite this second knockback, Edward found Sydney enchanting, and seriously considered uprooting himself from Melbourne and settling there. The expansive blue harbour was particularly attractive after the narrow brown Yarra. But Melbourne seemed to be doing better economically than it had been, and Edward felt he should return. He even had hopes that it would eventually become the capital of a federated Australia.[1] So did many others.

Once back in Melbourne, Edward continued to search for a publisher of his heretical tract. He went to Wilson and Mackinnon, printers in Collins Street. They weren't as concerned about the content of Edward's manuscript as with its bulk, and suggested that instead of publishing a book, he should divide it up and they could print and publish some cheap pamphlets. He agreed that these might be more digestible to readers and, bearing in mind

PRICE ONE SHILLING.

THE

REAL PLACE IN HISTORY

OF

JESUS AND PAUL.

BOOK I.—MIRACULOUS HISTORY OF JESUS.
BOOK II.—JESUS AND PAUL BOTH HONEST VISIONARIES.

BY

EDWIC ***, C.W., M.L.D.A., &c.

To be Completed in Four One Shilling Parts.

PART I.—BOOK I.

"TRUTH IS IMMORTAL AND SHALL LIVE, ERROR IS MORTAL AND SHALL DIE."
ANDREW JACKSON DAVIS.

MELBOURNE:
PUBLISHED BY THE AUTHOR, AND PRINTED BY ROBERT BELL, 97B LITTLE
COLLINS STREET EAST.
1867.

TO BE HAD OF ALL BOOKSELLERS.

Cole's pamphlet on Jesus and Paul, which scandalised Melbourne's clerical establishment the angry reactions of Robertson and Maddock, decided to give the pamphlets innocuous titles. He called the series 'Information for the People on the Religions of the World'; the first pamphlet was titled *A Sketch of the Religious Sects of all Nations*, and the second *A Sketch of the Sacred Scriptures of all Nations*. Both were priced at sixpence. He commissioned a cover illustration of a globe with ten latitudes underlining the words:

Advance
Knowledge
Let Prejudice Perish
Let Justice and Charity
Encircle the Earth
and
Extend
to the Men
of Every
Creed

The pamphlets did not sell. Customers for Edward's pies were encouraged to read them as they munched away, and some did, even occasionally engaging their minds as well as their mouths. But few parted with sixpence, and most of the pamphlets remained a forlorn unwanted stack on the pie cart.

Refusing to give up, Edward began to hawk his pamphlets around the neighbourhood. While doorknocking along the East Melbourne terraces, he came across a female occupant who suggested rather tartly that he would do much better selling books with catchy titles and entertaining contents rather than weighty religious pamphlets. Why, she said, she had a shelf full inside, and would he like to buy them? He would. He bought the lot for a shilling and trundled them back to his position in front of the market, then placed a handwritten sign above his wheelbarrow advertising 'Cole's Cheap Books'. He sold them all. It was early September 1865 and he was thirty-three years old.

Edward made 10 shillings selling books in his first week, 12 the next, and 10 again in the third—not as much as he earned selling pies, but a sustainable income and much more satisfying: in persuading passers-by to stop and read, then to buy, he engaged his and their intellects. When the managers of the Eastern Market told him he could not just camp indefinitely outside selling books, he rented a stall, Number 14. It was in a poor position in the gloomy depths of the market, but still accessible to likely customers. With a little more income, he rented a roomier and better-positioned stall, Number 8, and erected a sign: 'Read the Books. No one asked to Buy. All prices clearly marked.'

Amid the market's carnival atmosphere, the raucous cries of stall-owners spruiking their carrots, ducks, cabbages, rabbits, iced jellies and hot bowls of peas sprinkled with pepper, salt and vinegar, Edward sold his books. Initially, he acquired stock volume-by-volume from people like his first door-to-door customer who had offered him her shelf of books. One day, however, he was offered a job lot of redundant stock from a book trader for £17. His own inventory now expanded to over 600 books and 600 periodicals. Sales at the end of his first full month amounted to £15.12.0, of which he spent £13.7.7 on further stock and advertising, leaving a gross profit (without provision for rent or wages) of £2.4.5.[2] In the market, people were not inhibited, and they stopped to read and then to buy; his income rose accordingly.

Melbourne's economy was now as buoyant as the Eastern Market, boosted by an influx of British visitors. Queen Victoria's second son, Prince Alfred, the Duke of Edinburgh, arrived in November 1868 as commander of Her Majesty's Ship the steam frigate *Galatea*. Although abstemious and not given to excess of any sort, Edward probably witnessed from the fence-line of a paddock on the city's outskirts the notorious 'Free Banquet', to be hosted by Prince Alfred ostensibly for the poor of Melbourne. Public-spirited caterers supplied 12,000 pounds (5443 kilograms) of mutton joints, several gigantic cauldrons of potatoes, a whole bullock slowly turning on a spit, 4500 pounds (2000 kg) of plum pudding, 72 dozen pasties, 5000 pies, 600 pounds (272 kg) of fish, and 100 pounds (45 kg) of cakes and lollies. They also provided a wine 'fountain' that was designed to erupt from a 500-gallon (2273-litre) cask of good red.

In high spirits, 90,000 people attended—enough to fill today's Melbourne Cricket Ground—but the weather was very hot and blustery, and the crowd became fractious when the feast was delayed because the prince did not appear, being probably engaged at the time in what was euphemistically called the saddling paddock in Melbourne's red-light district. By 5 p.m., the tents holding the wine and food had been rushed and pulled down, food fights had begun, and the wine barrel had been attacked, with ruby streams liberally spraying the crowd. It was a total disaster.[3] Edward no doubt felt vindicated in his decision to move out of the food trade into selling books.

With more income from book sales, he moved into an even better stall, Number 1, facing onto Bourke Street. It was illuminated after dark by gaslights blazing from the Haymarket Theatre on the western flank of the Eastern Market down Bourke Street. Wishing to avoid the horse-drawn drays congesting the market laneways, many people flowed past his stall on the footpath of Bourke Street, some stopping to read, some to buy. According to Turnley, a gentleman on horseback would occasionally hail Edward, shouting out the title of the book he wanted, and, without dismounting, catch the book as it was flung up to him.[4]

Anticipating more customers, Edward bought job lots of new titles at rock-bottom prices, mostly reprints of popular novels. He installed a bargain table and hoisted a sign saying:

BOOKS, BOOKS, BOOKS
READ FOR AS LONG AS YOU LIKE. NOBODY ASKED TO BUY.
A FREE PEN WITH EVERY PURCHASE

As his business expanded, he needed help to fetch and carry an increasing number of books for a growing number of patrons. So he employed his first assistant, a bright fifteen-year-old lad, William Thomas Pyke, whom he invariably and formally addressed as 'Mr Pyke'; Pyke called Edward 'sir'.

As his bank balance accumulated, Edward's appetite for further business grew along with his craving for greater public attention. He needed to advertise—not the small, insignificant advertisements tucked away at the bottom of the miscellaneous columns of newspapers that had previously been all he could afford, but larger, attention-getting announcements. He chose as his main platform the Melbourne *Herald*, the city's only evening broadsheet. In addition to advertising prosaic lists of books—which was still essential—he needed to invent attention-getting gimmicks.

One of these concerned a tribe of people in New Guinea with tails. In 1873, New Guinea was still largely terra incognita. Spaniards and Portuguese had explored the island in the fifteenth century, but its colonisation by the Germans in the north and the British in the south, after Queensland unsuccessfully tried to annex it in 1883, was still a decade away. So Melbourne's reading public were at first taken in by Edward's fanciful story, which he launched in *The Herald* on Saturday evening, 23 August 1873. Under the headline 'Discovery of a Race of Human Beings with Tails', he began by quoting from Darwin's *The Descent of Man, and Selection in Relation to Sex* to the effect that early human progenitors were no doubt covered with hair, both sexes having beards and pointed ears and being capable of movement, and their bodies having a tail with the proper muscles. He continued:

> The startling announcement has just reached us of the discovery by a traveller of a race of men in the interior of New Guinea still possessing tails of an unmistakeable length …

The inhabitants of Etihwretep in carnival mode

Mr Thomas Jones, the talented and observant traveller in question, informs us that he arrived by ship at the native village of Etihwretep, on the north-east coast of New Guinea on the 24th December, 1871, with the intention of exploring the upper waters of the river Tramsderf, and the country thereabouts; that on the 3rd of January, having his outfit completed, he started in company with a European body-servant and a native guide and interpreter for the interior … After seventeen days of dangerous and arduous marching through the jungle, he reached the hill country, and in two more days arrived at a country where dwelt a community of people which filled him with astonishment, and the discovery of which will render his name immortal. Mr Jones found a community of men walking upon two legs, but bent forward, with a considerable amount of hair on their bodies, long arms, claw-like fingers, and real, tangible tails, more or less long.

Edward claimed the place in which the tribe was discovered was the valley of Eloc, and the natives the Elocwe or Elocweans. His column caused a mild sensation, then much amusement when readers realised that the name of the tribe was Cole's name spelt backwards. Many called at his bookstall the following Monday to confirm their suspicions. And what of the village Etihwretep and river Tramsderf? These were the names of Peter White and Fred Smart, two recent additions to Edward's staff, also spelt backwards—rather like a vastly amusing game invented by my younger sister, Susan, in Adelaide in the 1960s, when she called herself Nasus Ikswoniorb and her boyfriend Leahcim Tseb.

Edward was pleased at this public reaction, as was *The Herald*, whose circulation was considerably boosted by the advertisement. His fantasy continued and was embroidered in the right-hand front-page column day-by-day. The Elocweans attached feathers to their tails as fans in hot weather. On public outings, they formed a conga line with the oldest man going before and the next in age following, taking hold of his tail with one or both hands, the next in seniority the same, and so on to the youngest, who brought up the rear: rather like Dr Seuss's story written much later about the cats in Katzenstein. The Elocweans put their children's tails in sheaths to gradually form them into a fashionable shape. There were tail barbers and tail milliners, tail jewellers, and tailomancers to tell fortunes. The tail restorer of an Elocwean quack was so potent that when accidentally spilled on a severed dog's tail, the process reversed itself and grew a new dog.

Edward milked his saga for all it was worth, finally ending it in *The Herald* on Friday 21 November 1873 with Mr Jones's conclusion as to whether people are better with tails or without. Notwithstanding their occasional tribulations from diseased, jammed, frostbitten, burnt, scalded, rheumatic, crushed, mangled or sore tails, and the enormous cost of clothing, decorating and doctoring their tails, they were, Jones concluded, better off because of the numberless ecstatic delights, extra sensations and pleasures, mental and corporeal, provided by an extra member. Elocweans, concluded Jones, are, in consequence, the happiest people on earth.

Another story concerned roast pig. Published in *The Herald* on 19 March 1874, it held that roasting meat was discovered by accident in ancient China when the lazy son of a peasant accidentally burnt down the family cottage when his father was out working the fields. Trapped in the cottage were a sow and nine new-born piglets. All perished in the blaze, but the son, a greedy youth, tasted crackling for the first time as he was removing the burnt animals. Soon, peasants everywhere in China were burning down their houses and eating pigs left inside. This became rather expensive until they realised they could roast pigs without sacrificing houses.

Some pious Melbourne citizens deplored the vulgarity of Edward's advertising and his promotion of frivolous stories when, they fumed, not nearly enough people read the Bible.

But most went along with the fun. His book trade increased as they responded to his atrocious pun in *The Herald* that he had a great variety of tails, tayles and tales—Australian, Indian and other varieties—available at his bookstore. And in a crack at his detractors, he wrote the following and placed it in his *Herald* column:

In Vindication of Tale Reading

Many good persons hold that light reading is pernicious and ought to be discouraged. I, from taste, am not a reader of fiction, yet think that such reading, for all its abuses, is on the whole more beneficial, and brings more real good to mankind, than evil. On the ground that one of the main objects of man's existence on earth is to make himself innocently happy, from a pure humanitarian point of view, then I hold that tale reading is justifiable, and even commendable; for what a vast amount of harmless mental pleasure has accrued to millions of our race from the reading of Robinson Crusoe, Pickwick and Handy Andy alone, besides that gained from the multitude of other tales.[5]

Meanwhile, seismic changes were about to be made to the Eastern Market, Edward's base of operations in stall Number 1. The tipping point may well have been a fire in the market in 1871, which was described by an unknown writer in Melbourne's morning daily newspaper, *The Argus*, in the most disparaging terms:

… a dreary waste with an ugly looking gaol shrinking away in the farthest corner of it,[6] as if ashamed both of its purpose and of its appearance. Then hawkers, miscellaneous dealers and homeless new arrivals pitched their tents upon it, and spread their motley merchandise along the edge of the footpath to allure the attention of passers-by. One summer morning as I turned out of Spring-street into Bourke-street I saw a whiff of flame spring from one of the tents and flash from end to end with inconceivable rapidity. It is no exaggeration to say that by the time I reached Stephen-street the encampment was a heap of ruins, and the owners of the tents were surveying their blackened sites with such a look of incredulity and amazement that there was quite as much of the ludicrous as of the pathetic in the incident. After this, I think, no more tents were suffered to be erected; but hay and corn factors set up their sentry boxes on the scene of the fire; and then stall keepers were permitted to utilise the vacant ground; and there might be found the strangest assortment of damaged provisions to be met with outside of the New Cut, the Whitechapel-road or the High-street, Shoreditch. There were cheeses strong enough to waft their odour to Carlton, dried fruits that had been honeycombed

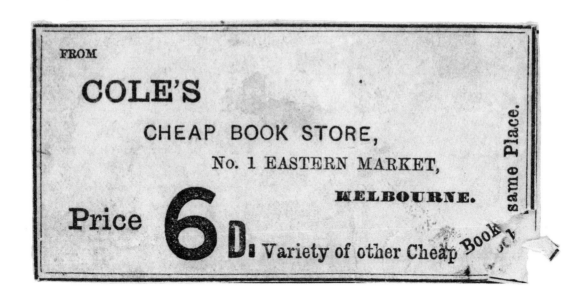

Receipt for a book purchased
at Cole's Eastern Market stall

by insects, salt fish of perdurable toughness, tins of jam and bottles of pickles with the shabbiest of anonymous labels, sides of bacon of wonderful antiquity, and a conglomerate of so-called dates which appeared to have been cemented together with paste blacking. Who bought those things? And, oh, by whom were they consumed? Sometimes I fancy that the vendors, finding no market for such unconsidered trifles, were driven to consume them themselves, and so perished miserably.[7]

Local architects Reed & Barnes won the tender to design a new market, and the construction firm Messrs Nation and Co. was contracted to build it at a cost of £77,223. The new market would better reflect the prosperity of Melbourne: it would be built of masonry and would have fifty-three stalls and extensive cellars, plus a fountain in which traders could wash their vegetables. It was completed in 1879 at a cost closer to £100,000. Much grander than the ragtag timber and corrugated iron structures it replaced, it was of late-Victorian design, of two storeys with high narrow arched windows on the upper floor crowned with square towers and finials. Verandas on the Bourke Street and Exhibition Street sides tended to cut down the interior light.

Edward maintained his book trade at the old market for as long as he could, but he needed a new venue when the wreckers forced him out. He wanted something altogether more splendid that would be a magnet for book shoppers—something like the Royal Arcade, diagonally opposite the Post Office on the corner of Bourke and Elizabeth streets, a meeting place for strollers and lovers, with tables and chairs and potted palms for atmosphere. He wanted a happy festive mood that would attract the public. He also wanted to remain in Bourke Street, which, as described by local writer Horace Perkins in 1880:

> literally swarms with people, who find attractions in the well-lighted and splendidly -stocked shops, or seek amusement in the many theatres and public halls that abound in the vicinity. Every taste is here suited. The strains of Italian opera mingle with the din of the Waxworks band, at which establishment the 'Kelly Gang', 'Wieberg', and 'Captain Moonlite' have recently been added; and it is but a step from the Theatre Royal to the fetid room, with its twelve billiard tables, where larrikins and loafers make cannons and winning hazards at the charge of sixpence a game. The cries of the trotter vendor—'only a penny each'—mingle with the screech of the peripatetic songstress, *'When other Lips and other "arts",'* and the blind seller of matches: 'only a penny a box'.[8]

Edward found what he wanted in a vacant building at 158 Bourke Street, several doors lower down from the market and west towards Russell Street. It had a frontage of 20 feet (6 metres) and a depth of 90 (27.4). It was very gloomy inside, but Edward believed that with proper lighting and an open design, it could work. In fact, it could become an arcade, a place to stroll about and examine the merchandise, not just a shop where one had to front up to a counter and ask a salesperson for a particular book.

On signing the lease with its owner, the well-known Sydney retail merchant Anthony Hordern, Edward persuaded Hordern to allow him to widen the entrance. He added pictures, gas jets and mirrors to give the hall brilliance, and open-fronted shelves and display cabinets along the walls to give customers direct access to the books, unimpeded by counters. In *The Herald* on 19 December 1873 appeared an advertisement announcing that Cole's Cheap Book Store would move from 1 Eastern Market to 158 Bourke Street, ten doors lower down.

Throughout 1874, Cole's Book Arcade thrived. So did other booksellers, such as Charlwood & Son of 7 Bourke Street East, George Robertson of Little Collins Street, and Samuel Mullen's lending library on Collins Street. With his flair for gimmickry, Edward could survive the competition. His promotional inventiveness increased. In addition to books, he sold novel 'catch lines'—from pincushions to paper flowers—and invested in copper coins. These he had made at Stokes & Martin, Melbourne's leading metalware manufacturers. He had his young assistants drop them around the city streets, where pedestrians would pick them up, mistaking them for currency. On them he had stamped 'A pencil and two good writing pens at Cole's Book Arcade'. At least some of the finders, he calculated, would also buy a book or two when claiming their prizes at the arcade.

He gradually expanded his use of coins for advertising, to gain admission to the arcade and to spread little moral homilies. Stokes & Martin became his regular supplier. Their first issue was of medium thickness; the second, in 1879, of copper, quite thick. The third, in the same year, was of medium brass with a gilt and white metal finish. From then until Edward's death in 1918, another dozen series of coins and tokens were issued, including humanitarian medals for his trip to Japan in 1903.[9]

Edward's inspired talent for promotion then went into overdrive. One Sunday he was visiting the Royal Botanic Gardens, established by his friend the government botanist, Baron von Mueller, to whom he had sent plants and seeds from Castlemaine in 1862 and during his voyage down the Murray in 1863.[10] During their meeting, a rainbow appeared in the sky above the Gardens.[11] What a dramatic emblem that would make for his arcade, Edward thought—embodying every colour, it was a sign of reconciliation, of the unity of humanity, a pledge of universal peace in a federated world. He promptly registered the rainbow as his legal trademark and engaged a team of house painters to render the whole front of his Bourke Street arcade white and then emblazon it with a brilliant arching rainbow. Every time they saw a rainbow in the sky, he reasoned, his reading customers would associate it with his arcade and be encouraged to come in and buy more books.

In this, Edward was ahead of the Russian physiologist Ivan Pavlov, who in the 1890s conditioned his dogs to salivate in response to a particular stimulus. But the idea was the same, as it is with many advertisers today: associate a product with something pleasant or status-building, and people will buy. Before the Commonwealth government–driven backlash against the evils of tobacco at the turn of the twentieth century, tobacco merchants were particularly adept at the game—cigarettes were associated with fast cars, high society, sexual attraction. The rainbow, regarded as God's covenant to humankind, attracted criticism from some of Melbourne's religious, but the vast majority of Edward's fans thought it lovely, and so did their children.

Embellishments to the book arcade continued. Cane chairs were strategically placed to allow customers to read at their leisure without pressure to buy. Massive brass columns were installed the length of the arcade to support a roof cleverly modified to accommodate a newly constructed light well; light reflected off the brass to add to the ambience. As Christmas of 1874 approached, Edward fitted his male staff out in scarlet jackets with Cole's Book Arcade embroidered on golden armbands—a sight that attracted admiring glances from some of the arcade's female customers. Dressed in his usual fusty black suit, Edward unobtrusively patrolled along the back of the arcade.

He continued his 'men with tails' fantasy by advertising shares in a fictitious public company—the Caudo-Homo Search and Exhibition Company—whose purpose would be to arrange a travelling world exhibition of a tailed man. An announcement was made in *The Herald* that several thousand shares were available at one shilling each, and that in the event of the company's success, each shilling invested would return to the holder £27.10.0. Some diverting correspondence ensued in *The Herald,* once again increasing the newspaper's sales. One correspondent complained that no profit would accrue if the exhibition moved to New Guinea, where tailed men were not unusual; the company's response was that in this special instance, the tailed man would act as the exhibitor of one of the company's remarkable tailless directors. Another correspondent complained that many European areas of the world 'were degraded enough through the admission of hordes of Chinamen without being (additionally) cursed with the presence of a more contemptible race'; the company replied at some length that all men were essentially equal, and none inferior to others because of skin colour. Things turned even nastier when a correspondent asserted that:

> I happen to know something of your company's manager … and I venture to say that in the whole of Australia … his match could not be found for variety and heinousness of crimes, and were it not for his superlative, his exquisite cunning, he would not be at large today attempting to concoct, yes! concoct, his swindling company.

And this was 150 years before Facebook! The company replied:

> Insults to our manager we shall treat with the silent contempt they deserve … (However) as this enterprising company is not properly supported and … all the money we have collected from shares is but two pounds seventeen shillings, and we have been unjustly abused, we shall now throw up the whole concern in disgust and conclude our existence by simply remarking that it was E.W. Cole of the Book Arcade, Bourke Street, that started the idea, and he naturally thought that if a number of people made a deal of money through his suggestion, out of simple gratitude they would come and spend a part of it on books; and now the next best thing to buying shares in the Caudo-Homo Search and Exhibition Company is to take the money you would otherwise have bought shares with and go and buy books or music at Cole's Cheap Book Arcade, 158 Bourke-street.[12]

Once more, most Melburnians took no umbrage. They enjoyed the eccentric ads and the indignant correspondence they stimulated, and wondered what Mr Cole would next find to amuse them. They did not have to wait long.

On 3 July 1875, the 'Books and Publications' column on the front page of *The Herald* ran an advertisement:

A Good Wife Wanted
Twenty Pounds Reward
Positively Bone Fide
I, Edward William Cole
of the Book Arcade
Bourke Street,
wish to obtain a person for a wife
with the following characteristics:-

SHE MUST BE A SPINSTER of
thirty five or six years of age, good
tempered, intelligent, honest, truthful,
sober, chaste, cleanly, neat, but not
extravagantly or absurdly dressy;
industrious, frugal, moderately
educated, and a lover of home.
Any respectable, well-intentioned
person who from the range of their
observation can conscientiously
recommend to me an unengaged
woman answering the above
description will, in the event of a
marriage taking place between us
in consequence of such information,
receive my sincere thanks, and the
above reward directly such marriage
takes place. This may be thought by
many an absurd, because unusual,
way of looking for a wife; and I am
quite sensible that I may be laughed
at, but the thoughtful will not laugh,
the most that they will

do in that direction will be to smile
good-humouredly, for they know
that whilst the best thing a man can
have is a good wife, and the worst
thing a bad wife, yet, in most cases,
a very irrational principle of selection
is followed, for that nineteen out of
every twenty of the unions that take
place originate from accident of life,
from a chance meeting at a ball,
at a relation's, at a friend's, at a
neighbour's &c. I take what I believe
to be the most reasonable course,
of looking wide around to find, and
when found, of ascertaining by
inquiry, the exact character a woman
bears in her neighbourhood, and
amongst those who know her, before
I enter into indissoluble intimacy with
her: and I have no more hesitation
in advertising for, and critically
examining into the character of
one who is to be my partner for life,
than I should have were I merely
advertising for a business partner:
and if, by advertising, I get a good,
a sensible, and a suitable wife
instead of an unsuitable one, which
I should very likely get in the usual
way, my temporary exposure is well
indemnified and my twenty pounds
well spent.

Lest the reader be confused or have an inexact understanding of what Edward wanted (although this would seem impossible with such a pedantically clear description), he then elaborated. Here is a summary:

SHE MUST BE SOBER, for a drink, insinuating drink, is a fearful curse. As a destroyer of domestic happiness it is indeed the worst of all—the curse of curses.

SHE MUST BE CHASTE, for let even a colourable supposition of unfaithfulness once arise, and frequently all domestic happiness is at an end. In the marriage state both parties owe it to each other to so conduct themselves to be, like Caesar's wife, above suspicion.

SHE MUST BE HONEST. The most inspired line of the poet asserts that 'an honest man is the noblest work of God' and in morals, a woman is a man. She also, if honest, is the noblest work of God, and who would not prefer to have the noblest work of God for a wife?

SHE MUST BE INTELLIGENT. Modesty doubtlessly forbids me to say it, but I have some intelligence myself, and therefore require an intelligent wife, and should be miserable with an unintelligent one.

SHE MUST BE CLEANLY, for cleanliness is necessary to comfort, is necessary to health, is necessary to gain the respect of all decent people, and in fact, as the wise man says, is next to godliness, or goodness itself, and is absolutely necessary to make a home happy.

SHE MUST BE INDUSTRIOUS, for industry occupies the mind, makes the time lighter, makes the food sweeter, makes the sleep sounder, makes the person healthier, makes the person wealthier, makes the person wiser, makes the person worthier, and makes the home happier.

SHE MUST BE NEAT IN DRESS, and not extravagant or absurd; and on this point I shall speak very plainly. One of the greatest curses of unhappy homes, and one of the greatest curses to the well-being of the civilised world is the inordinate, the most insane love of unnecessary dress in women. It has made, and does make millions of homes unhappy that might otherwise be happy; it has indirectly sent and is sending thousands and tens of thousands of striving honest men through the insolvency Court, and to prison for debt ... for there is not one man in a thousand but more or less sneers at, despises and hates the absurd chignons, ridiculously placed head-dresses, silly looking paniers or back saddles and dragging trains that disfigure and disgrace the lovely form of woman in our streets. Of all things men most like to see women neatly and sensibly dressed from head to foot, and their natural charms shown to the best advantage, and I, as one of them, like to see the same.

SHE MUST BE GOOD TEMPERED, for a sulky, a hasty, a scolding, a nagging or a fretting person is a curse in a house, while a good-tempered one is always a joy. [Twenty-four lines of cheesy doggerel about womanly virtues followed Edward's admonition about cheerfulness.]

Melbourne's reaction was galvanic. General public amusement at yet another of Mr Cole's stunts was matched by incredulity that the man could so expose his private matrimonial wishes. Indignation and moral censure flowed from the usual pious suspects. He was blaspheming the holy estate of matrimony! He was aping the heathen practice of purchasing a wife! But sales of *The Herald* increased, as did the crowd at Cole's Arcade. The Saturday evening following the advertisement was busier than any his rapidly growing staff could remember. Edward himself did not appear on the sales floor, but an assistant who bore him a vague resemblance, a man named Cuttleworth, was the blushing target of speculative regard from female customers. One of Edward's pie-stall customers offered to send him for a price a whole notebook of former girlfriends.

According to family legend, Edward received letters—some humorous, some critical—but only one he felt had possibilities:

Melbourne 5th July/75

Sir,
I have very carefully read your letter in *The Herald* and I think it is a very sensible one.

For my part, I think it is a very serious thing to get married, and if there were more thought as I do, I think there would be fewer unhappy unions.

I have been a little over twelve months in Victoria. I am a Tasmanian, and if ever you have visited that island you could not but remark the difference between the people there and here, so sociable and friendly. People here tell me I should not say I come from Tasmania because of unfortunate aspects of its history, but I will stick up for my island home as long as I have breath, for my family are highly respectable, and there has never been a stain on one of our names.

I thought I would tell you I was a Tasmanian in the first place, for you might be one of the narrow-minded ones, though I hardly think so by your sensible remarks. I have made the acquaintance of a few gentlemen in Victoria, and what I have met do not come up to my ideas of a good husband. I do not care so much for a pretty face (though I like to see one as well as most people). I would sooner have good sense and good temper any day. I am not pretty myself, for I am a little dark thing with dark eyes and hair, and nearly thirty years old.

I want someone to love and take care of me, someone I can look up to and respect, one who is good-tempered, sober, good-principled, industrious, honest, and kind, and I am sure it will not be my fault if I do not make him a good wife.

I have received a very good education, and have been brought up to do everything from making a pudding to playing the piano. I am rather hard to please, for I intend to look before I leap. You could not blame me for that. So if you think you would like to make my acquaintance you can do so by addressing a letter to

Tasman,
Post Office,
Melbourne

and I will see you if you wish it.[13]

Edward did wish it, but his nerve failed when he asked her to come to the arcade: he did not himself turn up. Taking matters into her own hands, she left a note with an assistant there, saying she'd meet him at seven o'clock that evening at the top of Collins Street in Spring Street. She would be wearing a dark dress and a black hat with a rose on the side.

They did meet at the appointed hour at the top of Collins Street. He found her to be plump and plain, and she found him to be sensible if uncharismatic. But they felt wonderfully at ease with each other as they strolled down Collins Street. He told her of his unconventional religious views, which she said in no way discouraged her from contemplating a lifetime union, although if they were to marry, she'd prefer a quiet ceremony in a church. Her name was Eliza Frances Jordan, and she told him of her family background. Her father was Charles Jordan, a timber merchant, formerly of Brander's Ferry in Melbourne, now a man of some substance living with his family in a house called 'Lauderdale' on several acres of ground overlooking the River Derwent in the Hobart suburb of New Town.

Eliza was staying in Melbourne with family friends, the Clarkes, also formerly of Hobart. Edward was invited to meet them for afternoon tea. Mrs Clarke put him at ease by saying

A couple made for each other, Edward and Eliza,
close to their wedding day in August 1875

she loved visiting Cole's Book Arcade and was frankly interested in meeting its proprietor. So were the rest of the Clarke family and several of their friends who, intrigued, gathered to meet this rather unconventional suitor for Eliza. Edward in turn took Eliza to meet a close friend and sophisticated confidant he had recently acquired, Joseph D'Ama Drew, a man of English, French and Canadian origins, and his wife. They took to Eliza as warmly as the Clarkes had taken to Cole.

Eliza, chaperoned by her married sister, then took Edward to Tasmania to meet her family. He found them welcoming, and realised that Eliza had her father's quiet sense of humour and easy congeniality.

And so they married, the unpretentious ceremony being performed by the Rev JH Gregory at All Saints Church of England in St Kilda on 10 August 1875. Edward's first shop assistant, young Mr Pyke, now sixteen, was charged with minding the arcade. After the service, Edward and Eliza took the train to Mack's Hotel in Geelong for their honeymoon. Word had gone around that the bookseller who had advertised for a wife in *The Herald* was about to consummate his resulting marriage at the hotel, and a small crowd was gathered at the station. The couple escaped unscathed, but according to family legend a couple of wags

HAPPINESS

READ

LENDING LIBRARIES

COLLINS ST.
6000 Volumes.

BOURKE ST.
2000 Volumes.

Mother

HAPPINESS

Mother

had strung up cowbells under their hotel bed, which tested Eliza's sense of humour to the full. She also set a Seidlitz powder fizzing when she used the chamber-pot.[14]

Back in Melbourne, the happy pair had a short dispute about where to live. Wanting to start married life outside the polluted city environs, Edward had rented a terrace house in Carlton, but Eliza, neither meek nor submissive, would have none of it. A perfectly serviceable apartment existed above the arcade at 158 Bourke Street, and if they cleared out the stock, it would suit her very well. She furnished it without frills but comfortably, and they installed a window in the roof for extra light.

As they were settling into domesticity, Eliza had to overcome one problem that was haunting her. A jilted and suicidal suitor had learned that she had married, but before throwing himself into the Yarra he implored her to have one last meeting with him. She discussed this with Edward, who thought she should meet him lest he do something foolish, but insisted on joining her at the meeting. The suitor was initially extremely hostile, but Edward calmed him down and he left them quite amicably after realising that Eliza had found a good match.

The arcade continued to prosper as new gimmicks were added to attract customers. One of the most ingenious comprised a couple of little puppets installed on a platform at the entrance. Dressed in sailor suits, they wound a windlass that with a clatter tipped over a seemingly endless succession of tin signs advertising books available inside, interspersed with short homilies about religion and morality. They included:

> All men are brothers. The people everywhere that you do not know are as good as the people that you do know.
>
> The government of right, the religion of goodness. United States of the World, 'tis coming. One government, one religion, one language before the year 2000.
>
> Let the world be your country and to do good be your religion.

Children asked their parents what made the little puppet men go round, and what made the signs tip over. Some parents hazarded the guess that a man was turning a handle hidden under the floor—but it was in reality a tap running over a waterwheel.

Two events followed in the summer and autumn of 1876. First, Edward went with his staff to a booksellers' picnic at the beach village of Mordialloc. Not a sportsman, he reluctantly agreed to take part in a game of cricket but was clean-bowled for a duck by WH Cooper,

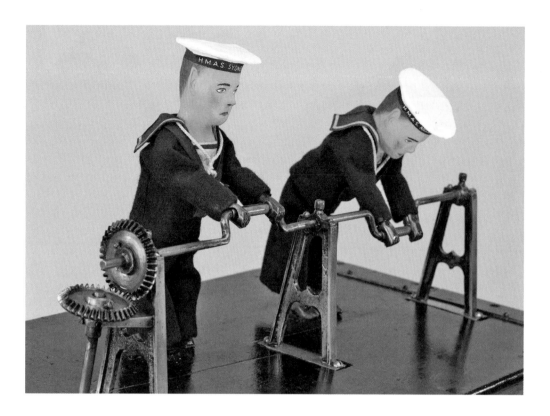

The sailors now reside in the Melbourne Museum, adjacent to the Royal Exhibition Building, Carlton

who later became a Test cricketer. Edward was not an adept sportsman, but he was good at making babies. The second event occurred on 13 April 1876, when his and Eliza's first child, Ada Belinda Cole, was born. Her initials were ABC. Maybe, mused Edward, we will get through the alphabet naming our children. They didn't, but, being a fertile and child-loving couple, had a further five, all born in Melbourne as Edward continued to manage his expanding book trade. They were Edward William Charles (Eddy), born 5 May 1878; Valentine Francis Stewart (Vally), 13 February 1880; Ruby Angelina, 10 February 1882; Pearl Adelia, 14 November 1883; and Ivy Diamond, 1 August 1885.

As his financial means grew, Edward attempted once again to move his family out of the heavily polluted environment of central Melbourne. According to Turnley, he even succeeded in doing so for a few months between 1881 and 1883, apparently boarding in a substantial house, one of seven adjoining properties called Bayview Terrace, in Princes Street, Fitzroy, close to the Exhibition Building and a few metres off Nicholson Street.[15] The house was a half-hour's walk down Nicholson Street, Spring Street and Bourke Street, which to Edward at the vigorous age of fifty-one would have been welcome morning exercise. Eliza tolerated his concerns for a while, but yearned to return to the cramped flat above the arcade at 158 Bourke Street; he eventually gave way.

COINS AND MEDALS

As soon as he became a bookseller in Melbourne, Edward was enthusiastic about advertising. He actively used the local press, including *The Argus, The Age* and *The Herald*, not only to advertise his books but to find bookcases for his arcades and staff to work in them. When he became more affluent he advertised for houses for his family to move to, possible new places of business and a wide range of furniture to equip those places, and domestic servants. And, of course, in *The Herald* of 3 July 1875, he famously advertised for a wife. Newspapers were not his only medium for publicity: he also printed calendars, bookmarks, postcards and stamps. Most unusual and prolific, however, were the coins and medals he had minted, although he was not the first merchant to do so.

The Royal Mint, the Bank of England and the treasuries of many countries had rules for use of currency in advertising, both notes and coins, throughout the nineteenth century. Most government authorities decreed that likenesses could be used, but nothing that approached counterfeiting. The US Treasury decided that one side of a paper note could resemble a dollar bill, but one side only. Many convicts owed their transportation to Australia to forgery, including Francis Greenway, who became the architect of several beautiful Sydney buildings.

READING AND THINKING BEING WISDOM

THE ELEVENTH COMMANDMENT
A NEW COMMANDMENT GIVE I UNTO YOU THAT YE LOVE ONE ANOTHER

CAUSES OF VARIATION IN MANKIND
MAN IS BUILT UP BY TWO CAUSES HEREDITY FROM HIS PARENTS AND THE SUM TOTAL OF HIS
ENVIRONMENTS SUCH AS FOOD CLOTHES SHELTER CLIMATE LOCALITY EDUCATION OCCUPATION ETC. MADE IN U.S.A.

BE YOU GOOD WILL BE AND HAPPY

COLE'S TEXT FOR A BILLION SERMONS
A KNOWLEDGE OF TRUTH IS BEST FOR HUMAN WELFARE THEREFORE TO OBSERVE ENQUIRE READ AND THINK IN ORDER TO FIND TRUTH IS THE HIGHEST DUTY OF MAN

CAUSES OF VARIATION IN MANKIND
MAN IS BUILT UP BY TWO CAUSES HEREDITY FROM HIS PARENTS AND THE SUM TOTAL OF HIS
ENVIRONMENTS SUCH AS FOOD CLOTHES SHELTER CLIMATE LOCALITY EDUCATION OCCUPATION ETC. MADE IN U.S.A.

FEDERATION OF THE WHOLE WORLD
DESIRABLE POSSIBLE AND INEVITABLE

RELIGION
THE THREE GRANDEST TRUTHS OF UNIVERSAL RELIGION ARE THE FATHERHOOD OF GOD THE BROTHERHOOD OF MAN AND PROGRESSIVE IMMORTALITY

BE GOOD AND YOU WILL BE HAPPY AND MAKE OTHERS HAPPY

ALL MEN ARE BROTHERS
THE PEOPLE EVERYWHERE THAT YOU DO NOT KNOW ARE AS GOOD AS THE PEOPLE THAT YOU DO KNOW

THE WORLD'S LANGUAGE
EVENTUALLY ONE LANGUAGE ONLY IS CERTAIN DESTINED TO PREVAIL THROUGHOUT THE WORLD AND AT THE RATE ENGLISH IS NOW SPREADING IT SEEMS TO SUPERSEDE ALL OTHER LANGUAGES IT IS BECOMING THE UNIVERSAL ONE

COLE'S FIELD OF GOLD AN ENCHANTING SIGHT OPENED JULY 1892 AT THE BOOK ARCADE MELBOURNE

FEDERATION OF THE WORLD
ONE GOVERNMENT ONE RELIGION ONE LANGUAGE ONE COINAGE BEFORE THE YEAR 2000

ALWAYS DO THAT WHICH YOU BELIEVE TO BE RIGHT

Edward's coins could not be mistaken for Australian or English currency, except by the dimly sighted. They bore on one side the legend 'Coles Book Arcade of Bourke Street' with the outline of a palm tree, which Edward thought attractive. It was established practice to plant palms in many colonial cities, not least in Melbourne. Palms were also a favourite of Edward's friend Ferdinand von Mueller, who planted them in the Melbourne Botanic Gardens; many are still there.

In the early days of his first arcade at 158 Bourke Street, Edward instructed his staff to scatter his coins at random around the city streets on their way home from work. He asked them to vary their routes to ensure the widest distribution. Apart from reminding finders where the coins came from so that they might pay his arcade a visit, Edward later used them as tokens for reward. One set of medals was imprinted with the promise that if handed in at his arcade, the donor would receive six 'easy writing pens' and 'two good pencils' at Cole's Book Arcade Melbourne. This idea was subsequently expanded to include his coins as discounts against purchases at the arcade. If, as happened on certain gala occasions at his big arcade in Bourke Street in and after 1883, the crowds seeking entrance became too unruly, Edward would have his staff sell the coins as the price of admission, usually for about threepence, thus encouraging the crowd to form a queue. The coins could then be used as tokens to be discounted against the price of a purchase once they were inside. This ploy was particularly effective on Melbourne Cup Day in November 1883, when crowds threatened to overwhelm police and staff at the opening of the new arcade in Bourke Street.

But Edward's medals had another purpose. From his beginnings as a bookseller in Melbourne he had energetically promoted his views about the evils of drink and tobacco, the virtues of a moral life, and the need to think clearly. He predicted a utopian world in which everyone would have access to decent food and clothing and the necessities of life. Crime would diminish and drunkenness would be rare. Good education would be available to all and the rights of women universally established. War would diminish as a way of settling differences between nations, and a world language based on a version of English would be modified to accommodate the best words of other languages.[16]

So, apart from their value in advertising his bookstores and their later use in crowd control, Edward used his coins to broadcast his enthusiasms. He would imprint them with uplifting messages and predict an optimistic future if certain rules of behaviour were followed. He believed that a great idea, even if conveyed in simple or ungrammatical language, was of more value than a dozen volumes of exquisite obscurities. His philosophy was similar to that of religious populists like John Wesley, who simplified the erudite and obscure practices of the established Christian churches to make them accessible to less educated worshippers. Aphorisms on the obverse of Edward's coins promoted in simple language such concepts as world federation, education, language, the dignity of labour, and the truth about religion and morality, as well as his pet themes about the equality of men, the perils of foolish expenditure, the evils of war and the coming of aviation. Some of them were the same or similar to those shown by the sailor puppets at the arcade's entrance. Here are samples, with punctuation adjusted for clarity.

On a united world:

One government, One religion, One language, One coinage before the Year 2000

The Whole World is the Fatherland of the Noble Minded

Federation of the whole world at the rate mankind is now progressing in literature, science, education, commerce, politics, morals, humanity, friendly intercourse and practical common sense—the early federation of the world is inevitable. Reader, do your best to help it on

On language:

The World's Language: eventually one language only is certain to prevail throughout the World and at the rate English is now spreading, it seems destined to supersede all others and become the Universal One

On morality:

Pure thoughts pure words pure deeds: Parsee Maxim

Be Good and you will be Happy and make others Happy

On drink and drugs:

Wasted wealth: The money spent on intoxicating drink, drugs, sheer foolishness and war would feed, clothe and educate the whole human race

On knowledge:

Educate the whole human race

For remember that the knowledge and goodness which you acquire in this world will be your only stock in trade to start with in the next

On the dignity of labour:

Labour ennobles a man. Idleness debases him

Work while you work, play while you play, and fairly earn and fairly take a recreation day

Labour is noble and best for all. It produces almost every blessing we enjoy. It gives us homes, food, clothing, luxuries, arts, learning. It profitably occupies our time and makes us healthier, wealthier, wiser, worthier, and happier

Wednesday is the Workers' Own.[17] Economise your time by working 48 hours in 5 days and so gain without loss the great boon of a whole recreation day—something for nothing

On race and colour:

Man's skin colour is caused by the sun. He degenerates in the enervating tropics. He evolves physically stronger in the bracing temperate regions

Causes of variation in Mankind are built up by two causes: heredity from his parents, and the sum total of his environment, such as food, clothes, shelter, climate, locality, education, occupation etc

On the future, aviation, commerce:

Could the foremost men of our time by some panoramic view be suddenly shown where on the path of progress the human race would be one hundred years hence, they would stare in blank astonishment; for everywhere we look, happily, we see evidence (that) is now diminishing the material distance which so long has divided the chief theatres of the world's commercial activity

I firmly believe that men will, in the immediate future, invent a machine to fly through the air as fast as a bird, and will finally succeed in obtaining a velocity beyond that of the swiftest bird that wings its way through the free vault of the heavens

Against war and armaments:

For while knowledge will bring about the unity of men and the wealth of nations, clothing the avenues of life with blossom and music and song till men shall revel in the glory of living, armaments, like some venomous reptile, which at the sign of friction shows its fangs; or some unscrupulous power become ambitious for the immediate acquisition of territory, springs at its neighbour's throat with all the ferocity characteristic of the barbarous ages

More coins and sayings—at top right is Cole's only coin in aluminium, cast to celebrate the coming of the air age and daughter Linda's flight with Harry Hawker

Throughout his innovative commercial life, Edward is estimated to have had over 300,000 coins minted, mainly by metallurgists Stokes & Martin of Melbourne, but also by firms in Britain, France and Japan. They were distributed widely not just in Australia and Britain and on the Continent, but in Japan and China and probably other parts of Asia. Some coins were pierced and used as pendants, like colonial Australia's 'holey dollars'. Others were used as 'alberts'—chains from vest pockets attached to fob watches. A Zulu warrior is said to have been found in South Africa wearing one of Edward's coins as a medallion around his neck with the inscription BE GOOD AND DO GOOD. Collectors appear not to have recovered any of the coins Edward had minted and distributed in Japan during his anti–White Australia policy visit in 1903, but the language barrier would have inhibited a thorough search.

Edward also gave away his coins as prizes. In advertising for public contributions to a book on humour he was compiling for the Melbourne International Exhibition of October 1880, he promised that 'a handsome gold medal, value £3.3s with proper incription (sic), will be given for the funniest piece sent in, and another gold medal, value £2.2s for the second best, and a gold locket, value £1.1s for the third best'.[18] He also packaged his coins in pillboxes with airtight lids, bought in bulk and labelled 'Boxes of Wisdom'. They were coated with gold-coloured lacquer and had a label in red or blue with white lettering. Inside the boxes were two aphorisms: either 'Reading and thinking bring wisdom' or a more lengthy one, 'The Happiness of Mankind, the Real Salvation of the World, must come about by every person in existence being taught to read and induced to think'. The boxes were also, of course, not-so-subtle encouragements to those who acquired them to visit Cole's Book Arcade and buy a book or three. But they delivered Edward's messages to readers who had not bought his early religious pamphlets.

Edward's coins were gradually lost or destroyed over the decades, and have become rare and valuable objects for collectors. Knowledge of their provenance was kept alive largely due to the efforts and enthusiasm of two contemporary coin enthusiasts, Alfred Chitty and Henry Williams. Chitty was born in England around 1850, the son of a leading London barrister. Apprenticed to a builder, he found an ancient coin on a London building site and caught the collecting bug. He arrived in Melbourne around 1870, joined the construction industry and went on to build around 300 houses in the Prahran area. He retired in 1910 to pursue his hobby as a coin collector, first at the South Australian Museum in Adelaide in 1927 and 1928, then for the next ten years in the 'coin room' of the State Library of Victoria.

The second enthusiast was Henry Williams, the 'Little Man', a long-serving and faithful department manager in Edward's arcade and one of the four trustees Edward chose to manage his estate after his death. In 1924, Williams collaborated with Chitty to produce a small handbook called *Incidents in the Life of E.W. Cole and a Collectors Guide and Catalogue to his Medals*. Their story is told in *A Handbook on E.W. Cole, His Book Arcade, Tokens and Medals* by George D Dean of Tarragindi, Queensland, published in 1988; Dean's book has informed much of what follows.

Edward's first coins were struck in 1879, when he was managing his expanding business, by Stokes & Martin (later Stokes and Sons), medallists of Melbourne. These coins, undated, were of gilded copper and were used to remind those who found them of Cole's first book arcade at 158 Bourke Street. Between 1879 and 1918, the year of Edward's death, the 300,000 coins and medals minted and distributed cost the arcade a total of £1500—an extravagance according to the budget-conscious Henry Williams, but worth their weight in promotion of the book business.

Altogether there were about fifty categories. Some were finished in copper or gold; others in silver, bronze and occasionally brass or, when commemorating the beginning of flight by heavier-than-air machines, in aluminium. A 'Japan Humanitarian' medal commemorating Edward's visit to that country was struck in 1903 to promote his anti–White Australia views. They were the only ones with a ribbon: of yellow with two black stripes. The likely sequence of issue is as follows:

1879: Cole's 'Text for a Billion Sermons'
1883: Medal marking the opening of Cole's big arcade in Bourke Street
1885: Medal commemorating the opening of Cole's Ornamental Exhibition
1890: Medal promoting Federation of the Whole World
1891–93: Medal proclaiming 'Wednesday the Workers' Own' (supporting Cole's campaign against early closing of newsagents and bookstores)
1893: Coin about the opening of Cole's Field of Gold—an optical illusion at the arcade
1898–99: All Men are Brothers (possibly a protest against Australia's involvement in the Boer War)
1903: His Japan Humanitarian medal
1914: The Coming of the Flying Machine (in aluminium)
1914–15: Medals on wasted wealth, alcohol, etc.
1918: A commemorative medal, its message a round-up of Cole's life and achievements, was instigated by Williams and produced four months before Cole's death. It was the last to be produced.

Ha Ha Ha.

7
COLE'S FUNNY
PICTURE BOOK

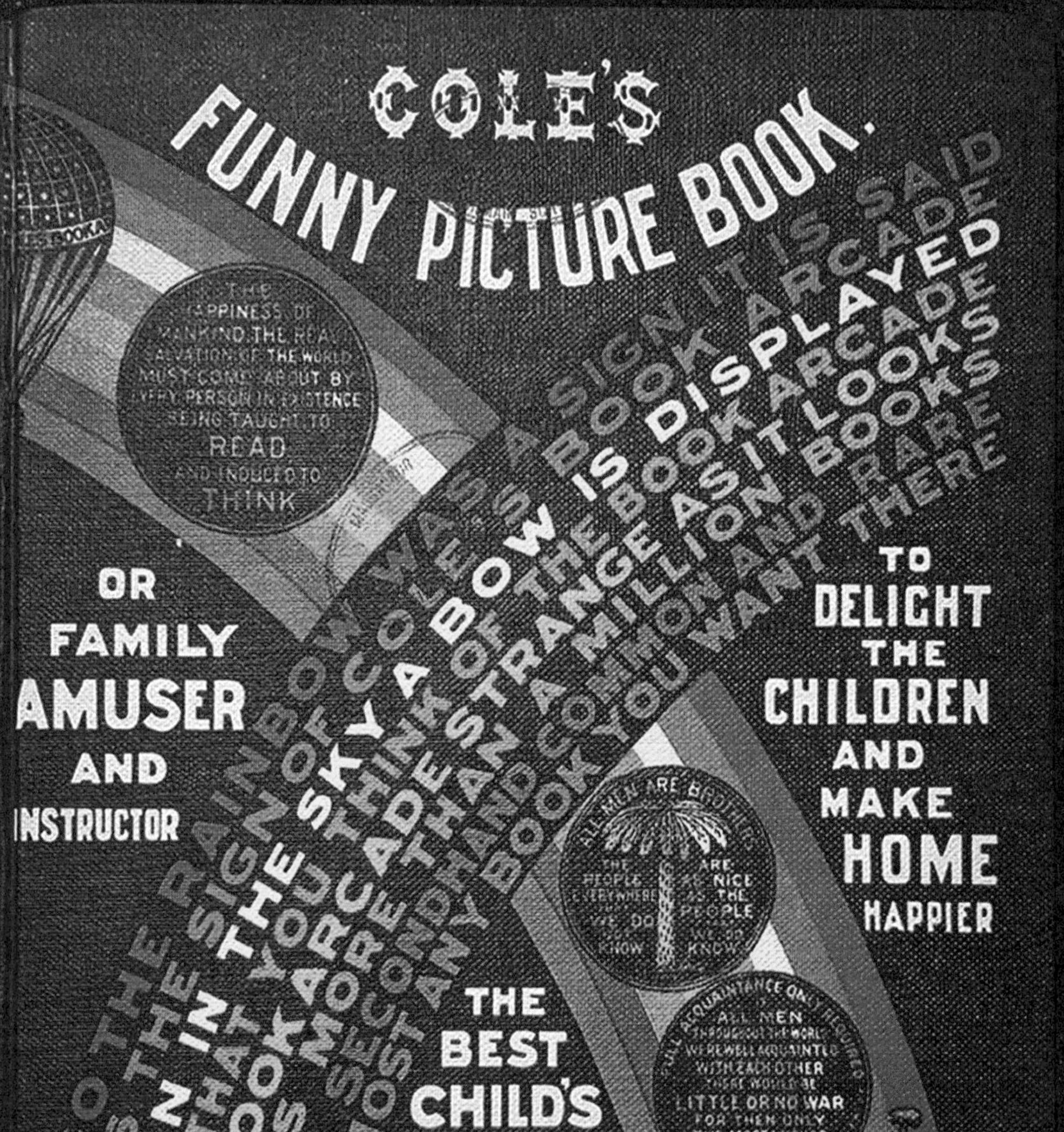

COLE'S FUNNY PICTURE BOOK.

THE HAPPINESS OF MANKIND, THE REAL SALVATION OF THE WORLD MUST COME ABOUT BY EVERY PERSON IN EXISTENCE BEING TAUGHT TO **READ** AND INDUCED TO **THINK**

A SIGN IT IS SAID
IS DISPLAYED
OF THE BOOK ARCADE
STRANGE AS IT LOOKS
A MILLION BOOKS
COMMON AND RARE
YOU WANT THERE

HOW A BOW WAS COLE'S SIGN OF THE SKY OF COLE'S
THINK YOU THAT THE ARCADE THAT SZ
AND SECONDHAND COMMON AND MORE THAN ANY BOOK

LONG AGO THE RAINBOW
NOW, 'TIS THE SIGN IN THE SKY
SO WHEN YOU
BE SURE THAT
COLE'S BOOK ARCADE
CONTAINS MORE SECONDHAND AND
NEW AND
CAN GET MOST ANY BOOK

OR FAMILY **AMUSER** AND INSTRUCTOR

ALL MEN ARE BROTHERS
THE PEOPLE ARE AS NICE EVERYWHERE AS THE WE DON'T PEOPLE KNOW WE DO KNOW

IF OUR ACQUAINTANCE ONLY INCLUDED ALL MEN THROUGHOUT THE WORLD, IF WE WERE WELL ACQUAINTED WITH EACH OTHER THERE WOULD BE LITTLE OR NO WAR FOR THEN ONLY THE MOST WICKED WOULD HAVE TO BE KEPT IN ORDER WORLD'S POLICE

TO **DELIGHT** THE **CHILDREN** AND MAKE **HOME** HAPPIER

THE **BEST CHILD'S** PICTURE BOOK IN THE WORLD

NO. 2

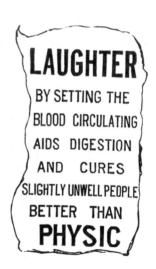

LAUGHTER BY SETTING THE BLOOD CIRCULATING AIDS DIGESTION AND CURES SLIGHTLY UNWELL PEOPLE BETTER THAN PHYSIC

Ask any mature Victorian if they have heard of Edward William Cole the bookseller, and the response is often a blank. But ask if they ever read his *Funny Picture Book* and favourable memories come flooding back. It was read to them as children, by parents, aunts, uncles and grandparents. They remember some of the illustrations, the rhymes and riddles.

A favourite is a pair of cartoons of 'The Whipping Machine for Flogging Naughty Boys', including John Hawking for talking, William Winning for grinning, George Highing for crying, Edward Daring for swearing, William Wheeling for stealing, Robert Hoaking for smoking, and Jonah Earls for chasing girls. In the first picture, a revolving cylinder with porcupine-like quills is turned slowly and with great effort by its inventor, Mr Snooks, while the line of pinioned boys baring their bottoms laugh at their frustrated teacher with his bow tie and birch cane as they say 'It don't hurt a bit', 'It'll dust my clothes' and 'Oh! what a joke'. However, the cylinder in the second cartoon is powered by Cole's patent steam-powered 'Gentle Persuader', and the boys are crying copiously into wooden buckets, promising a much more robust and sanctimonious-looking teacher that they will behave in future. Also illustrated is Cole's Electro-Micro Scolding Machine for Naughty Girls, priced at £5.5.0, which could severely scold 700 girls an hour.

The book is a richly grotesque collection of Victoriana, some of it frightening to small children, some of it maudlin and sentimental, but most of it enormously entertaining to delighted readers, whose numbers rapidly grew after the book was first published. It was Victorian-era Disneyland. It contained many moral and uplifting tales in chapters entitled Funny Land, Wonder Land, Baby Land, School Land, Teacher Land, Thinking and Reading Lands, Boy and Girl Lands, Sleep Land, Dialogue Land, Monkey Land, Temper, Pride and Greed Lands, Laziness and Stealing Lands. Edward employs cats, dogs, frogs, pigs, kangaroos, monkeys and rabbits to make his point. It is a grab bag of stories, rhymes, riddles, picture puzzles, poems, cartoons and moral tales, most of which were purloined

ABOVE *Cole's Funny Picture Books* on display in the Bourke Street arcade
OPPOSITE Cole's steam-powered flogging machine, more effective than his earlier hand-driven one at wringing repentance from recalcitrant schoolboys

by cutting and pasting from other sources, such as the English magazine *Punch*, which had been launched in London in 1841.[1] Edward had a gift for using curiosity and humour to capture the imagination of children and, once he had gained their attention, to put to them an intellectual challenge—a puzzle, a riddle, a cartoon with hidden characters—to draw a moral lesson.

The edition referenced in this chapter is the 70th, printed in 1965, at which stage over 870,000 copies in various editions of the book had been sold since it was first published in 1879. It begins rather eccentrically with a double page in full colour of ten varieties of Australian apples, which Edward swore by as a great benefit to health. They include Geeveston Fanny, Cox's Orange Pippin, Crofton Pearmain, Rome Beauty, Tasman's Pride, Granny Smith, Cleopatra, French Crab, Delicious and Jonathan. These are followed by another double-page full-colour illustration of the coats of arms of the six Australian states, together with a foreword written by Edward in which he extols Australia as the best country in the world—a fact, he says, that most Australians do not appreciate. It is, he observes, a continent rich in minerals, forestry and agriculture that could be made even better by the sowing of marram grass[2] and lupins in the drifting sands of Australia's deserts, where they would eventually decay and turn sandy wastes into fertile soil.

Apart from the material he enthusiastically lifted from others, Edward used the book as a vehicle to express many of his own feelings and beliefs. One concerned his obsession with heavier-than-air flight. He began with a riddle about a man in search of a particular but undefined article. Starting in Melbourne, the man travels in a huge assortment of vehicles around the world in search of it—on foot; by rowing boat, ox, horse, elephant, camel, yacht, junk, reindeer; on stilts; by paddle-steamer; in a rickshaw; on a tricycle; and by steam train. He calls on the governor of Victoria, the Rajah of Sarawak, 'His Dual Majesty Lord Paramount' of Japan, the Great Cham of Tartary, the 'Celestials' of China, the Grand Lama of Tibet, the Chief of the Greenland Esquimeaux (sic), the Mormon Prophet of Utah, the presidents of Brazil and Peru, the Sheikh of Timbuctoo, the Sultan of Zanzibar, the Custodian of the Precious Tomb of the Great Prophet, the Rao of Cutch, the Maharaja

Cole's Patent Whipping Machine for Flogging Naughty Boys in School.

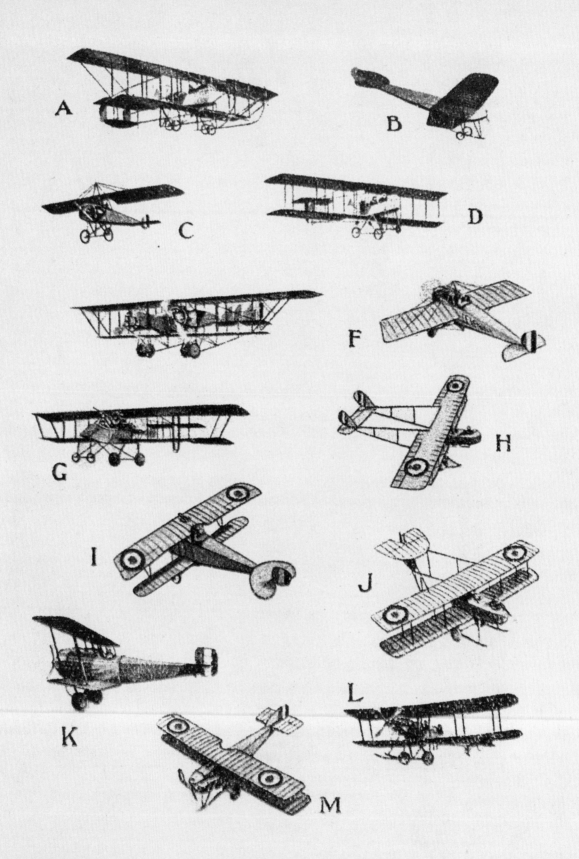

of Mysore and, by no means last or least, 'Her Royal and Imperial Majesty, the Queen of England, Empress of India, Sovereign of Canada, Australia, and 40 other countries, powerful and beloved ruler of the finest race of men and the largest, mightiest and grandest Empire the world has ever seen'. None, including Queen Victoria, have the faintest idea where the man might encounter the article he seeks.

Finally, the man returns to Melbourne, where he finds it staring in his face at Cole's Arcade—a FLYING MACHINE. Edward added his own homily about flight. In the second edition of the *Funny Picture Book* he included a sketch of a weird and completely unairworthy contraption with columns of umbrellas meant to suck into the air a platform controlled by a man in a top hat. It moved rather like an octopus propelling itself hydraulically through the water by squirting water through its nozzles. Since then he had remained fascinated by flight and in October 1882 he offered a £1000 reward to anyone who could propel a machine through the air by any means other than gas and land it in Bourke Street outside his arcade. No one ever claimed the reward, but Edward was finally vindicated in his predictions when people began to fly in the first decade of the twentieth century and one of them, Harry Hawker, took Edward's eldest daughter, Linda, up for a joy ride. Illustrations of thirty-six aircraft types designed before the First World War were included in later editions of the book.

Edward also gave full play to some of his pet aversions. On smoking, he wrote:

The following organs, fluids, functions, etc of the body, especially of the young, are frequently more or less affected by the use of tobacco: the blood, the heart, the nerves, the brain, the liver, the lungs, the stomach, the throat, the saliva, the taste, the voice, the eyes, the ears, the nose, the mouth, the tongue, the palate, the pancreas, the lips, the teeth, the bones, the skin.

Medical men and observing experts affirm that many diseases are caused or accelerated by the use of tobacco, among which are the following:- heart disease, consumption, cancer, ulceration, asthma, bronchitis, neuralgia, paralysis, palsy, apoplexy, indigestion, dyspepsia, diarrhoea, constipation, sleeplessness, melancholia, delirium tremens, insanity.

Tobacco using injures the unborn child by giving it a puny body and an imperfect start in life.

The following governments have passed laws against juvenile smoking:- Germany, Switzerland, Norway, Japan, Canada, Nova Scotia, New Brunswick, Prince Edward Island, British Colombia, the North West Territories, Cape Colony, New South Wales, Victoria, South Australia, Tasmania, and about 48 of the States and Territories out of 53.[3]

Edward's nineteenth-century outburst gave the lie to the twentieth-century claim of the tobacco industry that smoking did not injure health.

In earlier editions of the *Funny Picture Book*, Edward included his well-known saga of men with tails that had caused such amusement to readers of the Melbourne *Herald* in the 1860s and 1870s; it was dropped from later editions, but some of his other writings and thoughts remained. In his Reading Land and Drawing Land chapters, he included his view that a room hung with pictures was a room hung with thoughts, and that a single picture often conveyed more than volumes. He wrote that a good clear map of the world should be hung in every house in the world, 'for it is a most deplorable fact that 99 out of every 100 of the inhabitants, even of the civilised world, have a very poor conception of the geography and ethnology of the world'.

He included a quirky list of 555 names of girls and 555 names of boys, advising the reader that if they had more children than this they should call on Professor Cole at the Book Arcade and he would give them a supplementary list.

In a later edition, Edward added a full-page illustrated memorial to his second daughter, Ruby Angelina, who died of scarlet fever as a child, entitled 'Ruby Cole and her Clever Frog'. It showed Ruby in a fairy dress, with her frog playing his violin under a mushroom, and included the words: 'Sacred to the memory of our dear little Ruby, who departed this life March 27th 1890, aged eight years. She was intelligent, industrious, affectionate and sociable, and is deeply regretted by all who knew her.' There were also some poignant verses:

> There is no flock, however watched and tended
> but one dead lamb is there
> There is no fireside, howsoever defended
> but has one vacant chair.

> There is no death! What seems so is transition
> This life of mortal breath
> Is but a suburb of life elysian
> Whose portal we call death.

> She is not dead - the child of our affection -
> But gone unto that school
> Where she no longer needs our poor protection
> And God himself doth rule.

Another full page was devoted to his second son, Valentine Francis Stewart, but, curiously, there is no page about his other son, Edward, or his daughters Linda, Pearl and Ivy.

A typical piece of Edward's puckish humour was designed, like his people with tails, to amuse readers and entice them into the arcade:

Popular Errors

The commonly received notion that a man may marry his first cousin but not his second, is not true; but it is quite true that Cole's Book Arcade is in Bourke Street, Melbourne, about half way between Swanston and Elizabeth Streets. The rumour that a Yankee Gentleman has invented a machine to take the noise out of thunder has turned out not to be true; but it is quite true that Cole's Book Arcade is open from nine in the morning to ten at night, every working day of the year. The fact that Cole's Book Arcade contains 80,000 sorts of books is not the cause of the sea being salt—or coconuts containing milk, or the growth of big gooseberries, nor of the multitude of great big files told annually about a sea-serpent. It is not true that cats will suck the breath of children when they are asleep, but it is quite true that Cole's Book Arcade contains one interesting cat and 80,000 sorts of interesting books.[4]

In the business review section of *The Australian* on Tuesday 4 September 2018, journalist Andrew White reported in his 'Margin Call' column that Australia's richest man, Anthony Pratt, had posted a gif on Twitter combining a 'Happy Father's Day' wish with a call to the public to buy more Visy boxes. Pratt also promoted himself and his cardboard business— through learning the eccentric art of juggling. Perhaps he was inspired by Edward Cole, who used humour as well as fantasy to advertise his Book Arcade, including his import trade with England, as in this story:

The true History of the great Sea Serpent

John Smith was born in a swamp near Sydney about 5,000 years ago. He was hatched by a female bunyip from an immense 3-cornered egg which had fallen out of the moon. He had no relations—no brother, wife, sister or mother. Of shy disposition, he has made love to many mermaids, but remains a bachelor. He is exceedingly intelligent, can sing with a voice of tremendous compass from a sweet nightingale to the deepest tones of the largest organ. He believes in all the religions of the world. His whistle can be heard 100 miles [160 kilometres] away. He is 15 miles [24 km] long, 60 feet [18 metres] in diameter, has horny skin harder than steel and 5 feet [1.5 m] thick. He can travel at

200 miles an hour [320 km/h] and carry 120 times as much as *The Great Eastern*. A large eater, he has a whole whale for breakfast.

As a Carrier, the world-renowned sea serpent has been specially chartered to bring a fresh supply of books every week from England to Cole's Book Arcade in Melbourne; and also to show upon the coils of its body 2,000 rainbows, being so many copies of the beautiful sign of that establishment.

PS: Some people don't believe in the existence of the sea serpent, but if it did not exist, how could we have got his likeness and his history? That question is for unbelievers to answer.[5]

Despite Edward's own belief that every man is equal and the colour of his skin does not define his capabilities, and his fierce opposition to the Immigration Restriction Act of 1901, some of the illustrations in his *Funny Picture Book* are in today's terms overtly racist. An unsmiling Sambo slowly breaks into an enormous laugh through thick rubber lips across six illustrations as he reads a piece in Funny Land; seven little 'niggers' play with an axe and one cuts himself in two; there is a tale about Chinkey Chow-Chow the Chinaman and illustrations of a Scotsman, an Englishman, an Irishman, a 'Red Indian', an American and a Chinaman in grotesquely stereotyped clothes; in a cartoon, a group of Aboriginal people steal from white colonists; and there is an illustration of a rather glum Japanese schoolboy dressed in strange oriental garb with a 'scroll' inscribed with what the artist imagines are Japanese characters displayed on the wall behind him—quite obviously, the artist had no clue about Japan or its culture. It may never have occurred to Edward that these were racist stereotypes, and they would not have been seen as such by his contemporaries. He would probably have been mortified if someone with future vision told him they would be offensive and unacceptable in modern society.

Cole's Funny Picture Book broke new ground in Australia. Children's books were not printed locally before about 1841, and when they were, their content and culture were overwhelmingly English. When they gradually began to appear with Australian themes, the English artists who illustrated them knew as little about the Australian landscape as they did about the deserts of Mongolia. Only by the 1890s were Australian children's books becoming less derivative. A nucleus of gifted artists were encouraged by such journals as *The Bulletin* to produce black-and-white cartoons and illustrations. But Ethel Turner and her *Seven Little Australians*, May Gibbs and her gumnut babies, Mary Grant Bruce and her Billabong novels, Norman Lindsay's adventures of Bunyip Bluegum in *The Magic Pudding*, Dorothy Wall's *Blinky Bill*, Leslie Rees' Digit Dick, and the illustrations of Ida Rentoul Outhwaite and Pixie O'Harris were still decades away.

The compilation and production of *Cole's Funny Picture Book* was haphazard, although Edward's convictions about the need to present humorous books accessible to children was not. He put together the first compilation in one volume around 1876. This first edition, now practically unobtainable and priceless, measured 27.5 cm by 21.5 cm and had a limp cover with the title in black and gold inside a gold frame, decorated with a black and gold rainbow from the bottom left to the top right corner. Small print on the frame line reads: 'W. Detmold Binder'.

If an advertisement in the Melbourne *Herald* of 19 and 20 December 1879 is anything to go by, the book itself did not go on sale until that Christmas. Under 'Publications and Stationery', the advertisement reads:

CHRISTMAS BOOK, price 1s; by Post 1s 6d. Published this day at the Book Arcade. The Cheapest Child's Picture Book ever published in the World, under the name of COLE'S FUNNY PICTURE BOOK. It contains Baby Rhymes, Little Children's Stories, Boy Stories, Girl Stories, etc. etc. etc. E W COLE BOOK ARCADE Melbourne.

The volume contains barely half the content of later editions, and no accurate records exist of its sale. In subsequent editions, Edward made alterations and additions and then split the book into two volumes: *Cole's Funny Picture Book No. 1* and *Cole's Funny Picture Book No. 2*, both published in hardback.

Edward advertised an augmented edition of his *Funny Picture Book* in the Melbourne *Herald* on Tuesday 20 January 1880:

Cole's Funny Picture Book, price 1s; by Post 1s 6d

It contains all the choicest and most favourite of the nursery rhymes and tales, a variety of original and amusing reading, and fifty five select and funny pictures for the young. It also has a Supplement containing sixty of the most beautiful and instructive gems of poetry extant, suitable for the reading of other persons. I have tried to make it a book for the prattling infant—the five year old—the ten year old—the twenty year old—and the fifty year old, will alike be interested in, delighted with, and instructed by: and I have no hesitation in saying, that taking into consideration the favourite character of some parts, and the intrinsic worth of other parts, that it is one of the best books, and is certainly the CHEAPEST CHILD'S PICTURE BOOK in the WORLD, or that was ever in the world.

E.W. Cole
Book Arcade
Melbourne

Press reviews of the early editions were uniformly favourable. On 22 December 1882, the *Alexandra and Yea Standard, Gobur, Thornton and Acheron Express* reported:

We have received from Mr E.W. Cole his Funny Picture Book. It consists of 62 pages, well filled with nursery rhymes, entertaining anecdotes and numerous oddities, humorously illustrated. A previous edition of the same work, consisting of 12,000 copies, is said to have been entirely disposed of, and this success is certainly fully warranted. The book, which would make a highly acceptable Christmas or birthday present for a child is retailed at 1s 6d, or posted to any part of the colony for 2s.

On 28 December 1882, *The Argus* wrote:

> Mr E.W. Cole of the Bourke Street Arcade, has sent us Cole's Funny Picture Book, for which he claims that it is the funniest, the cheapest, and the best picture book for children in the world. The book is certainly a marvel of industrious compilation, and contains the most numerous collection of nursery rhymes and stories we have ever seen. The illustrations are most amusing, and altogether we are not surprised at the popularity of this capital book.

Edward separately compiled and published other children's books, many little more than pamphlets, and many later absorbed into one or other edition of the *Funny Picture Book*. He was obsessed with humour, or at least his brand of humour, which may have been laboured and derivative but was essential, he believed, as an aid to promoting education, enjoyment in life and good health. In a lengthy advertisement in *The Herald* on Saturday 17 July 1880 he announced:

> I, the undersigned, being desirous to prepare a first class Book of Fun for the Melbourne Exhibition, throw myself upon the liberality of the inhabitants of Victoria for funny contributions to the same. I propose to collect 1,000 pieces if possible from 1,000 persons in the following manner:- Any person in Victoria is requested to send by letter or postal card, addressed to E.W. Cole, Book Arcade, Melbourne, the choicest little bit of fun that they can remember ever having heard in their life— which made them laugh very much when they heard it, and which has always made others laugh very much when they have retold it.

Interestingly, the hugely successful Phillip Adams joke books published by Penguin in the 1990s and early 2000s were largely compiled from jokes requested by the author and publisher and sent in by people around Australia. Edward argued that:

> Good humour, seasonally applied, will dispel the dullest care. Mirth therefore is said to be the principal engine by which physicians batter down the walls of melancholy ... to exhilarate the heart has been the practice of every age and country, as the best means of preserving life ... Laughter is an external expression of joy. It is the most salutary of all the bodily movements, for it agitates both the body and the soul at the same time,

promotes digestion, circulation and perspiration, and enlivens the vital powers in every organ. Dr Fuller says:- 'Harmless mirth is the best cordial'. Henry Ward Beecher says:- 'Mirth is the sweet wine of human life'. Haywood says:- 'Man hardly hath a richer thing than honest mirth', and Carlyle, the prince of cynics, speaking of it in a moral aspect, says:- 'No man who has heartily and wholly laughed can be altogether irredeemably bad' … To sum up then, the chief benefits of laughter:- Laugh yourself heartily and you will feel better. Make your friend laugh and you will make him happier. Make your enemy laugh and he will hate you less. Make a stranger laugh and you will give him more confidence. Make the sorrowful laugh and you will lessen their grief. Make the despondent laugh and you will raise their hopes. Make the old laugh and you will make them feel younger. Make the child laugh and you will make it better tempered, better looking, more healthy, more happy and more loving.

Although his 'Book of Fun' did not see the light of day, Edward published six other books with humour as the theme during the 1880s and 1890s: *Fun Doctor, Fun Doctoress, Funniest Book But One, Funniest Song Book in the World, Funny Fun* and *Cole's Funny Music Book*.

Nor was this the end of the phenomenon. In 1976, fifty-eight years after Edward's death, his grandson Cole Turnley published a new *Funny Picture Book*, which he dubbed No. 3. The advertising blurb claimed:

It's true! After all these years, a brand new model … has been published. That old gent you see presenting it is 'Professor Cole', who ambled happily through its new pages of pictures, puzzles and poems; stories, sunshine and sea serpents; merriment, monkeys and marvels.

The six years' preparation of such a unique publication would never have been a practical commercial venture. It had to be a labour of love by the only person qualified to do it—Cole's journalist-grandson, Cole Turnley. The result is an editing miracle, so amazingly does the book manage to be entirely new while adhering so closely to the warm-hearted fun tradition of the old. At first glance, you would swear you were looking through one of the old books—[6]

To confuse the book's provenance further, a 72nd edition of *Cole's Funny Picture Book No. 2* appeared in 1992, alternatively known as the *Funny Picture Book No. 4*. It was enhanced and completed by Turnley and his daughter Merron Callum, and contained fresh contemporary material that the two of them compiled. The whipping machine for naughty schoolboys continued to be included. It was printed by the Book Printer/Globe Press in Maryborough, Victoria.

GETTING READY
TO GO TO
COLE'S BOOK ARCADE
FOR HIS
FUN DOCTOR

8
COLE'S BOOK ARCADE: TRIUMPHS OF MARKETING

BOURKE ST.

Bourke Street, 1895—the rainbow painted on the front of Cole's new second-hand book venture just visible on the lower left

By 1881, Edward was becoming a moderately prosperous merchant and a shrewd investor in Melbourne's commercial real estate. He maintained his small arcade at 158 Bourke Street, with its scarlet-clad salesmen and regular musical entertainment, but moved his second-hand book business to a supplementary location he leased at 232/234 Bourke Street East, just below Spring Street.

These premises had previously been occupied by Henry Tolman Dwight, a prominent early Melbourne bookseller and publisher who died in 1871. Dwight had hosted regular gatherings of Melbourne's literati, the core group comprising the poet Richard Henry 'Orion' Horne; the poet, jockey, police officer and politician Adam Lindsay Gordon; the bush poet Henry Kendall; and Victoria's attorney-general, Sir Archibald Michie, surrounded by a coterie of lawyers, doctors, clergy, journalists—a group of somewhat dissipated citizens united by the bonds of bookdom. Perhaps some of Dwight's literary aura hung around to add a degree of distinction to Edward's latest venture.[1]

To promote his new store, he put the following in *The Herald* on Friday 8 April 1881:

To lovers of old books, E W Cole begs to announce that he has opened a large SECOND-HAND Book Shop in Mr Dwight's old place, next to the White Hart, Bourke Street. Many thousands of books are already there, and more will continue to be added.

Meanwhile, the new Eastern Market was becoming a white elephant. During its lengthy construction, most of its tenants had moved to the Queen Victoria Market at the top of Elizabeth Street, and few were tempted to return, especially since the new market's logistics were all wrong. Instead of driving their drays full of produce into the market's interior under cover, market gardeners were required to stop in the street, exposing horse, driver and produce to traffic and weather. They also had to unload all their goods, whereas at the old

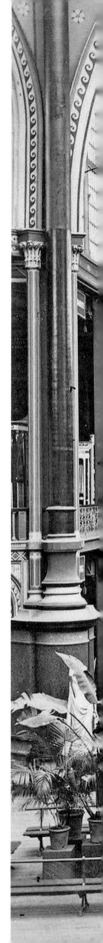

market they could unload under cover only what they anticipated selling, leaving on board the surplus for offering elsewhere. Furthermore, the new market's interiors were gloomy and pretentious compared to those of the Victoria Market.

Over its first two years of operation, under-utilisation drove down the Market Committee's hopes for a triumphant rebirth of their site. Observing this, Edward took a calculated risk: he offered to lease the *whole* market complex. After some prevarication, the committee agreed to a one-year trial lease, with a further two years if the first year proved successful—a total period from 1881 to 1883. The annual rent for the three years would be £2294.

If he could make the premises more attractive, Edward believed he could lure merchants back. He could also recapture the carnival atmosphere that had made its predecessor such a magnet for Melbourne shoppers. He was given grudging permission to enliven the market's gloomy archways. He painted all the walls for £350 of his own money and spent another £800 on showcases. He installed a printing press at stall number 13 in the basement. He added gas lighting pending the imminent arrival of electricity, and divided the untenanted area into a bazaar, salesrooms and a dairy produce arcade. Once the market got going, he planned to contract a professional band to play on Tuesday and Thursday evenings and Saturday afternoons. The Market Committee insisted that the extra lighting fixtures and some of the shop furnishings Edward installed at his own expense would have to be left behind at the termination of the lease.[2]

The Melbourne International Exhibition at the Royal Exhibition Building in Carlton Gardens had just wound up on 30 April 1881. Noting that it had lost money, Edward opportunistically advertised in the Melbourne *Herald* on 6 May 1881:

E.W. Cole, Book Arcade, having rented the Eastern market, begs to intimate to those who have goods in the Melbourne Exhibition, that he has a large amount of space to let, where advertising show cases can be stood, and goods sold.

Mr Cole intends to make every effort, by a collection of attractions, to allure the public into the building; and as the grand market is in the centre of a go-ahead city of 260,000, it cannot but succeed.

The produce market upstairs is steadily progressing.

The part intended to be devoted to the exhibition and sale of fancy goods and general merchandise, is in the lower basement lately occupied by the International Juvenile Exhibition.

German Court, Dresden China and Glassware in the
Great Hall, Melbourne International Exhibition, 1881

There are 40 open-fronted shops to let on this flat, at about 10s a week each,
and parties can, if they choose, sell in the shops, and rent a space in front of them
to stand their showcases on. Persons can also obtain space for open stalls. It is
also proposed to hold auction sales every day for the convenience of buyers and
sellers.

The building will be brilliantly lit with the electric light from the first of July, and
it will then be the favourite place of resort in the city.

For information about shops, stands, and all particulars, apply to E.W. Cole
at the Book Arcade.

||||||||||||||||||||||||||||||||||||||||||||||||||||||||||||||||||||||||||||||||||||||||||||||||||||||||||||||||||||||||||||||||||||||||||||||||||||||||||||||||||||||||||||||||||||||

To sweeten the proposal, Edward declared stalls rent-free for periods anywhere between two
weeks and six months, at the end of which stallholders could either pay a very moderate rent
or walk away without obligation. The word quickly got around and inquiries for stalls came
in rapidly. In an advertisement headed GRAND BAZAAR and SHOPS TO LET, he declared
the market suitable for all kinds of fancy ornamental and useful goods: toys; dolls; artificial flowers; millinery; baby linen; collars and ties; fancy boots; Italian, French, Japanese,

Chinese, American and Indian shops; general knick-knacks; music; catering; tobacconists; refreshments; confectionery; Indian tea; patent medicines; and herbalists.

Now to attract customers. Never one to understate his cause, Edward advertised on billboards and hired boys to put extravagantly worded circulars into every letterbox in the metropolitan area, with the message:

PROCLAMATION:

To the Inhabitants of the capital city of Melbourne and the visitors sojourning therein. GREETINGS! Long life, health, and much happiness to all of you, and be it known unto you that:-

Our city is the largest and grandest in Australia, and one of the finest in the world. That our market cost £100,000 to build, is one of the finest in the world, and is in the centre of the city; and whereas, the said market has for sundry reasons been slighted and neglected; but be it known unto all of you that this is contrary to the good sense and practice of all the world. In all ages, in all countries, the market-place has been the centre of attractions, a place for much trading, and a place for much meeting together to see and be seen.

Now verily it is absurd that we can act contrary to the good sense and experience of all the world, and allow our market to remain a byword and a reproach. Be it, therefore, ordered and ordained, fixed and established that from this day forward, every person who has nothing particular to do will do his or her duty and go to the market to buy, to see, and be seen, as of old.

And verily it is further recommended that everyone should so make their arrangements through the week as to be able without inconvenience, to do their duty, and cheerfully appear in person at our Grand Market and Meeting-place, every Saturday night.

Then look about and see your friends
The sights, and what to buy,
Enjoy yourselves for one sweet hour
Without a single sigh.
Next make your way to Cole's Arcade,
To buy a book for Sunday,
'Twill make you happy on that day,
and wiser on the Monday.[3]

Ignited by Edward's enthusiasm, the new Eastern Market filled and prospered. Clothing, fashion and leather traders from the International Exhibition vied with fruit, vegetable, meat and livestock merchants for the best stalls. Sideshow proprietors quickly followed. The first priority of customers was meat and dairy, fruit and vegetables, but many looked for other things and stayed on to be entertained by a growing number of sideshows: coconut shies, fortune tellers, jugglers, conjurers, a Punch-and-Judy show, six shooting galleries with rifles and live bullets, and a lady wrestler who challenged men to try to kiss her. She was felled by one man who in the process broke her jaw, possibly invigorated by sustaining a shilling shock from Madame Xena's Scientifically Controlled Electricity Machine Guaranteed to Double Male Virility.[4] From September 1881 Edward fulfilled his promise to hire a band, which played from 7.00 to 8.30 every Wednesday and Saturday night.

But all was not well. The City Corporation was not happy with Edward's vulgar sideshows, or with their returns from his rent. He was paying them £2294 rent per year—a miserly 2.5 per cent on their £100,000 capital outlay in building the new market. His sublessees were at the same time paying him a total of £10,000. Better, the corporation calculated, if they cut him out and took the rents directly from the subtenants. Sticking to their decision not to reimburse him for running expenses and maintenance, and giving him only minimal compensation for installing electric light and cabinetry, the corporation members voted not to extend Edward's lease beyond its three-year term—that is, beyond 1882.

According to Turnley, Eliza was extremely indignant at both the corporation's decision and her husband's decision not to fight it or even sue for compensation for all his installations. Edward's compromise was to assure her that he would walk away when the time came and make absolutely no effort to promote or maintain the market's popularity.[5]

While all this was going on, Edward was absorbed in two other things: continuing to attract customers to his dedicated Book Arcade with its brilliant rainbow front at 158 Bourke Street, and finding a newer and grander venue to replace it. He continued to bombard Melbourne with advertisements. Typical was one in *The Herald* on 22 September 1881. Within a border that endlessly repeated the words 'Cole's' and 'Saturday Night', the text was:

Book Arcade, strange as it looks
contains 20,000 sorts of books
New and second-hand
common and rare
you can get almost any that you want there.

Another appeared in *The Age* on 22 April 1882, intended to be sung to the tune of 'Mary Had a Little Lamb'. It contained twenty verses of morally freighted doggerel. To print the whole poem would test the reader's patience, but the last four verses carry the drift:

For all the books in all the world,
Are man's greatest treasure;
They make him wise and bring to him
by far his choicest pleasure.

They make his time pass happily
Through many weary hours
Amuse, compose, instruct his mind,
Enlarge his mental powers.

They give to him the greatest thoughts
Of all the good and wise
Preserved in books is knowledge vast
Which therefore never dies.

Books are the greatest blessing out,
The grandest thing we sell;
The joy they bring, the good they do,
No mortal tongue can tell.

As for premises for a grander arcade, Edward was searching for the ideal building, preferably still in Bourke Street, the centre of Melbourne's burgeoning retail and restaurant district. The street was colourfully described by contemporary writer Horace Perkins, as:

Melbourne's Oxford Street, or Cheapside, by day, and Piccadilly by night. Though not the most fashionable thoroughfare by day—which distinction must be accorded to Collins Street—it is yet, at all times, the busiest street, and at night it reigns supreme, without rival. The pavements are daily thronged with pedestrians, elegant equipages halt in numbers before the doors of favourite drapers and haberdashers, and the roadway is alive with vehicles of every description … Humanity, too, is seen under phases as varied as they are distinctive. The black coat and 'belltoppers' contrast strangely with the jumper, billycock hat, and roll of blankets that load the back of the 'swagman'. Jack ashore, not having joined the 'band of hope' jostles against the daintily-dressed Government official; and the Chinese hawker, with bamboo and basket, jogs along under the pressure of heavily-filled baskets of merchandise, which he maintains are 'welly good'. Vulgarity, in silks and golden ornaments, hustles past gentility in alpaca; and anonyma, in fur robes, shoulders with wealthy respectability in feathers and flowers. Newspaper runners, policemen, volunteers, country cousins, street arabs, bank-clerks, shopmen, and citizens in general make up, for the most part, the rest of the pedestrian personnel … Neither must mention be omitted of the three arcades, all of which are entered from Bourke Street—viz, the 'Royal', the 'Victoria' and the 'Eastern'.[6]

Edward had begun placing advertisements seeking new premises in Melbourne newspapers as early as 1880. One in *The Herald* of Saturday 21 February of that year specified what he wanted:

To Owners or Holders of Property in Bourke Street—Wanted to lease between Russell Street and the Post Office, an ERECTION, built or altered suitable for Cole's Book Arcade. A shell with open front, 30 or 40 feet [9 or 12 metres] wide, 150 feet [46 m] deep, three stories high and lighted from the top would be preferred, but a building of other dimensions might be made to suit. Rent not to exceed £100 per week. Address or apply to E.W. Cole, Book Arcade, Melbourne.

Throughout 1881 he put similar advertisements in *The Age*, *The Argus* and *The Herald*, always calling for a building of the same dimensions, always at the same rent ceiling, and invariably in Bourke Street. The low rent of £100 a week was a courageous call, occurring as it did at the beginning of the city's great land boom. For the 1880s was a decade of rapidly inflating real estate, based on wild speculation in land and the appearance of a multitude of building societies hoping to capitalise on the speculation. But Edward stuck to his guns. One of the city's decommissioned playhouses might be suitable if he could find one. Melbourne's first theatre, the Royal Vic, had opened in Bourke Street in 1842, followed by many more during the gold rushes of the 1850s and later, most in the eastern part of the city. Among them was Victoria Hall, also in Bourke Street, an ideal location and about the right size. But Edward was discouraged because it was relatively new and its owners would hardly agree to extensive alterations and a long-term lease.

In early 1883, he finally found what he wanted: the Spanish Restaurant, owned by Matthew Cantlon—by reputation an ex-convict who had made good in Melbourne's property market before returning to England in the 1870s. The restaurant was of three storeys, situated on the south side of Bourke Street between Swanston and Elizabeth streets. It had a generous frontage and extended back towards Little Collins Street to a depth of 120 feet (36.5 metres). It had been a popular eating house and hostelry during the post–gold rush days, but had fallen upon hard times as trade fell off during the late 1870s, and was about to be wound up.

Edward had found Cantlon's address and written to him late in 1882 to seek a lease, but heard nothing. At the beginning of 1883, however, Cantlon turned up in Melbourne without warning and approached Edward, who outlined with great enthusiasm his ambition to rebuild the restaurant and turn it into a book arcade.

According to Turnley, Edward and Eliza took Cantlon one Saturday night in late January on a tour of the Eastern Market followed by the hot spots of Bourke Street. Cantlon was impressed with the way Edward had turned the market into a raucous, energetic meeting place where Melbourne's population came to see and be seen and entertained under bright electric light hooked up to a dynamo attached to a steam engine. The trio then toured the Royal Arcade, on the corner of Bourke and Elizabeth streets, with its shining glass roof reflecting the light of numerous gas jets (later embellished with a large clock flanked by Gog and Magog, two giants who supposedly led an invasion of Britain, copied from the same figures placed at the Guildhall in London in 1708). By contrast, the Spanish Restaurant was a dull place indeed, but Edward assured Cantlon it could be rejuvenated as a mecca of books and other attractions. Cantlon was seduced by his certainty and enthusiasm and, on 27 January 1883, signed a lease at Edward's solicitor's office giving his lessee permission to alter the building at his own expense in any way he chose.[7]

Although no records can be found verifying the story of Cantlon's Saturday-night walking tour with the Coles, it is probably true. Turnley claims to have heard it first hand from his mother, Linda, Cole's eldest child, who apparently had a reliable memory. And historical evidence about Cantlon and his activities in Melbourne bear it out. First, Cantlon was very likely in Melbourne at the time. According to *The Australasian* of Saturday 18 November 1882, he and his wife disembarked in Melbourne from Britain on the *Kaiser-i-Hind* on 14 November 1882. Second, Cantlon had been a successful Melbourne property owner since the 1850s. His holdings—the subject of numerous news-paper reports—included hotels, boarding houses, wine and spirit wholesale depots, and pie shops.[8] One of his most famous establishments was the Bull and Mouth Hotel, a few doors east of his Spanish Restaurant in Bourke Street. He built it in 1850, replacing another drinking venue, the Eagle Inn.

Edward's ideas for a popular book arcade probably struck sparks of enthusiasm in Cantlon because of the popularity of his own establishments, even if Edward's arcade would be alcohol-free. William Kelly, an English traveller and writer, described a typical trading day at the Bull and Mouth sometime in 1853—reminiscent of Victoria's post–First World War licensing laws that created the notorious statewide 'six o'clock swill':

> The bar was really a sight for a stranger, with its close-packed crowd in front, skirted by outsiders, who were served over the hats of the inner ranks. Effervescing drinks frequently boiling over in the transit, and nobblers [small glasses of alcohol] overturn-ing in trayfuls on the brandy-proof heads of the indifferent multitudes. Whenever a man fell or retired, the gap was filled up like magic by a fresh customer, so that the demand

never flagged, the trade never ebbed, the fusillade never intermitted: 'Nobblers for five', 'Six ales', 'Round of old Toms!', 'Whiskeys neat', with only an ever-varying transportation in precedency, continued without ceasing, at the rate of one shilling all day long. The upper apartments were as fully occupied as those below if I might judge from the torrents of waiters of both sexes rushing down or sliding up in obedience to the law of demand and supply, the stairs positively dripping alcohol, and the oakum mat at the bottom squirting juices under every tread. The low atmosphere was one of spirituous essences, as dense as a Scottish mist, which I verily believe would inebriate a person of weak powers, and over it rolled, in murky curls, a thick fog of vile tobacco-smoke that would poison a rookery.[9]

Third, Cantlon's Spanish Restaurant had a long and colourful provenance. Writing in *The Age* in 1879, the bohemian journalist and poet Marcus Clarke thought it the best of the cheap eating houses in Bourke Street. He noted that it employed thirty-two persons in the house with nine cooks in the kitchen. One hundred beds were made up nightly, and it had its own billiard room. It had been founded by five Spanish brothers, the Parers (antecedents of the distinguished World War Two photographer Damien Parer). In the dining room were nineteen tables serving an average of 600 diners daily. On Cup Day, or other great holidays, it was patronised by 2000 customers. Five hundred pounds (227 kilograms) of fish, 600 eggs and 3000 pounds (1360 kg) of meat were consumed in a week, and it provided bed and meals at very good rates. Breakfast consisted of a choice of ham and eggs, steak, cutlets or sausages, plus tea or coffee, all for a shilling. For dinner a visitor could order pea soup for threepence, roast beef for sixpence, fruit pie or pudding for threepence, cheese for threepence, and English ale for threepence: total one and six. Clean and comfortable rooms could be had for a shilling a night. Bed and board plus three meals daily cost 20 shillings a week. Fresh meat and vegetables came from the Parers' own farm. They served quality Spanish wines imported from family members who owned vineyards in Spain; Clarke reckoned these to be far superior to colonial wines.[10]

The Parers disposed of the restaurant in 1868 to another Spanish landholder: their business partner, Augustus Barbeta, joint licensee with the Parers of Hosie's, a neighbouring hotel in Bourke Street. Barbeta in turn sold it to Cantlon, who leased the premises in 1883 to Edward.

Edward wasted no time in gutting and rebuilding the Spanish Restaurant to his specifications. His plan was to retain the external walls of bluestone masonry, and remove the interior floors and replace them with flying galleries around the walls, thus creating a hollow space from the ground floor rising through three floors. The building would be crowned by an arched roof of iron interspersed with two rows of glass panels, allowing natural light to flood all floors. It was visionary stuff, a forerunner of George McRae's magnificent Queen Victoria Building, the wonderful Romanesque Revival arcade of impressive proportions built on George Street in Sydney in the 1890s. I cannot find evidence that McRae was inspired by or emulated Cole's Arcade, but it is entirely possible that he travelled to Melbourne and saw the arcade in the 1880s before embarking on his own work—an intriguing thought.

Edward's plans were the butt of sarcastic jibes from his building contractor and associated tradesmen, who gloomily forecast it would all have to be done again 'the proper way'. Nonetheless, like enthusiastic 21st-century owner-builders in the BBC television series *Grand Designs*, Edward persisted. He rough-sketched his ideas on paper and put them to his architect, Mr TJ Crouch, who drew up plans comprehensible to the builders. Crouch added professional respectability to Edward's vision: he had already designed several of Melbourne's major public buildings, including the Blind Asylum, the Deaf and Dumb Asylum, the Homeopathic Hospital, and the Methodist Ladies' College in Barkers Road, Kew.

From 1 January 1850, all building in the City of Melbourne had been governed by an Act 'for regulating Buildings and Party Walls, and for preventing mischiefs by fire',[11] and alterations to them had to be officially approved. On 6 February 1883, a builder, CJ Verso of High Street, Northcote, gave notice to the Building Surveyor of the City of Melbourne that he intended to make alterations to premises at numbers 40 and 42 in Bourke Street for EW Cole Esq., using the services of TJ Crouch, architect.[12]

The building program was not without interruptions. In a letter to Eliza dated 4 March 1883 (she was resting with the children in Tasmania), Edward wrote:

> Everything goes on very comfortably in the shop. The new arcade has rather lingered in completion and there has been some difficulty about a wall, but matters are now arranged and the large hall was commenced yesterday but we cannot get it finished for six months so we shall be all the winter in the present shop. The contract was let for £4,800. I have two pillars cast to stand either side of the entrance, which weigh a ton each and they will have 400 pounds [181 kilograms] of brass on each of them. They are 18 inches [46 centimetres] thick and 12 feet [3.6 metres] high and will look very grand. Nothing like them in Australia. A neighbour, Mr Hosie, objected to our putting scaffolding on his roof but I went up to his farm about 20 miles [32 kilometres] from Melbourne and talked the matter over with him. I stayed all day and he was very hospitable and showed me over his farm and fed me up. He seems a very sensible man but has a keen eye for business … (Meanwhile) it takes me all my time seeing about the place

below. It requires the utmost vigilance to see that mistakes are not made and hundreds of pounds lost in an undertaking of such a nature and magnitude. It is not like an ordinary building that everyone can understand. It is as it were my own planning and invention and I must be on the spot to see the thing carried out. The City Council have given me notice about the drainage and the tax gatherer has been and rated it as a rental of £850 for the year so that rates will not be so heavy. One man has offered me £7 per week and £100 bonus for one of the shops. I intend to let them both for jewellers so that you will be able to pick out a jewel good and cheap.[13]

In a following letter of 11 March, however, he backtracked on his earlier view that things were settled with Hosie:

First the side wall of Hosie's was crooked, and after much negotiation with the agent, the lawyer, the owner of Hosie's property Mr Mears the late mayor, the building surveyor and others we got pretty well over that difficulty—when Mr Hosie objected to my putting a scaffold over his roof to raise and plaster the gable end to put a sign on! After a great deal of negotiation it was finally arranged that I should pay his lawyer, his architect, himself seven guineas in and give a bond of £2,500 that I would make his roof right if I damaged it. Next, his foundation is spread out under our ground, and we have to underpin it to make it safe. Next, another serious difficulty is just come upon me: the front of the building has shown signs of parting outwards! We are going to put props up to it in the morning so that we can tie it … but I am fearful that the present heavy rain may affect it before tomorrow … The foundation next to Hosie's is dug out right along his building and will be full of water in the morning … Altogether I am full of anxiety. I only hope this will prove to be one of the many times that things do not turn out so bad in the end as we feared.[14]

By mid-1883, construction difficulties had largely been solved and Edward had a canvas that would allow his vision of unique splendour full play. He now moved on to the fit-out.

Edward wanted a gala occasion for his arcade's opening, and chose Melbourne Cup Day 1883, Tuesday 6 November. Even back then, Cup Day was a prominent national race event. A popular story was that it had originated from a race organised in 1838 by squatters at Batman's Hill, where a series of bullock carts were drawn up as a grandstand, riders wore red and blue serge, the winning post was a discarded clothes prop, and bets were wagered in bottles of rum. The race day was moved to river flats on the Maribyrnong River in

Won by Martini Henry from New Zealand, the first non-Australian horse to win the event, Melbourne Cup, Tuesday 6 November 1883, also marked the grand opening of Cole's new arcade. Punters came in from Flemington to crowd the arcade.

1840, an area later known as Flemington. The *Port Phillip Gazette* of 7 March 1840 described the scene:

> … swept on one side by the river, on the other by a low ridge of undulating green hills, the site was particularly well chosen. The little plain itself was studded with tents and stands, above which floated the gay embroidering [sic] of a hundred flags; a band of willing if not superior performers lent their notes to mellow the harsh dissonance of a thousand voices, whose cheers and shrieks of excitement were borne well nigh to the silent and deserted streets of Melbourne.

The first officially designated Melbourne Cup race, held before 4000 onlookers in 1861, was won by an Australian bay stallion called Archer; he won again the following year. In 1864 the Victoria Turf Club and Victoria Jockey Club merged to form the Victoria Racing Club, and 'The Cup' became firmly established as the major race meeting of the Australian colonies. In 1865 Cup Day was designated a half-holiday for public servants and bank officials. By 1870, the crowd had swollen to 20,000; by 1880 to 100,000, the same as a well-filled Melbourne Cricket Ground on grand final day in the present Australian Football League. By the 1880s, Cup Day had developed its own legends about fortunes and reputations made or ruined in the betting ring. It had become a phenomenon to be discussed not only in racing pages, editorial pages, pictorial pages and fashion pages, but also to be denounced from pulpits and debated in parliament.[15]

On Cup Day in 1883, a new bluestone grandstand was opened at Flemington. Above was seating for 5000 people and below, large areas for tearooms, lunch rooms, ladies' retiring rooms and a vice-regal suite. More improvements for the general public were available on the hill. Flemington now more than matched in splendour any of the wonderful British racecourses about which the novelist Dick Francis later developed his plots. And 1883 was one of the most magnificent starts ever seen there: out of a field of twenty-seven, a New Zealand thoroughbred yearling named Martini Henri, sired by Musket out of Sylvia and starting at three to one, won the race. He was the first non-Australian horse to win the Cup. A visiting 'London Reporter' gushed:

As far as the eye could see (the scene) was one persistent area of human creatures, all alive and aglow with pleasure, mirth, and goodwill. Nothing could possibly give a more distinguished characteristic view of the various resources of this colony. ... The fun of the meeting was concentrated on the hill. I discovered when I strolled up there to take in the magnificent view ... There is nothing so amusing to a student of character and a disciple of custom than to watch 'yon amorous couple in their play', and it appeared to me that a considerable number of young people had come to the races to have a little quiet love-making. The climate here, no doubt, does open the female heart and make it more susceptible than in dull England.

The most interesting feature of the day was when the races were over and the horses went home ... What a splendid stud, and how intelligent they all looked. The brave

young Cup winner, Martini Henri, appeared to be perfectly conscious of his credit and renown.

The middle-class respectability which … is the mainstay of England was thoroughly represented on the Hill. Good, sober, honest, respectable people were there in abundance, and that self-complacent English look which your prosperous tradesman has was amply portrayed in their faces.

The general *bonhomie*, the universal kind-heartedness, the cheerful small-talk and the aspect of general content which the people had at large, says a great deal for the prosperity, solidity and future prospects of this colony … Victoria has every right to be proud of herself, and if her sons and daughter do blow a little bit, they have every reason and right to do so.

… The mother land must ere long adopt a different kind of political regime for these children, and a change will come over this country which will be better for both places. There is in the air even now a stirring breath of this sort. The national character here is changing, and the vivacity of Cup Day is one sure sign of the status of a people destined to prosper.[16]

During his literary tour of Australia in 1895, the celebrated American writer and humorist Mark Twain wrote: 'Nowhere in my travels have I encountered a festival of the people that has such a magnetic appeal to a whole nation. The Cup astonishes me.'[17]

Edward may have revelled in the bonhomie and nationalism at Flemington, but he was more concerned to transfer it to his arcade opening in Bourke Street. He risked censure from the race crowd with a provocative pre-opening advertisement he placed in *The Herald*: 'Cole's new book arcade will open on Cup Day. It is the finest sight in Melbourne and the grandest book shop in the world. Intellectual non-racing people are invited there instead of going to the races.'

But it worked. Not only did non-racing readers turn up, but half the Flemington crowd as well. Indeed, such was the congregation wishing to enter the arcade's brass portals that police had to be called to control them, and staff were instructed to sell coins at threepence each to those in the queues. The crowds continued to pour into the arcade for the remainder of the Spring Racing Carnival. It was a triumph of advertising and a triumph of presentation, and business had never been better.

**9
GROWTH AND
CONSOLIDATION**

Bourke Street looking west from Swanston Street,
Cole's Book Arcade on the southern side

So Edward got what he wanted: a book arcade right in the heart of Melbourne's most popular shopping and entertainment centre. On the southern side of Bourke Street between Elizabeth and Swanston streets, the arcade was flanked by Hosie's Restaurant and Shackleton's soda and milk shop towards Elizabeth Street to the west; and a watchmaker, a clothing company, the Bull and Mouth Hotel, a wine shop, a tobacconist and Victoria Hall towards Swanston Street to the east.[1] Behind the arcade were a jewellery store, a gasfitter and a decorator.

On the arcade's south-east flank was Sugden Lane, a busy alley with bootmakers, tobacconists, wine and spirit importers and a shooting gallery. To the south was Little Collins Street, from which, extending part way to Collins Street, ran Howey Place. Bought by property developer Henry Howey in 1837 for £128, it was eventually leased to Edward as a part-extension of the arcade through to Collins Street—about which more later.

It could reasonably be expected that popular enthusiasm for the arcade would simmer down following its successful opening on Cup Day in 1883. On the contrary, it increased. With strategically timed advertisements, Edward egged his readers on. On Saturday 15 December he placed a typically hyperbolic advertisement in *The Age*: 'People from all parts of Europe and America agree that Cole's New Book Arcade is the grandest Book Shop in the world. It is worth a shilling to see and all are invited to call and see it *FOR NOTHING*.' In *The Age* on Saturday 22 December he predicted that 'Ten thousand people will visit Cole's Grand new Book Arcade tonight, 20,000 his Market Fair' (the latter was in the Eastern Market).

With the installation of the books, the new arcade was ready for business. How did it look to its many customers? Above the bow-shaped veranda on Bourke Street was painted a splendid and garish rainbow illuminated by gaslight, a grander repetition of the trademark at

OPPOSITE The arcade's grand entrance
FOLLOWING PAGES Grand interior of the
arcade, taken from the second floor

the smaller arcade further up Bourke Street. Equally splendid were two impressively tall brass columns flanking the Bourke Street entrance. Customers flowed in through the wide entrance past the pillars. Other brass columns continued down the length of the vast hall, its dimensions enhanced by prolific use of mirrors, soft gaslighting and daylight penetrating the glass panels on the ceiling three storeys above. All added to the impression of unimpeded space.

The two little mechanical men in sailor suits turning windlasses with revolving moral tales and advertisements that had captivated customers at the entrance of the old arcade at 158 Bourke Street were reinstalled at the new premises. Greeting customers on the ground floor were 3000 large cedar drawers set against the walls and containing thousands of books, prominently and systematically labelled in categories such as CARPENTRY, DICTIONARIES, FASHION, FEDERATION OF THE WORLD, GARDENING, HUMANITY, MECHANICS, MEDICINE, PHILOSOPHY, RACE, RELIGION and SCIENCE. Unimpeded by counters and attendants, customers could help themselves to the books in the cabinets, or those in the shelves arrayed above them.

In the Melbourne *Weekly Times* of Saturday 15 December 1883, an anonymous visiting correspondent from London gave his impressions of the new arcade:

‘Forty thousand books’ is the large-type announcement that first fixes our bewildered eyes. Forty thousand books, with so many lines in each page, so many words in each line! What a stupendous lot of ‘copy’ to be waded through! What a quantity of ‘proofs’ to be corrected. What an amount (very probably) of exceedingly strong language to be expended before this colossal result was achieved! were my first and instinctive reflections.

I should first state that as the premises have only been some two or three weeks opened, it was not to be expected that things had got into their proper places yet. Indeed, when I recollected that a public library, not a hundred miles from our City, has existed for a quarter of a century, and is still an interesting labyrinth of mystery and confusion, I could not but think that this ‘Palace of Intellect’ has progressed wonderfully well. To be sure, the one is a Government Institution, and the other a private enterprise; but even making full allowance for this, the contrast is already strongly marked.

COLE'S BOOK ARCADE

FIRST
BOOK
ARCADE
OPENED
IN THE
WORLD.

A MILLION

COLE'S BOOK ARCADE

COLE'S
BOOK
ARCADE

The ground-floor of the establishment is devoted to new books, and some odds and ends of stationery, among which were conspicuous all sorts and conditions of year books and diaries, and a 'large and choice assortment' of Christmas cards, the harmless harbinger of Christmas. This new book department rather frightened me, I confess, as it had a sort of 'you may look, but you mustn't touch' air about it which repelled and disheartened me. They looked too fresh and *clean* to be enjoyable, did these gorgeously-bound dictionaries, these appalling 'works of reference', these spotlessly uncut and glaring novels. I ascertained that the 'upper gallery' was the second-hand department, and here I thought I could take up my selection, and settle down to a comfortable 'root' among the old familiar friends. A book to be thoroughly enjoyable should, like a coat, be old and well-worn; and accordingly I hailed with satisfaction the placard 'Books from 100 to 500 years old'. Like the laureate's Palace of Art, this was indeed 'a haunt of ancient peace'.

> For there was Milton like a seraph strong,
> Beside him Shakespeare, bland and mild:
> And there the world-worn Dante grasped his song,
> And somewhat grimly smiled.

I found the simple old 'Child's Guide to Knowledge', which gravely informs the infant that 'sal-volatile salt is an aromatic volatile salt, composed of sal-ammoniac, distilled with salt of tartar', and that '*assafoetida* is a valuable medicinal produced from an umbelliferous plant', and many other similar and suitable pieces of information, full of meaning and interest for the youthful mind. I found Mrs Markham's 'History of England' side by side with Pinnock's, and the 'Decline and Fall of the Roman Empire' cheek by jowl with an old Cambridge University Calendar, the parting from which suggests the last pitiful struggle in the unappreciated scholar's colonial experience. Here were 'works of fiction' which were 'loose'; there was 'theology', which was tight. Before me was Henry's 'Latin Arnold', with a long vista of retrospective horrors; behind me, a Greek 'Delectus' stood forth in bold relief, bringing back a flood of memories.

Adding to the cornucopia of books were the arcade's welcoming rest areas. An ordinance had been introduced by the city council in the 1870s to discourage public loitering in Melbourne's streets; external windowsills were set with iron spikes and street seating was removed. An old colonist, Mr WH Bilton, had complained: 'Try the Treasury, Parliament House, the Post Office steps, and "move on" from a constable will startle you, the same on steps of Banks and other buildings. I have searched and there is no resting place to be found, except, by great favour, Cole's Arcade.'[2] Edward wanted customers to come in and read without pressure to buy. Chairs and benches were set in quiet nooks amid a garden of giant ferns transplanted from the Dandenongs and the Yarra Valley, and other greenery banked up with tanbark and logs on either side of the seats, reminiscent of Eugene von Guerard's famous paintings of Ferntree Gully in 1857. The area became an oasis for weary shoppers and pedestrians wanting to read, take refreshments or simply rest.

By 1885, the Victorian economy was booming. The grain harvest was prolific, the price of wool was high, and railways were making a profit for the first time in the colony's history, although accompanied by much corruption. Melburnians were gaining in material prosperity—not just those who had made rich pickings in the goldfields, but upwardly mobile people in the middle classes. Wage-earners were also benefiting. A strike for higher wages and increased rations by convicts in the Liverpool district of New South Wales in 1822 had led to agitation for better pay and conditions across that colony and in breakaway Victoria. Stonemasons struck in 1856, then maritime workers, shearers and other workers in building trades. No longer was a fourteen-hour working day, six days a week, acceptable to the average worker. The demand was for an eight-hour working day followed by eight for leisure and eight for rest—the first such conditions approved in the world. It became a long battle between workers on the one hand and employers and their parliamentary mates on the other. Victoria did not extend the eight-hour day to all workers until 1916, the rest of Australia in 1920, but the flame had been lit much earlier.

Another phenomenon was the increased buying power of women. More and more women now worked in the city as secretaries, sales assistants and telephonists. With money of their own to spend, they were becoming a force in shaping the inventories of shops. Generous loans from proliferating banks and building societies enabled these women and their husbands to contemplate buying their own homes in the suburbs—and decorating them. The aesthetic movement of the 1880s inspired a fashion for blue-and-white china, and fans and paintings depicting exotic locations, particularly in Japan. The International Exhibition of 1880–81 displayed Japanese arts and crafts for the first time to Melbourne's buying public. Rather unkindly, a French art collector, Edmond de Goncourt, called the new Victorian enthusiasm for clutter 'bricabracomania', some kind of disease.[3]

Disease or not, Edward was onto it. Books would remain his main stock in trade, but just as he had made more money supplying lemonade to miners in Castlemaine than by mining himself, he could better profit by satisfying the emerging demands of homemakers than by speculating in Victoria's booming real estate market. Porcelain and glassware would become the second string to his arcade.

Not just a book store, but a garden for rest and reflection, just outside the Crinkled Paper and Fancy Goods Department—note the electric light bulb, top left, and Union Jack on the paper lantern, top right

He decided to sell ornaments not from another prosaic department in the arcade, but displayed in an 'Exhibition', and he had just the right space for it—his sun-filled third-floor gallery. The space was not suitable for the display of books, where their covers would warp and fade, but pottery, glassware, porcelain and ceramics were impervious to the sun's rays. Indeed, sunlight would embellish their colours and made them more attractive to customers than if displayed in artificial electric or gaslight.

In 1884, he installed a newfangled, water-powered passenger lift from the ground to the third floor—itself an attraction for customers. *The Argus* reported on 24 April of that year that it ascended upwards every five minutes. It may have been designed by Elisha Graves Otis, an American who began retailing his elevators as early as 1853, or invented and installed by Peter Johns, a Melbourne engineer who began by making presses for the wool industry and adapted his system to designing passenger lifts. Johns installed hydraulic lifts in Allan's Music Warehouse in 1877. Whatever its provenance, Edward's lift was water-driven, as Mrs Magruther reported in her regular column 'Round About Town' in *The Herald* on 18 January 1887:

> That there water supply as were playin' the very Dickins that afternoon, had turned off Mr Cole's water, and in consequence we could not go up in the lift. But we climbs the stairs, and there were the most beautifullest set of ornaments as ever I see and quite as good as any exhibition.

With the lift as an attraction to draw customers upwards, Edward set about turning the top floor into a gallery of beauty. He initially ordered his ceramics long distance by catalogue, but wanted to be more directly involved. He now had the money for a sea passage and accommodation and decided to travel 'home' to England and select further stock himself.

Who would manage the arcade in his absence? He had several long-serving, experienced and loyal department heads, but trusted none of them to carry on the business his way. He did not want to appoint a general manager 'to be humming and hahing and smirking to himself' at every new Cole eccentricity.[4] On 10 March 1886 he instructed his solicitor to draw up a power of attorney giving Eliza complete control of the business in his absence, including the power to pay bills, collect money from sales, operate his bank account, manage staff, and seek legal advice on any matter, including dealing with disputes.[5]

HOUSE ORNAMENTS

ORNAMENTS FOR WHAT·NOTS

ORNAMENTS FOR BRACKETS

ORNAMENTS FOR SIDE·BOARDS

ORNAMENTS FOR MANTEL·PIECES

ORNAMENTS FOR TABLES

ORNAMENTS FOR SHELVES

ORNAMENTS FOR WALLS

ORNAMENTS FOR ALL PARTS OF THE HOUSE

His business deckchairs thus arranged to his satisfaction, and assured of Eliza's willing-ness and capacity to shoulder the burdens of management, Edward embarked for England in March 1886. He would order more books and greeting cards, but his main mission was to see the factories where fine china was made bearing the names Wedgwood, Davenport, Royal Worcester, Royal Crown Derby, Royal Dalton, Sèvres and Minton. In an undated letter to Eliza, probably written shortly after his arrival in London in April or May 1886, he observed:

> Everyone is very polite and pleasant, much more polite than they are generally in the colonies. We [presumably Edward and his agent] live well at the hotels and generally drive from one pottery to another in a hansom or coach. When I reach Melbourne in about October we will have a grand ornament exhibition indeed and shall have all the gentry in in such numbers as ever have been seen in Melbourne or Australia. I believe we will have an immense rush at Cup and Christmas time to see the sight.[6]

In another letter, dated 13 May 1886, he wrote:

> My own dear wife,
>
> I was round the town buying glass and china. We have a better show than I have seen in any of the windows in London. Yet I find I can buy many things much cheaper in London than in Melbourne. We went to a place in town yesterday and saw Mr Robertson and Mr Petheric in Boltons, but they did not see me. Of course there is a great objection on the part of the wholesale houses that retailers should buy at first hand but in our case the time is come when we must do so to hold our own. I bought a parcel of goods from one of our regular houses last week and today I bought some at 20 percent cheaper at the very maker he bought them from. Tell Fred not to buy any Christmas cards whatsoever as I can buy them much cheaper in London from the makers.[7]

On 20 May, he wrote:

> I am now at the centre of Staffordshire after getting to Liverpool. I slept in the Grand Hotel with 600 rooms and went to the Liverpool Exhibition the next day. It had been

[*Continues on page 166*]

A SPECULATIVE FOOTNOTE

Several Chinese–Australian businessmen based in Sydney famously built lasting mercantile emporia in Shanghai, Canton and Hong Kong at the beginning of the twentieth century, many of which survive to this day. The businessmen were based in Sydney's Haymarket and were involved in the banana trade, with plantations in Queensland and Fiji. They included Ma Ying Piu, George Kwok Chin, James Kwok Lock, Liu Hing Choy Hing and William Liu.

Ma Ying Piu was a founding partner of the Wing Sang import-export business and exported bananas, Arnott's biscuits and IXL jams to China. He opened the Sincere Department Store in Hong Kong in 1900, then stores in Guangzhou and Shanghai. Others followed. Four department stores were built on Nanjing Road in Shanghai. What they had in common, apart from their vast size, was their emphasis on entertainment as well as shopping. Some were replete with exhibitions, cultural displays, art and calligraphy galleries, music, theatre and roof gardens. Some managed adjoining hotels where shoppers could stay. The latest inventions, escalators and lifts, were installed to increase customers' delight. Sometimes tickets were sold for admission, redeemable as discounts on the prices of goods in store.

The Sydney-based historian Peter Hack has shown that these Chinese–Australians were inspired to some extent by innovations in the Japanese department stores Shirokiya and Mitsukoshi. Shirokiya had ninety-eight speciality departments with the latest baby goods, sewing machines, exercise equipment, books and magazines, arts and crafts, household electrical goods and furs, as well as restaurants, an art gallery, a smoking room and a hairdresser. In addition, Mitsukoshi had lifts, escalators, central heating and a rooftop garden 'playground'.[8]

The Haymarket-based banana merchants took Japanese retail stores as their template in fashioning their Chinese-based department stores. They were also inspired by their Sydney neighbour, Anthony Hordern. Just up George Street from the Haymarket was Hordern's Palace Emporium, which opened with extensions in October 1881. There were two opening nights, as described by Hack: 'Each evening, 10,000 people passed through the spacious complex while being entertained by the Young Australian Band. This was a whole new shopping experience. It was like promenading through an exhibition. Shopping had become a pleasure.'[9]

The Palace burnt down in spectacular fashion on 10 July 1901, but a much larger Hordern store replaced it in September 1905, on land covering most of the city block bounded by Goulburn, George, Liverpool and Pitt streets. This new Palace Emporium inspired the Mas, Kwoks, Choys and William Liu in building their department stores in Shanghai.[10]

Anthony Horden's Palace Emporium in Sydney opened in 1881, an inspiration for Chinese–Australian emporia in Shanghai and Hong Kong and also possibly for Cole in Melbourne

Were they also inspired by Edward Cole's trailblazing retail efforts in his Melbourne Book Arcade? Circumstances suggest it. First, Edward's friend Quong Tart knew these merchants, especially Liu, who was a student of Christ Church St Laurence School in Pitt Street and fluent in Cantonese and English. Both Quong Tart and Liu were lifetime campaigners against Australia's immigration laws. Second, Liu worked as the English-speaking secretary of the Chinese Consulate in Melbourne from 1912 to 1914. He knew Cole's Book Arcade, passing it frequently when walking between the consulate in William Street and China Town in Little Bourke Street. Edward and Liu had similar interests in protecting Australian Chinese from unthinking prejudice, in advancing wellbeing in the Australian community, and in innovative marketing. It is reasonable to assume that in shaping his emporium in Shanghai, Liu not only took inspiration from Hordern's but also from Cole's Book Arcade in Melbourne. Cole's arcade was much smaller and its range of goods narrower than the behemoths of Mitsukoshi, Shirokiya and Anthony Hordern, but its sales principles and promotional techniques were the same.

opened by the Queen in great state about a fortnight before but it was not above half ready when we were there. Went on to Manchester which is thirty miles [48 kilometres] distant from Liverpool. Liverpool is a very black town larger than Melbourne. I have agreed with one of the potters to make a child's plate with our rainbow and a view of the arcade and the logo of the book arcade on it. Also a child's mug with an advertisement. Back to Derbyshire and saw the Crown Derby factory and showrooms, but all too dear. Then Stoke on Trent, another town in the centre of the Potteries.

Manchester next to London in importance in the British Empire; some splendid streets but a great number of factories makes it very black. I went to three different glass works and bought some at each for one third less than we buy it in Melbourne. Went on the *Great Eastern* which was lying round in a port in Wales and are about to fit it up as a large ballroom, theatre and bazaar and general exhibition. They expect a half a million people will visit it. Went on board—a huge ship from stem to stern she sadly wants painting, but it is an immense ship more than twice as long as the Royal Arcade and very wide. The theatre is held in one of the large compartments where the Atlantic cable was stowed away. I bought about 1,000 cheap novels last week at 9d each. Some will go as regular stock and some can be sold cheaper.[11]

The *Great Eastern* was the largest iron ship of its day, designed by Isambard Kingdom Brunel, a British mechanical engineer of great originality who designed the first transatlantic steamer. When Edward went on board, it was a showboat, a floating concert hall, also used as an advertisement for the chain of Lewis's department stores that originated in Liverpool in 1856. It never made a voyage, but when launched in 1858, its designers claimed it had the capacity to carry 4000 passengers from England to Australia without refuelling.

No record can be found of Edward visiting his childhood homes in Woodchurch and Rolvenden in Kent during this buying trip to England. He may have been too busy buying pottery in Staffordshire, Manchester and Liverpool for a side trip to Kent by coach. More likely, he had little wish to revive painful memories of his poverty-stricken youth or confront the unpleasant fact that he had no known father.

By all accounts, Edward's homecoming to Melbourne in October 1886 was greeted by family and staff with warmth and relief: warmth from his wife and children, who were glad to see their father bearing wonderful gifts; relief from his staff, who had been subject to

Ceramic plate commissioned by Cole during his trip to the United Kingdom in 1886

a stricter regime of surveillance and discipline under Eliza's management than they were accustomed to from their softly spoken boss. Absenteeism and lateness were down, and a few employees of whom Edward had not thought much but could not bring himself to sack had in his absence been let go by Eliza.[12]

Most of the new stock had arrived in Melbourne and been arranged on the top floor before Edward's ship docked at Port Melbourne. Embellished with backlit bowls of goldfish, clocks telling the times around the world, and a giant globe, the New! New! New! Ornament Exhibition proved to be every bit as popular as the arcade itself when it had opened on Cup Day 1883. In view of the press of customers eager to visit the exhibition, Edward reintroduced the purchase of medals as tokens for entry, just as he had done on that Cup Day.

Altogether, the arcade was a rejuvenating arena of sights and colours. If equipped with future vision, Edward would have seen that it resembled the deep interior stairwells of shopping arcades and soaring railed galleries of some of the Paris department stores of the twentieth century and the huge shopping malls of gigantic cruise liners of the early twenty-first century. Unlike them, however, his rails carried messages of Empire and uplifting morality: flags of different nations to celebrate Queen Victoria's Golden Jubilee of 20 June 1887, and a profusion of framed paintings interspersed with small-scale repetitions of Cole's rainbow accompanied by aphorisms, such as:

Do good and you will be happy and make others happy.
The reign of ignorance and force is going; the reign of knowledge and humanity is coming.
Labour ennobles a man, idleness debases him.

10
EDUCATION, LOSS AND GRIEF

OPPOSITE Another view of Cole's arcade taken from the north-western side of Bourke Street, with the state Parliament House clearly visible at the eastern end in Spring Street
RIGHT Sentimental image of mother and child, a repeated theme in Cole's narrative

Schooling in early colonial New South Wales was seen to be the responsibility of the clergy. Through voluntary exertion, ministers and priests of the main denominations conducted lessons in reading and writing for the children of their congregations. Children beyond their influence, including those living far from town settlements with their squatter parents or on the goldfields, were left illiterate.

As the number of children increased, the colonial government began to take an interest. Sir Richard Bourke KCB was the Irish-born governor of New South Wales from 1831 to 1837. A Whig, he encouraged the emancipation of convicts and helped bring forward the ending of penal transportation to Australia. He was also interested in providing state-based education to the children of settlers, free from the divisive demands of the different churches. On 10 October 1835, he wrote to the British Colonial Secretary of State for the Colonies, Lord Glenelg: 'I would earnestly recommend that a provision be made for schools in which children of different religious tenets may be instructed without distinction, on the plan now adopted in Ireland.'[1] (The Irish system had been adopted in 1831, replacing a clandestine system of illegal 'hedge schools' run by the Roman Catholic Church with secular state schools.)

Bourke's advice led to the NSW Public Schools Act of 1866, which became the model for public education in Australia. State schools run by government-trained teachers were established wherever there was a minimum enrolment of twenty-five students. Each school day had to include four hours devoted exclusively to secular education: two hours in the morning and two in the afternoon. Church schools continued to receive financial assistance from the government 'on condition those schools used the same curriculum and same text books as government schools, employed government-trained teachers, and restricted religious instruction to an hour a day'.[2] The Church of England had token objections to these restrictions on religious teaching, but was not too put out. The Catholic Church included religious indoctrination as a core part of its school curriculum, and it was strongly opposed to the restrictions. But the legislation had the support of a majority of the NSW Education Council—all Protestants—and the Act went through.

When the colony of Victoria separated from New South Wales in July 1851, its legislators felt that an inclusive school system should welcome children of any denomination or of none. The Victorian Education Act of 1872 adopted most of the substance of the earlier NSW Act, and stipulated that education throughout the colony must be secular, compulsory and free. All children between the ages of six and fifteen would have to attend state-run schools unless they could obtain proper education elsewhere, were ill or infected, or lived more than 2 miles (3.2 kilometres) from a school.

The legislation did not go down well with Edward Cole. He wanted his children educated in a less restrictive environment than one engineered by what he feared would be unimaginative bureaucrats. He worried that the new system would be boring and would stultify young minds. He wrote:

> There is a vast amount of precious time wasted, and a vast amount of mental and often physical suffering incurred through the teaching of a great deal that is valueless in our schools and college. Ten or twelve years of the best learning-time of the pupil are spent in gaining three parts of grain and nine of chaff—three parts of useful knowledge and nine of useless, and when the poor brain-wracked pupils leave school or college they go out into the world to swell the ranks of the 'ignorant-learned'.
>
> In their long, painful pupilage they have partially learnt a great deal of 'fashionable' knowledge that will be practically useless to most of them through life. But they have learnt little of useful knowledge, little of the wonderful world in which they live, little of the great human family to which they belong, little of the constitution and nature of their own wonderful minds and bodies, and little of a hundred other things, which, for their own benefit, and the benefit of the world at large, they ought to know. The curriculums and management of our schools and colleges could, and should, be vastly improved. What we want is not so much professors of Latin and Greek and Hebrew and Sanscrit and the rest, but professors of general and useful knowledge, sensible, necessary, useful knowledge which will tend to make every man and woman wiser, and healthier, and happier, and better, and encourage them to help, as much as in them lies, in the progress of the world by working for the betterment of all mankind.
>
> No person at present in the world is capable of learning one-tenth of the subjects taught in all the schools, and as most persons are not capable of learning some subjects

they should not be set to them … Teach persons to read and you put them in the best way to educate themselves, and you give them the key to the accumulated literature and knowledge of the world, and if there is anything in them they will go on learning in whatever direction they choose.

In civilised communities I think the best plan would be to teach every child the three essentials, reading, writing and arithmetic; and then I would bring in the *hobby* principle as much as possible, and let each pupil (of course under proper advice and direction) learn what they had an inclination for … and consequently in most cases were best adapted for. In each case it would become their hobby, which they would 'follow with zeal and delight', instead of with pain and weariness of the flesh … Every person we meet is deficient in some things, but proficient in some other things. Let us cultivate in all those faculties which are best worth cultivating, and in most cases that will constitute our happifying and well-paying *hobby*.[3]

On first glance, Edward's sentiments betray his own lack of a formal education, his suspicion and dismissal of the disciplines of languages and philosophy and the natural world that were never part of his own narrow and deprived education. As a poor child in Kent he had not been taught Latin and how it informs the pupil about the origins of English grammar, law and history, nor how knowledge of other languages can lead to an understanding of different cultures and ways of thinking, nor how philosophy enlarges the mind and gives access to the wisdom of great thinkers.

Meanwhile, he could not foresee that the new Victorian state school curriculum would very soon reach well beyond just reading, writing and arithmetic. After a period of stagnation in education during the 1890s depression, a royal commission was convened in 1899 under Theodore Fink, brother of the energetic land speculator Benjamin, and friend of Alfred Deakin. Although considerably younger than Edward, Theodore may well have made his acquaintance at the Victorian Eclectic Society, of which both were members. The outcome of the royal commission was the appointment of Frank Tate, Victoria's first director of education. Tate became the apostle of a child-centred pedagogy: he introduced his thoughts into infant schools, and broadened the primary school curriculum to include the manual arts (for example, metalwork and carpentry), elementary science, music, literature, history and physical education. He also initiated uniform procedures for teacher recruitment and training.

Perhaps it is ungenerous to see Edward's views as narrow and uninformed. Such a view fails to take into account his lively curiosity about religion, technology, geography, the immensity of the universe, the future of humankind. It also misses what must have been a

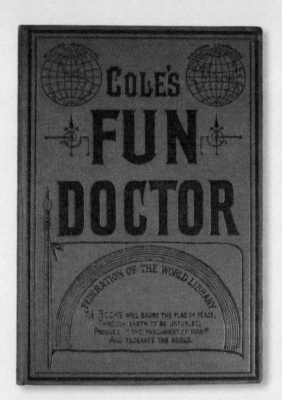

COLE'S
FUN
DOCTOR

FEDERATION OF THE WORLD LIBRARY

THIS BOOK WILL CAUSE THE FLAG OF PEACE, THROUGH EARTH TO BE UNFURLED; PRODUCE "THE PARLIAMENT OF MAN" AND FEDERATE THE WORLD.

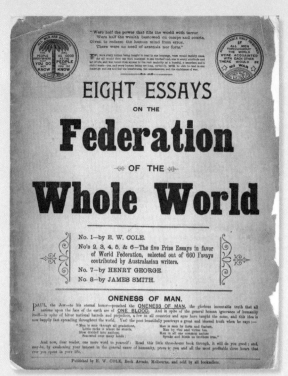

EIGHT ESSAYS
ON THE
Federation
OF THE
Whole World

No. 1—by E. W. COLE.
No's 2, 3, 4, 5, & 6—The five Prize Essays in favor of World Federation, selected out of 660 Essays contributed by Australasian writers.
No. 7—by HENRY GEORGE.
No. 8—by JAMES SMITH.

ONENESS OF MAN.

Published by E. W. COLE, Book Arcade, Melbourne, and sold by all booksellers.

A GOO
DIARY
BY THE AUTHOR
A BAD BOY'S DIA

E.W.COLE BOO

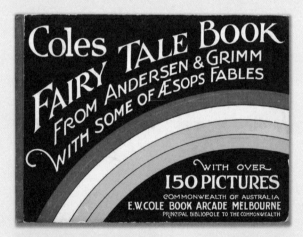

Coles
FAIRY TALE BOOK
FROM ANDERSEN & GRIMM
WITH SOME OF ÆSOPS FABLES

WITH OVER
150 PICTURES
COMMONWEALTH OF AUSTRALIA
E.W. COLE BOOK ARCADE MELBOURNE
PRINCIPAL BIBLIOPOLE TO THE COMMONWEALTH

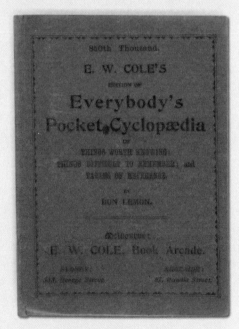

850th Thousand.
E. W. COLE'S
EDITION OF
Everybody's
Pocket Cyclopædia
OF
THINGS WORTH KNOWING;
THINGS DIFFICULT TO REMEMBER; and
TABLES OF EXCHANGE.

BY
DON LEMON.

E. W. COLE, Book Arcade.

FOURTH EDITION
20TH. THOUSAND
Pr
ALM
Useful,
CONT.
2,000 Very Ir

BOOK ARCADES,
PRINTED AND PUB.

Cole's
Handy
Reckoner

COLE'S
ENGLISH
DICTIONAR

A small selection of
Cole's astonishingly wide
range of publications;
a common theme being the
improvement of the mind

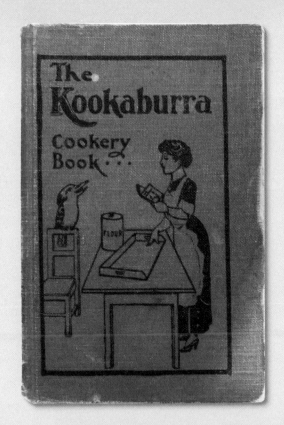

The Kookaburra Cookery Book...

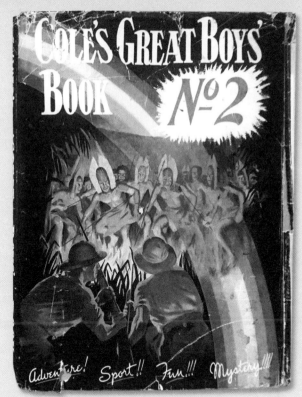

COLE'S GREAT BOYS' BOOK No 2

Adventure! Sport!! Fun!!! Mystery!!!!

1907.

...ive
...NAC
...Amusing.
...OF
...Very Funny Jokes.

300 items on the Blessing and the Curse of Tobacco.

...NEY & ADELAIDE.
...ADE, MELBOURNE.

Also

COLE'S INTELLECT SHARPENER AND FAMILY AMUSER CONTAINING 2000 CHOICE RIDDLES

AND 500 AMUSING PUZZLES & GAMES

Australian Edition.

The Best Poems of Ella Wheeler Wilcox

E. W. COLE.

major concern he had that to be effective, education must engage the interests of students and not be boring, but *fun*. This was the main idea behind his Funny Picture Books, and what made them so popular with generations of children. His other educational texts had the same theme, including his *Fun Doctor*, his *Colonial A1 Reciter, Cole's School Land* and *Cole's Intellect Sharpener and Family Amuser*, which contained '2,000 riddles and 500 amusing puzzles and games'. He made a bid to have a selection of his books included as part of the Victorian schools reading list, sending them to selected teachers with a note saying they would engage the attention of students and make reading more enjoyable. But the publisher George Robertson had already been designated by the Education Board as official supplier of textbooks and stationery to schools. Most teachers decided that Cole's books were trivial and refused to include them on reading lists for their charges.

As the 1880s progressed, Edward was beginning to realise that he would seriously have to consider the education of his own children. By 1883, he and Eliza had three daughters and two sons ranging in age from seven to one. Their sixth child, Ivy Diamond, was born in August 1885.

Before addressing education, however, Edward wanted to remove the children from the city, where open drains carried human and animal waste into the swamps of West Melbourne, and residents inhaled air that tasted of coal smoke and sewage. Eliza wanted to continue to live above the shop in Bourke Street, but over her objections he found a spacious flat in Fitzroy, to which they were all removed. Turnley names the address as 'Gayview Terrace',[4] but local archives show no such property in the area. However, there was a 'Bayview Terrace', which, according to the historical section of the Fitzroy Library, was owned by a Mr Edmund Gleeson. His property comprised seven substantial houses each of nine rooms, four of which took in boarders. Edward, Eliza and their four children at the time (Pearl and Ivy were yet to be born) were most likely boarders in one of these terrace houses.

Edward found a school in the area that seemed to offer the kind of mental stimulation he sought. Its curriculum was inspired by the revolutionary play-learning approach of the German educator Friedrich Froebel called *kindergarten,* which offered spiritual, physical and moral development, even for the very young. Froebel's system had crossed the Atlantic to the fledgling United States, where it was emulated and promoted in the 1860s by prominent educators such as Elizabeth Peabody and William T Harris, the supervisor of public schools in St Louis. The concept rapidly spread as industrialisation drew more and more mothers into factory work and clerical jobs and they enrolled their offspring in play schools and nurseries modelled on kindergarten principles. And, as with other new ideas worth emulating from Europe and the New World, kindergartens became established in colonial Australia.

However, after a couple of years, Linda, Eddy and Vally had not taken to their new kindergarten environment with much enthusiasm. They found it too earnest, too heavy—too German. Eliza used their boredom as a powerful argument for removing them from the school and, at the same time, to persuade a reluctant Edward to transfer the whole family back into the city. At her insistence, he had a flat built next to the porcelain and pottery exhibition on the third floor of the new arcade, overlooking Bourke Street. There was even space for a small garden where Edward could plant a nursery. The children were delighted. They had the run of the arcade and could watch the busy traffic come and go below them on Bourke Street, including the pretty ladies alighting from Cobb & Co. coaches across the road, and the occasional herds of sheep and cattle being driven to the city slaughterhouse or fresh pastures outside the city.

As for education, the children, Eliza assured Edward, could manage with private tutors. Edward gave in, and in his thorough way mounted an extensive advertising campaign for a suitable private teacher. After exhaustive interviews, he engaged a couple called McCormick who were familiar with kindergarten philosophy but also shared Edward's belief in children being stimulated to engage in free inquiry and reading.

Not that he left the children's education entirely in the hands of the McCormicks: he frequently exposed them to his friends and their libertarian views. One of the most notable was Joseph Symes, a rationalist and publicist who came to Melbourne from England in February 1884 at the invitation of the Victorian Secularists' Society. Contemptuous of what he termed 'dilettante free-thinkers' who flinched from publicising what he regarded as the cruelties and lies of Christianity, Symes started a secular Sunday school. He also agitated for free speech, an uncensored press, excursion trains and the opening of art galleries and public libraries on Sundays. The Lord's Day Observance Society and the Victorian government retaliated with three major and some minor prosecutions between 1885 and 1887. Unable to engage reliable counsel, Symes defended himself in the courts and routed his prosecutors. He bought a printing press and began a weekly newspaper called *The Liberator*. He stood for the Collingwood seat in the Victorian Legislative Assembly in 1889 on an ambitious policy platform of land nationalisation, a graduated income tax, abolition of colonial titles and governorships, Sunday holidays, legalised contraception, an end to discrimination against the Chinese, and home rule for Ireland, Scotland and Wales. He came last in the polls.[5]

Despite, or more likely because of, Symes' views, Edward welcomed his influence on his children's young minds. He told him they were free to choose any religion that took their fancy, or none at all. According to anecdotal evidence, this led to the children trying to shout each other down in a game in which they chose their religions: 'I bars being a Presbyterian!',

A Cobb & Co coach is drawn up outside the Royal Arcade, a light-filled shopping mall near the corner of Bourke and Elizabeth streets, the southern entrance of which is flanked by the mythic figures of Gog and Magog—surely an inspiration for Cole's arcade

'I bars being a Methodist!', 'I bars being a Hindu!', all capped by the eldest child, Linda, who shouted, 'I bars being a Joseph Symeser!'[6]

Edward loved his children very much and treated them with gentleness and respect. They were constantly entertained by his puckish sense of humour, the games he invented for them in the arcade, and the madcap expeditions he took them on in cable trams to the terminuses in outer suburbs, to Melbourne's parks and gardens, and by coach to fishing and swimming spots around Port Phillip Bay. He missed them keenly when he was away on buying trips, and pined for their company as well as his wife's. In a letter from London in 1886, he told Eliza:

> I should like to see them all and your dear self but ten thousand miles is a long way off. I was showing the photographs to a man a few days ago and he seemed to have a

very great opinion of Vally and said he had a fine frank open countenance. He does look a fine fellow. Dear little Ruby and Pearl also look fine. Ruby has a half sorrowful thoughtful expression upon her countenance. Popps looks a little independent but she is a good girl at learning her lessons and Eddy is good at making wagons and bird cages and catching fish. Do you remember what excitement there was at Mordialloc when he caught a fish?[7]

Edward spent much time in the arcade when the rest of his family went on holidays to Deloraine in Tasmania, to New Zealand, or to Lorne and Geelong in coastal Victoria. When holding the fort in Bourke Street he would regale them in letters written late at night with stories about their two family cats and how they caught rats and mice and would occasionally get sick after eating these rodents. He would enjoin both Eliza and the children to stay well, get plenty of fresh air and rest, go for expeditions and make mud pies. Hearing from Eliza how Vally had encountered a snake near their beachside holiday house in Geelong, he informed Vally how to tell if it was dangerous or not: if you eat a mushroom and don't die, it is not poisonous; if a snake bites you with the same result, you can conclude it is not venomous.

There is no evidence that Edward played favourites with the children, but he seemed to have a particularly soft spot for Ruby. When she was four years old, he wrote her a letter dated 30 July 1886 from London:

My dear little Ruby Angelina,

Ruby means red and so I write you a letter on red paper. Is it not pretty paper? I hope you and Pearl Adelia get on all right and play nicely together. I think I shall bring you a nice dolly that can say Mama and Papa, and some other things, perhaps a doll's house.

Goodbye my dear little Ruby from your affectionate Papa,
E W Cole.

As the children grew, they were a constant source of amusement and fascination to their father. Barely four years after he wrote the letter to Ruby, however, tragedy struck.

Eliza took Linda on an Edward-style voyage of education to New Zealand early in 1890, and the other children went down to Warrnambool with their governess-cousin, Lilly White. During their holiday, Ruby became uncharacteristically quiet and lacking in energy. Concerned, Lilly took the children by coach back to Melbourne, where Ruby seemed to

recover her good spirits. Lilly decided to resume their fresh-air holiday in a different but closer location, and they all went by coach to the home of a family friend, Mrs Lockstone, in what was then the outer Melbourne suburb of Camberwell.

Ruby seemed to rally, but then had a relapse. The doctor diagnosed scarlet fever, a streptococcal infection whose symptoms are sore throat, fever, swollen glands, headaches, swollen lymph nodes and rash—all effectively treatable today with antibiotics, but in the 1890s a leading killer of children. Edward urgently contacted Eliza, who returned with Linda from New Zealand on the first available ship. Ruby rallied once again, and her parents relaxed enough to leave her bedside to attend a public talk at the Exhibition Building by the celebrated American economist and philosopher Henry George, a radical advocate of a single tax.

But their relief was premature. Ruby lapsed into a coma and died on 27 March 1890, her grief-stricken parents by her side. According to Turnley, Edward did his best to console the family, but was himself devastated. Turnley's mother, Linda, recalled that until then she had never seen her father cry. In a vain effort to assuage his grief, Edward published a

RUBY COLE AND HER CLEVER FROG.

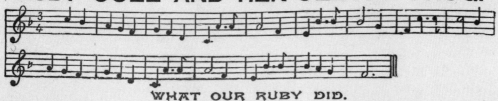

WHAT OUR RUBY DID.

SHE danced like a Fairy,
She sung like a Frog,
She squeaked like a Pig,
She barked like a dog.
    Oh yes! Oh yes! She did! She did!
    And Frog-gy played a tune.

She mooed like a Bullock,
She baaed like a Ram,
She leaped like a Goat,
She skipped like a Lamb—Oh yes!

She brayed like a Donkey,
She cried like a Hare,
She neighed like a Horse,
She growled like a Bear—Oh yes!

She munched like a Rabbit,
She gnawed like a Rat,
She popped like a Mouse,
She flew like a Bat—Oh yes!

She talked like a Parrot,
She quacked like a Drake,
She mewed like a Cat,
She hissed like a Snake—Oh yes!

She climbed like a Squirrel,
She flopped like a Seal,
She ran like a Deer,
She slid like an Eel—Oh yes !

She crept like a Tortoise,
She soared like a Lark,
She drank like a Fish,
She ate like a Shark—Oh yes !

She roared like a Lion,
She dived like a Whale,
She swam like a Goose,
She crawled like a Snail—Oh yes!

She croaked like a Raven,
She screeched like an Owl,
She cawed like a Crow,
She crowed like a Fowl—Oh yes!

She grinned like a Monkey,
She hummed like a Bee,
She buzzed like a Fly,
She jumped like a Flea—Oh yes!

Our dear little daughter once went to a children's ball
dressed as a fairy. She was proud of being a fairy, and
looked so nice that I put together the above nursery
doggerel to please her, and in honour of the event, little
thinking that she would so soon leave us for the other
world. It might be considered better by some to
remove this page, but as children like it I venture to
let it stand with this explanation.—E. W. C.

Sacred to the Memory of our dear LITTLE RUBY, who departed this life March 27th, 1890, aged 8 years. She was intelligent, industrious, affectionate
and sociable, and is deeply regretted by all who knew her.

There is no flock, however watched and tended
  But one dead lamb s there !
There is no fireside, howsoe er defended,
  But has one vacant chair !

There is no death ! what seems so is transition ·
  This life of mortal breath,
Is but a suburb of life elysian
  Whose portal we call death

She is not dead—the child of our affection—
  But gone unto that school
Where she no onger needs our poor protection
  And GOD himself doth rule.

full-page memorial to 'Ruby Cole and her Clever Frog' in the then-current edition of his Funny Picture Book.[8]

Tragic though Ruby's death was, Edward was lucky not to have lost more of his children. The Victorian age in Melbourne witnessed a huge rate of infant mortality from diarrhoea, diphtheria (called 'severe croup'), measles, typhoid, scarlet fever and 'convulsions'. Because of the unsanitary conditions in hospitals and doctors' contempt for cleanliness, many mothers and their babies died in childbirth. The medical science of paediatrics was unknown. Meanwhile, the medical 'profession' was infested with quacks and charlatans who also knew nothing of paediatrics. Their often phoney nostrums for adults contained opium, mercury, iodine, strychnine or zinc, and were claimed to cure, among other illnesses, rheumatism, palsy and dropsy. Holloway's famous pills and ointments were claimed to cure syphilis, while distilled eucalyptus oil was claimed to be an efficacious cure for infections of the mucous membranes of the stomach and bowel. Water pumped out of the Yarra River close by a tannery was marketed as miracle water: the only miracle was when its imbiber failed to succumb to dysentery.

This is not to suggest that Ruby Cole's doctor in Camberwell was a quack, or that he didn't try everything he could to save her life. But he had no answer to her illness, and in 1890, the city fathers had not done enough to alleviate the foulness of Melbourne's environment that created the conditions for such diseases—its filthy air, open sewers and infected water. They knew that an underground sewerage system was required, together with sufficient water from reservoirs to flush waste through the system, but these things cost money. An early reservoir built at Yan Yean in the 1850s proved entirely inadequate by the 1880s. An adequate water supply was not available until the Maroondah River was dammed above Healesville, and comprehensive underground sewerage not finished until 1898, when solid and liquid waste could be flushed out to sewage farms at Mordialloc and Werribee.

Of course, it was the same in other Australian cities, especially Sydney, whose harbour was an open sewer even well after work on the Bondi sewer had begun in 1888. When Sydney suffered an epidemic of bubonic plague in 1900, the Sydney Council established a Plague Department that set about cleaning up the filth in the inner suburbs and along the walls around Darling Harbour, which were daubed with excreta and where thousands of rats poked their heads out of holes.[9]

Edward had been right when he'd succeeded, against his wife's objections, to remove his family from Bourke Street to Fitzroy, even if only for a short three years. It is probably a pity that they did not continue to live there, although this may not have saved Ruby.

11
THE FIRST
GREAT
DEPRESSION

OPPOSITE Cole and the surviving members of his family seated in the arcade's fernery in the early 1900s—from left to right: Eddy, Ivy, Linda (standing), Vally, Eliza, Edward and Pearl

RIGHT If you want a saveloy, it will cost you a penny

Most people think of the 'Great Depression' as the dramatic fall-off in economic production that followed the collapse of shares on the New York Stock Exchange in October 1929. That collapse occurred at the end of a decade of ebullient post–First World War economic expansion in America's industrial sector. Feverish investment in speculative shares created a bubble that occurred at the same time as consumers accrued unmanageable debt on houses they had purchased on mortgage and consumption based on easy credit.

The stock market collapse had a disastrous flow-on effect throughout the United States and in most capitalist countries, including Australia. The Depression lasted through the 1930s, and the horrendous social consequences were graphically recorded by some of America's greatest contemporary writers, including Horace McCoy, John Dos Passos, John Steinbeck and Henry Roth.[1] Notwithstanding President Franklin D Roosevelt's extensive public works program, the Depression only came to an end as a result of rapid expansion in US war production leading up to the Second World War. Other depressions of lesser magnitude followed, just as other wars followed the Great War.

This chapter is concerned with a less-known economic depression that occurred in Australia in the 1890s. Many of its causes were similar to those of the Great Depression, and most of its effects were equal or more severe. Its most devastating effects were felt in Victoria.

After such a promising start on Melbourne Cup Day in 1883, how did Edward Cole cope with the depression? First, due to his singular way of doing business he was in reasonably good shape financially. Ever since his bank manager had foreclosed on the mortgage he held over Edward's first brick cottage in Castlemaine in the Victorian goldfields, Edward had held

[*Continues on page 189*]

THE LAND BOOM

During the 1880s, speculation in urban real estate in Melbourne was rife. Encouraged by the belief that the city was on an ever-expanding spiral of wealth, speculators began to buy land wherever it became available. They were generously financed by a plethora of banks and newly created building societies, whose officials believed that every family could buy a house and keep up the payments, whether in good times or bad. No one thought of losing their jobs. The building societies were financed by an army of opportunistic private investors who were being paid high rates of interest for the use of their money. The unshakable conviction was that it was impossible to lose money by investing in land—a misguided belief still commonly held in the twenty-first century.

From 1886, city and suburban land prices began to float upwards. In 1887 land in Surrey Hills rose from 15 shillings a foot (30 centimetres) to £15, in Burwood from £70 to £300 an acre (0.4 hectares). If a railway line could be put through from the city to a suburb, the value of the land there shot up. An estate in Fitzroy was bought by a syndicate in November 1887 for £18,000 and its estimated value rose to £28,000 when news of a railway line became known.

Corrupt members of the Legislative Assembly and Council influenced relevant authorities to construct rail or tram lines into areas bought by speculators. They then bought the land, and sold it when the transport plans were announced and the value of the land went up—a form of insider trading. In 1884, the Railway Construction Act, nicknamed the 'Octopus Act', authorised sixty-five new railway lines connecting Flinders Street Station to Spencer Street Station with an outer circle that meandered 30 kilometres through Brunswick to Fairfield, thence to East Kew and Hartwell, joining the country line to Gippsland at Oakleigh. It was a land speculator's paradise. By 1891, practically the entire Melbourne suburban railway system as it now exists had been constructed, assisted by notoriously corrupt Victorian businessmen and politicians.[2]

The bubble burst at the beginning of the 1890s. Nervous of overreach, British financial institutions began withdrawing funds from speculative real estate ventures in the colony. In 1891, seven leading British life insurance companies stopped putting money into colonial securities. Investors in Australian building societies panicked and withdrew their deposits. Fringe banks, followed by those in the mainstream, could no longer extend credit, and sixteen small banks and building societies collapsed in Melbourne. In 1892, 133 limited companies went into liquidation in Victoria alone. Many Victorian financial institutions, including several major ones, suspended trading.[3]

On 1 May 1893, the government of Victoria declared a five-day bank holiday in an attempt to stem the panic—a five-day bank holiday! That year, 14,000 houses in the Melbourne suburbs were vacated as mortgages were called in and landlords evicted tenants who could no longer pay their rent. The value of property fell and remained extremely low for many years. Thousands of title deeds were held by mortgagors, for the land and houses were hardly worth the expense of advertising them for sale.

AMONG THE WORKLESS—FEEDING THE HUNGRY.

The situation was exacerbated by general weakness in corporate governance, including by company directors who, although fine upstanding Christian gentlemen and pillars of their churches, were not above falsifying balance sheets, paying dividends on non-existent profits, or publishing misleading and optimistic forecasts about their investment companies. Their Calvinistic Presbyterianism justified their actions: God had chosen certain men to govern world affairs, and the fact that they had made fortunes was a sure sign they were among His elect. The less god-fearing could call on Darwin's theory of the survival of the fittest to justify their wealth. Fraud was not fraud. Misleading balance sheets were presented in order to maintain public confidence and prevent further losses. None of these self-serving rationalisations impressed Victorian judges. When their accounting practices were discovered, many offenders went to jail. Some committed suicide.[4]

The full extent of corporate crime in the 1880s and 1890s was curiously under-reported in the Melbourne press, except in *Table Talk*, a scandal sheet owned and edited by Maurice Brodzky. A historian and teacher of European languages, Brodzky was a brilliant and fearless journalist. He had some excellent sources deep within the corporate sector, including the lawyer and land acquisitor and speculator Theodore Fink, who somehow managed to avoid bankruptcy when the market crashed.[5] Launched in June 1885, *Table Talk* was immediately successful. It had a keen eye for scandal and a wide appreciation of the arts. In January 1892, it published a story about the theft of the speaker's mace that alleged that the 1.5-metre-long, silver-plated and ornately engraved staff had been stolen from Parliament House and secreted in a brothel somewhere in Little Lonsdale Street; it was never recovered. The story generated enough scandal and satire to keep Melbourne's society entertained for months.

Brodzky was a fierce advocate of the reform of company law and insolvency legislation, which was a long time coming, and then only after the full disaster of the depression had spent its force at the end of the decade. He himself became an exile in 1904 after becoming bankrupt as the result of a criminal libel case brought by a politician—the bane of every nineteenth-century newspaper proprietor. Brodzky was caught in the great San Francisco earthquake of 1906; he died in New York in 1919.

During his time in Melbourne, Brodzky was less concerned about the plight of Melbourne's poor than with corporate criminality. In the 1890s, the Victorian government provided no safety net for the unemployed. The only major public works project was the construction of the city's underground sewerage system, but this created a mere few thousand jobs. By 1893, a third of Melbourne's breadwinners were without work. If the legions of jobless could not find relief from churches, charities or benevolent relatives, they ended up on the streets, and their families with them. Many starved to death, especially the children—the only time in Melbourne's history when

this occurred on a major scale. Mothers turned to prostitution to try to feed their children: 10,000 sex workers plied the streets of Melbourne during the worst years of the depression.

During these travails, Melbourne society remained basically self-righteous; it could look on with equanimity as an unemployed labourer who stole bread to feed his starving family was jailed, yet tolerate the shameful jobbery of its politicians and financiers operating under the cloak of respectable commerce.[6]

an aversion to borrowing money. His business was free of debt. He would have agreed with Polonius's admonition:

> Neither a borrower nor a lender be;
> For loan oft loses both itself and friend,
> And borrowing dulls the edge of husbandry.[7]

Edward's considerable holdings in Melbourne were all leasehold, and he purchased merchandise for his arcade from his own capital. He had no encumbrances that could be called in. This is not to say that he was not susceptible to making special financial arrangements with his regular bank, the Bank of London, when asked to do so by its manager. In 1893 he was asked to transfer his four-figure cash holdings at the bank from a current account to a fixed deposit, against which he could borrow cash. He also agreed to a rather unusual arrangement of opening a 'personal valuables' deposit account that was independent of banking procedures, and from which he was able to continue to pay staff salaries. The arcade was not a public company or one against which shares had been floated. It owed no money and paid its way as it went along. Edward was in no debt to any bank, and his arcade was insulated against foreclosure.

Second, Edward had nurtured a unique management–staff philosophy. He was determined to provide a reassuring working environment for his 100-odd staff, to insulate them as far as he could from the viciousness of the depression. His strategy was twofold: assure staff that dismissing any of them would be a very last resort, and enlist their support in finding ways to combat the downturn in sales. He called for a 'team effort': find economies in all your daily duties, no matter how small or insignificant; use thumb tacks, stationery, pens and pencils sparingly; turn out electric lights in unoccupied rooms. He recorded:

> I took a memo book, went around and noted down 300 [expense] items, and printed them on paper with a margin, and then put a copy into the hands of 24 employees, asking them to read it carefully, and put down in the margin all other items of expense which they could think of. My object lesson largely gave them a clue right along the line to further items, and, with a few more that I thought of myself, they increased the number to 600. I then printed these 600, gave 100 employees each a copy with a piece of paper accompanying it, asking them to read it and put upon the paper any other items of expense, of any kind whatever, that they could think of current in the Arcade. The result was that 90 employees returned the paper, which when sifted out and totted up with the 600 already printed, amounted to 1,700 distinct items of expense … This thinking

about, and realizing, by the employees of the great and many expenses incurred in the carrying on of the trade has had a favourable influence throughout the Arcade, and things are going on much more satisfactorily than they were previously; and now, more than ever, I am confirmed in my previous conviction, that the employees should fully realise what all the working expenses total up to. This should always be a part of their trade education to induce them to do what is fair and just in their work.[8]

In what must have then been a novel concept in reverse assessment but is much in fashion today, Edward also invited his staff to list the faults of employers towards employees. He started the ball rolling by making his own list, which included:

1. working employees too heavily, 2. working them too long, 3. under-paying them, 4. tyrannising them, 5. undeservedly hurting their feelings by an offensive manner towards them. These five faults are the principal ones; some employers have none of them, while some have one or two or three or four, or all five of them.

Meanwhile, the faults of employees, said Edward, amounted to at least twenty-one: they could be 'unpunctual, dishonest, untruthful, intemperate, idle, unpersevering, thoughtless, careless, wasteful, unmethodical, untidy, wasteful, unuseful, immodest, disobedient, discontented, unamiable, impatient, disobliging, undutiful or foolish.'[9]

His staff filled in their questionnaires with circumspection. Several added the diplomatic footnote that they did not believe any of the listed failings of employers applied to Mr Cole.

Whether the questionnaires had any effect on staff performance is not known, but they may have diluted a resentful feeling among his employees that their boss had it made, and would do anything to keep profits coming in during trying times. Yet Edward's demonstrated goodwill towards his employees and his reluctance to sack them must have had a benign effect, as indeed must have his known beneficence to those few staff who stole books or indulged in other acts of petty crime.

Not so petty, but well known to his staff, was the way he treated one employee who stole the breathtaking sum of £1000 from the arcade to pay off gambling debts. Even with him, Edward was magnanimous. 'What good would he do in jail while his family starved?' he argued against Eliza's protests that he was being too soft. 'Better that I continue to employ him on the strict undertaking on his part that he would pay off the amount he stole while continuing to work for me.'[10]

Whether Edward's fight with the Victorian authorities over the Early Closing Act of 1896 was motivated by his concern for staff welfare or by self-interest could be interpreted

Some of the arcade staff in the fernery: at rear, second from right is
Syd Endacott; standing beside him is Frank Wilmot (Furnley Maurice)

either way—it was probably a mixture of both. An amendment had been made to the Act in
1897 to exclude booksellers on the basis that Cole's Arcade was a 'perfect free library' that
should not be made to close at 7 p.m. But the Act was amended back to its original form in
1898. The same year, Edward opened a petition that attracted 30,000 signatures asking for a
further exemption. He argued (the italics are his):

> That, in the passing of the 'Shops and Factories Act, 1885', the desire to keep the Book
> Arcade open largely influenced the Honourable Legislature to exempt Booksellers. That,
> since that time, the Book Arcade has been open until ten o'clock every night, having

been run with two relays of hands—*all working about eight hours*. That, there have been recitals of good music every afternoon and evening. That, free seats and largely free reading have been allowed, and that, the attendance has been greater during the whole time *than at any other literary and artistic institution in the world*. That, it has become world-renowned as a peculiar and useful Australian institution, different from any other; and many eminent travellers have spoken of it with high praise and as worthy of being copied in other countries.

Your petitioner humbly prays that, for the foregoing reasons and also because the large majority of the public desires that the said Book Arcade should remain open, your Honourable House will be pleased to so enact that at least the portion of the said Book Arcade, namely, that which extends from Bourke Street to Little Collins Street, shall be allowed to remain open as heretofore, and that your petitioner may be permitted to sell sufficient goods to pay his expenses.

And your petitioner will ever pray,
EDWARD WILLIAM COLE[11]

The Legislature made a compromise. It allowed Edward's book department to remain open till 10 p.m., but no other department. This resulted in Edward reluctantly shedding some staff, reflecting the still-subdued business environment of Melbourne at the end of the 1890s, ten years after the worst of the depression had passed.

Not that Edward was suffering particular hardship at this time himself. In 1897, he sent Eliza and eldest daughter Linda off to London to help celebrate Queen Victoria's Diamond Jubilee, followed by a grand tour of Europe. Linda was twenty-one at the time, and it was her first overseas trip. Eliza was interested but phlegmatic, Linda wildly excited.

A third factor that helped Edward survive the depression in relatively good shape compared to other city merchants was his counterintuitive instinct to expand the arcade in the teeth of economic adversity, rather than contract it. He began with technical innovations. He had already used telegraphy, established between Melbourne and Europe in 1872, to communicate with his buyers in England and on the Continent. He had also installed a telephone connected to a telephonic service first put in place in Melbourne in 1879—an expensive device, but an immense boon to professionals and commercial traders.[12] Australia's first telephone directory was printed in 1880, listing forty-three subscribers; the arcade's telephone number was 616.[13] Whether Edward installed vacuum tubes to transmit messages and cash around the arcade, or speaking tubes and electrically operated bells to facilitate communication between staff in different departments, is unknown, but he may well have done.[14]

Cole's musicians, sometimes augmented with other players,
kept customers entertained with popular classics and hymns

Electric lighting? Although he appreciated the advantages of good lighting for a reading public, Edward was initially not keen to install electricity in the arcade, preferring the softness of gaslight, especially when its luminosity was enhanced with a rigid but fragile mantle of metal oxide.[15] But the better the lighting, the more hours could be devoted to reading, which was no longer confined to daylight. Edward knew he would eventually have to bow to the inevitable, and envisaged a mix of gas and electricity throughout the arcade. In 1892 he had the ground floor electrified, though gas jets remained for emergencies. The same year he hired a Frenchman, Leon Chaviron, a specialist in optical illumination through electricity, to install a 'field of gold' on the right-hand Bourke Street entrance to the arcade. The field seemed to stretch right through Elizabeth Street and beyond.

Edward's ambition ranged far beyond the installation of modern technology. He appreciated the opportunities the depression provided for acquiring foundering businesses, and looked around at what might be available. His primary target was two bookstores owned by Edward Augustus Petherick. No simple bookseller, Petherick had acquired a sophisticated understanding of the book trade as an apprentice to the Victorian bookseller and stationer George Robertson, and for a time managed Robertson's bookstore in London. He later branched out and acquired a bookshop at 346 George Street in Sydney, on the corner of Market Street, and another at 67 Rundle Street, Adelaide. He was recognised as one of the great collectors of Australiana, and a reading room at the National Library in Canberra was subsequently named in his honour.

Neither his ability nor his prominence saved Petherick from the remorseless arithmetic of the depression, however, and he went bankrupt in 1894. Edward acquired his bookstores and stocks, but Petherick held onto his famed collection of Australiana and negotiated with the federal parliament's Library Committee for its acquisition 'in consideration of an annuity of £500 a year'. An agreement between the Petherick family and the Commonwealth was signed on 4 November 1909, and was confirmed by the Petherick Collection Act of 1911.[16]

Edward had his trademark rainbow painted across the front of Petherick's bookstores in Sydney and Adelaide, and appointed local managers. During visits he instructed the newly appointed managers to allow the public to read the stock without pressure to purchase. Whether they followed what they probably regarded as eccentric instructions incompatible with good business is not recorded. As Edward was out of sight and out of mind, it is likely they did not. Neither store acquired the fame of Cole's Arcade in Melbourne, although a model of the Sydney store was constructed in the 1950s by Jack Montgomery of the ABC, and continues to exist in Sydney's Powerhouse Museum as an example of the bookselling trade in and around Sydney's Market and George streets in the late nineteenth century.

In Melbourne, Edward continued to expand his grand arcade. Although deeply suspicious of bringing in outside talent at senior levels to help him run it, and accustomed to engaging young workers and training them to follow his methods, around 1890 he made two exceptions. One was Charles Bassett, a confident young Englishman who claimed to have worked in retail music stores in London and wanted to open a sophisticated music shop to expand the sheet-music department Edward had earlier established. The other was Ernest Ransome, a confectioner, who saw great potential for a splendid chocolate and confectionery shop in the arcade.

Undeterred by the fact that Joseph Wilkie and George Allan had run a successful music warehouse in Collins Street since the 1850s and now ran Allan's, a highly successful music store elsewhere in Bourke Street, Bassett persuaded Edward to let him open another one. It was located in a leased building facing Collins Street, where it would be insulated from the sound of the band that played regularly in the arcade in Bourke Street. He stocked the shop with string, woodwind and brass instruments and hired musically literate assistants to help sell them. He added a section for sheet music, including (an extra inducement) Edward's own musical publications, *The Thousand Best Songs in the World* and *The Funniest Song Book in the World*. Bassett proposed that his staff play selections from these.

Edward also agreed to Bassett ordering a German-made symphonion in a handsome mahogany cabinet. Similar to the cylinder nickelodeon invented in the 1890s, and forerunner of the jukebox of the 1940s, the symphonion activated a large perforated metal disc when a coin was inserted. Its musical repertoire was restricted to *The Blue Danube* and one or two other German favourites, but if its technical capacity could have extended to a more comprehensive music bank, Edward would have favoured hymns, popular songs and light classics—nothing, to his untutored mind, too 'heavy'. Bassett also persuaded Edward to import a mechanical egg-laying hen (again, operated by the insertion of a coin) from the same company that supplied the symphonion.[17] Both the symphonion and the hen are today displayed in a permanent exhibition called 'The Melbourne Story' at the Melbourne Museum in Carlton.

Edward leased a building on the arcade's western flank in 1893, knocked out a wall and opened what he called a 'Shilling Room' where, in order to attract cash-strapped shoppers, no article was priced above one shilling. To his chagrin, however, business was slow as customers were reluctant to be seen in a place that had the stigma of poverty. After giving the room a decent time to see whether customers would overcome their pride and frequent it in greater numbers (they did not), he turned part of it into a light-filled optical illusion for children called Wonderland. He installed a giant stuffed alligator, a 'Fairy Forest' and a 'World Beneath the Sea'—exhibitions designed by specialists who knew how to use lighting, reflective surfaces and optical illusions to enhance space and depth. He contracted the Melbourne glaziers Meadows and Company to supply warped mirrors that distorted the human form by making the thin fat, the fat skinny, the pretty plain and the plain attractive, and installed them

OPPOSITE TOP Quong Tart in front of his luncheon
rooms, possibly at 777 George Street, Sydney
OPPOSITE BOTTOM Cole's tea salon in the arcade,
inspired by Quong Tart's tea rooms

in a 'Funny Mirrors Room' from which erupted squeals of mirth from delighted customers. At around the same time, he added a stationery department stocking fine writing instruments; a fashion department; a perfumery for women; and a photography studio.

Edward had long entertained the idea of installing a sophisticated tearoom at the arcade. The inspiration to move ahead on this came when he and Eliza travelled to Sydney in the mid-1890s to see how his George Street bookstore was going, and to allow Eliza to attend a seance.[18] During the visit he met Quong Tart, a notable and well-respected businessman.

Any anti-Chinese feelings Sydneysiders may have had about Quong Tart were stifled by his very European-ness. An orphan from Canton who was adopted as a child by a Scottish miner on the goldfields of Braidwood in southern New South Wales, he went to the Scots College in Woollahra, spoke vernacular Australian English, occasionally wore a kilt, and played the bagpipes—'almost a white man', as some of Sydney's newspapers patronisingly observed. He owned and managed several high-class tea salons in Sydney, including one in a pavilion at Moore Park Zoo. A total abstainer from alcohol, like Edward, Quong Tart occasionally served tea without charge in the foyers of Sydney theatres. He was the patron of several sports and an advocate for Sydney's Chinese community, defending their rights especially during the anti-Chinese period leading up to Federation and the passage of the Immigration Restriction Act by Australia's first parliament. His grandest salon, the Elite Dining Hall, occupied two floors of the newly constructed Queen Victoria Building in George Street. In his advertisements, Quong Tart described the hall's decorations as 'celestial artistry with its marble reservoirs with gold carp, ferneries in rock, massive carvings and hand-painted mirrors'.[19]

Edward was captivated, and invited Quong Tart to consider opening a tea salon in Melbourne in partnership with himself. Quong Tart demurred, and suggested that Edward consider opening one of his own. To facilitate such a venture, he provided an introduction to his friend the Reverend Cheok Hong Cheong of the Episcopalian Mission to the Chinese in Victoria, and instructed Edward where and how to get the best imported teas.

And so it came about. On his return to Melbourne, Edward replaced what remained of the unsuccessful Shilling Room with a tea salon. With the permission of Harry Rickards, a well-known impresario, comedian and entrepreneur who ran Melbourne's Opera House,

he obtained the services of Rickards' foremost scenic artist, Harry Grist, to decorate the
walls of the salon. This Grist did with gay abandon, employing elaborate Chinese and Indian
themes. The salon was opened on Cup Day 1895. Select Indian and Chinese teas were served
on the finest china, accompanied by scones, cakes and sandwiches. According to Turnley's
rich fund of anecdotal evidence from his mother, Linda, the occasion was graced by the
presence of the American writer Mark Twain.[20]

In 1900, Edward added another attraction to the arcade: a monkey house. According to
Turnley, Edward had been intrigued by *The Speech of Monkeys*, a book by Richard Lynch
Garner, an American researcher who studied the language of primates, especially chimpan-
zees. Garner contended that monkeys' cries and grunts were more sophisticated than those
of other animals, and could be interpreted as a basic form of speech. When he and Eliza
visited Quong Tart in Sydney, Edward broached his interest in monkeys, and Quong Tart
took him to meet Mr AG Holmes, superintendent of monkeys at Moore Park Zoo, and his
remarkable ape Jacob, who appeared to recognise Holmes' instructions in English.[21]

Edward already had an aviary stocked with parrots at the end of the arcade's fernery,
including sulphur-crested cockatoos—one of which, to the amusement and occasional
scandal of visitors, regularly exercised its rudimentary and sometimes coarse English vocabulary. But now he wanted monkeys. He set about importing some mating pairs, and accommodated them in a light and airy storeroom on the second floor overlooking Bourke Street.
He outfitted their keeper, Gabe Mellot, with a scarlet-and-gold uniform and hired Grist to
paint jungle murals. The monkeys quickly became one of the main attractions at the arcade,
especially for mothers and their children.

Melbourne's property rentals had fallen dramatically during the depression, and remained
low well into the first decade of the twentieth century. Edward shrewdly took advantage of
his financial liquidity and leased several buildings adjacent to or behind the main arcade,
some of which were owned by his original lessor, Matthew Cantlon. He also rented a
three-storey building on the north side of Little Collins Street running parallel with the
arcade owned by Benjamin Fink, a well-known Melbourne property developer and the
brother of Theodore Fink, who had provided Brodzky, the owner of *Table Talk*, with such
juicy scandal about crooked entrepreneurs during the depression; and a building on the
arcade's western flank, presumably the former Hosie's Hotel.

The arcade emerges into Collins Street, its final extension

Edward also leased Howey's Lane running from Little Collins Street towards Collins Street, roofed it with glass (which still stands) and rented the building along its western flank as a magnificent toyshop whose wares were attractively displayed through a series of plate-glass windows along the side of the building. By the turn of the century that building, and another he leased between Howey's Lane and Collins Street, extended the arcade all the way through from Bourke Street to Collins Street. Some of Edward's leases had to be reissued in the late 1890s as his landlords re-registered their holdings under the Torrens Title, a South Australian invention named after Sir Robert Torrens, premier of that colony from 1857 to 1858, designed to simplify land registration and transfer and eliminate most grounds for property dispute.

12
COLE
AND WHITE
AUSTRALIA

Quong Tart, a distinguished, bagpipe-playing Chinese–
Australian entrepreneur, was an inspiration to Cole

Throughout the 1890s the six Australian colonies, all highly suspicious of each other, had held numerous meetings about how to achieve closer economic and social integration. Embraced by the free traders of New South Wales and grudgingly acknowledged by the protectionists in Victoria, measures such as the abolition of border tariffs and establishment of intercolonial free trade were really in the interests of all the colonies. So was the consignment to a federal government of such things as defence, railways, the movement of stock, post and telegraph, and immigration.

In 1889 Sir Henry Parkes, the 74-year-old premier of New South Wales, delivered an address at Tenterfield in the New England district of that colony saying the time had come for federation. 'The crimson thread of kinship', he said, 'runs through us all.' His call resonated to some degree with the other premiers, and they met with him in Melbourne in 1890 and agreed to hold a constitutional convention to draft a federal constitution. After a number of false starts—the premiers were more concerned about the prospect of depression than federation—a draft constitution drawn up by the convention was submitted to and approved by voters in Tasmania, Victoria, South Australia and, with qualifications, New South Wales. A second referendum was held in 1899 in which Queensland participated, and was accepted by all. Western Australia held its own referendum in 1900, and the Commonwealth of Australia was proclaimed on 1 January 1901 in Centennial Park, Sydney.[1]

Australia's first federal parliament was convened the same year in Melbourne, and the very first piece of legislation it passed was the Immigration Restriction Act, which virtually prohibited non-white immigration. The rationale for the Act included several factors, some of them fictitious, some exaggerated, none of them admirable. They included forestalling the invasion of 'teeming millions' from China and Japan, maintaining Australia's British nationhood through the 'racial purity' of White Australia, and preventing cheap 'coloured' labour from undercutting white wages.

Edward Cole was one of several articulate Australians at the time who vociferously opposed this racist Act. He was a universalist, an idealist, something of a humanist, who believed that all people are equal in intelligence and capability. He was convinced that the colour of their skin was all that distinguished humans one from another, and that pigmentation correlated directly to the proximity of their habitat to the equator: the closer to it they lived, the darker their skin; the further away, the lighter. Living proof of his theory, he claimed, was Simon Gabriel, a dark-skinned man he had hired as a turnstile operator at Wonderland in his arcade in 1890, but who by 1897 had turned 'white'. (Gabriel's parents were Portuguese, and he had inherited their swarthy complexion, which probably became pale after working out of the sun at the arcade for seven years.)

Edward extended his theory to all humankind—to Asians, Africans, Indians and Caucasians. While living in their own latitudes and geographic zones, they retained their natural skin colour, but if they migrated to other regions, he claimed, their skin would lighten or darken accordingly. Underneath, all people had the same fundamental human characteristics of intelligence, perceptiveness, capacity to learn, sensitivity and humour. If Edward was forensically challenged about his theory, history does not record, although he received many racist slurs in newspapers about his 'Jap'- or 'Chink'-loving ways.

Acculturation was another component of Edward's theory. If brought up in an Australian or English environment, he asserted, Chinese or Japanese or Africans would have exactly the same manners, sensitivities and communication skills as Europeans. He would have applauded Professor Henry Higgins' efforts in George Bernard Shaw's *Pygmalion* (first performed in 1913) to transform Eliza Doolittle from cockney flower seller to grand lady merely by changing her dress and speech. There is no evidence that Edward tested his views by examining the manners and accomplishments of whites living in non-white communities, but he probably would have if challenged. Humans, he would have said, are environmental chameleons, who survive by adapting to their surroundings.

Then came Edward's conviction, which would no doubt be condemned today as eccentric at best or racist at worst, that darker-skinned people could undertake manual labour successfully in tropical climates but white people could not. In 'The Better Side of the Chinese Character, Its Relation to a White Australia and the Development of Our Tropical Territory',[2] he described what he saw as Chinese qualities of thrift, intelligence, honesty, sobriety, cheerfulness, patience and capacity for hard work, particularly in hot areas.

Two tracts outlining in detail Cole's objections to colour prejudice in Australia, particularly against the Chinese, and how it will adversely affect the development of the country

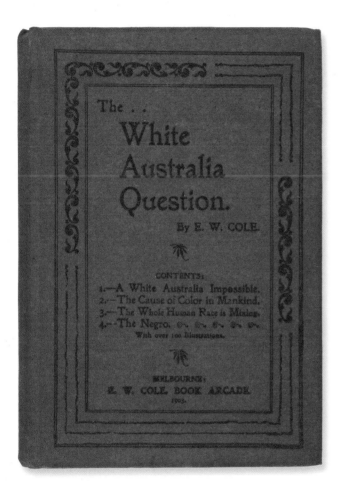

Along with other non-white people, they would be ideal settlers in the Northern Territory, where they could grow rice, rubber, sugar and tropical fruits. Edward's views were remarkably similar to those of the South Australian utopian Wilton Hack, who appealed to the Japanese and South Australian governments in 1876 to send a few hundred Japanese settlers to work as agricultural workers in the Northern Territory—a proposal rejected out of hand by the Japanese government.[3]

In their views, Edward and Hack were unwittingly or consciously supporting the policies of those in Whitehall, which moved workers across the giant chessboard of Empire to grow

A WHITE AUSTRALIA IMPOSSIBLE,

and for Very Important Reasons

UNDESIRABLE.

————o—··——

"We will not allow any Asiatics, or other Coloured People, to settle in any part of Australia." So say many Australians.

————o————

"God hath made of one blood all nations of men for to dwell on all the face of the earth." "Do unto others as ye would they should do unto you." These just and humanitarian doctrines were taught by two Asiatic, coloured men, Jesus and Paul.

Yes! The man who taught men to love one another—that the foreigner is our neighbour—and to do as we would be done by—the man who has influenced for good more of the human family, our white *selves included, than any other man that ever lived, the man whose doctrines are taught every week in the eight hundred thousand churches and chapels of Christendom—that man, under our* proposed *Alien law, would not be allowed to live in this country through being an Asiatic and a coloured man.* **Now, whatever may happen, or however we may reason, one thing is certain—that no man can support such a law and remain a Christian.**

crops, work in mines and earn profits for white people in inhospitable tropical colonies. This included transporting Pacific Islanders to Australia to work as little better than slaves in the sugar and cotton fields of Queensland and the Northern Territory. Edward apparently saw no contradiction here with his argument that 'all people are equal'. He may have envisaged non-white workers in Australia's tropics not as indentured labourers but as free citizens who owned and worked their own farms, as Hack proposed.

Edward's beliefs were reflected in the idealistic aphorisms featured on the coins he cast to promote his book business—about all men being brothers under the skin, the end of international conflict, world federation, one universal government, one religion, one language. He developed these beliefs further in a series of pamphlets published at his book arcade. In one of them, called *A White Australia Impossible*, he made the unanswerable point that Jesus was a 'coloured' man and that no one could support a law excluding Asiatic or coloured men from Australia and remain a Christian. In another, entitled *Humanity*, or the *Human Race at a Glance*, he exhaustively offered 560 representative portraits of all the races of humankind, emphasising their common humanity beneath their superficial differences.

Even before the federal parliament passed its Immigration Restriction Act in 1901, Edward, consistent with his beliefs, strongly opposed other measures to prevent non-whites from settling in Australia. He had first-hand experience of the unfair and sometimes brutal treatment of South African blacks by colonialists, and of the discrimination whites had imposed on Chinese miners at Castlemaine. The quiet and industrious Chinese had to put up with European miners they saw as:

> giants of six feet [180 centimetres] and more, rowdy and prone to use their ham-like fists when annoyed, greedy when faced with roasted beef which they devoured without ceremony, ever thirsty for foul-tasting beers and fiery rum, lacking in delicacy and refined taste, and clumsy in their demeanour ... And what did an intelligent Chinese make of a people who continually denounced fan tan [a Chinese card game] and opium, but spent vast sums on betting and alcohol?[4]

During the gold rush European miners attacked Chinese communities, including at Ararat in 1855, Daylesford and Buckland River in 1857, and Lambing Flat in 1861. In the main, Chinese settlers restrained their compatriots from violent retaliation, but they were not incapable of fighting back. Some literate Chinese citizens wrote carefully drafted petitions about these disturbances to the colonial authorities. Among them was Mei Quong Tart, the Canton-born businessman who inspired Cole to establish a tea salon in his Bourke Street arcade. On 9 December 1887, a letter from Quong Tart appeared in the *Sydney Morning Herald* objecting to: a £100 poll tax on Chinese proposed by the Anti-Chinese League; the prohibition of Chinese from working any mine until it had been abandoned by Europeans for three years; and the disenfranchisement of Chinese. Listing the occupations closed to Chinese people, he assured readers that they competed with Europeans only in such labour-intensive occupations as cabinet-making, gardening, mining, hawking and 'general dealing'. He ended his letter with a little sarcasm, saying he supported the league's proposal that a special tram car be put on for the use of the 'dirty, nasty Chinese', but suggesting that if all the dirty drunken Europeans were put in the same car, 'it would encourage cleanliness in both cases'.[5]

Quong Tart was patronisingly described by the *Sydney Mail* as the 'whitest Chinaman we know', while *The Bulletin* assured its readers that 'Quong Tart's Mongolian qualities are only skin-deep. He is a native of Australia and a loyal subject of Her Most Gracious Majesty the Queen … and a true Briton, expert at manly sports.' As previously mentioned, Quong Tart ran a successful business importing tea, and a fashionable teashop in Sydney. He played the bagpipes and knew how to fit in with hostile Australians until one of them attacked him. On 19 August 1902, he was savagely assaulted by an intruder in his office in the Queen Victoria Building. After a partial recovery he died from pleurisy at his home, Gallop House, Ashfield, on 26 July 1903 and was buried in the Rookwood Cemetery.[6]

Praise of Quong Tart was the exception that proved the rule. In 1888, which *The Bulletin* described as its 'Anti-Chinaman year' and which was the centenary of white 'settlement' of Australia, pronouncements against Chinese settlers became so vociferous that the Chinese were 'extremely reluctant to introduce relatives or friends from China'.[7]

Quong Tart was not the only resident Chinese to object to Australian discrimination laws. Others included a committee of Chinese in Australia chaired by the Reverend Cheong Cheok Hong that sent a petition of protest to Prime Minister Edmund Barton in 1901, supported by, among others, the See Yup Society and Chinese Empire Reform Association in Melbourne and Sydney. William Ah Ket, a Melbourne University law graduate, appealed to the governor-general against applying a dictation test to prospective Chinese immigrants. Under pressure from London, the test was introduced as a less blunt instrument than outright exclusion on grounds of colour and allowed immigration officers to impose on applicants a fifty-word test in any European language, not necessarily English.[8]

Australia's fear of Asia was initially focused on China but quickly broadened to include Japan. By the early 1890s, Japanese immigrants had begun to dominate Australia's pearl-fishing communities in Broome in the north-west and on Thursday Island at the top of Cape York. In his diary describing a voyage to Japan via Thursday Island in 1905, a Victorian parliamentarian and vociferous anti-Asian, Dr William Maloney, observed disapprovingly that 'the Japs, pearl fishers, beachcombers and traders, had run most of the niggers off, and with a sense of entitlement had established a cohesive patch of Japan on Australian territory'.[9]

The Queensland colonial government had a treaty with Japan for the entry of more than 3000 Japanese workers as canecutters, but other colonies wanted them excluded. Edward knew about this legislation and it would not have escaped his notice that the British, who had signed a Treaty of Commerce with Japan in 1894, were in the middle of negotiating a broader Anglo-Japanese Alliance[10] and would not take kindly to anticipated restrictive Commonwealth legislation. This was indeed the case. The Secretary of State for Colonies objected to any Australian legislation discriminating against Japanese on two grounds:

> First, any attempt to impose disqualifications on the base of origin embodies race and colour. Besides being offensive to a friendly power, (this) is contrary to the general conceptions of equality which have been the guiding principle of British rule throughout the Empire.
>
> Second, the Bill is objectionable as embodying a provision which is peculiarly offensive to Japan, a power with which His Majesty's Government is and earnestly desires to remain on friendly terms ... In excluding them it places them in the general category of Asian races, without any consideration being paid to their state of civilisation—a proceeding which is not agreeable to the Japanese Government, as the Consul in Townsville stated in his letter of the 6th November 1899 to the Chief Secretary.[11]

But the secretary of state's appeal fell on deaf ears. Legislation from Queensland and other colonies was overridden by the Immigration Restriction Act of 1901, which was applicable across the whole Commonwealth.

FOLLOWING PAGES Tom Robert's famous 1903 painting of the opening of the first Parliament of the Commonwealth of Australia in the Great Exhibition Hall in Melbourne on 9 May 1901 by HRH the Duke of Cornwall and York. One of the observers is Hisakichi Eitaki, acting Japanese consul general in Sydney (bottom left hand corner of the painting), who strongly objected to Japanese nationals being included under Australia's forthcoming restricted immigration laws.

Under the Qing in the nineteenth century, China was introspective, with little time, inclination or energy to protect the rights of any of its citizens who chose to work abroad. The imperial view was that emigration was akin to treachery, and that those who migrated cut themselves off from the ruler's care. Even if they had been more favourably disposed to help émigrés, however, the Chinese were mired in wars against Britain and France,[12] torn apart by internal rebellions, and humiliated by being forced to open over eighty treaty ports to British, French, Italian, German, Dutch, Japanese, Russian and American trading colonies under the American-inspired 1899 Open Door Policy. The scramble for foreign enclaves in China became particularly fierce after the Sino-Japanese War of 1894–95.

In 1887, the Chinese conducted a token inquiry into conditions of the Chinese community in Australia by sending two commissioners, General Wong Yung Ho and Consul U Tsing, to Melbourne and Sydney as part of a wider investigation into Chinese living in South-East Asia. They witnessed first-hand the racist anti-Chinese sentiment in the lead-up to the restrictive colonial legislation of 1888 and recommended establishing a consulate general, but were ignored by the conservative Tsungli Yamen (Chinese Foreign Ministry). The first Chinese consulate general in Australia was not established until 1909, in Melbourne.

In contrast, Japan's protestations were strong and direct. On instructions from Tokyo, Hisakichi Eitaki, the acting consul general in Sydney from 1898 to 1903, wrote frequent letters to British authorities before Federation complaining about the forthcoming Immigration Restriction Act, and after Federation to the governor-general, Lord Hopetoun, and to prime ministers Barton and Deakin. He also wrote assiduously to the Australian press, particularly the Melbourne *Argus* and the *Sydney Morning Herald*. Eitaki's efforts gained him public attention to such an extent that artist Tom Roberts painted his likeness among other foreign dignitaries into *The Big Picture*, his record of the opening of the first federal parliament by the Duke of Cornwall and York at the Exhibition Building in Melbourne on 9 May 1901. In one letter to Deakin, Eitaki wrote that 'the Japanese belong to an empire whose standard of civilisation is so much higher than that of Kanakas, Negroes, Pacific Islanders, Indians, or other Eastern peoples'.[13]

Eitaki also reported to Foreign Ministry officials in Tokyo, and they responded to him in Sydney and to the consul general in Melbourne. The official correspondence began with concern about colonial acts of exclusion in the 1880s and continued through to the federal Immigration Restriction Act of 1901. Letters between the Foreign Ministry in Tokyo and Japanese officials and honorary consuls in Australia during this period—an amazingly voluminous collection of indignant correspondence—are contained in nine large volumes in the Japanese Foreign Ministry archives.[14]

13
COLE GOES
TO JAPAN

A Japanese peddler of brooms and baskets made from bamboo and rice straw, 1901

The next part of our story concerns Edward's visit to Japan in 1903, and the significant part played in getting him there by a sympathiser in the Imperial Japanese Navy. His single-handed and quixotic crusade against the White Australia policy is little known in Australia, as is its background.

For two centuries before the Meiji Restoration in 1868, Japan had been cut off from Western influence by the Tokugawa Shogunate's isolation policy of *sakoku*. The country was dependent on agriculture, had little technology, and was controlled by hundreds of semi-independent feudal lords. Foreigners were forbidden entry, and to discourage the long sea voyages by Japanese seafarers common in pre-Edo times, Japanese shipyard managers were prohibited on pain of death from building vessels of more than 100 tonnes.

On Friday 8 July 1853, Japan's rural isolation was abruptly interrupted by the appearance in Tokyo Bay of a squadron of four American naval ships with sixty-one state-of-the-art cannon: the steamers *Susquehanna* and *Mississippi*, and sloops *Saratoga* and *Plymouth*. Their commander, Matthew C Perry, had been instructed by President Millard Fillmore to open trade links with Japan. All four breathed black smoke from tall funnels and could move through the water even when the wind was not blowing. These 'black ships' (*kurofune*) seemed vast and threatening to the Japanese. To reinforce his not-too-subtle message that reluctance to open its trade doors would result in selective destruction of Japan's towns, Perry promised to come back the next year with an eight-ship squadron bristling with even more guns. But with the beginning of the American Civil War, Washington lost interest for the time being in forcing open trade ports in the Orient.

Despite this, Perry's 1853 visit inflamed impatience among samurai clans with the Tokugawa policy of isolation. During the Japan civil war of 1868–69 (the *Boshin Sensō*, or War of the Year of the Dragon), the western clans of Chōshū, Satsuma and Tosha defeated the armies of Yoshinobu, last of the Tokugawa shoguns, and restored the throne to the young Emperor Meiji ('Enlightened Ruler'). Meiji and his advisers lost no time in transforming the country into a modern state. Envoys and technicians were sent to Europe and the United States to seek out the most enlightened ways of law, government, education, transport, communications, weapons and shipbuilding for the new Japan to emulate. The results of their efforts were impressive. By the time of Meiji's death in 1912, Japan had a centralised bureaucratic government, a constitution establishing an elected parliament (known as the diet), well-developed transport and communications, a highly educated population (still hierarchical but free from stultifying feudal class restrictions), a rapidly growing industrial sector, a powerful army and the third-largest navy in the world.[1]

Japan's scrutiny was not restricted to Europe and America: it included the southern colonies of Australia, particularly through the agency of its navy. Between the Meiji Restoration of 1868 and 1916, a surprising seventeen reconnaissance visits were made to Australian ports.[2] Invariably called 'training' visits, the ships also carried civilians and naval observers skilled in intelligence gathering. Among them were Shigetaka Shiga, who in 1887 found it odd that until then Japan had paid no attention to Australia, 'whose people were the bravest and most audacious of Anglo-Saxons'. 'Australia', he wrote, 'is like an egg. An egg is hatched, from which the young is born … it begins to think on its own, and then becomes an adult. Likewise colonies evolve into independence.'[3]

In 1892, Sub Lieutenant Takeo Hirose observed that 'Australia is rapidly on its way to independence … it may well become a second America in the Southern Hemisphere. How shall we Japanese react? What position are we going to adopt *vis à vis* Australia? I am not a politician, but a military man, and I am much concerned about this.'[4]

Kanjūrō Watanabe, a trained Foreign Ministry observer, was in Australia from August to December 1893. Visiting Charters Towers, Cooktown, Brisbane, Melbourne and Sydney, he was commissioned by the ministry to draw up an accurate report about Australia. His book *Gōshū tanken hōkokusho* (*Report on the Exploration of Australia*), became a guidebook for Japanese officers, businessmen, journalists and prospective immigrants. He saw little prospect for Japanese immigration except to Queensland and the Northern Territory.[5]

During the first decades of the twentieth century the Australian public openly admired visiting Japanese warships, their efficiency, and the superb training and discipline of their crews. Elaborate hospitality was offered them, including goodwill concerts, games, smokos, dinners, receptions, sporting competitions and free railway passes. Extravagant declarations of goodwill were made by Australian politicians and the media. A letter dated 7 May 1902 from the honorary Japanese consul in Melbourne, Alexander Marks, to the Japanese minister of state for foreign affairs, Baron Jutaro Komura, illustrates the point:

> The two training ships *Hiei* and *Kongo* left here today to Hobart Tasmania. All on board received the most kindly reception from the people of this country—and were entertained by all classes. Through my personal application, the railways of the State were at their disposal to travel through the country. In fact I cannot say enough for the consideration shown to Officers, Midshipmen and Crew—of both vessels. The orderly behaviour of the Sailors was remarkable. Not one case of drunkenness which impressed the people very much indeed. As compared to other men of war sailors.[6]

Praise indeed. But Japanese sailors could be forgiven for feeling puzzled by Australians' double standards. 'We are welcomed when we visit, but forbidden from settling here. Why?' was a question that must have been asked in many a Japanese wardroom. It was also a question that frequently occurred to Edward Cole: in many pamphlets and tracts he had made plain his abhorrence of White Australia.

The arrival of HIJMS *Hiei* and *Kongo* to Melbourne in 1902 was significant for several reasons. It was the first visit since the signing of the Anglo-Japanese Alliance on 30 January 1902; one of the first visits of a non–British Empire naval force since the establishment of the Commonwealth on 1 January 1901; and the first visit of such a force since the Immigration Restriction Act had received assent on 23 December 1901. The new Commonwealth was responsible for the visit, not individual colonies. A letter from Acting Consul General Hisakichi Eitaki to Prime Minister Edmund Barton dated 27 March 1902 informed Barton of the squadron's intended itinerary, including Thursday Island, Townsville, Sydney, Melbourne and Hobart from 3 to 30 April 1902. It caused quite a flurry among the prime minister's staff, and Barton took charge to ensure that everything was just so.

Now was Edward's opportunity to share his views with a sympathetic foreign audience. At a reception on the deck of *Hiei* in Melbourne on or about 20 April, he met its commander, Captain Tatsuto Iwasaki. A shrewd man with good English, Iwasaki gave Edward his undivided attention. He read Edward's pamphlets against White Australia and professed his absolute agreement that all men are brothers and that nothing distinguishes them but the colour of their skin. Iwasaki must have reported his discussions back to Tokyo, because shortly thereafter Edward received an invitation from Baron Tosuke Hirata, Minister for

[*Continues on page 222*]

THE FIRST JAPANESE WARSHIP

The first Japanese warship to visit Australia was HIJMS *Tsukuba*. Under the command of Captain Junzo Matsumura, it visited Brisbane and Sydney in 1878. Compared to later Japanese vessels, *Tsukuba* was primitive—an iron-framed, wooden-hulled steam-and-sail corvette with two rectangular boilers, purchased from Britain in 1870. With sails set and boilers going full blast, it was capable of 9 knots. It was equipped with four deck-mounted, breech-loading Armstrong guns and carried a crew of 301. Under different commanders, *Tsukuba* visited again in 1882 and 1886.

HIJMS *Hiei* and its sister ship, *Kongo*, separately visited Australia in 1891, 1894 and 1898, and together as a two-ship squadron in 1900 and 1902. Third-rated warships of the corvette class, they had more powerful engines and armaments than *Tsukuba* but still carried sails and rigging, and their single screws could only drive them at 13.5 knots.

A sea change followed in 1903, when Australian crowds welcomed to Australian shores HIJMS *Matsushima*, *Itsukushima* and *Hashidate*, three all-steel armoured cruisers. Each weighing over 4000 tonnes, they were equipped with twin triple-expansion steam engines capable of driving them at 16.5 knots, each carrying a single breech-loading 320mm Canet gun, a wide range of secondary armaments, the usual cohort of sea cadets, and a collection of civilian observers.

Japanese naval technology kept on advancing, in step with the best in Europe. HIJMS *Ibuki* was a heavy battle cruiser that together with the light cruisers HMAS *Sydney* and *Melbourne* protected a convoy carrying 20,000 Anzacs and 7500 horses from Fremantle to Egypt in late 1914. *Ibuki* represented the highest point in Japanese naval technology at the time. Driven by two geared Curtis steam turbines with twin shafts, and carrying two twin turrets of 12-inch guns and four twin turrets of 8-inch guns, it was launched at the Kure Naval Arsenal in 1907. In speed, armour and weaponry, it almost matched Jackie Fisher's HMS *Dreadnought*, which revolutionised European battleship technology and started a naval arms race with Kaiser Wilhelm II in 1906.[7] *Ibuki* was a much more potent escort than *Sydney*, and would have made shorter work of the German raider *Emden* that *Sydney* had left 'beached and done for' off Cocos Island on 19 November 1914. But, while welcomed by the Royal Australian Navy as a useful additional escort for troop ferries, *Ibuki*, like most Japanese assistance in the First World War, was in Japanese eyes

Imperial Japanese ironclad warship *Hiei*

not given proper respect. It was a sideshow, all but ignored, unable to demonstrate its superior war-fighting potential.

Russian commanders had laboured under the same deadly delusions before the Russo-Japanese War of 1904–05 as did British and Australian commanders before the Pacific War of 1942–45: the combat effectiveness of the Japanese navy was thought to be even below that of the Italian navy; Japanese navy pilots were seen to be near-sighted and poorly trained, as were Japanese infantry; and the Mitsubishi A6M Zero fighter was seen as no match for American-made Brewster Buffalo fighters being provided to British forces in Malaya.

Agriculture and Commerce. Edward was to be a special guest at the Osaka Trade Exhibition, a huge festival held between 1 March and 31 July 1903 to celebrate the expansion of Japan's international commerce in the wake of its victory over the Chinese in the Sino-Japanese War of 1894–95. Following his visit to Osaka, Edward and his family were invited to tour Japan. During the tour, Edward was to meet a variety of prominent men to discuss his objections to Australia's new immigration law.

Before embarking on his visit, Edward prepared a statement and request to his hosts:

The Federal Parliament of Australia having passed a law in December 1901 entitled the 'Aliens Immigration Restriction Act' by which it is intended to prevent all 'Coloured' persons from entering Australia and whereas Australia contains three million square miles [7.7 million square kilometres] an area about twenty times the size of Japan and only four millions of white inhabitants I consider it under such circumstances a mistake and wrong against humanity to pass retain and enforce such a drastic law.

Believing as I do that mankind everywhere of every nation, creed and colour are one in all the attributes of humanity and that as few partial and one-sided laws as possible should be passed, I expressed that opinion in a pamphlet entitled *A White Australia Impossible and for very important reasons Undesirable* in which I described the intelligence, industry, progress and power of the Japanese and argued that it would be impolitic and wrong to wound the susceptibilities of so advanced and deserving a nation.

The pamphlet was discussed in the Federal Senate during the passing of the bill—and has had a large circulation amongst the Australian public who have received it (to my astonishment) very favourably and a great number of newspapers have given favourable notices some of which accompany this statement.

At the first Federal election the cry for 'A White Australia' was almost unanimous and few electors seemed to think of the unfairness and impossibility of the thing and voted accordingly, but upon reflection a considerable and intelligent minority influenced by a higher sense of general human rights are against the act as it stands.

Fully believing that the present considerable minority in Australia who are against this restrictive law would greatly increase if the telling statistics and other facts about Japan were concisely and clearly laid before them (especially with the alliance now happily existing) and wishing to make such a report in a fresh edition of my 'White Australia Impossible' I respectfully ask the assistance of the government and heads of departments in this country to assist me in obtaining UP-TO-DATE facts and figures for that purpose upon the following or any other subjects that may be deemed expedient.

There followed an extraordinary list of requests from Edward for information about the number of cities, towns and villages in Japan and the land area capable of cultivation; and details of agriculture, roads, railways, electric lighting, manufactures, commerce, schools, shipping, banking, currency, post, military, naval, police, government, education, religion, emigration, crime and social evil.

Edward's request was sent on to Japan by Eitaki on 27 April 1903, with a covering letter. Almost as impressive as an ambassadorial letter of credence, it read:

> The Bearer, Mr E.W. Cole, is the proprietor of a large Book Arcade in Melbourne and is a gentleman of the broadest cosmopolitan sympathies. He has written several very able and most interesting works against the 'White Australia' doctrine, and is particularly well-disposed towards the Japanese. He is visiting the Osaka Exhibition and other parts of Japan, for the purpose of obtaining information for further publication in the same strain.
>
> I shall be grateful for any kindness or courtesy that may be extended to him while in Japan.

Accompanied by Eliza and their eldest and youngest daughters, Linda and Ivy, Edward embarked for Kobe on the Japanese passenger ship *Kumano Maru* in April 1903. On arrival the family was given a welcome fit for the most respected of foreign statesmen. They had an interpreter at their disposal, free accommodation at the most expensive Westernised hotels, a discreet security detail, travel by first-class rail between cities, and horse-drawn carriages within those cities. They were given press coverage, accompanied on some occasions with woodcut likenesses of their faces. In her diary of the visit, Linda described the great courtesy of their interpreter, Mr Shinosaki, as being exceeded only by his quiet initiative.

Throughout their travels, their every wish was accurately anticipated, with one exception in Tokyo. According to Linda, Shinosaki-san had taken Edward to a geisha house where an exquisitely coiffured and kimonoed young woman had eyed him provocatively over her fan and begun to stroke his beard. He had beaten a hasty retreat and Shinosaki had been forgiven for making an arrangement well beyond his brief. In wide-eyed wonder, Linda also described 'riding through Tokyo in the brougham of Kondo-san, President of Nippon Yusen Kaisha—a footman sitting beside the coachman, and at the back a postilion calling out what sounded like Heshe! [sic] to clear the roadway. And at every corner he would run ahead to make sure no ordinary mortals in the street were thinking of making their humble crossing—for WE were coming!!!!'[8]

コール氏（三面參照）

コール氏夫人

コール氏令嬢

一、澤村氏が軟化病を以て非傳染性の蠶病と爲せる根底より誤れり。軟化病の劇烈なる傳染性を有する事は古來より養蠶家の熟知せる所なれども、今念の爲に一二の知れ切つたる事實を擧ぐべし。即ち、眞に軟化病に罹りたる蠶兒の體液を取り、之を桑葉に塗抹して他の蠶兒に食せしむる時は忽ち軟化病に罹るを見る。然るに、眞に軟化病に罹りたる蠶兒の體液を取り他

とに其論文の全然誤謬なるを斷言せざるを得ざれば、茲に其論文の全然誤謬なるを悲む。

二、澤村氏が軟化病を以て草綠なる一種類の如く思ひて試驗ひたる是れ也。軟化病だ多くの地方に於て特殊の徵候を呈し其流行の勢も亦地方に依りて殺急の差あり。殊ずるに氏の研究の範圍に於て之を見て速かに發病せる者と爲す。

三、澤村氏が軟化病を以て草綠なる一種類の如き過常健康なる蠶兒の消食管内に在るものにして弱き軟化病蠶兒にのみ在り而て氏が濃室中に置きし時は發病し肛門に一層腐敗せる蠶兒の一層腐敗を早めたるを見て速かに發病せる者と思ひたると明らかなり。

末期に於ける狀態を呈する者なり。氏は常に斯かる狀態を見て軟化病を發したると思へるが如し。故に氏が從來或る學者バチルスさへを注射して軟化病を起すと爲せるも枯草バチルスの如き過常健康なる蠶兒の消食管内に在る者にして弱き軟化病蠶兒にのみ在りと云はざるべからず。氏が濃室中に負傷して置きし蠶兒の一層腐敗せしを見て遠かに發病せる者と思ひたるなり。

四、澤村氏が盆林の組織中に病菌の繁殖を見ると云ふ。其事實に無辜なる誤謬説にして此寄生を受けたるが爲に軟化病の病菌を食したる所々に於ける細菌の環狀を以て充滿し粘液を呈し、粘液を以て充滿したる部分あり。此部分を切片標本と爲して光鏡すれば、粘液の著しくニケレ取り内部に無辜なる細菌の集合を見る。是れ即ち軟化病の病竈として此寄生を受けたるが爲に種々の誤謬説を見る。軟化病に無辜なる細菌の集合を見る。

五、澤村氏が遊離酸素、亞硝酸鹽、若くはアンモニアの如きを蠶兒の肛門より注射して同樣の試驗を爲すに絶えて眞の軟化病を發する者を見ず。又劇しく軟化病を發したるを云はざるべからず。澤村氏が眞の軟化病を發する者あり。然れども絶えて水に混じ、之を桑栗と共に蠶兒に食せしむる時は多く軟化病を發する者を見ざるべからず。室内の塵埃に食せしむる時は多く軟化病を發したる者を見ざるべからず。

ALL MEN ARE BROTHERS
THE PEOPLE EVERYWHERE
THAT WE DO NOT KNOW
ARE AS GOOD
AS THE PEOPLE
THAT WE DO KNOW
FEDERATION OF THE WORLD
MADE AND ISSUED IN JAPAN
BY E.W. COLE
BOOK ARCADE MELBOURNE 3G
AUSTRALIA MEIJI 36

世界萬民皆兄弟

Also in wide-eyed wonder, Edward recorded many impressions, including the following diary note:

> You don't go to bed—the bed comes to you. It is much easier that way, and in Japan the easiest way is the only way—nor does it matter which part of the house you are in—you may be in a friend's house, a tea house, a hotel—if you are drowsy the bed will come in and be spread before you at a moment's notice—if you are visiting, your host will determine your inclination and beg you to honour his house by taking a nap therein—clap his hands and call out 'Futon motte kudasai'. In a moment his wife will be toddling in with a bundle in her arms much larger than herself—a huge thickly wadded quilt, the 'Futon', which she rolls out over the Tatami, the straw mattresses covered with finely woven bamboo that is upon all floors in Japanese rooms.[9]

Among newspapers, the *Yomiuri Shimbun* maintained a running commentary on Edward's visit, including his character and beliefs, whom he met, and where he stayed. On 16 September 1903, it reported in detail on a reception given in his honour by Gentaro Kodama, the minister for home affairs. Edward told the gathering:

> 'It is narrow-minded that the Australian government prevents Japanese from entering Australia because they are coloured. Some newspapers think that I am Jewish but I am genuinely English. (laughter) Jesus is Jewish and he made Europe civilised. Australians must be grateful to him. It is unreasonable that Australia excludes Japanese because they are of a different race.'[10]

Everywhere Edward went during his three-month visit his message was the same: universal brotherhood and opposition to Australia's Immigration Restriction Act. His presentation was accompanied by the most flattering regard for Japanese economic, technical and social achievements, and an active curiosity to learn as much as he could. He even had a bilingual 'Justice Medal' struck during his visit. About the size of a 10-sen silver coin, it carried the inscription 'All Men are Brothers'. He gave medals to several of his Japanese hosts. In response, he was given access to some of the most prominent men in the land. They included judges, ministers, company presidents, provincial governors, newspaper editors, city mayors and prominent military officers in the army and navy.

If Edward's records of conversation accurately reflected what was said to him, his interlocutors all had the same message: we disapprove of the White Australia policy, which is morally outrageous, and we wish Japanese to be excluded from it; Australia is a vast country that should take more settlers; and Japan has an overabundant population, and many Japanese people would like to resettle in Australia.

Some also apparently held views about humans' skin colour remarkably similar to those of Edward. For example, Mr Toraichiro Yokoyama, mayor of Nagasaki, told him that all the human beings on earth are of one race, and the colour of the skin, which is caused by the sun, makes no difference. Baron Eiichi Shibusawa, president of the Tokyo Chamber of Commerce, told him 'our people are brown in the south and light in the north, and the white people in warm Australia will get brown in a hundred years and black in a thousand years'. Baron Yoshimoto Hanabusa, vice-minister of the Imperial Household Agency, said, 'Man is man, colour is nothing. People up north are light, down south they are dark.'

But others whom Edward met insinuated into their comments a degree of threat. President Renpei Kondo of the shipping company Nippon Yusen Kaisha, whose coachman had so impressed Linda, told him that 'the area of Australia is large with few inhabitants, while that of Japan is small with many inhabitants; therefore it is absolutely necessary for the Japanese to emigrate to Australia, and elsewhere where there is habitable land.' More was heard of the Japanese 'Lebensraum' argument in the decades that followed.

Mr Gozo Noma, a member of the Diet House of Representatives, told Edward that he had brought the matter before the House, and all members agreed the Act was an insulting action towards Japanese people. They would sooner fight Australia and America on this issue than fight Russia on the vexatious territorial question. (In fact, they did fight Russia two years later, but America and Australia not for another thirty-eight years.)

In a prescient forecast of Japan's Greater East Asia Co-Prosperity Sphere, Baron Gentaro Kodama, governor-general of Formosa, told Edward that some Japanese would 'like to annex the whole of the Indian Archipelago [sic], and so form an immense island empire with its hundred million coloured and kindred inhabitants; and with its powerful fleet and army to begin with, such an ambition could be realised if [your] Commonwealth keeps its narrow, exclusive and blind policy of a White Australia'. Kodama's implication was that Australia could well find itself within such a sphere of Japanese influence.

Marquis Hirobumi Ito, one of the originators of the Japanese constitution and a philosopher and friend to Emperor Meiji, told Edward in no uncertain terms that Australia had made a big mistake in closing its doors against Japanese:

They might possibly discover their error should any national calamity, such as for instance an invasion by a foreign enemy, give Japan an opportunity to prove her friendship by coming to their rescue with an army and fleet. For the present, it seems to me that they suffer from a plethora of politicians engrossed in local matters. A little extension of their vision beyond the confines of their territory will not do them harm.[11]

Three observations can be made about Edward's discussions in Japan.

First, his message of racial equality was not unique. Other foreigners, including other Australians, had tried to impart the same message. A contemporary of Edward's, Henry James Black, born in Adelaide in 1858, had 'crossed the gap' and settled in Japan in 1865 as a child of seven with his father, a Scottish journalist. An orator and public performer of *rakugo* (popular narration combining elements of philosophy, politics, stories and bawdy jokes), Black frequently held forth to his Japanese audiences about the unimportance of racial differences: 'After all, human feelings are universal and everyone has the same heart.'[12] Edward may have met Black in Japan, although there is no record of such an encounter in Black's biography.[13]

Second, taken as a nation, the Japanese are among the most exclusive of human beings. Their society is intricate and their language layered with arcane manners and meanings that *gaijin* struggle to master. Even as their current birthrate falls along with their population, popular resistance to open immigration remains. The shock of defeat and American occupation after the Pacific War leavened such exclusivity, but only to a degree. How much stronger their sense of uniqueness must have been during the Meiji Restoration. While striving to emulate Western statecraft and technologies, the Japanese saw themselves as infinitely superior to other Asians, especially the Chinese. How galling it was for rednecked colonial *arrivistes* in Australia to lump them in the same exclusionary category. It is very doubtful that many of Edward's interlocutors were sincere in agreeing with him that every person is equal under the skin.

A third observation is that recurring visits by increasingly sophisticated and powerful Japanese warships sent Australians a mixed message. On the one hand there was popular admiration for the ships and their crews, who were well mannered, well turned out and courteous to a fault. On the other hand was increasing concern about Australia's vulnerability to sea attack, as some of Edward's interlocutors rather silkily implied in 1903. The Anglo-Japanese Alliance of 1902 was all very well, but Australians suspected that if the crunch came, Japan would overturn the alliance's provisions and demand territories to its south, even as far as Australia. Mix this with a demonstration of Japanese naval superiority against the Chinese in 1894, and an even more comprehensive victory over the Imperial Russian Fleet at Tsushima in May 1905, and agitation for a navy of Australia's own inevitably grew.

During their roundabout return sea voyage to Australia, the Cole family visited China and some Pacific neighbours. According to Linda's diary, 'Splendid notice about Pa in the *North China Daily News*', and 'We are anchored in the Malacca Straights [sic]. Pa had an interview with the Governor, Sir John Sweetman, and is later to have an interview with the Sultan in his Palace!!!'[14]

On the family's arrival in Sydney on 25 November 1903, Edward asked after his Sydney friend Quong Tart and was appalled to learn that he had recently died after being bashed senseless with an iron bar and robbed.

The Coles returned to a huge welcome by family and friends in Melbourne. Edward took every opportunity to publicise his visit, especially the overwhelming response he had received condemning White Australia. Adding asides he had picked up from his Japanese hosts, he elaborated on his earlier work by listing twenty 'strong reasons' why White Australia was impossible. Some are dogmatic, others erroneous, but all are worth recording:[15]

The sun causes men's skin tone. It is white in Australia's south, brown in the north. A White Australia across the continent is therefore impossible

It is impossible to inhabit the Australian tropics with Whites, which enervates their bodies, particularly women and children

Every seventh person in Australia is already coloured or partly coloured

In every country in the world, people of all races are mixing their blood; the same will happen in Australia

Asians are no more or less insanitary than Whites. In fact, the Japanese, who bathe every day, are among the cleanest people on earth

White Australia will make us disliked by all coloured people of the world

It will make us a laughing stock for attempting to carry out an unnatural and impossible policy

Jesus, an Asian and coloured man, taught that all men are brothers

Paul, another Asian and coloured, taught that all men were of one blood

Men's better nature will not permit such a selfish policy

No human legislation can permanently set aside universal kinship and brotherhood

More frequent overseas travel will make Australians realise that humans are everywhere alike

The English government and people are against such a policy

Before long every country on earth will be free for respectable men to live

Australians will themselves relax and finally abolish such a selfish law

The power of commerce will break down the policy, especially as we export our agricultural produce to Java, Japan, China and other countries

India's 300 intelligent and industrious millions are bound to want to immigrate here,
either as friends or forcibly

So will 400 million Chinese

So, with their powerful fleet and army, will 46 million Japanese

So will 30 million Javanese, who have every right to oppose Australia's dog-in-the-
manger claims

Edward also published an exhaustive report on Japan's education system, literature, transport, post and telegraph, the value of its mineral and marine products, its tax system and
the competence and strength of its military forces, in the hope it would lead Australians to
a better, more sympathetic understanding of this extraordinary nation and its people. His
efforts received little positive response, and much that was negative. A particularly nasty
comment appeared in April 1905. Headed 'A Jap Joke', it went on:

Cole, the Chow crank, in his latest spasm, gives an account of a dinner given to him
when in Japan by Captain Iwasaki of the battleship *Yashima*. Cole asked how many
foreigners they had on board as engineers etc. This, he says, was considered a joke, and
went into the papers. Poor fatuous fool. He cannot even now see that the cuter Japs
laughed at his folly. Would they employ foreigners? As poor old King Billy would say,
'No Plurry fear'. Cole is the evangel of foreign scum, and continually yelps for Australia
to take to its white bosom the Chows, Japs, Hindoos, and all the vile stinkards of the
earth. There is coal for Cole when his mission is done.[16]

Racism and a sense of threat are a poisonous mixture in official minds. Japan was already
turning into a feared potential enemy. In his first comprehensive statement about Australia's
defence since Federation, Prime Minister Deakin said in 1905 that Australia was now within
striking distance of sixteen foreign naval stations, the strongest being at Yokohama: 'Japan
is at her headquarters so to speak, next door, while the Mother Country is many streets
away.'[17] Two political campaign groups were set up in the wake of Japan's victory over Russia:
William Morris Hughes' National Defence League, and the Immigration League founded by
Richard Arthur. Deakin was involved in both. Their belief was that 'the only doctrine these
races respect is force. Our White Australia legislation is so much waste paper unless we have
rifles to back it up.' Both groups also wanted an Australian navy, one not subject to priorities
determined by London.

PREVIOUS PAGES Cole's staff welcome the family home
OPPOSITE Cole's massive lending library—'Read a
book while having a massage and manicure'

Australia's official distaste for Japan reached a low point during the 1919 Paris Peace Conference at the end of the First World War when Prime Minister Billy Hughes successfully sought to have a Japanese-sponsored 'racist equality clause' removed from the Protocol to the Covenant of the League of Nations. Japan's proposal was perfectly reasonable—an amendment to Article 21 of the Treaty that would have guaranteed equal treatment for Japanese in Australia. It declared:

> The equality of nations being a basic principle of the League of Nations, the High Contracting Parties agree to accord as soon as possible to all alien nationals of states, members of the League, equal and just treatment in every respect making no distinction, either in Law or in fact, on account of their race or nationality.

In rejecting the amendment, Hughes declared that 'ninety five out of every one hundred Australians reject the very idea of equality'. Makino Nobuaki, head of the Japanese delegation, said, 'We are not too proud to fight, but we are too proud to accept a place of admitted inferiority in dealing with one or more of the associated nations. We want nothing but simple justice.'[18] The poison spread. Japan left the league of which it was not an equal member on 24 February 1933. The denouement was Japan's invasion of European colonies in South-East Asia in 1942 and unbridled savagery against European and Australian prisoners of war on the Burma Railway and elsewhere from the fall of Singapore in early 1942 until Japan's defeat in September 1945.

In 1919 at Versailles, the Allies attempted to appease the Japanese (who were outraged by Australia's 'Little Digger') by handing them the German treaty ports in China. This was a betrayal of China, which had sent the Chinese Labour Corps to the Western Front to assist the Allies and eventually entered the First World War on the Allies' side on the understanding that the German territories in China would be handed back to China after the war. It resulted in the anti-imperialist May Fourth Movement in China, when students protested about the government's weak response to the Treaty of Versailles and helped sow the seeds of the Second World War.

Revisiting earlier Australian agitation, the British decided in 1909 to allow the country its own navy provided it fell under British command during hostilities. The first two units were the torpedo-boat destroyers *Yarra* and *Parramatta*, which arrived from British shipyards in November 1910. Another, *Warrego*, was built in Australia and joined them in 1913. By the outbreak of the First World War in 1914, the Australian navy comprised a battle cruiser, three light cruisers, three destroyers and two submarines. It was a puny force compared to Japan's sea fleet, which was ten times bigger, but one that made the hearts of Australian witnesses in the Domain swell with pride as its main contingent steamed into Sydney Harbour on Saturday 4 October 1913—first the battle cruiser *Australia*, escorted by the light cruisers *Sydney, Melbourne* and *Encounter*, and then the three destroyers. Thanks to the Anglo-Japanese Alliance, the Japanese fleet was on Australia's side. (Not so in the Pacific War, as many Australian warships and crews found to their cost.)

If Edward Cole could be resurrected in the twenty-first century, what a surprise would await him. The racist poison that so much infected white Australian zealots during his lifetime has generally passed. He would not find the federation of the world, which he predicted would occur before the year 2000, but he would find a broad and unselfconscious Australian acceptance of multinationalism across the land—a blending of races, languages and cuisine.

More particularly, if he embarked on the right Qantas flight from Haneda or Narita bound for Sydney in the northern autumn of 2019, he would find it crowded with Japanese middle and senior high school kids, the girls in sailor suits, the boys in high-collared, buttoned-up black jackets, excited at the prospect of homestays with welcoming and hospitable Australian families across the country.

And on reaching Australia, he would find in Sydney, Melbourne and other sizeable cities large Chinese, Japanese, Korean and Vietnamese communities, and smaller ones from almost every Asian country and some African countries, all for the most part blending productively and harmoniously with earlier Anglo-Celtic and European settlers. Skin colour in 2019, he would find to his delight, but not to his surprise, is largely irrelevant. Anticipating such a change, the prescient writer and journalist Donald Horne took 'Australia for the White Man' off the masthead of *The Bulletin* in 1960 when he was appointed editor.

14
LOSING
CONTROL

Throughout the 1910s and until old age slowed him down, Edward Cole remained dedicated to improving and expanding his arcade, the goose that continued to lay him golden eggs. He first aimed to consolidate his holdings on Bourke Street and extend them through to Collins Street.

Before the turn of the century, Edward had never bought property, always leasing it—thus saving himself from the dangerous vulnerability of mortgaged debt and foreclosure. But with post-depression land prices still low, he began to make opportunistic property purchases. The first was in 1906, when he bought for cash a shop aligned with the back of his Bourke Street arcade on Collins Street, but still with buildings in between. It had a frontage of 10 metres and a depth of 40. He followed this up by buying, again for cash, a factory between the arcade and his new Collins Street holding; it connected the Collins Street building to the back end of Howey Place.

After an expensive and complicated conversion that involved wall reinforcement, he installed in the factory a heavy printing press that could turn out all the advertising material, pamphlets and tracts he wanted. He engaged a master printer named Griffiths, later to be replaced by another printer, WA Comeadow (who went on to become a prominent Melbourne city councillor), and a bright young apprentice, Charlie Probert.[1] According to rumour, it was Comeadow who originally suggested the idea of holding an annual 'Moomba' festival in Melbourne, now a fixture in the city's calendar.

Despite many approaches, the owners of the building flanking the western side of Howey Place were not prepared to sell to Edward. He cajoled them into leasing it to him, and persuaded the Melbourne City Council to allow him to cover the whole alley with a glass gable roof inspired by his light-flooded arcade on Bourke Street. He then turned the western side of Howey Place into a flamboyant and colourful toy department with plate-glass windows.

He also installed there the confectioner Ernest Ransome, an energetic young man who used his considerable marketing skills to display a wide range of chocolates, nuts and sweets

under attractive lighting. Ransome purloined the mechanical hen from the head of Cole's music department, Charles Bassett, who had reservations about the machine because he felt it lowered the tone of his part of the establishment. Ransome reinstalled it at the entrance of his confectionery department and drew even more sweet-toothed customers to sample his wares.

Edward installed a wholesale store above the toys and sweets, and a lending library on the opposite side. The library had a rival in a well-established lending library on Collins Street run by Melville, Mullen and Slade, but like Cole's music department, which had to compete with the long-established music store Allan's, the library ran successfully.

To keep the customers coming, Edward frequently introduced additional novel attractions to the arcade. He expanded his ever-popular orchestra. Harry Shepherd, a capable violinist, was the leader, augmented by a pianist, harpist, woodwind and brass players, and someone on chimes. According to the recollections of Sydney J Endacott, one of Edward's department managers, the orchestra supplied a satisfying feast of music from its stand on the second-hand department floor, with, at Edward's insistence, at least one popular hymn during each session. He hired a palm-reading gypsy, and a woman conversant with Japanese origami (the art of folding paper into flowers and cranes and other shapes).

Edward sometimes opportunistically snapped up job lots of unsaleable merchandise from merchants who had bought it in the hope of making a quick fortune. Arthur Tilley was a rather desperate soap trader who could not find a market for a shipment of Brazilian soap he had shipped to Melbourne—Edward bought several tonnes of it for £10. To the consternation of some of his floor managers, he had the soap dumped in the middle of the ground floor of the arcade and provided hammers, chisels and trowels to customers to scoop or hack out as much as they could carry away for sixpence in paper bags he provided. He got rid of the soap within a fortnight and made a satisfactory profit on his £10 outlay. On another occasion, he acquired a large stock of 4711 Eau de Cologne perfume. With its light citrusy aroma, the lavender water was popular with women customers, and he used it to open an entirely new perfumery department.[2]

Edward wanted customers to treat the arcade from Bourke Street to Collins Street as a continuous promenade, much as today's department stores do. To encourage them, he invited Indian traders to set up booths along the Howey Place thoroughfare. But they argued and fought and aggressively pursued customers to such an extent that Howey Place was nicknamed Battle Alley. The traders were more an irritant than an attraction, and Edward asked them to leave after a few months.

Department repairing fountain pens and selling
fine writing instruments and artists' supplies

By the mid-1910s, the arcade's expansion was complete. It had sixteen departments, all of them proudly listed on Cole's elaborate letterhead. They included new books, second-hand books, a circulating library, a wholesale book department, stationery and fancy goods (the latter were items such as ribbons, brooches and cheap jewellery that were meant to please the fancy of those possessed of delicate and refined taste), pictures and frames, ornaments, glass and china, music books and instruments, printing and rubber stamps, a photographic studio, toys, 'crinkled paper', a tea salon, perfumes and toilet requisites, a mail order department, and Wonderland—a miniature Disneyland before its time.

Edward was eager to advertise this magnificence far and wide. He hired Charles Scudamore, a full-time professional sign-writer, who went around touching up the trademark rainbows adorning the main store with a special luminous paint. Scudamore added rainbows at either end of 'Cole's Walk' in Howey Place, a new rainbow billboard at Flinders Street Station, and several other billboards on embankments of the suburban railway network where trains slowed down before entering stations. Edward also planned to erect a large rainbow over Mount Sugarloaf, an extinct volcanic cone near the country town of Camperdown in Corangamite Shire, 120 kilometres west of Melbourne. But he was unable to get approval from the owner of the land, Sir William Clarke, a wealthy stock breeder, philanthropist and leader of colonial society who was unimpressed by what he considered to be Edward's vulgarity.

As one of his drawcards, Edward continued to keep monkeys in the arcade as an attraction to the general public. They remained popular, but what he had not anticipated was their lack of inhibition in copulating in front of their mainly youthful audience. Children watched such activities with grave concentration, but their mothers and nannies were scandalised. The Melbourne City Council, which already had misgivings about the public health aspects of a monkey cage in a shopping arcade, now had a moral weapon as well. In October 1910 the menagerie received a visit from sanitary inspectors, who noted a few broken floor tiles and microscopic gaps in the skirting and wall joinery that they claimed could harbour rats. In December that year, a representative of the council wrote to Edward informing him that 'in view of the unsatisfactory condition of this portion of the premises and the objectionable nature of the exhibition, I am directed to request that you will make arrangements as early as possible to discontinue the exhibition'.[3]

240

Not one to submit meekly to bureaucracy's demands, Edward began a campaign of prevarication and resistance. In 1912 an anonymous author, probably Edward himself, extolled the virtues of the monkey house, reporting what the monkey keeper had told him:

> We are permitted to keep 13 little monkeys on condition that the place must be scrupu-lously clean … our monkeys draw the whole of Australia to the Arcade says the keeper, swept 7 times during the day, cleaned 3 times daily, fresh sawdust every morning, too much work he says, and while I was there I did not notice the least little smell, really it is a credit to the keeper to have his department so clean.[4]

By 1913, however, the situation became untenable when William Rudd, a young boy from Burnley, stuck a finger into the cage and was bitten. *The Argus* reported that the finger was so badly crushed that the major portion of it had to be amputated.[5] Most of the monkeys were donated to the Melbourne Zoo, although Edward kept a few as personal pets to enliven his retirement.[6]

Edward's decision to close the monkey house had been earlier made easier when he himself had been attacked by an enraged father monkey when playing with one of its baby offspring. His scalp had been badly torn, requiring many stitches.

Eliza, along with daughter Pearl, witnessed the attack on Edward's scalp and was shocked by the blood on his snow-white beard. The episode possibly hastened a minor heart attack she suffered shortly afterwards. She seemed to recover, and the pair went off to recuperate at a guesthouse among the stately country homes of Mount Macedon, some 65 kilometres north-west of Melbourne. But according to family accounts, Eliza grazed her shin on the iron bedstead at their lodgings and promptly returned to Melbourne for medical treatment. Doctor (later Sir) Henry Maudsley performed an operation but did not use anaesthetics because of the weak condition of Eliza's heart. It did not help, and her leg became paralysed. Her condition rapidly deteriorated. Pearl and Ivy were urgently summoned by their father to return to Melbourne from a holiday in New Zealand, and did so just in time to be at Eliza's bedside when she died on Thursday 16 March 1911.[7]

Edward, now seventy-nine, was initially inconsolable. It was a wrenching loss. His spouse, his best friend, the companion who had sustained him through many challenging times with her unreserved admiration for his writing, his business judgement, his sense of humour, had gone. How could he possibly maintain the energy he needed to supervise the running of the arcade? Quite suddenly, questions arose about whether he could or should continue to live by himself above the arcade, and where he should live if not there. His children were also concerned about the future management of the business. Would their father lose his sharpness, his drive, and slip into old age and senescence? His sons Eddy and Vally, now in their early thirties, had shown not the slightest interest in taking over, and some years before Eliza's death Edward had appointed her, his half-brother John Watson and his old friend and confidant Joseph D'Ama Drew as trustees. They may have been able to manage things sensibly, but D'Ama had died in 1906, and now Eliza was gone too.

As these concerns mounted, Edward was persuaded by Pearl and Ivy to take a circuit-breaker and go with them to Sydney to look around and visit his bookshop in King Street. He did so, and found the manager, Ted Smith, in efficient control but uninterested in Edward's unique method of inviting customers to read the merchandise without pressure to buy. Pearl also took him on a paddle-steamer cruise down the Murray to revisit his and George Burnell's old haunts during their photographic expedition in 1862, and then on to Adelaide, where his bookshop in Rundle Street was being jointly run by Benjamin Beck and RJ Manderville. Like Smith in Sydney, neither Beck nor Manderville shared Edward's ideals or standards, but they were managing efficiently enough.[8] Beck's bookshop remained in Adelaide for many years.

Back in Melbourne, Edward tried to resume his orderly life, writing and managing his arcade while living above it. But his grief at Eliza's death and his worry over future management of the business had taken their toll and he suddenly suffered a stroke that paralysed his left side and slurred and thickened his speech. Melbourne journalists wrote obituaries to the passing of a great man, but, like those of Mark Twain's demise, they were greatly exaggerated. Edward recovered some of his former vigour and was greeted throughout the arcade by words of cheer and encouragement from staff and customers, although most noticed that he was stooped and had difficulty moving his left leg. Dr Maudsley had a frank talk to him: unless he retired from the day-to-day running of the arcade, and unless he moved out of the flat and found somewhere with fresh air and a clean environment in which to enjoy life, the doctor would not be responsible for his health or even the continuation of his life.

Alexander and Coiler McCracken were cousins.[9] Their fathers, Robert and Peter McCracken, were the founders of a small Melbourne brewery that was eventually bought out in 1907 by Carlton & United. The brewery was located at the western end of Little Collins Street, and owed its success to the cousins' use of sterile methods of microbial fermentation to produce clear-coloured and sharp-tasting ales and stouts that were measurably superior to other local beers.

As Melbourne's population exploded from the gold rush on, the McCrackens rode the wave. By the turn of the century they had made a fortune selling their beers to over 100 pubs in the Melbourne metropolitan area. They also made names for themselves in sporting activities and civic duties, mainly in Essendon where they lived, including rowing, cricket,

lacrosse, cycling and golf, and in what was called the Poultry, Dog, Pigeon and Canary Society. In particular, Robert, his son Alexander and nephew Coiler virtually founded the embryonic Essendon Football Club. Robert became president, Alexander secretary and Coiler captain of the team in the 1870s. Known jocularly as 'The Same Old', Essendon played its first serious football match against a team from Carlton in 1873 on a paddock at Ailsa, a McCracken property in Ascot Vale. One authority claims the team shared the paddock with a local community of Aboriginal people, who used it for their corroborees.[10]

Despite their wealth and social prominence, the McCracken cousins were dogged by bad fortune. Coiler's father, Peter, had invested heavily in a private railway line between Melbourne and Essendon in 1858. But Essendon was one of Melbourne's early dormitory suburbs, and the company went broke after three years because no one used the train between the morning rush hour to work and the evening return to Essendon. Also, its single steam engine frequently broke down. The line was officially closed in July 1864 with great financial loss to its shareholders; it wasn't reopened until January 1871.

Two years before the great depression of the 1890s, the notorious Melbourne financier Benjamin Fink offered to buy the McCracken brewery. For the right to float the brewery on the stock market as a £2 million public company, he offered the McCrackens £250,000. They saw it as a chance to redeem the financial loss they had suffered from the railway, but none of the McCrackens anticipated the depression or knew how unreliable and unprincipled Fink was.[11]

Imbued with a false sense of newfound wealth after the brewery float, Coiler McCracken hired Melbourne architects Lawson and Grey of 144 Elizabeth Street to design him a spectacular residence on land he owned in Leslie Road, Essendon. Construction was carried out under the supervision of Mr WK Noble, contractor, between 1890 and 1892. A pretentious monolith of Doric design with Corinthian columns, 'Earlsbrae' boasted a billiard room, smoking room, drawing and dining rooms, large vestibule and ornate staircase ascending to several bedrooms, changing rooms, boudoirs and bathrooms. Above them was a spacious promenade deck on the flat roof for the residents to take the evening air. In the grounds were also a scullery, servants' quarters and stables, as noted by AD Pyke in his history of the building:

The mansion was to be the embodiment of all things held dear: ancestry, opulence, culture and refinement—above all, family. The title of the building, conceived long before work began, was a dual symbol combining the concept of a merchant aristocracy and the family name of Earle—the maiden name of Coiler's grandmother—passed down in perpetuity. Impressed by the speculators' blandishments in 1886, which extolled the sloping land of the Riverview estate for its 'excellent drainage qualities', its 'health and scenic beauty' and its 'close proximity to the Saltwater River', Coiler added the Scottish suffix 'brae', signifying a hillside bordering a riverside plain.[12]

Earlsbrae later was bought by the Anglican Church and turned into a girls school, of which more later. It is worth noting in passing that Earlsbrae was not the only stately Melbourne mansion with such a provenance and episcopal lineage. 'Raheen', the Italianate pile in Studley Park Road, Kew, built by another beer baron, Edward Latham of the Carlton Brewery, was sold to the Catholic Church as the extremely comfortable residence of Daniel Mannix and four other Catholic archbishops. It is now the home of Visy cardboard boss Anthony Pratt.

Coiler McCracken and his family lived at Earlsbrae for ten years from 1892. It was not a happy time. Coiler was a Victorian disciplinarian, withdrawn from his children and dogged by financial anxiety as Fink kept delaying paying dividends on the floated brewery. In 1902, Coiler moved his family to a farm he had purchased at Lilydale in the Yarra Valley, 35 kilometres north-east of Melbourne, and put Earlsbrae on the market for lease. In the next ten years it attracted three sets of short-term tenants. Between tenancies, it alternated ignominiously as a warehouse.

According to one report, on 4 November 1911 Edward Cole and his family, Earlsbrae's fourth and final tenants, rented the property for seven guineas a week. But another more believable version is that Edward bought it outright from Coiler McCracken, who came down from Wagga Wagga in New South Wales to give him a guided tour. Edward's youngest daughter, now Mrs Ivy Rudd, recalled the occasion:

> He was very much a McCracken, and aware of it, constantly exclaiming 'I built this, and I built that', which I found disconcerting. He exuded confidence, but was by no means overbearing or pushing. There was a young lady friend with him—it was certainly not his wife—whom I instantly disliked. She seemed to have him under her thumb, and ordered him about a great deal. Mr McCracken wanted a large figure, but the property was in a deplorable condition. Father beat him down to £6,000.[13]

Edward immediately set about repairs, including to the sewerage system, which was malfunctioning. Almost overnight, Earlsbrae was infused with energy and life, providing endless gossip among the neighbours. The grounds were transformed into a zoo, with a small marmoset, a bulldog, a tame kangaroo, and a large aviary filled with a variety of noisy and colourful birds. There was also a lavish flower garden in the shape of a rainbow. Other animals were left there by casual visitors, including a cheetah that Edward called Leo. Fearing for their chooks and children, several neighbours drew the line at the cheetah and caused it to be transferred to the Melbourne Zoo.

Inside the house, Edward fitted mirrors on the walls of his second-storey bedroom so that he could enjoy the view while lying in bed. A stuffed polar bear in a nickel cage in the entrance hall greeted startled visitors. Dominating the broad staircase was a large oil painting by Nathan Hughes entitled *The Great Tichborne Trial*, celebrating the criminal trial of the notorious Victorian imposter Arthur Orton, claimant of the Tichborne estates.[14] Ornate fireplaces and stained-glass windows installed by Coiler McCracken were brought back to splendid life.

Although generally preoccupied with enjoying Melbourne's social life and finding partners, Edward's children were all assigned rooms at Earlsbrae. They spent much of their time there and welcomed friends, acquaintances, the wealthy, the famous and the merely curious who came to open house parties. Did Edward maintain a visitors' book? If so, it seems to have been lost to posterity. What signatures there might be of men and women who, too poor to buy books for their early education, used the arcade as a free library! Men like Walter Murdoch, who in a letter of 3 October 1961 to one of Coles' senior staff, Sydney Endacott, recalls how he gained his education at three institutions—the University of Melbourne, the Public Library of Victoria, and Cole's Book Arcade, whose stooped proprietor would appear in his shabby broadcloth coat, his scruffy top hat and his scraggly beard as Murdoch wandered around the arcade; athletics coach Percy Cerutty, who left school at twelve and would spend his lunchtimes during city employment reading books at the arcade for free; future Australian prime minister Robert Menzies, who was rumoured to have read law books at the arcade he could ill afford to buy during his University of Melbourne law course; and artist Lionel Lindsay, a regular Saturday morning borrower who picked up a copy of Philip Gilbert Hamerton's book on etchings for a shilling and taught its techniques to his brother Norman.

During all the gaiety, the children kept a protective eye on their ailing father. He was suffering in ways they may not fully have comprehended. The shell shock suffered by soldiers in the trenches along the Western Front is today clinically recognised as post-traumatic stress disorder. Similarly, the anxiety and depression Edward must have suffered on leaving the arcade would today be accurately described as relevance deprivation syndrome.

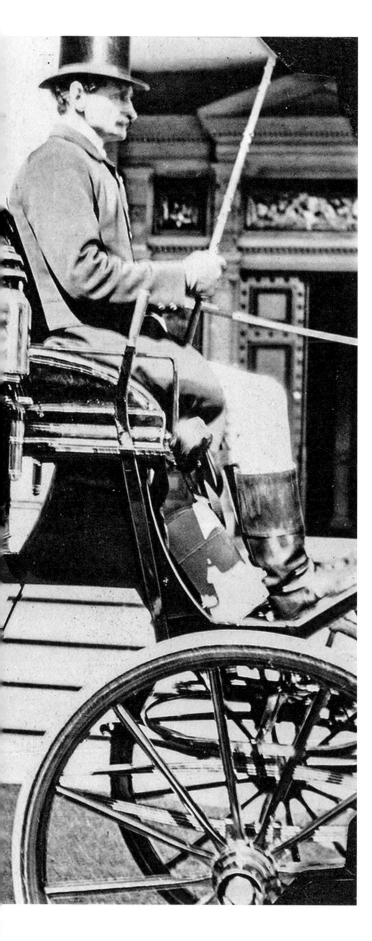

Cole in his fine brougham about to set out from Earlsbrae on one of his increasingly infrequent trips to the Bourke Street arcade to see how things were going

Edward fought his depression with characteristic stubbornness. He purchased a fine brougham and a strong young horse, hired a coachman, and in top hat and morning coat, and, frequently accompanied by one of his daughters and his marmoset, drove the 10 kilometres into the city about twice a week to keep an eye on the arcade. There he anxiously watched his managers going about their business, usually without seeking any guidance from him. Hearing disturbing rumours that some were carelessly overbuying stocks of books, which could not be sold and had to be written off, Edward summoned one of the managers to his office. The atmosphere between master and employee was vividly captured by Linda, who related it to her son Cole Turnley:

The message boy who had gone to summon the man came back to say he would be along presently.

I remember that I was indignant at his cheek, but Pa was always very tolerant, and he said to us [Linda and Edward's assistant—and husband of his daughter Ivy—Rupert Rudd] that the man after all had a responsible job, or something like that. But then a whole hour passed and Pa sent for him again, and this time the boy came back to say he would be up as soon as he had time. And at this Pa became stern, as he so very seldom did, and the boy almost ran out the door with the message that the manager's presence was requested in Mr Cole's office immediately.

He arrived in a few minutes saying, 'Yes, Mr Cole, what was it you wanted?'

And Pa said 'I wanted to see you, my lad, an hour ago … '

He said, 'Yes, I know, I was extremely busy.'

'Yes, the boy brought me that message,' Pa said. 'But to justify keeping me waiting an hour I would have liked to have more explanation than that.'

He said, 'Yes, well, but I can't tell every message boy what business I happen to be engaged in.'

And Pa said: 'If it were so private you could have given the boy a sealed note.'

He didn't know what else to say after that, and just tightened his lips, and he just said, 'Well, what exactly did you want to see me about?'

Pa got Rupert Rudd to hand him a paper and he said, 'I noticed five hundred copies of this title have been ordered, and another five hundred copies last month. Did you know that?'

He looked at the order, and at the earlier one which Rupert Rudd had also produced, and he stood there just saying, 'H'm … '

My father never believed in wielding his authority in an unpleasant way and he didn't do so now. He just said, 'I'm more than ever obliged to trust to your responsibility in

Cole with eldest daughter Linda in his study at
the arcade, possibly during the First World War

these things, my lad. You must try to honour my trust—you and the other managers. I'm
not sure if it will surprise you to know that this is not an isolated case.'

That is all I can remember Pa saying then, except to tell him to go back to his duties;
but I do remember thinking what cheek when he took out his watch as much as to say he
still resented having to have bothered with this interview at all.

I'm not sure, but I imagine Pa had talks with his other managers individually, because
no one seemed unduly surprised when he called them all to his office for a general meeting [with Linda and Rudd again present].

We could all see that he was upset. He so detested anything unpleasant like this. But he
told them that in all the years of the Arcade, the only times he had resorted to an overdraft
at the bank was for the purchase of the Arcade's freehold properties. 'But we're now for
the first time facing an overdraft simply to meet extravagant stock purchases,' he said.

And he then dropped his bomb-shell.

From that day forward, he said, all orders from every department would have to be
collated into lists for his personal consideration and approval.

Henry Williams, 'The Little Man', Cole's fourth trustee, widely disliked by staff as an unctuous flatterer

One of them put on a very cynical expression and said something about that being scarcely practical, and Pa said, 'Nevertheless, my lad, that is what will have to be done.'[15]

At first, it was done. But as the months slipped by, it became 'understood' among his managers that Edward only needed to concern himself with major orders, and fewer and fewer of the minor ones were sent for approval to what staff called his 'Parthenon' at Essendon. Whether he was becoming too vague to notice or felt that maintaining strict discipline was too taxing, Edward let the transgressions slip by.

The laxity made him increasingly keen to get another board of trustees in place. Of the original three—Eliza, Joseph D'Ama Drew and John Watson—only John survived. Whom could he appoint who was both competent and trusted to continue to manage the arcade according to his values? Among his own family, Linda was the only one interested and competent enough to oversee the business. His secretary and son-in-law Rupert Rudd would also do. So would Charles White, manager of his bank, the London, who had competently managed the financial affairs of the arcade for many years. Who else? Of all his department managers, Frank Wilmot, whose pseudonym as a well-known poet was Furnley Maurice, was one of the most intelligent and capable, but in private correspondence and conversations he had severely criticised Edward's management of the arcade during the depression:

Some institutions waste hundreds of pounds upon mere superficial and almost useless purposes, and yet complain if an employee wastes a half-penny-worth of wrapping paper. Undoubtedly, economy is necessary; but example is the best teacher, and it is

252

UNDER THE RAINBOW

human nature to look upwards for our guidance, the heads of businesses cannot justifiably complain, if they, themselves, are participators in that shortcoming for which they are bouncing their inferiors.[16]

Edward's choice of a fourth trustee was Henry Williams. Known as 'the Little Man', he was a pillar of the Methodist Church and a capable employee who had been originally hired at the start of the depression in 1891. His appointment as trustee was controversial within the arcade, as many other managers considered Williams an unctuous flatterer who had wormed his way into Edward's favour. But to Edward he was loyal and trustworthy. Edward simply chose not to hear the grumbles of his other department heads, and the four new trustees were duly noted in a codicil to his will.

There was more trouble with staff. Around 1912, the arcade's bank balance slipped into deficit as managers failed to refer orders to Edward and continued to over-order. They did so through either carelessness or misplaced optimism about potential sales; or—a darker possibility—they may have been on the take, earning secret commissions from London traders.

Things came to a head at another senior staff meeting at which Linda and Rupert Rudd were again present. Edward said that from now on he would warn all main suppliers that he would not pay for goods ordered without his signature, and would not approve payment of overbought consignments. In Linda's words to Turnley:

> Someone gave an incredulous laugh—Pa raised his voice the one and only time I can remember. 'How dare you laugh at me!' he said. He was white and trembling. 'I've tolerated that sort of laughter, though seldom to my face, following any unusual idea I ever had to build up Cole's Book Arcade. I won't tolerate it now that I'm forced to announce an unusual idea to save it.' Then, after an embarrassed silence, he asked them in his old, quiet voice, kindly to return to their departments.
>
> He presently called one particular manager back and showed him a copy of an order on a London publisher. Its value was over a thousand pounds. 'You must cable them and cancel it,' he told him.
>
> 'Oh,' he said, 'look here, we can't do a thing like that, Mr Cole.'
>
> Pa said, 'We can and we will do that. There will be no more of my instructions going in one ear and out the other. You will cable cancelling that order or I will send a personal cable disowning responsibility for payment.'[17]

The order was cancelled.

As if staff disloyalty wasn't enough, Edward had to contend with accusations relating to some of the material he sold and advertised during the First World War. An anti-war poem he published in his *Book Buyers' Guide* in September 1914 was inoffensive enough:

May peace her power extend,	And may all nations see
Foe be transformed to friend;	That men should brothers be,
Our nation's power depend	and form one family,
On war no more!	The wide world o'er.[18]

But as the shocking slaughter on the Western Front continued into 1917, Australian paranoia about Germany increased, exposing anything that might be considered subversive. In an undated and anonymous letter sent to the director-general of recruiting early in 1917, the author, signing himself as 'One Who Knows', referred to a satirical poem and an anti-conscription article published in *Cole's Book Buyers' Guide* of 13 February 1917. The writer described the arcade as a 'regular hotbed of disloyalty'. The offending poem was entitled 'Sing a Song of Europe':

Sing a Song of Europe	The General in the background
Highly civilised;	Is issuing commands;
Four and twenty nations	The King is in his palace
Wholly hypnotised.	Grabbing foreign lands.
When the battles open	The Bankers in the counting house
The bullets start to sing!	Are busy multiplying;
Isn't that a silly way	The Common People at the front
To act for any King!	Are doing all the dying.[19]

A referendum on conscription in Australia had been defeated in October 1916, but under enormous pressure from Britain for Australia to field more troops, Prime Minister Billy Hughes agreed to hold another in December 1917. The anti-conscription article was authorised by Edward's assistant WT Pyke, but was probably written by Edward. It read:

<hr>

Think!!
Which way would the Kaiser like you to vote?
The Kaiser would like you to vote yes
Why?

Because 'Yes' at once pulls Australia down to the level of Germany.

Australia wants population. Five million cannot hold a continent. We must aim at doubling or quadrupling our population as soon as possible. Australia must have good Europeans from every country in Europe if she is to develop her manifold magnificent resources—and incidentally keep the Asiatic out.

But Europeans who leave the old world to escape bad old-world conditions will not come here if we have Conscription. They will choose the United States, Canada or South Africa—countries which Mr Hughes knows well will not permit Conscription to send soldiers over the seas.

Australia's magnificent Volunteer Army of 300,000 free men includes descendants and natives of every European country, including Germany. Proportionately it is a contribution equal to three millions from the United Kingdom, or ten millions from Russia—and recruits are still coming in. What a magnificent advertisement for a country on the outposts of civilisation, twelve thousand miles from the centre of conflict.

Volunteerism has not been a failure. It has been a gigantic success. Don't besmirch Australia and Australian heroes by voting 'Yes'.

BE not like dumb driven cattle—Vote NO[20]

The article shows a puzzling aberration from Edward's anti–White Australia policy, but he may have sacrificed this principle in order to gain maximum support to defeat conscription. There is no record that he was hauled in by the authorities to explain either the poem or the anti-conscription pamphlet, and he probably wasn't. But further incidents occurred.

On 4 April 1917, a Lieutenant Colonel TC Alston wrote to the Intelligence Section at Victoria Barracks complaining of Bolshevik literature at Cole's Book Arcade, including a book entitled *Bolshevism: What the Russian Workers Are Doing* by Maurice Blackburn, a politician and socialist lawyer who established the legal firm of Maurice Blackburn & Co. in Melbourne in 1919 (still going strong today); Blackburn was a pacifist who took a strong stance against the war and opposed conscription. In a reply of 5 May 1919, a captain in the Intelligence Section, General Staff, dismissed Alston's concerns, saying that it was known that literature of a socialist and bolshevist nature was for sale at the arcade, as well as literature concerning militant unionism; the letter said that the same class of literature was for sale in other shops, and since they were not prohibited publications, there was nothing the Intelligence Section could or would do.[21]

There was more static concerning trading with the enemy. On 18 April 1917, Edward received a letter from Sir Robert Randolph Garran, solicitor-general of the Commonwealth of Australia. He had the honour to inform Edward 'that attention has been drawn to the fact that some little time since you exposed for sale certain goods bearing the enemy trade marks which had been suspended, namely "4711" Eau de Cologne and Lead Pencils and Crayons, made by Faber and L. and C. Hardtmuth'. This, Garran informed Edward, was an offence under Section 4 of the Patents, Trade Marks and Designs Act 1914–15.

In another exchange, Edward informed Garran that the ship *Adelaide* had carried twenty -three cases of toys from Hamburg, that the ship had been interned in Portuguese West Africa for two years before reaching Melbourne on the *Cunene*, and that the goods in question had been seized by Customs but then sold again to Edward on the undertaking that he would remove all German trademarks. He had done so, and Garran told him that 'under the circumstances there is no objection to their sale'.[22]

Towards the end of the war, Edward was inspired by the temperance movement, and by Lord Kitchener's prohibition against sending liquor to servicemen in France, to write a 200-page tract entitled *The Evils of the Drink Traffic*. Although he had spent much of his retirement reprinting many of his earlier books and pamphlets, this was among the very last articles he wrote. It drew together some of his earlier writings against booze, but was aimed at soldiers:

> The khaki uniforms mingle in the crowded bars. The hour grows late. No one behind or before the bar says a warning word about the last train to the camp. When the bars close the last train has gone, and the money gone—perhaps. If it has not, with self-control gone and passion excited, there are havens—not of refuge—in the dark places of the city, the ways where to go down to destruction. *The Age* described a hundred 'drink-besotted soldiers' taking part in a Melbourne riot. In some cases the 'wet' canteen in camp started the drink habit. The public house has confirmed and strengthened it. The liquor traffic has done injury to hundreds of our young soldiers of a worse character than that inflicted by German bullets.[23]

At the time he wrote it, the article probably deterred neither the liquor trade nor the propensity of soldiers to drink, but it sold well during the closing stages of the war, going through six printings. Along with pressure from a growing temperance movement, it may have been influential in prompting the passage through Victoria's parliament in 1916 of legislation compelling hotels to close their bars at 6 p.m. as a wartime austerity move. The other states followed suit. Despite the unsavoury nature of Australia's notorious 'six o'clock swill', the legislation was not repealed in Tasmania until 1937, in New South Wales until 1947, in Victoria until 1966 and in South Australia, the last state to do so, under Premier Don Dunstan, until 1967.

15
FLIGHT
OF FANCY

OPPOSITE The dashing Harry Hawker with his
Sopwith Tabloid, in Melbourne for demonstration
flights, including one with Linda Cole
RIGHT Cole's wildly impractical early conception
of a flying machine

Cole's Flying Machine.

Oh! I have slipped the surly bonds of Earth
And danced the skies on laughter-silvered wings;
Sunward I've climbed, and joined the tumbling mirth
Of sun-split clouds,—and done a hundred things
You have not dreamed of—wheeled and soared and swung
High in the sunlit silence. Hov'ring there,
I've chased the shouting wind along, and flung
My eager craft through footless halls of air …

Up, up the long, delirious burning blue
I've topped the wind-swept heights with easy grace
Where never lark, or even eagle flew—
And, while with silent, lifting mind I've trod
The high untrespassed sanctity of space,
Put out a hand, and touched the face of God.[1]

Edward Cole was fascinated by the possibility of men flying—not in balloons that had been carrying people aloft for decades, but in heavier-than-air machines. He no doubt knew about Leonardo da Vinci's Renaissance-era ornithopter, in which the pilot lay on a board in the centre of a complex wooden structure and furiously pedalled a crank connected to a rod-and-pulley system that flapped a set of wings. He was probably also aware of da Vinci's attempts to design a helicopter. His own early concept of a flying machine—a series of vertically arrayed umbrellas propelling aloft a top-hatted man on a platform by pushing air downwards like an octopus squirting water through its ventricles—shared some of the same principles.

[*Continues on page 262*]

THE DREAM OF FLIGHT

No one achieved controlled flight in a heavier-than-air machine until the beginning of the twentieth century, and then only through painful, sometimes disastrous trial and error. Every aviator's dream was to fly higher and faster over longer and longer distances in the shortest possible time.

On 17 December 1903, Wilbur and Orville Wright mastered the first step when they flew their biplane *Flyer 1* for twelve seconds over a distance of 36.6 metres at Kitty Hawk in North Carolina. *Flyer 1* had an elevator in front of two doped fabric wings, two pusher propellers spinning in opposite directions to avoid the effects of torque, and an undercarriage of bicycle wheels. It was powered by an engine they built themselves. With the aid of a wind tunnel they had constructed to test the aircraft's aerodynamics, they solved the problem of three-dimensional flight. They could ascend, descend and change horizontal direction by leaning into a turn as one would if riding a bicycle. In 1908, they carried out demonstration flights in France and negotiated contracts there and in the United States to share their technology.

In Europe, the first decade of the twentieth century was a time of collaborative aviation invention. Among the French inventors were Charles and Gabriel Voisin, who sustained a flight in 1907 of six seconds in their powered machine—half canard, half box kite held together by piano wire. Another Frenchman, Louis Blériot, who had made a modest fortune constructing motor-car headlights, flew his Blériot XI monoplane, equipped with a 25-horsepower (19-kilowatt) motor,

across the English Channel from Calais to Dover in 1909, collecting a £1000 prize from London's *Daily Mail*. He went on to win many trophies at European flying festivals. In Germany, Hans Grade flew his first aircraft in 1908. By 1910 he had established his first pilot school and aircraft factory and exported his designs across Europe and into Asia. Another German aircraft firm, Albatros-Flugzeugwerke, owned by Walter Huth and Otto Wiener, soon followed. It supplied many of Germany's aircraft in the First World War.

In September 1910, the American newspaper baron William Randolph Hearst offered a $50,000 prize to the first pilot who flew his own machine across the United States. It was won by a colourful cigar-smoking entrepreneur, Calbraith (Cal) Rodgers, who piloted his flying machine, *Vin Fiz* (named after a grape-soda drink manufactured by his commercial backer, Armour—a Chicago-based meat-packing company), across the North American continent from Shepherd's Bay in New York State to Long Beach, California. Backed up by a ground support team, Rodgers navigated his way along 6809 kilometres of railway lines, taking 82 hours of flight spread over 84 days with 70 stops.

With its vast distances, Australia was another logical place to develop air travel. Among its enthusiastic aviation pioneers was John Robert Duigan (1882–1951), who with his brother Reginald conducted more or less successful flying experiments during the first decade of the twentieth century on their property at Mia Mia, 209 dusty kilometres north-west of Melbourne near the Victorian

Harry Houdini getting airborne over Digger's Rest,
30 kilometres north-west of Melbourne

goldfields. Robert ordered a four-cylinder engine from Europe and bolted it to an airframe he had copied from a Henry Farman design from France. The craft's elevator was in front of the pilot, its rudder and ailerons between the wings, with a single vertical stabiliser on the tailplane. Take-off across a ploughed wheatfield was rough going, so Robert fitted shock absorbers to the undercarriage. On 7 October 1910, before six witnesses, he was the first Australian to fly an Australian-built aircraft. His flight was 180 metres.

A few foreign aviators brought their machines to Australia to make demonstration flights. They included Colin Defries, an English racing-car driver, who in 1909 brought with him a Wright Flyer and gave semi-successful flights of around 100 metres on Australian racecourses. Too short in duration, none were officially recognised as particularly successful.

In March the same year, the famous Hungarian escape artist Harry Houdini brought his French Voisin biplane to Australia at the invitation of the Aerial League of Australia. He had purchased the machine in Hamburg for a reputed $5000. On 18 March 1909, he made a series of controlled flights at Digger's Rest in Victoria, not far from the goldfields at Castlemaine. His longest flight lasted three-and-a-half minutes. He is also reputed to have made other controlled flights on the Rosehill Racecourse in western Sydney.

Edward must have realised that the main flaw in da Vinci's designs, and his own, was that a man simply did not have the muscle power to lift himself and a flying machine into the air. An engine would be necessary. Prompted by this thought, he offered a £1000 reward in 1882 to any man who could fly such a machine over Melbourne and land it in front of his arcade in Bourke Street:

> I, the undersigned, firmly believe that as man has already made machines to run over the land and float over the water faster than the swiftest animal, so shortly he will make machines to fly through the air as fast, and finally faster, than the swiftest birds do now. And I hereby offer a bonus of £1,000 to any person who shall (in consequence of said bonus) within the next two years, invent a flying machine, to go by Electrical, Chemical, Mechanical, or any other means, except gas, a distance of 100 miles [161 kilometres], and shall come and stop in front of the Book Arcade, Bourke Street, Melbourne, Australia, as easily and as safely as a carriage stops there now.[2]

Unless the Victorian police cleared Bourke Street from Queen Street to Swanston Street as a landing strip, the only flying machine that could have done this would have been a helicopter.

Harry George Hawker, the son of a blacksmith, was born at Moorabbin in Victoria in 1889. A slight, quietly spoken boy, he left school at eleven and worked in a Melbourne garage helping to build motor-car engines. In 1901 he became a trainee mechanic with the bicycle manufacturer Hall and Warden, then road-tested Oldsmobile motor cars assembled in Melbourne from knockdown components imported from the United States. In 1905 Hawker joined the Tarrant Motor and Engineering Company as a qualified mechanic, and then went to England. He first worked for the Commer Car Company, then Mercedes and Daimler, and finally for the Sopwith Aviation Company.

In 1912, Hawker collaborated with Fred Sigrist, foreman of the Sopwith company, to build a Sopwith-Wright biplane. In December of that year, the company built another biplane, the short-winged Tabloid, so-called because of its small size. Because of its speed and agility it caused a sensation when it first appeared. It had side-by-side seating for two in a single cockpit. Originally equipped with a Gnome Lambda rotary engine of 80 hp (60 kW), it could achieve speeds up to 92 miles per hour (148 kilometres per hour) and a rate of climb that allowed it to reach 1200 feet (366 metres) in one minute. Its nose was covered in streamlined aluminium with two vents to allow air to cool the engine, and it had an endurance of two-and-a-half hours carrying a pilot and one passenger. A seaplane variant with floats and a larger engine—a French-made Monosoupape of 100 hp (70 kW)—won the Schneider

Trophy in 1914, a race for seaplanes along a triangular course founded by Jacques Schneider, a French financier, balloonist and aviation enthusiast.[3]

Having just missed winning a £5000 *Daily Mail* competition to fly around the British Isles, Hawker shipped a Tabloid to Australia in April 1914 to give paid demonstration flights. In Melbourne, he based his demonstrations in a paddock at Elsternwick. One of his first passengers was Edward Davis Millen, a New South Wales senator from 1901 to 1923 and minister for defence under Joseph Cook from 24 June 1913 to 17 September 1914. Millen was closely involved in the government's response to the outbreak of war and supervised the recruiting and equipping of 20,000 men for the Australian Imperial Force. After the Cook Liberal government lost the election in September 1914, he became leader of the Opposition in the Senate.

Millen, being a man of some imagination, must have seen the military advantages of using an aircraft like the Tabloid as a fast aeroplane patrolling a battle space. So did the British Ministry of War, which shortly after the conflict broke out ordered thirty-six Tabloids for the newly formed Royal Flying Corps, the air arm of the army. Tabloids were used for photo reconnaissance and, later, as fighters. Millen would also have been intrigued to know that on his return to England, Hawker continued to work for the Sopwith Aviation Company until it went bankrupt, then formed the Hawker Engineering Company. After Hawker's death in an aeroplane accident in 1921, the company designed and built the Hurricane, a low-winged monoplane armed with eight Vickers machine guns—one of two mainstay fighters of the Royal Air Force that played a major part in the defeat of Germany's Luftwaffe during the Battle of Britain in 1940–41.

Edward was intrigued by Hawker's arrival in Melbourne, and hearing that he was a friend of his printer, Charlie Probert, called Probert into his office to ask whether Hawker would be interested in taking his daughter Linda on a joy flight. Probert inquired, and returned to say yes and that the fee would be £35. Edward promptly wrote a cheque to Hawker for that amount and the flight was arranged for Friday 13 February 1914.

Linda was wildly excited about her forthcoming flight with the dashing Harry Hawker, and scoffed at the idea that 13 February was an unlucky day. Her scorn would have been reinforced had she known that it was also the birthday of a famous female American aviator, Nancy Harkness Love. Love became a stunt pilot in the 1930s and then joined a group of courageous women civilian pilots who throughout the Second World War ferried all sorts of untested US military aircraft from their factories direct to military airfields, where male air force pilots were nervously waiting to learn to fly them. Many of these male pilots gasped in disbelief as a brand-new four-engined bomber or sleek single-seater fighter taxied to a stop outside their hangars and a young woman emerged from the cockpit and nonchalantly asked for a cup of coffee. It was a shock to their systems, a powerful wake-up call to realign their prejudices. Some never did; others lionised the women and wanted them in their squadrons.

According to Linda's son Cole Turnley, her take-off with Hawker was from a public golf course in Elsternwick. Through Probert, Edward had asked Hawker to fly Linda over Earlsbrae in Essendon, where he would be waiting to witness the flyover from a deckchair on the roof. But instead, Hawker avoided the city and flew her over Port Phillip Bay via Sandringham, Brighton and St Kilda. Nevertheless, Linda was able to regale her father with a full description of the panoramic view she had of the bay, the city and the distant mountains—Mount Macedon to the west and the Dandenongs to the east.[4]

Elsternwick is about 10 kilometres from Moorabbin, where an airport was later developed and named in honour of Harry Hawker. Instructions drafted by an unnamed writer in 1920 for pilots flying aircraft from such airfields showed how primitive things were:

- Don't take the machine into the air unless you are satisfied it will fly.
- Never leave the ground with the motor leaking.
- Don't turn sharply when taxiing. Instead of turning sharp, have someone turn the tail around.
- In taking off, look at the ground and the air.
- Never get out of a machine with the motor running until the pilot relieving you can reach the engine controls.
- Pilots should carry hankies in a handy position to wipe off goggles.
- Riding on the steps, wings, or tail of a machine is prohibited.
- Learn to gauge altitude, especially on landing.
- In case the engine fails on take-off, land straight ahead regardless of obstacles.
- No machine must taxi faster than a man can walk.
- Do not trust altitude instruments.
- If you see another machine near you, get out of the way.
- Never run motor so that blast will blow on other machines.
- If flying against the wind and you wish to fly with the wind, don't make a sharp turn near the ground. You may crash.
- Don't attempt to force a machine onto the ground with more than flying speed. The result will be bouncing and ricocheting.
- Pilots must not wear spurs while flying.
- Do not use aeronautical gasoline in cars or motorcycles.
- You must not take off or land closer than 50 feet [15 metres] to the hangar.
- Never take a machine into the air until you are familiar with its controls and instruments.
- If an emergency occurs while flying, land as soon as possible.

Captioned as a Sopwith 'Scout' biplane photographed at Aldershot, this is more likely a Sopwith Tabloid of the kind Harry Hawker took to Australia. The Tabloid had a distinctive aluminium cowling folded around the engine intake.

Linda's flight no doubt came as a satisfying vindication for Edward in the last decade of his life (as well as a relief that she was safe): he had long prophesied that air travel would become a common means of transport in the twentieth century. He had predicted that it would compress the tyranny of distances and promote international understanding—that, in a word, it would bring humankind together. He must have keenly followed the astonishingly rapid development of aviation technology in the decade preceding the First World War— from the fragile machines of Wilbur and Orville Wright and the Europeans to machines that were developed a mere couple of years later, such as the Tabloid, which could quickly and reliably fly for hours at high altitudes.

But Edward would also have been troubled to see the quick adaptation of aircraft to shoot at each other and drop the occasional hand-held bomb on enemy trenches along the Western Front in the First World War, and the heavy twin-engined Gotha bombers of the Luftstreitkräfte that began to drop bombs on England in 1915. Had he lived long enough, he would have been appalled to witness Junkers Ju-87 Stuka dive-bombers of the Luftwaffe

Condor Legion deliberately targeting civilians during the Spanish Civil War; and sickened by industrial-scale bombing in the Second World War by German and Allied air forces in Europe, by the deliberate fire-bombing of wooden and paper houses in Tokyo and Yokohama by General Curtis LeMay's US Army Air Corps in 1945, and the atom-bombing of Hiroshima and Nagasaki bombers in the closing stages of the Pacific War.

On a lighter note, he could not have foreseen the surprising capacity of a fledgling Australian aircraft industry to build capable aircraft during and after World War Two—military aircraft such as the Wirraway and Boomerang, the Beaufighter, the P-51 Mustang and, later, the F-86 Sabre fighter with its powerful Avon jet engine; or our capacity to design and build civil aircraft adapted to crop dusting such as the Transavia Airtruk, or for air ambulance work such as the GAF Nomad for the Flying Doctor Service.

Edward would have been amazed at the rapid advances in passenger aircraft, from fragile biplanes with uncertain reliability in the 1920s through amphibious aircraft such as the Short Empire flying boats in the 1930s that took off from Rose Bay in Sydney, Australia's first international airport, and reduced a trip to London from forty days by ship to ten days by air.

He would have admired the capacity of American aeronautical engineers to quickly adapt military aircraft, such as the Douglas DC-3 and DC-4, to civilian use after the Second World War and marvelled at the rapid pace of improvements in aeronautical engineering from the 1960s through to the turn of the century—from long-range aircraft such as the graceful three-finned, piston-engined Lockheed Constellation through the British prop-jet aircraft Vickers Viscount and the American Lockheed Electra, to the invention in the 1950s and 1960s of pure-jet, pressurised, swept-wing aircraft such as the British Comet, American Douglas DC-8, Convair 880 and Boeing 707. He would have been thunderstruck at the advent of supersonic passenger aircraft such as the Anglo-French Concorde and the Russian Tupolev Tu-144, and marvelled at the development of gigantic wide-bodied jets such as the Boeing 747, Douglas DC-10, Lockheed Tristar and Anglo-British Airbus 380.

Finally, Edward may before his death have modified his chauvinistic views about the subordinate role of women if he had known about the future exploits of female pilots such as Amelia Earhart, Amy Johnson, Nancy Bird Walton and Margaret 'Peggy' McKillop Kelman. He may have also marvelled at the fact that although no female pilot was allowed to fly an aircraft in Australia until 1927, more and more women pilots are flying commercial aircraft in Australian skies today.

All this would have been entirely compatible with his belief that through aviation, humankind would move effortlessly around the globe and, in doing so, establish peace and world federation.

16
THE END OF INSPIRATION

Cole in his front garden at Earlsbrae. Note the flower bed in the shape of a rainbow surrounding him.

Surrounded by family and friends, Edward Cole died in his bed at Earlsbrae on the bright summer morning of Monday 16 December 1918. His last sight, in his bedroom mirrors, was of the riotous blooms of his floral rainbow on the front lawn. He was eighty-six years old.

No specific cause of death was identified by his doctors, but he had been weakened by the stroke he suffered two months after Eliza's death in 1911, which had left him with a limp, vagueness, slurred speech and failing eyesight. He also suffered from chronic indigestion, which resulted in minor surgery at Earlsbrae two weeks before his death.

He kept assuring his anxious sons and daughters—Linda, Eddy, Vally, Pearl and Ivy—that he was all right, but his physical and mental condition continued to deteriorate. He lost his determination to persevere with his weekly routine of creative writing and commuting into the city from Essendon by brougham to keep tabs on the arcade. During the final months of his life, he would sit in silence for long periods in his bedroom or talk to himself or his pet marmoset about matters that still concerned him. He was worn out—from semi-paralysis, old age and the huge effort throughout that year and the preceding one of reprinting many of his major works into three deluxe volumes, the *Selected Works of E.W. Cole.* There was unprecedented demand for these works among his buying public, due as much as anything to the disruption of book imports from England when many ships on the Australia route were sunk by German U-boats in the latter stages of the war.

Edward was buried beside Eliza and their daughter Ruby in Boroondara Cemetery in the eastern Melbourne suburb of Kew the morning after his death. Nearly the entire staff of the arcade attended. One newspaper reported:

> The funeral of the late Mr E.W. Cole, which took place on Tuesday morning, was attended by a large number of mourners, including many intimate friends, and

practically the whole of the Book-arcade employees. The cortege left the late residence of the deceased, 'Earlsbrae Hall', Leslie Street, Essendon, at 10am en route to Boroondara Cemetery. Following the hearse was a motor car laden with wreaths from the employees of the arcade, personal friends and public bodies, the private brougham and motor car of the deceased, four mourning coaches and a number of motor cars and other vehicles. The remains were interred in the Church of England portion of the cemetery. The pall bearers were Messrs W. T. Pyke, W. Bassett, C. J. Smith, H. Williams, A. F. Turnley, C. W. White, M. C. Dunlop and J. Hischson.[1]

Edward's death was big news, and not just in Melbourne. It received wide press coverage throughout Victoria, in other cities of Australia, in New Zealand and as far as London. Melbourne's mainstream papers, including the *Australasian, Age, Argus, Herald, Leader, Weekly Times, Table Talk, The Graphic* and *Truth,* covered his passing with generous and comprehensive obituaries. So did the local and country press, including the *Upper Murray and Mitta Herald, Echuca and Moama Advertiser and Farmers' Gazette, Essendon Gazette and Keilor, Bulla and Broadmeadows Reporter, Spectator and Methodist Chronicle,* and *Castlemaine Mail.* They all described in great or less detail the highlights of his life: the poverty of his youth in England, his adventures in South Africa, prospecting for gold in Victoria, his voyage down the Murray, his struggle to establish himself as a bookseller and self-taught philosopher in Melbourne, his novel and highly entertaining search for a wife, his writings on religion and moral issues, his Funny Picture Books, his predictions about science and the human race, his inventive capacity for self-promotion and, above all, his rise to prominence as one of Melbourne's most successful booksellers. On 19 December 1918, the *Upper Murray and Mitta Herald* gave the essentials: 'He was a fine old character, animated by a great love for his fellow man. He was a most industrious maker of books. His juvenile books are household words throughout Australia.'

Edward's will, dated 22 November 1911, was read to his family, trustees and beneficiaries by his solicitors shortly after his death. He had appointed three trustees of his estate—his friend Joseph D'Ama Drew, his eldest daughter, Ada Belinda Cole, and his long-time loyal employee, Henry Williams. But as D'Ama Drew had predeceased him, he had added a protocol on 5 October 1917 appointing two additional trustees: Charles White, his long-standing bank manager, and Rupert Clark Ffrench Rudd, his son-in-law and former private secretary, thus bringing the number of trustees to four.

The will bequeathed *The Great Tichborne Trial,* the large oil painting hanging in the entrance of Earlsbrae, to Ada Belinda. To each of his four trustees he left £50. To his sons, Edward William Charles (Eddy) and Valentine Francis Stewart (Vally), he left £2000. The rest of his estate was to be converted into money and held by the trustees on trust for his living children, to be distributed in equal shares on their reaching twenty-one years of age.[2] As all his children were in their thirties or forties when he died, they received their inheritances straight away.

Apart from holding funds for the children until they reached twenty-one, the trustees were directed to manage the arcade 'until the expiration of the lease'. But as Edward had purchased the main Bourke Street site shortly before his death, the October 1915 codicil directed them 'to carry on the business of the Book Arcade for 21 years from the date of my death, or more or less as they judge expedient'. This was a broad and vague brief, giving unassailable discretionary powers to trustees who were singularly ill-equipped to exercise them. But Edward had chosen his trustees not for their business acumen or temperament, or their likelihood of surviving him by a number of years, but simply because of their closeness to him and the likelihood that they would continue to practise his singular business methods.

However, none of them had the qualities that had made Edward such a successful businessman—his single-mindedness, his willingness to embrace risk, his innovation and self-centredness, and his refusal to delegate (apart from to Eliza when he went on the buying trip to England in 1886). Their lack of cohesion and motivation soon began to show. White's heart was not in it: he had liked Cole and been his trusted banker, but did not share his vision of how to run a book arcade and would have been more comfortable managing a conventional business. He resigned soon after Edward's death.

Of the remaining three trustees, Williams—Cole's 'Little Man'—became a lightning rod for staff resentment. Senior managers had little respect for his capabilities, and frequently and flagrantly ignored his directives. They became adept at dividing and ruling—confusing his instructions and appealing to the other trustees, Linda and Rudd, confident that they would side with them against Williams. Several resigned, including WT Pyke, Edward's longest-serving employee, a man he had relied on to understand and support the strategy he had developed to attract customers at his first arcade in upper Bourke Street in the early 1870s. Pyke asserted that he could no longer work under such management, or lack of it, and in a letter to Linda wrote sadly of forfeiting a lifelong dream of 'an ideal book business with a lecture hall and scholarships attached and ideas at present undreamt of—in an enlightened future when nine people out of ten buy books instead of one in ten as at present'.[3]

Needing their jobs, many staff clung to the sinking ship. Most maintained their integrity and did honest work but, taking advantage of the laxity and confusion of senior management, some became outright crooks, drawing their wages without turning up for work, or overbuying stock and diverting it to suburban businesses they started on their own.

Greatly worried about these and other malpractices, Linda hired a public accountant, Mr E Pyke (no relation to WT Pyke), to carry out a full investigation of the arcade and make recommendations about what should be done. At the beginning of his report to Linda, he said he had been stonewalled by Rudd and Williams, who he thought strongly resented his investigations. He then described in detail the growing practice of department heads of overbuying and discounting stock, and recommended that a general manager independent of the trustees be engaged at a generous salary to strictly supervise future buying. Linda agreed, but could not shift Rudd or Williams from their refusal to cooperate. So nothing constructive could be done. The probate papers show that Edward was no stickler for record-keeping. He wasn't providing annual returns to the registrar-general under the Victorian Companies Act, and his business wasn't a company.[4] Adding to his short-sightedness, he had given his trustees absolute power to act as they saw fit, and neither Rudd or Williams saw as fitting the appointment of a new overseer.

The situation continued to deteriorate. Apart from corrosive mismanagement, the arcade was losing space. Edward had in 1905 bought the building facing Collins Street, and later, the Bourke Street arcade, but he never succeeded in converting the leaseholds he held on buildings flanking Howey Place, or two other properties linked to the arcade—one beside the Bourke Street section and one beside the Collins Street property. When these leaseholds expired soon after his death, the trustees were unable to persuade the owners to renew them. Some departments were downsized or moved to other spaces; others simply disappeared, including Wonderland and the Smiling Gallery. The funny mirrors were sold to Luna Park, where they were installed in the Giggle Palace. The aviary went the same way as the monkeys, and the fernery, much valued by tired shoppers as a restful sanctuary, was converted into an extension of the Little Man's own stationery department.[5]

Other things remained for the time being, including the two tin sailors cranking out their moral messages at the front of the store, and the orchestra, which now played in the afternoons but not at night, as booksellers were no longer exempt from six o'clock closing. The great German symphonion remained in the music department but was seldom played, as Charles Bassett had installed a row of gramophones with sound tubes to enable customers to listen to records they intended to buy without disturbing others.

The arcade staggered on, with department profit-and-loss statements sometimes rigged to show continuing viability by failing to depreciate the value of large quantities of dead stock—a ploy taken by department managers, often without the knowledge of the trustees. But they eventually found out the true situation. At a tense meeting to discuss the 1928 balance sheet, the three trustees decided, with their solicitors, and with unaccustomed unanimity, to wind things up. The family were saddened by the imminent closure of the arcade; so were many of its customers who, over decades, had taken such pleasure in shopping and being entertained there.

Taking a much-needed rest—Cole
with his dog in January 1916. He
was equally partial to cats.

According to Turnley, it stopped commercial trading at the end of June 1929, ten years
after Edward's death,[6] but photographic evidence shows that its doors stayed open until
27 July 1931, presumably in order to get rid of as much heavily discounted remaining stock
as possible.[7]

After closure, all freehold was sold. The main arcade building from Bourke Street to Little
Collins Street was snapped up by the retail company GJ and AW Coles and Co. (no relation
to Cole) for the sum of £200,000, which in 2019 terms would approximate more than AU$80
million. It was a shrewd acquisition on two counts: the arcade was in the epicentre of the city's
retail sector, and the company could bask in the reflected goodwill of Edward's name, even
though its name ended with an 's'. The new owners felt no need to spell out that they were not
related. Their new building was known as Store Number 12, Bourke Street, Melbourne.

Bill Rudd, Edward's grandson who died in 2019, had a wonderful story concerning the Coles brothers and Edward, the Prince of Wales. During his visit to Australia in May 1920 to thank Australia for its contribution to the Great War, Prince Edward explained that his regal crest was a crown and feather under which was his motto, 'Ich Dien' (I serve). George Coles replied, 'Yes, Your Highness, we have a similar motto. Ours is "Nothing over half a Crown", and underneath is another motto, "Cafeteria", which means "Serve Yourself".[8] This exchange took place six years after the Coles brothers established their first store, in Collingwood in April 1914, and ten years before they purchased the arcade in 1930. Coles was acquired by Wesfarmers in 2007, then de-merged in 2018. Today there are 807 Coles supermarkets around Australia.

Edward's property on Collins Street was sold to the chemists Simpson and Davenport for £54,000—in today's terms around AU$20 million. These sums alone show how financially well-endowed Edward's surviving five children became for the rest of their lives. Sadly, they lacked business experience in how to run a simple bookstore, let alone a huge arcade with sixteen departments. Edward had never seen fit to get them to work in the arcade on procuring stock, in sales or in accounts.

Indeed, the manner and extent of the secondary education of Linda, Eddy, Vally, Pearl and Ivy is something of a mystery, and remained so to Ivy's son, Bill Rudd. He knew only about Ivy:

> I regret to send you a nil answer to your question of the education of the children of EWC.
>
> It would be entirely in his character NOT to immerse his children in such a formality. I never heard my mother mention schooling, nor of the inevitable after school functions that follow, yet both my parents were keen to give my sister and myself the best education possible.
>
> I was sent to Melbourne Grammar and Melbourne University. My sister to Merton Hall (now known as Melbourne Girls' Grammar).
>
> At her request—after getting her matriculation—my mother graduated as a first class linguist at a 'Finishing School for Young Ladies' at Lausanne Switzerland.
>
> I never heard my Aunt Pearl nor Uncle Eddy or Val speak of their school days.

UNDER THE RAINBOW

COLE'S
FASHIO
CORNE
E. W. COLE MUSIC PUBLIS

OPPOSITE Books on one side, plants for sale
on the other—ground floor of the arcade
facing south towards Collins Street
FOLLOWING PAGES Everything must go:
closing down sale in 1931, a poignant time

Perhaps it's rather ironic that I was actually born at 'Earlsbrae Hall' gifted by EWC in his will to the Anglican Church becoming 'Lowther Hall'—shortly to celebrate its centenary.

Most cordially,
Bill Rudd[9]

(Bill was mistaken on this last point. Earlsbrae was sold, not gifted, to the Anglican Church: see page 281.)

Neither Eddy nor Vally wanted to run the arcade, and neither of them had been motivated to do his 'patriotic duty' and enlist in the Australian Imperial Force during the Great War. Their father probably shared Mark Twain's view that patriotism was the last refuge of the scoundrel. Eddy married a Melbourne woman, Alice Minnie Hearn, and settled down to a life of gentility, while Vally tried his luck on the London stage and married a young British actress, Eva 'Tessy' McTavish.

The two youngest daughters, Pearl and Ivy, were close. Ivy embraced married life and domesticity and produced several children, the first two of whom, twin girls, tragically died when they were less than a year old. A boy, Bill, followed, and at the time of writing he was still living, but passed away at the age of 102. By contrast, Pearl became an energetic bon vivant, attracted to travel and romance. According to Bill Rudd, one of her favourite destinations was Monte Carlo. He described her as a living example of the reverse of the old naval adage about sailors having a girl in every port. Bill reckoned that she left a host of admirers wherever she went, an English admiral among them.

Edward's first-born, Linda, was the only sibling sufficiently concerned to try to save the arcade. In 1915 she married Angus Oliver Frances Turnley, a widower with several children by his first marriage. He was also editor of *Truth*, Melbourne's most scurrilous weekly newspaper, which often featured lascivious stories about local personalities. Their union was not enthusiastically embraced by Linda's siblings, who did not approve of Turnley's background, but Edward himself had time for Turnley, who beneath his bluff exterior as a leading figure in Melbourne's 'yellow' press was sensitive and well-read. He shared Edward's vision of a federated world and had thoughtfully read Edward's essays *The Real Place in History of Jesus and Paul* and *In Defence of Mental Freedom*.

Linda and Angus Turnley married in December 1916 and produced a son, Edward Cole Turnley, who later wrote *Cole of the Book Arcade,* a definitive biography of Cole.[10] Linda opened a small bookshop and lending library at 255 Swanston Street, which she called Cole's Arcade in a sentimental attempt to keep the memory of Edward alive and public goodwill flowing. But her husband's own death and the Great Depression coincided in 1931, and the venture staggered and died. The shop closed its doors for the last time on the evening of Friday 7 July 1939. The last customer was the brilliant left-arm test bowler Leslie O'Brien 'Chuck' Fleetwood-Smith, who purchased a copy of *How to Play Cricket* by Jack Hobbs. Fleetwood-Smith is reported to have said, 'My prospects for test batting in the coming series should improve.'[11]

The story of the 'last sale' made news across the country, including in *The Age* and *The Argus* in Melbourne, *The Mail* in Adelaide, the *Albany Advertiser*, the *Perth Daily News*, even the Burnie *Advocate* and Dubbo *Liberal and Macquarie Advocate.*

Free of the chaotic interference from the Melbourne trustees, the branches in Sydney and Adelaide continued to function profitably for a time. But the trustees eventually sold them: the Adelaide branch to its managers, Beck and Manderville, who in turn sold it to Rigby Limited, and the Sydney branch initially to Edward's daughter Ivy in partnership with an accountant named Charles Dunlop. However, the Sydney business began to slide and was closed in 1924.

Before his death, Edward had transferred the title to Earlsbrae to Linda, Pearl and Ivy. Linda was keen to sell it, Pearl was indifferent, and Ivy wanted to live there until she realised how much its upkeep would cost her—a daunting task with twenty-four rooms to dust and clean and a lack of domestic servants available in postwar Melbourne. The three women were aware that at one stage their father had wanted to bequeath the property to a charity or the Church of England, but they insisted on selling it, at least for a nominal sum. They were also aware that the Reverend Lowther Clarke, Anglican archbishop of Melbourne and a friend of their father in his later years, had his eye on the property as a possible future school for girls.

Lowther Clarke arrived in Melbourne in February 1903 and was enthroned as Melbourne's first Anglican archbishop in 1905. According to his parishioners, he was a rather pompous individual who lacked a sense of humour and was unaccustomed to accommodating the views of others. Some of them called him a magnificent procession of one. He was nevertheless an eloquent spokesman for sectarian education, especially Anglican. He was keenly aware that in 1918 the majority of children in Melbourne attended secular state schools, and of the rest, most went to Catholic schools. Only 3700 attended Anglican schools. Clarke wanted to establish a network of strategically placed Anglican schools around Melbourne, and one of his targets was Earlsbrae in Essendon. Largely through his efforts, the Church in Melbourne eventually established Tintern, Korowa, Ivanhoe Girls' Grammar and Firbank, as well as Trinity Boys Grammar School.

When the Cole daughters put Earlsbrae on the market in April 1919, Clarke was well placed to make a bid, being a fairly regular, if not altogether welcome, guest for tea. As Ivy recalled:

> Before Father died, the archbishop would always include us in his little courtesies whenever he visited. But later on his attentions were rather gallant. He would arrive in ceremonial style and plant a kiss on each of our cheeks. I must say that for an archbishop he seemed an odd mixture—on the one hand an English gentleman with impeccable drawing-room manners; on the other, a pushing go-getter who did very much as he liked.[12]

Honouring their late father's wish to let Earlsbrae go as a profitless transaction, the daughters offered it to Clarke for £6500. Ivy observed that:

> The Archbishop must have been aware that he was getting an extraordinarily handsome bargain. But it was a case of the Church crying poor. I think he was reluctant to give up hope that the mansion might be donated. When it became obvious that payment was inevitable, he suddenly asked, 'Will you settle for £5,000 cash?' Of course we refused.[13]

After some polite bargaining, a sales contract was closed with the Anglican Church on 5 November 1919 for the asking price of £6500. Earlsbrae then became Lowther Hall, a well-known and respected Anglican girls' school that still operates today.

I do not believe I could have satisfactorily completed Edward Cole's biography without seeing his final resting place.

I make the pilgrimage on a calm, sunny early autumn morning in 2019. I fly from Sydney to Melbourne and board a number 48 tram heading east up Collins Street bound for North Balwyn. An obliging young passenger scrolls through her smartphone and advises me to get off at stop number 37. And there it is: Boroondara General Cemetery, behind a high brick wall on High Street. An obliging caretaker sitting behind a desk in an ornate administrative building with a clock tower at the cemetery's entrance uses her felt-tip pen to pinpoint the Cole plot on a crowded map of graves.

I follow the map past hundreds of monuments testifying to the love so many grieving families needed to express about their dearly departed. There are simple crosses on slightly sunken graves; stone angels with outspread wings, staring beseechingly at the sky; granite obelisks and sombre tombstones. There are extravagant mausoleums, mainly, it seems, of Greek and Italian families, with portraits of their deceased and words about their many virtues carved into granite walls and finished in gold. Time and geological subsidence have done their silent work: some of the taller statues and obelisks lean drunkenly towards or away from each other.

Among all this crowded confusion, I find the Cole family plot. Not all of Edward's family are buried here. His eldest child, Ada Belinda (Linda), is buried with her first husband, Angus Turnley, at Brighton General Cemetery. His youngest daughter, Ivy Diamond, is interred with her husband, Rupert Rudd, at Melbourne General Cemetery in Carlton, where their grave is said to be a replica of Cecil Rhodes' tomb in Rhodesia (now Zimbabwe)— Rhodes was one of Rudd's heroes. But the rest of the family are at Boroondara.

The plot is an unostentatious rectangle of plain gravel of perhaps 36 square metres. It is bordered by a black-painted wrought-iron fence about a metre high. In the plot's centre, behind an urn of flowers, is an open book carved in granite with the word 'FATHER' on the left-hand page, and 'Edward William Cole, born 4th Jan 1832, passed away 16th Dec, 1918' on the right. Directly behind the book in the shape of a white stone shield is a memorial to Edward's wife, Eliza Frances, 'who passed peacefully on to a richer life on 15 March, 1911'.

Lined up on the left-hand side of Eliza's stone along the back fence are three other white stone shields marking the deaths of Edward's son Eddy and his wife Alice, who died in 1946 and 1964 respectively; Ruby and Frances Rudd, the twin infant daughters of Ivy and Rupert Rudd, who died at the age of one month on 24 July 1916; and John Joseph Ruel, a beloved friend of the Cole family, who died in April 1965.

On the right-hand side of Eliza's are stones marking the deaths of Edward's second son, Valentine, in 1941, and his sister Ruby, the latter of whom died of scarlet fever as an eight-year-old on 27 March 1890; little Esme, infant daughter of Eddy and Alice, who died at eleven months on 19 June 1913; and finally a shield marking the deaths of Pearl Adelia, Edward's second-youngest daughter, who never married, on 21 May 1977, and her sister-in-law Eva Cole, the wife of Vally, on 17 March 1953.

I leave the cemetery in a gloomy frame of mind, thinking about the permanence of death, the great equaliser, which reduces even the most charismatic characters to insignificant piles of dust. But as I wait for my tram back into the city, I am uplifted by recollections of Edward's essay *God and the Universe*, in which he described the millions and millions of celestial bodies in the infinite distances of space. And I can see him looking down on me, laughing among the stars.

EPILOGUE

A lovely  s**e**gn ap**Q**s above the

On retirement from the Australian Foreign Service in 1998, I wrote my first book, *A Witness to History,* about the life and times of my grandfather Robert Arthur Broinowski,[1] clerk of the federal Senate from 1939 to 1942. I only met him once, because after he divorced my grandmother Daisy in 1926, she forbade her two sons from mentioning him, let alone seeing him. The younger son was my father, Philip. But after writing about his life, I felt I knew Robert rather well, and in my final chapter I briefly brought him into the present and played mind games with his ghost.

Like Edward William Cole, Robert was an autodidact with literary pretensions. He was a poet of no great distinction. One of his friends was Frank Wilmot, a department manager in Cole's Book Arcade who wrote under the pseudonym Furnley Maurice. Although forty years younger than Edward, Robert must have met him on a number of occasions at various literary soirees in Melbourne during the 1910s. They had much in common.

Having devoted two years to researching Edward's life for this book, I feel I know him, too. I have been intrigued by his writings—not only his tracts on religion and his Funny Picture Books that made him such a popular figure in Victorian Melbourne, but his predictions about the course of human affairs in his essay 'Federation of the World'. In it he predicted that the federation of Australia would be followed by the federation of the world, that English would become a universal language, that advanced education would inform the masses, that disease would be brought under control by scientific discoveries in medicine, and that universal suffrage would prevail throughout the world. On world federation, he wrote:

> Federation of the Australian Colonies has been much discussed, and is much in favour; Federation of the British Empire has been somewhat discussed, and is somewhat in favour ... but [as to] the Federation of the Whole World ... while a few minds in many countries and through the ages have believed more or less strongly in the brotherhood and final unity of man, the great mass of mankind have not thought on it at all. For myself, about thirty years ago, from general reading and conversation I formed an idea

that all the religions in the world were in the main essentially and strikingly similar. I ... made a comprehensive search in universal history and universal literature; and came out with the thorough conviction not only of the essential mental, moral, and religious oneness of the human mind, as shown in the world's literature, but of the entire, complete, and absolute oneness of the human race. Upon this conviction, and strengthened by the later significant progressive signs of the times, my theory of World Federation is built.[2]

What an interesting experience it would be to bring Edward back to life in 2019, just as I did with my grandfather, and review with him what has taken place in the 100 years since his death.

So I do, and the following is what transpires.

I meet Edward on the steps of the Victorian State Library in Swanston Street, the place where as a young man he feverishly read all the texts he could find on religion before writing his radical essay *The Real Place in History of Jesus and Paul* that upset so many clerics in the 1860s. He is wearing his customary black frockcoat and top hat, which attract mild stares of curiosity from passers-by. But he seems younger than his eighty-six years. His beard is not yet grey and his step is sprightly. It seems as if the 100-year sojourn since his death has done him good.

He says he is delighted to meet the grandson of a former acquaintance and poet. I explain that he has become quite famous since his death, and that many people have recorded their views about him, including academic and essayist Walter Murdoch, two of his department managers (Frank Wilmot and Syd Endacott), the Olympic coach Percy Cerutty, the bookseller and e*nfant terrible* of Adelaide literary circles Max Harris, and his own grandson Cole Turnley, Linda's first-born, who in 1974 wrote a comprehensive biography called *Cole of the Book Arcade*. A Melbourne writer, Lisa Lang, has written another biography, *Chasing the Rainbow*, and a novel about him, *Utopian Man*. Hilary Bell, daughter of the famous Shakespearean actor John Bell, and a composer, Phillip Johnston, have even written a musical about him, yet to be performed, called *Do Good and You Will Be Happy*.

Edward wryly remarks that being resurrected is as good as being present at his own funeral: he can hear and see what people really think of him.

Before we talk, he wants to stroll around Melbourne to observe its changes. He marvels at the smooth and almost silent trams, the streamlined motor cars, the macadamised streets free of horse manure and open drains, and the opulence of the goods displayed in so many department stores—including David Jones, which occupies the site of his arcade in Bourke Street, having replaced the Coles store that originally replaced the arcade.

Edward is fascinated with Melbourne's pedestrians, especially the informality of their dress and how all of them seem to be absorbed with tiny hand-held devices, either talking loudly into them or reading messages on their screens. The men are without hats, coats or ties, the women without hats, gloves or apparently even the corsets that cinched their waists into an unnatural slimness, which Edward wrote disapprovingly about as a young man. And the mixture of races! Asians, Indians and even Africans seem to outnumber Caucasians, especially on the streets around RMIT and the University of Melbourne. I explain that the federal government in the early 1970s abolished the Restricted Immigration Act that he found so objectionable. Since then, as many migrants to Australia have come from Asian countries, particularly China, as they have from Europe. I say that many Australians pride themselves on being part of a genuine multicultural society and tell him about the catchy song, a signature tune of the national airline, Qantas, that ends with the words: 'I am, you are, we are Australian'.

Edward is keen to revisit some of his old haunts, including the General Post Office on Elizabeth Street; the Royal Arcade at 335 Bourke Street close to Elizabeth Street, with its clear glass ceilings that inspired the skylights in his own arcade; Parliament House in Spring Street; and the City Baths at the top of Swanston Street. He wants to see modern bookstores, so we go to Dymocks in Collins Street and take the tram up Swanston Street to Carlton and walk to Readings on Lygon Street. He notes that neither of them displays the inducements he used to attract customers, such as brass pillars, marionettes with quotations and aphorisms, quiet reading places or tearooms. 'Not even an orchestra, a monkey or a funny mirror!' he exclaims. I point out that Australian bookstores are no longer carnivals. The pickings of booksellers are lean as their customers are distracted by television and social media, and they have to watch their budgets. But the stores, especially Readings, do hold regular book launches, and the literary public flock to them.

We finish our walk at Ross House, a community-based library and study centre in Flinders Lane where I have a room booked for several hours. Edward doesn't need corporeal refreshments, so I get straight to my objective of taking him through his predictions about human behaviour since he departed Earth in 1918. It is an awkward moment. I don't want to expose too brutally the fallacy of some of his predictions about the brotherhood of humankind. How can I tactfully describe some of the uncomfortable realities?

I explain that after his death, people everywhere were sickened by the slaughter of the Great War. Barely a year after the Armistice, the League of Nations was established to renounce war and settle disputes by arbitration, and in 1928 the Kellogg-Briand Pact was negotiated to renounce war as an instrument of statecraft. If international affairs had remained stable, these developments could conceivably have led to peace, or even the federated world that Edward confidently predicted.

But the league was institutionally weak because despite the fact that the US president, Woodrow Wilson, had proposed its formation, it was out of favour with the American people and they voted against joining it. Furthermore, its member states found they were powerless to prevent territorial takeover and conflict. Japan invaded Manchuria in 1930 and walked away from the league in 1933; Italy invaded Ethiopia in 1935; the Spanish Civil War began in 1936; and Germany, which had become a fascist dictatorship under Adolf Hitler, used the war to test and demonstrate the effectiveness of its tanks, aircraft and bombs against the civilian population.

The European situation deteriorated further when Hitler invaded Austria, Czechoslovakia and Poland. Too late and with too little resolution, Britain finally decided to stand up to him and declared war on Germany on 3 September 1939. The Second World War began, with the Axis powers of Germany, Italy and Japan on one side and the Soviet Union, Britain and its colonies and dominions, and eventually the United States on the other. After enormous destruction and death, including the genocide of six million Jews in Hitler's gas chambers, the war ended in Europe in May 1945. On 6 and 9 August the same year, President Harry Truman dropped two atom bombs, one on Hiroshima, the other on Nagasaki, instantaneously killing hundreds of thousands of soldiers and civilians alike. Many more died from radiation in coming months and years. With the fall of China to communist forces in 1949, the acquisition of an atom bomb by the Soviet Union the same year, and the outbreak of the Korean War in 1950, the Cold War—the most dangerous period in the postwar decades—began.

We pause while Edward absorbs these developments. He has many questions, which I do my best to answer, but I am keen to press on and complete the story.

I resume by observing that just as the League of Nations was created in response to the bloodletting in the First World War, so the United Nations was created after the Second. Its aims are the same: to prevent war through negotiation and cooperation. The UN has much larger membership than the league had. Its Security Council has five permanent members: China, Russia, Britain, France and the United States—the victors in the war—and its General Assembly has 193 member states. It has many weaknesses but is a genuine international forum that gives each of its members, many of which are comparatively new countries liberated from postwar colonialism, a voice to express their opinions. There has also been a proliferation of regional groupings, such as the European Union, the Association of Southeast Asian Nations (ASEAN), the African Union, and the Community of Latin American and Caribbean States. But none of these adds up to the global federation Edward envisaged.

He wants to know about Britain. Has it remained strong? Is it still the leader of a great empire? I tell him that it lost much of its power and prestige in the 1940s and 1950s as it faced enormous costs associated with the Second World War and its colonial possessions gained independence. Meanwhile, Australia, which fought as a loyal member of the British Empire in every British war until the Second World War, changed its military allegiance to the United States when, in 1942, the British Navy was unable to stop Japan from occupying the Malayan Peninsula, Indonesia and parts of New Guinea. Since then, Australia has fought in most of America's wars, including in Korea, Vietnam, Afghanistan, Iraq and Syria. In none of these wars has the United States been victorious, and none has guaranteed a safer environment for Australia.

I go on to other developments in the twenty-first century. I tell Edward about the attack on the New York World Trade Center by terrorists in 2001, mainly from Saudi Arabia and Egypt. The incumbent United States president, George W Bush, suspected that Afghanistan and Iraq had accommodated training centres for the terrorists, which gave him the excuse to invade Afghanistan in 2001 and Iraq in 2003 as the leader of a 'Coalition of the Willing'. The results were disastrous, especially for Iraq, which lost all social cohesion. Afghanistan remained a corrupt mess, and growing numbers of refugees sought asylum in other Middle East countries, particularly Jordan and Lebanon, as well as in Europe. In 2011, they were joined by refugees from countries across North Africa who began resisting the corruption and violence of their own governments in what was known as the 'Arab Spring'. The situation spiralled almost out of control as racial intolerance towards refugees took hold in many European countries, and fundamentalist Islamists initiated terrorist attacks in European cities and in their own and neighbouring countries, targeting sects against which they held grudges.

I explain to Edward that although isolated from the trouble spots by thousands of kilometres of land and sea, Australia has not escaped them. In the past decade, thousands of asylum seekers have fled across Asia to Indonesia, where they have hired boats in an attempt to reach Australia. It has suited both major political parties to inflame popular phobias about 'boat people' and amplify the damage to society these 'queue-jumpers' would cause if they reached Australia. As a disincentive to keep others from trying, many of those who did arrive have been imprisoned in offshore camps on Christmas and Manus islands and Nauru, with governments asserting that these people will never be allowed to settle in Australia. The fact that a number of asylum seekers drowned in their attempt to reach Australian shores has provided a moral justification by politicians to 'stop the boats'. Meanwhile, occasional attacks by Muslim extremists, goaded by Australian military action in the Middle East, have prompted the politicians to draft draconian terrorist laws and create an anti-terrorist military and security industry.

We ponder this deterioration of social tolerance. Edward, who had such high hopes for humanity, is shocked and disappointed at how bad the situation has become. He seeks more clarification, which I do my best to supply, and there is silence as he digests my explanation.

Before turning to predictions of his that have come true, I need to get one more of his assumptions out of the way: that 'all savage and barbarous races will be subjugated by more advanced nations, civilised, and then, like grown-up children, allowed the rights of equals'.[3] Today, I tell him, no one speaks in such terms, which are seen as racist and condescending. Countries needing economic assistance are categorised as 'developing'; they need economic assistance, not 'nurturing'; and their rights cannot be withheld until they 'grow up'. Such colonial concepts are out of date. Inhabitants of developing countries are no more capable of savagery than those of countries seen as being more 'advanced'. Germany was the home of Beethoven and Brahms and Goethe but its government was still capable of murdering six million Jews. Edward can see, he says with a wry smile, that many Victorian precepts became quickly outmoded with decolonisation.

'Have none of my predictions come true?' he asks with some impatience. Indeed they have, I reply.

The 'masses', as he called them, have generally become better educated in most countries, although fundamentalist Islamists still prohibit the education of women wherever they can. Literacy and numeracy have generally improved with the assistance of UN agencies and private not-for-profit groups. Irrigation and scientific cultivation are applied throughout food-producing countries, and are assisted in developing countries by specialised international agricultural agencies, including the Food and Agriculture Organization. Due to modern medicines, human pandemics have virtually disappeared, although if anti-vaccine fanatics insist on not inoculating their children, the diseases could return. Today, Edward's young daughter Ruby would never be permitted to die from scarlet fever.

I quote his prediction back to him that a network of railways, telegraphs, telephones and later inventions will cover the entire earth, bringing all nations closer together. All this has come true, I say, and his 'later inventions' include linkages through space via geo-stationary satellites, a concept he finds astounding but quite believable. The invisible internet gives everyone a dictionary, an encyclopaedia, a camera and a mouthpiece.

I remind him of his prediction that 'the reasonable rights of women will be established throughout the world'.[4] I detect a qualification here: it's a bit like saying, in his advertisement for a wife in 1875, that she must be 'moderately educated'. What does he mean by 'reasonable' concerning women's rights? According to whom? Before he can reply, I say that any response he gives will likely be unsatisfactory to modern women. In most countries they have come a long way since Victorian times. I explain the revolutionary change in women's lives that was brought about by reliable contraception. But women want the same rights as men, and despite female agitation for equality since the suffragettes demanded the vote, they still don't have them—certainly not in terms of equal pay, corporate promotion or seats in parliament.

Edward takes my point, and reminds me that in his age, men were conditioned to think of women as the weaker sex. On reflection, he concedes that his own wife, Eliza, proved the exception to this assumption: she was the only one he considered tough-minded enough to manage the arcade and its staff in his absence—the men were not up to it. His daughter Linda also had qualities of courage and perseverance not usually attributed to women in his day. The alacrity with which she accepted a flight with Harry Hawker in his frail biplane proved that point.

Triumphant among the accuracies of his predictions, I remind Edward, has been aviation: that 'flying machines will be in general, passing and re-passing over every spot on earth; that men will travel by these or some other means to the Antipodes in a week'.[5] We only have a couple of hours left of his resurrection, so I hustle him down to Spencer Street Station where we catch a red double-decker bus to Melbourne Airport. I take him up to the international departure lounge and he is amazed at the number of enormous aircraft on the tarmac, which, I explain, can each carry up to 400 passengers as far as London or Los Angeles in eighteen hours or less without stopping. Destinations from the airport also include practically every major city in Asia, and many others in Europe and Africa.

The reliability and cheapness of international aviation has also increased knowledge among travellers about the world, especially tourists who take advantage of package flights to selected destinations in Asia, Europe, Africa and Latin America. But has this in turn increased their tolerance of different cultures and drawn people closer, as Edward predicted? Certainly not in terms of laying the foundation for world federation, but it has certainly reduced ignorance and insularity among the travelling public.

As we step outside the terminal, Edward says farewell. He has found our discussion extremely illuminating, and would have modified his optimism about human federation if he had been prescient enough to see what was coming after 1918. But his faith in the essential goodness of humankind has not been severely dented, and he is determined to revise his predictions. After all, he reminds me as his corporeal form begins to fade, he has all the time in the world, and out of it, to do so.

APPENDIX

His Imperial Majesty's Japanese Naval
Visits to Australia 1878 to 1916

1878: *Tsukuba* – visited Brisbane, Sydney under command of Captain Matsumura

1881: *Ryujo* – Sydney, Melbourne, Hobart – Captain Fukushima

1882: *Tsukuba* – Melbourne, Hobart – Commander Kasama

1886: *Tsukuba* – Sydney – Captain Fukushima

1887: *Ryujo* – Adelaide, Melbourne, Sydney – Captain Yoshijima

1891: *Hiei* – Sydney, Melbourne – Captain Mori

1894: *Kongo* – Sydney – Captain Arima

1898: *Kongo* – Brisbane, Sydney, Melbourne, Darwin – Captain Nashiwa

1900: *Kongo* and *Hiei* – Thursday Island, Brisbane, Sydney, Melbourne – captains Imai (*Kongo*) and Enchi (*Hiei*)

1902: *Kongo* and *Hiei* – Thursday Island, Townsville, Newcastle (instead of Sydney because of an outbreak of the plague there), Melbourne – captains Ijichi (*Kongo*) and Iwasaki (*Hiei*)

1903: *Matsushima, Itsukushima* and *Hashidate* – Adelaide, Melbourne, Sydney, Thursday Island, Townsville – Rear Admiral Hikonojo Kamimura commanding the squadron on the flagship *Hashidate* with captains Ijichi (*Matsushima*), Matsumoto (*Itsukushima*) and Iide (*Hashidate*)

1906: *Matsushima, Itsukushima* and *Hashidate* – Thursday Island, Townsville, Melbourne, Sydney – Rear Admiral Hayao Shimamura commanding the squadron on the flagship *Hashidate* with captains Okumiya, Tsuchiya and Ishibashi respectively

1907: *Matsushima, Ikutsushima* and *Hashidate* – Brisbane, Thursday Island – Vice Admiral Sadayasu Tomioka commanding the squadron with Captains Nomaguchi, Nawa and Yamagata respectively

1910: *Aso* and *Soya* (originally named *Bayan* and *Variag*, these ships had been part of the Russian fleet and were 'battle trophies' of the Russo-Japanese War of 1904–05) – Thursday Island, Townsville, Brisbane, Sydney, Hobart, Melbourne, Fremantle – Rear Admiral Hikojiro Ichiji in command aboard the flagship *Aso* with captains Sato (*Aso*) and Suzuki (*Soya*)

1912: *Aso* and *Soya* – Sydney, Townsville – Rear Admiral Sadakichi Kato in command with captains Nakajima and Hiraoka respectively

1913: *Azuma* and *Soya* – Fremantle, Melbourne, Hobart, Brisbane, Thursday Island – Rear Admiral Sojiro Tochinai in command with captains Inamura and Horiuchi respectively

1914: Super Dreadnought *Ibuki* – Fremantle, Perth (to escort Anzacs to Egypt) – Captain (later Vice Admiral) Morihide Tanaka in command

1915: *Aso* and *Soya* – Fremantle, Melbourne, Hobart, Sydney, Brisbane – under the command of Rear Admiral Tomojiro Chisaka on board the flagship *Aso*

1916: *Iwate* and *Azuma* – Fremantle, Melbourne, Hobart, Sydney, Brisbane – both under the command of Rear Admiral Tatsuo Matsumura

NOTES

Chapter 1: Life in Kent

1. See Preface and Bibliography for comprehensive references to Turnley and his book.
2. Cole Turnley, *Cole of the Book Arcade*, Cole Publications, 1974, p. 8.
3. From 'The Happifying Gardening Hobby', an article by Cole in praise of gardening from his compilation *The Cosmopolitan Reasoner*, published in 1900.
4. Lisa Mendes, *EW Cole: The Early Years*, unpublished, p. 10.
5. The others are Berkshire, Buckinghamshire, Essex, Hertfordshire, Surrey and Sussex.
6. 'Dungeness A' comprised two Magnox reactors each of 219MW, which went on line in 1965. They reached the end of their serviceable life in 2006. 'Dungeness B' has two advanced gas-cooled reactors each of 615MW, connected to the national grid in 1983 and 1985 respectively.
7. Captain Swing was the figurehead of the movement, a mythical character named after the swinging stick of the flail used in hand threshing.
8. The rich and conservative classes still hold such suspicions. Consider former Australian treasurer Joe Hockey's infamous 'lifters and leaners' budget speech to the Australian parliament in June 2014, and former British prime minister David Cameron's slashing of social services in the UK in 2010.
9. 4 November 1810.
10. As recorded in Edward's personal correspondence in response to a request to name his siblings.
11. It was called an 'Indictment Roll' in those days because it was literally a long scroll of papers.
12. England was the only Protestant European country not to have some form of divorce law in place by the end of the sixteenth century. To obtain a legal divorce required a private Act of Parliament, something only the rich could afford. Pre-1858 laws governing divorce and bigamy were accordingly lax, and divorce in the modern sense was rare.
13. This marriage would have occurred during the latter part of Amos's term, and was entirely possible because convicts in Van Diemen's Land were given limited freedom, even in certain cases living in rented accommodation in towns.
14. This voyage was related in harrowing detail by the ship's surgeon, Mr JR Roberts; transcription courtesy of the Port Arthur Historic Site Female Factory Research Group.
15. Not John Watson, as mistakenly claimed by Cole Turnley (p. 8).
16. Turnley, p. 8.
17. Ibid.
18. From official marriage records uncovered by researcher Lisa Mendes.
19. Turnley, p. 10.
20. Ibid.
21. Ibid.
22. An emigration notice appeared in the Cape of Good Hope Government Gazette in June 1850 concerning *Dalhousie*'s arrival. Among its passengers listed as 'Single Men' was one Edward Cole, labourer.

Chapter 2: Cape without hope

1. The terms for the Cape Colony were substantially the same as those offered at the time for employment in the Australian colonies.
2. The *Cape of Good Hope Exchange Gazette and General Advertiser* of 27 June 1850 lists 'Cole, Edw., Male, Single, Labourer, arrived in Cape Town on 23 June 1850' aboard the *Dalhousie*. According to accompanying Ship Notes, 'The undersigned IMMIGRANTS having arrived in the Colony by the "Dalhousie", any persons desirous of engaging their services are requested to apply at the Depot without delay. JOS RIVERS, Immigration Agent, Cape Town 25 June 1850.'
3. *Cape of Good Hope Government Gazette* No. 2328, 11 July 1850.

4   The barks *Grindlay* and *Amphritrite* were both abandoned and sank at the end of June 1850 while sailing along South Africa's southern coast.

5   Cole Turnley, *Cole of the Book Arcade*, Cole Publications, 1974, p. 11.

6   Carol Victor, chief librarian at the Africana Library in Port Elizabeth, points out that the town's hospital was not constructed until 1856. Her claim is supported by the *Port Elizabeth Yearbook and Directory of 1899*, which states that the provincial hospital, built on Hospital Hill, was only formalised in 1856 by an Act of Parliament.

7   Turnley, pp. 10–11.

8   Karoo is a South African term describing the semi-desert regions of the country without precise geographical definition—a bit like 'outback' in Australia. Kloofs are steep-sided wooded ravines or gullies. The ones Edward explored could have been anywhere.

9   Diary of Charles Kent, Albany Museum, Grahamstown, p. 7.

10 Ibid., pp. 5–6.

11 Richard Marshall, *A Social and Cultural History of Grahamstown, 1812 to c1845*. MA thesis, Rhodes University, p. 18.

12 Allen Cawood, *Chronicles of Cawood: The Ancient Family of Cawood of Cawood Yorkshire—1000 years ago and Reminiscents about their Descendants* (unpublished), donated to the Settlers' Museum and now held in the archives of the Albany Museum, Grahamstown, pp. 14–15.

13 Diary of Charles Kent, Albany Museum, Grahamstown, p. 6.

14 Turnley, p. 11.

15 Cawood, Chapter 6, p. 22.

16 Philip Le Feuvre, *Cultural and Theological Factors Affecting Relations between the Nederduitse-Gereformeerde Kirk and the Anglican Church (of the Province of South Africa) in the Cape Colony 1806–1910*. PhD thesis, University of Cape Town, 1980, p. 10.

17 Turnley, p. 11. The fact that perhaps two relatives had martial backgrounds does not prove Edward did—Amos Cole's brother, George Cole, was in the 35th Regiment of Foot (East Sussex) and a Chelsea pensioner; Harriet's uncle Richard Gilbert may also have been forced to join the army in 1804 instead of being transported following a conviction of larceny.

18 The Cape Mounted Rifles were deployed in the Sixth Frontier War (1834–35), siege of Durban (1842), Seventh Frontier War (1846–47), Eighth Frontier War (1850–53) and Basuto War (1850–52).

19 Turnley, 1974, p. 12.

20 A brigantine is a two-masted vessel in which the foremast is square-rigged and the mainmast bears a fore-and-aft mainsail and square-rigged topsail. A schooner is a ship of two or more masts, all with fore-and-aft rigged sails.

21 *The Montreal Gazette* also reported that *Sebim* never returned to its home port but was sold at auction in Melbourne for £1200 (presumably in 1852 or 1853) and used by its new owners over the next sixteen years for trading between Australia, New Zealand and the Pacific Islands. It eventually caught its keel on a reef near Christmas Island (Kiritimati) in the South Pacific and was a total wreck.

22 Turnley, p. 12.

Chapter 3: Early Melbourne and the goldfields

1   Edward M Curr, *Recollections of Squatting in Victoria, Then Called the Port Phillip District (from 1841 to 1851)*. 2nd edn. Melbourne University Press, 1965 (originally published by George Robertson in 1883), pp. 4–6.

2   The latest evidence is that Aboriginal people have inhabited the continent for 65,000 years, not 40,000 as earlier thought.

3   *Sydney Morning Herald*, 6 July 2017, pp. 1, 6.

4   As well as Batmania, the settlement had previously been called Barebrass, Bareport, Barekeep and Bareberp.

5   Douglas Wilkie, 'Earth, Wind, Fire, Water—Gold: Bushfires and the Origin of the Victorian Gold Rush', *History Australia* 10(2), 2013, pp. 95–113.

6   There were some later breathtaking discoveries, including the 'Welcome Stranger', a huge alluvial nugget of 97.14 kilograms (3123 troy ounces) found on 5 February 1869 at the foot of a tree at Moliagul, 14 kilometres north-west of Dunolly in Victoria.

7   Geoffrey Blainey, *The Rush that Never Ended*, Melbourne University Press, 1963, p. 49.

8   CF Yong, *The New Gold Mountain*, Raphael Arts, 1977, pp. 1–4.

9   The Chartists were a working-class movement founded in England in 1836 to gain political rights and influence for workers. They quickly established roots in Australia, particularly on the Victorian goldfields through the Ballarat Reform League.

10 Blainey, p. 58.

11 Rod Fraser, *The Champion of the Seas,* Pilgrim Printing Services, 1999.

12 According to the Castlemaine Historical Society in a letter of 25 May 2017 to the author.

13 Cole Turnley, *Cole of the Book Arcade*, Cole Publications, 1974, p. 17.

14 Ibid., p. 18.

15 His tenders were accepted at a municipal council meeting in October 1858: from records held by the Castlemaine Historical Society.

16 Turnley, p. 20.

17 Geoff Hocking (ed.), *Early Castlemaine: A Glance at the Stirring Fifties—The Municipal Council, 1851–1863*. Original text written in 1908 by Frank McKillop. New Chum Press, 1998.

18 Fanny Lincoln, *The Burnell Family*, Reliance, 1948.

19 From 'Artists who drew with light', in *When, Where, Why and How It Happened: History's Most Dramatic Events and How They Changed the World*, Reader's Digest, 1997, pp. 214–15.

Chapter 4: Voyage down the Murray

1 From Cole's self-published article 'Greater Melbourne and the Federal Capital'; no date given but probably after 1898, the date on which a photo accompanying the article was published.

2 Greg Ryan, 'Albury: The "Federal City"', *Albury and District Historical Society Bulletin* 577, April 2017, p. 6.

3 Cole Turnley, *Cole of the Book Arcade*, Cole Publications, 1974, p. 23.

4 Edward M Curr, *Recollections of Squatting in Victoria, Then Called the Port Phillip District (from 1841 to 1851)*. 2nd edn. Melbourne University Press, 1965 (originally published by George Robertson in 1883), p. 231.

5 Susan Priestley, *Echuca: A History*. Rev. edn. Australian Scholarly Publishing, 2009, p. 5.

6 Curr, pp. 235–6.

7 Helen Coulson, *Echuca-Moama: Murray River Neighbours*. McCabe Prints, 1979, p. 3.

8 Ibid., p. 13.

9 Ibid., p. 29.

10 AE Orchard, 1999, 'A History of Systematic Botany in Australia', in *Flora of Australia*, Vol. 1, 2nd edn. Available at Australian National Herbarium, Canberra.

11 Ken Orchard, *Regional Botany in Mid-nineteenth-century Australia: Mueller's Murray River Collecting Network*, reprinted from *Historical Records of Australian Science*, 11(4), Australian Academy of Science, 1997.

12 Turnley, p. 25. Historically, Turnley's suggestion of Calvinist bigotry may be wide of the mark. In many country towns as well as in Sydney, debate had raged between the Baptists and worshippers of the Church of Christ over doctrine, and Wentworth may have been part of this. But the town held both a Protestant and a Roman Catholic church, and there is little historical evidence that the majority of its citizens thought photography a sin. Perhaps Cole and Burnell simply approached the wrong people when they tried to promote their services.

13 Nick Brodie, *1787*, Hardie Grant, 2016, p. 128 et seq.

14 Curr, pp. 175–7.

15 Turnley, p. 24.

16 The writer was probably EW Andrews, one of the proprietors of the *South Australian Register*, who took a keen interest in the Murray and had earlier been among the official party on board the paddle-steamer *Lady Augusta* on its inaugural voyage up the river to Archibald Campbell's Gannawarra Station in 1853. From Ken Orchard's paper (see note 10).

17 Turnley, p. 26.

18 Ibid.

19 Turnley writes that Edward undertook this research at 'the South Australian Institute, the fine new building standing beside open fields that flanked much of North Terrace, and housed the Art Gallery, Museum, and—chief attraction for Edward—the Public Library' (p. 27). However, this building was not completed until 1863, so Edward's research must have been done at whatever temporary building housed the colony's book collection before the South Australian Institute was completed.

20 Turnley, p. 28.

Chapter 5: Poverty and heresy

1 Cole Turnley, *Cole of the Book Arcade*, Cole Publications, 1974, p. 28.

2 Letter dated 25 January 1861, in private papers held by State Library Victoria.

3 Turnley, p. 28.

4 Andrew May, *Melbourne Street Life*, Australian Scholarly Publishing, 1998, p. 155.

5 Turnley, p. 36.

6 EDWIC, *The Real Place in History of Jesus and Paul*, self-published, 1867, p. 9.

7 Ibid., p. 47.

8 Al Gabay, *The Mystic Life of Alfred Deakin*, Cambridge University Press, 1992, p. 39.

9 Ibid.

10 Judith Snodgrass, *Presenting Japanese Buddhism to the West*, University of North Carolina Press, 2003, pp. 86–7.

11 *Anacalypsis*, as quoted in Wikipedia: https://en.wikipedia.org/wiki/Godfrey_Higgins (accessed on 27 July 2019).

Chapter 6: The art of self-promotion, or How to sell books

1 Cole Turnley, *Cole of the Book Arcade*, Cole Publications, 1974, p. 33.
2 John Holroyd, *The Australian Book Trade*, Braidwood Press, 2015, p. 159.
3 Knight, JG (comp.), *Narrative of the Visit of His Royal Highness the Duke of Edinburgh to the Colony of Victoria, Australia*, Mason, Firth and Co., 1868.
4 Turnley, p. 37.
5 Ibid., p. 41.
6 Presumably this is the 'old female gaol situated within the market area' referred to in *The Argus* of 13 May 1859 during redevelopment in that year.
7 'The Eastern Market', *The Argus*, 11 April 1871.
8 Horace Perkins, *Melbourne Illustrated and Victoria Described*, 3rd edn, Walker, May and Co., 1880, pp. 3–4.
9 See the feature text for more on Cole's coins and medals.
10 'A large assortment of seeds of the more ornamental bushes of the Murray Desert was recently presented to the gardens by Mr E W Cole of Castlemaine', *The Argus*, Saturday 2 August 1862, p. 4. Cole was recognised as a donor of seeds and plants in the annual report of the government botanist and director of the Botanic Gardens, as reported in *The Argus* of Tuesday 26 May 1863, p. 7.
11 Turnley, p. 44.
12 Ibid., p. 45.
13 Ibid., p. 49.
14 Ibid., p. 52.
15 Ibid., p. 69.
16 These ideals were summarised by Cole Turnley in his foreword to George D Dean, *A Handbook on EW Cole, His Book Arcade, Tokens and Medals*, GD and GF Dean, 1988.
17 In one of his frequent articles on social engineering, Cole devised a new working week in which people worked a bit longer on Monday, Tuesday and Thursday through Saturday, and took a midweek break on Wednesday, which he called 'Recreation Day'. He believed that workers worked more efficiently when they were able to take a break. The idea never came to anything.
18 *The Herald*, 17 July 1880, p. 1.

Chapter 7: Cole's Funny Picture Book

1 Copying from other sources seemed acceptable at the time. To my knowledge, Cole was never sued for breach of copyright.
2 Marram is a long and densely swarded perennial grass with stems 120 cm high, widely planted as a sand-dune stabiliser.
3 EW Cole, *Cole's Funny Picture Book No. 1*, 70th edn. EW Cole, 1965, p. 203.
4 Ibid., p. 125.
5 Ibid., p. 196.
6 Printed on the inside back cover of the 70th edition of *Cole's Funny Picture Book No. 1*, 1965.

Chapter 8 Cole's Book Arcade: Triumphs of marketing:

1 Ian F. McLaren, 'Dwight, Henry Tolman (1823–1871)', Australian Dictionary of Biography, National Centre of Biography, Australian National University, http://adb.anu.edu.au/biography/dwight-henry-tolman-3460/text5289, published first in hardcopy 1972, accessed online 20 July 2019.
2 John Holroyd, *The Australian Book Trade*, Braidwood Press, 2015, p. 163.
3 Cole Turnley, *Cole of the Book Arcade*, Cole Publications, 1974, p. 62.
4 Ibid.
5 Ibid., p. 65.
6 Horace Perkins, *Melbourne Illustrated and Victoria Described*, 3rd edn, Walker, May and Co., 1880, pp. 2, 3.
7 Turnley, p. 70.
8 The *Melbourne Daily News* of 4 July 1850 reported that Cantlon owned a successful wine and spirit wholesale depot, and the *Port Phillip Gazette and Settler's Journal* of 20 April 1850 recorded that he had successfully tendered to open a pie shop in Bourke Street to be called the Bull and Mouth.
9 Museums Victoria: text derived in part from research gathered by Patricia Draper, 1997.
10 Marcus Clarke in *The Age*, 26 July 1879, p. 6.
11 Public Record Office Victoria archives.
12 Public Record Office Victoria catalogue.
13 Manuscripts/papers from EW Cole 1875–1903, State Library Victoria.
14 Ibid.
15 Andrew Lemon, *The History of Australian Thoroughbred Racing, Vol. 1*, Classic Reproductions, 1987, p. 293.
16 Turnley, p. 75.

17 Maurice Cavanough, *The Melbourne Cup 1861–2000*, Crown Content, 2001.

Chapter 9: Growth and consolidation

1 From *Standard Plans of the City of Melbourne*, prepared in January 1888 for fire insurance companies by Mahlstedt and Gee, Surveyors and Draftsmen.
2 Andrew May, *Melbourne Street Life*, Australian Scholarly Publishing, 1998, p. 77.
3 Jane Elise Rhodes, *Spectacular! Spectacular! Cole's Book Arcade, Melbourne, 1863–1927*. MA thesis, University of Melbourne, 2008, pp. 63 et seq.
4 Cole Turnley, *Cole of the Book Arcade*, Cole Publications, 1974, p. 88.
5 Australian Manuscripts Collection, La Trobe Library, State Library Victoria.
6 State Library Victoria Papers 1875–1903, MS 10111, Box 4394.
7 Ibid.
8 Peter Hack, *The Art Deco Department Stores of Shanghai*, Impact Press, 2017, pp. 17–20.
9 Ibid., p. 18.
10 Correspondence between Peter Hack and the author, November 2018.
11 State Library Victoria Papers.
12 Turnley, p. 89.

Chapter 10: Education, loss and grief

1 Edward Sweetman, Charles R Long and John Smyth, *A History of State Education in Victoria*, Education Department of Victoria, 1922.
2 Stephen Dando-Collins, *Sir Henry Parkes*, Random House, 2013, pp. 232–3.
3 Cole Turnley, *Cole of the Book Arcade*, Cole Publications, 1974, p. 76. Edward may have found that his views on childhood education resonated with the spiritual and holistic Steiner method, but that didn't begin to be used in any practical sense until after 1919; Edward died in 1918.
4 Ibid., p. 69.
5 FB Smith, 'Symes, Joseph (1841–1906)', Australian Dictionary of Biography, National Centre of Biography, Australian National University, http://adb.anu.edu.au/biography/symes-joseph-4681/text7745, published first in hardcopy 1976, accessed online 20 July 2019.
6 Turnley, p. 94.
7 Australian Manuscripts Collection, La Trobe Library, State Library Victoria.
8 Turnley, p. 96.
9 Personal notes from historian Peter Hack.

Chapter 11: The first Great Depression

1 See Horace McCoy's *They Shoot Horses, Don't They?* (1935), John Dos Passos's *USA Trilogy* (1938), Henry Roth's *Call It Sleep* (1934), John Steinbeck's *The Grapes of Wrath* (1939).
2 Michael Cannon, *The Land Boomers*, Melbourne University Press, 1967, p. 86.
3 Other colonies were affected but not as badly as Victoria, because of the crash of its 1880s land boom.
4 For the full catastrophe, see Michael Cannon, *Life in the Cities*, Nelson, 1986, Chapter 48, 'Church, Society and State'.
5 Cannon, 1967, p. 133.
6 Ibid., p. 48.
7 From William Shakespeare's *Hamlet*, Act I, Scene 3.
8 Cole Turnley, *Cole of the Book Arcade*, Cole Publications, 1974, p. 106.
9 Ibid.
10 Ibid., p. 107.
11 Ibid., p. 132.
12 Encyclopaedia of Melbourne Online: The City Past and Present, 'Telephone'.
13 Turnley, p. 73.
14 Miles Lewis, *Australian Building: A Cultural Investigation*. Available at http://mileslewis.net/australian-building/.
15 The mantle was invented by Carl Auer von Welsbach, a chemist who had studied under Robert Bunsen in the 1880s. See Encyclopaedia of Melbourne Online: The City Past and Present, 'Light and Power'.
16 CA Burmester, 'Petherick, Edward Augustus (1847–1917)', Australian Dictionary of Biography, National Centre of Biography, Australian National University, http://adb.anu.edu.au/biography/petherick-edward-augustus-4393/text7159, published first in hardcopy 1974, accessed online 13 July 2019.
17 Turnley, pp. 100–1.
18 Ibid., pp. 112–14.
19 Ibid., p. 114.
20 Ibid.
21 Ibid., p. 126.

Chapter 12: Cole and White Australia

1 Graeme Davison, John Hirst and Stuart Macintyre (eds), *The Oxford Companion to Australian History*, Oxford University Press, 1998, pp. 243–4.
2 Published as a stand-alone article in or around 1903 by Cole's Book Arcade, Melbourne.
3 Louise Renfrew, 'Wilton Hack and Japanese immigration into the Northern Territory 1876–1877',

BA (Hons) thesis, Department of History, University of Adelaide, 1992.

4   Robert Travers, *Australian Mandarin*, Kangaroo Press, 1981, p. 29.

5   Alison Broinowski, 'Chinese Remonstrances', in Wenche Ommundsen (ed.), *Bastard Moon: Essays on Chinese-Australian Writing*, Otherland Literary Journal, 2001, pp. 12–13.

6   EJ Lea-Scarlett, 'Mei Quong Tart (1850–1903)', Australian Dictionary of Biography, National Centre of Biography, Australian National University, http://adb.anu.edu.au/biography/mei-quong-tart-4181/text6719, published first in hardcopy 1974, accessed online 20 July 2019.

7   Chung-ming Yuan, *Awakening Conscience: Racism in Australia*, Lung Men Press, 1983, p. 54.

8   AT Yarwood, *Asian Migration to Australia*, Melbourne University Press, 1964.

9   W Maloney, *Flashlights on Japan and the East* (in collaboration with Francis Myers), Will Andrade, 1905.

10 The Anglo-Japanese Alliance of 30 January 1902, negotiated between British Secretary of State Lord Lansdowne and Japanese Minister in London Hayashi Tadasu, effectively ended Britain's policy of 'Splendid Isolation'.

11 Letter of 14 May 1901 from J Chamberlain, HM Secretary for the Colonies, to Lord Lamington, Governor of Queensland, supporting abolition of the Queensland Sugar Works Guarantee Acts of 1893–95, but equally applicable to the Commonwealth Immigration Restriction Act of 1901. Source: Diplomatic Archives, Japanese Foreign Ministry, Tokyo.

12 The first of the Opium Wars was fought against Britain from 1839 to 1842; the second, against Britain and France, was fought from 1856 to 1860. China lost both.

13 Neville Meaney, *Towards a New Vision*, UNSW Press, 2007, p. 99.

14 As shown to the author during a research visit to the Japanese Foreign Ministry archives in Tokyo on 30 October 2017.

Chapter 13: Cole goes to Japan

1   Behind only those of Britain and the United States of America.

2   Many more followed, almost up to the Second World War, but they do not concern us here.

3   From Shiga's book *Nan'yō jiji* (Diary of a Sea Voyage), held in the National Archives of Japan, quoted in Henry Frei, *Japan's Southward Advance and Australia*, Melbourne University Press, 1991, p. 54.

4   From Takeo's personal record of a southern voyage he made in 1892 on board HIJMS *Hiei*: Frei, p. 55.

5   Frei, p. 56.

6   Correspondence held by the Japanese Foreign Ministry archives, accessed by the author on 1 November 2017.

7   *Ibuki* carried four 12-inch guns and eight 8-inch guns; *Dreadnought* carried ten 12-inch guns.

8   Cole Turnley, *Cole of the Book Arcade*, Cole Publications, 1974, p. 138. It is unlikely the postilion was warning pedestrians that Cole was coming. More likely, he was warning that a coach was coming—a courteous warning of Japanese coachmen at the time.

9   Australian Manuscript Collection, State Library Victoria, MS 10111, PAC-10036457.

10 Translated from the *Yomiuri Shimbun* by Mariko Yamamoto.

11 Letter dated 16 September 1903 and hand-delivered to Cole while he was in Japan.

12 Alison Broinowski, *The Yellow Lady*, 2nd edn. Oxford University Press, 1996, p. 48.

13 Ian McArthur, *Henry Black: On Stage in Meiji Japan*, Monash University Publishing, 2013.

14 Turnley, p. 138.

15 Ibid., p. 141.

16 *Sydney Sportsman*, 19 April 1905, p. 1.

17 Comment made in an interview with the Melbourne *Herald* on 12 June 1905. This was shortly after the Battle of Tsushima Straits in May 1905, which had sent shock waves around the world. Deakin's comments were reported in the Australian press (in the *Daily Telegraph*, *The Mercury* and the Adelaide *Chronicle*, among others) for the next week or so—see Neville Meaney, *Fears and Phobias*, National Library of Australia, 1996, p. 4.

18 Nobuaki's quote was widely reported around the world and in Australia: see, for example, 'Japanese Peace Mission', *World's News* (Sydney), 28 June 1919, p. 9, and Paul Gordon Lauren, 'Human Rights in History: Diplomacy and Racial Equality at the Paris Peace Conference', in Michael L. Krenn (ed.), *Race and US Foreign Policy from 1900 through World War II*, New York, 1998, p. 111 (footnote).

Chapter 14: Losing control

1   Cole Turnley, *Cole of the Book Arcade*, Cole Publications, 1974, p. 117.

2   Ibid., p. 157.

3 Jane Elise Rhodes, *Spectacular! Spectacular! Cole's Book Arcade, Melbourne, 1863-1927*. MA thesis, University of Melbourne, 2008, p. 76.
4 Public Record Office VPRS 3181/P1 Town Clerk Correspondence Unit 95, 1912/3140.
5 Public Record Office VPRS 3183/P1 Town Clerk Correspondence Unit 132 1912/7405.
6 Rhodes, p. 78.
7 Turnley, p. 165.
8 Ibid., pp. 165-6.
9 Coiler's name is misspelt in some sources as Collier.
10 AD Pyke, *The Gold, the Blue: A History of Lowther Hall*, Council of Lowther Hall Anglican Grammar School, 1983, p. 10.
11 Ibid., p. 18.
12 Ibid., p. 19.
13 Ibid., p. 27.
14 Turnley, p. 167.
15 Ibid., p. 170.
16 Ibid., p. 161.
17 Ibid., p. 172.
18 Ibid., p. 175.
19 *Cole's Book Buyers' Guide* no. 75, 13 February 1917, p. 1: MP 16/1, 1917/747, National Archives of Australia.
20 MP16/1, 1917/747, National Archives of Australia.
21 MP16/1, Y1919/179, National Archives of Australia.
22 A 3201, TE 325, National Archives of Australia.
23 Turnley, p. 176.

Chapter 15: Flight of fancy

1 John Gillespie Magee Jr, *High Flight*, 1941.
2 Cole Turnley, *Cole of the Book Arcade*, Cole Publications, 1974, p. 68.
3 Radko Vasicek, 'Schneider Trophy Race', *Aviation History*, September 2002.
4 Turnley, p. 173.

Chapter 16: The end of inspiration

1 *The Leader,* 21 December 1918, p. 34. The funeral was also reported in *The Herald*, 17 December 1918, p. 1 and *The Age,* 18 December 1918, p. 10.
2 Public Record Office Victoria, Series Title: Wills, description 168/337, VPRS 7591, consignment number P0002, unit number 613.
3 Cole Turnley, *Cole of the Book Arcade*, Cole Publications, 1974, p. 180.
4 Observation on 28 August 2018 of Abigail Belfrage, who looked at the probate records.
5 Turnley, p. 181.
6 Ibid., p. 182.
7 'Last Trading Day of the Arcade', a photograph from the Melbourne *Sun,* 27 July 1931.
8 From private reminiscences of Bill Rudd.
9 Email from Bill Rudd to the author on 22 December 2018.
10 Published in 1974.
11 *The Mail*, 8 July 1939, p. 23.
12 AD Pyke, *The Gold, the Blue: A History of Lowther Hall*, Council of Lowther Hall Anglican Grammar School, 1983, p. 57.
13 Ibid.

Epilogue

1 Richard Broinowski, *A Witness to History: The Life and Times of Robert Arthur Broinowski*, Melbourne University Press, 2001.
2 Cole Turnley, *Cole of the Book Arcade*, Cole Publications, 1974, p. 102.
3 From Edward's essay 'Federation of the World', quoted in Turnley, pp. 83-4.
4 Ibid., p. 84.
5 Ibid.

BIBLIOGRAPHY

Bell, Lucy and Johnston, Philip. *Do Good and You Will Be Happy: A Musical*. Unpublished; © Hilary Bell and Philip Johnston.

Blainey, Geoffrey. *The Rush that Never Ended*. Melbourne University Press, Parkville, Vic., 1963.

Bock, Ian. *Remembering Melbourne 1850–1960*. Royal Historical Society of Victoria, Melbourne, 2016.

Boehm, EA. *Prosperity and Depression in Australia, 1887–1897*. Clarendon Press, Oxford, 1971.

Brodie, Nick. *1787: The Lost Chapters of Australia's Beginnings*. Hardie Grant, Richmond, Vic., 2016.

Broinowski, Alison. *The Yellow Lady: Australian Impressions of Asia*. 2nd edn. Oxford University Press, Melbourne, 1996.

—— 'Chinese Remonstrances', in Wenche Ommundsen (ed.), *Bastard Moon: Essays on Chinese-Australian Writing*, Otherland Literary Journal, Kingsbury, Vic., 2001.

Broinowski, Richard. *A Witness to History: The Life and Times of Robert Arthur Broinowski*. Melbourne University Press, Carlton, Vic., 2001.

Cannon, Michael Montague. *Life in the Cities*. Australia in the Victorian Age series, vol. 3. Nelson, West Melbourne, 1975.

—— *The Land Boomers: A Study of the 1880s Boom in Victoria and the Men and Companies who Profited by It*. Melbourne University Press, London, 1967.

Casson, Mark. *The Entrepreneur: An Economic Theory*. 2nd edn. Edward Elgar, Cheltenham, UK, 2003.

Cavanough, Maurice. *The Melbourne Cup 1861–2000*. Crown Content, Melbourne, 2001.

Cawood, Allen. *Chronicles of Cawood: The Ancient Family of Cawood of Cawood Yorkshire—1000 Years Ago and Reminiscents about their Descendants*. Unpublished, Albany Museum Grahamstown.

Cole, EW. *Cole's Funny Picture Book No. 1*. 70th edn. EW Cole, Melbourne, 1965.

—— *The Lies We Tell*. EW Cole, Melbourne, 1917.

Coulson, Helen. *Echuca-Moama: Murray River Neighbours*. McCabe Prints, Wangaratta, Vic., 1979.

Curr, Edward M. *Recollections of Squatting in Victoria, Then Called the Port Phillip District (from 1841 to 1851)*. 2nd edn. Melbourne University Press, Melbourne, 1965. Originally published by George Robertson, Melbourne, 1883.

Dando-Collins, Stephen. *Sir Henry Parkes: The Australian Colossus*. Random House, North Sydney, 2013.

Darwin, Charles. *On the Origin of Species by Means of Natural Selection, or, The Preservation of Favoured Races in the Struggle for Life*. J Murray, London, 1859.

Davison, Graeme, John Hirst and Stuart Macintyre (eds). *The Oxford Companion to Australian History*. Oxford University Press, Melbourne, 1998.

Dean, George D. *A Handbook on EW Cole, His Book Arcade, Tokens and Medals*. GD and GF Dean, Tarragindi, Qld, 1988.

EDWIC (EW Cole), *The Real Place in History of Jesus and Paul*, self-published, Melbourne, 1867.

Endacott, Sydney J. 'Recollections of Cole's Book Arcade, 1899 to 1929'. *Victorian Historical Journal*, 32(3), 1962, p. 140.

Fowler, C de K and Smit, GJJ. *History for the Cape Senior Certificate and Matriculation*. Maskew Miller Limited, Cape Town, n.d.

Fraser, Rod. Extract from *Champion of the Seas Gazette*, 21 October 1854, in Rod Fraser, *The Champion of the Seas*, Pilgrim Printing Services, Glen Waverley, Vic., 1999.

Frei, Henry. *Japan's Southward Advance and Australia: From the Sixteenth Century to World War II*. Melbourne University Press, Carlton, Vic., 1991.

Gabay, Al. *The Mystic Life of Alfred Deakin*. Cambridge University Press, Cambridge, 1992.

Griffiths, Phil. 'The roots and consequences of Australia's fear of Japan'. Honours history essay, Macquarie University, 1998.

Hack, Peter. *The Art Deco Department Stores of Shanghai: The Chinese-Australian Connection*. Impact Press, Edgecliff, NSW, 2017.

Hattendorf, John B (ed.). *The Oxford Encyclopedia of Maritime History, Vol. 2: Factory Ship-Navies, Great Powers—Japan*. Oxford University Press, Oxford, 2007.

Hocking, Geoff (ed.). *Early Castlemaine: A Glance at the Stirring Fifties—The Municipal Council, 1851–1863*. Original text written in 1908 by Frank McKillop. New Chum Press, Castlemaine, Vic., 1998

Holroyd, John Percy. *The Australian Book Trade: A Bookseller's Contribution to Its History*. Braidwood Press, Fairfield, Vic., 2015.

Howarth, Stephen. *Morning Glory: A History of the Imperial Japanese Navy*. Hamish Hamilton, London, 1983.

Hudson, Wayne. *Australian Religious Thought*. Monash University Press, Clayton, Vic., 2016.

Japanese Navy History Association. *Japanese Navy History*, vol. 11, Navy History Association Tokyo, 1995.

Knight, JG (comp.). *Narrative of the Visit of His Royal Highness the Duke of Edinburgh to the Colony of Victoria, Australia*. Mason, Firth and Co., Melbourne, 1868.

Lang, Lisa. *EW Cole: Chasing the Rainbow*. Arcade Publications, North Fitzroy, Vic., 2007.

—— *Utopian Man*. Allen & Unwin, Crows Nest, NSW, 2010.

Le Feuvre, Philip. *Cultural and Theological Factors Affecting Relations between the Nederduitse-Gereformeerde Kirk and the Anglican Church (of the Province of South Africa) in the Cape Colony 1806–1910*. PhD thesis, University of Cape Town, 1980.

Leckey, John. *Low, Degraded Broots? Industry and Entrepreneurialism in Melbourne's Little Lon, 1860–1950*. Australian Scholarly Publishing, Kew, Vic., 2004.

Lee, Robert. *Transport: An Australian History*. UNSW Press, Sydney, 2010.

Lemon, Andrew. *The History of Australian Thoroughbred Racing, Vol. 1: The Beginnings—to the First Melbourne Cup*. Classic Reproductions, Melbourne, 1987.

Lewis, Miles. *Australian Building: A Cultural Investigation*. Available at http://mileslewis.net/australian-building/.

Lincoln, Fanny. *The Burnell Family: Three Generations in Australia*. Reliance, Adelaide, 1948.

McArthur, Ian. *Henry Black: On Stage in Meiji Japan*. Monash University Publishing, Clayton, Vic., 2013.

Madgwick, RB. *Immigration into Eastern Australia, 1788–1851*. Longmans, Green, London, 1937.

Maloney, W. *Flashlights on Japan and the East: Notes and Observations on a Trip by the 'Taiyuan', March to June 1905* (in collaboration with Francis Myers). Will Andrade, Melbourne, 1905.

Marshall, Richard. *A Social and Cultural History of Grahamstown, 1812 to c1845*. MA thesis, Rhodes University.

May, Andrew. *Melbourne Street Life: The Itinerary of Our Days*. Australian Scholarly Publishing, Kew, Vic., 1998.

Meaney, Neville. *Fears and Phobias: EL Piesse and the Problem of Japan, 1909–39*. National Library of Australia, Canberra, 1996.

—— *Towards a New Vision: Australia and Japan Across Time*. UNSW Press, Sydney, 2007.

Mendes, Lisa. *EW Cole: The Early Years*. Unpublished research by the author's research assistant in Kent, England.

Metrowich, FC. *Frontier Flames*. Books of Africa, Cape Town, 1968.

Muir, Marcie. *A Bibliography of Australian Children's Books*. Andre Deutsch, London, 1970.

Perkins, Horace. *Melbourne Illustrated and Victoria Described*. 3rd edn. Walker, May and Co., Melbourne, 1880.

Priestley, Susan. *Echuca: A History*. Rev. edn. Australian Scholarly Publishing, North Melbourne, 2009.

Pyke, AD. *The Gold, the Blue: A History of Lowther Hall*. Council of Lowther Hall Anglican Grammar School, Essendon, Vic., 1983.

Rhodes, Jane Elise. *Spectacular! Spectacular! Cole's Book Arcade, Melbourne, 1863–1927*. MA thesis, University of Melbourne, 2008.

Roe, Jill. *Beyond Belief: Theosophy in Australia 1879–1939*. UNSW Press, Kensington, NSW, 1986.

Russell, Penny. *Savage or Civilised? Manners in Colonial Australia*. New South, Sydney, 2010.

Sansom, Ian. *The Norfolk Mystery*. Fourth Estate, London, 2013.

Schama, Simon. *A History of Britain, Vol. III: The Fate of Empire 1776–2000*. Bodley Head, London, 2009.

Schumpeter, Joseph. *The Theory of Economic Development*. Harvard University Press, Cambridge, MA, 1934.

Serle, Geoffrey. *The Rush to be Rich: A History of the Colony of Victoria, 1883–1889*. Melbourne University Press, Melbourne, 1971.

Snodgrass, Judith. *Presenting Japanese Buddhism to the West: Orientalism, Occidentalism, and the Columbian Exposition*, University of North Carolina Press, Chapel Hill, NC, 2003.

Sweetman, Edward, Charles R Long and John Smyth. *A History of State Education in Victoria*. Education Department of Victoria, Melbourne, 1922.

Travers, Robert. *Australian Mandarin: The Life and Times of Quong Tart*. Kangaroo Press, Kenthurst, NSW, 1981.

Tulloch, Alexander. *The Little Book of Kent*. History Press, Stroud, UK, 2011.

Turnley, Cole. *Cole of the Book Arcade: A Pictorial Biography of EW Cole*. Cole Publications, Hawthorn, Vic., 1974.

Turnley, Cole (ed.). *Cole's Funny Picture Book No. 3*. EW Cole, Melbourne, 1951.

Walker, David. *Anxious Nation: Australia and the Rise of Asia 1850–1939*. University of Queensland Press, St Lucia, Qld, 1999.

Wilkie, Douglas. 'Earth, wind, fire, water—gold: Bushfires and the origin of the Victorian gold rush', *History Australia* 10(2), 2013, pp. 95–113.

Wilson, AN. *The Victorians*. Norton, New York, 2004.

Yarwood, AT. *Asian Migration to Australia: The Background to Exclusion, 1896–1923*. Melbourne University Press, Melbourne, 1964.

Yong, CF. *The New Gold Mountain: The Chinese in Australia, 1901–1921*. Raphael Arts, Richmond, SA, 1977.

Yuan Chung-ming. *Awakening Conscience: Racism in Australia*. Lung Men Press, Hong Kong, 1983.

Other Sources

Castlemaine Historical Society

PICTURE SOURCES

Abbreviations

Cole's album	Henry Williams, *Cole's Book Arcade: Album of Photographs*, Papers of Edward William Cole, MS 10111, SLV, 1923
MV	Museums Victoria
NGV	National Gallery of Victoria
SLNSW	State Library New South Wales
SLSA	State Library of South Australia
SLV	State Library Victoria
Turnley	Cole Turnley, *Cole of the Book Arcade*, Cole Publications, Hawthorn, 1974

All illustrations and decorative motifs are from Cole's Funny Picture Books 1 and 2. Artists' and photographers' are names supplied where known. iv plate, c. 1886, MV; vi–viii Cole's album; x–xi provenance unknown; 3 Gordon Gibbs, *Woodchurch*, 1910; 4 Turnley; 5 A. Ridley, date unknown; 7 De Luan/Alamy; 8 Classic Images/Alamy; 13 Garner, *Ashford, Kent: Market day*, from G. Shepherd and H. Gastineau, *Virtue's Picturesque Beauties of Great Britain in a Series of Views*, 1829, G. Virtue, London; 17 John O'Connor, *From Pentonville Road looking west: evening*, 1884, Museum of London; 19 Nash, Haghe and Roberts, *Dickinson's Comprehensive Pictures of the Great Exhibition of 1851*, 1854, British Library; 20 provenance unknown; 22 Thomas William Bowler, *Market Square, Port Elizabeth*, 1864, Nelson Mandela Metropolitan Art Museum; 26 *Xhosa warrior, 8th Cape Frontier War, 1850–53*, 1861, National Army Museum, London; 31 *SS Great Britain, Sydney Cove*, 1852, SLV; 32 S.T. Gill, *Queens Wharf, Melbourne, West End, in the 'Fifties'*, 1905, SLV; 34 Richard Daintree, *Castlemaine, Victoria*, c. 1858, NGV; 39 Atkinson and Atkinson, *Arrival of the first gold escort, William Street, Melbourne 1852, by an eye witness*, 1852, SLNSW; 42 top S.T. Gill, 'Diggers on Way to Bendigo/S.T.G.', from *The Victorian gold fields during 1852 & 3, comprising forty original sketches by S.T. Gill*, 1869, SLV; 42 bottom S.T. Gill, *Prospecting*, 1865, NGV; 43 provenance unknown, c. 1855; 44 *Kangaroo hunting*, D. de Rienri del, 1863; 46 S.T. Gill, *Forest Creek, Mt Alexander*, 1852, SLV; 49 S.T. Gill, *A Bendigo mill 1852*, c. 1865, NGV; 53 Turnley; 56 George Burnell, *Rowing boat used by G. Burnell and E.W. Cole*, 1862, SLSA; 58 Turnley; 60 Samuel Calvert, *Echuca 1865*, 1865, SLV; 65 George Burnell, *Rowing boat used by G. Burnell and E.W. Cole*, 1862, SLSA; 68 George Burnell, *River steamers at the Mannum Wharf*, 1863, SLSA; 71 Turnley; 74 *Bourke Street, looking west from Spring Street*, 1858, SLV; 76 Nicholas Chevalier, *English mail day at the post office, Melbourne*, 1862, SLV; 79 J.B. Philp, *The Eastern Market, from top of Whittington Tavern*, 1863, NGV; 82 *Bourke Street*, 1860, SLV; 86–7 J.W. Lindt, *Eastern Market, Bourke St. E. [Melbourne, Vic.]*, 1876, SLV; 92 Turnley; 94 1867, SLV; 101 Edward Gilks, *From Cole's Cheap Book Store, No. 1 Eastern Market, Melbourne*, 1851, SLV; 109 Turnley; 110 Cole's album; 112 F. Ziegler & Sons, *Cole's Book Arcade 'Little Men' or 'Little Sailors'*, c. 1883, photographer Rodney Start, MV; 113 Turnley; 113–17 medals, c. 1885, photographer Jon Augier, MV; 122 Cole's album; 124 Turnley; 134 *Bourke Street*, 1895, SLV; 136 Ludovico Hart, *Great Hall, Melbourne International Exhibition*, 1880–81, MV; 138 Ludovico Hart, *German Court, Melbourne International Exhibition*, 1880–81, MV; 147 David Syme & Co., *The Race for the Melbourne Cup: Rounding the Turn by the River*, 1883, SLV; 152 *Bourke Street, 1880s*, MV; 155 Cole's album; 156–7 Spencer Shier, *Cole's Book Arcade*, c. 1883–1903, SLV; 160–2 Cole's album; 165 *View of Anthony Horden Emporium*, 1921, National Museum Australia; 166 Cole's album; 168 c. 1886, MV; 170 *Bourke Street, Melbourne, Victoria*, 1890, SLV; 178 Clifford Williams, *View of Bourke St., Melbourne (Vic.)*, 1900, SLV; 180 Turnley; 184 Cole's album; 187 J. Macfarlane, *Among the Workless—Feeding the Hungry*, 1892, SLV; 188 Turnley; 191–3 Cole's album; 195 *Cole's Mechanical Hen*, c. 1889, MV; 196 *Symphonion*, c. 1889, MV; 199 top *Quong Tart outside luncheon rooms, possibly at 777 George Street*, 1886–98, Tart McEvoy papers, Society of Australian Genealogists; 199 bottom Cole's album; 200 Cole's album; 202 *Collins St., Melbourne*, 1908, SLV; 204 *Quong Tart, ca. 1880s*, 1880, SLNSW; 207–08 E.W. Cole, *The White Australia Question*, 1903, MV; 212–13 Tom Roberts, *Opening of the First Parliament of the Commonwealth of Australia by H.R.H. The Duke of Cornwall and York (Later King George V), May 9, 1901*, 1903, oil on canvas, British Royal Collection; 216 *Basket and broom peddler*, 1901, Kjeld Duits Collection/MeijiShowa; 221 *Japanese Ironclad Hiei*, date unknown, Kjeld Duits Collection/MeijiShowa; 224 top Turnley; 224 bottom *Federation of the World*, medal, 1903, MV; 230–44 Cole's album; 248–9 unknown provenance; 251–2 Turnley; 258 Bain News Service, *Harry Hawker*, 1919, US Library of Congress; 261 Marc Pourpe, *Harry Houdini airborne in his Voisin at Diggers Rest*, 1910, SLNSW; 265 *Sopwith Scout Biplane*, 1915, US Library of Congress; 268 Turnley; 273 from Henry Williams, *E.W. Cole: Founder of the Book Arcade, An Appreciation*, Book Arcade Printing Department, Melbourne, 1916; 275–9 Cole's album.

INDEX

THE MIEGUNYAH PRESS
This book was designed and typeset
by Pfisterer + Freeman
The text was set in 10½ Minion
with 15½ points of leading
The text is printed on 120 gsm Woodfree
This book was copyedited by Katie Purvis

Richard Broinowski was born and raised in Melbourne. He gained a law degree from the University of Adelaide and a Master in Public Administration from Harvard. During a long career as a diplomat, he became Ambassador to Vietnam, the Republic of Korea and to Mexico, the Central American Republics and Cuba. He is a past general manager of Radio Australia and was president of the New South Wales branch of the Australian Institute of International Affairs. In 2019 he was appointed an Officer in the Order of Australia for his advancement of Australia's diplomatic, trade and cultural relations. He lives in Sydney with his wife Alison. This is his fifth book.

THE MIEGUNYAH PRESS
An imprint of Melbourne University Publishing Limited
Level 1, 715 Swanston Street, Carlton, Victoria 3053,
Australia
mup-contact@unimelb.edu.au
www.mup.com.au

First published 2020
Text © Richard Broinowski, 2020
Design and typography © Melbourne University Publishing
Limited, 2020

 A catalogue record for this book is available from the National Library of Australia

9780522876222 (hardback)
9780522876239 (ebook)

The EW Cole Foundation has commissioned this book, as well as working with the City of Melbourne to erect an illuminated sign as a replica of the sign in Cole's Book Arcade to commemorate Cole's contribution to Melbourne's commercial culture. It is hoped this will be installed in Howey Place, the site of the Book Arcade.